KU-533-245

ACCOUNTING INFORMATION SYSTEMS

Transaction Processing and Controls

J. L. Boockholdt, PhD. CPA, CMA

Samford University
Birmingham, Alabama

Boston   Burr Ridge, IL   Dubuque, IA   Madison, WI   New York   San Francisco   St. Louis
Bangkok   Bogotá   Caracas   Lisbon   London   Madrid
Mexico City   Milan   New Delhi   Seoul   Singapore   Sydney   Taipei   Toronto

Irwin/McGraw-Hill

A Division of The McGraw·Hill Companies

ACCOUNTING INFORMATION SYSTEMS

Material from Uniform CPA Examination Questions and Unofficial Answers, Copyright © 1982, 1983, 1984, 1985, 1986, and 1988 by the American Institute of Certified Public Accountants, Inc., is reprinted (or adapted) with permission.

Material from the Certificate in Management Accounting Examination, Copyright © 1972,1973,1974, 1975, 1976, 1977, 1978, 1979, 1980, 1981, 1982, 1983, 1984, 1985, 1987, 1988, 1989, 1990 and 1991 by the National Association of Accountants, is reprinted (or adapted) with permission.

Material from Certified Internal Auditor Examinations, Copyright © 1984, 1985, 1986, 1987, and 1988 by the Institute of Internal Auditors, Inc., 249 Maitland Avenue, Altamonte Springs, Florida 32701, U.S.A., Reprinted with permission.

2 3 4 5 6 7 8 9 0 DOC/DOC 9 3 2 1 0 9

ISBN 0-256-21885-4

Vice president and editorial director: *Michael W. Junior*
Publisher: *Jeffrey J. Shelstad*
Associate editor: *Stewart Mattson*
Editorial assistant: *Jennifer Jackson*
Senior marketing manager: *Michelle Hudson*
Project manager: *Christina Thornton-Villagomez*
Production supervisor: *Scott M. Hamilton*
Senior designer: *Crispin Prebys*
Designer: *James E. Shaw*
Supplement coordinator: *Rose M. Range*
Compositor: *GAC Shepard Poorman Communications*
Typeface: *10/12 Times Roman*
Printer: *R. R. Donnelley & Sons Company*

Library of Congress Cataloging-in-Publication Data

Boockholdt, James L.
    Accounting information systems : transaction processing and controls /
 J.L. Boockholdt.—5th ed.
        p.   cm.
    ISBN   0-256-21885-4
    Includes bibliographical references and index.
    1. Accounting—Data processing.   2. Transaction systems (Computer
 systems).   3. Electronic data interchange.   I. Title.
 HF5679.B597   1999
 657ʹ.0285dc—21   98-06855

http://www.mhhe.com

To the Student

Today, an accounting graduate who lacks an understanding of computers begins a career with a major handicap. Computer-based accounting systems have taken over the routine summarizing and processing of accounting information. Accountants now function as the designers, controllers, managers, and users of these systems. Your chances of career success will be greater if you understand how to function in these capacities.

Why Study This Text

This text is intended to help you gain the knowledge you need. It is the result of many years' experience both in practical accounting and in university-level teaching. Much of the material is not covered in other courses in your business curriculum, so you should master it now.

Previous students' responses to this material have been favorable. They consistently say that "This is what we need to know about how accounting is done in the real world." By the end of this course, you will understand the relevance of an accounting information systems course to your own career.

Objectives of the Text

This text does not simply repeat material covered in courses in management, computer science, or management information systems. It identifies the distinct information systems knowledge required by accountants, and it incorporates accurate, understandable, thoroughly tested material that addresses those specific needs. It recognizes how you, as an accounting graduate, will use your systems knowledge.

Accounting Information Systems prepares you for three types of accounting careers. As a *management accountant,* you will use information systems and will participate in project teams that develop them. As an *auditor,* you will evaluate accounting system controls and examine system outputs. As a *consultant,* you will design and implement new accounting systems. In each career, you will work with systems using both older technologies and those implementing newer, state-of-the-art methods. Perhaps you do not yet know which direction your accounting career path will follow. With this text, your AIS course will prepare you for any of them.

To the Instructor

As an instructor in accounting information systems, you have a difficult job. You must structure your AIS course in an environment characterized by

- *Changing technology:* The methods for implementing accounting procedures change yearly. And unlike your colleagues teaching tax, financial accounting, or auditing, you have no authoritative organization to inform you of these changes.
- *Changing students:* The students you meet each term are more computer literate than those you taught in the previous term. More knowledgeable students means you cannot afford to rely on teaching materials that soon become obsolete.
- *Changing role for accounting:* Accountants are no longer just professionals who prepare financial reports. Accountants now serve as advisers and interpreters of management information—information that is both financial and operational. Your students must be prepared for this role.
- *Inaccurate perceptions:* Many students feel that AIS is not a "real" accounting course but merely another course in management, MIS, or computer science. You must establish the relevance of your AIS course to their career goals.

The fifth edition of *Accounting Information Systems* is written with these problems in mind. It emphasizes systems as an accounting discipline yet minimizes the opportunity for technological obsolescence.

Using the Text

This text is intended for both undergraduate and graduate AIS classes. It assumes that students have taken one-term introductory-level courses in accounting and in information technology. If you teach an undergraduate AIS course, you will probably omit some of the chapters. In a graduate class, you can proceed at a more rapid pace and may want to cover the entire book. In either case, you can adapt its content to the needs of your students.

Key Features

The fifth edition retains the features that contributed to the popularity of the preceding editions. These include

- *Accounting Emphasis Throughout:* The book begins by providing a systems perspective on some traditional accounting topics. The technical chapters use accounting applications as examples. The chapters on system development emphasize the role of auditors and accountants.
- *Modular Organization:* The text is adaptable to the needs of your institution, yet it is not so fragmented that planning your course becomes difficult. The suggested sequence of chapters on the following page will help you in preparing a syllabus that reflects your personal preferences regarding course content.
- *Exercises and Real-World Cases:* Each chapter contains a variety of questions, exercises, and cases. These are sequenced by difficulty and incorporate many questions from past professional exams. Each chapter ends with one or more cases that show how real companies implement the major concepts presented in the chapter.
- *Technological Completeness:* Because accountants work with both old and new systems, accounting students must learn older technologies as well as state-of-the-art processing methods. This text shows how accounting is practiced using manual systems, mainframe-based ("legacy") systems, and computer networks. Your students will have the background to understand any system they see in practice.

SUGGESTED SEQUENCE OF CHAPTERS

Chapter Number	Chapter Topic	Suggestions
1 ↓	Accounting Model	Cover Chapters 1–2 for a systems perspective on financial and managerial accounting.
2 ↓	Managerial Accounting Systems	
3 ↓	Systems Concepts	You may begin with Chapter 3 and cover Chapter 16 here.
4 ↓	Systems Tools	Cover the tools you will use in your class.
5→ 6→ ↓ ↓ 7 ↓ 9← 8←	System Development Methodologies	Cover Chapters 6–8 for a system development emphasis. Cover Chapter 12 here for a database design emphasis.
↓ 10→11→ ↓ ↓ 13←12←	Computer Software and Configurations Data Storage and Processing	A summary of material from other courses. Cover Chapters 11 and/or 12 for a technical emphasis.
↓ 14 ↓ → → ↓ ↓ 15 ↓ ← ← ↓	Internal Control Information System Controls Data Security and Integrity	Chapters 13–14 contain basic knowledge for all accountants. Cover Chapter 15 for a control emphasis.
16→17→ ↓ ↓ 18 ↓ 20← 19←	Transaction Cycles	Cover Chapters 17–20 to emphasize transaction cycles.

Improvements in the fifth edition include

• *Practice Examples:* Most chapters contain an insert entitled "AIS in Practice." This provides a concise example of how a real company has implemented the concepts described in the chapter. These add realism because your students will recognize many of the companies. Examples from outside the United States give an international dimension to your course.

• *Updated Technology:* This edition contains new material on recent technological changes, such as client/server computing, electronic commerce (including EDI, intranets, and extranets), and object-oriented systems.

• *Expanded Coverage of Database Design:* A new chapter describes the process of implementing database management systems. You can cover it early in the term and then assign a database design project to your students.

• *Updated Discussion of Internal Control:* The internal control chapter covers the material from the perspective of current auditing standards and the Committee of Sponsoring Organizations (COSO). This is the perspective required for your students to succeed on professional exams.

• *Improved Writing Style and Pedagogy:* This edition incorporates many comments from adopters and reviewers of the previous editions. Their suggestions make the text easier for your students to read and for you to use.

• *Web-Site Supplement:* Through the Irwin/McGraw-Hill site on the World Wide Web, you can access the home page for this text. It contains technological updates and links to other sites that your students will find educational. It also contains material from prior editions of this text that has been omitted from the current edition.

Organization

The text contains five major parts. Incorporating selected chapters from each part allows you to adapt the text to your specific needs. The suggested chapter sequence diagram shows you how to do this.

• *Accounting and Systems Concepts:* Chapters 1 and 2 provide a systems perspective on financial and managerial accounting. These chapters establish for your students that they are in an accounting course—one that is relevant to their career objectives. If you wish, you may skip these chapters and begin with Chapter 3, "Systems Concepts and Accounting." If you use an accounting software package in your course, you may wish to cover Chapter 16, "Accounting Transaction Cycles," immediately after Chapter 3. This provides your students with a theoretical basis for understanding what the package does. In Chapter 4, "Systems Tools," you can cover only those techniques that are important for your students.

• *Developing Accounting Systems:* Chapter 5 provides an overview of system development and can be covered either early or late in the school term. Chapters 6 through 8 emphasize system design and describe the development process in detail. Early coverage of this material allows you to assign a major project, such as *Your Company Project,* to your students. If you wish, you may omit Chapters 6 through 8 without loss of continuity.

• *Technology of Accounting Systems:* Chapter 9 reviews basic material on computer software and discusses state-of-the-art topics such as expert systems, electronic commerce, object-oriented systems, and computer networks. It omits basic descriptions of computer hardware that students know prior to entering this course. Chapter 10 contains an overview of data storage and processing methods that is basic to much of the later material. Chapters 11 and 12 cover these topics in more detail; either chapter can be omitted without loss of continuity. Chapter 11 covers the traditional data files used in legacy systems. Chapter 12 describes the process of database design. You may cover it after Chapter 5 and then assign a database design project. This chapter may be covered with or without Chapters 6 through 8.

• *Controls:* Chapter 13, "Internal Control," describes the subject from the viewpoint of auditing standards and the COSO report. Chapter 14 provides detailed coverage of controls in computerized systems, also from the perspective of auditing standards. Data security and integrity are the focus of Chapter 15, which discusses fraud, describes the impact of networks and database management systems, and uses computer-related crimes to illustrate the results of security weaknesses. This chapter also describes how auditors evaluate security and integrity—allowing you to cover relevant topics from EDP auditing without assuming that your students have prior auditing knowledge.

• *Processing Accounting Transactions:* Chapter 16 provides an overview of transaction cycles. The remaining chapters, 17 through 20, contain in-depth coverage of transaction processing systems, organized by cycle. Late coverage of this material ensures that by the time you get to these chapters, your students know enough about technology and controls to understand how the systems work. These chapters also provide a thorough introduction to the auditing course, which many students subsequently take.

Supplements

The *Instructor's Lecture Guide* contains a *lecture outline* for each chapter. You can make transparencies from the lecture outlines to use in your lectures. The guide also contains a *transparency master* for some of the illustrations referred to in the lecture outlines.

Also in the *Instructor's Lecture Guide* is an excellent test bank prepared by Professor Julian Lowell Mooney of Georgia Southern University. It contains an expanded selection of multiple-choice and true/false questions and problems. You may obtain it from McGraw-Hill Customer Service in Windows or MacIntosh form by requesting the Computest feature. It includes advanced features such as allowing the instructor to add and edit questions on-line, save and reload tests, create up to 99 versions of each test, attach graphics to questions, import and export ASCII files, and select questions based on type, level of difficulty, or keyword. The program allows password protection of saved tests and question databases, and is networkable.

The *Solutions Manual* is complete and incorporates the suggested solutions to professional exam questions. It is organized so that you can easily remove the solution to an individual exercise or case.

The *AIS Web Site* contains technological updates and links to other relevant Web sites. If you used material in a prior edition of this text that has been omitted from this one, you will find it at the Web site. This includes material on cost-benefit analysis of internal controls, control flowcharting, data structures, and the basics of computer hardware.

Permission has been received from the Institute of Certified Management Accountants of the Institute of Management Accountants to use questions and unofficial answers from past CMA examinations. We are also indebted to the American Institute of Certified Public Accountants and the Institute of Internal Auditors for allowing us to adapt and use material from past CPA and CIA examinations.

Many students made innumerable suggestions and criticisms that greatly improve the book. The most appreciation is due to the reviewers who critiqued all editions of the book. Each of you, as you read the text, can identify your personal contributions to it. The reviewers for this edition were

Paul Goldwater
University of Central Florida

Judith Welch
University of Central Florida

William Cummings
Northern Illinois University

Venkataraman Iyer
Georgia College

Charles Caliendo
University of Minnesota

Barry Williams
King's College

Ronald Rasch
Auburn University

Brad Tuttle
University of South Carolina

Sean Chen
Clemson University

Thomas Harris
Prairie View A & M University

Scott Summers
University of Missouri/Columbia

Byoung Bae
Temple University

Randolph Coyner
Florida Atlantic University

Troy Hyatt
University of Northern Iowa

Ram Sriram
Georgia State University

Thanks very, very much to each of you.

Jim Boockholdt

C O N T E N T S

PART II

DEVELOPING ACCOUNTING SYSTEMS

1   A MODEL FOR PROCESSING ACCOUNTING INFORMATION

Learning Objectives

1. To learn the objectives of accounting information systems.
2. To review the steps in the accounting cycle.
3. To review how accounting information systems produce reports for external use.

Introduction

The study of accounting information systems analyzes how events affecting an organization are recorded, summarized, and reported. These events are recorded using that organization's *system* of human and computer resources, summarized using *accounting* methods and objectives, and reported as *information* to interested persons both within and outside of the organization.

This chapter describes a conceptual model for recording, processing, and reporting these events to external parties. You should be familiar with this model from your introductory accounting course. If so, much of the material in this chapter will be a review. The next chapter will show how this model is adapted for reporting within the organization. The remainder of the book details how this conceptual process is implemented.

Organizations

Accounting information systems exist in many forms of organizations, whether proprietorships, partnerships, corporations, nonprofit foundations, or households. While the complexity of each accounting information system differs, each is similar in three important ways. Each contains a similar structure (of human and computer resources), similar processes (the use of accounting methods), and similar purposes (to provide information).

This book, like most accounting textbooks, uses as an example one type of organization: the profit-seeking, publicly owned corporation engaged in manufacturing and selling goods. The structure, processes, and purposes of the accounting information systems are more complex in the manufacturing corporation than in the others. You can readily adapt what you learn about this type of corporation to the circumstances of the other types listed earlier.

Events Affecting an Organization

The events that affect any organization are a result of its interactions with its environment, which includes economic, social, political, and regulatory entities. Accounting information systems record, summarize, and report events arising from these interactions. The events to be processed depend on the scope of the organization's accounting information systems and the nature of the events.

Human and Computer Resources

A system of human and computer resources records, processes, and reports events from the organization's environment. When the system contains only human resources, it is a *manual system*. If it uses only computer resources, it is a *computer system.* When it uses both human and computer resources, it is a *computer-based system.*

Most organizations today use computer-based accounting information systems. This book offers comparisons of manual and computerized methods for recording, processing, and reporting events. However, both methods are important, because each organization's computer-based system has a different mix of computerized and manual methods. Furthermore, many computer and manual systems employ the same procedures. In these cases, understanding manual methods makes it easier to master computerized ones.

Accounting Methods and Objectives

All accounting information systems record, process, and report events using accounting methods to achieve accounting objectives. These objectives determine the system's scope, which in turn determines the nature of the events and the method of accounting. However, all systems record events in money and use the same conceptual accounting process.

Scope of the System and Nature of the Events

For the publicly held corporation, the accounting information system's scope must comply with generally accepted accounting principles (GAAP). GAAP is necessary to produce financial statements intended for parties external to the organization. With GAAP, any event that has a determinable monetary impact on the organization must be recognized as an accounting *transaction.* A system whose objective is to record, process, and report past transactions as financial statements in accordance with GAAP is a *financial accounting information system.*

Usually the scope of an organization's system for processing data is broader than that required by GAAP. For example, when an accounting system includes budgetary forecasts, it recognizes future transactions and estimates their monetary impact. Whether short-term annual budgets or long-term ones, budgets provide vital financial information for managing the organization. Budgeting and other such accounting systems intended primarily for use within the organization constitute *managerial accounting information systems.*

Both the financial and the managerial systems are components of the organization's *management information system* (MIS). The MIS is the combination of people, procedures, and machines intended to provide information for management decision making. It recognizes events beyond those of a purely financial nature. Chapter 2 discusses managerial accounting information systems, and you will read about management information systems in Chapter 3.

AIS in Practice

Chartwell Reinsurance Company, a subsidiary of Chartwell Re Corp., writes property and casualty reinsurance for specialty, regional, marine, aviation, and global insurance companies. Its accounting requirements are complex. It files GAAP financial reports with the U.S. Securities and Exchange Commission, statutory accounting reports with insurance regulatory authorities, and a third type of report with selected tax agencies. Growth through acquisition made its accounting system inadequate. The old system was unable to support growth or multiple currencies, and it handled consolidations poorly.

Management purchased new financial software from an external vendor. Chartwell's accountants then adapted it to the company's needs. They created a new chart of accounts, new forms, and new reports, and they loaded two years of historical data into the new system. Once the system was functioning, users could create their own reports, query the system for information, and modify existing functions. The new system was implemented quickly and placed in the hands of accountants many duties that had traditionally been done by the company's information technology group.

Illustration 1–1 depicts an accounting information system as two overlapping circles. The left circle represents the financial accounting information system, which produces information for external reporting according to GAAP. The right circle is the managerial accounting information system. Its objective is internal reporting, and it uses the accounting methods preferred by management. Each is a component of the management information system.

The area where the two circles overlap shows how these two systems share certain components. For example, GAAP requires that the total accounting information system maintain data on accounts receivable. Management uses these data to decide which customers are creditworthy. Thus, these data are used for both external and internal

ILLUSTRATION 1–1

Scope of the Accounting Information System

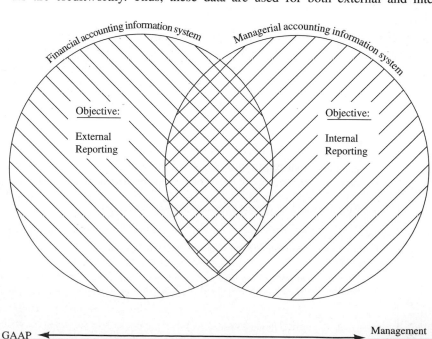

Financial accounting information system — Managerial accounting information system

Objective: External Reporting

Objective: Internal Reporting

GAAP ← → Management preference

reporting. Within the limits specified by GAAP, management exercises its preference when determining how to calculate the Allowance for Doubtful Accounts. In this way, the accounts receivable component is a part of both the financial and the managerial information systems.

The Accounting Process

The accounting process begins when an economic event is recognized by an accounting information system, which records the economic event as an accounting transaction. This book illustrates how the system's human and computer components process a transaction.

For financial accounting information systems, the activities that process a transaction constitute the *accounting cycle*. Conceptually, the accounting cycle consists of the following six steps.

Journalize.   The first step in the accounting cycle, *journalizing* is recording the transaction. Someone analyzes the event, determines the accounts it affects, identifies whether each account is debited or credited, and enters the transaction chronologically in a journal.

Illustration 1–2 is an example of a general journal whose sample entries reflect some common transactions. Most organizations also use several special journals

ILLUSTRATION 1–2

A General Journal

		GENERAL JOURNAL			Page 1
\<colspan=2\> Date	Accounts and Explanation	Ref.	Debit	Credit

Date		Accounts and Explanation	Ref.	Debit	Credit
Sept.	1	Cash		100,000	
		Capital Stock			100,000
		Issued capital stock for cash.			
	2	Land		20,000	
		Building		60,000	
		Cash			15,000
		Notes Payable			65,000
		Purchased land and building financed in part by a long-term note.			
	3	Equipment		72,000	
		Cash			72,000
		Cash purchase of equipment.			
	4	Supplies Inventories		6,000	
		Accounts Payable			6,000
		Supplies purchased from General Chemical Corporation on account.			
	5	Cash		60,000	
		Services to Be Rendered			60,000
		Advance payment by Delta Aircraft Company for contract signed.			
	8	Accounts Payable		6,000	
		Cash			6,000
		Paid General Chemical Corporation in full.			
	10	Prepaid Insurance		300	
		Cash			300
		Purchased one-year fire insurance policy.			

designed to record specific types of transactions. Common special journals include the cash receipts journal, the cash disbursements journal, the payroll journal, and the sales journal.

Each organization has a *chart of accounts,* which is a list of all account titles maintained in the accounting system. In journalizing an event, the accountant must choose accounts from this list. An analyst establishes this list at the time the accounting information systems are created. Illustration 1–3 contains a sample chart of accounts.

ILLUSTRATION 1–3

A Chart of Accounts

Account Title	Account Number
Current assets:	
Cash	110
Accounts Receivable	130
Research Fees Receivable	140
Supplies Inventories	160
Prepaid Insurance	180
Property, plant, and equipment:	
Land	210
Building	220
Accumulated Depreciation—Building	230
Equipment	240
Accumulated Depreciation—Equipment	250
Current liabilities:	
Accounts Payable	310
Income Taxes Payable	330
Wages and Salaries Payable	340
Interest Payable	350
Cash Dividends Payable	360
Services to Be Rendered	380
Long-term debt:	
Notes Payable	410
Stockholders' equity:	
Capital Stock	510
Retained Earnings	550
Revenue and Expense Summary	590
Revenue:	
Revenue from Services	610
Expenses:	
Salaries Expense	710
Supplies Expense	720
Depreciation Expense—Equipment	730
Depreciation Expense—Building	810
Insurance Expense	820
Other Administrative Expenses	890
Interest Expense	910
Federal Income Taxes	950

ILLUSTRATION 1–4

The Ledger Page for an Account

				Account Title			Account Number
Date	Description	Ref.	Debit	Date	Description	Ref.	Credit

Post. In *posting,* the second step, an accounting information system transfers journal entries to ledgers. A ledger is a summary, by account, of all transactions affecting that account. Thus, after posting, transactions are recorded by account rather than in chronological sequence. This step makes it possible to summarize the effects of all the events affecting the organization. Illustration 1–4 shows a page from a manual system's ledger.

Most organizations also use subsidiary ledgers, which contain detailed information explaining the general ledger's control account total. Common subsidiary ledgers include the accounts payable subsidiary ledger, the property ledger, and the stockholders' ledger.

Illustration 1–5 shows the results of posting to general ledger accounts the transactions journalized in Illustration 1–2.

Modern organizations produce many kinds of events that result in several different types of transactions. Computer-based systems devote extensive resources to journal-

ILLUSTRATION 1–5

Accounts after Posting

Cash				110
Sept.	1 (1)	100,000	Sept. 2 (1)	15,000
	5 (1)	60,000	3 (1)	72,000
			8 (1)	6,000
			10 (1)	300

Supplies Inventories		160
Sept. 4 (1)	6,000	

Prepaid Insurance		180
Sept. 10 (1)	300	

Land		210
Sept. 2 (1)	20,000	

Building		220
Sept. 2 (1)	60,000	

Equipment		240
Sept. 3 (1)	72,000	

Accounts Payable			310
Sept. 8 (1)	6,000	Sept. 4 (1)	6,000

Services to Be Rendered		380
	Sept. 5 (1)	60,000

Notes Payable		410
	Sept. 1 (1)	65,000

Capital Stock		510
	Sept. 1 (1)	100,000

izing and posting these transactions. Accounting information systems that concern the journalizing and posting steps constitute the *transaction processing systems*. You will learn how several transaction processing systems work later.

Prepare a Trial Balance.   This is step three in the accounting cycle. During any accounting period, accounting information systems journalize and post a large number of transactions. Prior to producing accounting reports, the system summarizes the effect of all the events in a ***trial balance***. Illustration 1–6 shows a sample trial balance.

Prepare Adjusting Entries.   The fourth step in the accounting cycle is the preparation of ***adjusting entries***. Sometimes accountants make these journal entries at the end of a reporting period to match the expenses of the period with the revenues generated by them. Other adjusting entries correct previous errors in journalizing transactions. An accountant or bookkeeper prepares adjusting entries, records them in the journal, and posts them to the ledger. These alter the account balances shown in the trial balance.

ILLUSTRATION 1–6

A Trial Balance

ALPHA RESEARCH CORPORATION
Trial Balance
September 30, 1998

Account Number	Account Title	Debit	Credit
110	Cash	$ 62,700	
130	Accounts receivable	1,200	
140	Research fees receivable	4,000	
160	Supplies inventories	5,100	
180	Prepaid insurance	275	
210	Land	20,000	
220	Building	60,000	
230	Accumulated depreciation—building		$ 500
240	Equipment	72,000	
250	Accumulated depreciation—equipment		1,200
340	Wages and salaries payable		600
350	Interest payable		314
380	Services to be rendered		55,000
410	Notes payable		65,000
510	Capital stock		100,000
610	Revenue from services		12,200
710	Wages and salaries expense	6,600	
720	Supplies expense	900	
730	Depreciation expense—equipment	1,200	
810	Depreciation expense—building	500	
820	Insurance expense	25	
910	Interest expense	314	
		$234,814	$234,814

ILLUSTRATION 1–7

An Income Statement

ALPHA RESEARCH CORPORATION
Income Statement
For Month Ended September 30, 1998

Revenue from services		$12,200
Expenses:		
Wages and salaries expense	$6,600	
Supplies expense	900	
Depreciation expense—equipment	1,200	
Depreciation expense—building	500	
Insurance expense	25	
Interest expense	314	
Total expenses		9,539
Net income		$ 2,661

Prepare Accounting Reports.   The fifth step in the accounting cycle is preparing the accounting reports. This task is easier if the system first prepares a second trial balance. Because its debit and credit totals reflect the adjustments made in step four, accountants call it the adjusted trial balance. From the adjusted trial balance, accountants prepare the reports.

Illustrations 1–7 and 1–8 show two reports—the income statement and the balance sheet—that, according to generally accepted accounting principles, must be produced by a financial accounting information system. Managerial accounting information systems, which are broader in scope, produce additional reports. The next chapter describes some of these.

Close the Books.   After preparing the accounting reports, accountants prepare the accounting records for the next reporting period. This includes the posting of closing and reversing journal entries.

Closing entries transfer balances from revenue and expense accounts into the Income Summary account. The balance in this account, which equals Net Income, is then transferred to the Retained Earnings account, leaving zero balances in these accounts in preparation for the next period.

Accountants also post reversing entries, so called because they are the reverse of the accrual and deferral adjusting journal entries made earlier. These reversing entries reset the balances in accrual and deferral accounts at zero and ensure that expenses and revenues of the prior period are not included in those of the following period.

Illustration 1–9 summarizes the six steps performed by a financial accounting information system when executing the accounting cycle.

Technology and Accounting Information Systems

The discussion so far has reviewed the accounting process in nontechnological terms. In older accounting systems, journals and ledgers are bound volumes in which bookkeepers manually record journal and adjusting entries. An accountant then manually prepares trial balances and reports using a large worksheet.

ILLUSTRATION 1–8

A Balance Sheet

ALPHA RESEARCH CORPORATION
Balance Sheet
As of September 30, 1998

Assets

Current assets:			
Cash			$ 62,700
Accounts receivable			1,200
Research fees receivable			4,000
Supplies inventories			5,100
Prepaid insurance			275
Total current assets			73,275
Property, plant, and equipment:			
Land		$ 20,000	
Building	$60,000		
Less: Accumulated depreciation	500	59,500	
Equipment	72,000		
Less: Accumulated depreciation	1,200	70,800	
			150,300
Total assets			$223,575

Liabilities and Stockholders' Equity

Current liabilities:			
Notes payable (portion due within year)			$10,000
Wages and salaries payable			600
Interest payable			314
Services to be rendered			55,000
Total current liabilities			65,914
Long-term debt:			
Notes payable (portion due after one year:			
secured by land and building)			55,000
Stockholders' equity:			
Capital stock, par $100, 1,000 shares outstanding		$100,000	
Retained earnings		2,661	
			102,661
Total liabilities and stockholders' equity			$223,575

In modern systems, journals and ledgers take the form of computer records. Computer programs post entries and prepare the accounting reports. Accountants control this process by providing inputs and by determining how these programs work.

Conceptually, the accounting process is identical regardless of the technology employed, which is why introductory accounting courses concentrate on journals and ledgers. This is actually a *technology-independent* view of the accounting process. It provides a model for how accounting data are processed in modern systems. For the rest of your career, you will encounter rapidly changing technologies for processing information. You will understand more easily how these new technologies work if you can relate them to this model.

ILLUSTRATION 1–9

Steps in the Accounting Cycle

1. **Journalize.** Identify the economic event and record it chronologically as an accounting transaction.
2. **Post.** Transfer transaction totals from the chronological record to summaries maintained by account.
3. **Trial Balance.** Prepare periodically a list of accounts and the balances in them.
4. **Adjusting Entries.** Make journal entries to recognize accruals, record deferrals, or correct errors.
5. **Reports.** Prepare accounting reports from the adjusted trial balance.
6. **Close.** Prepare the accounting records for the next reporting period.

As computers have been adapted for accounting, a terminology has evolved that is specific to computerized processing. These terms, introduced in Illustration 1–10, are a *technology-dependent* way of describing the concepts reviewed in this chapter. The study of accounting information systems will be easier if these terms are learned now.

Why Study Accounting Information Systems?

In the past few decades the study of accounting information systems has become important for all accountants. Prior to computerized processing, accounting systems used manual technologies that were much easier to understand. Microcomputers, however, have made computers practical for even the smallest organizations. Because almost every organization today uses computers to process accounting data, it is necessary to understand not only the conceptual process but also the technologies used in the process.

Accountants will work with computerized accounting systems in one of three ways: Auditors must know how to review computer-based systems and to plan and execute audit procedures using them. A management accountant will work daily with computerized systems and participate in project teams that develop new ones. Many accounting students also become management consultants or systems analysts. These accountants

ILLUSTRATION 1–10

The Accounting Process Using Computer Technology

The Accounting Concept	When Implemented on a Computer Is Called
Journals	**Transaction Files**
General	Journal voucher file
Special	Cash receipts file
	Voucher file
Ledgers	**Master Files**
General	General ledger master file
Subsidiary	Inventory master file
	Property master file
Journalizing	**Data Entry**
Posting	**File Update**

work full-time developing new accounting systems. Regardless of your career path, you must understand both the process and the technology. This text makes it easy to achieve this understanding.

Summary

The study of accounting information systems concerns events affecting an organization. These events are recognized and recorded by a system of human and computer resources, processed using accounting methods and objectives, and reported as information to interested parties. Most organizations use computer-based accounting information systems, which rely on both manual and computerized processing.

Financial accounting systems are accounting information systems of limited scope. These systems must conform to generally accepted accounting principles for external reporting and must implement the six steps in the accounting cycle. Financial accounting systems that journalize and post transactions are the transaction processing systems. More broadly defined, accounting information systems also produce reports for internal management purposes.

The accounting cycle, as described in this chapter, is a technology-independent process. The purpose of the study of accounting information systems is to learn how these accounting processes work using computer technology.

Key Terms

adjusting entries   Accounting entries made at the end of a financial reporting period to record accruals and deferrals and to correct previous errors.

computer-based system   An accounting system that uses both human and computer resources when processing transactions.

computer system   An accounting system that uses only computer resources when processing transactions.

financial accounting information system   An accounting system that records, processes, and reports past transactions in accordance with generally accepted accounting principles.

journalizing   The process of initially recording a transaction.

management information system   The combination of people, procedures, and machines intended to provide information for management decision making.

managerial accounting information system   An accounting system that records, processes, and reports financial information for internal use in accordance with the preferences of management.

manual system   An accounting system that uses only human resources when processing transactions.

posting   The process of transferring information recorded in a journal to a ledger.

transaction   The monetary record of an economic event affecting an organization.

trial balance   A summary of all the accounts in a general ledger and the balances in those accounts.

Questions

1–1. How does a transaction differ from an event?

1–2. How does a budgetary accounting information system differ from a historical accounting information system?

1–3. Why is it important to understand both the process and the technology associated with accounting information systems?

1–4. The journal is sometimes known as a book of original entry. Suggest a reason for the journal's being so known.

1–5. A company paid $3,000 to an attorney retained to render legal services to the company. Under which conditions would each of the following analyses be appropriate?

a. Legal Expenses	3,000	
Cash		3,000
b. Prepaid Legal Fees	3,000	
Cash		3,000
c. Accounts Payable	3,000	
Cash		3,000
d. Legal Fees Payable	3,000	
Cash		3,000

1–6. What is the balance of the following T-account?

4,000	2,000
240	330
1,200	150
700	

Is it more likely to be an asset account or a liability account? Which entry is likely to be the first one made?

1–7. What is the balance of the following T-account?

500	400
1,500	500
400	350
	1,500

Is it more likely to be an asset account or a liability account? Can you deduce the order in which these entries were made?

1–8. A sales representative suggests that a copy of the company's annual report be sent to a customer intending to place a large order.
   a. What information is generally contained in an annual report of a manufacturing company?
   b. What advantages and disadvantages would a company have in allowing its prospective customers to have copies of its annual reports?

1–9. In which order are assets normally listed in the balance sheet of a manufacturing or merchandising company? Why?

1–10. What accounting information might be needed by the following?
  a. A newspaper boy who maintains a stand at the corner of Broadway and Main Street, two busy streets in the downtown area.
  b. A newspaper girl who has a daily route in her neighborhood.
  c. A regional distributor of magazines.

1–11. Would accounting reports become more important when business enterprises are managed by professional management groups?

1–12. What is the purpose of preparing adjusting entries? How often must they be prepared? Could they be made on a daily basis? Under which circumstances would it be desirable to prepare them on a daily basis?

1–13. What are the differences between a manual system, a computer system, and a computer-based system?

1–14. Distinguish between the scope and the objectives of the following accounting information systems:
  a. Financial accounting information system.
  b. Managerial accounting information system.
  c. Budgetary system.
  d. Inventory system.

Exercises and Cases

1–15. TRANSACTIONS AND EVENTS

Sun Belt Market Research, Inc., was incorporated in May 1998. Selected transactions for the month of May are as follows:

1998		
May	4	Entered a contract to survey consumer reaction to Pour-Ease Flour for the Lone Star Milling Company. An advance payment of $100,000 was made by the company.
	5	Entered a contract to design a paper tissue box for the Big D Paper Products Corporation.
	15	Completed a research project on consumers' reaction to stainless steel razor blades for the Ever-Clean Corporation. A report was submitted. Cash payment of $20,000 was received for services rendered.
	15	Paid Computer Applications Associates $1,000 for computer time used to analyze data for the report submitted to the Ever-Clean Corporation.
	25	Made a formal presentation of the paper tissue box design to the management of the Big D Paper Products Corporation. The design was accepted. An invoice in the amount of $8,000 was submitted for services rendered.
	31	Paid salaries for the month, $18,000.
	31	Received a bill from the telephone company for telephone and telecommunication services for the month, $1,200.
	31	Received payment of $8,000 from the Big D Paper Products Corporation.

Required:

For each of the preceding events,

a. Determine if the event should be recorded as an accounting transaction. If so, identify the journal to be used and show the accounting entry.
b. Determine if the transaction should be posted to a subsidiary ledger. If so, identify the ledger.

1–16.   TRANSACTIONS AND EVENTS

Citywide Blueprint Service Company was organized in June 1998. Selected transactions for the month of June are as follows:

1998		
June	1	Leased a Blueprint-O-Matic from the BOM Corporation. The agreement called for a basic monthly charge of $50 plus 20 cents for each page of blueprint reproduced.
	4	Entered a contract to provide blueprint services for the Irving Engineers at a flat fee of $150 per month. The fee for the month of June was collected on signing the contract.
	15	Deposited cash of $500 for blueprint services rendered to various customers during the first two weeks of June.
	22	Completed a special reproduction assignment for the Oxford Engineering Consultants. The work was delivered. An invoice for $600 was submitted.
	30	Paid salaries for the month, $1,000.
	30	Reported to the BOM Corporation that 1,500 blueprint reproductions were made during the month.
	30	Received payment of $600 from Oxford Engineering Consultants.
	30	Received an invoice from Cornerstone Service Station for gasoline and oil used in the delivery truck for the month of June. The amount was $200.
	30	Deposited cash of $545 for blueprint services rendered to various customers during the second half of June.

Required:

For each of the preceding events,

a. Determine if the event should be recorded as an accounting transaction. If so, identify the journal to be used and show the accounting entry.
b. Determine if the transaction should be posted to a subsidiary ledger. If so, identify the ledger.

1–17.   ACCOUNTING REPORTS

The trial balance of the School for the Nineties, Inc., listing their accounts in alphabetical order, follows. The school was organized on September 1, 1998.

SCHOOL FOR THE NINETIES, INC.
Trial Balance
September 30, 1998

Accounts payable	$	100
Accumulated depreciation—classroom equipment		50
Accumulated depreciation—laboratory equipment		200

Capital stock		10,000
Cash	$15,080	
Classroom equipment	6,000	
Depreciation on classroom equipment	50	
Depreciation on laboratory equipment	200	
Instructional supplies expense	50	
Insurance expense	30	
Interest expense	70	
Laboratory equipment	12,000	
Notes payable		10,000
Prepaid insurance	270	
Prepaid rent	1,200	
Rent expense	400	
Salaries expense	2,800	
Tuition collected in advance		14,000
Tuition earned		4,000
Utilities expense	200	
	$38,350	$38,350

Required:

Close the books and prepare the following reports:

a. An income statement for the month ended September 30, 1998.
b. A balance sheet as of September 30, 1998.

1–18. *ACCOUNTING REPORTS*

The Columbus Pioneers Football Club, Inc., was organized on July 1, 1998, after receiving a franchise from the Transcontinental Professional Football League. The account balances as of September 30, 1998, follow in alphabetical order:

Accounts payable.	$ 10,000
Accumulated depreciation—automobiles	3,000
Administrative expenses	4,000
Advance ticket sales.	120,000
Advertising expense.	30,000
Automobiles.	40,000
Capital stock.	600,000
Cash and marketable securities	609,000
Depreciation on automobiles	3,000
Footballs and other supplies on hand.	50,000
Footballs and other playing field expense	10,000
Insurance expense	3,000
Players' per diem expenses on away games	5,000
Prepaid insurance.	9,000
Prepaid rent	40,000
Rent expense	20,000
Revenue from away games	60,000
Revenue from exhibition games	50,000
Revenue from home games	500,000
Salaries expense—office staff	80,000
Salaries expense—professional staff.	300,000

Ticket printing expense	15,000
Travel expense	75,000
Visiting teams' share of gate receipts.	50,000

Required:

Close the books and prepare the following reports:

a. An income statement for the month ended September 30, 1998.

b. A balance sheet as of September 30, 1998.

1–19.   ADJUSTING ENTRIES

The trial balances related to Data Teleprocessing Service as of October 30, 1998, follow. The trial balance on the left was prepared before incorporating the effects of adjusting entries for the month of October. The effects of these adjusting entries were included in the trial balance on the right.

DATA TELEPROCESSING SERVICE
Trial Balance
October 30, 1998

	Before Adjustments		*After Adjustments*	
Cash	$ 50,000		$ 50,000	
Accounts receivable	4,000		4,000	
Notes receivable	1,000		1,000	
Allowance for doubtful accounts	—			$ 190
Office supplies on hand	6,000		4,000	
Land	15,000		15,000	
Building	60,000		60,000	
Accumulated depreciation—building	—			250
Computer	180,000		180,000	
Accumulated depreciation—computer	—			3,000
Accounts payable		$ 85,000		85,000
Service fees received in advance		22,000		19,000
Taxes payable		—		5,000
Interest payable		—		218
Notes payable		45,000		45,000
Capital stock		30,000		30,000
Additional paid-in capital		80,000		80,000
Retained earnings		40,000		40,000
Revenue from programming consultation		5,000		6,000
Revenue from computer time rental		30,000		32,000
Salaries expense	15,000		15,000	
Maintenance expense	2,000		2,000	
Telephone and telecommunication expense	1,500		1,500	
Depreciation on computer	—		3,000	
Office supplies expense	—		2,000	
General expense	2,500		2,500	
Depreciation on building	—		250	
Bad debts expense	—		190	
Interest expense	—		218	
Tax expense	—		5,000	
	$337,000	$337,000	$345,658	$345,658

Required:

Prepare adjusting entries as reflected in the changes between the two trial balances.

1–20.   ADJUSTING ENTRIES

The trial balance of the Trans-World Storage and Moving Company as of March 31, 1998, is as follows:

TRANS-WORLD STORAGE AND MOVING COMPANY
Trial Balance
March 31, 1998

Cash	$11,700	
Prepaid rent	10,000	
Trucks	60,000	
Accumulated depreciation—trucks		$ 2,500
Accounts payable		1,200
Storage fees collected in advance		3,000
Capital stock		70,000
Retained earnings		3,000
Revenue from moving services		11,000
Revenue from storage services		1,000
Salaries expense	7,000	
Gasoline expense	1,000	
Maintenance expense	500	
Utilities and office expense	1,500	
	$91,700	$91,700

Data and information related to adjusting entries for the month ended March 31, 1998, are as follows:

1. The monthly rent was $1,000.
2. The estimated useful life of trucks was four years.
3. Many clients chose to pay several months' storage fees in advance. Based on individual service records, storage fees earned for the month amounted to $600.
4. Storage fees for some other clients were due on days other than the first of each month. Based on individual service records, storage fees earned from these clients for the month amounted to $1,500.

Required:

a. Prepare adjusting entries for the month ended March 31, 1998.
b. Deduce the date on which trucks were purchased.

1–21.   JOURNAL ENTRIES AND ADJUSTING ENTRIES

The Metropolitan Summer Light Opera Festival was organized to stage four musical shows during the summer of 1998. Each show was to last three weeks, and a three-week accounting period was adopted. Selected transactions during the first weeks of the festival are as follows:

1998		
June	1	Paid rent for 12 weeks, beginning June 9. The weekly rent was $1,000.
	2	Placed an advertisement in newspapers announcing the dates and programs of the festival. The expense was $200; cash was paid.
	3	Granted Theater Concessions, Inc., the privilege of selling refreshments during the 12-week festival in return for 5 percent of gross receipts payable within three days after the conclusion of each three-week period.
	4	Purchased liability insurance for the 12-week period at a total cost of $600. Payment was to be made when policy was received.
	5	Four "Program Notes," one for each show, were printed at a total cost of $400. Cash was paid.
	7	Season tickets to the festival, totaling $60,000, were sold. The season tickets permitted holders to attend each of the four shows on specified dates.
	9	The first musical show, "The East Side Story," had its premiere. Cash sale of tickets to the performance amounted to $1,400.
	28	The first musical show closed with this performance. Received a report from Theater Concessions, Inc., that total refreshment sales for the three-week period amounted to $20,000.

Required:

For each of the preceding events,

a. Determine if the event should be recorded as an accounting transaction. If so, identify the journal to be used and show the accounting entry.

b. Determine if the transaction should be posted to a subsidiary ledger. If so, identify the ledger.

c. Prepare the proper adjusting journal entry for June 28.

1–22. THE ACCOUNTING PROCESS

The following events relate to KQST-TV, a television broadcasting station:

1998		
July	1	KQST-TV, Incorporated, was organized with the issuance of capital stock for cash, $500,000.
	2	Received a franchise to operate a television broadcasting station from the Federal Communications Commission. The franchise was valid for three years. The cost of acquiring the franchise, mainly attorney's fees, amounted to $3,600. Cash was paid.
	3	Purchased land, valued at $40,000, and office building, valued at $240,000. Cash was paid.
	7	Purchased transmitting and broadcasting equipment at a total cost of $90,000. Cash was paid.
	8	Signed the Adams, Jackson, and Smith Company as the station's national advertising representative. Commission rate was set at 10 percent of revenue generated.
	9	Received a three-year insurance policy, effective July 1. Total premium was $2,400. Cash was paid.
	10	Signed with the Inter-American Broadcasting Company as a member of its network. Cost of such participation was to be determined at the end of each month.
	11	Signed various sponsors of television programs. Advance payments by some sponsors amounted to $100,000. All sponsors were referred by the Adams, Jackson, and Smith Company.
	15	Sold 100 spot announcements at $100 each to the Metropolitan Arrowjet Company to advertise the new Arrowjet food processors. Settlement was to be made at the end of each

month. This account was secured by the station's own marketing staff and did not involve the Adams, Jackson, and Smith Company.

16   The station began broadcasting.

31   Paid salaries for the month, $50,000.

31   Received an invoice from the Inter-American Broadcasting Company for program participation for the month of July. The amount was $10,000. Payment was to be made before August 10.

The following data are relevant to adjusting entries for the month ending July 31:

1. The life of the office and broadcasting building was estimated at 10 years.
2. The life of the transmitting and broadcasting equipment was estimated at three years.
3. Of the $100,000 advance payments, services amounting to $80,000 had been rendered.
4. Services amounting to $40,000 had been rendered for those sponsors who signed but did not make advance payments.
5. Eighty spot announcements were made for the Metropolitan Arrowjet Company.
6. Taxes expense was estimated at 50 percent of income before taxes.

Required:

a. Prepare journal entries for the month.
b. Post to accounts.
c. Take a trial balance.
d. Prepare and post adjusting entries for the month.
e. Take an adjusted trial balance.
f. Close the books and prepare an income statement for the month.
g. Prepare a balance sheet as of July 31.

1–23.   BALANCE SHEET

On March 1, 1998, Balboa Bay Cruise, Inc., was organized with the issuance of capital stock to stockholders for cash of $30,000. The company then acquired the assets of the Lido Isle Boating Company for $45,000. The assets consisted of an inland vessel valued at $40,000, a franchise to operate a cruise business valued at $4,000, and office equipment valued at $1,000. In payment for these assets, Balboa Bay Cruise paid cash in the amount of $20,000 and issued a noninterest-bearing note for $25,000. The note was to be paid in five annual installments of $5,000 each. The vessel was put into service on March 18, 1998, Palm Sunday, the opening of the tourist season.

The season closed on September 3, 1998, Labor Day. Extremely busy during the season, management did not maintain formal records. All cash received during the day was deposited with the bank the following business day; all bills were paid by check immediately on receipt.

From memorandum notes written on check stubs, it was determined that improvements costing $5,000 were made on the vessel; full payment was made in cash on the completion of each improvement. A portable ticket stand was acquired for $1,000 cash. Two motor boats were also purchased at a total cost of $20,000; settlement was made with $10,000 in cash and $10,000 in a note due one year hence on May 1.

On September 15, after the payment of all bills, the bank balance was $16,000.

Before proceeding further, management decided to prepare a balance sheet as of September 15, 1998, based on the previous information.

Required:

a. What was the status of assets and liabilities as of March 1, 1998, after the transaction with the Lido Isle Boating Company was begun?

b. What was the status of assets and liabilities as of September 15?

c. What reservation(s), if any, do you have with respect to amounts carried in the balance sheet as of September 15?

1–24. A COMPUTER-BASED SYSTEM

General Mills, a multidivision food products company based in Minneapolis, has experienced the benefits a large company can derive from using personal computers in its financial reporting process.[1] The company appointed a team from its financial reporting and information services departments to design an automated year-end accounting package. Its objectives were to speed up the consolidation process, increase accuracy, reduce the need for overtime, and make the year-end effort less burdensome.

The Manual System

Historically, collecting and consolidating annual financial results for year-end reports had been a time-consuming manual process. The financial reporting department had to collect the results of approximately 110 separate reporting entities. Then they spent a significant amount of time manually verifying the results. They reviewed and refooted each consolidation schedule to confirm that the amounts were recorded correctly. These reviews had to be accomplished during a one-week time frame and took nine people to complete, including outside help and substantial overtime. The consolidation process itself had to be completed during the same week. With help from an outside department, it required 12 people.

The Computer-Based System

The design team decided to implement the new system on personal computers (PCs) using a spreadsheet package that was common in the company. They developed a menu-driven system in which accountants entered the annual information from divisions and subsidiaries into financial schedules. After verifying the data for consistency, a consolidation software package combined it into a single database. This contained the information used to develop most of the financial schedules and footnotes included in the annual report and SEC Form 10-K.

The main system disk includes a worksheet file containing menus and macro instructions that drive the system. The main menu consists of the following options:

---

[1]Adapted from Earl E. Robertson and Dean Lockwood, "Tapping the Power of the PC at General Mills," *Management Accounting*, August 1994, p. 46. Copyright by Institute of Management Accountants (1994), Montvale, N.J. 07645. Used by permission.

Header Entry (to enter the organization's identification), Table of Contents (to show schedule names), Data Entry, Validation (to correct obvious errors), Print, and Quit. Each main menu selection also contains several submenu selections.

The system accommodates 83 schedules including a balance sheet and a profit and loss statement. Most of the schedules compare totals to the financial statements as a way of verifying the results.

With the new system, the department starts the financial statement section of the annual report several months before year-end. Shortly after the annual meeting of share-holders, they alter the previous year's annual report in preparation for the new year. Employees shift or drop columns of data as necessary, and update wording to conform to the new year-end. New statements issued by the Financial Accounting Standards Board are reviewed for applicability. If necessary, a draft of the necessary disclosure is put in place for use in the financial reports.

The Results

The new system allows easy changes to financial documents, provides for changes in the number of accounting entities and schedules, and provides input to the corporate tax department's automated tax return system. Consolidation occurs automatically and takes one minute to complete. The most time-consuming task is the one hour required to print the schedules. This consolidation system is just one example of how personal computers have changed General Mills' accounting processes and have saved the company both time and money.

Required:

a. What problems were the new computer-based accounting system intended to correct?
b. What are the similarities between the old and new systems? What are the differences?

2   Managerial Accounting Systems

Learning Objectives

1. To discover methods of providing top-down and bottom-up information flows.
2. To learn about the information systems that produce reports for internal use.
3. To understand how account codes are used to produce accounting reports.

Introduction

Chapter 1 described the scope of accounting information systems, including managerial and financial ones. It also introduced financial components, called *transaction processing systems*. This chapter describes the managerial accounting information systems that are used for responsibility accounting. These systems provide top-down and bottom-up information flows.

Information Flows

Accounting information systems recognize events, record them, summarize them, and report accounting information. This sequence of activities constitutes a *flow* of data and information. Those who receive this information are parties both internal and external to the organization. They use it for management or investment purposes.

In managerial accounting information systems, information flows in two directions. A *top-down flow* originates from events that occur at the top management level in an organization. Systems record these events, summarize them, and report them to employees at lower levels. Accounting information systems provide a *bottom-up flow* when events occur at the lower levels. These are recorded, summarized, and reported to top management. The budgeting and responsibility reporting systems provide these flows.

Top-Down Information Flow

An organization's budgeting system provides a top-down information flow. This accounting information system produces periodic budgets, which provide managers with quantitative statements of the organization's plans covering the next budgetary period. By establishing and coordinating measurable goals for the organization's segments, budgets help achieve overall organizational objectives.

An effective budgeting system is designed to work within the organization's structure. It requires that top management develop policies concerning the organization's objectives, communicate these policies with policy statements, and set performance goals for the organization.

Organization Structure.   An organization's structure provides the environment through which information flows. For the budgeting system to function properly, this environment must have several characteristics: (1) the organization must establish a structure that distinguishes each of its segments; (2) it must issue a clear statement of authority and responsibility for the manager of each segment; (3) each employee should report to only one higher-level manager; and (4) top management should clearly define all superior–subordinate relationships among employees. Most corporations adopt a structure that has these characteristics.

Top management communicates the organization's structure by using organization charts and job descriptions. Organization charts identify segments and communicate superior–subordinate relationships. Job descriptions assign responsibility to employees for specific tasks. Illustration 2–1 shows a typical organization chart for a manufacturing corporation.

Another form of top-down information flow is the policy statement used by top management to communicate their responsibilities to employees.

Policy Statements.   A company's ***policy statements*** identify top management's expectations concerning the behavior of the organization's employees. They provide guidelines for employees on how to carry out specific duties contained in job descriptions. To be effective, policy statements must be both comprehensive and enforceable.

One common policy statement is the code of conduct, a document that describes the ethical standards employees are expected to follow. For example, the code of conduct for one major national corporation establishes ethical policies in six areas:

1. Compliance with laws and regulations, including
   a. Antitrust and trade regulation.
   b. Election campaign laws.
   c. Securities regulations pertaining to the use of insider information and the trading of securities.
2. Relationships with government officials.
3. Proper recording of funds, assets, and disbursements.
4. Outside activities that represent a conflict of interest.
5. Subsidiaries and affiliate companies.
6. Reports and assurances.

In the code of conduct's introduction, this company's top management communicates both the purpose of the code and management's intent to enforce these policies. Illustration 2–2 presents this introduction to the code of conduct.

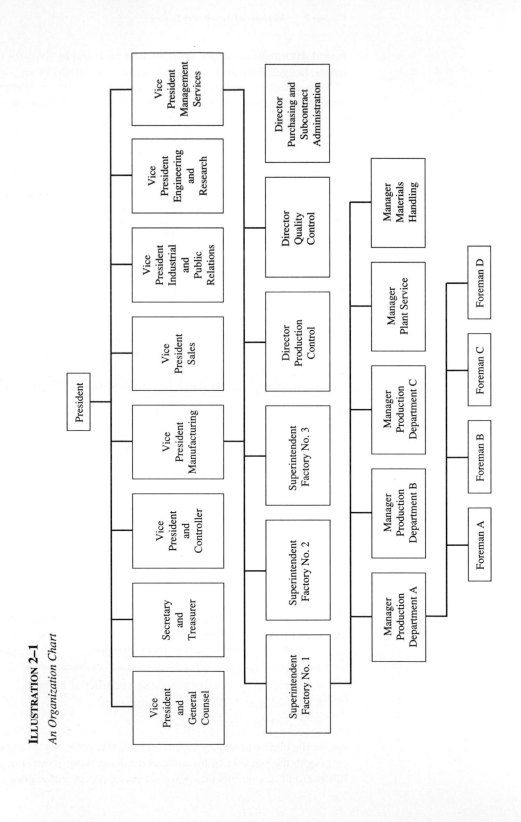

ILLUSTRATION 2–1
An Organization Chart

24

ILLUSTRATION 2–2

The Introductory Section of a Code of Conduct

1. INTRODUCTION AND EXPLANATION

The purpose of this Code is to state the principles of business ethics and conduct which the Board of Directors expects management and other employees to follow in dealings on behalf of the Company with government, the general public, customers, suppliers and fellow employees and to avoid personal activities which might conflict with the Company's interests. These principles relate to compliance with laws and regulations (with special emphasis, because of particular importance to our operations and their complexity which requires constant vigilance to insure compliance, on those relating to antitrust, political activities, relationship with government officials and securities regulation); proper recording of funds, assets and disbursements; conflicts of interest and outside activities; and use of inside information.

These principles are to be strictly adhered to at all times and under all circumstances. The Board of Directors will maintain continuing supervision of compliance with this Code to assure that the Company conducts itself in a manner consistent with its *obligations to society and its stockholders.* This will include the establishment of procedures whereby compliance may be monitored and key employees will periodically affirm in writing that they have adhered to these principles. Violations will result in disciplinary action including, in proper cases, discharge from employment.

Source: Phillips Petroleum Company, *Code of Business Ethics Conduct and Responsibility* (Bartlesville, Okla.: n.d.), p. 7. Used with permission.

Performance Goals.   An effective budgeting system requires that management establish performance goals for each segment of the organization. Top management then communicates these goals to managers of the segments by issuing periodic budgets. Such a system, called a ***performance budgeting system,*** coordinates segment performance goals so that, if each segment meets its goals, then overall organization objectives are met.

Organization Objectives and Departmental Goals.   Many corporations state their objectives using a measure such as residual income or return on invested capital. The performance budgeting system translates these objectives into goals that are meaningful at the subsidiary, division, and department levels. At the lower levels of the organization's structure, performance goals are stated in more detail and become more specific.

As an example, consider a corporation with an invested capital of $17 million. Assume that one of top management's overall company objectives is a return on invested capital of 11.8 percent. One way to achieve this performance goal is with sales of $30 million. Illustration 2–3 demonstrates how the budget system determines the expenses and working capital needed to achieve this objective. Illustration 2–4 shows how the budget system translates this company objective into performance goals at the vice presidential, regional, and local sales office levels.

Methods of Developing Departmental Goals.   When top management establishes departmental goals for lower-level managers, the performance budgeting system is an *authoritative* system. Accountants use this term because the system relies on the authority of top management to motivate employees to achieve the goals.

As an alternative, many companies allow managers at lower levels in the organization to participate in developing their own performance goals. When this occurs, the

ILLUSTRATION 2–3
Corporate Performance Objectives

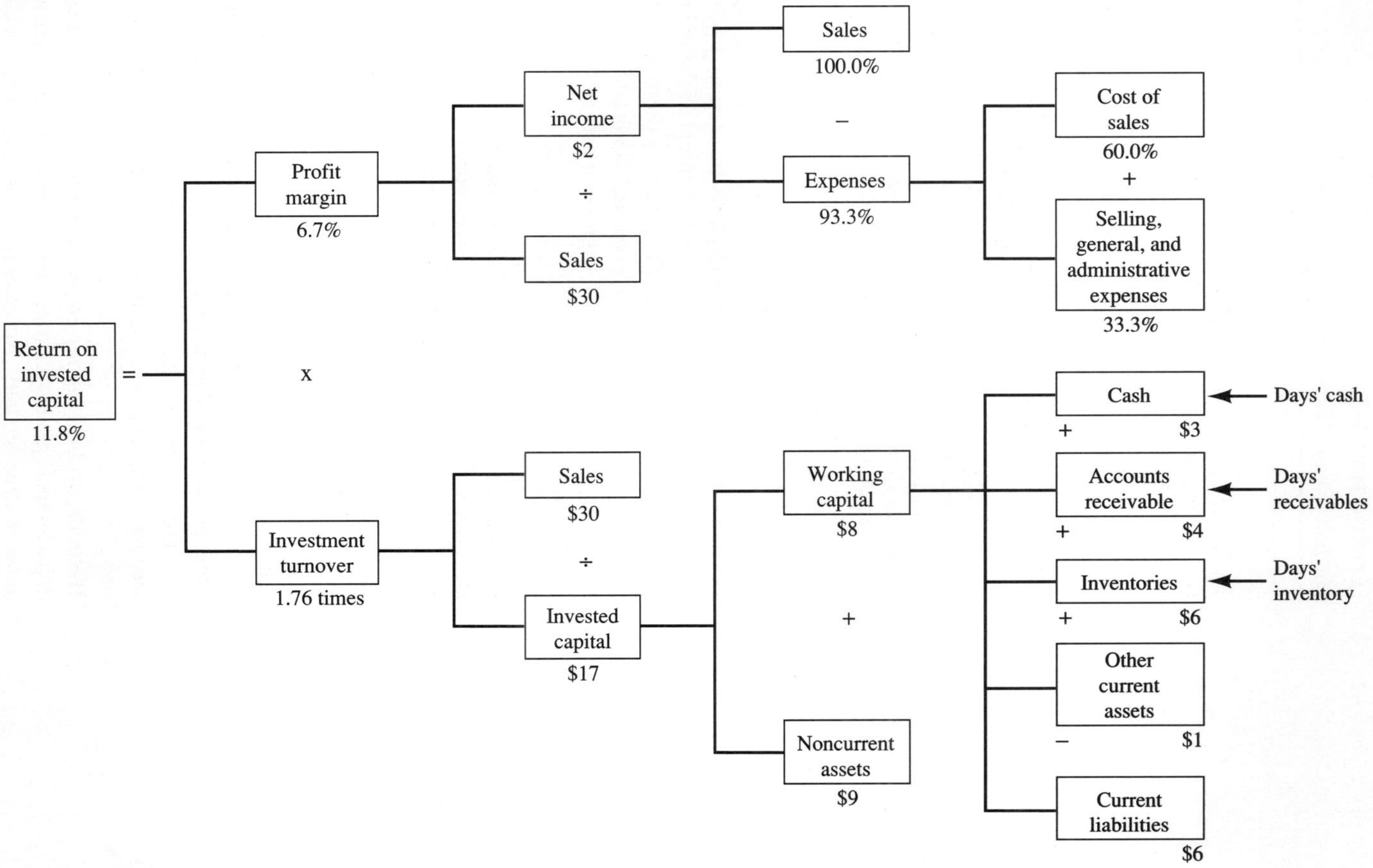

Note: Dollar amounts are in millions of dollars.

ILLUSTRATION 2–4

*Top-Down Flow of
Performance Goals*

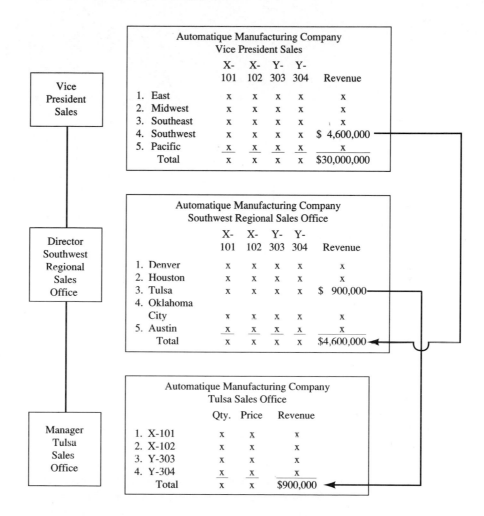

company uses a *participative* budgeting system. Many accountants believe that when individuals participate in developing their own goals, they are more motivated to achieve them. This means that they work harder and perform better. However, even when participative budgeting is used, lower-level performance goals are established to achieve desired overall company performance. Supervisors and subordinates negotiate these goals to satisfy the objectives of top management.

Organizational structure, policy statements, and performance goals begin at the top management level and are transmitted to lower levels in the company. They represent top-down flows in the communication of accounting information. As this information flows to successively lower levels, it becomes more specific and detailed. This process, called *information amplification*, is shown graphically in Illustration 2–5.

**Bottom-Up
Information Flow**

Bottom-up information flows originate with events occurring at the lower levels in the organization structure. The system that records these events, processes them, and reports them to managers at higher levels is the ***responsibility reporting system.*** Often

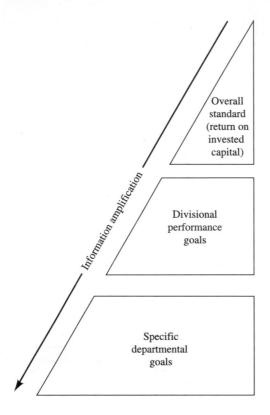

companies implement systems that provide for both responsibility reporting and performance budgeting. In this case, they have ***responsibility accounting systems.***

Responsibility reporting systems record performance measures at each segment in the organization. These performance measures may be monetary, such as dollars of revenue or expense, or they may be statistical, such as hours worked or units produced. In a responsibility accounting system, reports compare these performance measures with the performance goals established by the budgeting system. The organization then evaluates its managers by whether actual performance differed from budgeted goals.

Responsibility Centers.   Responsibility accounting systems accumulate performance measures and performance goals at the lowest level in the organizational hierarchy. Accountants refer to these organizational units as ***responsibility centers***.

In rare cases, a low-level responsibility center consists of only one person. More frequently, it is a department consisting of a supervisor and several employees. Assume, for example, that the plant service department in Illustration 2–1 consists of a supervisor and 10 service personnel. That supervisor and the 10 personnel together constitute a low-level responsibility center.

Responsibility centers also exist at each higher level in the organizational structure. A higher-level responsibility center consists of a manager and all the responsibility centers reporting to that manager. The organization assigns this manager authority and responsibility over all lower-level responsibility centers below the manager in the

---

AIS in Practice

Lockheed Martin Corporation is headquartered in Bethesda, Maryland, and employs more than 190,000 people. Its 200 operating companies implement defense, aerospace, and systems integration projects for U.S., state, and local governments and commercial organizations. A challenge for its finance department is to provide adequate budget information to managers all over the world. They need fast information, especially near budget deadlines.

A team of three accountants at corporate headquarters is implementing a new budgeting system that links all corporate operating departments and managers worldwide. It provides for electronic submission and review of financial plans during budget development and cost reporting. It allocates corporate overhead costs across operating companies and produces a variety of reports on costs incurred by project. Future plans include integrating general ledger data with other sales and profit data, providing a source of information for ad hoc analysis by managers of the company. Lockheed Martin believes that its managers can make more efficient use of capital if they can access more accurate cost information, earlier.

---

organization chart. In Illustration 2–1, the superintendent of factory no. 1 is in charge of a second-level responsibility center. Other higher-level responsibility centers include individual sales regions and the engineering and research division.

Cost, Profit, and Investment Centers.   For some responsibility centers, the only existing monetary performance measure is the amount of costs incurred at the center. For example, the manager of production department A controls the costs incurred in that department. Top management evaluates this manager's performance by comparing the actual costs incurred to those budgeted for that month. This department is a type of responsibility center called a *cost center*. Illustration 2 6, parts A and B, shows examples of higher-level cost centers.

Some responsibility centers, such as sales offices, regions, or divisions, generate revenue. In these cases, the responsibility accounting system determines the profit produced by the center by subtracting the costs incurred from the revenue generated. Accountants call such a responsibility center a *profit center*. Illustration 2–6, part C, contains an example. Top management evaluates the performance of a profit center manager by comparing actual profits with those budgeted during each budgetary period.

A responsibility center is known as an *investment center* when its manager not only controls the center's costs and revenues but also helps determine the amount of investment owners make in it. For example, large corporations decide each year how much profit should be reinvested in each subsidiary. If the manager of a subsidiary requests a portion of these retained earnings, then top management evaluates the subsidiary by how well it provides a return on them. At the president's level in the organization chart, the entire company is an investment center.

In designing a responsibility accounting system, an analyst assigns each manager to a responsibility center, each of which is either a cost center, a profit center, or an investment center. The analyst then develops procedures to produce, at the end of each budgeting period, a performance report for every responsibility center.

ILLUSTRATION 2–6

High-Level Responsibility Centers

A. A cost center at the factory level

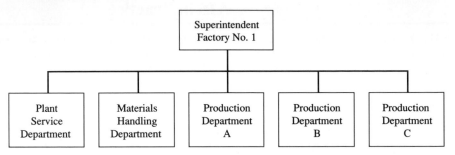

B. A cost center at the vice presidential level

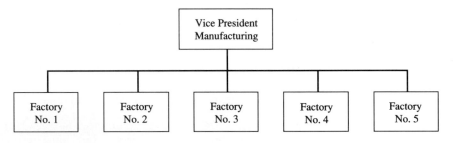

C. A profit center

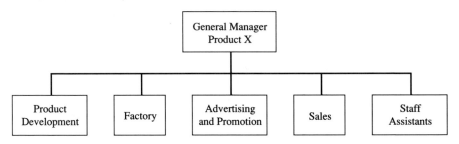

D. An investment center

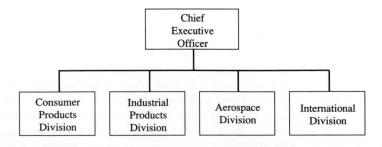

ILLUSTRATION 2–7

A Performance Report

AUTOMATIQUE MANUFACTURING COMPANY
Cost Report—Factory No. 1
Month of February 1998

	Actual Cost	Budget Allowance	Variance
1. Factory supervision	$ 500	$ 500	$ 0
2. Plant services	120	110	(10)
3. Materials handling	200	180	(20)
4. Production department A	2,400	2,500	100
5. Production department B	3,120	3,100	(20)
6. Production department C	1,500	1,250	(250)
7. Total cost incurred during the period	$7,840	$7,640	$ (200)
8. Unit cost	$ 7.84	$ 7.64	
9. Number of units	1,000		

Performance Reports.   All accounting information systems produce information; a responsibility accounting system communicates this information in ***performance reports.*** The information disclosed on a performance report depends on the performance measures controlled by the manager.

The manager of a cost center controls its costs; the performance report for that cost center discloses the budgeted and actual costs attained for the budgetary period. Frequently it also shows the difference between these amounts, called a *budget variance*. In managerial accounting courses you learn how to analyze this variance to explain its source. Illustration 2–7 contains a sample performance report for a cost center at the factory level.

Sometimes accountants develop budgets that analyze costs into fixed and variable categories. Because this allows the responsibility accounting system to produce *flexible* budgets, accountants call this variance a flexible budget variance. Flexible budgeting is useful for cost centers at the lowest level, where the output of the center is easily measured in nonmonetary terms. Illustration 2–8 shows a cost center performance report for production department B. It discloses budgeted amounts based on fixed and variable costs. This report produces better information for evaluating the manager than does one using a nonflexible, or *static* budget.

A performance report at higher-level cost centers summarizes the budgeted and actual costs of all the centers below it. This shows the costs controlled by the manager of the higher-level cost center. For example, in Illustration 2–7, performance of the superintendent of factory no. 1 is evaluated by the budget variance incurred in factory supervision, plant services, materials handling, and production departments A, B, and C. The total of these costs is shown on one line in the performance report of the cost center at the next higher level. In Illustration 2–9, the cost total for factory no. 1 is one line on the vice president for manufacturing's performance report.

ILLUSTRATION 2–8

A Performance Report with Nonvariable and Variable Budget Components

AUTOMATIQUE MANUFACTURING COMPANY
Cost Performance Report—Production Department B
Month of February 1998

	Budget Components		Budget Allowance This Month	Actual Performance This Month	Variance
	Nonvariable	*Variable*			
0. Equivalent units of production				1,000	
Controllable costs:					
1. Supplies and small tools	—	$0.015	$ 15	$ 60	$(45)
2. Power	—	0.200	200	190	10
3. Labor	$ 550	2.420	2,970	3,000	(30)
Total			$3,185	$3,250	$(65)
Uncontrollable costs:					
4. Depreciation, taxes, insurance	$1,750	—	$1,750	$1,750	0
Total processing cost incurred in the department (lines 1–4)	$2,300	$2,635	$4,935	$5,000	$(65)

Performance reports for profit and investment centers are similar. Totals at lower-level centers become line items at the next higher profit or investment center. However, for these responsibility centers, the responsibility accounting system discloses four totals: total budgeted revenues, total actual revenues, total budgeted costs, and total actual costs. These may be disclosed on up to four separate performance reports for each center (see Illustration 2–10).

Responsibility accounting systems produce performance reports at each responsibility center in the organization. At a high-level center, the reports summarize budgeted and actual costs and revenues for each center at the next lower level. At each successively higher level, the reports become less detailed, less specific, and more highly summarized. In this way, bottom-up information flow accompanies a process of *data reduction*. Illustration 2–11 shows this process graphically.

Data Accumulation

Responsibility accounting systems provide top-down and bottom-up information flows. The system produces a performance report for each responsibility center summarizing budgeted costs and revenues to provide top-down flow, and actual costs and revenues for bottom-up flow.

A system summarizes totals for budgeted costs, budgeted revenues, actual costs, and actual revenues, for each responsibility center and for each month of the year. A

ILLUSTRATION 2–9

*Responsibility Reporting
by Cost Centers*

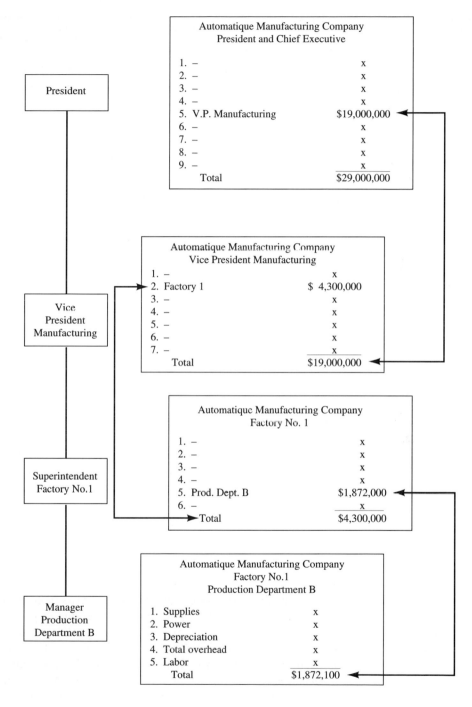

ILLUSTRATION 2–10

Responsibility Reporting by Profit Centers

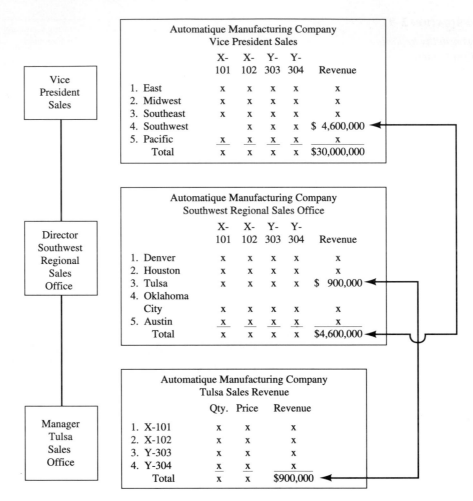

large company may have hundreds of responsibility centers, so the system produces a lot of totals. The system accumulates this much data by the processes of ***classification*** and ***coding.***

Classification and Coding

The system *classifies* transactions when it groups them by responsibility center and by account from the chart of accounts. For example, during a particular month, the system may classify $910 of labor expenditures as production department A's Wages and Salaries expense. In a manual system, an accounting clerk performs this classification function. In a computer-based one, either a person or a computer program may do it.

The system *codes* a transaction when it assigns to it a combination of characters that distinguishes the classifications to which it belongs. To continue the example, the accounting clerk who classifies the transaction may consult a chart of accounts and determine that wages and salaries transactions are coded with the number 710. The clerk enters that number and the amount into the computer, and the computer adds that amount to the total of wages and salaries in the general ledger.

ILLUSTRATION 2–11

Data Reduction

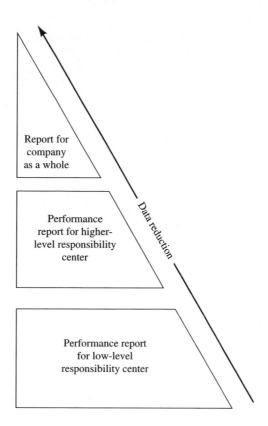

A responsibility accounting system classifies a transaction in two ways: first, according to the proper account in the chart of accounts, and second, according to the responsibility center. The system then codes the transaction using the proper account code for that account and the proper responsibility code for that responsibility center.[1]

Responsibility Codes.   A responsibility accounting system duplicates the chart of accounts for each responsibility center. When journalizing a transaction, the system debits or credits the appropriate financial statement account, such as Equipment, Raw Materials Purchases, or Salaries and Wages. However, it makes this entry in the account for the center that has control over the event generating the transaction. This is the center responsible for it. The system is able to maintain the large number of totals by assigning a unique code to each responsibility center.

When designing a responsibility accounting system, an analyst develops a coding scheme similar to that in Illustration 2–12. In this example, each responsibility center has a four-digit code. By examining this organization chart carefully, you can see a pattern in how these ***responsibility codes*** are assigned.

---

[1]For an extended description of coding methods, see the monograph *Classifying and Coding for Accounting Operations* by Germain Boer (Montvale, N.J.: National Association of Accountants [now the Institute of Management Accountants], 1987).

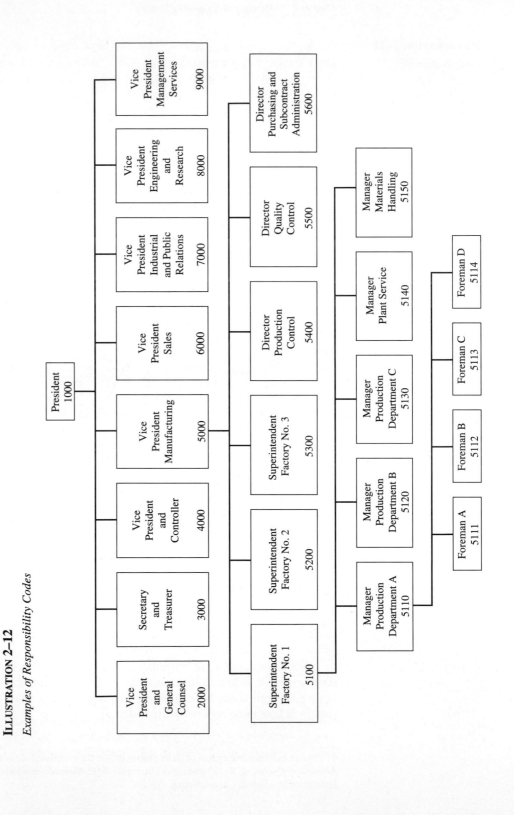

ILLUSTRATION 2–12
Examples of Responsibility Codes

At the vice presidential level, each code contains a nonzero digit followed by three zeros. At the factory level, each responsibility center has a code containing two nonzero digits and two zeros. The first of these nonzero digits comes from the code of the higher responsibility center. Thus, the superintendent of factory no. 1, who has a code of 5100, reports to the vice president of manufacturing (code 5000). Furthermore, the manager of production department B, with a code of 5120, reports to the superintendent of factory no. 1 (code 5100), and so on. Using this method, the responsibility center with the most zeros in its code is at the highest level in the organization structure.

Account Codes.   In a financial accounting system, each account in the chart of accounts has a unique *account code.* For example, each account in the chart in Illustration 1–3 contains a three-digit account code. The account code structure in a responsibility accounting system combines a responsibility code with an account code. This structure uniquely identifies each account in the chart of accounts for each responsibility center.

For example, assume that the financial statement account Wages and Salaries has an account code of 710. Using the responsibility codes of Illustration 2–12, wages paid to people working for foreman A of department B are debited to account 5111-710. The salaries paid to workers in the office of the manager of production in department A are charged to 5110-710. The salaries of any sales personnel working in the office of the vice president for sales are recorded in account 6000-710, and so on. This is how the responsibility accounting system maintains a separate chart of accounts for each responsibility center.

A chart of accounts is a table of account names and account codes. You could make a similar table containing a list of responsibility centers and responsibility codes. Combining these two tables creates another table that shows the coding structure in a responsibility accounting system (see Illustration 2–13).

In Illustration 2–13, each row contains all the account balances for one responsibility center. Each column represents one financial statement account and contains the balances in that account for all responsibility centers. (To simplify things, only two financial statement accounts are shown, and many responsibility centers are omitted.) The illustration shows that in production department B, foreman A controlled total Wages and Salaries expense of $1,850 and Supplies expense of $110. Wages and salaries of $910 were incurred in the office for production department A. In a similar way the responsibility accounting system records revenues under the revenue account codes for a profit center. It records asset purchases under the asset account codes for an investment center.

This chapter has demonstrated how responsibility accounting systems record actual costs and revenues by responsibility centers. Similar procedures are used to record performance goals in a budgeting system.

Budget Codes.   A budgeting system records performance goals for each financial statement account at each responsibility center by using *budget codes.*

When designing the system, an analyst adds one digit to the account code to distinguish between budgeted and actual amounts. For example, assume the digit 0 indicates actual amounts and the digit 9 signifies budgeted amounts. The actual Wages and

ILLUSTRATION 2–13

Account and Responsibility Code Structure

Responsibility Center		Account Codes				Total Cost by Responsibility Unit
Code	Description	Other Accounts	710 Wages and Salaries	720 Supplies Expense	Other Accounts	
1000	President	$x	$ x	$ x	$x	$ x
—	....	x	x	x	x	x
—	....	x	x	x	x	x
2000	Vice president counsel	x	x	x	x	x
—	....	x	x	x	x	x
—	....	x	x	x	x	x
3000	Secretary-treasurer	x	x	x	x	x
—	....	x	x	x	x	x
4000	Controller	x	x	x	x	x
5000	Vice president manufacturing	x	x	x	x	x
5100	Factory no. 1	x	x	x	x	x
5110	Production department A	x	910	x	x	x
5120	Production department B	x	x	x	x	x
5121	Foreman A	x	1,850	110	x	4,560
—	....	x	x	x	x	x
5200	Factory no. 2	x	x	x	x	x
—	....	x	x	x	x	x
6000	Vice president sales	x	x	x	x	x
—	....	x	x	x	x	x
—	....	x	x	x	x	x
7000	Vice president industrial relations	x	x	x	x	x
—	....	x	x	x	x	x
8000	Vice president engineering	x	x	x	x	x
—	....	x	x	x	x	x
9000	Vice president management services	x	x	x	x	x
—	....	x	x	x	x	x
—	....	x	x	x	x	x
—	Total cost by account	$x	$ x	$ x	$x	$ x

Salaries expense for production department A is recorded in account 5110-0-710. The budget account, with code 5110-9-710, contains the budgeted Wages and Salaries for this cost center.

ILLUSTRATION 2–14

Use of Budget Codes

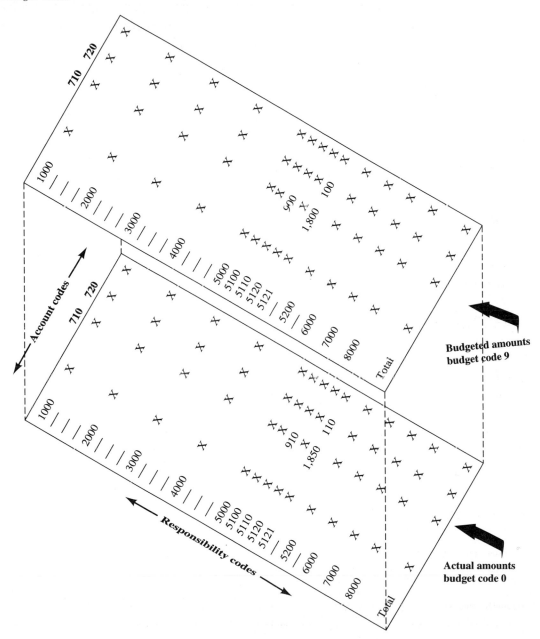

    Illustration 2–14 shows budgeted costs and revenues as another table identical in
structure to that used in recording actual transactions. Using the table, what are the budgeted Wages and Salaries expense for foreman A? What is the Wages and Salaries
expense variance?

Financial Reporting and Responsibility Accounting   The performance reports produced by a responsibility accounting system are useful for managerial purposes. However, their form and content are inadequate for financial accounting because they do not comply with the disclosure requirements of generally accepted accounting principles. An accounting information system must produce both financial statements and responsibility reports from the data accumulated by the system.

ILLUSTRATION 2–15

Converting from Performance Reports to Financial Statements

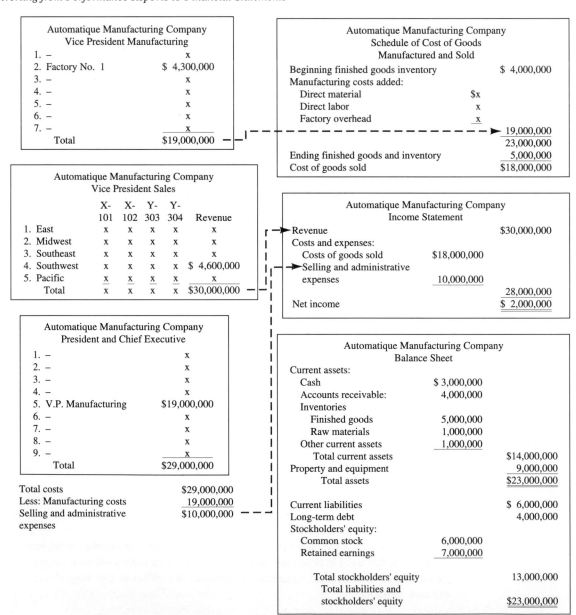

To produce financial statements at the end of a reporting period, the system classifies the totals in each financial statement account by financial statement category. These totals are represented by the columnar totals in Illustration 2–13. In this example, the total of Wages and Salaries expense on the income statement includes $910 from department A and $1,850 from foreman A of department B. According to GAAP, the system should classify these as indirect labor on the income statement. To produce responsibility reports, the system summarizes the row totals from this illustration into performance reports for each responsibility center. The report for foreman A would disclose total costs of $4,560. This includes $1,850 of wages and salaries, $110 of supplies, and $2,600 in costs associated with other financial statement accounts. Illustration 2–15 shows how performance reports and financial statements interrelate.

Due to the number of individual records processed by such a system, maintaining them on paper in bound journals and ledgers is extremely difficult. For this reason, systems like those described in this chapter are most efficient when implemented with computer-based systems.

Summary

Managerial accounting information systems provide both top-down and bottom-up information flows. Organization charts, policy statements, and performance budgeting systems provide a top-down flow. Responsibility reporting systems record performance measures at each level in the organization and summarize them in reports to managers at higher levels. This provides a bottom-up information flow.

An accounting information system that provides both performance budgeting and responsibility reporting is a *responsibility accounting* system. By using a separate chart of accounts for each responsibility center, this system produces performance reports that disclose budgeted and actual performance. Responsibility accounting systems also produce information for financial reporting that complies with generally accepted accounting principles. However, responsibility accounting is practical only in computer-based systems.

Key Terms

account code   A number uniquely identifying a general ledger account. It enables the accounting system to summarize amounts recorded in that account.

bottom-up information flow   Information that originates from events occurring at lower levels in an organization. The information system reports them to people at higher levels.

budget code   A number uniquely identifying the budgeted amounts for a responsibility center. It enables the accounting system to disclose comparisons of actual and budgeted amounts on a performance report.

classification   The process of determining in which financial statement account and responsibility center an accounting transaction should be recorded.

coding   The process of assigning a group of numbers or letters to an accounting transaction. These letters distinguish the financial statement account and the responsibility center to which that transaction belongs.

performance budgeting system   A managerial accounting information system that communicates budget goals from top management to lower-level managers in the organization.

performance report   A report produced by a responsibility accounting system. It discloses financial measures showing the performance of the manager in charge of a responsibility center.

policy statement   A written communication from top management that identifies its expectations for the behavior of the organization's employees.

responsibility accounting system   A managerial accounting information system that provides both responsibility reporting and performance budgeting.

responsibility center   An organizational unit where a manager controls financial measures recorded and reported by a managerial accounting information system. It may be either a cost center, a profit center, or an investment center.

responsibility code   A number uniquely identifying a responsibility center. It enables the accounting system to summarize financial measures for the center.

responsibility reporting system   A managerial accounting information system that communicates to top management the results of events occurring at lower levels in the organization.

top-down information flow   Information that originates from events occurring at the higher levels in an organization. The information system reports them to people at lower levels.

APPENDIX
CODING STRUCTURES

This chapter showed how a managerial accounting system uses account and responsibility codes to classify transactions. You may encounter other ways to encode transactions during your career; this appendix discusses them in more detail.

Accountants frequently participate in the development of new accounting systems. When they do this, they help to determine a method for classifying coding transaction data. System designers call these methods the *coding structures.*

Importance of the Coding Structure

An accounting system uses codes to classify, summarize, and retrieve data. For example, when a system records a transaction, it makes debit and credit entries in accounts. Accounting personnel identify the accounts using financial statement account codes. When a payroll system identifies employees to be paid by employee account codes, it records payroll expenses by expense account codes. Accounts receivable systems record and classify sales and customer payment transactions by customer account codes. When systems produce totals, they summarize totals using codes.

The coding structure should be adaptable to changing needs within a company. It should not require replacement as the company grows or as the nature of its business changes. For example, a three-digit employee code becomes inadequate once a company hires more than 999 employees. If a company enters a new industry, it requires new financial statement account codes. Accountants in the company should be able to create them by adding to the old chart of accounts.

The choice of a coding structure is a long-term decision because changes to it are difficult to make. Once employees learn a method, changing to another one requires retraining. Furthermore, producing comparable information from data coded in different ways requires different systems; maintaining redundant systems is expensive and inefficient. For these reasons, accountants participating in system design must choose an appropriate coding structure.

Types of Coding Structures

Many different ways of encoding information exist. The coding structures most commonly used for accounting are sequential codes, block codes, group codes, and mnemonic codes.

Sequential Codes.   A sequential code assigns unique identifiers to data items in sequence. Accountants commonly assign them to the documents processed by an accounting system. These include checks, sales orders, requisitions, purchase orders, invoices, and receiving reports.

Easy-to-use sequential codes enable an accountant to keep a record of documents on hand and to identify their unauthorized use. These codes are appropriate when the only way to categorize data items is by time. For example, checks issued by a cash disbursement system have unique identifying numbers assigned in increasing sequence. A check with Check No. 10034 was issued immediately before Check No. 10035. Materials Inventory Requisition No. 2667 was completed sometime after Requisition No. 2487.

Some people call sequential codes *serial* codes. Although useful in many circumstances, they are less flexible than block codes.

Block Codes.   An elaboration of a sequential code is a block code. When creating a block code, the system designer reserves certain adjacent numbers in the sequence for certain classifications. For example, in Illustration 2–13 all transactions coded with responsibility codes in the block

5000–5999 apply to the production area of the organization. The 6000 block refers to sales, the 7000 block to industrial relations, and so on.

The chart of accounts in Illustration 1–3 contains the following blocks of account codes:

Account Category	*Block*
Current assets	100–199
Property, plant, and equipment	200–299
Current liabilities	300–399
Long-term debt	400–499
Stockholders' equity	500–599
Revenue	600–699
Expenses	700–999

The system designer assigned codes sequentially to accounts so that the first digit indicates the financial statement classification. Each block contains unassigned numbers to allow future expansion of the chart of accounts. For example, if the company issues bonds, they may decide to add account number 420 (Bonds Payable) in the long-term debt block.

Group Codes.   A group code is an extension of a block code in which the position of each character in the group has significance. The position represents a different characteristic of the data classification. They are commonly used as account codes.

Earlier, this chapter discussed encoding accounting transactions using block codes. In the example, an account code has the form XXXX-X-XXX. Using this structure, the first four digits constitute the first group. They identify the responsibility center controlling the transaction. The second group contains one digit and designates either actual or budgeted amounts. The third group contains three digits and identifies a financial statement account. Using this method, a transaction coded 5110-0-710 represents an actual expenditure (code 0) for salaries and wages (code 710) in production department A (code 5110).

Often group codes are structured so that the interpretation of each succeeding digit depends on the digit immediately to its left. In Illustration 2–13, responsibility code 5121 represents foreman A of production department B. In this code, the first digit 1 represents factory no. 1, the digit 2 indicates department B within factory no. 1, and the last digit 1 identifies transactions for foreman A. When used in this way, some people call these codes *hierarchical* codes.

Group codes are flexible because analysts can readily add or delete groups when coding a new characteristic is required. Furthermore, a design team can reassign the meaning of a group without affecting other groups. A person familiar with the structure can interpret the significance of a code from the position of the digits.

Group codes sometimes become long and difficult to remember. Clerks unaccustomed to the group coding structure may make mistakes in recording them. Mnemonic codes help them avoid this problem.

Mnemonic Codes.   Mnemonic coding structures identify data items with combinations of letters and numbers. The design team chooses the combination so that clerks can more easily remember the associated data item. Companies may use them when developing customer or product codes.

For example, to avoid data entry errors by sales clerks, a design team may choose to develop mnemonic codes for customers. The code that identifies each customer is a shortened version of the customer's name. If the code allows six letters or numbers, clerks may assign the code "A&B" to A&B Furniture Company. Merchandise Market, Inc., may have the identifier "MERMKT."

In a proper application, mnemonic codes prevent errors in data entry. If there are many similar data items, however, the mnemonics may also be similar. This would confuse clerks and cause errors. For example, if customers are individuals rather than businesses, different individuals are likely to have similar names. These could produce a set of customer codes that are confusing because of their similarity. Furthermore, many alphabetic characters have similar sounds (e.g., B, P, D, T) that introduce confusion when speaking mnemonic codes.

As a part of their daily activities, accounting personnel code accounting transactions and interpret these codes. When the coding structure is logical and easy to use, they are less likely to make errors that produce misleading accounting reports. This is why accountants help to determine the method of coding transactions during the system development process.

Questions

2–1. Would a well-prepared organizational chart provide answers to each of the following questions?
   a. To whom am I accountable?
   b. Who has the most seniority?
   c. What is the chain of command down to me?
   d. What is my position in the organization?
   e. Who is responsible to me?

(CIA Adapted)

2–2. In the introductory portion of the policy statement shown in Illustration 2–2:
   a. Which groups of employees are covered by the policy statement?
   b. Which major areas of employee conduct are discussed?
   c. What are the potential consequences of a violation of employee conduct?

2–3. How does a performance budget differ from a cost standard?

2–4. How does the concept of cost controllability vary with the organizational level?

2–5. Why is a return-on-investment figure not usable as a performance standard for a cost responsibility group?

2–6. Ernest R. Breech, former chairman of the board of the Ford Motor Company, once observed: "While many companies believe they have good financial control systems, all too few really do. Many companies confuse a large volume of paperwork and reports with good financial control." What are your views?

2–7. In Illustration 2–9, can you deduce the number of vice presidents who report to the president?

2–8. "A performance budget prepared using the flexible budgeting technique is tantamount to setting standards subsequent to performance. It is not acceptable." Do you agree? Explain your position.

2–9. "We have an annual budget, but it is not much help because it is always wrong. Sales do not turn out as expected. Materials go up in cost. Production people work overtime. After only one month our budget is out of date." How could a flexible budget help in a situation like this?

(CIA Adapted)

2–10. A company sets its target volume at 100,000 units for the year. At that level, indirect labor cost is estimated at $150,000, of which $30,000 is nonvariable. Actual volume turns out to be 115,000 units, and actual indirect labor cost turns out to be $166,000.

    a. How do you evaluate this performance without the benefit of flexible budgeting?

    b. How do you evaluate this performance with flexible budgeting?

    c. What additional analysis would make information in question *b* even more meaningful?

2–11. "Controllability is relative rather than absolute. In this imperfect world, there are degrees of control. Furthermore, it may often be joint and indivisible." What are the implications of these statements to the analysis of variances disclosed in responsibility reports?

2–12. Standard costs and variance analysis are said to be applications of the principles of management by exception. Why is this so?

Exercises and Cases

2–13. *REPORT OF PROFIT RESPONSIBILITY GROUPS*

Quad-Cities Enterprises is organized on a product basis with profit responsibility. Both product divisions A and B have four departments. During the month of September 1998, the factory of each product division produced 10,000 units of goods and the sales department of each product division sold 10,000 units of goods. Operating data for the month are as follows:

	Product A	Product B
Sales revenue	$40,000	$40,000
Costs and expenses:		
Factory	15,000	12,000
Engineering and research	2,000	5,000
Marketing	10,000	8,000
Staff assistant	1,000	2,000
Divisional manager's office	2,000	3,000

Required:

a. Prepare a profit report for the month of September 1998 for each of the product divisions.

b. Comment on the performance of these divisions.

2–14. *REPORT OF A COST RESPONSIBILITY GROUP*

Harbour Industries is organized on a functional basis with cost responsibility. Its manufacturing division, under the supervision of a production manager, has four service departments and three production departments. Data for these departments and for the production manager's office for the month of November 1998, a month in which 3,000 units were produced, are as follows:

	Materials	Labor	Manufacturing Overhead
Production department A	$10,000	$15,000	$ 7,000
Production department B	2,000	18,000	9,000
Production department C	1,000	16,000	8,000
Service department W	—	—	4,000
Service department X	—	—	6,000
Service department Y	—	—	5,000
Service department Z	—	—	10,000
Office of production manager	—	—	11,000

Required:

Prepare a cost responsibility report for the manufacturing division for the month of November 1998.

2–15.   COST PERFORMANCE REPORT

The budget components of manufacturing overhead items incurred in production department M of the Homewood Manufacturing Company are as follows:

Supplies	$ 0.20	per unit produced
Power	0.35	per unit produced
Repairs	0.02	per unit produced
and	200.00	per month
Indirect labor	0.73	per unit produced
and	600.00	per month
Depreciation and taxes	2,000.00	per month

During the month of September 1998, the department produced 4,000 units and incurred the following costs:

Supplies	$ 850
Power	1,380
Repairs	320
Indirect labor	3,600
Depreciation and taxes	2,000
	$8,150

Required:

Prepare a cost performance report for the department for the month of September 1998, with columnar headings similar to those shown as Illustration 2–8.

2–16. COST PERFORMANCE REPORT

At the basic research department of Omega Research Corporation, the consumption of research chemicals is found to be $40 per day for the nonvariable portion and $11 for each hour of research activities undertaken. Chemicals consumed and research hours worked during the first week in June 1998 are as follows:

	Chemicals Consumed	Hours Worked
June 4, Monday	$ 500	45
June 5, Tuesday	650	55
June 6, Wednesday	800	65
June 7, Thursday	700	58
June 8, Friday	550	47
Total for the week	$3,200	270

Required:

Prepare a report for the manager of basic research department for the week ended June 8, 1998. Use the following columnar headings:

			Favorable (Unfavorable) Variance	
Day of Week	*Budget Allowance*	*Actual Consumption*	*For the Day*	*Week to Date*

2–17. RESPONSIBILITY ACCOUNTING

The manager of the assembly department of Richardson Manufacturing Company receives a monthly report in the following format:

1. Direct labor	$xxx
2. Material spoilage	xxx
3. Overtime premium	xxx
4. Reassembly	xxx
5. Supplies and small tools	xxx
6. Department manager's salary	xxx
7. Depreciation of plant building	xxx
8. Plant superintendent's office—allocated	xxx
9. Maintenance department cost—allocated	xxx
10. Factory administrative cost—allocated	xxx
Total	$xxx

Required:

a. Rearrange the format of this report so that cost items controllable by the manager of the assembly department are separately listed and totaled from those not controllable by that manager.

b. Assume that five departments report to the plant superintendent: machining, assembly, and finishing (production departments), and maintenance and general factory (service departments). Identify those cost items controllable at the level of the plant superintendent that are not controllable by the manager of the assembly department.

2–18. RESPONSIBILITY ACCOUNTING

The manager of production department F of the Wagner Manufacturing Company received the following cost and production report for November 1998 from the accounting department:

WAGNER MANUFACTURING COMPANY
Production Department F
Cost and Production Statistics Report
Month of November 1998

		Percent of Factory
Production Statistics		
1. Number of materials requisitions made	250	10
2. Number of employees in the department	30	12
3. Number of direct labor hours worked	5,000	11
4. Square feet of floor space occupied	3,000	20
5. Number of units produced	4,000	15
Cost Data		
6. Cost of materials requisitioned	$20,000	15
7. Materials handling, allocated on the basis of cost of materials requisitioned	450	
8. Storeroom, allocated on the basis of number of requisitions made	750	
9. Total material cost (lines 6 to 8)	21,200	
10. Total direct labor cost.	11,000	
11. Power	1,000	
12. Building occupancy, allocated on the basis of floor space occupied	1,500	
13. Supplies and small tools	200	
14. Departmental supervision	1,200	
15. Depreciation, insurance, and taxes on machinery	3,000	
16. Factory supervision, allocated on the basis of number of employees	1,800	
17. Inspection, allocated on the basis of number of units inspected (100% inspection)	600	
18. Personnel welfare and first aid, allocated on the basis of direct labor hours worked	275	
19. Total manufacturing overhead (lines 11 to 18)	9,575	
20. Total manufacturing cost (lines 9, 10, and 19)	$41,775	
21. Unit cost of goods manufactured	$10,444	

Required:

a. Deduce the number of service departments involved, and establish the departmental cost of each of these departments.

b. Prepare a cost report for production department F for the month of November 1998 with the costs incurred in the department and those allocated to the department clearly labeled and subtotaled.

2–19.   FLEXIBLE BUDGET

The Jason Plant of Cast Corporation has been in operation for 15 months. Jason employs a standard cost system for its manufacturing operations. The first six months' performance was affected by the usual problems associated with a new operation. Since that time the operations have been running smoothly. Unfortunately, however, the plant has not been able to produce profits on a consistent basis. As the production requirements to meet sales demand have increased, the profit performance has deteriorated.

During a staff meeting at which the plant general manager, the corporate controller, and the corporate budget director were in attendance, the plant production manager commented that changing production requirements made it more difficult to control manufacturing costs. He further noted that the budget for the plant, included in the company's annual profit plan, was not useful for judging the plant's performance because of the changes in the operating levels. The meeting resulted in a decision to prepare a report that would compare the plant's actual manufacturing cost performance with a budget of manufacturing costs based on actual direct labor hours in the plant.

The plant production manager and the plant accountant studied the cost patterns for recent months and volume and cost data from other Cast plants. Then they prepared the following flexible budget schedule for a month with 200,000 earned production hours that at standard would result in 50,000 units of output. The corporate controller reviewed and approved the flexible budget.

	Amount	Per Direct Labor Hour
Manufacturing costs:		
Variable:		
Indirect labor	$160,000	$0.80
Supplies	26,000	0.13
Power	14,000	0.07
		$1.00
Nonvariable:		
Supervisory labor	64,000	
Heat and light	15,000	
Property taxes	5,000	
	$284,000	

During the month of November 1998, when 220,000 actual direct labor hours were used in producing 50,500 units, actual cost data were as follows:

Indirect labor	$177,000
Supplies	27,400
Power	16,000
Supervisory labor	65,000
Heat and light	15,500
Property taxes	5,000
	$305,900

Required:

a. Explain the advantages of flexible budgeting over fixed budgeting for cost control purposes.
b. Prepare a cost report, showing variances, for the month of November.

(CMA Adapted)

2–20. POLICY STATEMENT

The Leather Corporation plans to offer a one-day course to its management employees in the finance and accounting areas. The topic will be the increased responsibilities of the corporation for the quality and accuracy of its financial information system and the information derived from the system. One of the segments is a review of Leather Corporation's proposed code of professional conduct for corporate financial and accounting personnel; it has been developed as a consequence of recent events.

Required:

Identify and discuss the provisions that probably should be included in Leather Corporation's proposed code of professional conduct regarding the relationship of the corporate financial and accounting personnel with

a. Other members of corporate management.
b. Shareholders.
c. The general public.

(CMA Adapted)

2–21. DELMARVA COAST HOSPITAL

The Delmarva Coast Hospital is located in a well-known summer resort area. The area's population doubles during the vacation months (May–August), and hospital activity more than doubles during these months. The hospital is organized into several departments. Although the hospital is relatively small, its pleasant surroundings have attracted a well-trained and competent medical staff.

An administrator was hired a year ago to improve the business activities of the hospital. Among the new ideas he has introduced is responsibility accounting. This program was announced along with quarterly cost reports supplied to department heads. Previously, cost data were presented to department heads infrequently. Excerpts from the announcement follow:

> The hospital has adopted a "responsibility accounting system." . . . Responsibility accounting means you are accountable for keeping the costs in your department within the budget. The variations from the budget will help you identify what costs are out of line and the size of the variation will indicate which ones are the most important. Your first such report accompanies this announcement.

The first report received by the laundry supervisor is shown as Exhibit 2–1. The annual budget for 1998 was constructed by the new administrator. Quarterly budgets were computed as one-fourth of the annual budget. The administrator compiled the budget from analysis of the prior three years' costs. The analysis showed that all costs

EXHIBIT 2–1

Case 2–21

DELMARVA COAST HOSPITAL
Performance Report—Laundry Department
July–September 1998

	Budget	Actual	(Over) Under Budget	Percent (Over) Under Budget
Patient days	9,500	11,900	(2,400)	(25)
Pounds of laundry processed	125,000	156,000	(31,000)	(25)
Costs:				
Laundry labor	$ 9,000	$ 12,500	$ (3,500)	(39)
Supplies	1,100	1,875	(775)	(70)
Water, water heating,				
and softening	1,700	2,500	(800)	(47)
Maintenance	1,400	2,200	(800)	(57)
Supervisor's salary	3,150	3,750	(600)	(19)
Allocated administrative costs	4,000	5,000	(1,000)	(25)
Equipment depreciation	1,200	1,250	(50)	(4)
	$ 21,550	$ 29,075	$ (7,525)	(35)

Administrator's comments: Costs are significantly above budget for the quarter. Particular attention needs to be paid to labor, supplies, and maintenance.

increased each year, with more rapid increases between the second and third year. He considered establishing the budget at an average of the prior three years' cost, hoping that the installation of the system would reduce costs to this level. However, in view of the rapidly increasing prices he finally chose the previous year's costs less 3 percent for the 1998 budget. The budgeted activity level measured by patient days and pounds of laundry processed was set at the previous year's volume, which was approximately equal to the volume of the past three years.

Required:

a. What are your views concerning the method used to construct the budget?
b. What information should be communicated by variations from budget?
c. Does the report effectively communicate the level of efficiency of the laundry department?

(CMA Adapted)

2–22. *PROFIT PLAN REPORT*

Kenbart Company decided to place increased emphasis on profit planning and on analyzing results as compared to its plans. A new computerized profit planning system has been implemented to help in this objective.

The company employs contribution margin reporting for internal reporting purposes and applies the concept of flexible budgeting for estimating variable costs. The

EXHIBIT 2–2

Case 2–22

KENBART COMPANY
PROFIT PLAN REPORT
MONTH, YEAR

	MONTH				YEAR-TO-DATE			
			OVER (UNDER)				OVER (UNDER)	
	ACTUAL	*PLAN*	*$*	*%*	*ACTUAL*	*PLAN*	*$*	*%*
SALES								
VARIABLE MANUFACTURING COSTS								
RAW MATERIALS								
DIRECT LABOR								
VARIABLE OVERHEAD								
TOTAL VARIABLE MANUFACTURING COSTS								
MANUFACTURING MARGIN								
VARIABLE SELLING EXPENSES								
CONTRIBUTION MARGIN								
FIXED COSTS								
MANUFACTURING								
SALES								
GENERAL ADMINISTRATION								
INCOME BEFORE TAXES								
INCOME TAXES								
NET INCOME								

following terms were used by Kenbart's executive management when reviewing and analyzing actual results and the profit plan:

- *Original Plan*—Profit plan approved and adopted by management for the year.
- *Revised Plan*—Original plan modified as a consequence of action taken during the year (usually quarterly) by executive management.
- *Flexed Revised Plan*—The most current plan (i.e., either original plan or revised plan, if one has been prepared) adjusted for changes in volume and variable expense rates.
- *YTD Actual Results*—The actual results of operations for the year.
- *Current Outlook*—The summation of the actual year-to-date results of operations plus the flexed revised plan for the remaining months of the year.

Executive management meets monthly to review the actual results as compared to the profit plan. Any assumptions or major changes in the profit plan usually are incorporated on a quarterly basis once the first quarter is completed.

An outline of the basic profit plan report designed by the data processing department is reproduced in Exhibit 2–2. This report is prepared at the end of each month. In addition, this report is generated whenever executive management initiates a change or modification in its plan. Consequently, many different versions of a company profit plan exist that make analysis difficult and confusing.

Several members of executive management have voiced disapproval of the profit plan report because the Plan column is not well defined and varies in meaning from one report to another. Furthermore, no Current Outlook column is included in the report. Therefore, the accounting department has been asked to work with the data processing department in modifying the report so that users can better understand the information being conveyed and the reference points for comparison of results.

Required:

a. What advantages are there to Kenbart Company having its profit plan system computerized?
b. Redesign the layout of the profit plan report so that it will be more useful to Kenbart's executive management in its task of reviewing results and planning operations. Explain the reason for each modification you make in the report.
c. Which types of data would Kenbart Company be required to capture in its computer-based files to generate the plans and results which executive management reviews and analyzes?

(CMA Adapted)

2–23.   ORGANIZATIONAL CHART

Thirty years ago four friends started a business that manufactured wooden office furniture. Executive responsibilities were divided among them as shown in Exhibit 2–3.

Their business experienced phenomenal growth and now comprises three product lines, nine factories, and 15 sales offices geographically dispersed throughout the United States. The company has always been departmentalized on a functional basis. However, the company is now considering a proposal to restructure the organization as reflected in Exhibit 2–4.

Required:

Analyze the proposed organizational chart and answer the following questions:

a. Which type of departmentation is being suggested for:
 1. The entire enterprise at level one?
 2. The manufacturing operation at level two?

EXHIBIT 2–3

Case 2–23

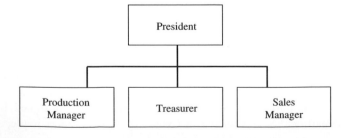

EXHIBIT 2–4

Case 2–23

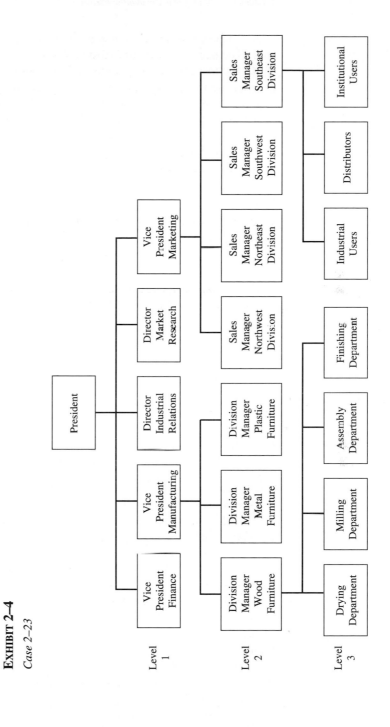

3. The marketing operation at level two?
4. The marketing operation at level three?
5. The manufacturing operation at level three?

b. What are the principal advantages of the suggested departmentation plan for the manufacturing operation at:
1. Level one?
2. Level two?

c. Why would the departmentation plan suggested for manufacturing at level two be inappropriate for marketing?

d. What are the principal advantages of the suggested departmentation plan for the marketing operation at level two?

e. What rationale supports keeping finance, industrial relations, and market research centralized at level one?

(CIA Adapted)

2–24.   CODING STRUCTURES

Franklin Flooring is a manufacturer and distributor of carpet and vinyl floor coverings. The company's home office is located in Springfield, Illinois, with its mills and manufacturing plants spread throughout the Midwest. Franklin's total sales last year exceeded $300 million.

Retail showrooms are Franklin's primary customers. However, many major corporations buy Franklin's products directly, and large construction companies purchase carpet and floor covering on contract with Franklin at reduced rates for use in newly constructed homes and commercial buildings. In addition, there is a company-owned retail outlet at each plant where overruns, seconds, and discontinued items are sold; these are Franklin's only retail sales. The company has divided the sales market into seven territories—New England, Mid-Atlantic, Southeast, Great Lakes, South Central, Southwest, and Northwest. Each sales territory is divided into 5 to 10 districts with a salesperson assigned to each district.

Franklin manufactures over 200 different varieties of carpet. The carpet is classified as commercial or residential and is sold under four brand names with up to five subproduct lines under each brand. The subproduct lines indicate the different grades of quality; grades are measured by type of tuft and number of tufts per square inch. Each subproduct line of carpet can have up to 15 different colors.

Approximately 180 varieties of vinyl floor covering are produced, which are also classified according to commercial or residential use. There are four separate brand names (largely distinguished by the type of finish), up to eight different patterns for each brand, and up to eight colors for each pattern.

Franklin's current accounting system is adequate for monitoring the sales by product; however, in-depth analysis of more specific market factors is limited as the information is not available. In order to improve the planning process and overall decision making, the accounting systems department has been asked to design a sales analysis code that would make this information easily accessible. The code should permit Franklin to prepare a sales analysis that reflects any and all of the company's operating characteristics.

Required:

a. Briefly define and give an example of each of the following coding structures:
   1. Sequence coding
   2. Block coding
   3. Group coding
b. Identify and describe at least three general factors that should be considered before a coding system is designed and implemented.

(CMA Adapted)

2–25.   TRANSACTION CODING

Ollie Mace has recently been appointed controller of a family-owned manufacturing enterprise. The firm, S. Dilley & Co., was founded by Sam Dilley about 20 years ago, is 78 percent owned by Dilley, and has served the major automotive companies as a parts supplier. The firm's major operating divisions are heat treating, extruding, small parts stamping, and specialized machining. Sales last year from the several divisions ranged from $150,000 to more than $3 million. The divisions are physically and managerially independent except for Dilley's constant surveillance. The accounting system for each division has evolved according to the division's own needs and the abilities of individual accountants or bookkeepers. Mace is the first controller in the firm's history to have responsibility for overall financial management. Dilley expects to retire within six years and has hired Mace to improve the firm's accounting system.

Mace decided that he will need to design a new financial reporting system. It should

1. Give managers uniform, timely, and accurate reports on business activity. Monthly divisional reports should be uniform and available by the 10th of the following month. Companywide financial reports also should be prepared by the 10th.
2. Provide a basis for measuring return on investment by division. Divisional reports should show assets assigned to each division and revenue and expense measurement in each division.
3. Generate meaningful budget data for planning and decision-making purposes. The accounting system should provide for the preparation of budgets recognizing managerial responsibility, controllability of costs, and major product groups.
4. Allow for a uniform basis of evaluating performance and quick access to underlying data. Cost center variances should be measured and reported for both operating and nonoperating units (including headquarters). Also, questions about levels of specific costs should be answerable quickly.

A new chart of accounts, it appears to Mace, is essential before getting started on other critical financial problems. The present account codes used by divisions are not standard.

Mace sees a need to divide asset accounts into six major categories: current assets, plant and equipment, and so on. Within each of these categories, he sees a need for a maximum of 10 control accounts. Based on his observations, he concludes that 100 subsidiary accounts are more than adequate for each control account.

No division now has more than five major product groups. The maximum number of cost centers Mace foresees within any product group is six, including operating and nonoperating groups. He views general divisional costs as a nonrevenue-producing product group. Altogether, Mace estimates that about 44 natural expense accounts plus about 12 specific variance accounts would be adequate.

Mace is planning to implement the new chart of accounts in an environment that includes both manual and computer-based systems. Therefore, the chart of accounts should facilitate the processing of transactions both manually and by machine. Efforts should be made, he believes, to restrict the length of the code for economy in processing and convenience in use.

Required:

a. Design a chart of accounts coding system to meet Ollie Mace's requirements. Your answer should show the number of digits in the coding system and the purpose of each digit. You should explain the coding method you have chosen and the reason for the size of your code elements. Explain your code as it would apply to asset and expense accounts.

b. Use your chart of accounts coding system to illustrate the code needed for the following transactions:
   1. In the small parts stamping division, $100 was spent on cleaning supplies. The expenditure was requested by Bill Shaw, supervisor in the polishing department of the Door Lever Group.
   2. A new motorized sweeper has been purchased for the maintenance department of the Extruding Division. Its cost is $13,450, and it is coded as an asset acquisition.

(CMA Adapted)

2–26.   TRANSACTION CODING[2]

Budget Rent a Car Corporation is the world's third largest car and truck rental company. It has revenues of $2.3 billion and employs more than 25,000 people in 118 countries. It operates more than 1,000 locations in the United States, of which 40 percent are corporate owned. Increasing competition has required its accounting department to gather nonfinancial information and integrate it with financial information. This allows management to perform more analysis of business segment profitability and of Budget's competition.

To meet expanded reporting requirements, the department changed from a two-dimensional chart of accounts to an eight-dimensional one. The old chart contained ten-digit account codes identifying the dimensions *location* and *cost center.* The new chart uses 30-digit numbers and identifies the following dimensions:

- Location code
- Department code
- Major account group

---

[2]Reprinted with permission from Management Accounting. Copyright by Institute of Management Accountants, Montvale, N.J., April 1996.

- Minor account group
- Product line
- Source of reservation
- Project number
- Project phase

The database includes 3 gigabytes of data, 20 vehicle classes, 1,700 accounts, and 26,000 names.

Current Information Needs

Nonfinancial information is essential for decision making in the vehicle rental business. Market forces vary widely between locations, depending on the size of the market, proximity to an airport, source of the vehicle reservation, and several vehicle rental options. Because of this, managers in the corporate office need information by business segment.

By providing nonfinancial segment information, the accounting department aids in making profitability decisions. For example, they determined that business with certain tour operators in Florida is unprofitable because of the operators' preferences for low-cost vehicles during peak season.

Future Plans

The accounting department would like to expand its nonfinancial reporting to aid in other decisions. For example, they would like to be able to analyze the market for rentals to international visitors; to identify the relative profitability of truck rentals for household moves, both local and cross-country; and to gather information on competing rental companies at each Budget location.

The accounting department hopes to implement its information gathering and analysis capabilities at the local level. This will provide managers at individual locations the ability to analyze better their competitive climates and to forward this information to the corporate level. The accounting department's role is critical, because it provides the specialized data analysis that the company needs to succeed in its fiercely competitive global marketplace.

Required:

a. For what kinds of management decisions does the Budget system *currently* provide information?
b. For what kinds of decisions should the system be able to provide information *in the future?*
c. For each decision you identify in *b,* suggest some dimensions on which the system should be able to collect data.

3 SYSTEMS CONCEPTS AND ACCOUNTING

Learning Objectives

1. To learn selected concepts from the theory of systems.
2. To apply these selected concepts to the processing of accounting transactions.
3. To learn about those systems that include accounting information systems.
4. To review the systems approach to problem solving.

Introduction

Accounting processes offer mechanisms for recording and summarizing accounting information, and they provide both top-down and bottom-up information flows. This chapter explores the theoretical basis for these processes. Some relevant concepts from systems theory are described and applied to the processing of accounting information. This will provide a framework for the study of accounting information systems.

Systems Theory

In their daily activities, accountants frequently encounter references to many different kinds of *systems:* the public transportation system, the digestive system, the solar system, a high-fidelity stereo system, and communications systems. What is a system? And what do all these systems have in common?

Characteristics of Systems

Given the wide variety of systems, the concept is hard to define. West Churchman has proposed the following definition: "A *system* is a set of parts coordinated to accomplish a set of goals."[1] According to this definition, any system, whether a computer system or one of those mentioned above, has three characteristics: (1) *component parts,* or those tangible features that can be seen, heard, or felt; (2) a *process,* whereby the parts are coordinated in a defined way; and (3) *goals,* or those objectives toward which the component parts are coordinated. Although process and goals are intangible, they are just as

---

[1]C. West Churchman, *The Systems Approach* (New York: Dell, 1968), p. 29.

important as the tangible parts. How this definition applies to accounting systems will become clear later.

Subsystems and Supersystems.   The parts of a system may themselves constitute different systems, each having all of a system's characteristics. Lower-level systems are called *subsystems,* each of which also represents a process whereby component parts are coordinated to achieve a set of goals. Although a subsystem's goals are different from those of the higher-level system, they should be consistent with them. A subsystem is also a part of a higher-level *supersystem,* or a system of systems.

What constitutes the supersystem, the system, and the subsystem depends on one's point of view. For example, one may view the public transportation system as a supersystem consisting of an airline system, a rail system, and a system of highways. An objective of each of these subsystems is to move people or goods using a certain form of technology. These subsystem goals are consistent with the goals of the supersystem, which include movement from one location to another.

Boundaries and Interfaces.   Systems are also characterized by the *boundaries* separating them from other systems. The boundaries of subsystems help to identify the system's component parts. In some cases, such as the airline or rail systems, these boundaries are distinct and easy to identify. In others, system boundaries may be imprecise, such as in many business and economic systems. One of the more difficult tasks in designing information systems is identifying the boundaries, or limits, of a new information system.

Whenever subsystem boundaries meet, system *interfaces* are created. An interface occurs where systems or component parts connect. For example, an interface between the highway and airline systems is the airport terminal, which enables a traveler to arrive by auto at the airport, enter the terminal, and then use the airline system. This interface enables the public transportation system to move people from one location to another more efficiently.

Interfaces are often designed to provide *decoupling* between component parts or subsystems. Therefore, components operate independently, so that the timing of the operations of one component does not rely on the operations of another. For example, air travelers can arrive early for their flights, knowing they will have a comfortable place to wait. The terminal has decoupled arrival by bus from departure by plane.

Accounting system interfaces are designed to provide various degrees of coupling between system components. Many examples are discussed later.

Types of Systems   Although systems have many different forms, they have certain characteristics in common. Systems theory recognizes four basic types of systems. Any system will fit in one of the following categories:

Closed Systems.   A *closed system* is totally isolated from its environment. There are no external interfaces, the system has no effects outside of its boundaries, and the environment has no effect on the processes within the system.

The closed system is a theoretical rather than a practical concept, because all systems interact with their environment in some way. Airline and bus systems, for example, are affected by weather, congestion, worker strikes, or accidents.

Relatively Closed Systems.   A *relatively closed system* reacts with its environment in a known and controlled way. The system contains interfaces with the environment, and it controls the effects of the environment on its process. The interactions consist of system *inputs* if they flow from the environment to the system; interactions flowing in the opposite direction are called *outputs.*

A well-designed system limits, but does not eliminate, its susceptibility to the environment. Airline companies use radar and other devices to operate in adverse weather and to avoid accidents. Proper scheduling and labor negotiations can limit the effects of congestion and strikes on the airline system.

Open Systems.   An *open system* is one in which the system's interaction with the environment is not controlled. Besides having inputs and outputs, an open system has *disturbances,* or uncontrolled inputs, that affect the processes within the system. Disturbances to the airline system, for example, may include icy runways.

Well-designed systems minimize the impact of disturbances. System designers anticipate the things that can go wrong in the environment and create processes and interfaces to control them. For example, to prevent the buildup of ice, airport runways can contain heating elements. In accounting information systems, internal controls protect system processes against disturbances from the environment. An inadequate design is one in which designers gave insufficient thought to potential disturbances, thus producing an open system.

Feedback Control Systems.   In *feedback control systems,* a portion of system output is returned as an input to the system. A system may be designed to provide feedback to help the system attain its goals. Automatic guidance systems in airplanes are examples of feedback control systems. They measure the plane's current heading, compare it to a desired heading, and adjust the plane's controls to correct for differences.

Many accounting systems are designed to provide feedback for control purposes. Responsibility reporting systems provide feedback to managers about their performance in achieving organizational objectives. Managers can then make decisions that adjust the inputs to processes, which helps them attain their systems' goals.

Supersystems may have different types of subsystems; for example, a relatively closed system may have component parts that are relatively closed, open, or feedback control systems. The diagrams in Illustration 3–1 represent the four types of systems.

Accounting Information Systems

Given these basic systems theory concepts, this section outlines how systems theory applies to processing accounting transactions. This section presents the characteristics of an accounting system, the subsystems that constitute it, and the supersystems of which it is a part.

Accounting as a System

A well-designed accounting system is an example of a relatively closed system. This system has processes that convert inputs to outputs and utilizes internal controls to limit the effects of its environment on the system.

The inputs to an accounting system are the economic events that become accounting transactions. These include selling goods for cash, selling goods on credit, or

ILLUSTRATION 3–1

Types of Systems

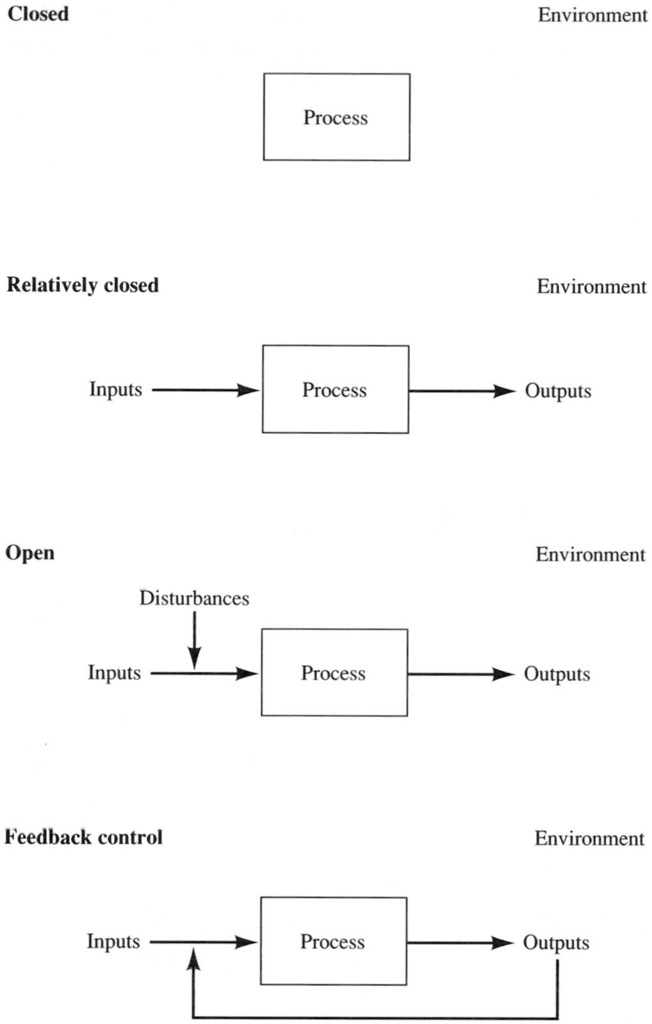

Closed   Environment

```
         ┌──────────┐
         │          │
         │ Process  │
         │          │
         └──────────┘
```

Relatively closed   Environment

Inputs ────────▶ │ Process │ ────────▶ Outputs

Open   Environment

Disturbances

Inputs ────────▶ │ Process │ ────────▶ Outputs

Feedback control   Environment

Inputs ────────▶ │ Process │ ────────▶ Outputs

incurring an expense. The processes in an accounting system record an economic event as a transaction, journalize and post transactions, and summarize transactions in various reports. The outputs of this system are accounting documents and reports such as financial statements or responsibility reports. Illustration 3–2 shows the accounting system as a relatively closed system.

In the accounting system, internal control measures help to prevent or detect disturbances from the environment. For example, footing and crossfooting is a common bookkeeping technique used to disclose arithmetic errors; computerized systems usually require temperature-controlled rooms because they malfunction more frequently when exposed to extremes in temperature; and microcomputer owners often use surge protectors to eliminate the effects of changes in the power source. Many other examples of potential disturbances and the measures necessary to control them are discussed in the chapters about internal control.

ILLUSTRATION 3–2

The Accounting Process as a Relatively Closed System

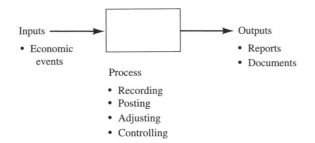

Inputs

• Economic
  events

Process

• Recording
• Posting
• Adjusting
• Controlling

Outputs

• Reports
• Documents

Subsystems of the Accounting System.   The accounting system has component parts that are themselves systems. Data processing personnel commonly speak of the accounting system as composed of *application systems.* An application system is a set of procedures and computer programs that perform a specific accounting objective. For example, the process of calculating amounts owed to suppliers and then printing checks for those amounts is a *cash disbursements* application.

Many auditors, on the other hand, prefer to think of the accounting system as a set of *transaction cycles.* These auditors identify in a client specific sets of economic events that normally follow each other in a cyclical way. In the expenditure cycle, for example, XYZ Food Company needs a raw material, corn, for its manufacturing process. XYZ locates a grain company that sells the corn on credit. XYZ receives the corn and mails the grain company a check in payment. At the conclusion of this process, the grain company may sell to XYZ Food Company again, producing a cycle of economic events. Each economic event generates an accounting transaction, and this set of transactions forms a transaction cycle. Using transaction cycles enables the auditor to evaluate the effects of internal controls in the accounting system.

As the preceding example demonstrates, the cash disbursements application is a part of the expenditure cycle. Any application system is not only a subsystem of the accounting system but also a subsystem of a specific transaction cycle.

Thus, the accounting system is a supersystem consisting of a responsibility accounting system and a transaction processing system. The transaction processing system is composed of transaction cycle subsystems. A transaction cycle is a system composed of subsystems that are application systems. Each is an example of an accounting information system.

Most auditors identify the following four transaction cycles:

1. *Revenue cycle.* Accounting transactions resulting from economic events that produce revenue for the accounting entity.
2. *Expenditure cycle.* Accounting transactions caused by the economic events necessary to acquire material and supplies for the accounting entity.
3. *Conversion cycle.* Accounting transactions recorded when converting purchased inventory into salable finished products.
4. *Financial cycle.* Accounting transactions that record the acquisition of capital from owners and creditors, and the use of that capital to acquire property necessary for generating income.

ILLUSTRATION 3–3

The Expenditure Cycle

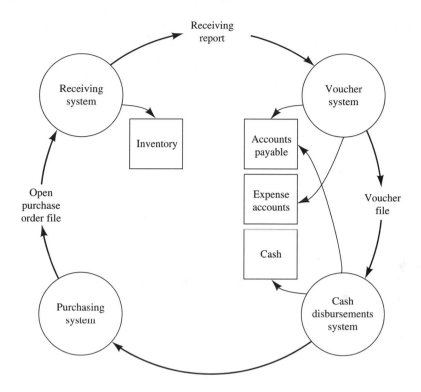

Another chapter describes the application systems that constitute each of these transaction cycles. As an example, the expenditure cycle is shown in Illustration 3–3. This cycle contains four major application systems: purchasing, receiving, voucher, and cash disbursements. These systems impact four major general ledger account categories: cash, inventory, accounts payable, and asset or expense accounts.

Boundaries.   Illustration 3–4 shows the boundaries of the accounting transaction processing system in a manufacturing firm. Its boundaries separate this system from the other systems in its environment. Some of these include vendors, employees, customers, and stockholders and creditors who provide capital. Other systems that are also a part of the accounting system include the budgeting system and the responsibility reporting system.

Sometimes the boundaries of a transaction cycle are not clearly defined. Many auditors think that the property application system is a part of the financing cycle; others include it in the conversion cycle. Similarly, some treat the payroll application system as a separate cycle, rather than including it in the expenditure cycle. General ledger accounts that are affected by two cycles or by two or more applications are a part of each cycle or application.

Interfaces.   Most systems have interfaces that provide means of interaction with the environment. The interface is a link at which a transaction exits one system and enters another. In the accounting system, an interface can be general ledger accounts, docu-

ILLUSTRATION 3–4

The Accounting Transaction Processing System and Its Cycle Components

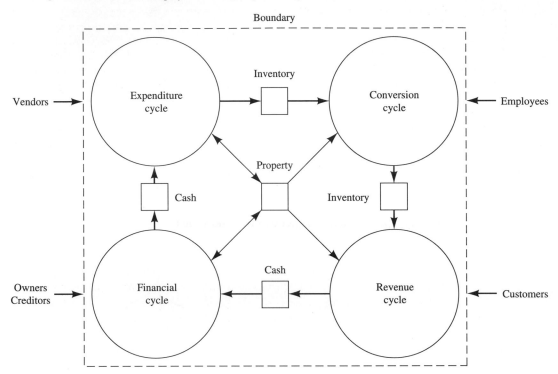

ments, or computer records that contain data flowing between applications. For example, in the expenditure cycle, the receiving report (a document) provides an interface between the receiving system and the voucher system. Illustration 3–3 shows this document used as an interface.

Decoupling.   Decoupling is often provided by the files in an accounting system. Decoupling allows individual application systems to operate independently, so that an output of one system does not immediately become an input to another system.

In the expenditure cycle, the purchase order is an interface that provides decoupling between the purchasing and receiving systems. When an order has been placed with a vendor by the purchasing system, information regarding that order is stored in an open purchase order file. This information remains in the file until the merchandise requested in the order is received. At this time the information provides an input to the receiving system. Illustration 3–4 shows how inventory and cash accounts in the general ledger provide decoupling between transaction cycles.

The receiving and voucher systems, on the other hand, are tightly coupled by the receiving report. Whenever a receiving report is issued by the receiving system, it quickly becomes an input to the voucher system.

The designer of an accounting system must decide where decoupling or coupling is useful during development of the system. Too much decoupling between applications, for example, can result in inconsistent data. This can cause the system to produce mis-

---

AIS in Practice

Mersey Docks and Harbour Company is the second largest port operator in the United Kingdom and ranks in the top 250 of the *Financial Times* top 500 firms. The company operates the ports of Liverpool, Sheerness, and Chatham in England, runs shipping lines serving England, Ireland, and Holland, and has interests in stevedoring, warehousing, and property development in these areas.

Mersey purchased and installed a general ledger software package on its mainframe computer in 1982. As the company diversified, maintaining a top-level view of the state of the business became difficult. So in 1991, the company added fixed assets, job costing, and accounts payable subsystems. In 1995 it implemented subsystems that process accounts receivable, purchase order, inventory control, and fund accounting. Currently the system has around 200 users on-line, including accountants, clerks, and sales, credit, and legal personnel. Management believes that the additional modules give them better control of their business, free them from the mechanical aspects of accounting, and allow them more time to manage the business and look for improvements.

---

leading reports. A later chapter describes how the use of a database management system can overcome this problem.

The accounting transaction processing system illustrates many of the characteristics identified in systems theory. As you may suspect, accounting information systems are subsystems within a larger supersystem. This supersystem is the organization's management information system (MIS).

Accounting as a Subsystem

An organization's information system has objectives that extend beyond those identified for accounting systems. This section uses systems concepts and terminology to examine the management information system and its subsystems. Also discussed are various goals for an MIS and different information systems needed to achieve these goals. This discussion clarifies the role of accounting information systems in an organization.

Decision-Making Activities

Henry Lucas defined a management *information system* as "a set of organized procedures that, when executed, provides information to support decision making and control in the organization."[2] The goal of any part of the information system, then, is to help the decision-making process. Analyzing decision-making activities helps you to understand the role of the subsystems that make up the information system.

Robert Anthony developed an approach for categorizing the decision-making activities within an organization.[3] Having identified three levels of such activities, he stated that decision making differs so significantly between these levels that different information systems are needed at each level. These levels are strategic planning, management control, and operational control.

> Strategic planning is the process of deciding on the objectives of the organization, on changes in the objectives, on the resources used to obtain these objectives, and on the policies that are to govern the acquisition, use, and disposition of these resources.

---

[2]Henry C. Lucas, *Information Systems Concepts for Management,* 2d ed. (New York: McGraw-Hill, 1982), p. 8.

[3]Robert N. Anthony, *Planning and Control Systems: A Framework for Analysis* (Boston: Harvard University Graduate School of Business Administration, 1965), pp. 24–67.

Management control . . . is the process by which managers assure that resources are obtained and used effectively and efficiently to accomplish the organization's objective.

Operational control . . . is the process of assuring that specific tasks are carried out effectively and efficiently.

These three levels are often illustrated as a hierarchy of decision-making activities. Management control activities are undertaken to achieve objectives identified during strategic planning. Similarly, the tasks executed at the operational control level are identified with specific management control activities. In this way, operational control information systems support management control information systems, which in turn support those systems used for strategic planning. The pyramid in Illustration 3–5 represents this hierarchy of decision-making activities.

Strategic Planning.   Strategic planning activities are the primary concern of top management, which normally includes the president or chief executive officer and the vice presidents of major divisions of the organization. In their jobs, they identify major markets and product lines for the organization during the long-range planning process. In large corporations, long-range planning staffs advise top management concerning these decisions; top management then communicates these objectives to lower-level managers. Information systems for strategic planning help evaluate possible organization objectives and provide top-down information flows. They are used by top management and those people who advise top management. These are sometimes called *executive information systems.*

Management Control.   Management control activities are primarily the concern of an organization's middle management, which includes those men and women in charge of factories, sales regions, and administrative and engineering activities. Middle managers want to operate their segments of the organization efficiently while achieving the objectives identified by top management. The decisions made by middle management are sometimes called *tactical decisions,* because they implement strategy identified at the higher level. Middle managers rely on the budgeting and responsibility reporting systems of the accounting system.

ILLUSTRATION 3–5

Managerial Activity Levels

Operational Control.   Operational control activities are implemented by department heads and supervisers, the lowest-level managers in an organization. Their aim is to achieve those specific tasks assigned to them by middle management. For example, the manager of an accounts payable department may report to a controller or chief accountant in middle management. One task of the accounts payable manager is to pay the organization's bills promptly. In achieving this task, the manager coordinates the activities of several accounts payable clerks. The manager and clerks routinely use the voucher and cash disbursement systems of the accounting transaction processing system.

Decision Problems and the Activity Level

Different activities are performed at various managerial levels in an organization. The managers at each level face different decisions. Those made by top management evaluate many alternatives and require the knowledge and judgment acquired by many years of experience. At lower organizational levels, decision makers face fewer alternatives. These decisions are made within the constraints established at higher levels and affect three categories of problems. Differences in decision problems between levels create differences in the kinds of information systems that are needed.

Unstructured Problems.   The problems faced by top management are usually unstructured; many alternatives are available but there is little guidance concerning the best one to pursue. For example, among all the possible new markets or new products, top management must choose those that the organization can deliver successfully within existing human and financial constraints. These decisions impact the long-term success of the organization and may affect decisions at the management control level for 20 years or more. Some activities at the management control and operational control levels are also unstructured, but these are less frequent and less far reaching.

Information systems that solve unstructured problems must have certain characteristics. These systems process data that are largely predictive—long-term forecasts about technology, demographics, and market demand—and that consist of estimates that are relatively inaccurate and highly summarized. The data are obtained mostly from external sources, such as public databases, economic statistics, and predictions of future trends. Because the decision-making process is unstructured, the information system must be quickly and easily adaptable to new decisions or to new data inputs. Information systems that fit many of these characteristics are sometimes called *decision support systems.*

Structured Problems.   The decisions that managers face at the operational level are significantly different. At this level, managers are assigned specific tasks by middle management and are often given clear directions about how to carry out each task. For example, an accounts payable manager may be instructed to pay all bills when due but to take purchase discounts whenever they are offered. The problem faced by the manager is a structured one—determining the payment date given the preceding rules. Other structured decision problems are faced by middle and top management, but these become less common at the higher levels.

Information systems needed for structured problems are different because they concentrate on processing historical data from within the organization. These systems are highly detailed and, in that they are both historical and internal, are usually accurate. Since the manager knows in advance what kind of information is necessary to make the decision, a system can be designed to provide what is needed. Data sources for this system can be identified in advance and used repeatedly. The system's adaptability is less important for these structured decision problems than it is for most unstructured ones.

Semistructured Problems.   Many decisions management faces cannot easily be classified as structured or unstructured. Middle managers receive a set of objectives, but have some freedom in choosing how to attain them. Thus, middle managers frequently are required to make decisions about semistructured problems. For example, top management may assign production quotas and profit objectives to a middle-level factory manager. The manager must then acquire materials, hire and train workers, and schedule production to meet these objectives. He or she must exercise judgment in selecting the quality of materials, the number of employees, the amount of training, and the proper production schedule. Semistructured decisions also exist at the operational and strategic planning levels.

Information systems used for semistructured decisions tend to combine the characteristics of systems used for structured and unstructured decisions. For example, in selecting the quality of materials to purchase, a factory manager may use both historical data (on the quality of a finished product) and predictive data (the anticipated sales for a product of low or high quality); he or she may also use externally produced data (purchase prices) as well as data from internal sources (standard quantities of material).

Illustration 3–6 classifies these decision problems by management activity level and provides examples of information subsystems useful in each area. It provides examples of structured, semistructured, and unstructured problems at all three levels of decision making.

ILLUSTRATION 3–6

Decision Problems and Managerial Activity Levels

	Operational control	Management control	Strategic planning
Structured	Accounts payable Cash disbursements	Responsibility accounting	Tanker fleet mix Warehouse and factory location
Semistructured	Inventory control Production scheduling	Budget preparation	Mergers and acquisitions
Unstructured	Cash management	Personnel management	New products R & D planning

Source: Reprinted in adapted form from G. Anthony Gorry and Michael S. Scott Morton, "A Framework for Management Information Systems," *Sloan Management Review,* Fall 1971, p. 59, by permission of the publisher. Copyright 1971 by the Sloan Management Review Association. All rights reserved.

Accounting transaction processing systems that provide information for decision making appear in the upper left-hand box of the illustration; these are structured decisions at the operational control level. Examples of problems in the lower right-hand box include new-product and research and development planning decisions. These decisions tend to be unstructured because they are infrequent, many alternatives are available, and they have long-range implications for the organization. This places them at the strategic planning level. Systems at this level are decision support and executive information systems. In the upper right-hand box examples include tanker fleet mix and warehouse and factory location. These are infrequent decisions with long-term implications and are thus at the strategic level. Yet structured methods using computerized linear programming procedures aid in making these decisions. A course in quantitative methods in management covers these procedures.

The example information subsystems in Illustration 3–6 vary significantly in their characteristics. Systems that are at the top and on the left side in the illustration tend to be more frequently used but have less significant financial implications for the organization. At the bottom and on the right are systems that serve less frequent needs but have a more significant impact when used. This shows how management information systems must satisfy a broad range of needs for information.

A Spectrum of Management Information Needs

Like all systems, the management information system is composed of many subsystems, each of which is an information system designed to satisfy management's decision-making needs. But each of these systems must be tailored to the structured, semistructured, or unstructured problems faced by a manager at each of the three levels. This section examines some conclusions about accounting systems as subsystems of the management information system.

Accounting Information Systems.   The three accounting information systems are the transaction processing system, the budgeting system, and the responsibility reporting system. Each is a component of the management information system that provides information for decision making at all levels of an organization.

The *transaction processing system* is the most structured component of the management information system; it provides information used by clerical and managerial personnel at the operational level. Because it is structured, and because most organizations require transaction processing systems that are similar in nature, we can describe standard processes for these systems. You will learn the details of these systems when the book examines the accounting transaction cycles.

The *budgeting system* allows top management to communicate corporate objectives to all managers in the organization. It provides for the top-down information flows described in Chapter 2. A budgeting system utilizes both internal and external data, is predictive in nature, and involves estimates that are frequently imprecise. Thus, it is used in semistructured decision processes involving management control activities.

The *responsibility reporting system* summarizes historical data on a periodic basis and provides the bottom-up information flows described in Chapter 2. It is an example of a highly structured information system that is useful for management control.

These three accounting information systems provide information for structured or semistructured decisions at the operational and management control levels. Because

ILLUSTRATION 3–7

*The Spectrum of
Management Information
Needs*

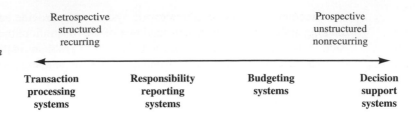

accounting systems are more structured, they are more highly developed in most organizations. They are also more standardized across different organizations than other information systems.

Decision Support Systems.   Whereas accounting information systems are highly structured and most useful at the lower organizational levels, decision support systems are most useful at the higher levels. At the strategic level decisions are unstructured, and decision styles may differ significantly among managers. Furthermore, a specific decision problem may occur only once. Thus, information systems developed for this level often are decision-specific. Once the decision is made, the information system used for it is no longer applicable in its current form. For subsequent decisions, the system must be modified or discarded, a development that has major implications for the design of information systems.

In considering the nature of decision problems and the management activities at various levels, there is a spectrum of management information needs. At one end of the spectrum are the highly structured, recurring, retrospective needs satisfied by the accounting transaction processing systems. At the other end of the spectrum are the unstructured, nonrecurring, prospective needs that must be met by decision support systems. All other systems, including those identified in Illustration 3–6, exist somewhere along this spectrum of management information needs, as shown in Illustration 3–7.

The Systems Approach

This chapter has shown how systems theory provides a structure for the study of systems, and how to apply the theory in accounting and management information systems. Systems theory also provides a structured way of planning and implementing changes to these systems: the *systems approach* to problem solving. The systems approach views the organization as a system with a defined objective. It recognizes the system–subsystem relationships in the organization and coordinates subsystem goals to achieve the overall objective. In this way, it takes the viewpoint of the organization as a whole.

Organizations frequently initiate changes to information systems in response to a perceived problem. Managers have learned that the systems approach is an effective way to evaluate potential solutions to the problem. They employ *systems analysts* who apply the systems approach to business problems. For example, if a budgeting system provides inadequate or incorrect information, management will assign a group of employees, including accountants, systems analysts, and others, to identify the source of the incorrect information and to recommend a solution. When applying the systems approach, the group performs the following tasks.

Define the Objective

After identifying the problem, the group then defines the objective of the system that contains it. Frequently, a problem exists because people do not clearly understand the system's objectives.

For example, among the possible objectives for a customer service department are the following: (1) to aid customers in quickly finding merchandise; (2) to resolve all customer complaints about product quality or service. If the customer service manager perceives the first as the objective when the second is the true objective, then problems will arise in resolving customer complaints.

During the information system design process, systems analysts first analyze existing systems to identify the relevant organizational objectives. Then they look for a solution to the information system problem.

Explore Alternative Solutions

Next, identify a range of alternative solutions to the problem. After defining the objective, identify as many ways as possible to achieve it; then carefully consider the advantages, disadvantages, costs, and benefits of each alternative. Many people mistakenly choose the first solution that occurs to them, when perhaps a better, less obvious solution exists. Analysts avoid this error by recording each of the alternatives, researching them, and carefully describing the analysis of each. After this process, analysts can make intelligent, objective choices. Professional systems analysts use design tools such as flowcharts, interview notes, and questionnaires to create working papers that help them explore and document alternatives.

Take a Broad Viewpoint

Examine the problem and solution alternatives from the viewpoint of the entire system, rather than limiting the analysis to the subsystem presenting the problem. This characteristic of the systems approach recognizes that supersystem and subsystem objectives may differ. An alternative that achieves subsystem objectives may be inadequate from the viewpoint of the larger supersystem. For example, a customer service manager can resolve every complaint by fully satisfying every unhappy customer, but in some companies this may be inconsistent with the company's desire to earn a profit and remain in business. A better solution is a compromise that adequately addresses both supersystem and subsystem objectives. Because of their knowledge of business information needs, systems analysts are able to evaluate trade-offs between the objectives of an organization and those of its subunits.

Obtain Varied Perspectives

Finally, analyze alternatives from several different viewpoints or perspectives. The information system design process accomplishes this using a *project team*. Because the members of a project team have varied backgrounds, each may contribute ideas that would not occur to other team members. Frequently, such a project team is directed by a systems analyst experienced in the use of the systems approach. Other members may include accountants, computer technicians, or internal auditors. The use of a project team accomplishes the same purpose as getting a friend's advice. A friend's perspective may suggest ideas that would never occur to you otherwise.

ILLUSTRATION 3–8

Applying the Systems Approach

1. **Identify the problem.** Evidenced by a decision-making situation.
2. **Define the objective.** Develop a clear understanding.
3. **Explore alternative solutions.** Identify both quantitative and qualitative costs and benefits.
4. **Take a broad viewpoint.** Examine the system as a whole rather than its subsystems.
5. **Obtain varied perspectives.** Using a project team encourages creative solutions.

The Systems Approach—an Example

Consider the problem of a new college student who must identify a place to live while at school. Many students take the easiest approach and apply for a room in a university dormitory. However, a student applying the systems approach may select a different alternative.

The student applying the systems approach first determines his or her objective. A student who likes to sleep late may wish to maximize convenience to the classrooms. If so, an on-campus dormitory may be best. But a student wishing a quiet place to study may select an off-campus location. A student wishing to minimize costs may live with parents or a relative. Students may want to be near a good friend, may desire especially luxurious or private accommodations, or may need to be within easy walking or commuting distance. Regardless, the choice of living accommodations depends on the student's objectives.

After determining the objective, the student can identify the alternative that best achieves the objectives. This requires that the student determine availability, cost, affordability, desirability, preferences of friends, and distance from the campus. The student should record his or her objective and list the alternatives that best fulfill it. When there are multiple objectives, the student must consider trade-offs between them and identify an alternative that satisfies the most important ones.

When applying the systems approach to information system design, organizations consider the problem from different perspectives by using a project team. The student choosing living accommodations can obtain different perspectives by consulting parents, university officials, friends, and other students who have made the same decision.

The systems approach is a useful way to approach any problem or decision-making situation. Illustration 3–8 summarizes the steps in applying the systems approach. Chapter 5 describes some alternative ways of using it in information system development.

Summary

This chapter presented many of the concepts underlying systems theory and applied these concepts to accounting systems and to management information systems. Systems exist at many different levels; supersystems are made up of components, or subsystems, that are also systems. Each system is defined by a boundary and interacts with other systems through interfaces at the boundary. Sometimes the interface provides decoupling, which affects the system's operations. Systems are developed by a procedure utilizing the systems approach to problem solving.

Accounting information systems are subsystems of the management information system and are used to make structured and semistructured decisions at the operational and management control levels. The accounting information systems discussed in this chapter were the transaction processing system, the budgeting system, and the responsibility reporting system. The transaction processing system is composed of four subsystems called transaction cycles. Each transaction cycle is composed of one or more accounting application systems.

Key Terms

application system   A set of procedures and computer programs that perform a specific accounting objective.

closed system   A system totally isolated from its environment.

decision support system   An information system that provides information primarily at higher organizational levels to aid decisions that are usually unstructured. Although it may rely on accounting information, a decision support system is ordinarily not an accounting information system.

decoupling   A feature that sometimes exists at system interfaces, allowing the systems to operate independently.

feedback control system   A system in which a portion of its output is returned as an input.

information system   A set of organized procedures that, when executed, provides information to support decision making and control in an organization.

interface   The connection between two systems occurring at the boundaries of the systems.

open system   A system in which its interaction with its environment is not controlled.

relatively closed system   A system that reacts with its environment in a known, controlled way.

subsystem   A component part of a system that is itself a system.

system   A set of parts coordinated to accomplish a set of goals.

systems approach   A way of approaching a problem that recognizes the system–subsystem relationships in any problem situation and provides a structured method for solving the problem.

transaction cycle   The accounting transactions recording an organization's economic events that normally follow each other in a cyclical way. There are four transaction cycles: the revenue cycle, the expenditure cycle, the conversion cycle, and the financial cycle.

transaction processing system   An accounting information system that provides information for structured decisions primarily at the operational level. It also provides information that is summarized and used by other information systems.

Questions

3–1. What is the definition of a system?

3–2. How does a system differ from a supersystem? From a subsystem?

3–3. Which four systems are recognized by systems theory? Of these, which is the most common in your environment?

3–4. What are the three components of an accounting information system?

3–5. What are the inputs to an accounting information system? The processes? The outputs?

3–6. How does a system boundary differ from a system interface?

3–7. What is the purpose of decoupling?

3–8. What are the levels in management's hierarchy of decision-making activities? What are the distinctions between them?

3–9. How can you characterize the decision problems that commonly face top management? Middle management? Operating management?

3–10. Accounting information systems are more standardized than other information systems. At which decision levels are these systems most useful? Which decision problems do accounting systems address?

3–11. What are the steps in the systems approach to problem solving?

Exercises and Cases

3–12.   SUBSYSTEMS AND SUPERSYSTEMS

Identify the subsystems and supersystems in each of the following groups of systems:

a. Inventory system, management information system, transaction processing system, accounting information system.
b. Solar system, Jupiter, universe, human race, Earth.
c. Computer system, information system, central processing unit, computer user, floppy disk drive.
d. Air conditioner, electrical system, headlights, radiator, steering system, automobile.

3–13.   APPLYING SYSTEMS CONCEPTS

Think of one system that has not been discussed in this chapter.

a. For this system, identify each of the following:
  1. Objectives.
  2. Inputs.
  3. Processes.
  4. Outputs.
  5. Levels.
  6. Boundaries.
  7. Interfaces.
  8. Decoupling.

b. Which controls can you suggest that would limit the impact of disturbances to this system?

3–14.   PREVENTIVE AND DETECTIVE CONTROLS

In a system, controls are used either to prevent or to detect disturbances. Identify each of the following as either a preventive or a detective control:

a. Footing and crossfooting.
b. Temperature-controlled computer room.
c. Personal computer surge protector.
d. Highway speed limit.
e. Police radar unit.
f. Proctor for an examination.

3–15.   ACCOUNTING ENTRIES AND TRANSACTIONS

In an introductory accounting course, you learn proper accounting entries for certain transactions. The following accounting transactions produce these entries; for each, identify the transaction cycle of which it is a part.

a. Cash sale.
b. Credit sale.
c. Obtain long-term bank loan.
d. Purchase materials.
e. Pay debt.
f. Sell stock.
g. Manufacture product to inventory.
h. Pay employees.

3–16.   MANAGEMENT ACTIVITIES AND DECISION-MAKING LEVELS

Classify each of the following management activities by decision-making level. Identify each as either strategic planning, management control, or operational control.

a. Assign worker to factory task.
b. Develop production schedule.
c. Authorize construction of new factory.
d. Hire factory personnel.
e. Acquire manufacturing subsidiary.
f. Select new product for development.
g. Bill customer for product.

3–17.   JOB POSITIONS AND DECISION LEVELS

The following positions are typical in a manufacturing company. For each job, decide whether the position's decisions are primarily strategic, management control, or operational.

a. Corporation president.
b. Accounts payable supervisor.
c. Controller.
d. Chief accountant.

   e. Factory manager.

   f. Vice president, manufacturing.

   g. Shop foreman.

   h. Product line sales manager.

   i. District sales manager.

3–18. *MANAGEMENT DECISIONS AND DECISION LEVELS*

Look at the following list of typical management decisions. First, classify each decision as either a structured, semistructured, or unstructured decision. Second, suggest the level of the job position that normally makes the decision.

   a. Accept an order from a customer.

   b. Promote an employee.

   c. Expand sales to an overseas market.

   d. Allocate capital to divisions for reinvestment.

   e. Approve an adjusting journal entry.

   f. Post an adjusting journal entry.

   g. Approve a purchase order to an existing vendor.

   h. Terminate an employee.

3–19. *SYSTEMS APPROACH*

The following are some decision problems that students commonly face. Describe how you would apply the systems approach to each situation.

   a. High school student selecting a college or university.

   b. College student selecting a method of transportation.

   c. College student selecting a profession.

   d. College student selecting a graduate school.

3–20. *SYSTEMS APPROACH*

Greenleaf University has a beautiful, tree-shaded campus located in a wealthy residential part of a city of 500,000. The blending of architecture with its natural surroundings impresses students and visitors alike. Unfortunately, this creates a problem for university administration: Many more students would like to live on the campus than the university can accommodate.

Currently, on-campus residential housing can accommodate only about half the student body. The director of housing estimates that about 1,000 additional students would choose to live on campus if adequate rooms were available at a reasonable cost. They can build additional dormitories, but this requires that the university destroy much of the scenery that makes it such a pleasant place to live and work. Current dormitory rooms on campus rent for $1,000 per year, double occupancy. The director of university planning estimates that, if new dormitories were built, rates for these rooms would be 20 percent higher.

Required:

Describe how you would apply the systems approach to the decision problem facing Greenleaf's administration.

3–21.   PROJECT TEAMS

Mega-Systems, Inc., is a large company that manufactures and markets office information processing systems. Mega-Systems has consistently been innovative and profitable. From its corporate headquarters and manufacturing facilities in the Midwest, the company has developed a regional system for marketing and servicing its products. The regions are operated as profit centers because regional managers have significant amounts of authority within their territories. The regional organizations consist of an accounting and budget department, a personnel and training department, and several area offices that market and service the products. The regional organization provides accounting and personnel services for area offices. Each of these offices consists of sales, service, and administrative departments headed by managers who report to the area manager.

The Los Angeles area office has departed from the standard organizational structure by establishing a branch office to market and service the firm's products in the San Diego area. This office is headed by a branch manager who reports to the area manager. Sales and services for the remainder of the Los Angeles territory are handled by the Los Angeles area sales manager and service manager, respectively. A partial organization chart showing the relationships among the Western Region, Los Angeles area, and San Diego branch offices is presented in Exhibit 3–1.

The San Diego branch office was opened over a decade ago and was very profitable until the past two years, when it has had declining profits; the most recent two quarters showed losses. The Los Angeles area manager and the Western Region manager have concluded that a project team with people from the regional office, the area office, and the branch office should be established to identify San Diego's problems and make recommendations to correct them. The manager of the Western Region, in consultation with the Los Angeles area manager, appointed the following people to the project team with Richard Moore named chairperson:

Western Region office
John Overton, budget supervisor
Sally Miller, training director
Los Angeles area office
Richard Moore, administrative department manager
San Diego branch
David Alworth, branch manager and sales manager
Tim Smithson, assistant branch manager and service manager
Robert Tishman, salesperson
Harry Bend, serviceperson

Required:

a. A project team, such as the one illustrated for Mega-Systems, Inc., is a group of individuals who contribute their particular skills to accomplish a given objective. Characteristics of members of the group can influence the functioning and effectiveness of it. Identify some of these characteristics.

EXHIBIT 3–1

Case 3–21

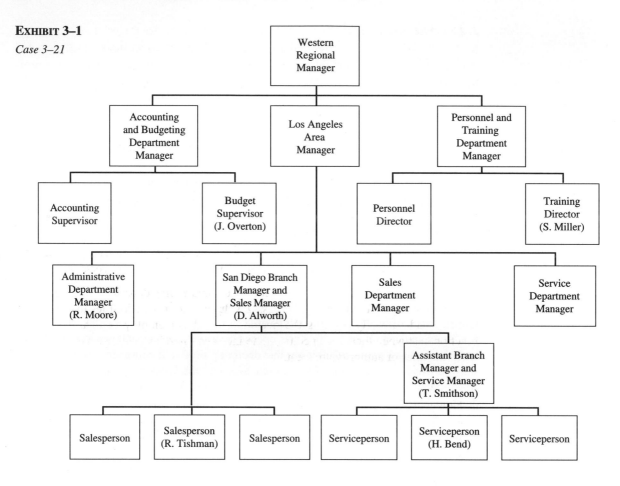

b. What sources of conflict can you foresee arising among the members of this group because of its composition? Do you think it can achieve its objective?

c. What contribution would a person who holds a position as budget supervisor make in a project team such as this one?

(CMA Adapted)

3–22.   *A BOOKKEEPING DEPARTMENT*

Linda Fry is the supervisor for the bookkeeping department of Medford Bank and Trust. The department processes 10,000 to 15,000 checks and related items daily. Six clerical employees perform this work under Fry's direct supervision.

The sequence of events in preparing canceled checks for processing by the book-keeping department is as follows:

1. Checks are processed through the proof department, where the dollar amount is microencoded onto the check and a record of the transaction is input to computer records.

ILLUSTRATION 4–1

Good Interviewing Techniques

1. Make an appointment for the interview in advance. Employees you wish to interview appreciate this courtesy, and it makes your job easier.
2. Arrive for the interview on time. Thank the other person for taking time to talk to you.
3. Prepare a list of questions in advance. Keep the list in front of you during the interview, and take notes on the person's answers and comments. Questionnaires are useful for this purpose.
4. Dress appropriately for the interview. If the other person wears a suit, do the same. If he or she is attired for physical work, you should be more casual. Overdressing may intimidate the other person.
5. Ask direct questions and obtain answers to them. Often the person may digress, and you may have to return the discussion to the original question.
6. Be courteous and do not interrupt the other person. Sit at an angle with the person. Sitting directly in front may be interpreted as a confrontational position.
7. When finished, thank the person again. Request permission to ask additional questions later if needed.
8. After the interview, find a quiet place to review your notes. Elaborate on what you wrote, write other comments you remember that the person made, and write your conclusions. Transcribe any abbreviations you used during note taking. These facts could be hard to remember later.

Flowcharting

Charts are widely used by auditors and systems analysts because they concisely summarize ideas that may require many words to express. One of the most useful forms is the *flowchart,* which describes the relationships among sequential processes. There are a variety of flowcharts, including system, program, and document flowcharts. Before studying these, first become acquainted with the standard flowchart symbols.

Standard Flowchart Symbols

For most purposes, accountants use standard flowchart symbols recommended by the American National Standards Institute (ANSI), the International Organization for Standardization (ISO), and International Business Machines Corporation (IBM). The symbols are limited in number and yet broad enough to describe most systems. There are three kinds of symbols: basic, programming, and systems.

Basic symbols are flexible in their applications and are important to know because they are used frequently. They are used with any of the programming or systems symbols. Illustration 4–2 explains the five basic flowchart symbols.

Illustration 4–3 shows the symbols related to programming. Programmers use them, along with the basic symbols, to describe the logic of computer programs. Accountants encounter these four programming symbols when reviewing program documentation for accounting systems.

The third kind are systems symbols, which accountants use to document reviews of internal control and to describe the operations of a proposed information system. Although some basic and programming symbols are interchangeable with certain systems symbols, the latter have more specific meanings. For example, the *input/output* symbol, a basic symbol, may signify any form of computer output. However, a *document,* a *display,* or a *magnetic tape* systems symbol may suffice. Good flowcharting technique is to use the more specific representation whenever possible. Illustration 4–4 contains 14 systems symbols.

ILLUSTRATION 4–2

*Basic Flowcharting
Symbols*

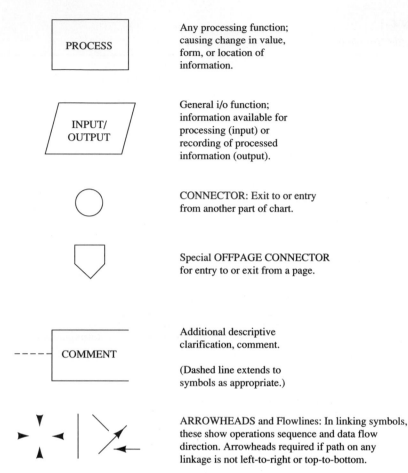

PROCESS — Any processing function; causing change in value, form, or location of information.

INPUT/ OUTPUT — General i/o function; information available for processing (input) or recording of processed information (output).

CONNECTOR: Exit to or entry from another part of chart.

Special OFFPAGE CONNECTOR for entry to or exit from a page.

COMMENT — Additional descriptive clarification, comment.

(Dashed line extends to symbols as appropriate.)

ARROWHEADS and Flowlines: In linking symbols, these show operations sequence and data flow direction. Arrowheads required if path on any linkage is not left-to-right or top-to-bottom.

Since these standard flowchart symbols have many applications throughout this book, being able to recognize them is essential. The three kinds of flowcharts that accountants use are discussed on the following pages.

System Flowcharts

A *system flowchart* is a pictorial representation that shows the relationships between processes. Flowlines represent the sequences of processes, and other symbols represent the inputs and outputs to a process. Accountants use system flowcharts to describe the computerized processes, manual operations, and inputs and outputs of an application system.

A properly drawn system flowchart alternately uses two kinds of symbols. A symbol representing an operation, such as the *process, manual operation,* or *auxiliary operation* symbol, is preceded by a symbol showing the input to the operation. It is followed by another symbol for the output. This output may be an input to another operation. Thus, the system flowchart contains alternate layers of data identification and operation identification. In this way the flowchart specifies each process in the system

ILLUSTRATION 4–3

Programming Symbols

A decision or switching-type operation that determines which of a number of alternative paths followed.

Instruction modification to change program—set a switch, modify an index register, initialize a routine.

One or more named operations or program steps specified in a subroutine or another set of flowcharts.

A terminal point in a flowchart: start, stop, halt, delay, or interrupt; may show exit from a closed subroutine.

and the inputs and outputs for the process. The direction of flow in a flowchart should proceed from top to bottom and from left to right.

Illustration 4–5 contains a well-drawn system flowchart that depicts part of an accounts receivable application. It begins with a *manual input* symbol. This shows the input of individual sales transactions to a computer program depicted by a *process* symbol. The output of the process is a computer file represented by the *online storage* symbol. This is the input to the next process. The last process, update customer master file, has two inputs and three outputs.

Program Flowcharts

A system flowchart represents each computer program in an accounting application by the *process* symbol and its accompanying verbal identification. Although this provides a high-level description of a system, it does not describe how individual computer programs work. Computer programmers do this by drawing program flowcharts.

A ***program flow diagram*** shows in detail each processing step of a computer program. Similar to a system flowchart, a program flowchart uses flowlines to show the sequence of these steps. The lines proceed from top to bottom and left to right across the page. A *terminal* programming symbol both starts and stops the flow. Complete documentation for an accounting system includes program flowcharts for all programs identified on the system flowchart. Often each program consists of several modules, or segments. In this case, there is a flowchart for each module.

Illustration 4–6 shows a flowchart for one program from Illustration 4–5. It is the update customer master file program, which posts sales transactions to customers'

ILLUSTRATION 4–4

Systems Flowcharting Symbols

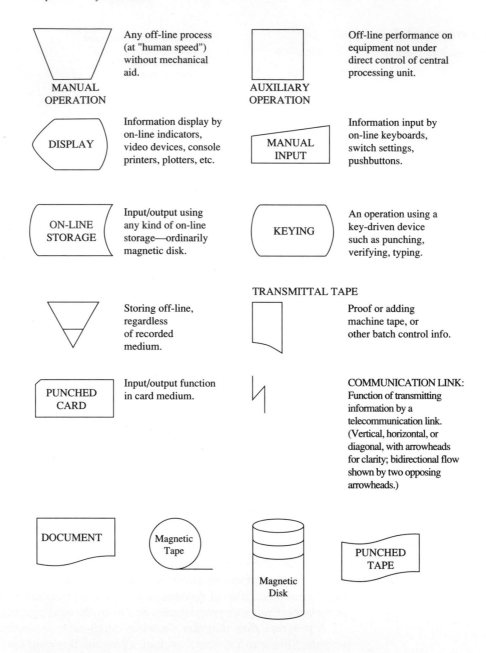

MANUAL OPERATION — Any off-line process (at "human speed") without mechanical aid.

AUXILIARY OPERATION — Off-line performance on equipment not under direct control of central processing unit.

DISPLAY — Information display by on-line indicators, video devices, console printers, plotters, etc.

MANUAL INPUT — Information input by on-line keyboards, switch settings, pushbuttons.

ON-LINE STORAGE — Input/output using any kind of on-line storage—ordinarily magnetic disk.

KEYING — An operation using a key-driven device such as punching, verifying, typing.

Storing off-line, regardless of recorded medium.

TRANSMITTAL TAPE — Proof or adding machine tape, or other batch control info.

PUNCHED CARD — Input/output function in card medium.

COMMUNICATION LINK: Function of transmitting information by a telecommunication link. (Vertical, horizontal, or diagonal, with arrowheads for clarity; bidirectional flow shown by two opposing arrowheads.)

DOCUMENT

Magnetic Tape

Magnetic Disk

PUNCHED TAPE

accounts in the accounts receivable subsidiary records. This program reads one sales transaction from a transaction file containing records of all sales. Next it reads the master file containing customer accounts until it finds the account number of the customer receiving the sale. The program adds the amount of the sale to the customer's outstanding balance; then it processes the next sales transaction in the same way. When all transactions are recorded, the program stops.

ILLUSTRATION 4–5

A System Flowchart

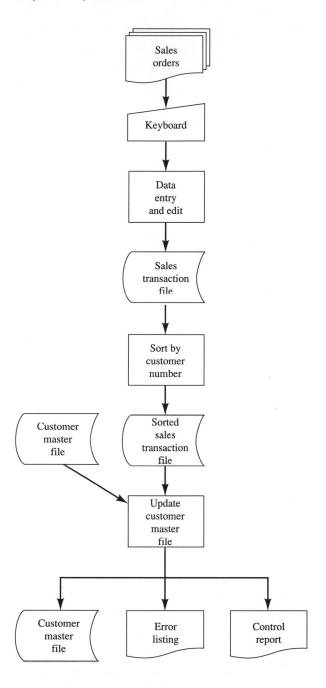

Accountants may examine program flowcharts when evaluating the internal control of a computer-based system. If flowcharts don't exist, they may use automated program flowchart generators. These are computer software packages that read an existing computer program and produce a flowchart of it. Sometimes accountants also program a

ILLUSTRATION 4–6

A Program Flowchart

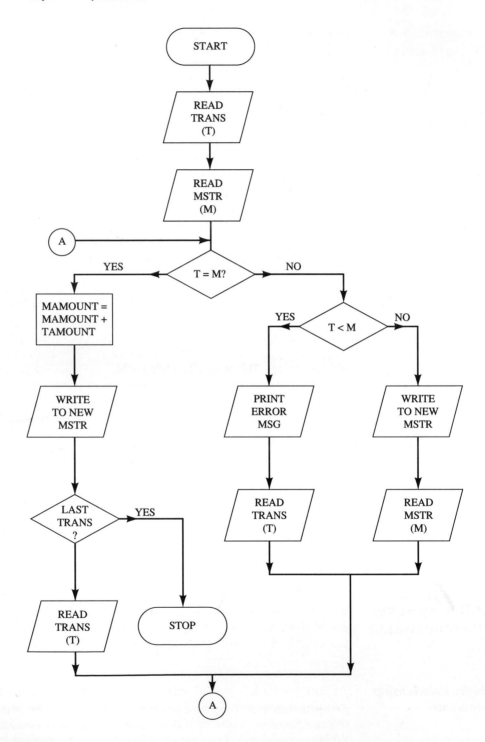

system. In this case, they draw flowcharts to describe how their programs work. Software is available to aid in this process also. Another flowchart accountants use frequently is the document flowchart.

Document
Flowcharts

While a system flowchart shows the flow of data between processes, a ***document flowchart*** emphasizes the flow of documents between organizational units. Auditors use them when documenting a client's internal control procedures. Systems analysts also use them to describe noncomputerized procedures when designing a new system.

When drawing a document flowchart, divide the page into columns separated by vertical lines. Each column represents an organizational unit, such as a department, office, or employee. An operations symbol within a column indicates that the unit performs an operation. When a document moves from one department to another, the flowchart shows this by a flowline connecting the document symbol in each department. Flowlines start in the upper left corner of the page and proceed down and to the right.

Illustration 4–7 contains a document flowchart showing procedures to accept and fill a sales request from a customer. The order department receives the customer's order; from it they make four copies of an internal document, the sales order. These are sent to the shipping department, which includes copy 4 as a packing list with the goods when shipped. Copy 2 of the sales order returns to the order department, and copy 3 goes into off-line storage. This is usually a filing cabinet. The letter P in this symbol indicates that this is a permanent file. (Analysts may also use the letters A for alphabetic, N for numeric, and T for temporary in this way.) Copy 1 of the sales order goes to the billing department, which prepares a three-part invoice. Invoice copy 1 is mailed to the customer; invoice copies 2 and 3 go to the accounts receivable department.

A document flowchart is most useful for describing noncomputerized procedures. Both document flowcharts and system flowcharts are necessary to adequately describe a computer-based accounting system. For example, in the sales order entry system of Illustration 4–7, accounts receivable receives two copies of the invoice and records the sale in the customer's account. If they use a noncomputerized system, they record the sale on a ledger page. If they use a computerized system, the system flowchart of Illustration 4–5 describes a possible set of procedures.

Other Systems Documentation

Besides flowcharts, accountants use other forms of documentation to describe accounting information systems. They include entity-relationship diagrams, data flow diagrams, system charts, structure charts, and decision tables.

Entity-Relationship
Diagrams

An ***entity-relationship (E-R) diagram*** depicts the associations between items of data stored in a computer system. Analysts create them in the process of data modeling during systems development. Different conventions exist for drawing them, but usually a box represents a type of data and a line connecting boxes indicates the nature of the relationship. Illustration 4–8 represents one way of doing this.

AIS in Practice

Hewlett-Packard Corporation (HP) designs, manufactures, and services equipment and systems for measurement, computation, and communications. Headquartered in California, the company employs 112,000 people. It has design and manufacturing facilities in 18 countries and sales offices worldwide. Annual revenues approximate $40 billion.

HP has information system (IS) facilities at both corporate and divisional levels. Believing that user involvement is vital to the success of a new system, the HP division at Boise, Idaho, used its accountants in the design of a new financial information system. Two groups were involved from the finance area: forecasting and reporting. With the help of IS professionals, these accountants learned how to develop data models using entity-relationship diagrams. They designed a database that is used by both financial reporting and in forecasting systems. The database not only satisfies current information requirements but is flexible enough to meet the division's unforeseen needs.

This illustration shows six entities: customer, invoice, invoice item, customer order, customer order item, and inventory stock. The computer stores data about each entity in its memory. Lines show relationships between these entities, and the words and symbols on a line describe the relationship. For example, the top line shows three relationships: that the customer places the customer order, that for each customer there may be many orders, and that each order applies only to one customer. System designers need this information when they decide how to store data in the computer.

An E-R diagram represents an entity with a rectangle containing the entity's name. A line connecting two rectangles represents a relationship between two entities. At each end of the line a small symbol shows the nature of the relationship. If this symbol is a bar perpendicular to the line, it means "only one." If the symbol is a crow's foot, it means "one or more." Some modeling conventions use a small circle next to the other symbol to indicate the possibility of no occurrence.

Above the line to the left, the analyst concisely describes in words the relationship that the left entity has with the right entity. Below the line to the right, the analyst describes the relationship that the right entity has to the left entity. The chapter on implementing database management systems discusses E-R diagrams in more detail.

Data Flow Diagrams

Data flow diagrams use a small number of simple symbols to represent the flow of data between processes, data stores, and external destinations. They differ from flowcharts because they emphasize the flow of data rather than the flow of documents or records containing data. In other words, data flow diagrams show logical rather than physical flows. Because fewer symbols are involved, people using data flow diagrams must be more careful in selecting verbal descriptions to communicate their ideas.

Data flow diagrams are useful for describing data flows at varying levels. For example, a systems analyst using this technique can show data flows between organizational units, between individuals within a unit, between computer programs within a system, or between modules within a computer program. Early in the system development process, analysts draw data flow diagrams at a high level with little detail. As development proceeds, they refine them to show more detail. Ultimately, they completely specify data flows in the new system.

ILLUSTRATION 4–7

A Document Flowchart

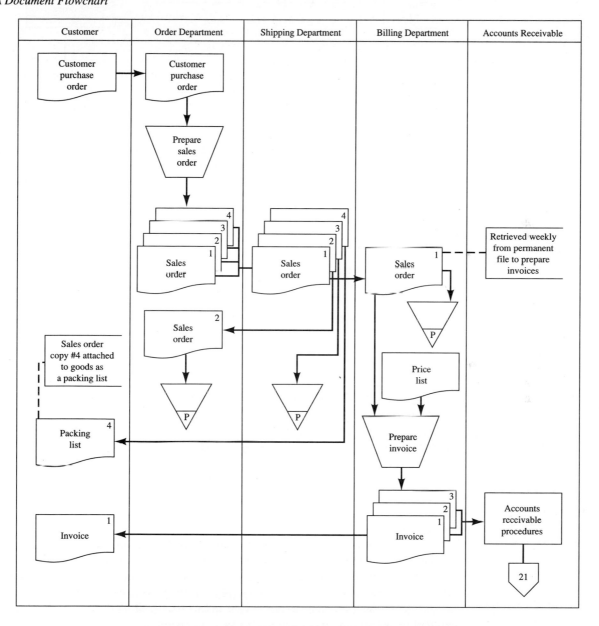

Data flow diagrams exist in different forms. In the DeMarco-Yourdon symbol set, a circle represents a process, a square indicates an external destination for data (such as a customer, a supplier, or an employee), a rectangle that is open on two sides represents a data store, and arrows represent the flow of data. Each flow begins at a destination or store, goes through a process, and terminates at a destination or store.

ILLUSTRATION 4–8

*An Entity-Relationship
Diagram*

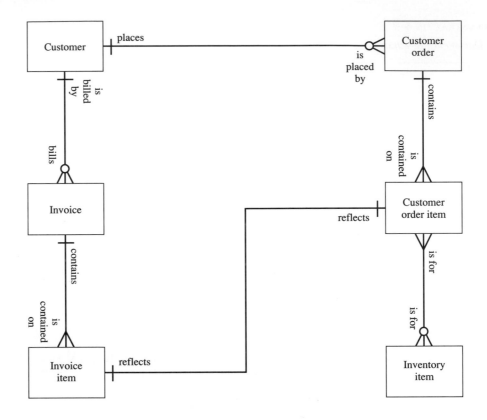

Illustration 4–9 shows a data flow diagram for a sales order entry application. In this diagram, a customer's order for goods is recorded in a sales order file. After an order is filled, it is recorded in a sales journal and an accounts receivable subsidiary file. Posting to the general ledger occurs from the sales journal.

Data flow diagrams differ from flowcharts in several ways. Although each uses symbols to represent processes, data flow diagrams do not show the *sequence* of processes, as do flowcharts. Thus, a single data flow diagram may show several processes operating in parallel. As Illustration 4–9 shows, recording and filling orders may take place simultaneously.

Furthermore, in a data flow diagram, the arrows connecting processes with destinations or stores indicate nothing about the timing of the processes. A single data flow diagram may contain processes that occur daily (such as recording and filling customer orders in Illustration 4–9), or monthly (posting them to a general ledger). Finally, because data flow diagrams do not have symbols representing decisions, they cannot explicitly represent the *if* occurrences or looping operations that are common in flowcharts.

System Charts

A *system chart* provides a graphic representation of the equipment configuration of a computer system. By convention, a system chart shows input devices to the left and output devices to the right. The example in Illustration 4–10 shows input by three

ILLUSTRATION 4–9

A Data Flow Diagram

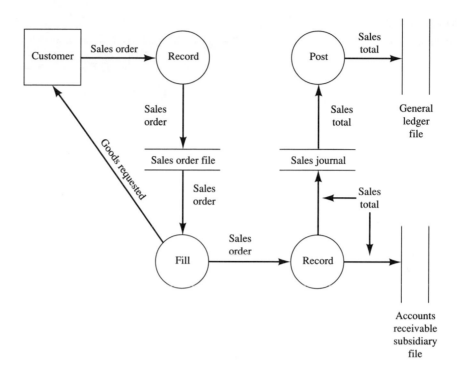

remote and one local keyboard data entry devices. The outputs are a video display and the *document* symbol, which indicates a printer. This system chart uses the *process* symbol to represent the central processing unit, and the *magnetic disk* symbol for an information storage device. A system chart for an actual system also contains verbal descriptions of the equipment.

Structure Charts

Many companies develop programs in modules. Each computer program is a module composed of a set of smaller modules. Individuals develop and test each one individually and then test all of them together. When using a modular approach to program development, many organizations use structure charts to document the programs.

A *structure chart* identifies each of the modules making up the program and shows the hierarchy between them. This hierarchy exists because a high-level module may cause the execution of one or more lower-level modules. On the structure chart, each module is represented by a rectangle. The hierarchical relationship between modules is shown by the levels on the chart. Modules execute in sequence from top to bottom and from left to right. Illustration 4–11 contains an example of a structure chart.

Decision Tables

Another useful systems tool is the preparation of *decision tables.* These offer a concise way to summarize outcomes of complex decisions, and they provide a tabular representation of the logic in a program flowchart. Decision tables offer advantages over flowcharts when there are a large number of alternatives; however, they do not disclose the sequences.

ILLUSTRATION 4–10

A System Chart

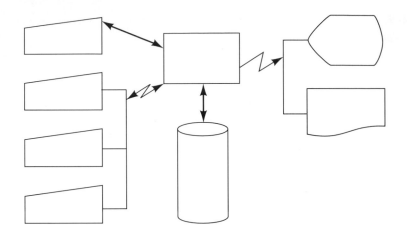

A decision table is a matrix divided into three sections. The left half of the decision table contains two sections, a list of *conditions* and a list of *actions.* The right half contains several columns. Each column represents a *rule,* which is a combination of conditions and actions. Each rule shows the action taken whenever a combination of conditions occurs. An accountant could use a flowchart to show the information contained in a decision table; however, the flowchart is difficult to follow when a large number of conditions and actions are present.

To illustrate the use of decision tables, consider a common decision in an inventory application. In a computer-based system, either a clerk or a computer decides whether to place an order to replenish inventory. For each inventory item, the following six conditions determine the action taken:

1. Is the current inventory level below the reorder point?
2. Was the item sold during the previous month?

ILLUSTRATION 4–11

A Structure Chart

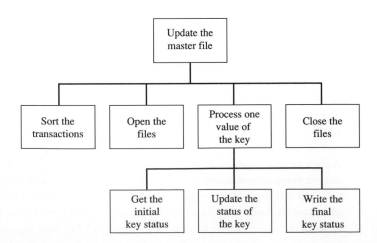

3. Has the inventory reached a critical point below the reorder point?
4. Is the item currently being produced?
5. Will the item be sold in the future?
6. Are sales of the item profitable?

Illustration 4–12 shows a flowchart of this decision. It contains six decision symbols, one representing each condition. It also contains two process symbols, one for each possible action. Notice how awkward the flowchart is, and compare it to the decision table in Illustration 4–13.

This decision table shows the six conditions in the upper left portion, called the *condition stub*. The two actions are in the lower left portion, the *action stub*. The upper right portion of the decision table, known as the *condition entry*, contains seven rules. For each rule, if a condition is present, the intersection of the row and column contains a Y. If not, it contains an N. The lower right portion, the *action entry*, shows the action resulting from each condition. Each rule in the decision table corresponds to one logic path through the flowchart.

With some combinations of conditions, when certain conditions are irrelevant to the decision, the condition entries for these combinations are blank. For example, only one condition is relevant to rule 1. Whenever the inventory level exceeds the reorder point, no order is placed regardless of any other condition. The decision table indicates this by leaving blank the rows for the other conditions in the condition entry. By custom, the simplest rule is listed first and the most complex last, producing a triangular shape for the contents of the condition entry.

When should decision tables be used? Whenever there are more than three conditions, a decision table is valuable. It summarizes the logic more clearly and concisely than a flowchart, making it easier for someone to identify errors or omissions. The blanks in the condition entry clearly identify irrelevant combinations of conditions not readily identified in a flowchart.

When developing accounting systems, many programmers and analysts use both decision tables and flowcharts. They create the decision table first to ensure that all conditions are considered. They then draw the flowchart showing the sequence in which conditions are evaluated. This approach ensures that all possibilities are described in complex situations.

Accountants use flowcharts and decision tables when developing new systems and when reviewing old ones. Systems analysts use data flow diagrams and structure charts when developing systems, and auditors review them during an audit. The next section describes Gantt charts and network diagrams, two tools used to manage large system development projects.

Project Management Tools

A successful system is one that is completed within a reasonable period of time. System development projects require from a few months to a few years to complete; they almost always require more time than originally expected. Evaluation of the manager in charge of a development project is based on whether the project is implemented on time and within the budget. Project management tools help to accomplish these goals.

ILLUSTRATION 4–12

Flowchart for an
Inventory Decision

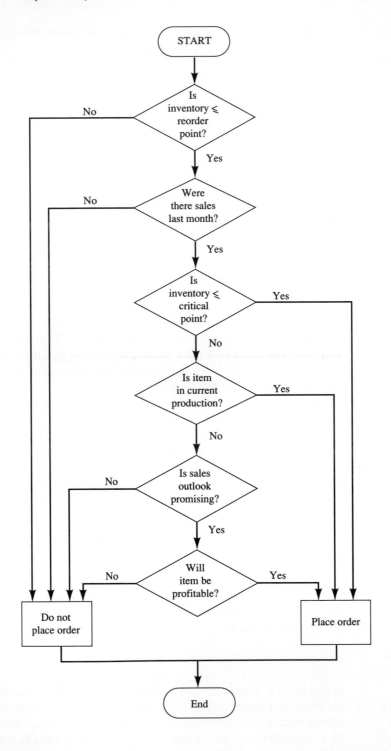

ILLUSTRATION 4–13

A Decision Table

	Inventory-Replenishment Decision Rules						
	Rule 1	Rule 2	Rule 3	Rule 4	Rule 5	Rule 6	Rule 7
Conditions:							
1. Inventory ≤ reorder point	N	Y	Y	Y	Y	Y	Y
2. Sales last month		N	Y	Y	Y	Y	Y
3. Inventory ≤ critical point			Y	N	N	N	N
4. Item currently in production				Y	N	N	N
5. Sales outlook promising					N	Y	Y
6. Profit from sales satisfactory						N	Y
Actions:							
1. Place production order			X	X			X
2. Do not place production order	X	X			X	X	

Two project management tools that aid in the timely completion of development projects are Gantt charts and network diagrams. The following example project will help you understand how these techniques work.

An Example Project

Developing a new accounting system consists of many different tasks and requires coordinated efforts by many people. Project management techniques are especially helpful in managing this process.

Project management tools require an analyst to divide the project into distinct activities. Each activity has measurable outputs and a clearly defined beginning and end. The analyst also estimates the time required to complete each task and determines the sequences that they follow. A time budget summarizes this information.

Illustration 4–14 contains a time budget for the activities of the implementation phase of the system development life cycle, which is described in a later chapter. For now, concentrate on learning the project management tools.

This system development project requires 12 implementation activities. Activity A, *establish policies*, requires an estimated one month from start to finish. Because it has no preceding activity, it can begin at any time. Activity D, *train personnel*, requires one and one-half months and cannot begin until activities B and C are complete. Illustration 4–14 shows the estimated times and preceding activities for each of the other 10. Analysts use a Gantt chart to manage the implementation phase of this project.

Gantt Charts

A **Gantt chart** is a form of graph developed by Henry L. Gantt in the early 1900s. On a Gantt chart, the horizontal axis represents elapsed time and the vertical axis contains a list of activities. A horizontal line connects the beginning and ending times for each activity. The chart schedules the activities so that each begins after the end of all preceding ones.

Illustration 4–15 is a Gantt chart for the implementation activities of Illustration 4–14. It shows that activity A, *establish policies,* is completed before activities B, C, E,

ILLUSTRATION 4–14

Time Budget for Implementation

	Activity	Estimated Duration in Months	Preceding Activity
A	Establish policies	1	—
B	Select personnel	3	A
C	Prepare user manuals	3	A
D	Train personnel	1½	B, C
E	Develop programming standards	½	A
F	Code programs	5½	E
G	Test systems	1	F, J
H	Convert files	½	G
I	Prepare site	2	A
J	Install equipment	1	I
K	Parallel operations	3	D, H
L	User review and sign-off	½	K

and I are begun. The last activity, *user review and sign-off,* ends after 12 months have elapsed.

Gantt charts are easy to develop and to interpret. They show the precedence of activities more clearly than time budgets, and they indicate the total elapsed time required for the project. For these reasons they are widely used to manage system development projects.

An organization can alter the duration of a project by changing the resources allocated to it. For example, by assigning more programmers to activity F, *code programs,* the project manager decreases the time required for this activity. This possibly decreases the implementation time for the system. However, from the Gantt chart the manager cannot determine if this would occur. Other project management tools using network techniques provide this information.

Network Diagrams

Widely used *network techniques* include PERT and CPM. These methods for managing large projects are similar and were developed about the same time. The United States Navy created Program Evaluation and Review Technique (PERT) and first applied it to develop a missile. E. I. du Pont de Nemours created Critical Path Method (CPM) to manage the construction of a chemical plant. Many variations of these two techniques now exist, and computer software packages to implement them are widely available.

These approaches represent the project as a network of nodes and arcs. In PERT, an arc represents an activity of the project, and nodes signify the beginning or end of an activity. The sequence of the arcs shows the sequence of the activities. Labels identify durations, starting times, and stopping times for activities. A CPM network is similar, except that nodes represent activities. Illustration 4–16 contains a PERT diagram for the activities of Illustration 4–14. One variation of PERT specifies the probabilities of the estimated times. The diagram helps determine the probability that a project will be completed by a specified date. A case at the end of this chapter illustrates probabilistic PERT.

ILLUSTRATION 4–15

A Gantt Chart

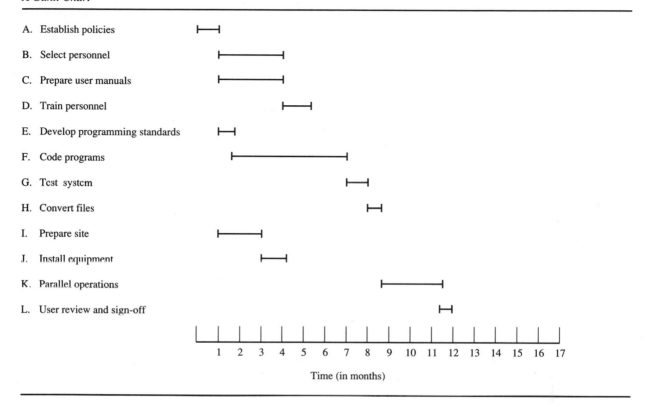

Most computer programs implementing PERT represent each arc as an arrow and identify it by its beginning and ending nodes. They number the nodes so that the node at the point of an arrow is always higher than the one at the tail. This is how you specify the sequence of activities to the PERT program. In Illustration 4–16, the arc representing activity A begins with node 1 and ends at node 2. Its estimated duration is one month.

Label E identifies an activity's earliest possible start time, also called its *optimistic time*. Label L shows the latest possible start time without delaying the project's completion, or the *pessimistic time*. For activity D, *train personnel,* the early start time is the fourth month of the project. If this activity begins later than 7 months into the project, the project will not be completed within 12 months.

The difference between the early start time (E) and the late start time (L) for an activity is its *slack*. An activity's slack is the amount of additional time the activity can require without delaying the project. For activity D in Illustration 4–14, the slack is three months. This activity can require up to four and one-half months to complete without delaying the project.

The major advantage of network techniques is that they identify the *critical path,* which is the sequence of project activities that requires the longest elapsed time. These are the activities that determine the duration of the project. If any activity on the critical path is delayed, the entire project is delayed.

ILLUSTRATION 4–16

A PERT Network Diagram

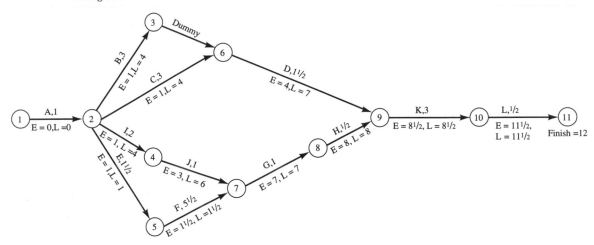

You can easily identify the activities on the critical path because they are the ones that have no slack. For these activities, the early start time E equals the late start time L. In the PERT diagram of Illustration 4–16, the critical path contains activities A-E-F-G-H-K-L. The total duration of these activities is 12 months, which equals the duration of the project.

Network diagrams are useful in managing system development projects because they enable the project manager to predict the effect of reallocating resources. The manager may transfer resources from an activity with slack to one on the critical path. Called *crashing,* this often decreases the time required to complete the project. In the implementation phase example, the project manager may reassign personnel from activity D, *train personnel,* to activity F, *code programs.* This decreases the duration for activity F, shortens the critical path, and decreases the time required for the project.

For complex projects, network techniques are difficult to implement without the aid of a computer. Fortunately, software programs that implement them are readily available. Illustration 4–17 shows the output of a PERT computer program used to analyze the project of Illustration 4–14.

Summary

This chapter describes nine techniques for developing and reviewing accounting systems. They are flowcharting, entity-relationship diagrams, data flow diagrams, system charts, structure charts, decision tables, Gantt charts, network diagrams, and interviews.

ILLUSTRATION 4–17

Output of a PERT Computer Program

```
PROJECT:  System Implementation
DATE:  01-30-1998
```

No.	Act	Description	Begin Event	End Event	Optimist Time	Likely Time	Pessimist Time
1	A	Establish Policies	1	2	1.00	1.00	1.00
2	B	Select Personnel	2	3	3.00	3.00	3.00
3	C	Prepare User Manuals	2	6	3.00	3.00	3.00
4	E	Develop Prog Stds	2	5	0.50	0.50	0.50
5	I	Prepare Site	2	4	2.00	2.00	2.00
6	M	Dummy Activity	3	6	0.00	0.00	0.00
7	J	Install Equipment	4	7	1.00	1.00	1.00
8	F	Code Programs	5	7	5.50	5.50	5.50
9	D	Train Personnel	6	9	1.50	1.50	1.50
10	G	Test Systems	7	8	1.00	1.00	1.00
11	H	Convert Files	8	9	0.50	0.50	0.50
12	K	Parallel Operations	9	10	3.00	3.00	3.00
13	L	Review & Sign Off	10	11	0.50	0.50	0.50

```
PROJECT:  System Implementation
```

Act	Description	Expected Time	Early Start	Early Fin.	Last Start	Last Fin.	Slack Time
A	Establish Policies	1.00	0.00	1.00	0.00	1.00	0.00
B	Select Personnel	3.00	1.00	4.00	4.00	7.00	3.00
C	Prepare User Manuals	3.00	1.00	4.00	4.00	7.00	3.00
E	Develop Prog Stds	0.50	1.00	1.50	1.00	1.50	0.00
M	Dummy Activity	0.00	4.00	4.00	7.00	7.00	3.00
I	Prepare Site	2.00	1.00	3.00	4.00	6.00	3.00
J	Install Equipment	1.00	3.00	4.00	6.00	7.00	3.00
F	Code Programs	5.50	1.50	7.00	1.50	7.00	0.00
D	Train Personnel	1.50	4.00	5.50	7.00	8.50	3.00
G	Test Systems	1.00	7.00	8.00	7.00	8.00	0.00
H	Convert Files	0.50	8.00	8.50	8.00	8.50	0.00
K	Parallel Operations	3.00	8.50	11.50	8.50	11.50	0.00
L	Review & Sign Off	0.50	11.50	12.00	11.50	12.00	0.00

```
CRITICAL PATH
  A E F G H K L


Time of critical path
  12.00
```

Flowcharts provide graphic representations of sequential processes. System flowcharts summarize the processes of a system and show their inputs and outputs. Program flowcharts describe in detail how computerized processes work, showing the logic of computer programs or modules. Document flowcharts are useful when describing non-computerized procedures. An entity-relationship diagram describes the relationships between the items of data stored in a computer system. A data flow diagram shows flows of data between processes, files, and destinations. A system chart uses flowchart symbols to represent the components of a computerized system. A structure chart shows relationships between modules in a computer program.

Decision tables summarize the outcomes of complex decisions involving many alternatives. They enable an auditor or analyst to examine the consequences of all alternatives, but they do not show sequences. For this reason, decision tables are frequently used with program flowcharts to describe complex situations.

Gantt charts and network diagrams are useful for managing system development projects. Gantt charts are easy to create and read but provide less information than network diagrams. Network methods such as PERT or CPM enable a project manager to reallocate resources to decrease the project's duration. They normally are implemented using computer software packages.

Accountants and analysts frequently use interviews to gather data. Good interviewing skills are acquired through practice.

Key Terms

data flow diagram   A diagram that shows the flow of data between processes, files, and external destinations.

decision table   A matrix that summarizes the outcomes of complex decisions. It contains a list of conditions and a list of actions under each condition.

document flowchart   A flowchart that emphasizes the flow of documents among organizational units.

entity-relationship diagram   A diagram that identifies the data items, or entities, stored in the computer memory, and describes the relationships between these entities.

flowchart   A diagram showing the relationships between sequential processes.

Gantt chart   A project management tool that represents a project by a graph. The duration of an activity is represented by the length of that activity's line on the graph.

network techniques   Project management tools that include PERT and CPM. They represent a project by a network of arcs and nodes. The sequences of the arcs show the sequences of the activities in the project.

program flow diagram   A flowchart that shows in detail the logic steps within a computer program.

structure chart   A diagram showing the hierarchy of the modules making up a computer program.

system chart   A graphic representation of the equipment configuration of a computer system.

system flowchart   A flowchart that describes the computerized processes, manual operations, inputs, and outputs of an application system.

Questions

4–1. What are the distinctions between each of the following?

    a. System chart
    b. System flowchart
    c. Program flowchart
    d. Document flowchart
    e. Data flow diagram

4–2. What are the alternating layers in a system flowchart?

4–3. The output from one operation has been omitted in Illustration 4–5. Can you identify what it is?

4–4. Why should an accountant know how to read and to draw a

    a. System chart?
    b. System flowchart?
    c. Program flowchart?
    d. Document flowchart?
    e. Data flow diagram?

4–5. What are the components of an entity-relationship (E-R) diagram?

4–6. What advantages do decision tables have over program flowcharts? What disadvantages?

4–7. Can you identify the difference between a Gantt chart and a network diagram? What is it?

4–8. How does a PERT network diagram differ from a CPM network diagram?

4–9. What does each of the following symbols represent? Identify each as a basic, a systems, or a programming flowchart symbol.

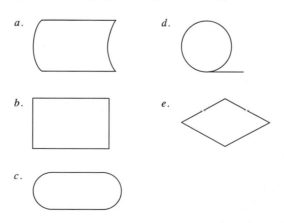

a.

b.

c.

d.

e.

4–10. Identify each of the following symbols. In your own words, describe what it represents.

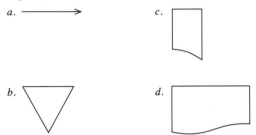

a.   *c.*

b.   *d.*

4–11. Below is an entity-relationship (E-R) diagram for a system that issues drivers' licenses. The letters *a* through *f* on the diagram stand for relationships between the entities. Identify each relationship indicated by the letters *a* through *f*.

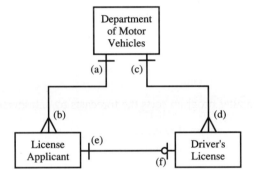

Exercises and Cases

4–12.   SYSTEM FLOWCHART

Illustration 4–5 contains a system flowchart. Redraw this flowchart using only the basic symbols. Which way of diagramming the process is more descriptive?

4–13.   GANTT CHART

While reviewing an existing system, an accountant discovers the following document, entitled Project Analysis.

Activity	Project Analysis Time in Weeks	Preceding Activity
A	3	—
B	3	A
C	7	A
D	4	A
E	2	B
F	4	B
G	1	C,E
H	5	D

Required:

Prepare a Gantt chart for Project Analysis.

4–14.   NETWORK DIAGRAM

The accountant's supervisor, after reviewing the solution to Exercise 4–13, wants to know how long Project Analysis requires for completion.

Required:

a. With the data given in Exercise 4–13 for Project Analysis, develop a PERT network diagram.
b. What is the earliest completion time for Project Analysis?
c. What is the earliest time that activity G can begin?

(CIA Adapted)

4–15.   SYSTEM FLOWCHART FOR CARD INPUT

Abacus Corp. has a computer-based sales forecasting system, developed in the 1960s, that uses punch-card data entry. The procedures below are followed in their system:

a. Sales forecasts are submitted by salespersons.
b. Forecasts are keypunched into computer cards.
c. Computer cards are read into the computer and stored in a magnetic tape file.
d. A computer program sorts the forecasts by salesperson, and a sales forecast report is prepared.
e. A computer program sorts the forecasts by product code, and a sales forecast report is prepared.
f. The dollar amount totals produced by steps *d* and *e* are compared.

Required:

Prepare a system flowchart for this sales forecasting system.

4–16.   SYSTEM FLOWCHART FOR ON-LINE INPUT

Brewster, Inc., employs the following procedures in connection with budgetary control over research activities:

a. Budget projections are entered into a computer at a keyboard and stored on a magnetic disk.
b. Data from expense voucher forms are entered into the computer and stored on a magnetic disk.
c. The computer sorts, or resequences, the budget and expense information by expense account number.
d. Weekly expense transactions, listed by account, are available on inquiry at a computer terminal.
e. A monthly expense summary report is prepared.
f. A monthly budget analysis report is prepared.
g. A year-end budget summary report is prepared comparing actual and budgeted expenses.

Required:

Prepare a system flowchart for this budgeting system.

4–17.   PROGRAM FLOW DIAGRAM

A program in a payroll system must determine if old age, survivors', and disability insurance (OASDI) should be deducted from employees' pay. One module in the program begins with the employee's gross pay for the current pay period (determined in another module) and calculates the OASDI deduction, if any. This module executes the following procedures:

a. Deduct the employee's gross pay up to the last pay period from $32,400.
b. Test the result. If it is negative or zero, there are no more deductions to be made for the year. The computer transfers to a module that calculates net pay. If the result is positive, proceed to the next step.
c. Compare the result of step *b* with the gross pay for the current period, and select the smaller of the two amounts as the basis for calculating OASDI.
d. Multiply the amount selected in step *c* by 6.7 percent, and store the product.
e. Branch to the module that calculates net pay.

Required:

Prepare a program flowchart for the preceding module.

4–18.   DECISION TABLE

Prepare a decision table for the program module described in Exercise 4–17.

4–19.   STRUCTURE CHART

A program in a cost accounting system must calculate an overhead allocation rate each month. Overhead data and job cost data are stored in separate disk files. The last record in the overhead data file is signified by a dummy record with account code 999. The last record in the job cost file is another dummy record with Job No. ZZ999. The program executes the following procedures:

a. Read a record from the overhead file.
b. Compare the account code on the record with the number 999. If they are equal, the last overhead data record has been read, and the computer proceeds to step *d*. If the account code is not 999, the computer proceeds to step *c*.
c. Add the amount on the overhead data record to a total of overhead costs. Return to step *a*.
d. Read a record from the job cost file.
e. Compare the job number on the job cost data record to the number ZZ999. If they are equal, the computer branches to step *g*. If they are unequal, proceed to step *f*.
f. Add the labor hours recorded on the job cost record to a total of labor hours. Then branch to step *d*.
g. Divide the total of the overhead data by the total of the labor hours. Print the result.
h. Stop execution.

Required:

Prepare a structure chart for this overhead allocation program.

4–20.   DOCUMENT FLOWCHART

Using the customer's purchase order as the authority, the order entry section prepares a six-part prenumbered sales invoice. A seventh part is prepared if it is a special order.

After preparation, the order entry section sends part 5 to the credit department for credit approval and part 6 to the customer as acknowledgment; other parts are temporarily filed numerically.

After approving the credit, the credit department returns part 5 to the order entry section, where it is filed numerically. At the same time, parts 1 and 2 are sent to the billing department, part 3 to the warehouse, and part 4 to the shipping department. When a seventh part is prepared, it is sent to the production department.

Required:

Prepare a document flowchart for these procedures.

4–21.   E-R DIAGRAM

Consider the procedures described in Exercise 4–20.

a. Identify the entities about which management wishes to collect data.
b. Describe the relationships between the entities you identified in part *a*.
c. Draw an entity-relationship diagram for this system.

4–22.   DATA FLOW DIAGRAM

Prepare a data flow diagram for the procedures described in Exercise 4–20.

4–23.   DOCUMENT FLOWCHART

At the end of each day, the accounts receivable section prepares a control total showing the total amount debited to various accounts receivable accounts for the general ledger clerk. Independently, the billing clerk summarizes all sales on account during the day and prepares a journal voucher, which is sent to the general ledger clerk.

The general ledger clerk compares the amount shown on the control total with that shown in the journal voucher and attaches the former to the latter. An entry is then made in the sales journal. Finally, the journal voucher is filed numerically.

Required:

Prepare a document flowchart for these procedures.

4–24.   E-R DIAGRAM

Consider the procedures described in Exercise 4–23.

a. Identify the entities about which management wishes to collect data.
b. Describe the relationships between the entities you identified in part *a*.
c. Draw an entity-relationship diagram for this system.

4–25.   DATA FLOW DIAGRAM

Prepare a data flow diagram for the procedures described in Exercise 4–23.

4–26.   NETWORK DIAGRAM

The following data were estimated during planning for a system design effort:

Activity	Duration (in Weeks)	Predecessor Activity
A	10	none
B	8	none
C	30	none
D	12	A
E	15	A
F	14	B
G	15	D
H	20	E,F
I	5	C

Required:

a. Draw a PERT network diagram for this project.

b. Identify the critical path.

c. What is the earliest project completion time?

d. Find the slack time for each activity.

e. Discuss what the project team manager can do if the system design must be completed within 40 weeks.

(CIA Adapted)

4–27.   *PROGRAM FLOWCHART*

The Metal Container Corporation was engaged in the manufacture of metal containers for the food industry. Although it began as a regional supplier, swift expansion mostly through acquisitions and mergers made it a national company with several dozen plants from coast to coast. Annual sales were about one quarter of a billion dollars.

Management Problems

Although there were only a few companies in the metal container industry, competition, particularly in customer service, was extremely keen. This generally meant attempting to meet customers' unexpected needs on very short notice and allowing customers to cancel orders on the slimmest of pretexts. This policy, coupled with the inherent seasonal nature of the business, meant wide fluctuations in production and, worse yet, a large inventory of slow-moving items. Out of an inventory balance of $50 million, about 20 percent, or $10 million, was judged to be slow moving. Although the controller was fully aware of the situation and prepared monthly reports listing these slow-moving items by plant and by product specifications, his efforts generated few results. Both the percentage figure and the dollar amount had shown consistent monthly increases during the past several years. Because the company was in need of funds for further expansion, the president's attention was attracted by the sizable inventory. The company's plan to convert to a more sophisticated computer system afforded him the opportunity to ask the advice of a management consultant.

Production Scheduling

In the course of his study, the management consultant came across plant managers' production schedules that reflected each plant's plan to meet expected sales needs for each month of the coming year. Because the plant managers' performance was evaluated mainly on the basis of their ability to service these sales needs, they tended to carry large inventories and to be overcautious about responding to any decreases in sales forecasts. Both factors, of course, contributed to the company's high inventory position and increased its vulnerability to slow-moving items.

Since proper production scheduling provided an attractive avenue to a reduction of inventories, the consultant pursued the matter further. He felt that what top management considered the preferred manner of production scheduling was reflected accurately by the following:

a. Inventory is to be no lower than 50 percent and no higher than 75 percent of the sales forecast for the following month.
b. Production is to be scheduled in such a way that the planned inventory at the end of each month falls within the range just indicated.
c. The normal workload is a five-day, eight-hour-a-day workweek.
d. If the normal workload results in too much inventory, the workweek may be reduced to a four-day, three-day, two-day, or even a one-day workweek.
e. If the normal workload results in inadequate inventory, the workweek may be extended first by working 9, 10, 11, or 12 hours a day for a five-day week, then by working Saturdays, then by working Saturdays and Sundays, and then by working two shifts a day. The extended day options (working 9, 10, 11, or 12 hours a day) are also available to weekend or two-shift operation.
f. If around-the-clock operation for a month still results in inadequate inventory, the production schedule of the preceding months is to be revised to allow inventory accumulation in these months.

With this set of rules, the consultant prepared some production schedules and compared them with those prepared by plant managers. Invariably, schedules prepared by the consultant showed inventory positions of about 20 percent less than those indicated in plant managers' schedules.

Because of these favorable findings, the consultant suggested that the preparation of production schedules be computerized. He even prepared a program flowchart to be used by the company's programming staff for this task.

Required:
a. How would you have prepared the program flowchart?
b. Would a decision table be useful in this situation?

4–28.   *PROBABILISTIC NETWORK DIAGRAM*

Whitson Company has just ordered a new computer for its accounting information system. The present computer is fully utilized and no longer adequate for all of the financial applications Whitson would like to implement. The present accounting system applications must all be modified before they can be run on the new computer. Additionally, new applications that Whitson would like to have developed and implemented have been identified and ranked according to priority.

Sally Rose, manager of data processing, is responsible for implementing the new computer system. Rose listed the specific activities to be completed and determined the estimated time to complete each activity. In addition, she prepared a network diagram to help coordinate the activities. The activity list and network diagram are presented in Exhibit 4–1.

EXHIBIT 4–1

Case 4–28

Activity	Description of Activity	Expected Time Required to Complete (in Weeks)	Variance in Expected Time (in Weeks)
AB	Wait for delivery of computer from manufacturer	8	1.2
BC	Install computer	2	.6
CH	General test of computer	2	.2
AD	Complete an evaluation of personnel requirements	2	.8
DE	Hire additional programmers and operators	2	1.6
AG	Design modifications to existing applications	3	1.2
GH	Program modifications to existing applications	4	1.4
HI	Test modified applications on new computer	2	.4
IJ	Revise existing applications as needed	2	.6
JN	Revise and update documentation for existing applications as modified	2	.4
JK	Run existing applications in parallel on new and old computers	2	.4
KP	Implement existing applications as modified on the new computer	1	.6
AE	Design new applications	8	3.2
GE	Design interface between existing and new applications	3	1.8
EF	Program new applications	6	2.6
FI	Test new applications on new computer	2	.8
IL	Revise new applications as needed	3	1.4
LM	Conduct second test of new applications on new computer	2	.6
MN	Prepare documentation for the new applications	3	.8
NP	Implement new applications on the new computer	2	.8

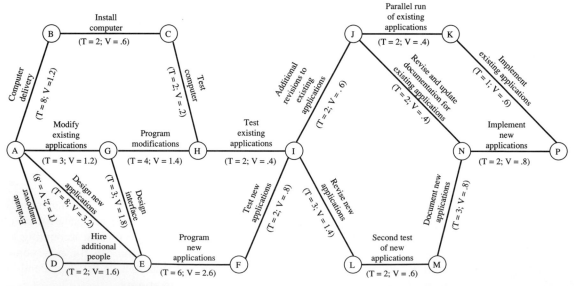

T = Expected time in weeks to complete activity
V = Variance in expected time in weeks

Required:

a. Determine the number of weeks required to fully implement Whitson Company's accounting information system on the new computer.

b. Identify the activities critical to completing the project.

c. Determine the slack time for one activity.

d. Whitson Company's top management would like to reduce the time necessary to begin operation of the system.

1. Which activities should Sally Rose attempt to reduce to implement the system sooner? Explain.

2. Discuss how Sally Rose might proceed to reduce the time of these activities.

e. The general accounting manager would like the existing accounting information system applications to be modified and operational in 22 weeks.

1. Determine the number of weeks required to modify the existing accounting information system applications and make them operational.

2. What is the probability of implementing the existing system applications within 22 weeks? Use the following table in your calculations.

Table of Areas Under the Normal Curve

z	Area	z	Area	z	Area
0.1	.540	1.1	.864	2.1	.982
0.2	.579	1.2	.885	2.2	.986
0.3	.618	1.3	.903	2.3	.989
0.4	.655	1.4	.919	2.4	.992
0.5	.692	1.5	.933	2.5	.994
0.6	.726	1.6	.945	2.6	.995
0.7	.758	1.7	.955	2.7	.997
0.8	.788	1.8	.964	2.8	.997
0.9	.816	1.9	.971	2.9	.998
1.0	.841	2.0	.977	3.0	.999

(CMA Adapted)

5   SYSTEM DEVELOPMENT PROCESSES

Learning Objectives

1. To discover alternative methods for creating accounting information systems.
2. To understand the qualities of a successful information system.
3. To learn the phases that make up the system development life cycle.
4. To learn alternative methods for developing information systems.

Introduction

Accountants commonly apply the systems approach in the development of new information systems. Many organizations implement the systems approach in a formal process called the *system development life cycle*. This chapter introduces this formal process and variations of it.

Accountants need to know about system development for two reasons. First, they participate in project teams that design accounting systems. Second, auditors review and make suggestions for new systems prior to their implementation. The details of the development process are described more fully in the chapters that follow.

The Objective of System Development

Unlike systems that occur naturally, accounting information systems must be created. Accountants have been creating accounting systems for hundreds of years; the double-entry system originated in Italy before Columbus discovered America. But the relatively recent adoption of computer technology in accounting has forced accountants to be more attentive to the methods used in developing accounting systems.

In the past 40 years, accountants have had both successes and failures in implementing the double-entry system on computers. Because all accountants are likely to participate in developing a new accounting system, how can one avoid participating in a failure? Which steps are necessary to successfully implement an accounting system? The implementation of a successful system is the objective of any system development process.

AIS in Practice

The State of California recently terminated a system development project after a $100 million investment. The system, the State Automated Child Support System (SACSS), was intended to maintain data on child-support payments from parents in the state's 58 counties. After four years, it was working in only 17 counties. Users complained that the system was flawed from the beginning, relying on DOS-based software and dumb terminals. According to users, the system erased $17,000 in back child-support payments from one account. The whole project moved so slowly that it was out-of-date by the time it was installed. Another problem that users cited was a conflict between the state's interest in a statewide system and counties wanting to do things in their own ways.

Abandoning the project left counties trying to repair old systems or find new ones to monitor child-support payments. Some even reverted to paper-based systems.

The Qualities of a Successful System

No accounting information system is completely successful or totally unsuccessful. In this context, success is a relative quality: A system is successful if it achieves most of the goals set out for it. In general, an accounting information system is successful if it achieves four objectives. First, it should produce correct and timely information. Second, it should be developed within a reasonable amount of time. Third, the system should meet the organization's needs for information. And finally, users should be satisfied with it. These qualities, and some methods of achieving them, are summarized in Illustration 5–1.

Correct and Timely Information.   In an accounting system, errors and fraud are the two sources of incorrect information. The double-entry system prevents or detects many of the errors that humans can make in manually processing accounting data. Because of this, double-entry systems are implemented on computers even though computers are less likely to make these kinds of errors. The use of computers, however, creates the

ILLUSTRATION 5–1

Achieving the Qualities of a Successful System

Quality	Achieved by
1. Correct information	Have adequate internal control
2. Timely information	Choose a processing method suited to the user's needs
3. Reasonable time for development	a. Properly define the scope of the system
	b. Use project management techniques
4. Satisfy the organization's needs	
a. Current	Get steering committee approval for new systems projects
b. Future	Have a long-range systems master plan
5. User satisfaction	a. User input in setting policies
	b. User support for projects
	c. Active user participation in projects
	d. User responsibility for the system

possibility of other errors and makes it easier for a dishonest person to use the accounting system to conceal fraud.

A successful accounting system has **internal controls** that prevent and detect errors and fraud. Accountants and auditors frequently participate in system development processes because they, more than most other professionals who work with computers, are knowledgeable about internal control. Adequate internal control is necessary for implementing a successful accounting information system.

Information is considered *timely* if it is available to its user when needed for decision making. Some of the earlier computerized accounting systems fell short of this objective. In these systems, information in computerized ledgers was updated weekly or monthly, even though employees needed current information daily. For example, suppose inventory issues and additions are posted only on Fridays. A customer asks a salesperson about the availability of a particular product on Wednesday. The salesperson can tell the customer that goods were in stock on the previous Friday but cannot say that the goods are available when the customer wants them. This accounting system provides information that is untimely. More modern processing methods avoid this shortcoming. Timely information is provided by adopting a transaction processing method that meets the needs of the system user.

Time Required for System Development.   Another quality of a successful accounting system is that its development should be completed in a reasonable period of time. Many large accounting systems require three or more years to complete. Companies that have used computers for many years can tell horror stories of systems that were never completed. Excessive time for development results in excessive costs that may cause the system's costs to exceed its benefits.

What can be done to avoid this kind of system failure? First, system designers learn to limit the scope of any new system to a size that can be developed within a reasonable time. In the terminology of systems theory, they define the boundaries of the system and limit their efforts to those components within the boundaries. Even though procedures outside the boundaries may need changing, these needs are addressed at a later date. For example, accountants seldom attempt to change an entire transaction cycle. Instead, they identify the application system within the cycle that most needs to be improved. Then they complete a new version of that application system before proceeding to another system within the cycle.

Second, system design teams learn to use project management techniques such as budgets, Gantt charts, and PERT or CPM diagrams. These methods require that the designers identify in advance all activities required by the development effort and the estimated times and costs for each activity. Designers can monitor actual elapsed time and costs, comparing them to those expected. Then they can change either the scope of the system or the resources assigned to the effort before an excessive amount of time elapses.

Satisfy the Organization's Needs.   A third quality of a successful system is that it meets the needs of the organization implementing it. The system should provide information that is both meaningful and relevant to its users. Because developing accounting systems can be expensive and time consuming, they should be useful for many years. Thus, any new system should satisfy not only the current needs of the company but also anticipated future needs. An appropriate system design satisfies the organization's current needs; adequate system planning helps to identify future needs.

Most organizations have management committees that provide short- and medium-range planning for new information systems. Frequently called the *information system steering committee,* this group considers and approves new systems on a project-by-project basis. When approving the final design for a new system, they try to ensure that current information needs will be met.

To produce successful systems, organizations should also engage in long-range systems planning. This type of planning examines information requirements at a broader level than a project-by-project analysis allows. It may be accomplished by members of a corporate long-range planning staff or by a system planning group within an MIS department. This *long-range systems planning group* identifies long-range information resource requirements and develops a system master plan for new systems. The master plan is based on overall corporate goals, on proposed new products, on new markets the firm will enter, and on future critical tasks within the firm's operations.

Whether a system is intended for a transaction processing application or for aiding in management decisions at a less-structured level, adequate system planning is necessary if it is to be considered a success.

User Satisfaction with the System.   A system is usually considered to be successful if its users are satisfied. In fact, many systems professionals consider user satisfaction as the strongest indicator of success. The user may be a clerk inputting data into a component of a transaction processing system. He or she may be an operating manager reviewing reports from a responsibility accounting or budgeting system. In either case, user satisfaction indicates that the system provides information that is correct and timely enough to satisfy the user's needs.

Frequently, designers of a new system conduct an evaluation of it months after it starts operation. Major objectives of this *post-implementation review* are to determine if intended users are relying on the system and to find out whether they are happy with its operations and outputs. By using surveys and interviews, they can determine if users are satisfied with the system.

Gaining User Acceptance

Often organizations allocate time and money to develop a new system only to find that users are unwilling to use it. In other situations, employees or managers use the new system grudgingly because no other is available. In some cases, users deliberately sabotage a new system, making it inoperable. A system can be technically sound, designed to be consistent with the organization's needs, and produce correct and timely information. Yet employees may prefer to use an older system, a manual system, or an informal one.

Users may resist a new system for several reasons. Sometimes personnel may feel an economic threat due to the fear of losing a job. In other cases, the threat is simply to the user's ego or status. For example, in the past many managers were unwilling to use computer terminals. Using the keyboard requires typing, which, they believed, was a secretarial task. Sometimes a new system changes an employee's job in an undesirable way. The job may have added complexity or become more rigid due to a time schedule established for the new system. Occasionally a person may feel more insecure because of the formality introduced by using computer-generated reports rather than those humans produce. Many people simply oppose any change in their work routines.

System designers have learned to anticipate these problems and to take steps during system development to gain users' acceptance of the new system. The right kind of user involvement in the development process encourages user acceptance.

User Input in Setting Policies.   The information systems steering committee should involve users. The steering committee should have representatives from top management and from all the major information systems user departments: accounting, marketing, production, engineering, internal audit, and others. Each representative should be a high-ranking manager within a department and may be the head of the department. The manager in charge of the MIS group (frequently called the *chief information officer* or CIO) should also serve on this committee. Large corporations may have several such committees—one at the top management level composed of divisional vice presidents, others within the company's operating divisions or subsidiaries.

The steering committee provides user input into the selection of new systems for development. Just as important, the committee establishes priorities for those system projects that are approved. Every manager thinks that his or her pet project is the most important one! On the steering committee, a manager has to convince other managers of the importance of the project. Illustration 5–2 lists the primary responsibilities of a typical steering committee.

User Support for Projects.   System designers must enlist user support for development projects in progress. All managers and supervisors should be sold on the project's value to their departments. If the superiors openly support a new system, subordinates will have difficulty resisting it after implementation. In developing a successful accounting system, sales ability and good interpersonal skills are as important as technical skills.

Active User Participation in Projects.   Users not only should be sold on the value of a new system project but should also be active participants in the design process.

A multidisciplinary *project team* handles most projects. Members of the team come from varied backgrounds, and each contributes unique skills to the design process. Accountants usually participate in the design of an accounting system, and so do personnel from the affected operating departments. For example, the design of an order

ILLUSTRATION 5–2

Responsibilities of the Information Systems Steering Committee

1. Review and approve for further study all projects requested by operating departments or the MIS department.
2. Review and approve the MIS department's work program and determine priorities for projects.
3. Review periodic progress reports on active systems projects.
4. Review and approve proposed plans for system implementation.
5. Review periodically the MIS department's budget.

entry system requires someone from sales. The design of a cost accounting system requires input from production. Frequently these personnel are temporarily relieved of their normal duties and assigned full-time to the project. Any project team also has people from the MIS department who are experienced in the design and development process. These include systems analysts, programmers, documentation specialists, and technical consultants.

The project team should provide user input to the development process throughout. User representatives should be involved not only in developing specifications for the system but also in coordinating the project, in performing cost–benefit analyses, and in planning the final implementation of a new system.

User Responsibility for the Implemented System.   One objective of user involvement throughout a project's life is to have a manager in the affected user area assume responsibility for the implemented system. Ideally, a user representative on the project team is the person with this responsibility. Of all employees in the affected user department, someone from the project team is most likely to feel responsible for the success or failure of the new system.

This manager then becomes the internal advocate for the new system. He or she can help train other users, answer questions or resolve problems in the user department, and serve as a contact person with the MIS department on technical problems.

Relevance for the Accountant

How is this relevant to an accountant? Why is an accountant concerned with the success of a system or the degree of user involvement?

In most organizations, accountants use more computerized information systems than any other professional group. Thus, accountants are user representatives on many project teams when older accounting systems are replaced. As the ultimate benefactors of a new accounting system, accountants have a personal concern for its accuracy and efficiency.

Also, accounting systems are pervasive throughout any organization. Actions by all operating departments cause inputs to the accounting transaction processing system. Companies with good budgeting and responsibility reporting systems find that these directly affect the decisions of managers. Often managers hold accountants responsible for inaccuracies or inequities designed into these systems.

Accountants are the auditors of these accounting systems. Auditors want systems that produce accurate, reliable information so that they can rely on them during the audit process. For this reason, internal auditors sometimes participate in developing them.

The discussion in this section has highlighted the importance of the system development process from the accountant's perspective and some of the behavioral concerns in system development. The next section presents some methods for developing successful accounting information systems.

The System Development Life Cycle

Information systems contribute to management decisions at the strategic planning, management control, and operational levels. As organizations change, managers at all levels face new decisions and acquire new needs for information. Thus, information systems must change to meet these new needs. The evolution of most accounting systems follows a distinct cyclical pattern commonly called the ***system development life cycle***

(SDLC). This cycle is evident in accounting systems because these information systems have been in use for a long time.

The system development life cycle describes how an information system progresses from its conception as an idea, through the development process, and into routine operation. Typically, the cycle begins as a manager recognizes a need that existing information systems do not satisfy. This manager may propose a solution or may want a problem studied by someone else who can suggest possible solutions. Management appoints a study team to apply the system study process to the problem. The study team may increase in size and may implement a new information system as a solution to the problem. This solution may be used for many years before another manager recognizes some other need for information that the system does not satisfy. Then the cycle begins again.

Components of the SDLC

SDLC components include systems planning, analysis, design, implementation, and operation. Three of the components—analysis, design, and implementation—compose the system development process and may require a few months to a few years. The fifth component, operation, may last for decades. For example, one major oil company has used the same payroll accounting system for over 30 years. In the mid-1950s, this system required approximately two years to develop.

Illustration 5–3 shows the cyclical nature of systems analysis, design, implementation, and operation. They exist within the context of systems planning, which is done as a part of the organization's overall long-range planning.

Systems Planning.   Ideally, system development takes place within the context of a systems master plan that coordinates new information system development projects with the company's long-range plans.

Many companies employ a staff of strategic planners who advise top management and who identify and suggest long-range goals, such as new markets, new product lines, or new lines of business. If a company is to achieve these goals, its systems must provide relevant information. Members of the strategic planning staff work with senior MIS and accounting personnel to develop the systems master plan. Before beginning new development projects, these people ensure that the new projects are consistent with the master plan.

ILLUSTRATION 5–3

The System Development Life Cycle

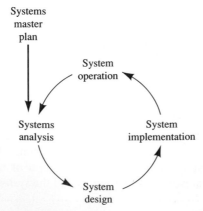

Systems Analysis.   *Systems analysis* is the process of examining an existing information system and its environment to identify potential improvements.

Systems analysis may begin for a variety of reasons. In some cases, it may be an outgrowth of the systems planning process. A long-range planning group may identify a need for information at some time in the future and may incorporate that need in a systems master plan. The information systems steering committee then appoints a system study team to investigate possible ways of supplying this information. The system study may or may not lead to the development of a new information system.

Many times, systems analysis begins at the request of the manager of a user department. This manager identifies a need for information that is currently not supplied. He or she prepares a proposal for a new or modified information system and submits it to the steering committee. The committee considers the seriousness of the problem, the feasibility of the proposal, the current workload of the MIS development staff, and the relative importance of competing proposals. The steering committee then may decide to appoint a study team to examine the proposal in more detail. The study team may consist of one or more systems analysts and user department representatives.

Systems analysis is initiated for three reasons. The first and most frequent reason is that an existing system is not functioning as required. For example, a small-business accounting system may have been adequate at the time of its acquisition, but the growth of the business now produces bottlenecks in the processing of transactions. In this case, systems analysis begins to *solve a problem* with an existing system.

The second reason a system study team may be appointed is a *new requirement* for information. A new requirement may be identified by a long-range systems planning staff or may result from legal or competitive changes in the business environment. For example, in response to competition, many companies choose to analyze past accounting data on sales by customers to plan future marketing programs. Periodically, changes are made in tax laws that increase reporting requirements to the government by banks, brokerage firms, and publicly held companies. Companies have invested substantial sums in new systems to satisfy these requirements.

Third, sometimes organizations initiate systems analysis to take advantage of a *new technology*. The existing system may be functioning satisfactorily, but since its implementation, technological change introduced new methods that are more efficient. For example, many retailers have attached labels containing computer-readable bar codes to their goods. Cash registers can read the bar codes, and sales are immediately shown in inventory records. In this way, inventory records are kept current. Illustration 5–4 summarizes these reasons for initiating systems analysis.

ILLUSTRATION 5–4

Reasons for Initiating Systems Analysis

1. *Problem Solving*. An existing system does not meet its objectives.
   Example: A small-business system has been outgrown.
2. *New Requirement*. Information that was not needed before.
   Example: Reporting dividends and interest paid to comply with tax laws.
3. *New Technology*. Better methods are now available.
   Example: Point-of-sale data entry to computer system.

Sometimes the systems analysis study team concludes that a new information system is a possibility. They stop studying the problem and start to address potential solutions that include new forms of technology, new sources for required information, or more efficient procedures. When this occurs, there are two activities in systems analysis: the activity of examining existing systems, the *preliminary survey,* and that of examining potential solutions to the problem, the *feasibility study.* The feasibility study begins the process of developing a new system.

System Design.   During *system design,* the team translates recommendations made in systems analysis into a form that can be implemented.

Usually the study team performs a cost–benefit analysis during systems analysis. If a new system appears cost-effective, the chief information officer (CIO), with input from the steering committee, appoints a design project team. This team may include members of the original system study team and additional systems analysts and user department personnel. The project team reviews the work of the study team during systems analysis, reexamines their proposed solutions, and begins to define a new system in gradually increasing detail.

In large projects, system design consists of two distinct phases. During *preliminary design,* the first phase, a system is created conceptually. The project team starts with the objectives of the system and identifies the major processes, data, and reports needed to achieve those objectives. At the conclusion of preliminary design, the project team prepares a report for the steering committee. This report describes a proposed new system in general terms.

If authorized by the steering committee, the project team then begins the second phase, *detailed specification* of the new system. During this process, the team identifies in detail how the system will work. The purposes of all computer programs and manual procedures are identified, all documents and reports are designed, all files are described, and the necessary internal controls are identified. Accountants and internal auditors can make significant contributions to the detailed specification of a system because of their training and knowledge in internal control.

By the conclusion of detailed specification, an organization has made a significant commitment in time and money to a new system. A sizable, detailed paper description of the system is created and submitted to the steering committee for approval. Thus, the committee has another opportunity to change the proposed system, or stop it, before additional resources are devoted to the project.

System Implementation.   Once the information systems steering committee approves the detailed specifications for the new system, its implementation begins. During *system implementation*, the project team is enlarged to include programmers and clerical personnel from user departments. Many activities occur simultaneously to convert the paper description produced during design into a working information system.

The most time-consuming activity during implementation is computer programming. The programmers assigned to the project team code, debug, and test each computer program that was identified in the system design documentation. Frequently, programs provide inputs to other programs. When this occurs, the programs must be tested together to ensure that interfaces are compatible. System designers call this process *acceptance testing.* When all programs are tested in conjunction with manual procedures, they call it *system testing.*

Some organizations avoid much of the programming by purchasing software packages. Programs are available that perform most accounting transaction processing applications. These can be modified by programmers to suit the organization's needs.

During implementation, personnel are trained in the new system and, if necessary, new personnel are hired. Any required new equipment is acquired and installed. Any new forms or supplies required by the system are ordered.

The entire project team and many user area personnel participate in the final implementation activity, *system conversion.* During this activity, all data stored in the files of the old system are recorded in the form specified by the new system. Operation of the new system then begins.

Many activities can occur during system implementation, but all activities are not necessary for each new system. For example, existing equipment may be adequate so that the purchase of new equipment is unnecessary. Also, many of the activities can take place simultaneously. Frequently, for example, user training begins immediately after the detailed specifications are approved, while programming is taking place.

System Operation.   System conversion does not terminate the system development process. Several months after operation of a new system begins, the post-implementation review of *system operation* occurs. During this review, members of the design team, frequently with the aid of an internal auditor, examine the operation of the new system. The purpose of the review is to determine if the system meets its objectives. It identifies problems that need correction and provides feedback to the design team concerning the success of the system.

Another activity, *system maintenance,* takes place during the operation phase. These are the tasks that are necessary to correct errors in the system design or to make minor changes to the system because of changes in its environment. System maintenance includes both changes to equipment (hardware maintenance) and changes to computer programs (software maintenance). Although it is not a part of the system development process, system maintenance is necessary for the operation of an information system.

Formal System Development Methodologies

Several formal system development methodologies incorporate the components of the system development life cycle. These methodologies decompose systems analysis, system design, and system implementation into distinct phases like those previously described. They impose their own design tools and standards on the SDLC.

These methodologies require formal reports to management at the end of each phase. These reports describe the status of the project and show the project team's suggestions for the new system. Usually one or more members of the team make a presentation to the steering committee apprising them of the project's progress.

The end of a phase provides a checkpoint for management; each checkpoint is an opportunity to review and evaluate the proposed system. Management can identify changes to the proposal, stop further consideration of the proposal, or authorize initiation of the next phase.

Structured Systems Analysis and Design.   During the 1970s, many organizations adopted formal system development methodologies based on the concepts of *structured analysis* and *structured design.* Several of these exist, and they differ in the details of their techniques.[1]

Structured analysis techniques rely on the use of data flow diagrams rather than flowcharts. Data flow diagrams force the analyst to focus on the *logical system,* what the system does or should do, rather than the *physical system,* how the system works. Advocates of structured methods argue that this causes the analyst to define user requirements more accurately by not prematurely worrying about technology. This, they believe, improves the creativity of the analyst.

Structured design techniques develop computer programs as a top-down hierarchy of modules. Each module is a segment of computer code that serves only one function. Structure charts (or similar diagrams) describe these programs. Programs developed in this way are more easily written and tested. They also are easier to modify later because they minimize connections between modules.

Information Engineering.   *Information engineering* is an approach that includes many of the tools and techniques of structured analysis and design. It provides a comprehensive framework for meeting the information needs of an organization. When an organization uses information engineering, a study team first develops a strategic systems plan. This plan then determines the objective of subsequent analysis and design activities. It replaces older, project-by-project approaches to developing systems with a structured, orderly one.

Information engineering requires that analysts begin by analyzing the data needs of the business first. They create methods for determining that these needs are met adequately. Then they determine the processes to provide the data. In this way, information engineering is *data-driven* rather than *process driven.*

A similar approach, *business process reengineering,* goes even further. Rather than look at existing business needs, it requires study teams to examine and redesign fundamental business processes. Their objective is to determine if those processes can be significantly improved even if it means changing current organization units and systems. Reengineering directs the attention of the organization toward finding better processes and then computerizing them, rather than simply computerizing existing processes. Some companies have shown major increases in efficiency by employing this approach.[2]

CASE Tools.   Many formal methodologies make extensive use of *computer-aided software engineering* (CASE) tools. These software packages automate many of the processes required during system development. Different CASE tools serve different purposes: They aid in drawing data flow diagrams or flowcharts; they maintain records concerning data files, inputs, and outputs; they aid in project management; they generate computer code; and they maintain system documentation.

---

[1]For a more detailed description of structured techniques, see J. L. Whitten and L. D. Bentley, *Systems Analysis and Design Methods,* 4th ed. (Burr Ridge, Ill.: Irwin McGraw-Hill, 1997), p. 312.

[2]For a more comprehensive discussion of this subject, see Michael Hammer and James Champy, *Reengineering the Corporation: A Manifesto for Business Revolution* (New York: Harper Business, 1993).

ILLUSTRATION 5–5

What CASE Tools Do

SDLC Phase

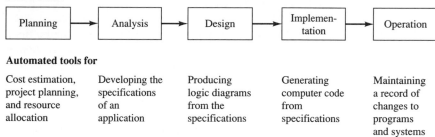

Automated tools for

| Cost estimation, project planning, and resource allocation | Developing the specifications of an application | Producing logic diagrams from the specifications | Generating computer code from specifications | Maintaining a record of changes to programs and systems |

CASE tools increase the productivity of personnel assigned to project teams and at the same time improve the quality of the new systems and of their documentation. Management accountants are likely to work with CASE tools when they participate in the development of accounting systems. Auditors are likely to review the documentation produced by CASE tools.

Illustration 5–5 summarizes the functions performed during the SDLC by comprehensive CASE tools.

Formal system development methodologies impose structure and discipline on the development process and aid in the timely completion of a system. They are most successfully applied in the creation of large transaction processing applications; many organizations consider them a necessity for such a system. Illustration 5–6 presents an example of such a formal, phased approach.

Rapid Application Development

Large system development projects may require years and cost millions to complete. When an organization's needs for information change rapidly, such a system may become obsolete before it is completed. To avoid this problem, some organizations have adopted newer approaches that produce working systems much more rapidly.

Called *rapid application development* (RAD) methods, these approaches attempt to deliver high-quality systems quickly and at low cost. Small project teams implement

ILLUSTRATION 5–6

A Phased Approach to System Development

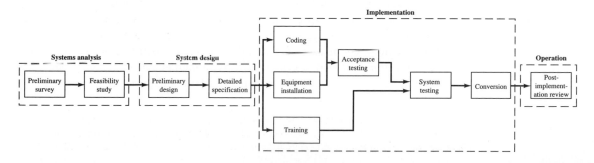

RAD projects, and they minimize costs by using CASE tools and whenever possible by reusing existing computer code and other system components. They shorten development time by omitting the decision checkpoints and management approval processes of formal SDLC methodologies.

A RAD Project

A RAD project typically consists of four stages. In the first, requirements planning, the team conducts a review of the business functions and data closely affected by the proposed system. This review yields an outline of the system's functions and its costs and benefits. In the second stage, user design, key users define the detail of the business functions and the data associated with the new system. They determine inputs and outputs of the system and program critical procedures in it. They also prepare a plan for implementing the system. During construction, the third stage, the project team completes the system, demonstrates the system to users, and modifies its design as necessary. Cutover, the final stage, turns the operational system over to its final users and provides training to them.

RAD Techniques

The structure of a RAD project sounds similar to a project using a traditional SDLC approach. However, the project team uses several techniques to make the RAD project proceed faster. These are user workshops, prototyping, timeboxes, reusable components, and developmental tools.

User Workshops.   Traditional projects rely heavily on interviews with users affected by a new system. Although an effective way to gather information, conducting many interviews is time consuming. As an alternative, RAD methods employ *user workshops.*

The workshop is a meeting of all key people involved in a project, both users and information systems professionals. A professional facilitator conducts the meeting and promotes an open discussion and free flow of ideas. The facilitator helps the group to achieve its objectives and agree on its results. A user workshop may produce in one meeting ideas that would require days or weeks of interviews and analysis.

Prototyping.   *Prototyping* is an iterative process that avoids the structure and the periodic formal approval process of the traditional approaches. It relies on the development of a prototype, or working model, of the new system.

The project team quickly creates a high-level, nondetailed working model of the system. Users are then allowed to repeatedly revise the system, its outputs, or its inputs, until they are satisfied with it. Once users are satisfied with the system, the design team creates an actual production system patterned after the prototype.

Illustration 5–7 identifies and describes the suggested steps in one approach to prototyping.[3] Other approaches minimize the involvement of systems analysts by having the ultimate users of the system learn the tools and create the design.

Prototyping may be used successfully with RAD methods because these are relatively small transaction processing systems implemented with state-of-the-art technology. These systems have a limited number of users who become closely involved in

---

[3]John Connell and Linda Brice, "Rapid Prototyping," *Datamation,* August 15, 1984, pp. 93–100. Used by permission.

ILLUSTRATION 5–7

Suggested Steps in Prototyping

1. *Analysis.* Create an incomplete paper model of the system based on preliminary interviews with users.
2. *Database development.* Create a test database for use in prototyping. Using a relational database management system, the prototype can be easily changed.
3. *Menu development.* Describe the menus that will guide the user of the system. A menu identifies functions to be performed.
4. *Function development.* Describe the functional modules that execute the processes in the system. These may include, for example, data entry and report generation.
5. *Prototype iteration.* Using software development tools, create each module. This produces a working model of the system that a user can easily modify. Make changes to the prototype until the user is satisfied.
6. *Detailed specifications.* Refine the system as necessary to make it efficient in creating a production system. Complete the documentation for the system.

---

the design effort. Prototyping can be advantageous whenever it is difficult to specify in advance the precise data processing needs of a system. It is extensively used for developing decision support systems because the prototype can be customized to a decision maker's preferences and decision style.

Timeboxes.   A *timebox* is a fixed time period at the end of which the project team must deliver a working system. If necessary, the team must narrow the scope or reduce the functions performed by the system in order to complete it on time. This avoids the common mistake when prototyping of overspecifying the system prior to developing code. Advocates of timeboxes assert that it is better to produce a working system early and then progressively to improve it than to wait months to complete a comprehensively specified project.

Teams complete RAD projects typically within timeboxes of two to four months. If using RAD with a large project of, say, a year's duration, they must break it up into a succession of several timeboxes. A typical large system development project consists of three or four small RAD projects.

Reusable Components.   Components of a system include computer programs, forms, display screens, documentation, and paper reports. RAD works best when there is an existing library of such components that were developed for use in earlier systems. The project team is able to draw from this library to obtain components similar to, or in some cases identical to, those required for the current system under development.

Creating a new system from preexisting designs in this way is much faster than recreating each component for each new system. Because reusable components are used many times, they are likely to have been tested thoroughly and less likely to contain errors. Furthermore, they present a consistent interface to users, making the new system easier to learn and use.

Developmental Tools.   Rapid application development requires the use of appropriate high-level developmental software tools. CASE tools, discussed above, are invaluable with a RAD approach. Other tools, discussed in later chapters, include report generators, display screen generators, fourth-generation languages, and a relational database management system.

Tools of these kinds are widely available for use on both desktop and mainframe computers. Whereas project teams can create prototypes quickly using high-level developmental tools, creating a prototype in a procedural language (such as COBOL) is usually too time consuming and expensive.

This chapter has shown how organizations adapt the system development process using RAD techniques in order to shorten development time. Another new approach that promises this and other advantages is object-oriented development.

Object-Oriented Development

Traditional system development processes and the RAD approach described above focus on identifying what the system does. With these approaches, development teams identify what people or machines do and figure out ways to do these things better.

Object-oriented development, in contrast, focuses on the objects, or elements, of the system. An *object* is a computer representation of a person, place, or thing. Development teams identify the relevant objects, the knowledge associated with each (its related data, called *attributes*), and the functions each must provide (its *methods* that must be programmed). With object-oriented systems, these are all stored together in the computer so that another person or program cannot obtain this knowledge without using the object's own methods.

This radically different approach, like RAD, requires the use of appropriate software development tools. It is intended to shorten development time, increase the reliability of the resulting systems, and make maintenance of the system easier. Object-oriented systems are described in more detail later in this text.

Auditor Involvement in System Design

Sometimes auditors participate in the system development process. Because of their training and auditing experience, auditors have special skills to contribute to the process of developing an accounting system. Usually the auditors are one or two *internal auditors* employed by the company. Internal auditors' other duties include reviewing all the operations of the company and making recommendations to management for improving them. By participating in the SDLC, internal auditors can make suggestions during design, when changes to a system are easier.

Occasionally an *independent auditor* may be asked to participate as well. The independent auditor is a firm of certified public accountants that renders an opinion on the financial statements produced by the accounting information system. The independent auditor may assign this system design duty to a member of its information system consulting staff.

Ideally, most auditor involvement in the SDLC occurs during the system design phase. Auditors review the detailed specifications for the system proposed by the project team. They are also heavily involved in the implementation phase, during system testing and conversion. After completion of the development process, and during the operations phase, auditors participate in reviews of the system. Illustration 5–8 identifies the role of the auditor in each phase of the SDLC.

ILLUSTRATION 5–8

Auditor's Role in the Development Process

Systems Analysis Phase
Provide audit reports on systems being examined to the study team.

System Design Phase
Review the proposed design:
1. *Reports*. Identify information needed in reports for control and auditability.
2. *Processing steps*. Suggest control procedures.
3. *Equipment selection*. Ensure that those selected conform to existing company policies.
4. *Data files*. Determine that data will be accurate and complete, and will provide the ability to audit the system.

System Implementation Phase
During system testing, review adequacy of test data and results of tests.

Review plans for conversion to ensure that accurate data are maintained during changeover to the new system.

System Operation Phase
During the post-implementation review, assess the adequacy of internal controls in the operational system.

As this illustration shows, much of the auditors' work in the system development process is concerned with *auditability* and the *controls* in the system. An audit trail ensures that the system is auditable; controls are the measures adopted to safeguard assets and to ensure accurate and reliable data.

The Audit Trail

Auditors review a system to decide if it provides the information needed to conduct an audit. Called the ***audit trail,*** this information is included in the reports produced by the system.

An accounting system records, categorizes, and summarizes transactions to produce reports such as financial statements. The audit trail enables an auditor to begin with a summary balance on the financial statement and trace through the accounting records to the individual transactions that make up the balance. It also allows an auditor to trace from individual transactions to the summary totals. For example, journal entry numbers, posting references, or document numbers are included in reports to provide an audit trail.

The audit trail is important because it enables an auditor to evaluate the accuracy of financial statement amounts and to determine the sources of errors in summary reports.

Controls

The independent auditor relies on controls while examining the financial statements, and the internal auditor evaluates controls as a service to management. As a result, auditors are more knowledgeable about controls than are most project team members.

A system that includes good control measures produces accurate, reliable reports. The accounting records stored by such a system are secure from damage or theft. Good internal controls aid in gaining user acceptance and are necessary for a successful system. During the SDLC, auditors review the system design and make suggestions identifying controls that should be included.

Summary

This chapter provides an overview of the processes used in developing accounting information systems. The objective of system development is to create a successful information system. Experience shows that the most successful information systems are those created with the right kind of user involvement.

System development is a part of the system development life cycle. This cycle contains four components that exist in the life of any information system: analysis, design, implementation, and operation. Phased development methodologies attempt to create successful systems by requiring periodic reviews of a project proposal during the development stage of the life cycle. Alternatives to these methodologies, rapid application development and object-oriented approaches, are intended to shorten development time and decrease costs. Auditors participate in system development by reviewing the controls and the audit trail in proposed systems. Their purpose is to ensure the adequacy of internal controls.

Key Terms

audit trail   Information, including journal entry numbers, posting references, and document numbers, that is included on the outputs of an accounting system. They allow an auditor to identify the individual transactions that make up an account balance.

information system steering committee   A group composed of the chief information officer and managers from computer user departments. Among other duties, this committee considers and approves new information system development projects.

internal controls   The features of an accounting system that prevent or detect errors and fraud. They help it to produce accurate information.

object-oriented development   An approach to developing information systems that is intended to decrease development time and costs and to make system maintenance easier. It requires identifying the basic elements, or objects, relevant to the system.

project team   A group of employees with varying backgrounds who are assigned responsibility for developing a new information system.

prototyping   An iterative system development process in which a small project team quickly develops a working information system and allows users to modify it until they are satisfied with it.

rapid application development   An approach to developing information systems that is intended to decrease the time and cost of development. It avoids the extensive decision checkpoints and approval processes of formal system development life cycle methods.

system design   The second phase of the system development life cycle. The process of translating the recommendations made during systems analysis into a form that can be implemented.

system development life cycle   The evolutionary pattern followed by most accounting systems. It consists of four phases: systems analysis, system design, system implementation, and system operation.

system implementation   The third phase of the system development life cycle. The process of converting the description created during system design into a working information system.

system operation   The last phase of the system development life cycle. The period of time during which a working information system provides information for decision making and control.

systems analysis   The first phase of the system development life cycle. The process of examining an existing information system and its environment for the purpose of identifying potential improvements.

Questions

5–1. Explain what is meant by a successful information system.

5–2. In a large organization, who performs long-range systems planning? Medium-range? Short-range?

5–3. What can happen when employees refuse to accept a new information system?

5–4. Identify some reasons why employees refuse to accept new systems.

5–5. What can be done to gain user acceptance of a new system?

5–6. Why should an accountant be concerned about the success of an information system?

5–7. Explain why we say that the life of an information system follows a cycle.

5–8. Define the following terms:
   a. Systems analysis.
   b. System design.
   c. System implementation.
   d. System operation.

5–9. What are some of the reasons for initiating systems analysis within an organization?

5–10. In which ways are the preliminary description and the detailed specification of a new system similar? In which ways do they differ?

5–11. Which activities take place during system implementation?

5–12. What are the advantages of using a formal system development methodology?

(CIA Adapted)

5–13. Why should auditors participate in the system development process? On which features do they concentrate their efforts?

5–14. What is an audit trail? Why is it important?

5–15. When might prototyping be useful in developing an accounting information system?

Exercises and Cases

5–16.   ACTIVITIES AND PHASES

Identify the phase of the system development life cycle in which each of the following activities is performed:

a. Feasibility study.
b. Post-implementation review.
c. System conversion.
d. Detailed specification.
e. Preliminary survey.
f. Preliminary design.
g. Equipment acquisition.

5–17.   SDLC PHASES

The phases of a system development life cycle project are analysis, design, implementation, and operation. You can identify analogous phases for most projects that you undertake. Identify the activities that occur in each phase in each of the following projects:

a. Writing a term paper.
b. Purchasing a personal computer.
c. Choosing a college to attend.
d. Planning a vacation over spring break.
e. Selecting a job after graduation.

5–18.   STEERING COMMITTEE

A company president is perplexed by requests for computers from three different areas of the firm. The EDP manager (who reports to the vice president of services) wants $4.5 million to upgrade the mainframe computer. The vice president of engineering wants $500,000 to replace a minicomputer. The vice president of finance wants $100,000 to purchase microcomputers.

The company doubled its sales over the past five years, but profits increased only 50 percent. The added sales volume strained the firm's computer resources. Payroll, accounting, inventory, and engineering functions are computerized; other tasks are manual.

The firm is organized by business functions and has vice presidents for manufacturing, marketing, engineering, finance, personnel, and services. The president wonders if an information systems steering committee is needed.

Required:

a. Prepare an executive memorandum, to be signed by the president, creating an information systems steering committee. In this memo, you should outline its objectives, responsibilities, and composition.
b. Justify your recommendations concerning its membership and the selection of its chairperson.

(CIA Adapted)

5–19. *PROTOTYPING*

GEM Corp. wants to develop a decision support system to be used in strategic planning through the analysis of varied and often complex alternatives. Potential users have been directed to identify specifically their information requirements in a manner similar to that utilized for recently developed general ledger and accounts payable applications. However, responses to this new request are vague and the project appears to be stalled. Users are having trouble comprehending the tasks required of them in the new system, and the system project team has no experience with systems of this kind.

Because of these problems, GEM's management has concluded that a prototyping approach would be preferable to the system development life cycle approach that was used for the recently developed general ledger and accounts payable applications.

Required:

a. Identify the steps for prototyping an application system.
b. Identify the advantages of prototyping in developing applications that have a high degree of uncertainty as to requirements.
c. Identify some disadvantages of prototyping.
d. Decide whether prototyping should have been used to develop the general ledger and accounts payable applications, and explain your response.

(CIA Adapted)

5–20. *USER SATISFACTION*

Five years ago, Black Motors, an international automaker, contracted with Blue Computer Company for minicomputers to support the data processing for its 30 largest U.S. dealers. Black Motors has 1,400 dealers in the United States. Three years ago, the dealers began using the Blue computers under long-term leases. The Black Motors Computer Support Group (CSG) is responsible for applications software. Altogether, each dealer spends about $5,000 a month on hardware and software rental.

When the Blue systems were first proposed, CSG sent to the dealers specifications of what the systems would and would not do. The dealers were pleased with the proposed capabilities and agreed that the proposed system would serve their needs.

The dealers gradually came to realize, however, that the Blue computer systems did not live up to the CSG's promise. At a meeting two years ago, the dealers formed a committee composed of dealer representatives to address the problems. The software problems seem to have begun three years ago when Black Motors moved its corporate staff, including the CSG, from the East Coast to the Midwest. Many of its programmers declined to move, impairing the CSG's ability to support the Blue systems.

Two years ago, the CSG began upgrading the computer systems used by all but the largest 30 dealers with minicomputers from Green Computer Company. To support these systems, most CSG personnel work on software for the Green computers. Software programs for the Green and Blue computers are incompatible but perform similar functions.

Three months ago, the CSG sent the 30 largest dealers a letter assuring support for the Blue systems for the next four years and promising a decision about long-term support. The dealers remained skeptical and have been talking about legal action to force the CSG to comply with its original agreement.

Required:

Given the foregoing difficulties, explain what the CSG should do to improve computer system support for the 30 largest dealers. Include in your explanation the reasons for the actions you suggest.

(CIA Adapted)

5–21.   *OBTAINING USER ACCEPTANCE*

The B&B Company manufactures and sells chemicals for agricultural and industrial use. The company has grown significantly over the last 10 years but has made few changes in its information gathering and reporting system. Some of the managers have expressed concern that the system is essentially the same as it was when the firm was only half its present size. Others believe that much of the information from the system is not relevant and that more appropriate and timely information should be available.

Dora Hepple, chief accountant, has observed that the actual monthly cost data for most production processes are compared with the actual costs of the same processes for the previous year. Any variance not explained by price changes requires an explanation by the individual in charge of the cost center. She believes that this information is inadequate for good cost control.

George Vector, one of the production supervisors, contends that the system is adequate because it allows an explanation of discrepancies. The current year's costs seldom vary from the previous year's costs (as adjusted for price changes). This indicates that costs are under control.

Vern Hopp, general manager of the Fine Chemical Division, is upset with the current system. He has to request the same information each month regarding recurring operations. This is a problem that he believes should be addressed.

Walter Metts, president, has appointed a committee to review the system. The charge to this System Review Task Force is to determine if the information needs of the internal management of the firm are being met by the existing system. Specific modifications in the existing system or implementation of a new system can be considered only if management's needs are not being met. William Afton, assistant to the president, has been put in charge of the task force.

Shortly after the committee was appointed, Afton overheard one of the cost accountants say, "I've been doing it this way for 15 years, and now Afton and his committee will try to eliminate my job." Another person replied, "That's the way it looks. John and Brownie in general accounting also think that their positions are going to be eliminated or at least changed significantly." Shortly afterward, Afton overheard a middle-management person saying about the task force, "That's all this company thinks about—maximizing its profits—not the employees." He also overheard a production manager in the mixing department say that he believed the system was in need of revision because the most meaningful information he received came from Brad Cummings, a salesperson. He stated, "After they have the monthly sales meeting, Brad stops by the office and indicates what the sales plans and targets are for the next few months. This sure helps me in planning my mixing schedules."

Afton is aware that the problems of paramount importance to be addressed by his task force are (1) to determine management's information needs for cost control and decision-making purposes and (2) to meet the behavioral needs of the company and its employees.

Required:

a. Discuss the behavioral implications of having an accounting information system that does not appear to meet the needs of management.

b. Identify and explain the specific problems B&B Company appears to have with regard to the perception of B&B employees concerning the
1. Accounting information system.
2. Firm.

c. Assume that the initial review of the System Review Task Force indicates that a new accounting information system should be designed and implemented.
1. Identify the concerns B&B employees have about the new system.
2. Discuss how B&B's management can address each of these concerns.

(CMA Adapted)

5–22.   *INITIATING SYSTEM DEVELOPMENT*

Kelly Petroleum Company has a large oil and natural gas project in Oklahoma. The project has been organized into two production centers (petroleum production and natural gas production) and one service center (maintenance).

Maintenance Center Activities

Don Pepper, maintenance center manager, has organized his maintenance workers into work crews that serve the two production centers. The maintenance crews perform preventive maintenance and repair equipment both in the field and in the central maintenance shop.

Pepper is responsible for scheduling all maintenance work in the field and at the central shop. Preventive maintenance is performed according to a set schedule established by Pepper and approved by the production center managers. Breakdowns are given immediate priority in scheduling so that downtime is minimized. Thus, preventive maintenance occasionally must be postponed, but every attempt is made to reschedule it within three weeks.

Preventive maintenance work is the responsibility of Pepper. However, if a significant problem is discovered during preventive maintenance, the appropriate production center supervisor authorizes and supervises the repair after checking with Pepper.

When a breakdown in the field occurs, the production centers contact Pepper to initiate the repairs. The repair work is supervised by the production center supervisor. Machinery and equipment sometimes need to be replaced while the original equipment is repaired in the central shop. This procedure is followed only when the time to make the repair in the field would result in an extended interruption of operations. Replacement of equipment is recommended by the maintenance work crew supervisor and approved by a production center supervisor.

Routine preventive maintenance and repair of breakdowns of automotive and mobile equipment used in the field are completed in the central shop. All repairs and maintenance activities taking place in the central shop are under the direction of Pepper.

Pepper has records identifying the work crews assigned to each job in the field, the number of hours spent on the job, and parts and supplies used on the job. In addition, records for the central shop (jobs, labor hours, parts, and supplies) have been maintained. However, this detailed maintenance information is not incorporated into Kelly's accounting system.

Pepper develops the annual budget for the maintenance center by planning the preventive maintenance that will be needed during the year, estimating the number and seriousness of breakdowns, and estimating the shop activities. He then bases the labor, part, and supply costs on his plans and estimates and develops the budget amounts by line item. Because the timing of the breakdowns is impossible to plan, Pepper divides the annual budget by 12 to derive the monthly budget.

All costs incurred by the work crews in the field and in the central shop are accumulated monthly and then allocated to the two production cost centers based on the field hours worked in each production center. This method of cost allocation is used on Pepper's recommendation because he believes that it is easy to implement and to understand. Furthermore, he believes that a better allocation system is impossible to incorporate into the monthly report due to the wide range of salaries paid to maintenance workers and the fast turnover of materials and parts.

The November cost report for the maintenance center provided by the accounting department appears below.

OKLAHOMA PROJECT
Maintenance Center Cost Report
For the Month of November 1998
(dollars in thousands)

	Budget	Actual	Petroleum Production	Natural Gas Production
Shop hours	2,000	1,800	—	—
Field hours	8,000	10,000	6,000	4,000
Labor—electrical	$ 25.0	$ 24.0	$ 14.4	$ 9.6
Labor—mechanical	30.0	35.0	21.0	14.0
Labor—instruments	18.0	22.5	13.5	9.0
Labor—automotive	3.5	2.8	1.7	1.1
Labor—heavy equipment	9.6	12.3	7.4	4.9
Labor—equipment operation	28.8	35.4	21.2	14.2
Labor—general	15.4	15.9	9.6	6.3
Parts	60.0	86.2	51.7	34.5
Supplies	15.3	12.2	7.3	4.9
Lubricants and fuels	3.4	3.0	1.8	1.2
Tools	2.5	3.2	1.9	1.3
Data processing	1.5	1.5	.9	.6
Total	$213.0	$254.0	$152.4	$101.6

Production Center Managers' Concerns

Both production center managers have been upset with the method of cost allocation. Furthermore, they believe the report is virtually useless as a cost control device. Actual costs always seem to deviate from the monthly budget, and the proportion charged to each production center varies significantly from month to month. Maintenance costs have increased substantially, and the production managers believe that they have no way to judge whether such an increase is reasonable.

The two production managers, Pepper, and representatives of corporate accounting have met to discuss these concerns. They concluded that a responsibility accounting system could be developed to replace the current system. In their opinion, a responsibility accounting system would alleviate the production managers' concerns and accurately reflect the activity of the maintenance center.

Required:

a. Explain the purposes of a responsibility accounting system, and discuss how such a system could resolve the concerns of the production center managers of Kelly Petroleum Company.

b. Identify the behavioral advantages generally attributed to responsibility accounting systems that the management of Kelly Petroleum Company should expect if the system were effectively introduced for the maintenance center.

c. Discuss the procedures that the production managers should follow to initiate systems analysis for a new responsibility accounting system. What approval processes would the system pass through before being fully implemented?

d. Responsibility reports are created during system design. Describe a report format for the maintenance center that would be based on an effective responsibility accounting system, and explain which, if any, of the maintenance center's costs should be charged to the two production centers.

(CMA Adapted)

5–23.   *SYSTEM DEVELOPMENT PROCEDURES*

Mickie Louderman is the new assistant controller of Pickens Publishers, a growing company with sales of $35 million. She was formerly the controller of a smaller company in a similar industry, where she was in charge of accounting and data processing and had considerable influence over the entire computer center operation. Prior to Louderman's arrival at Pickens, the company revamped its entire computer operations center, placing increased emphasis on decentralized data access, microcomputers with mainframe access, and on-line systems.

The controller of Pickens, John Richards, has been with the company for 28 years and is near retirement. He has given Louderman managerial authority over both the implementation of the new system and the integration of the company's accounting-related functions. Her promotion to controller will depend on the success of the new accounting system.

Louderman began to develop the new system at Pickens by using the same design characteristics and reporting formats that she had developed at her former company. She sent details of the new accounting system to the departments that interfaced with accounting, including inventory control, purchasing, personnel, production control, and marketing. If they did not respond with suggestions by a prescribed date, she would continue the development process. Louderman and Richards determined a new schedule for many of the reports, changing the frequency from weekly to monthly. After a meeting with the director of computer operations, she selected a programmer to help her with the details of the new reporting formats.

Most of the control features of the old system were maintained to decrease the initial installation time, while a few new ones were added for unusual situations. However, the procedures for maintaining the controls were substantially changed.

Louderman appointed herself the decisive authority for all control changes and program testing that related to the system, including screening the control features that related to payroll, inventory control, accounts receivable, cash deposits, and accounts payable.

As each module was completed by the programmer, Louderman told the department to implement the change immediately in order to incorporate immediate labor savings. Instructions accompanying these changes were incomplete, and specific implementation responsibility was not assigned to departmental personnel. Louderman believes that each operations person should "learn as they go," reporting errors as they occur.

Accounts payable and inventory control were the initial areas of the system to be implemented, and several problems arose in both areas. Louderman was disturbed that the semimonthly runs of payroll, which were weekly under the old system, had abundant errors and required numerous manual paychecks. Frequently, the control totals of a payroll run would take hours to reconcile with the computer printout. To expedite matters, Louderman authorized the payroll clerk to prepare journal entries for payroll processing.

The new inventory control system failed to improve the carrying stock level of many items, causing several critical raw material stock-outs that resulted in expensive rush orders. The primary control procedure under the new system was the availability of ordering and usage information to both inventory control personnel and purchasing personnel by terminals. This allowed both departments to issue purchase orders on a timely basis. The inventory levels were updated daily, so the previous weekly report was discontinued by Louderman.

Because of these problems, system documentation is behind schedule and proper backup procedures have not been implemented in many areas. Louderman has requested budget approval to hire two systems analysts, an accountant, and an administrative assistant to help her implement the new system. Richards is disturbed by her request since her predecessor had only one part-time employee as his assistant.

Required:

a. List the steps Mickie Louderman should have taken during the design of the accounting system to ensure that end-user needs were satisfied.
b. Referring to Louderman's approach to implementing the new accounting system,
   1. Identify and describe the weaknesses.
   2. Make recommendations that would help Louderman improve the situation and continue with the development of the remaining areas of the accounting system at Pickens Publishers.

(CMA Adapted)

5–24.   PROTOTYPING

Superior Oil Company has completed a substantial prototyping project in its materials department, resulting in increased efficiency, cost savings, and large numbers of happy users. This project created a tubular information system (TIS) for use in inventory control.[4]

---

[4]Adapted from T. R. Young, "Superior Prototypes," *Datamation,* May 15, 1984, p. 152. © 1984 by Cahners Publishing Company. Used by permission.

Companies exploring for oil and gas need a lot of tubular goods—steel casing and oil tubing. The casing keeps the well bore clear during drilling, and the tubing conducts the crude oil from the producing formation when the well is completed. Capital investment in inventories of these items can be significant; a single 18,000-foot well, for example, requires about $7 million worth of tubular goods. Inventory management is complicated by fluctuations in both drilling demand and steel availability. Incorrect purchasing decisions result either in excessive inventories tying up unnecessary amounts of capital or out-of-stock material. Both conditions are costly to Superior Oil.

Past materials control at Superior had been based on a tubular availability report (TAR). The system producing this report had plenty of limitations: It provided no inquiry capability, its information was out-of-date, unreliable verbal inputs were used, and it contained no controls or audit trails. This was unsatisfactory to Matthew Seltzer, the materials manager. He discussed the problem with William Cooper, the CIO, who agreed to support development of a new system using prototyping methods. They decided to use the old TAR system as an operating prototype.

The design process started with a half-day team effort to create an overall materials system plan tying TIS to the purchasing system. The team consisted of two staffers from MIS and one from the materials department. The plan contained block diagrams of the intended relations among the inventory, purchasing, fixed assets, accounts payable, and general ledger systems. It allowed the design team to draw boundaries around the existing purchasing system and the projected TIS, thereby identifying all interfaces with related systems. The outgrowth of this meeting was a project proposal.

The project proposal called for construction of a production system to manage tubular materials. The system would be constructed by the MIS professional staff in close cooperation with the user's organization. The principal software used would be NATURAL, a high-level language that greatly eases access to the database. A user representative was dedicated full-time to the project during system design and implementation. The materials department was particularly motivated—and rightly so—because they regarded the development as their project.

The development process included three stages: The first was initiated by the statement of management objectives covering system boundaries and capabilities. User participation was high during this stage as the specifications for the system were worked out and prototype screens and reports were developed.

To get started, one MIS team member created a number of images of the computer display screens to handle keyboard data input and file inquiry. Users were asked to evaluate the screens and to resolve differences of opinion among themselves. As the users worked with the screens, they realized that certain necessary features had not been included in the initial screen designs. In the course of a day, the entire first draft set of screens was reviewed. The following day, the user group returned and found that a fully revised set of screens had been constructed by the MIS programmers using NATURAL. The revised versions incorporated the new requirements identified during the previous session.

The evolution of screen designs moved along quickly until a set of screens was developed that satisfied user requirements. The screens' convenience in use, vocabulary, and format was also satisfactory. None of the users had ever experienced such response from the MIS department. The reaction was highly favorable, and the materials control users began to warm to the idea of building their own system. Because user involvement was intense, they felt a personal identification with the system being created. As a result, their acceptance of the system was well formed by the end of the first stage.

The second stage primarily consisted of system construction by the supporting MIS organization; user participation dropped back to a consulting capacity. Equipment was selected, programming was completed, and preliminary documentation was produced.

The final stage began with a management review and commitment to system implementation in field operation. A team was formed for implementation, and user involvement accelerated with operational testing of the prototype. When testing was completed, the new system was installed at all field locations. Then work began on Mod II, the inevitable next phase in development that occurs as new needs are discovered through use of the system.

TIS went on-line seven months following the project's start. Management's evaluation of the project indicated that this would have taken approximately 20 months using conventional development methodologies. According to Materials Director Seltzer, TIS contributed directly to inventory reduction of $100 million over a 10-month period. Further savings result from the fact that purchasing a proprietary system would have cost more than twice the price of in-house development. The systems available for purchase were inappropriate for Superior Oil's business because they were intended for manufacturing companies and were difficult to adapt to the oil drilling environment. Seltzer was well satisfied with the decision to use prototyping methods for system development. "It went like a train!" he was heard to say.

Required:

a. Who were the users of this information system? Which actions were taken to gain their acceptance of the new system?

b. Would you call this a successful system? Explain why.

c. Which characteristics made the tubular information system a likely candidate for prototyping?

5–25.   *USER INVOLVEMENT*

When the Human Resources (HR) Department at **Blue Cross/Blue Shield of New Jersey** decided to change to a personal computer–based system, they did so in spite of opposition from the Information Systems (IS) Department.[5] HR invited IS representatives to its meetings with vendors, but after two such meetings IS quit attending, so HR proceeded without them. (The IS Department wanted to enlarge its mainframe system instead of installing personal computers.) HR managers met with vendors, chose an application package, trained themselves in development tools, modified the package, and installed the hardware and software.

The process took five months and was accomplished by three groups: a management team, a user team, and a systems team. The *management team* included the vice president of human resources and three HR directors. Though not directly involved in design, it was accountable for the project's success. The *user team* consisted of seven direct users of the new system. They configured the application package to meet the

---

[5]Copyright (December 9, 1996) by Computerworld, Inc., Framingham, MA, 01701. Adapted from Computerworld.

department's needs and devoted between 10 and 15 percent of their time to the project during the development process. The *systems team* worked full-time on the project, serving as advisers to the user team, approving its configuration, coordinating the project, and doing most of the training. It consisted of several department managers within HR.

When the old mainframe system was switched off, the 60 HR Department employees began using the new system to manage the company's 4,000 active employees and 18,000 retirees. The project was completed at a cost of 70 percent of its $1 million budget. Six people could not adapt to the new system and either resigned, were fired, or were transferred to other departments.

Management is pleased with the results and plans to create a similar system for financial reporting. One of the big benefits was that users programmed the system to the exact needs of the department. The knowledge they acquired became valuable when Blue Cross/Blue Shield of New Jersey combined with sister companies in Delaware and Connecticut. The HR staff was asked to add the new companies to the system.

Required:

a. In this project, who performed the role that is ordinarily performed by IS personnel?

b. Can you suggest reasons why the Information Systems Department was opposed to this change?

c. What implications does this situation have for the future?

5–26.   *YOUR COMPANY PROJECT—PART I*

In this assignment you will design and develop a computerized accounting system for a small business. To program your system, you may use a software package or language of your choice, or your instructor may select one for you. The system should produce a minimum of two reports: a balance sheet and an income statement. Each of these should conform to GAAP disclosure requirements. You may produce any other management reports that you feel are appropriate for your company.

To complete the project, you should do the following:

a. Choose a small company with which you are familiar, or create a company in an industry that interests you.

b. Develop a chart of accounts for this company. This chart of accounts should contain each of the accounts shown below, plus other accounts that are appropriate for your company. At a later date you will be given opening balances for these accounts and a list of transactions for posting. You should develop your system to process any such transaction.

c. Turn in the following to your instructor by the deadline:

1. A set of financial statements, after updating your general ledger file with the transactions to be handed out later.

2. A documentation package for your system. This should include a description of manual and computerized procedures, source documents, and examples of management reports and display screens.

d. Your instructor may choose to have you make a presentation to the class describing your system. In your presentation you should discuss

1. System inputs.
2. System outputs.
3. Manual and computerized processing steps.
4. Advantages and disadvantages of using your language or package for this application.

Your project will be evaluated for the

a. Efficiency and completeness of your system.
b. Quality of the documentation provided for your system.
c. Clarity and effectiveness of your presentation.

General Ledger Accounts to Be Included in Your System

Cash
Prepaid Expenses
Office Equipment
Accumulated Depreciation—Office Equipment
Office Buildings
Accumulated Depreciation—Office Buildings
Accounts Payable
Wages and Salaries Payable
Common Stock
Retained Earnings
Revenue
Wages and Salaries Expense
Office Supplies Expense
Utilities Expense
Depreciation Expense

Note: This project requires that, if you use a spreadsheet package, your system must include macros. If you complete it in a database package, you must use command modules. Your documentation package must include listings of all programs, macros, and command modules used.

6   SYSTEMS ANALYSIS

Learning Objectives

1. To discover which activities take place during the first phase of the system development life cycle.
2. To learn how to conduct a preliminary survey.
3. To know how to perform a feasibility study.
4. To understand the criteria that determine the feasibility of a proposed accounting information system.

Introduction

The previous chapters provided some useful tools for system development and an overview of system development processes. The next chapters go into more detail about the phases that constitute the system development life cycle (SDLC).

The first part of this chapter reviews the relationship between systems analysis and the other phases of the SDLC. Then it describes two systems analysis processes, the preliminary survey and the feasibility study. The chapters that follow present the activities that take place during the design and implementation of a new information system.

Systems Analysis

Systems analysis is the process of examining an existing information system and its environment to identify potential improvements. The information systems steering committee begins systems analysis in response to a request from a manager or from a long range systems planning group. As discussed in Chapter 5, systems analysis may begin for three reasons: (1) to solve a problem with an existing system; (2) to satisfy a new requirement for information; or (3) to implement a new form of technology. Illustration 6–1 shows the relationship between systems analysis and the other phases of the SDLC.

In an information systems department, highly skilled employees called *systems analysts* coordinate systems analysis activities. A good systems analyst has a thorough

141

ILLUSTRATION 6–1

The Systems Analysis Phase

Systems analysis

knowledge both of computer processing methods and of business needs for information. A systems analyst is also skillful at applying the *systems approach* to problem solving.

The systems analysis phase of the SDLC represents an application of the systems approach to an organizational problem. During this phase, a multidisciplinary project team examines the problem from the perspective of the entire organization. They sometimes call this process the *preliminary survey*. During their examination, the project team identifies possible solutions to the problem that may, or may not, require the use of a computer. As they explore these alternatives, they may identify this process as the *feasibility study*.

The Preliminary Survey

The *preliminary survey* consists of an evaluation of an existing system or systems. Performed by a team of analysts from MIS and user departments, it has four objectives:

1. To acquire an understanding of an existing application system.
2. To develop good relationships with users of the system.
3. To collect data that are potentially useful in system design.
4. To identify the nature of the problem being investigated.

The System Study Proposal

The information systems steering committee initiates the preliminary survey in response to a *system study proposal*. Usually this proposal comes from an operating manager. Sometimes it comes from the long-range systems planning group or from top management. If the proposal has merit, the committee appoints a system study team to conduct the survey.

Reasons for the Proposal.   Sometimes an operating manager initiates a system study proposal after identifying a problem with an existing system. The manager wants a study team to investigate the problem and to consider the need for changes to the system. Often an organization outgrows an existing system, and because of this growth the system develops *insufficient processing capacity*. This problem occurs, for example, in noncomputerized accounting systems that develop backlogs of unprocessed accounting transactions. Changes in the organization can also cause *erroneous processing* of transactions. For example, a business may reassign responsibility for entering sales orders from professional to clerical personnel. If the clerical personnel are unfamiliar with the customers or the product line, they may record many sales orders incorrectly. Sometimes a system is simply *not functioning as intended*. For example, a

---

AIS in Practice

The need for systems analysis sometimes arises from unusual sources. For many international companies, the **European Monetary Union** (EMU) creates new reporting requirements that were unanticipated when their information systems were developed. On January 1, 1999, a new currency (the "Euro") will be used in certain European countries for bookkeeping and noncash transactions. Then in 2002, Euro currency will be issued and individual currencies retired in these countries. In the meantime, accounting systems must process amounts in both European and local currencies.

EMU rules require that when countries convert from one local currency to another, they convert first to the Euro and display the result to six significant figures. This requires changes not only to accounting data and applications but also in computer fonts in order to accommodate the Euro's new symbol. Major software vendors have already addressed the problem. Some maintain records in as many as three currencies simultaneously. Companies that develop their own software must appoint project teams to study the problem and identify feasible solutions.

---

computerized responsibility accounting system may not provide meaningful performance measures for operating supervisors. A manager may submit a study proposal for a new system that provides better information for motivation and control. Finally, many proposals are submitted to correct *processing inefficiency*. In this case, a manager feels that a new system can produce significant cost savings.

Other reasons for initiating a system study proposal include the existence of new information requirements. These can arise for either *legal* or *competitive* reasons. For example, some companies transact business with governments on a "cost plus" basis. The company's revenues from a government contract are its costs, plus a percentage of costs determined in advance and recorded in the contract. In such a situation, the company is legally obligated to maintain detailed records of its costs of production. Other organizations want to keep detailed cost records for good cost control. This helps them to acquire business from competitors. Additional new information requirements may be identified by a systems planning group as a part of long-range strategic planning.

Many times operating managers or long-range planners may submit a system study proposal to implement a new technology. For example, during the 1970s most organizations ceased using punched cards for inputting transactions to computerized systems. On-line computer terminals replaced keypunches because the terminals provide an *improved data entry* method. For the same reason many companies today use cash registers as data entry devices. Accountants call these *point-of-sale systems* because they record the transaction data immediately when the sale occurs.

Another technological development provides *terminal reporting* capability. This allows managers to receive informative reports at terminals or personal computers whenever they desire, rather than when reports are printed as a part of routine processing by older systems. Systems with terminal reporting capability often enable managers to produce ad hoc reports. With ad hoc reporting, managers not only receive the reports at terminals but also can select the information to be reported and rearrange the reports to their own preferences.

Implementing a new technology is an appealing reason to initiate a preliminary survey. However, a system that uses the latest technology is sometimes not

ILLUSTRATION 6–2

Reasons for a System Study Proposal

Problems with an Existing System
Insufficient processing capacity.
Erroneous processing.
Not functioning as intended.
Processing inefficiency.

New Requirement for Information
Legal.
Competitive.

Desire for New Technology
Improved data entry.
Terminal reporting capability.
Ad hoc reporting capability.

cost-effective. Costs and benefits of a proposed new technology are evaluated during another activity of systems analysis, the feasibility study. Illustration 6–2 summarizes these reasons for submitting a system study proposal.

Project Initiation.   The information systems steering committee consists of the chief information officer and a representative from each user department. A user department is one that uses significant computerized applications. The committee meets on a regular basis, perhaps weekly or monthly, to review and evaluate project proposals. Among these proposals are system study proposals from managers and planners who wish to initiate preliminary surveys.

In deciding which proposals merit further study, the committee establishes priorities for the MIS staff. If the proposal arises from problems with an existing system, the committee evaluates the seriousness of the problem. Processing backlogs or excessive errors may require prompt correction and often require overtime work or temporary clerical help. Less serious problems, such as those represented by minor inefficiencies, may be deferred. A proposal in response to a need for new information requires the committee to evaluate the time frame associated with the need. Frequently, new laws or competitors require prompt action by the committee. Priorities for proposals that implement a new technology depend on the expected costs and benefits associated with the technology. In some cases, potential benefits justify a high priority for a study proposal.

Once the steering committee assigns a priority to each system study proposal, it approves the most important ones for further investigation. The committee then forms a system study team to examine the environment of the problem, the new information requirement, or the new technology.

The System Study Team

A *system study team* consists of one or more systems analysts and user personnel. An experienced systems analyst is in charge of the team. User personnel may be professional or clerical employees from the affected user department who have some experience or training with the system. These may include engineer: duction managers or supervisors, or sales managers or clerks. For an accountant or experienced accounting clerk may represent the on the study team.

A common problem in forming a study team is getting adeq.. input. Each user member of a study team has full-time duties within the department. user member must be relieved of at least some of these duties to participate in any system project. User personnel who are knowledgeable about an existing system's shortcomings are likely to be valuable employees. A manager frequently hesitates to release a valuable subordinate, even temporarily, for assignment to a study team. For example, the production supervisor who best understands the shortcomings of a responsibility accounting system is probably one who uses it. Because of the supervisor's responsibilities in the department, a production manager may resist having this supervisor assigned to a study team. The information systems steering committee must ensure that the managers of user departments support the project and allow key personnel to participate.

Scope of the Preliminary Survey

The purposes of the preliminary survey include developing an understanding of existing applications and available resources. This is primarily a process of gathering facts about the way the organization currently operates. In conducting the survey, the system study team determines the following information about the existing system:

Data Flows.   The study team gathers facts about the flow of data within the system and across interfaces to other systems. Data flow can take the form of documents, oral communications, or computer records. The study team identifies each of these items used in the system and determines what data is contained on each, who initiates the data, and who receives it.

Effectiveness.   The study team evaluates the effectiveness of the existing system. An effective system adequately achieves its goals; to measure effectiveness, the team must first clearly define the goals of the existing system. Then the team gathers data about the system that can be used to measure effectiveness. This data can be objective, such as descriptive statistics on system operations, or subjective, such as users' opinions about the system's usefulness. Often a manager proposes a system study to investigate a problem with an existing system's effectiveness. During the preliminary survey, the study team can evaluate the source of the manager's dissatisfaction.

Efficiency.   In gathering data about an existing system, the study team looks for ways to improve the system's efficiency. Although efficiency may be difficult to measure, the team can sometimes compute efficiency as the ratio of system outputs to system inputs. At other times, the team calculates a ratio of outputs to cost of inputs. Sometimes the steering committee initiates a system study because of inefficiencies in an existing system; this makes the study team's evaluation of efficiency especially important.

Internal Controls.   The study team also evaluates internal controls in the existing system. Internal controls are the measures taken by the organization to safeguard assets, to ensure accurate data, to promote efficiency, and to encourage compliance with management's policies. Frequently, poor internal control can cause a system to record erroneous transactions and to generate incorrect accounting or management reports. The adequacy of its internal control also influences the system's effectiveness and efficiency. Accountants have special expertise concerning internal control and are assigned to study teams for this reason.

During the preliminary survey, the system study team gathers data on information flows, effectiveness, efficiency, and internal controls in the existing system. In this process, the team identifies both strengths and weaknesses in the existing system. Systems analysis may result in the design and implementation of a new system. If so, the old system's strengths should be retained in the new one. During the system design phase, a project team also corrects any serious weaknesses found during the preliminary survey.

Using Systems Tools

During the preliminary survey, the study team uses many of the systems tools presented earlier. Members of the team review existing documentation, conduct interviews, and use work measurement techniques to understand how the current system operates. They take notes during these activities and include them in the study team's working papers. They use data and process modeling techniques to document their conclusions. They may review reports provided by internal or independent auditors.

Documentation Review.   Three kinds of documentation concern the study team: organizational, individual, and processing documentation.

The study team examines documentation describing the organization's structure and accounting procedures. This information includes organization charts, the chart of accounts, and departmental budgets for recent years. Organizational documentation describes the environment of the problem as well as the new requirement or new technology that caused the proposal. Budgets and organization charts may indicate sources of a problem or may affect the feasibility of possible changes to a system. A chart of accounts aids in understanding the budget, and its structure affects the nature of proposed system changes.

The study team also looks at all available documentation concerning how individuals perform their jobs. These include job descriptions, procedures manuals, performance standards, and computer operating instructions. This individual documentation is often highly detailed, and examining it is a tedious process. Yet in this documentation study team members find precise descriptions of individual tasks that may help identify the source of a problem. Frequently a new information requirement or new technology requires changes to these tasks, and gathering data on existing tasks makes later development activities easier.

Another type of documentation examined by the study team is processing documentation. This provides information on interfaces between individual tasks and between these tasks and the computer. Processing documentation shows how computerized and manual procedures interact; it includes flowcharts, sample forms, and sample reports. By examining flowcharts, the study team identifies the sequence of tasks that make up a system. The sequence, rather than the individual tasks, may require change to correct a problem. Sample forms identify the data that the system collects, and sample reports illustrate the information it provides. Frequently, these must be changed to satisfy a new requirement for information or to implement a new technology.

ILLUSTRATION 6–3

Documentation Reviewed During the Preliminary Survey

Organizational Documentation

Organization chart. A diagram showing superior and subordinate relationships.

Chart of accounts. A list of accounts in the general ledger.

Department budgets. Projected costs and revenues summarized by responsibility centers. These may be compared to actual costs and revenues.

Individual Documentation

Job description. Identifies for each clerical and supervisory position the specific tasks, procedures, and responsibilities assigned.

Procedures manual. A document that identifies and describes tasks constituting each noncomputerized procedure required by a system. It also identifies the job description performing each procedure.

Performance standards. Expected measures of efficiency, quality, or quantity for a task or procedure.

Computer operating instructions. A document describing tasks assigned to a computer operator.

Processing Documentation

Flowcharts. A graphic representation of sequential processes.

Sample forms. One of each kind used for data input by the system.

Sample reports. One of each kind produced by the system.

Illustration 6–3 summarizes the three types of documentation gathered during the preliminary survey. Unfortunately, the study team may find that much of this documentation has become obsolete. For example, if the system under study is old, then existing flowcharts, procedures manuals, and job descriptions may no longer accurately describe the system. An examination of existing documentation provides a way to begin data gathering. This data must be updated by further procedures. These procedures may include interviews, data modeling, process modeling, questionnaires, and work measurement techniques.

Using Interviews.   After collecting documentation, the next step in the preliminary survey of an existing system is conducting interviews. Members of the study team first interview the manager in charge of the affected user department. In this interview, the team not only learns the manager's perspective on the problem but also attempts to gain the manager's enthusiasm and support. The cooperation of all affected user employees is important to the success of the study, and this cooperation is easier to attain if employees realize that their bosses support it. After interviewing the manager, members of the study team then conduct interviews with key supervisory and clerical personnel.

In conducting interviews, the study team encourages the interviewees—whether managers, supervisors, or clerks—to describe their job functions. This allows the study team to learn how existing documentation is out-of-date. The team also learns the interviewee's opinions concerning the problem, the information requirement, or the technological change that initiated the study. Even though supervisors or clerks may have limited perspectives on a problem, often they can offer insight regarding its source, its potential solutions, or the difficulties inherent in providing new information or introducing a new technology. While conducting an interview, the study team member may take notes or collect examples of completed forms for later review.

Interviews aid in gaining user acceptance if management decides to introduce a new system later. They also provide the study team with the information needed to understand how an existing system operates. The study team uses data modeling, process modeling, decision tables, questionnaires, and work measurement techniques to improve their understanding of the system.

Data Modeling.   Using the information gathered from the documentation review and interviews, the study team creates models of the data used by the system. *Data modeling* is a technique for organizing and documenting the organization's data. It does this independent of how the data will be processed to produce information.

When done properly, data modeling helps to ensure that the data processed by the system are accurate and up-to-date and meet all of the current information requirements. The data are also organized so that future requirements can be met by easily modifying existing data forms. Future information systems evolve around the data without requiring major changes to the data.

One popular approach to data modeling uses entity-relationship (E-R) diagrams. These were introduced in Chapter 4, on systems tools. An E-R diagram identifies the items of data used by a system and shows the associations between those items. It represents an item of data (an entity) with a rectangle and associations between data items (the relationships) with lines between rectangles.

For example, the applications making up an accounting information system are entities. The nature of the transactions flowing between applications defines the relationships between applications. The general ledger entity summarizes transactions from other applications, but the other applications post transactions to the general ledger. The E-R diagram in Illustration 6–4 depicts the entities and relationships in an accounting system. Illustration 6–5 shows examples of relationships typically found during data modeling.

Process Modeling.   The study team also creates process models to document the existing system. *Process modeling* is a technique for organizing and documenting a system's processes, outputs, inputs, and data. Different methods exist for producing process models, but the most common one today uses data flow diagrams. The chapter on systems tools introduced this technique.

A data flow diagram shows the flow of data between processes, files, and external destinations. One method of drawing them uses circles to represent processes, squares to signify external destinations for data, rectangles (open on two sides) for data stores, and arrows for data flow. These symbols show the process performed by a system without identifying the technology used in the processes.

Older systems may have been developed using flowcharts rather than data flow diagrams. A flowchart is a graphic representation of sequential processes and may be a system or document flowchart. Analysts drawing flowcharts specify by their choices of symbols a form of technology.

Because data flow diagrams show logical rather than physical flows, they allow analysts more creativity. Analysts are forced to think about *what* is done rather than *how* it is done. This enables them to identify problems easier and develop better solutions. An analyst who is preoccupied with details of technology may overlook users' needs for information until late in the system's development, when it is expensive to correct.

ILLUSTRATION 6–4

*E-R Diagram of an
Accounting System*

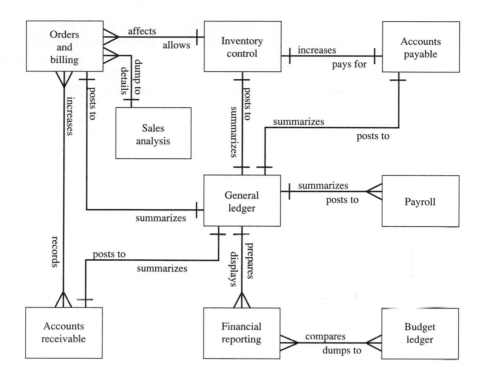

Omitting technological details also makes easier the analysts' communication with users, who may not understand the technology. For these reasons, data flow diagrams have generally replaced flowcharts as a systems analysis tool.

As an accountant, you may encounter either form of process model. Regardless of the approach, the systems study team uses process modeling for three purposes: summarizing, documenting, and analyzing. The diagrams are an efficient way to summarize

ILLUSTRATION 6–5

Examples of Relationships Between Entities

Appears on	←→	Is for
Contains	←→	Is contained on
Drives	←→	Is driven by
Employs	←→	Is employed by
Governs	←→	Is governed by
Holds	←→	Is held by
Orders	←→	Is ordered by
Owns	←→	Is owned by
Manufactures	←→	Is manufactured by
Rents	←→	Is rented by
Requests	←→	Is requested by
Returns	←→	Is returned by
Services	←→	Is serviced by
Supplies	←→	Is supplied by

what the study team learns from interviews and documentation reviews. For example, during interviews an analyst accumulates many pages of interview notes. The notes from each interview describe the views of an individual employee. The analyst then summarizes this information into a form that describes operations from the viewpoint of the organization as a whole. Data flow diagrams make this task easier for the analyst.

Data flow diagrams also allow the study team to document how the existing system works. Those produced during the preliminary survey update older documentation that may no longer be correct. If the systems analysis phase is followed by the design of a new system, new diagrams of the old system are useful in design and conversion. New diagrams also demonstrate to management and the steering committee that the study team has adequately examined the existing system.

Data flow diagrams are valuable once the study team has gathered all its data. At this point, the team begins to analyze the existing system to identify problems or potential improvements. A data flow diagram contains a concise description of the processes making up a system. The analyst can see the effects of changes more easily than when notes, narratives, or other forms of documentation are used. In fact, many experienced analysts find that the process of diagramming itself helps identify problems or produce ideas for new systems.

Using Questionnaires.   A study team may also use questionnaires during a preliminary survey. A questionnaire may be used in two ways; either an analyst or user department personnel can complete it.

Sometimes the study team develops a questionnaire for its members to use when conducting interviews. The questionnaire lists facts that should be identified or answers that should be obtained by the analyst during the interview. The analyst uses it as a guide to ensure that all necessary data are gathered. When used in this way, the questionnaire is developed by an experienced systems analyst. Then the study team can use less-experienced members to conduct interviews without fear of omitting important information.

At other times, the study team desires information or opinions from a large number of user personnel. The team may allow the users to complete a questionnaire rather than interview each user individually. This approach is efficient when the study team has examined the system and identified specific information requirements. For example, the team may want to gather descriptive statistics concerning user satisfaction or frequency of usage; a questionnaire used in this way may save significant time and cost. However, substituting a questionnaire for interviews may cause the team to omit important information. It does not allow the analyst to ask probing questions, nor does it encourage an interviewee to volunteer information.

Work Measurement.   Sometimes the study team uses questionnaires in conjunction with work measurement studies. While other techniques used by the study team identify tasks occurring in the system, a *work measurement study* determines the magnitude or quantities of these tasks.

For example, an analyst may find through interviews or documentation reviews that an accounts payable clerk prepares a batch control slip. The analyst, however, does not know how frequently this occurs, nor does the analyst know how much time this task requires. The analyst asks the clerk to complete a questionnaire each day showing how much time was required to complete each batch control slip. After several days' questionnaires are available, the analyst computes an average elapsed time for the task. As an alternative, the analyst may choose to time the task over several repetitions using a stopwatch. Industrial engineers refer to this work measurement technique as *time and motion study.*

Another approach to work measurement counts the number of outputs from a task or system, such as forms completed or reports produced. This enables a study team to compute measures of efficiency by the number of outputs per employee or unit of time.

Regardless of the approach taken, the system study team normally undertakes some form of work measurement. This is especially important when the preliminary survey results from problems regarding system efficiency, or when the team uses a cost–benefit analysis to determine the feasibility of developing a new system.

Audit Reports.   The study team may choose to examine reports written by auditors prior to the study. These reports may be prepared by internal auditors or by independent auditors.

As part of their duties, internal auditors perform ***operational audits*** of departments or segments of the organization. In the operational audit, the internal auditor analyzes the operations of the department and identifies weaknesses or potential improvements. At its conclusion, the internal auditor writes a report to management describing them.

The independent auditor writes a *management letter* to top management during the audit of the financial statements. This letter describes weaknesses in internal control that the auditor identified during the audit. The independent auditor provides it as an additional service; the management letter is not a part of the standard independent audit report.

Frequently, an operational audit report or a management letter describes weaknesses and makes suggestions useful to the study team. The auditor may have examined the system under study, and the auditor's evaluation helps the team identify a problem. The auditor's suggestions may be included in the design of a new system.

These are the procedures used during the preliminary survey. The information systems steering committee initiates this activity to gather data about an existing system. However, sometimes the steering committee decides that obtaining this data is unnecessary. By omitting it, the organization fails to receive the benefits of performing a preliminary survey.

Benefits of the Preliminary Survey

The preliminary survey provides three major benefits. First, it provides an objective evaluation of the situation that produced the system study proposal. Objectivity is attained by appointing to the study team individuals who initiated neither this proposal nor other competing proposals. The study team is directed by a systems analyst who has no daily interaction with the system and is skilled in applying the systems approach. By objectively evaluating the existing system, the system study team may conclude that it is operating satisfactorily. They may decide that a minor modification to the existing system, rather than a new system, is adequate.

A second benefit of the preliminary survey is that it provides necessary information. At the conclusion of systems analysis, the information systems steering committee may decide that a new system is warranted. If this occurs, much of the information gathered

ILLUSTRATION 6–6

Benefits of the Preliminary Survey

1. *Provides an objective evaluation.* A study team may decide that a new system is unnecessary.
2. *Provides design information.* Data could be useful in design and implementation, should a new system be authorized.
3. *Aids in gaining user acceptance.* Users are involved from the beginning of the system development life cycle.

during the preliminary survey is useful during the system design and implementation phases. While examining the existing system, the study team determines the resources of personnel and equipment that are available for a new system. The team identifies strengths in the old system that should be retained, and weaknesses that should be eliminated. At the conclusion of the implementation phase, the organization converts from the old system to the new one. The data gathered about the old system's files, procedures, and forms make this conversion process easier.

And finally, the preliminary survey facilitates gaining user acceptance of a new system. The survey requires significant personal contact between the system study team and user personnel. Knowing that they have provided inputs to the new system, users are more likely to work to make it succeed. Illustration 6–6 summarizes the benefits of performing a preliminary survey.

During the preliminary survey, the study team gathers data concerning the system. After producing working papers to document their conclusions, they begin the process of examining in detail potential changes to the system. This process is the feasibility study.

The Feasibility Study

The preliminary survey consists of an examination of existing systems. In contrast, during the *feasibility study* the system study team examines alternatives that are potential changes to existing systems. In the feasibility study, the study team specifies the objectives and scope of the new system under consideration. Then they examine each alternative in detail and eliminate from consideration those clearly infeasible.

Objectives of the System

Before examining the feasibility of a system change, the study team identifies the objective or objectives of the system. This is necessary if they are to apply the systems approach. The information system steering committee initiates systems analysis because an existing system is not meeting its objectives, or because new objectives have been identified for it. During the preliminary survey, the study team may find that the objectives of an existing system are not clearly defined. During the feasibility study, these are specified. Then in determining the feasibility of an alternative, the study team considers whether a proposed change achieves these objectives.

Scope of the System

During the preliminary survey, the system study team examined a problem. They gathered and analyzed data relevant to the problem from throughout the organization.

During the feasibility study, the problem is known, objectives are defined, and the study team evaluates possible solutions. In doing this, the study team must restrict their analysis to factors relating to the problem. They define the scope of the system to include only those components relevant to achieving the objectives of the system. In the terminology of systems theory, they establish the boundaries of the system that is to be changed. Then they restrict their efforts only to those components within these boundaries.

Defining the scope of the system is frequently a difficult task. During the preliminary survey, a study team may find many problems that need correction or many opportunities for technological improvement. They may wish to correct all the problems or make all the improvements immediately. Such a major system development effort is unlikely to be completed within a reasonable time period and will probably be unsuccessful. An experienced systems analyst recognizes the need to select the most critical needs and implement solutions to them first. Another study team can address less critical needs later.

Defining System Scope—an Example

The following example shows how to define the scope of a system. XYZ Company is considering a contract to produce 10,000 widgets for the government. The selling price for the widgets is equal to their production cost, plus 10 percent. The latter provides XYZ's profit on the transaction. However, XYZ must improve its cost accounting system to comply with government requirements.

XYZ appoints a study team to evaluate the existing cost accounting system and to identify the changes needed. The team determines that the system's objectives are to record costs for the direct material and direct labor used in producing the widgets and to allocate to the widgets their share of factory overhead. XYZ's payroll system is a manual one and can provide data concerning direct labor costs for the widgets. However, purchases of materials and supplies are recorded by a computerized accounts payable system that is inadequate for cost accounting purposes. The accounts payable system is incapable of recording the costs of material for the widgets separately from the costs of material for other products. The study team concludes that a new cost accounting system would be unsuccessful without a new accounts payable system. The company cannot develop two major systems simultaneously with the resources currently available to it.

How should the study team proceed? They should first identify the system that has the most critical need. Then they should define the scope of their study to include only this system and identify alternative ways to satisfy this need. The most critical system is the accounts payable system because it must be changed before the cost accounting system can provide accurate information. Once an adequate accounts payable system is functioning, another project team can develop a job costing system that complies with government cost accounting standards. At some later date, XYZ Company may decide to computerize its payroll system to increase processing efficiency.

This example illustrates the interactions that occur between the components of the accounting transaction processing system. These interactions require that, as accounting systems evolve, study teams carefully define boundaries for these components before implementing improvements. Once the study team determines the scope of a system, it then considers the feasibility of changes to it.

Determining
Feasibility

During the preliminary survey, the study team identifies a problem and possible solutions to it. These solutions may include minor changes, major changes, or completely new systems. After establishing limits to the scope of its efforts, the study team evaluates the feasibility of solution alternatives. For an alternative to progress beyond the systems analysis phase, it must be feasible in four ways: technical, operational, time, and economic.

Technical Feasibility.   This feasibility criterion concerns the state of technology in the computer industry and the technological capabilities of the organization. In evaluating *technical feasibility,* the study team determines whether computer software and equipment that allow implementation are available from manufacturers.

This is the easiest feasibility criterion to evaluate. MIS representatives on a study team usually are knowledgeable about the capabilities of available equipment. Their knowledge can be supplemented by advice from outside consultants. Technical and trade journals keep team members up-to-date regarding the state of technology.

Predicting the success of a technology in an organization is more difficult. This requires evaluation of a second feasibility criterion, the operating feasibility.

Operating Feasibility.   In considering the *operating feasibility* of an alternative, the study team determines if a proposed system change could enable the system to meet its operating objectives. An alternative that fails to do so is discarded.

Technological change often occurs faster than employees can adapt to it. Sometimes a system alternative is unsuccessful if employees feel threatened by the new technology, or if they feel that it makes their jobs less important or enjoyable. In other cases, a new technology may require capabilities that existing personnel lack. For example, using a computer keyboard requires typing skills that some factory workers may be unwilling to learn.

A significant factor in determining operating feasibility is user satisfaction. If users are dissatisfied with a system, it does not meet its objectives. When users are dissatisfied with a system, they fail to use it. Or, even worse, they may sabotage it, making it ineffective or inoperable. Thus, when a study team performs the feasibility study, they must consider any behavioral or social implications of a system change on the people who work with it.

Another issue examined by the study team is the expected performance of the system alternative. Many system studies are initiated to overcome problems with processing backlogs or to implement a new technology that improves performance. For example, a new system may complete the accounting cycle more quickly than an old one and thus eliminate the backlog. It may allow more data entry operators to use it simultaneously. The study team compares the performance of a system alternative to that desired. A system that does not meet performance expectations is eliminated from further consideration.

When analyzing operating feasibility, the study team answers the following questions:

- Do top management have the vision, support, and commitment to the new system?

- Are employees willing to accept the changes caused by the new system?
- Will all affected managers have input into the design of the new system?
- Can the organization ensure an orderly transition to the new system?
- Is the organization willing to accept the organizational changes brought on by the new system?

Time Feasibility.   In evaluating this feasibility criterion, the study team determines if the alternative can be implemented within a reasonable length of time. They compare the time needed to implement it with the company's needs for the system. If the company started a system study to implement a new technology, it may be willing to go through a lengthy development process, maybe two or three years, to gain the technology. If the study resulted from a critical problem with an existing system or an immediate need for information, the company wants an alternative that can be implemented quickly.

In determining *time feasibility,* the study team predicts the time needed to design and implement the new system. This time frame is affected by four factors: (1) The team estimates the equipment delivery time. Sometimes purchasers wait from several months to a year for the delivery of equipment. (2) The team must project the software delivery time. If computer programs are available for purchase, the system can be implemented much more quickly than if programs must be written. The team also estimates (3) the training time for users and (4) the time for conversion to the new system. These will be longer if the system requires a major technological change than if it requires only a minor change to an existing system. The study team considers these factors and compares implementation time to the time allowed by the company.

Economic Feasibility.   In analyzing this criterion, the study team determines whether the proposed change will benefit the organization financially. Their objective in evaluating *economic feasibility* is to find out whether the change is worth making. Many system development projects last from two to three years and cost millions of dollars to implement. During the feasibility study, the team makes preliminary calculations to determine whether the benefits received are worth the costs.

Before a study team recommends initiation of system design, the proposed system or system change must satisfy all four feasibility criteria. If an alternative is infeasible on any of these grounds, then the alternative is not considered further. Illustration 6–7 summarizes the four criteria for feasibility.

ILLUSTRATION 6–7

Evaluating System Feasibility

Technical feasibility. Can it be implemented?
Operating feasibility. Will it achieve its objectives?
Time feasibility. Can it be implemented within a reasonable length of time?
Economic feasibility. Are the benefits worth the costs?

Determining
Economic
Feasibility

The system study team determines the economic feasibility of a system by comparing the projected costs of a system change with its projected benefits. Estimating economic feasibility is useful during systems analysis even though at this stage all costs are approximate. If the steering committee decides to proceed with the development project, the team formed for system design develops a more accurate appraisal of costs and benefits later.

In estimating economic feasibility, the study team distinguishes between *annual* costs or benefits and those that occur only once, the *one-time* costs or benefits. Annual costs include the costs of operating the system, such as operating salaries, supplies, and utilities. One-time costs include equipment and salaries of the system development team. A new system may produce an annual cost savings or annual additional revenue; this becomes the annual benefit.

Determining Costs.   The expected costs of an alternative can be projected in advance with some accuracy. Members of the study team who worked on previous development projects use past costs as guidelines. Actual costs of developing previous systems are modified to reflect differences between the old one and the proposed one. Modifications are made based on differences in scope, differences in technology used, the experience of project team members, and inflation. Everyone involved recognizes the inaccuracy of such a cost projection. However, an estimate may be off by 100 percent or more and still be usable. Such an estimate is better than no estimate at all.

What if no one on the study team has experience with a system similar to the proposed one? When a proposed application or technology is unfamiliar to the study team, the wisest and safest course is to engage a consultant. Many accounting firms, for example, employ specialists in this area. They have wide ranges of experience, and their advice can easily be worth the cost of obtaining it. The costs of implementing a successful system are high, but these costs produce benefits; the costs of producing an unsuccessful system are equally high but may produce no benefits. The wise study team recognizes its limitations.

Determining Benefits.   Before an information systems steering committee proceeds with a development project, members want to know that its benefits justify its costs. Usually benefits can be identified easily in qualitative terms. The study team can state with confidence that a new system will, for example, eliminate a backlog, improve the company's competitive position, or improve decision making. However, such vague statements are insufficient during the SDLC. The study team must estimate in monetary terms the financial benefits from the new system or system change.

The nature of the system application determines the accuracy of this benefit estimate. The financial benefits of certain systems can be projected quite accurately, while for other systems the projection may be little more than a guess. The reasons for these differences in accuracy become apparent in the context of the three levels of decision-making activity: strategic planning, management control, and operational control.

Strategic Planning.   At the strategic planning level, top management makes decisions about the organization's objectives and the policies necessary to achieve them. Information systems aid in decisions about the introduction of future products or product lines, the entrance into future markets, and the acquisition of factories, subsidiaries, or companies. The payoffs from these decisions may be realized 5 to 25 years or more in the future. Furthermore, these payoffs are affected by future events that a study team cannot anticipate in the present. When the team evaluates the economic feasibility of these information systems, their estimates of financial benefits are very inaccurate.

Management Control.   Decisions at this level are made to accomplish the organization's objectives effectively and efficiently. Information systems used in management control include responsibility accounting and budgeting systems, and systems used in personnel management. Some of these provide benefits that are difficult to quantify; nevertheless, estimation is easier than at the strategic planning level. The benefits from these systems occur from one to five years after implementation. Because fewer unexpected events occur during this time period, the study team can predict the financial benefits of such a system more accurately.

Operational Control.   Decisions at the operational control level ensure that specific tasks are carried out properly. Examples of information systems at this level include accounting transaction processing, inventory control, and cash management systems. For these applications, benefits often result from cost savings that are easily projected. Their payoffs may be immediate and can be estimated with accuracy. In many organizations, the largest and most expensive systems are developed at the operational control level. Organizations make these investments because they feel confident that the projected financial benefits can be attained.

Determining Financial Benefits—an Example.   XYZ Company is considering the development of a computerized inventory control system to replace its current manual one. The average cost of finished goods inventory during the most recent year was $10 million. A consultant has determined that a computerized system would allow inventories to decrease to an average of $8 million while maintaining the same level of customer service. XYZ finances its inventories with a line of credit at its bank, which charges an interest rate of 10 percent per year. What are the expected financial benefits to XYZ Company from the computerized inventory system?

This proposed operational control system allows XYZ to reduce its inventory level by $2 million. The inventory carrying cost for XYZ Company is 10 percent. The financial benefit resulting from the computerized system is as follows:

Current average inventory	$10,000,000
Possible average inventory with the new system	8,000,000
Decrease in average inventory	2,000,000
Inventory carrying cost	× .10
Annual savings in inventory carrying costs	$ 200,000

XYZ Company could save $200,000 per year by implementing the computerized inventory control system. This savings constitutes interest that XYZ does not pay due to excessive inventory.

Comparing Costs and Benefits.   The study team evaluates the economic feasibility of a new system or system change by comparing its costs with its benefits. In many cases, such as the previous example, these costs and benefits can be estimated accurately. The next step is to compare the costs with the benefits by using one of three methods: net cost or benefit, return on investment, or discounted cash flow.

Net Cost or Benefit.   The simplest way to compare costs and benefits is to subtract one from the other. When benefits exceed costs, the study team calculates the net benefit. If benefits are less than costs, the result is a net cost. Many people refer to this calculation as *cost–benefit analysis.*

   This form of analysis is appropriate when the study team is comparing annual costs with annual benefits, or one-time costs with one-time benefits. However, the method may produce incorrect conclusions if, for example, one-time costs are subtracted from annual benefits. Doing so ignores the time value of money; discounted cash flow methods are better for this comparison.

Return on Investment.   Some companies evaluate economic feasibility using return on investment (ROI). One way of computing ROI is to divide annual benefits from a system by the one-time costs of developing it. If there are annual costs, these should be subtracted from the annual benefits first.

$$\text{ROI} = \frac{\text{Annual benefits} - \text{Annual costs}}{\text{One-time development costs}}$$

   ROI is a popular measure but, like cost–benefit analysis, it ignores the time value of money. Discounted cash flow methods overcome this disadvantage.

Discounted Cash Flow Methods.   These methods of comparing costs and benefits recognize the importance of the *timing* of cash flows as well as their *magnitudes.* Many new systems require a major one-time investment of cash during development and produce smaller annual benefits over many years. The value to an organization of the annual benefit received this year is greater than an identical annual benefit received 10 years in the future. Because of this, the money saved or received over an extended period of time has *time value.* Other accounting courses teach methods of evaluating projects, such as investments in new systems, that are called *capital budgeting models.* These methods consider the time value of money and include such techniques as the internal rate of return, the net present value, and the present value index. Illustration 6–8 shows calculations of the net benefit, ROI, and net present value for the XYZ Company example.

Report to Management

At the conclusion of the feasibility study, the system study team prepares a report of its findings. This **system study report** may vary in length from a few pages to a bound volume. The study team submits this report to the information systems steering committee and may provide copies to interested parties in top management, the long-range systems planning group, and user departments.

ILLUSTRATION 6–8

Example of Comparing Costs and Benefits for a New System

Example: XYZ Company estimates that a computerized inventory control system produces an annual savings of $200,000. The system will be used for eight years. XYZ's cost of capital is 10 percent. Projected costs for the system are as follows:

Annual cost:	Salaries	$ 70,000
	Utilities	20,000
	Supplies	10,000
	Total	$ 100,000
One-time development costs:	Equipment	$ 100,000
	Computer programs	350,000
	Conversion costs	50,000
	Total	$ 500,000

The present value of an annuity of $1 for 8 years at 10% is 5.335.

Net benefit =

Annual benefits	$200,000
Less: Annual costs	100,000
Net annual benefit	$100,000

Return on investment =

Net annual benefits	$100,000
Investment	500,000
ROI (100,000/500,000)	20%

Net present value =

Present value of benefits:		
$200,000 × 5.335		$1,067,000
Less: Present value of costs:		
Annual $100, 000 × 5.335	533,500	
One-time	500,000	
Total		1,033,500
Net present value		$ 33,500

The form of the system study report varies depending on the preferences of company management. Some managers like to see elaborate detailed analysis in the report, which they can skim or read in depth if necessary. Other managers prefer to have an executive summary in the first two or three pages, followed by pages of thorough analysis. With this approach, a busy manager quickly determines the study team's conclusions and has detailed information available to answer questions. Regardless of the form of the system study report, it should contain the information summarized in Illustration 6–9.

The system study report begins by describing the impetus for the study. This information is contained in the original system study proposal written by a manager and submitted to the steering committee. Because several months may have elapsed between the proposal and the report, the description is repeated. The impetus for the study may have been a problem with an existing system, a new requirement for information, or the desire to implement a new technology. The system study report then restates the objective of the study as it was identified by the steering committee.

ILLUSTRATION 6–9

Contents of a System Study Report

1. Describe the problem, information need, or desired technology.
2. State the objective of the system study.
3. Describe procedures followed in the preliminary survey.
4. Identify the constraints on the problem solution.
5. Discuss the two or three best system alternatives:
    • Identify the solution, its objectives, and its scope.
    • Describe advantages and disadvantages.
    • Summarize financial costs and benefits.
    • State major assumptions.
6. Make a recommendation.

The report also describes briefly the procedures followed in the preliminary survey. It identifies the departments and existing systems that were reviewed, and it discusses how tools such as questionnaires or work measurement techniques were employed. The report then provides a concise statement of the problem identified by the study team. It also includes a description of the constraints, or limitations, on possible solutions to the problem.

Most of a system study report is devoted to discussions of alternative solutions to the problem. In the report, the team identifies the two or three most promising solutions and describes them in detail. These solutions may include minor changes to existing systems, major overhauls of existing systems, or replacing an old system with a completely new one. The discussion lists the advantages, disadvantages, costs, and benefits of each solution. It also contains a summary of the major assumptions made by the study team in evaluating the alternatives.

Most important, the system study report contains the study team's final recommendation, which may be to implement one of the alternatives, to take no further action, or to delay action until some time in the future.

Frequently, members of the system study team present their findings to the steering committee and members of top management. Their presentation is an oral summary of the information contained in the system study report. It may include numerous graphs, charts, and other visual aids. This gives the managers an opportunity to ask questions about the study and to evaluate the competence of the study team. At the conclusion of this presentation, the steering committee makes a decision regarding the team's recommendations.

Outcomes of Systems Analysis

The systems analysis phase has three possible outcomes. The outcome is selected by the steering committee with input from top management. It is based on the recommendations of the study team.

Do Nothing.   The information systems steering committee may decide that no further action is warranted. Perhaps the problem is not as serious as originally thought, the need

ILLUSTRATION 6–10

Possible Outcomes of Systems Analysis

Do nothing. Problem is not serious or resources are unavailable.
Modify existing system. A less costly solution that may provide satisfactory results.
Design a new system. Existing systems cannot solve the problem.

for new information no longer exists, or the new technology is not cost-efficient. Often the committee will simply delay further action until some time in the future when more resources are available. Any change to information systems requires a commitment of MIS and user department personnel. The committee must allocate existing analysts and programmers to the needs that are currently most critical.

Modify an Existing System.   The committee may decide that a satisfactory solution can be attained by modifying an existing application system. This outcome may be chosen because it requires fewer resources and can be accomplished more quickly than developing a new system. It often represents a compromise; though not ideal, this solution is satisfactory and can be implemented at lower cost.

Design a New System.   Sometimes the committee concludes that the problem or need is serious enough to require a completely new system. This occurs when the committee believes that an existing system is outdated and that a modification would be unsatisfactory or not worth the cost. A new system is desired to solve the problem. They then authorize the formation of a system design team that creates a paper description of a new system. This marks the beginning of the system design phase of the system development life cycle. Illustration 6–10 summarizes the outcomes of the systems analysis phase.

Summary

Systems analysis is the first phase in the system development life cycle. An application of the systems approach, it is the process of evaluating existing systems and identifying recommendations for improvement.

Systems analysis begins with a system study proposal submitted by a manager to the information system steering committee. The steering committee appoints a system study team to investigate the need identified in the proposal. The study team conducts a preliminary survey of existing systems and identifies problems in them. Then in the feasibility study, the team evaluates alternative solutions to the problems.

The study team prepares a system study report for management that summarizes the results of its analysis. The report may be accompanied by an oral presentation of recommendations. Based on the study team's report, the steering committee may decide to appoint a design team and begin the system design phase.

Key Terms

economic feasibility   A feasibility criterion that concerns whether or not the benefits from a system alternative are worth the costs.

feasibility study   A systems analysis activity during which a study team examines alternatives that are potential improvements to an existing system.

operating feasibility   A feasibility criterion that concerns whether or not a proposed system alternative can meet its objectives.

operational audit   A study performed by internal auditors to analyze the operations of a department and to identify improvements.

preliminary survey   A systems analysis activity during which a study team evaluates existing systems.

systems analyst   An employee who participates in system development project teams. This employee is skilled in computer processing methods, recognizes business needs for information, and understands the systems approach to problem solving.

system study proposal   A written request from a manager asking that a study team be formed to analyze a system problem.

system study report   A report submitted to top management and the information systems steering committee summarizing the results of systems analysis.

system study team   One or more systems analysts and computer user personnel who are responsible for conducting systems analysis.

technical feasibility   A feasibility criterion that concerns whether or not a system alternative can be implemented given the technical capabilities of the organization.

time feasibility   A feasibility criterion that concerns whether or not a system alternative can be implemented within a reasonable time.

work measurement study   A study intended to determine the magnitude or quantities of tasks performed in an existing system.

Questions

6–1. What are the steps in the systems approach to problem solving discussed in Chapter 3? How are they applied during systems analysis?

6–2. How does the preliminary survey differ from the feasibility study?

6–3. What are the objectives of a preliminary survey?

6–4. Who initiates a system study proposal? For which reasons?

6–5. A preliminary survey is a process of gathering data about certain features of an existing system. What are these features?

6–6. Why is it sometimes difficult to get adequate user input on a system study team?

6–7. Which procedures does the system study team use in conducting a preliminary survey?

6–8. What are the advantages of conducting a preliminary survey?

6–9. What is the first step in performing a feasibility study?

6–10. In a feasibility study, a system study team evaluates possible solutions to an information system problem. What forms can these solutions take? Which of these forms requires a continuation of the system development process?

6–11. Can you distinguish between the four feasibility criteria? Which do you think is the easiest to determine? The hardest?

6–12. Discuss the advantages and disadvantages of three ways to compare costs and benefits of a proposed system solution.

6–13. Describe the contents of a report to management prepared at the conclusion of systems analysis.

Exercises and Cases

6–14. *ECONOMIC BENEFITS AND DECISION LEVELS*

Using the following three levels of decision-making activity, identify some possible financial benefits from a new information system that provides information at each level. Classify each as either easy or difficult to determine.

a. Operational control.
b. Management control.
c. Strategic planning.

6–15. *SYSTEM STUDY TEAM*

A systems analysis study team frequently includes representatives from user departments in the organization. These employees provide knowledge to the team about how the existing system operates. Identify by job positions which employees might be assigned to a system study team that conducts a preliminary survey on

a. A payroll system.
b. An accounts receivable system.
c. An inventory system.
d. A cost accounting system.

6–16. *PRELIMINARY SURVEY*

What are the possible shortcomings of studying an existing system before designing a new one to replace it?

6–17. *ACTIVITIES IN SYSTEMS ANALYSIS*

Each of the following activities may be performed during the development of a new system. Which are done as a part of the systems analysis phase?

a. Interviews are conducted with operating people and managers.
b. The complete documentation of the system is obtained and reviewed.
c. Measures of processing volume are obtained for each operation.
d. Equipment sold by various computer manufacturers is evaluated for its capability, cost, and availability.
e. Work measurement studies are conducted to determine the time required to complete various tasks or jobs.

(CMA Adapted)

6–18.   DETERMINING FEASIBILITY

The following five conclusions were drawn by a system study team as part of a feasibility study. For each conclusion, determine which of the four kinds of feasibility is being evaluated.

a. A proposed system is attainable, given the existing technology.
b. The chief information officer is able to coordinate and control the activities of the MIS department.
c. An adequate computer site exists for the proposed computer system.
d. The proposed system could produce economic benefits that exceed costs.
e. The system could be effectively used within the operating environment of the organization.

(CMA Adapted)

6–19.   ECONOMIC FEASIBILITY

Newton Enterprises has no experience with computer-based systems. When considering the acquisition of a new computer, they gathered the following information as part of a feasibility study:

Total initial cost for acquiring a computer system	$150,000
Annual operating costs when computerized	60,000
Annual operating costs for the existing system	90,000
Discount factor	30%
Estimated useful life of a computer-based system	3 years

Required:

Evaluate the economic feasibility of the proposed computer-based system.

6–20.   ENTITY-RELATIONSHIP DIAGRAM

Exhibit 6–1 contains an entity-relationship diagram.

Required:

a. Describe in your own words what is represented by this diagram.
b. Describe the relationships between the entities in each pair in Exhibit 6–1.

6–21.   DATA FLOW DIAGRAM

Exhibit 6–2 contains a data flow diagram.

EXHIBIT 6–1

Exercise 6–20

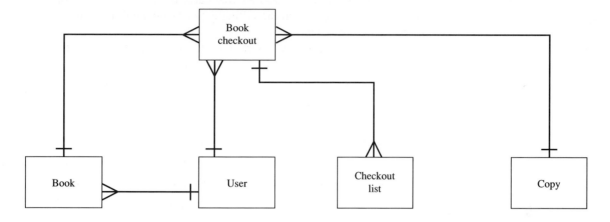

Required:

a. In this diagram identify each
  1. process
  2. data store
  3. data flow
  4. external destination
b. Describe in your own words the process depicted in Exhibit 6–2.

6–22.   SYSTEM FLOWCHART

After a shipment is prepared, the shipping department prepares a three-part shipping notice form. The first copy is included with the goods sent to the customer as a packing

EXHIBIT 6–2

Exercise 6–21

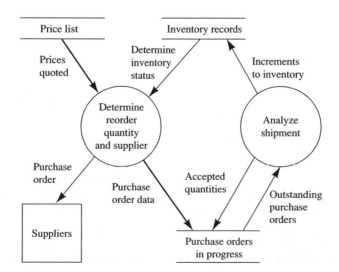

slip. The second copy is forwarded to the billing department. The third copy is sent to the accountant. When the billing department receives the second copy of the shipping order, it uses that information to prepare a two-part sales invoice. The second copy of the shipping order is then filed in the billing department. The first copy of the sales invoice is sent to the customer. The second copy of the sales invoice is forwarded to the accountant. Periodically, the accountant matches the copy of the shipping order with the copy of the sales invoice and files them alphabetically by customer. Before doing so, however, the accountant uses the copy of the sales invoice to post the sales entry in the subsidiary accounts receivable ledger.

Required:

Prepare a system flowchart summarizing these procedures.

(CIA Adapted)

6–23.   DATA FLOW DIAGRAM

Prepare a data flow diagram for the procedures described in Exercise 6–22.

6–24.   SYSTEM FLOWCHART

The Alaska branch of Far Distributing Company has substantial annual sales, which are billed and collected locally. Its procedures for handling cash receipts are as follows:

Cash collections on over-the-counter sales and COD sales are received from customers or the delivery service by the cashier. On receipt of cash, the cashier stamps the sales ticket "paid" and files a copy for future reference. The only record of COD sales is a copy of the sales ticket given to the cashier to hold until the cash is received from the delivery service.

Mail is opened by the secretary to the credit manager, and remittances are given to the credit manager for his review. The credit manager then places the remittances in a tray on the cashier's desk. At the daily deposit cutoff time, the cashier delivers the checks and cash on hand to the assistant credit manager. She prepares remittance lists, makes up the bank deposit, and takes the deposit to the bank. The assistant credit manager also posts remittances to the accounts receivable ledger cards and verifies the cash discount allowable.

Required:

Prepare a system flowchart summarizing these procedures.

(AICPA Adapted)

6–25.   DATA FLOW DIAGRAM

Prepare a data flow diagram summarizing the procedures described in Exercise 6–24.

6–26.   STEERING COMMITTEE

Information systems steering committees composed of high-level personnel have come into increasing use in many organizations for making key decisions regarding data processing.

Required:

a. List four responsibilities of a steering committee for information systems.

b. Give two reasons why it is desirable for a steering committee to perform these responsibilities rather than the chief information officer.

(CIA Adapted)

6–27.   *INTERVIEWING EXERCISE*

In this exercise, you will practice your interviewing skills. You are to play the role of Brad (or Brenda) Buttons, a recent college graduate. You have been hired as a staff accountant by a prominent local CPA firm, Tick, Mark & Total.

TM&T has a physician client, Dr. Pat Clark, who has been in solo practice for about two years. She currently uses a manual accounting system but is considering computerization. You have been assigned to conduct a preliminary survey of Dr. Clark's accounting system. The results of your survey are important to your firm because they could result in further consulting revenues. If she decides to computerize, you will be advising her on how to proceed.

You have made an appointment to interview Dr. Clark's office manager, Rhonda Redman, in order to discuss the physician's desires and needs. You will keep your appointment during a future class period, so you should come prepared to take notes on the interview. Prior to the interview, you should review (1) the interviewing tips in Illustration 4–1 and (2) the discussion of the scope of a preliminary survey in this chapter.

6–28.   *SYSTEMS SURVEY AND ANALYSIS*

Business organizations are required to modify or replace a portion or all of their accounting information systems to keep pace with growth and to take advantage of improved information technology. Modifying or replacing an information system, especially if computer equipment is involved, requires a substantial commitment of time and resources. When an organization undertakes a change in its information system, a series of steps or phases is taken. The steps or phases included in a systems study are

> Survey of the existing system.
>
> Analysis of information collected in the survey and development of recommendations for corrective action.
>
> Design of a new or modified system.
>
> Equipment study and acquisition.
>
> Implementation of a new or modified system.

These steps or phases tend to overlap rather than to be separate and distinct. In addition, the effort required in each step or phase varies from one system change to another, depending on such factors as extent of the changes or the need for different equipment.

Required:

a. Explain the purpose and reasons for surveying an organization's existing system.
b. Identify and explain the activities and techniques commonly used during the systems survey and analysis steps for an accounting information system.
c. The systems survey and analysis steps are often carried out by a project team composed of a systems analyst, a management accountant, and other persons in the company who would be knowledgeable and helpful in the system study. What

would be the role of the management accountant in these steps for an accounting information system study?

(CMA Adapted)

6–29.   MANUFACTURING CONTROL SYSTEM—PART I

Lockheed Austin Division (LAD) was formed in August 1981 by Lockheed Missiles & Space Company, Inc., of Sunnyvale, California.[1] Headquartered in Austin, Texas, LAD began operations in June 1982 with 30 employees, mostly scientists and engineers who worked on projects for the U.S. military. By 1984 the division had grown to over 2,000 people engaged in the development and manufacture of Navy and Air Force communications and surveillance systems.

LAD had become a melting pot of people, projects, and systems that had been added gradually with little planning or coordination. As a result, there was no integrated information system that allowed everyone access to the same information. If a worker in one department had a question about a project or operation, he had to go to several other departments for answers. Most of the systems being used in Austin were based in Sunnyvale, so employees at LAD had little input into how they worked. Furthermore, LAD couldn't operate unless the Sunnyvale computers were operating. In this environment, LAD could not predict when it was going to deliver its products. It had problems meeting schedules and budgets, and it was about to lose its competitive position in the marketplace.

At this point, LAD management formed a study team to examine the situation. They proceeded with a project that led to a computer-integrated operations support system (OSS) that would allow communication between all areas at LAD. Using structured analysis techniques, the team proceeded to decompose business processes by function. Starting at a high level, they exploded major processes to lower levels of detail. They gathered information on transaction volumes for data entry and outputs for all functions affecting the manufacturing processes. This provided a mechanism to discover, document, and review LAD's information needs and served as a foundation for subsequent activity.

LAD management felt that using technology to manage their processes was critical to the company's competitiveness. So they made the commitment—from the top down—to move ahead with the project as quickly as possible.

Required:

a. How did the history of Lockheed Austin Division contribute to its lack of competitiveness?

b. How did management react to the problems facing LAD?

6–30.   CORPORATE CONSOLIDATION SYSTEM—PART I

Several years ago at **R. J. Reynolds Industries, Inc.** (RJR), the corporate accounting group, which is responsible for developing consolidated and line-of-business financial statements, was facing difficulties in developing the financial information reported to

---

[1]This case, as well as its continuation in Chapters 7, 8, and 19, is adapted from C. Kenneth Howery, Earl D. Bennett, and Sarah Reed, "How Lockheed Implemented CIM," *Management Accounting,* December 1991, p. 22. Copyright by Institute of Management Accountants (1991), Montvale, N.J. 07645. Used by permission.

the corporation's stockholders and executive management.[2] Management concluded that the accounting system being used to consolidate the financial information from the operating companies for reports to management and stockholders was rapidly becoming inadequate because of RJR's internal growth and expansion and the increasing requirements of public reporting.

The Environment

R. J. Reynolds Industries, Inc., is a diversified, worldwide corporation with 1977 consolidated net sales and revenues of $6.4 billion. It serves as the parent company for seven subsidiaries each of which is a major line of business. Because RJR deals in a multicountry and multi-industry environment, any actions taken by financial management that might affect the corporation as a whole must reflect consideration of not only the current lines of business but also the possibility of future growth and acquisition.

The old consolidation system was a converted autocoder general ledger program built around a series of card sorts. The system could no longer handle RJR's growth or generate financial reports in the time frame and manner required in the 1970s. Also, the addition of new reporting entities resulting from acquisitions was an extremely time-consuming process that entailed preparing a series of new header cards for the various card sorts.

Another problem grew out of the increase in public reporting requirements from expanded Securities and Exchange Commission (SEC) regulations and accounting pronouncements issued by the Financial Accounting Standards Board (FASB). The growth in reporting requirements is illustrated by comparing R. J. Reynolds's 1968 and 1977 annual reports. In 1968 the annual report had 28 pages, including 6 pages of financial statements and notes. The notes to the financial statements were confined to one-half page. In 1977 the report was expanded to 64 pages with financial statements covering 17 pages and 14 pages of notes. Overall, the accounting information requirements both within and outside of RJR had grown tremendously over the past years. The corporate accounting staff was being asked to respond to questions faster and to make the financial information more useful to management and stockholders.

In recognition of the growth of the corporation and the changing public reporting environment, the corporate accounting group undertook a study to develop a response to the growing financial information requirements. The study resulted in the installation of a general ledger system in corporate headquarters to handle consolidation accounting and reporting. The general ledger system, when installed in corporate accounting, was named the corporate consolidation system (CCS).

The New System

CCS was designed to allow the corporate accounting department to keep its analysis records on the computer, to handle routine transactions automatically and systematically, to produce and change reports without systems assistance, and to maintain a

---

[2]This case, as well as its continuation in Chapters 7 and 8, is adapted from James H. Wood, "How RJR Put Its New MIS On-Line," *Management Accounting,* April 1979, p. 17. Copyright by National Association of Accountants (1979), Montvale, N.J. 07645.

database that can be accessed by other systems and departments. It processes the financial statements and selected account analyses of each of the reporting entities and consolidates them into the total corporate statements, with statements of earnings and balance sheets for each individual reporting company in a line of business. In addition, certain selected schedules for SEC Form 10-K are prepared using the statistical capabilities of CCS.

The system contains a variable report writer which gives a user in the accounting department the ability to request, design, and implement required reports, including budgeting and exception reports. CCS has an allocation feature for financial and statistical accounts which can support recurring journal entries, budgeting, consolidations, and distributions. Capability is provided for data entry and inquiry from terminals. Automatic consolidations and support for unlike charts of accounts are provided by CCS. Multiple regional user groups for the general ledger cover both domestic and international markets.

Justification

To justify CCS, the corporate accounting group had to estimate what its payout would be. The project team identified time savings as the principal justification for providing analytical capabilities at user terminals.

During closing in consolidation accounting, managers need to focus their attention on account fluctuations and at the same time to have the capacity to research backup data while a question is still current. Commonly an accounting staff member is asked a question, provides an answer, and immediately is asked a second question. Terminal access capability gave the accounting staff the power to handle this iterative questioning process. Its short response time allows accountants to verify input and output several times before presenting finished financial statements to management.

By using this terminal input and display feature, technical corrections and last-minute input of corrections are immediately processed and errors corrected. The accountant receives an immediate response to coding errors and usually can correct them on the spot.

Additionally, multiple users have access to the same updated financial database at the same time. As an example, someone within the financial organization may ask a question concerning the balances with the CCS database. An accountant at a terminal can give the answer, with assurance that all other users have access to the same financial data. Corporate accounting no longer had to type, copy, and distribute a financial statement every time a question was asked.

Required:

a. What were the changes that initiated this system study?

b. What were the objectives of the corporate consolidation system?

6–31.   *YOUR COMPANY PROJECT—PART II*

For the company selected for your project in Exercise 5–26, perform the following:

a. Identify one person who has accounting responsibilities in the company you have selected.

  1. Conduct an interview with this person.
  2. Document the results of your interview.
b. Conduct a preliminary survey for your company. Document the results of your survey.
c. Conduct a feasibility study for your company. Document the results of your study.
d. Prepare a system study report for your company.

7   SYSTEM DESIGN

Learning Objectives

1. To learn the activities that take place during the second phase of the system development life cycle.
2. To discover how to create a preliminary system design.
3. To understand how to develop the detailed specifications for an accounting information system.
4. To learn how auditors participate in the system design process.

Introduction

The previous chapter described the activities of the systems analysis phase of the system development life cycle (SDLC). At the conclusion of systems analysis, a system study team makes a recommendation to the information systems steering committee.

If the decision is to continue the development project, the steering committee appoints a project team to begin the system design phase. This design team consists of the systems analysis study team supplemented by accountants and systems analysts.

The system design team begins by identifying the major features of the new system. Then, after receiving the steering committee's approval, they specify in detail the system's characteristics. These activities are called *preliminary system design* and *detailed specification*. Following these activities, the design team begins the implementation phase. Illustration 7–1 shows the relationship of the system design phase to the other phases in the SDLC.

Importance of System Design

System design is the process of developing specifications for a proposed new system from the recommendations made during systems analysis. During the design phase, the project team produces working papers containing these specifications. The documentation contained in the working papers provides management with descriptions of the inputs, outputs, and processes of the proposed system.

ILLUSTRATION 7–1

The System Design Phase

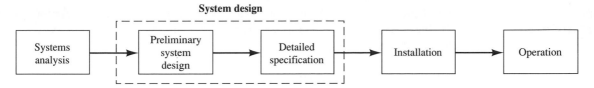

Performing a thorough system design provides two significant benefits: First, it gives management and the information systems steering committee opportunities to approve or disapprove the system before proceeding with implementation. During design the team can make changes or stop development of the system. Second, the design documentation provides the project team with an overview of how the system works. Careful attention to design allows the project team to identify inefficiencies in processing, inconsistencies with other systems, weaknesses in internal control, or other problems. Changes are much easier to make while the system is still in the design phase. Substantial effort devoted to design usually pays off later with easier implementation and a more successful system.

Preliminary System Design

System design is a process of starting with a set of objectives, identifying general methods of achieving those objectives, and gradually making those methods more specific and more concrete. Many organizations choose to break this process into two activities separated by a management decision point. The first of these activities is *preliminary system design.*

A study team identifies system objectives in the systems analysis phase. During preliminary system design, a design team develops a logical description of the proposed system. This gives management the opportunity to determine whether the proposed system meets its objectives prior to detailed specification. The team creates a documentation package that identifies the scope, the system requirements, and the resource requirements of the proposed system.

Statement of Scope

During preliminary design, the project team first defines the scope of the new system. This process is sometimes simply a restatement of the scope established during systems analysis. In that phase, however, the study team defines system scope for purposes of estimating feasibility. During preliminary system design, the project team defines scope for the purpose of creating a new system. The design team defines boundaries by identifying the interfaces between the proposed new system and other systems in its environment. They may have to redefine the boundaries of the system to avoid changes to other existing systems.

The new system's boundaries must be comprehensive enough to achieve the system's objectives. Yet if boundaries are set too broadly, the system development project becomes so large that it is difficult to implement successfully. One way to determine the limits of the current design project is to identify procedures that do not change when the new system is implemented. Any procedures that are not subject to change are beyond the boundaries of the new system.

During preliminary design, the design team identifies features necessary for the system to achieve its objectives. These are the requirements that the proposed system must provide and include outputs, data, processes, inputs, and policies.

Outputs.   The design team first determines the outputs that the system should produce. They address two issues: (1) the information content of the outputs and (2) the form of the outputs. When the proposed system must provide new or different information, the design team must determine both the form and the information content of the outputs. When the information content does not change, the team determines only the form of the outputs.

Information Content.   A new system is proposed for one of three reasons: (1) to satisfy a new information requirement, (2) to solve a problem with an existing system, or (3) to implement a new technology. When a new system is developed to satisfy a new reporting requirement, the information it provides is unavailable from existing systems. The design team ensures that the new system's outputs provide information to satisfy the requirement. For example, in designing a cost accounting system, the team may decide that an output should summarize the costs of production for a specific batch of widgets produced under government contract.

If a proposed system is to solve a problem with an existing system, the information content of system outputs may change to correct the problem. For example, a billing system may provide an inadequate audit trail. In creating a new billing system, the design team includes new information on its outputs that allows an auditor to trace individual transactions into the accounts. If the reason for the system is to implement a new technology, the information content of its outputs need not change. In this case, the outputs may take a new form.

Form.   When selecting the form of the outputs, the design team decides how the information should be presented. This may be in the form of reports printed routinely, or it may be a computer terminal display that a clerk uses for data entry. Sometimes the team creates a system that produces reports or displays on an *ad hoc,* or as-needed, basis. The system does not provide outputs routinely but rather allows a manager or user to obtain them on request. For a routine output, the study team must decide how frequently to produce it. They give each report or display a unique name and identifying number and decide who in the organization receives it. When the purpose of system development is to implement a new technology, the form of system output sometimes changes even though its information content does not.

Data.   The system's data records provide the information contained in reports or displays. After determining the information content of system outputs, the design team identifies the data necessary to produce them.

The design team updates the data models produced during systems analysis. They develop the models in more detail and may decide that additional data entities are required beyond those identified earlier. They also identify the desired attributes for each data entity. A *data attribute* is a characteristic that describes a data entity in some way of interest to the user of the system. For example, one example of an entity is CUSTOMER. Characteristics of CUSTOMER that are of interest include name, address, credit limit, and account balance. The design team specifies these as attributes of the CUSTOMER entity during preliminary design.

At this point in the SDLC, the design team makes preliminary decisions about which data files are required, which storage medium to use, and how to organize the data.

Processes.   The working papers produced during preliminary system design identify the processes required by the system. These processes may be manual procedures or computer programs.

During systems analysis, a study team produces process models to show existing processes. During preliminary system design, the design team uses these as a basis for process models to show how the proposed system will work. When the organization uses a structured design methodology, they describe processes with data flow diagrams. This allows the design team to concentrate on the logical processes independent of the technology used in implementing them. In other organizations, the design team develops system flowcharts to show the sequence of the processes and how they produce the reports and displays from *source documents* and data records.

The design team also determines those measures necessary to provide good internal control in the proposed system.

Inputs.   Inputs to the system provide the sources of the data contained in system files. Commonly used inputs include forms such as sales orders, requisitions, and payroll timecards. System users record on these forms information describing accounting transactions. The system converts this information into computer-readable form and summarizes it in data files.

Systems analysts call these forms *source documents* because they provide the source for all data items used by the system. Sometimes transactions are entered directly into a system without using a document. This occurs, for example, when a computer terminal is also a cash register in a point-of-sale system.

During preliminary system design, the project team identifies each source document with a name and form number, determines where it originates, estimates its volume, and decides how its information is converted into computer-readable form. They may also identify methods of data entry that do not use source documents.

Policies.   Sometimes a new system requires that management adopt new policies for it to be successful. For example, users of a manual system have flexibility in deciding when to perform many of their job tasks. However, if the manual system is replaced by a computerized one, user activities are constrained by the computer operating schedule. Management may adopt policies that dictate when users perform their duties so the computerized system can operate efficiently.

If new policies are required by a proposed system, management wants to know about them before authorizing the system's development. Policies may have a detrimental effect on employee morale and turnover. Management considers these effects when evaluating the costs and benefits of a system.

At this stage, the design team develops descriptions of outputs, data, inputs, processing steps, and policies without attention to specific detail. Their purpose is to identify only the essential features of the system. The preliminary system design allows the design team to assess more accurately the resources required to implement the proposed system and the benefits it could provide. Illustration 7–2 summarizes the system requirements determined during preliminary system design.

Resource Requirements

During preliminary system design, the design team identifies the financial resources required to successfully implement and operate the system. They determine the additional computer software and equipment that are necessary. They estimate the costs to complete development of the system and produce a schedule for completion. They estimate the ongoing costs to operate the system after implementation is complete. Because system requirements have been specified, these estimates are more accurate than those prepared during the feasibility study. The design team then performs another evaluation of the proposed system's costs and benefits and summarizes their conclusions in a report to management.

Software Resources.   Software is the set of programs that control the operations performed by the computer equipment. Once the design team identifies the necessary features for the system, they choose one of four alternative sources for the software.

ILLUSTRATION 7–2

System Requirements Identified During Preliminary System Design

---

Outputs. Reports and terminal displays.
   Name and number
   Information content
   Form
   Frequency
   Receiving person

Data items. Manual and computer records.
   Name and number
   Storage medium
   Content
   Data organization method

Inputs. Source documents and direct data entry.
   Document name and number
   Originating person
   Volume estimate
   Conversion method

Processes. Procedures and computer programs.
   Data source
   Outputs produced
   Internal controls

Policies established by top management.

In-House Development.   With this alternative, the organization's own employees write the computer programs required by the system. A large system contains many programs, and numerous users or programmers are added to the design team to complete in-house development.

Sometimes the chief information officer (CIO) also uses *contract programmers*. Contract programmers are employees of another firm who work for the organization only for the duration of the project. Using them is sometimes an efficient way to supplement the MIS programming staff.

In-house development has the advantage that the project team controls development of the programs. Thus, the programs specifically meet the organization's needs, and the system is more acceptable to the users who work with it. However, for accounting applications other sources are ordinarily less expensive.

Software Development Companies.   Some companies are in the business of producing and selling software packages. These packages are computer programs that provide commonly needed applications, such as payroll, inventory, or general ledger applications. Software development companies employ systems analysts and programmers to develop packages, and a sales staff to market them. They may sell software directly to an MIS department or through computer stores or software brokers.

Packages are designed to satisfy the needs of many organizations, so any package probably is less acceptable to users than a system developed in-house. Because a package may be sold to hundreds or thousands of buyers, each shares in its development costs. Thus, the cost of obtaining a package is much less than the costs of in-house development.

Computer Manufacturers.   Most manufacturers of computer equipment also produce and sell software. This software is intended for use on the manufacturer's product line and includes both application programs and system software. System software provides basic functions that control the computer and its peripheral devices. It includes operating systems that schedule the operations of the computer, file management programs that control data storage, and utility programs that perform frequently needed functions, such as sorting or printing files. In some cases, systems software is available only from a manufacturer, while the manufacturer's applications software competes with that of software development companies. Some systems software is necessary for the equipment to function; its costs are part of the initial acquisition costs of the system.

Users' Groups.   A users' group is a club formed by individuals and organizations that own a particular brand of equipment or software. Members of the group exchange software at low cost, exchange advice, and frequently publish newsletters or operate computerized bulletin boards. A computerized bulletin board consists of an operating computer connected to a telephone line. Anyone can call the telephone number of the bulletin board on a computer modem and leave or receive messages. Members frequently exchange programs in this way.

In the early days of management information systems, users' groups were valuable as a source of business application programs. Today, users' groups primarily benefit users of small computers. If you own a personal computer, joining a users' group provides you with an inexpensive source of programs and advice.

Internal and External Sources.   The possible sources for the programs in a new system are in-house development, software development companies, computer manufacturers, and users' groups. During preliminary system design, the design team chooses between in-house development and buying a software package from a source external to the organization. This is an example of the make-or-buy decision that you study in managerial and cost accounting courses.

Illustration 7–3 summarizes five considerations in choosing between in-house development or an external software package. Normally, gaining user acceptance is easier and fewer modifications are required when programs are written internally. However, installation time and costs are less when a package is purchased. Furthermore, with an external package, the design team can review the quality of its instruction manuals prior to purchase. If this documentation is inadequate, the team does not select the package.

Equipment Resources.   After determining system requirements, the design team evaluates the need for computer equipment. In some cases, a new computerized system can be implemented without the acquiring of additional hardware. This is true when excess capacity exists on current equipment and no new technology is needed by the new system. Where hardware is needed, the design team identifies a source for it during preliminary system design. The five alternative ways in which an organization can acquire computer equipment follow.

Purchase.   Organizations frequently choose to purchase the additional equipment required by a new system. An organization with existing equipment may have a preferred manufacturer and may be knowledgeable about equipment that is available.

ILLUSTRATION 7–3

Considerations in the Make-or-Buy Decisions for Software

User Acceptance
In-house. Programs customized to users' preferences.
External package. Users adapt to requirements of externally written programs.

Required Modifications
In-house. No modifications required.
External package. Modifications may be necessary to make software acceptable.

Installation Time
In-house. Measured in months or years.
External package. Measured in weeks or months.

Quality of Instruction Manuals
In-house. Time pressures may discourage preparation of good documentation.
External package. Documentation available for review prior to purchase.

Installation Cost
In-house. Costly; all costs absorbed by one system.
External package. Less costly; developmental costs absorbed by many systems.

Because of this knowledge and experience, the firm is willing to make the investment required by a purchase. Purchasing may provide tax benefits to profit-making businesses. However, this alternative requires a large initial cash outlay. Furthermore, in later years the equipment may become obsolete, and the organization may have difficulty selling it.

Lease or Rental.   Many organizations choose to rent or lease computer equipment. A lease is a rental of the equipment for a length of time fixed by a lease contract. The acquiring organization contracts with a bank or leasing company that provides the equipment in return for a monthly rental fee. Computer equipment leases commonly extend from two to five years. By leasing or renting, the acquiring organization avoids the initial large cash outlay of a purchase. However, the total of the lease or rental payments over several years exceeds the purchase cost of the same equipment. Leasing or renting allows the organization to avoid many risks of technological obsolescence that a purchaser incurs.

Service Bureau.   A ***service bureau*** is a business that provides computer services to other organizations for a fee. The service bureau owns its computer equipment and provides programs for many accounting transaction processing applications. An organization records accounting events on its own source documents and then delivers them to the service bureau. The service bureau converts the transactions into computer-readable form, processes them, and returns them along with accounting reports to the organization. A service bureau is a good alternative for an organization that has no experience with computerized data processing. It can obtain many of the advantages of computerization without establishing an MIS department. However, the organization is restricted to only those applications that the service bureau provides. And if the number of transactions is large, using a service bureau is an expensive alternative.

Remote Batch.   Remote batch processing results from a modification of the procedures used by a service bureau. With remote batch, the organization installs at its own location equipment that converts accounting transactions into computer-readable form. Its employees accumulate transactions into batches, convert them into computer files, and transmit these files over telephone lines to a computer at another location. The company that owns the computer then processes them and returns system outputs over telephone lines to a printer. This process is faster than using a service bureau, but the organization must employ data entry personnel and operate computer equipment. Many organizations first use a service bureau and then progress to remote batch processing. Later they establish an MIS department and lease, rent, or purchase their own equipment.

Timesharing.   Timesharing services are provided by companies that own large computers accessible by telephone lines. To use a timesharing service, an organization acquires terminals at its location and connects them to telephone lines with modems. This enables the organization to use the computers at a remote location as if they were located in the same building. A user at a terminal dials the telephone number of the computer to connect with it. The user can write and debug computer programs, enter data from source documents, or execute programs on the remote computer. Use of a timesharing service provides access to a computer just as if the organization owned it. The organization can develop its own applications, provide its own data entry, and control its own processing. Furthermore, the organization avoids the risk of obsolescence of the computer. However, extensive use of a timesharing service is expensive. For processing many transactions, owning or leasing a computer is usually less costly.

Economic Resources.   After identifying the equipment and computer software needed for the proposed new system, the design team estimates the costs to acquire them. Because the system's requirements have been identified, this cost estimate is more accurate than that developed during the feasibility study. The design team more accurately projects the benefits from it as well.

Costs.   Costs associated with a computer system include both the initial cost of development and the annual recurring costs of operation. After preliminary system design, the initial costs include the computer system (equipment and software), computer housing

ILLUSTRATION 7–4

Costs and Benefits for a Proposed Computer Purchase

Return on Investment Analysis

Initial cost:

Probable purchase price of equipment	$180,000
Installation, including air conditioning and cabling, estimated at 6% of price	12,000
Software, estimated at 40% of price	72,000
Training, estimated at 20% of price	36,000
Total initial cost	$300,000

Annual operating costs:

Salaries of MIS personnel	$104,000
Power, supplies, repairs, estimated at 20% of personnel cost	21,000
Facilities maintenance, estimated at 7½% of purchase price	14,000
Total annual operating cost	$139,000
Less salaries of clerical workers displaced by computer	267,000
Annual savings	$128,000
ROI ($128,000/$300,000)	43%

Present Value Analysis

(Assume five-year life and cost of capital = 20%)

Year	Annual Savings	Discount Factor	Present Value of Savings
1	$128,000	.833	$ 106,624
2	128,000	.694	88,832
3	128,000	.579	74,112
4	128,000	.482	61,696
5	128,000	.402	51,456
Present value of benefits			$ 382,720
Present value of costs			(300,000)
Net present value			$ 82,720

(air conditioning and special wiring), and the remaining costs of development (detailed system specification, implementation, and the post-implementation review). Annual recurring costs include salaries of MIS personnel, hardware maintenance, software maintenance, computer supplies, and utilities.

Benefits.   Benefits vary depending on the nature of the system. Salary reductions for clerical personnel, decreases in inventory carrying costs, and decreases in interest expense are easily quantifiable. Benefits that are more difficult to estimate may include better customer service and more informative management reports.

Illustration 7–4 shows an evaluation of the costs and benefits for a proposed computer system to replace a manual one. Using both return on investment and net present value measures, the change is a desirable one.

The design team may consider the alternative of leasing the equipment rather than purchasing it. Illustration 7–5 shows an economic analysis of this alternative. In this example, leasing is more desirable than either purchasing a computer or retaining the existing system.

ILLUSTRATION 7–5

Costs and Benefits for a Proposed Computer Lease

Return on Investment Analysis

Initial cost:

Installation	$ 12,000
Software	72,000
Training	36,000
Total initial cost	$120,000

Annual operating costs:

Salaries of MIS personnel	$104,000
Power, supplies, repairs	21,000
Computer rental	43,200
Total annual operating costs	$168,200
Less salaries of clerical workers displaced by computer	267,000
Annual savings	$ 98,800
ROI ($98,800/$120,000)	82%

Present Value Analysis

(Assume five-year life and cost of capital = 20%)

Year	Annual Savings	Discount Factor	Present Value of Savings
1	$98,800	.833	$ 82,300
2	98,800	.694	68,567
3	98,800	.579	57,205
4	98,800	.482	47,819
5	98,800	.402	39,718
Present value of benefits			$259,609
Present value of costs			120,000
Net present value			$175,609

Report to Management

At the conclusion of preliminary system design, the design team describes its recommendation in a report to management. The report consists of an executive summary and the documentation package created by the design team. They submit it to the information systems steering committee. They may also submit it or present it orally to top management.

The executive summary begins with a statement of the objectives and scope of the system. This is followed by a concise description of the system using system tools. The report then details economic analyses similar to those in Illustrations 7–4 and 7–5. Next comes a description of any anticipated policy changes or implementation difficulties. Finally, the design team states its recommendation either to halt further design efforts or to proceed with detailed specification of the system.

Detailed Specification

The system design phase of the SDLC consists of two activities: The first of these, preliminary system design, provides a high-level, conceptual description of how the system should work. At its conclusion, the steering committee evaluates the proposed system. During the second activity, *detailed specification,* the design team creates a detailed description of the system on paper. Auditors review these specifications and suggest needed changes to internal control measures and to the audit trail. Finally, the design team submits the specifications to the steering committee for review and approval.

Three major functions occur during detailed specification. First, the design team specifically defines the requirements for the system. These requirements identified during preliminary system design include outputs, data, inputs, and processing steps. After the requirements are defined, the team is ready to select a source for the software and a source for the hardware.

The sequence of these functions varies. For example, an organization may identify during preliminary design a specific software package that satisfies the specifications developed during requirements definition. In this case, they must acquire hardware compatible with the software, so the software selection decision precedes the hardware selection decision. In other circumstances, the organization may already have a major investment in a certain kind of hardware that they wish to continue. They will purchase or develop software compatible with that hardware, and the hardware decision precedes the software decision. In either case, requirements definition precedes the other two functions.

Requirements Definition

During preliminary system design, the design team identifies the logical requirements for the proposed system. These include system outputs, data, processes, and inputs. Prior to implementation, these must be specified in detail. The design team does this during *requirements definition,* the first major function of detailed specification.

Output Specification.   Outputs are the display screens and reports produced by the system. In preliminary system design, the design team identifies them by name and number and determines their information content. During detailed specification, the design team decides how each screen or report looks. They produce sample screens and reports, called *screen layouts* and *report layouts,* and include these examples in the documentation package for the proposed system. Users have the opportunity to examine them and suggest improvements prior to implementation. Illustrations 7–6 and 7–7 contain a sample screen layout and a report layout, respectively.

ILLUSTRATION 7–6

A Display Screen Layout

SECTION: CORRECTION TRANSACTIONS INPUT/UPDATE	NUMBER: 5.1
SUBJECT: Screen: Suspended Batch Master Batch Identification Inquiry	DATE ISSUED:

```
SCREEN 40-212         * * * GENERAL LEDGER SYSTEM * * *
                  * * SUSPENDED BATCH MASTER BATCH IDENTIFICATION INQUIRY * *

          --- KEY ---
SELECT   POSTING BATCH                             EFF        BATCH
         CO  DATE  NO  SOURCE    SEQ    OPER   STAT DATE       TOTAL

   -     035 07/98 0102  M002    H1400  A24    ENT  07/98         10,000.00
   -     035 07/98 0103  M002    H1400              07/98         10,000.00
   -     035 07/98 0104  M002    H1400              07/98         10,000.00
   -     035 07/98 0105  M002    H1400  A24    ENT  07/98         10,000.00
   -     035 07/98 0106  M002    H1400  A24    ENT  07/98         10,000.00
   -     035 07/98 0107  M002    H1400              07/98         10,000.00
   -     035 07/98 0108  M002    H1400              07/98         10,000.00
   -     035 07/98 0109  M002    H1400  A24    ENT  07/98         10,000.00
   -     035 07/98 0110  M002    H1400  A24    ENT  07/98         10,000.00
   -     035 08/98 0400  M001    H8000  A24    ENT  06/98         10,000.00
   -     035 08/98 0401  M001    H8000              06/98         10,000.00
   -     035 08/98 0402  M001    H8000              06/98         10,000.00

SELECT NEXT ACTION: PF1 = RETURN TO MENU
                    ENTER 'S' UNDER 'SELECT' TO GO TO BATCH ENTRY/SUMMARY
                    PRESS ENTER FOR NEXT PAGE
```

SUSPENDED BATCH MASTER BATCH IDENTIFICATION INQUIRY SCREEN

List of Suspended Batches

DART RESOURCES

ILLUSTRATION 7-7

A Report Layout

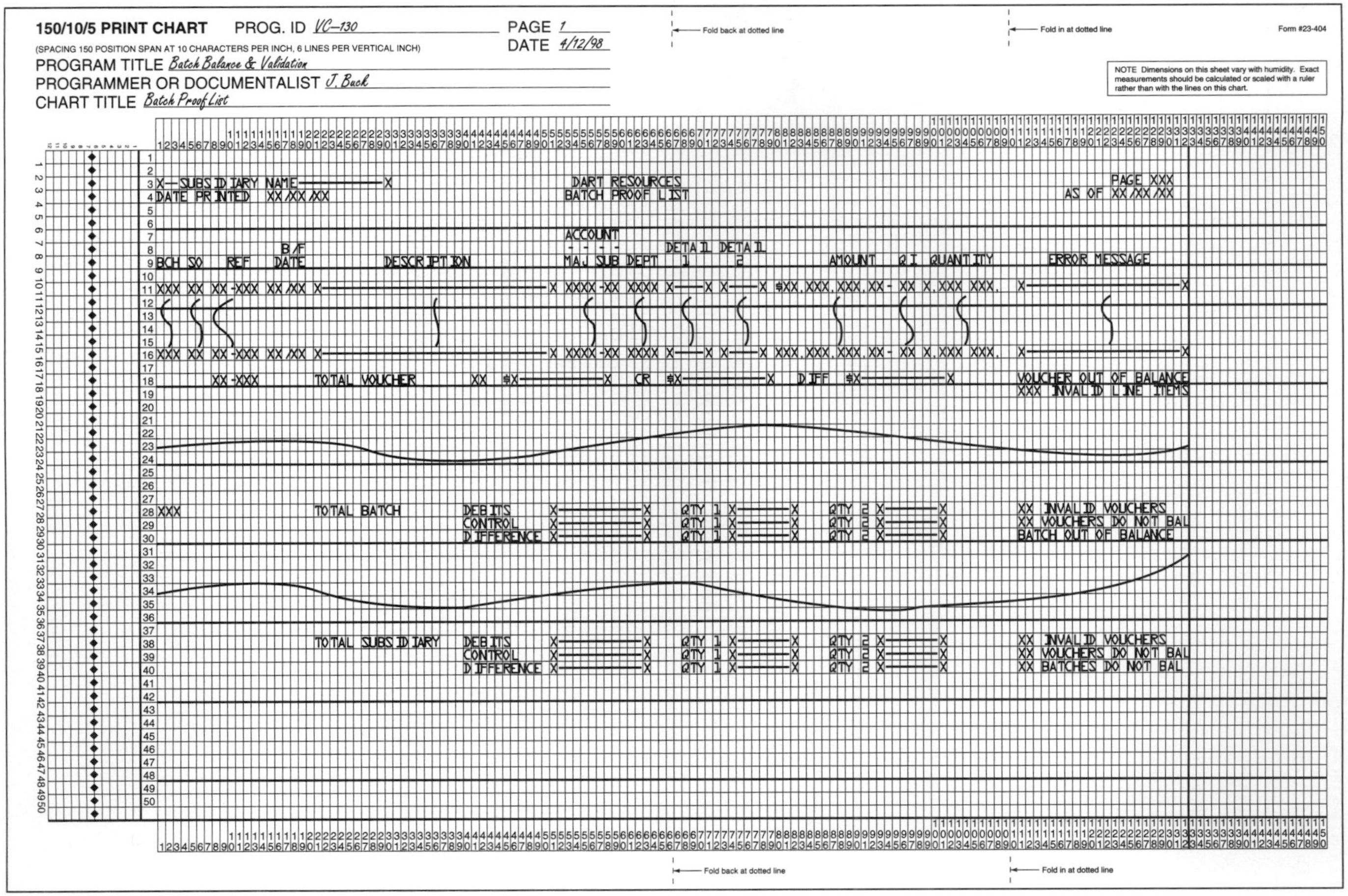

Data Specification.   Data records contain the data summarized and presented in reports and display screens. Manual files in cabinets or desks store data on records made of paper. Computer files store data in records written magnetically on computer disks or tape.

During detailed specification, the design team finalizes the data models produced during analysis and preliminary design. They describe each data entity in detail, listing its purpose, its attributes, and the way the data are organized. For computerized records, this includes producing a record layout showing the arrangement of all its data attributes.

For each data record, the design team estimates its number of occurrences and specifies retention and backup procedures. Retention procedures identify how long a copy of the data must be maintained for tax and audit purposes. Backup procedures describe how frequently backup, or spare, copies of the data are made. They are internal control measures that prevent loss of data when the original record is accidentally destroyed. Illustration 7–8 contains a sample record layout.

Input Specification.   Inputs include the source documents and magnetic media on which data are initially recorded by the system. During preliminary system design, the design team identifies each input and its source and estimates its volume. During system specification, they determine how each source document looks. They produce sample documents that show the arrangement of the data and include these in the design documentation. Users review these samples and suggest changes to them prior to implementation. For magnetic data input, such as in point-of-sale systems, the design team decides how the data are converted into a magnetic record. Illustration 7–9 contains a sample form produced during system specification.

Computer Program Specification.   Prior to detailed specification, the design team identifies each process and shows its relationship to other processes with system flowcharts or data flow diagrams. In requirements definition, a systems analyst from the team produces a programming work package containing a written description of each program. A programmer uses this package later when coding the program. The work package contains a description of the program's logic, its inputs, and its outputs.

Program Narratives.   In some organizations, the work package contains a program narrative describing the program's purpose, how frequently it executes, the computer data records that it accesses, and the inputs and outputs of the program. Inputs are magnetic computer records; outputs may be computer records, reports, or display screens. The narrative also describes the internal control measures to be coded into the program. Illustration 7–10 is an example of a program narrative. If the program is complex, the narrative may be accompanied by a program flowchart.

When the organization uses a structured design methodology, the design team does not use flowcharts. Instead, the programming work package contains structure charts and logic specifications. One effective way of specifying program logic uses *pseudocode*.

Structure Charts.   Structured methodologies utilize structure charts to describe a program. A structure chart identifies each of the modules making up the program and

ILLUSTRATION 7–8

A Computer File Record Layout

SECTION: FILE DOCUMENTATION	NUMBER:
SUBJECT: Record Layout, Journal Entry Transaction Record	DATE ISSUED:

SYSTEM NAME   On—Line General Ledger

FILE NAME   Journal Entry Transaction File

FILE DESCRIPTION   Contains all detail transactions to be
                       posted to the General Ledger

STORAGE MEDIA   Disk - 3380

FILE ORGANIZATION Indexed—sequential

FILE KEYS:

  PRIMARY   Group Number

  SECONDARY   None

MODULE NAMES
WHERE USED   ADD001, CHG001, DEL001, RPT001, RPT002

```
            1111111111222222222233333333334444444444555555555566666666667777777777 8
12345678901234567890123456789012345678901234567890123456789012345678901234567890
9999XXXXXXXXXXXXXXXXXXXXXXXXXXXS9999999.99XXMM/DD/YY9999XXXXXXXXXXXXXXXXXXXXXXXXXXXX
|ACCOUNT|←————ACCOUNT DESCRIPTION————→|←—AMOUNT—→|DR/|←—TRANSACTION—→|←-GRP-→|←————FILLER————→|
| NUMBER |                                        |CR |   DATE       | NUM |
                                                 |CODE|
```

DATA NOTATION: 9 — NUMERIC
                    P — PACKED NUMERIC
                    X — ALPHANUMERIC
                    C — CHARACTER
                    S — SIGN (+ OR —)
                    N — NULL SURPRESSION
                   MM — MONTH
                   DD — DAY
                   YY — YEAR

DART RESOURCES

ILLUSTRATION 7–9

A Sample Input Form

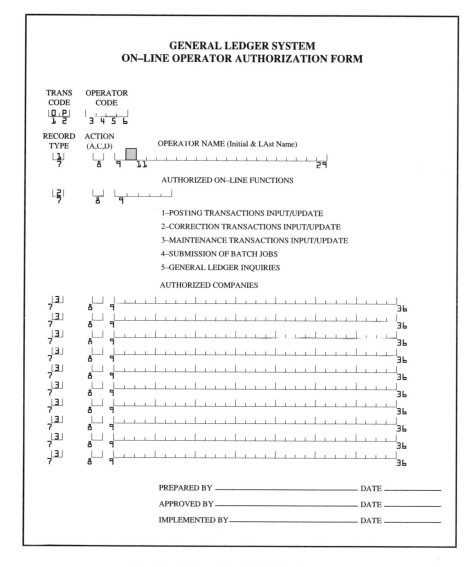

SECTION: COMPUTER SYSTEM INPUTS	NUMBER: 9.1
SUBJECT: Input Form: On–Line Operator Authorization Form	DATE ISSUED:

GENERAL LEDGER SYSTEM
ON–LINE OPERATOR AUTHORIZATION FORM

TRANS   OPERATOR
CODE   CODE

RECORD   ACTION
TYPE   (A,C,D)   OPERATOR NAME (Initial & LAst Name)

AUTHORIZED ON–LINE FUNCTIONS

1–POSTING TRANSACTIONS INPUT/UPDATE
2–CORRECTION TRANSACTIONS INPUT/UPDATE
3–MAINTENANCE TRANSACTIONS INPUT/UPDATE
4–SUBMISSION OF BATCH JOBS
5–GENERAL LEDGER INQUIRIES

AUTHORIZED COMPANIES

PREPARED BY ——————————— DATE ————
APPROVED BY ——————————— DATE ————
IMPLEMENTED BY ————————— DATE ————

ON–LINE OPERATOR AUTHORIZATION FORM

Form Number C-3

DART RESOURCES

ILLUSTRATION 7–10

A Program Narrative

SECTION: VALIDATION	**NUMBER:** VC±130
SUBJECT: Batch Balance & Validation	**DATE ISSUED:** 5/98

PURPOSE: Balance batches and vouchers within entities and
balance forward dates. Check the basic validity of
certain fields. Print Batch Proof List.

LOGIC OUTLINE:

I.   Balancing
     A.   By batch:
         1.   Control on: debits
                              Quantity 1
                              Quantity 2
         2.   Balance debits and credits for entire batch
         3.   Require separate batches for each:
                 ± Company
                 ± Source
                 ± Balance Forward Date
         Assume new batch if one of these changes within an
         input batch.

II.   Basic Validation
     A.   <u>Batch No.</u> ± numeric
     B.   <u>Reference</u> ± numeric, first two digits between 1 and 12
         inclusive (first two digits signify month)
     C.   <u>Source</u> ± numeric, valid within B/F Date. Source must
         be for an accounting transaction to be posted to a future period.
     D.   <u>Line Item Number</u> ± numeric
     E.   <u>B/F Date</u> ± numeric and valid first two digits between 1
         and 12 inclusive. B/F Date must remain constant within
         a voucher. If it changes or is invalid, generate an
         error message for each line item in the voucher. This
         will cause the entire voucher to be rejected in VC±190.
     F.   <u>Trans±Date</u> ± numeric and possible date
     G.   <u>Amount</u> ± numeric or blank
     H.   <u>Quantity Type</u> ± 1 or 2
     I.   <u>Quantity Fields</u> ± numeric or blank

III. Other Processing
     A.   If amount is coded = blank, make it 0 so that it can be
         added in subsequent programs.
     B.   Print <u>Batch Proof List</u> report (see Report Layout for
         details).

DART RESOURCES

shows their hierarchical relationships. This hierarchy exists because a high-level module may cause the execution of one or more lower-level modules. On the structure chart, each module is represented by a rectangle. The hierarchical relationship between modules is shown by the levels on the chart. Not only is the structure chart useful in specifying the logic of a program but it is also a good form of documentation after programming is complete.

Illustration 7–11 contains a structure chart produced by a CASE tool. It shows the modules required to produce payroll. On this chart, the small arrows represent data flows (in the form of records) between the modules.

Pseudocode.   Sometimes a project team uses pseudocode to describe modules. *Pseudocode* is an informal language that uses English-like statements representing the actions performed by computer language instructions after the module is programmed. Pseudocode allows a programmer to describe how the module works without paying attention to the syntax of a computer language. Later the pseudocode statements are translated into a language understandable by the computer. Pseudocode facilitates the development of the logic; it also enables another person to understand more readily how the program works. Illustration 7–12 provides a sample of pseudocode.

Manual Procedures.   Virtually all systems, even technologically advanced ones, require processes performed by people. Members of the design team identify these manual procedures for a proposed system during preliminary system design. During detailed specification they record each procedure in a procedures manual, usually a loose-leaf notebook containing a one-page narrative description of each procedure.

The procedure description, written by an analyst on the design team, identifies the job category of the person who performs the procedure. It lists the documents prepared and the reports or display screens used, as well as the steps necessary to carry out the procedure. The analyst estimates the frequency of the procedure and may illustrate it with a document flowchart. After reviewing this procedure description, users may suggest changes to it. Illustration 7–13 provides an example of a procedure description.

User Interfaces.   The design team creates user interfaces for the system. *User interfaces* are the conversations that occur between the user and the system and usually result in data input, output, or both. They are products of the project team's decisions concerning outputs, inputs, computerized processes, and manual ones. In many systems, a user interface is a series of display screens. The system prompts a user for data attributes on these screens, and the user responds by entering them.

The design team attempts to create user interfaces that make the system easier to use. This not only makes users more satisfied with the system, but it also decreases data entry errors and produces more accurate information. Through experience, analysts have identified some ways to make a system easier to use. If you are a personal computer user, you have seen examples: menus, help screens, windows, icons, and function keys. Illustration 7–14 summarizes guidelines for designing these and other user interfaces.[1]

---

[1]For a more thorough treatment, see J. L. Whitten and L. D. Bentley, *Systems Analysis and Design Methods*, 4th ed. (Burr Ridge, Ill.: Irwin McGraw-Hill, 1998), p. 482.

ILLUSTRATION 7–11

A Structure Chart

SECTION: PROGRAM DOCUMENTATION	NUMBER:
SUBJECT: Structure Chart, P–100–PAYROLL	DATE ISSUED:

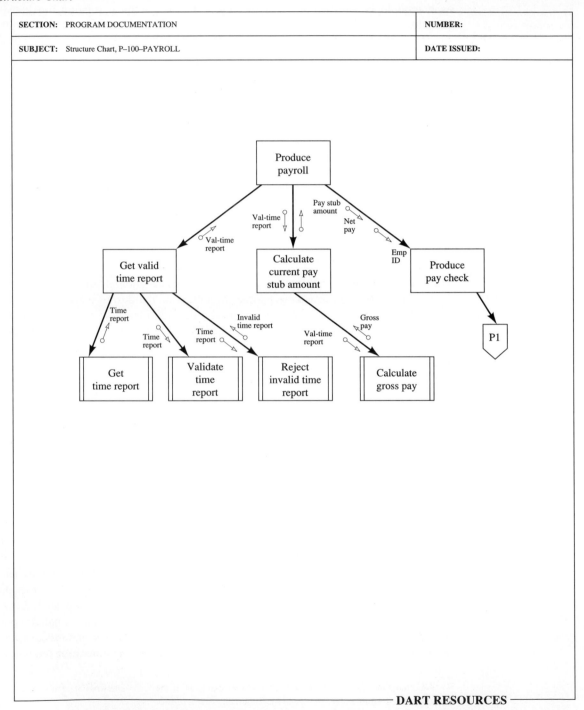

ILLUSTRATION 7–12

Pseudocode

SECTION: PROGRAM DOCUMENTATION	NUMBER:
SUBJECT: Pseudocode, B–100–PROCESS–RECORDS module	DATE ISSUED:

```
        If Oldmaster account number = Transaction account number
             PERFORM Change Masterrecord Module
             ENDPERFORM
             PERFORM Read Transactionfile Module
             ENDPERFORM
             GO TO EXIT
        ENDIF
        If Oldmaster account number > Transaction account number
             PERFORM Missing Masterrecord Error Module
             ENDPERFORM
             PERFORM Read Transactionfile Module
             ENDPERFORM
             GO TO EXIT
        ENDIF
        If Oldmaster account number < Transaction account number
             MOVE Oldmaster record to Newmaster record
             PERFORM Create Masterrecord Module
             ENDPERFORM
        ENDIF
        EXIT
```

In requirements definition, the design team specifies the contents of all data records, manual procedures, and computer programs. They also decide how all forms, display screens, and reports should look, recording these decisions in their working papers. Users, managers, and steering committee members review these working papers, identify problems they expect with the system design, and suggest possible improvements. At the conclusion of requirements definition, a thorough description of the proposed system exists on paper. The design team then selects the computer hardware and programs required by the system.

Equipment Selection   During preliminary system design, the design team identifies the computer equipment necessary to implement the proposed system. During system specification, they select a source for this equipment. They identify possible suppliers by studying trade journals and subscription services. Then they evaluate these vendors as possible sources for the equipment.

ILLUSTRATION 7–13

A Procedure Description

SECTION: CORRECTION TRANSACTIONS INPUT/UPDATE	**NUMBER:** 5.2
SUBJECT: Screen: Batch Entry/Summary for Correction Transaction	**DATE ISSUED:**

I.   PURPOSE

The purpose of this procedure is to describe the Batch Entry/Summary for Correction Transactions screen — Screen 40-212

II.   GENERAL FUNCTIONS

A.   Display Function. This function displays a suspended batch header and suspended line items (posting transactions). In addition, any corrections to the batch header information or to the line items' information is also displayed.

B.   Input Function. This function edits correction data to the suspended batch header information and edits correction data to suspended line items' data. If the correction data are valid, this function creates a correction transaction.

C.   Update Function. This function edits changes to a previously input correction to the suspended batch header's data and edits changes to previously input corrections to line items' information. If the changes are valid, this function updates the correction transactions.

D.   Finalize Function. This function finalizes a batch of correction transactions. A finalized batch is ready to be processed into a Batch Front-End Edit and Validation Job. After it has been successfully processed into a Batch Front-End Job, it is deleted from the On-line Transaction File. Neither the batch header correction data nor the correction transaction data of a finalized batch can be updated; however, a finalized batch can be un-finalized.

E.   Un-finalize Function. This function un-finalizes a previously finalized batch. An un-finalized batch will not be processed into the Batch Front-End Job until it is finalized again. An un-finalized batch's corrections to header data can be updated, its corrections to line items can be updated or deleted, and new line items can be added.

F.   Delete Function. This function deletes a correction transaction to a suspended line item.

G.   Transfer Function. This function transfers to the following screens at the operator's request:

1.   Main Menu screen.
2.   Suspended Batch Master Batch Identification Inquiry screen.

DART RESOURCES

ILLUSTRATION 7–14

Guidelines for User Interface Design

Guideline	Example
1. The system should always tell the user what to do next.	The screen always shows a menu of available options.
2. Succeeding displays should always show the same type of information or data in the same area of the screen.	The menu is always on the top row of the display screen.
3. A display should be used to communicate only one idea.	A menu option allows input of data attributes for only one entity at a time.
4. Information should stay on the screen long enough that users can read them.	The menu remains on the screen until the user has selected an option from the menu
5. Use display features to emphasize important things, but use them sparingly.	Blinking, highlighting, and reverse video help to guide the user but distract if overused.
6. Where data must be entered, default values should be specified in the design and displayed in the proper field of the display screen.	In word processing, the default drive on a personal computer is the hard disk. The software displays this disk identifier when requesting a drive selection.
7. The system should anticipate the errors a user is likely to make.	Before you can terminate a program, the program asks, "You have not saved your changes. Are you sure you want to quit?"
8. A display screen used for data entry should look like the form from which a user is entering the data.	If data are on the lower corner of the form, they should be entered on the lower left corner of a data entry screen.

Subscription Services.   *Subscription services* provide an efficient way to determine the kinds of equipment available. These services come from companies that monitor changes in the computer industry. They maintain contact with equipment and software suppliers and gather information when new products are released. These services then compile this information into loose-leaf notebooks; subscribers to the service purchase notebooks and receive updates whenever information on a new product becomes available. Different subscription services exist for different products. Some services describe large computer systems; others cover small business computers, peripheral equipment used with a computer, and software.

Subscription services summarize many equipment sources in a way that makes comparisons easy. The study team reviews the equipment specifications described in the notebook and identifies the models most suitable for the proposed system. Then they contact equipment sellers directly to negotiate prices and delivery dates.

Evaluation of Equipment Vendors.   Two common approaches exist for evaluating vendors. Under one approach, the design team establishes a minimum configuration for the hardware required by the system. They identify the quantity and specifications of all the computers and peripheral equipment needed. They summarize this in a *request for quotation (RFQ)* mailed to potential vendors. In the RFQ, the design team asks the vendor to quote a price for this configuration. This approach relies on the expertise of the design team.

Using the second approach, the design team establishes performance specifications for the proposed system. They describe these in a *request for proposal (RFP)* that goes

ILLUSTRATION 7–15

Criteria for Equipment Evaluation

Equipment performance. Difficult to measure properly.
Adaptability. Includes expandability and compatibility.
Vendor support. Quality of technical help.
Availability. Affects the implementation schedule.
Cost. Tangible costs of installation and operation.

---

to vendors. Each vendor then proposes a configuration for the hardware that meets these specifications and quotes a price for it. This approach is useful when the design team lacks the experience or time to develop its own configuration. However, because a vendor sometimes overstates the capabilities of its equipment, the second approach may result in inadequate configurations.

Criteria for Equipment Evaluation.   The design team uses five criteria to evaluate equipment sources and examine proposals from vendors: equipment performance, adaptability, vendor support, availability, and cost. Illustration 7–15 summarizes these criteria.

Equipment Performance.   The design team wants to acquire equipment that performs adequately. During system specification, they may compare performance of equipment from alternative vendors. Unfortunately, making meaningful predictions of equipment performance in a particular application is difficult. Manufacturers publish performance specifications for each model they manufacture. For example, computers are described by a *MIPS* number, the number of millions of instructions per second that they can process. For magnetic disk drives, manufacturers specify the *mean access time* to retrieve data stored on them. In determining these numbers, manufacturers assume operating conditions for the equipment that may be unrepresentative of an accounting application. Manufacturers' performance specifications are useful in comparing equipment, but they do not reflect expected performance in practice.

Sometimes a ***benchmark*** is used as a measure of performance. A benchmark is a computer program written to represent a typical application, such as computing payroll. The design team runs a benchmark program on two or more different computers and compares execution times. The system that requires the least time is the better performer. Data provided by benchmarking are useful whenever the benchmark program is similar to programs in the proposed system.

Adaptability.   Organizations investing thousands or millions of dollars in systems want them to be useful for many years and adaptable to changing needs. As the organization grows, the system must be able to grow; thus, adaptability of the system requires expandability for the equipment. The system should also be compatible with other equipment and software that may become available later.

Many computers are not expandable into faster, more powerful systems. Some purchasers have found that although their performance is adequate at the time of acquisition, these computers cannot add memory or peripherals or upgrade processors when needed. Similarly, purchasers of less popular brands of computers have few sources for software or peripheral equipment. As a result, costs are higher and the selection is smaller. A wise design team purchases a brand compatible with a variety of other brands.

Vendor Support.   Most organizations that acquire new computer equipment require technical help from the seller. A design team should select a vendor that has the ability and desire to provide this help. Adequate vendor support facilitates the activities performed during the implementation phase of the SDLC.

Vendor support reflects both the capabilities and the desires of the seller. A vendor with technicians in the local area can provide more help than one who must bring in technicians from some other region. Some vendors make backup computers available or service equipment at the data center, while others do not. A supplier who wants to maintain good customer relations can be relied on to keep promises and to aid customers in resolving implementation problems.

Evaluating vendor support is a subjective task. A design team does it by talking to each vendor's current customers and relying on their experience.

Availability.   The design team must choose a supplier that can provide the equipment at the time it is needed. Some new or popular models of computers are difficult to get and may be unavailable for several months. This can delay many activities of the implementation phase and be costly to the organization.

Sometimes a purchaser inserts a penalty clause in the purchase contract. This entitles the purchaser to a discount if equipment is not delivered on time. If a vendor refuses to accept such a clause, the purchaser should interpret this unwillingness as an admission of uncertainty regarding the delivery date.

Cost.   A final factor in the selection of computer equipment is its cost, not only the initial cost of purchase and installation but also the ongoing costs of operation. Equipment that requires special air conditioning or cabling is more expensive than equipment that is simply plugged into a source of electricity. Although the design team always considers these tangible costs, they are seldom the only criterion for equipment selection.

The other four criteria for equipment evaluation have implied costs that are difficult to estimate. There are costs for slow performance, for lack of adaptability, for poor vendor support, and for waiting on equipment that is unavailable. Usually a design team makes no attempt to estimate these costs. Instead, they identify equipment sources that are adequate in each of these areas; then they select equipment from these sources that is available at the lowest cost.

Software Specification

During preliminary system design, the design team evaluates possible sources for computer software. These are either custom programs written in-house or an external software package. Some organizations prefer a hybrid approach, in which they purchase a package written by another company but modify it to suit their own needs.

During detailed specification, the design team makes a final decision concerning the source of the software. If they choose in-house development, they must create a software development plan. If they choose to purchase an external software package, they must select the package and then plan to make any necessary modifications.

Planning Software Development.   When the programming for a new system is done in-house, it is likely to be the most time consuming and most expensive undertaking in the implementation phase. Adequate planning for software development enables the design team to avoid excessive costs during programming, to ensure its timely completion, and to achieve a more orderly system conversion. A software development plan contains estimates of time requirements, assigns personnel to programming tasks, and describes software standards.

Estimate Time Requirements.   After the programs have been described in detail, the design team can estimate the time required to develop each one. In developing a program, the programmer writes the code, debugs it, develops data to test the program, tests it, and produces documentation for it. In some cases the programmer also determines the logic of the program. The design team categorizes programs according to their complexity and then estimates the time required to develop each program. From these estimates, the team calculates the total time required for programming.

Assign Personnel.   During the implementation phase, the MIS department assigns programmers to the project team. These programmers may be employees in the MIS department, or they may be consultants or contract programmers from outside the organization. The design team estimates the number of programmers needed and arranges to have them assigned to the project. Some organizations create programmer teams, with each team led by a chief programmer. Other personnel such as data entry clerks, documentation specialists, and technicians may also be needed during implementation. The design team identifies these people and schedules their services as well.

Software Standards.   The CIO adopts standards in the form of a set of rules for programmers to follow in coding their programs. These software standards ensure consistency in programming style between programmers working on different systems. This aids in debugging the programs and makes later changes to them easier. Software standards describe acceptable ways to structure programs and to name variables and segments of programs.

Usually organizations adopt standards that provide for *modularity* in program structure. This divides each program into segments, or modules, with standardized ways of passing data between modules. Individuals on a programmer team are assigned different modules; more experienced programmers work on the more complex ones. Modularity aids later changes to the system because changes are restricted to one or a few modules. *Structured programming* is an example of a popular approach to achieving modularity. The next chapter describes it in more detail.

AIS in Practice

Sento Technological Innovations, Inc., provides state-of-the-art products and services to the information technology and computer networking industries. Sento stock became publicly traded in 1996, and the company reported revenues of $18 million in 1997.

Upon going public, management realized that its off-the-shelf accounting software program was inadequate. They needed a system that could process data from Sento's four divisions, provide an audit trail, and generate management reports. Management decided to purchase

software and then customize it. They identified three evaluation criteria: (1) ability to handle growth, (2) performance under a high transaction load, and (3) adaptability to Sento's business processes.

Management narrowed their choices to four packages and subjected these to hands-on testing. Their final selection impressed them with its modularity, which allowed them to reconfigure it easily. Furthermore, it allowed users to easily create custom display screens.

Software Acquisition.   During detailed specification, the design team defines the requirements for the proposed system. Most accounting transaction processing systems have similar requirements. For example, the requirements for a wholesaler's inventory control system are probably very much like those for any other wholesaler. The requirements for a cash disbursements application are identical for most businesses. Thus, the design team may find that an existing software package meets most of the requirements for the proposed system. A cost-effective alternative is to purchase the package and then, if necessary, modify it. The design team follows a seven-step procedure in selecting a package for acquisition. If you own a personal computer, you will find this procedure useful in buying your own software.

Review the Requirements.   The design team first reviews the requirements specified during requirements definition. These include reports, display screens, files, and manual procedures for the proposed system. The package chosen by the team contains as many of these requirements as possible. Reports and display screens provide the information needed for management control and operational decisions, so a software package should produce the essential information content of these outputs. Manual procedures show the capabilities of personnel who work with the system. Any proposed software package should require similar capabilities. After reviewing the requirements, the design team gathers data about existing software packages.

Identify Available Packages.   The design team identifies the software packages currently being marketed for this application. Computer magazines and subscription services are useful sources of information concerning available packages. The design team also may contact consultants and computer stores or talk to software development companies directly. Trade publications routinely publish descriptions of newly released software packages and some publish surveys summarizing the features of those available for a particular application. Others survey their readers and summarize users' experiences with software. Reviewing these information sources provides the design team with a list of software packages that could possibly satisfy the proposed system's requirements.

Narrow the Choice.   By eliminating clearly unsuitable packages, the design team narrows the list to three to five serious candidates. Many packages on the list likely do not execute on the computer hardware selected for the system. Others do not provide the essential information requirements defined by the design team. Still others are not compatible with existing application systems or software and are rejected from further consideration. The design team then evaluates the remaining candidates in detail.

Perform Detailed Comparisons.   The design team contacts the companies that sell the remaining packages. They may request that vendor sales representatives make presentations concerning each package. They obtain as much detailed information as possible about each, including user's manuals, installation instructions, other documentation, and copies of purchase or lease contracts. They then perform a detailed examination of this documentation to identify the advantages of each alternative.

For example, some software vendors provide the programs in a high-level language. This *source code* version of the programs enables the design team to modify the software to suit the requirements. Other vendors provide software only in *object code,* the computer's machine language that cannot be easily changed. Some vendors agree to aid in the installation process or to make changes desired by the design team. Other vendors provide a toll-free telephone number for technical advice. Some vendors only sell their packages, while others lease them or finance a sale. The design team considers these factors before making a software acquisition decision. The design team also solicits the opinions of current users of the packages.

Talk to Users.   Someone from the design team should contact CIOs at other organizations that use the package. This provides an objective appraisal of the package's strengths and weaknesses. In this way the design team learns of weaknesses or installation difficulties not evident from documentation.

An external user can also evaluate the quality of the vendor's support for the package. They can describe their experiences in implementing it, and identify problems with the package that no salesperson will mention. External users can evaluate the qualitative factors representing vendor support. These include prompt delivery and the availability of 24-hour consulting support.

If the design team knows no current user of the package, they ask the vendor for a list of current customers. A member of the team then contacts parties selected from the list. The design team realizes that users from a vendor-provided list may not be objective.

Conduct Benchmark Tests.   If possible, the design team conducts benchmark tests of the software. As mentioned earlier, benchmarks are used to evaluate equipment. In evaluating software, the team borrows a copy of each software package. They execute each, using copies of actual data files on computer equipment similar to that proposed for the system. Any package that completes processing in significantly less time is a preferred one. In this way the design team sees how the package performs under conditions similar to those during operations.

In practice, conducting benchmark tests may be impracticable. Identical equipment may be unavailable, or actual files may not exist for the system. Benchmarks conducted with different equipment or different files may be misleading and the design team cannot rely on them. Whenever they are appropriate, benchmarks may provide conclusive evidence for the software acquisition decision.

Select a Package.   After considering the detailed comparison of advantages, the discussions with users, and the results of benchmark tests, the design team selects a package. Frequently a single software package appears clearly preferable. In other cases, the design team makes subjective evaluations between two or more packages with contrasting advantages. By following this procedure, the design team conducts a thorough evaluation of available packages. Illustration 7–16 summarizes the software acquisition steps. Organizations frequently find that purchasing software is a desirable alternative for proposed accounting systems. Even when modifications are necessary, a software package is less costly than in-house development. Furthermore, a package with many current users has had most of its problems discovered and eliminated. With in-house programming, the project team almost always encounters difficulties during implementation requiring last-minute changes to programs. When an organization's requirements are unusual, or users cannot be satisfied by existing packages, then in-house development is necessary. Each alternative is considered by the design team during detailed specification.

Report to Management   At the conclusion of detailed specification, the design team prepares another report to management. This report is similar to that produced at the end of preliminary system design. It contains an executive summary that describes the objectives, scope, and major features of the system. It also contains a copy of the documentation package created during detailed specification.

This report differs from the earlier one because of the amount of detail it provides. At the end of detailed specification, descriptions of the outputs, processing, files, and inputs to the system are specified exactly. The design team has identified the necessary computer equipment and programs, and sources for them are selected. Costs of installing and operating the system are known with accuracy, so this report contains a better projection of costs and benefits for the system.

The information systems steering committee and interested members of top management review the report. They may request an oral presentation of recommendations by the design team. After considering these recommendations, they may halt further

ILLUSTRATION 7–16

Steps in Software Acquisition

1. *Review the requirements.* Define these requirements during detailed system specification.
2. *Identify available packages.* Identify packages being marketed for this application.
3. *Narrow the choices.* Eliminate those not satisfying system requirements.
4. *Perform a detailed comparison.* Evaluate thoroughly the features of each package.
5. *Talk to users.* Interview people experienced with the package.
6. *Conduct benchmark tests.* Execute the package on the actual computer equipment.
7. *Select a package.* Make a choice based on features, interviews, and tests.

development efforts, suggest changes in the design, or appoint a project team to proceed with the implementation phase.

Auditor Involvement in System Design

Many design teams obtain auditor involvement in the design process. Auditors are skilled in evaluating the auditability and controls in a system, and provide an independent appraisal of it. Auditors' suggestions that are difficult to implement in an existing system are more easily designed into a new one. Usually internal auditors participate, although sometimes independent auditors or consultants from the audit firm participate as well.

Auditors are normally not members of the design team, although they conduct a detailed review of the system during the system design phase. Auditors perform two major functions: They evaluate the detailed specifications of the system to recommend improvements, and they consider how to introduce audit modules into the system's programs.

Specifications Review

Auditors review the detailed specifications of the new system to evaluate the adequacy of its audit trail and of its internal controls.

The audit trail is produced by information contained in the reports and files of the system. It provides the ability to trace an individual transaction through the system into a financial statement amount, or to trace from an amount in the financial statements to the transactions making it up. When a report discloses a journal entry number, a posting reference, or a document number, it is creating an audit trail. Good bookkeepers produce an audit trail in a manual accounting system; similar procedures are needed in a computerized one. Because systems analysts and programmers are not experts concerning these procedures, an auditors' review of system specifications is important.

A new system should also have adequate internal controls. In a computerized system, these include the measures taken to prevent or detect erroneous data and to secure data from theft or unauthorized change. In reviewing controls, auditors examine the proposed procedures for data backup and data retention, and for correcting erroneous transactions detected by the system. These procedures are essential for ensuring accurate and secure accounting information.

When reviewing system specifications, auditors examine in detail the reports, the processing steps, and the data described during requirements definition. They also review the computer equipment selected by the design team.

Reports. Auditors examine the proposed reports to verify that they include information needed for auditability and control. Each report that produces summary totals should identify the sources of the detailed amounts. For example, a report that discloses journalized transactions should identify document numbers for all the transactions. A printout of a ledger should indicate a source for all journal postings making up the ledger balance. These enable an auditor to trace from a ledger total to an individual transaction. Batch and control totals should also be included on many reports to ensure that no transactions are omitted during processing.

Processing Steps. In the design documentation package, program narratives and procedures manuals describe the processing steps. After reviewing these, auditors suggest additional control procedures. For example, auditors may suggest that a clerk accumulate documents into batches and take an adding machine total of all transaction amounts in the batch. This batch total is input to all computer programs that process the batch. The programs are coded so that, in addition to normal processing, they compute control totals of all transactions in the batch. Each program compares the batch total to its control total and discloses any difference in a control report.

Data Files.   Auditors also review the data specifications for the new system. They evaluate the control measures ensuring the security and accuracy of the data and verify that data items included in the file provide an audit trail. They determine that specified backup procedures allow reconstruction of data should they be destroyed. They ensure that retention procedures satisfy audit and legal requirements.

Equipment Selection.   In reviewing the equipment selected by the design team, auditors provide an independent appraisal. They examine equipment choices to ensure that the hardware selected can fulfill management's desires. They evaluate the capacity of the equipment and determine if it is sufficient—but not excessive—for the needs of the system. In some organizations, MIS quality assurance personnel rather than auditors perform this function.

Audit Modules

Many modern systems do not contain the kind of audit trail that auditors prefer. Some of these systems enter a transaction into the system and immediately post it to a ledger, with no record on paper of intermediate processing steps. Thus, auditors cannot establish the reliability of the system by simply examining evidence provided in its reports by the audit trail. To determine that such a system is producing accurate data, auditors introduce audit modules into the system's programs.

An *audit module* is a segment of an accounting application program that enables auditors to examine transactions in magnetic form as they are processed by the program. An audit module may, for example, allow for examining transactions for a special characteristic such as a high monetary value. Transactions that have this characteristic are summarized in a file for later review by an auditor. The use of audit modules is discussed further in the chapter on data security and integrity.

Audit modules are difficult to add to programs in existing systems. However, if created during system design, they can be implemented at reasonable cost. During the review of design documentation, auditors look for opportunities to embed audit modules into the system's programs.

Summary

System design is a process of starting with a set of system objectives and selecting ways to achieve those objectives. It is an outgrowth of the recommendations made at the end of systems analysis. As design proceeds, the features of the proposed system are gradually refined and made more specific.

The system design phase of the systems development life cycle contains two activities: During the first, preliminary system design, the design team identifies the outputs, processes, inputs, and data for the system in a high-level, conceptual form. In the second, detailed specification, the design team defines these precisely. Each activity terminates with a report to users and management. These reports give them opportunities to suggest changes to the proposed system, or to halt further system development. If the information systems steering committee wishes to proceed with system development, they appoint a project team for the implementation phase of the SDLC.

Auditors become involved in system design near the end of the design phase. They review the documentation created by the design team and suggest ways to improve auditability and control in the proposed system. They also may include audit modules in the system's programs.

Key Terms

ad hoc report   A report produced as needed at irregular intervals rather than periodically.

benchmark   A test of the performance of either computer hardware or software.

detailed specification   An activity performed during system design in which a project team creates on paper a detailed description of how an information system should work.

preliminary system design   An activity performed during system design in which a project team develops a conceptual description of a proposed system.

pseudocode   An informal language that uses English-like statements to represent the actions performed by a computer program.

request for quotation (RFQ)   A letter prepared by a design project team that identifies a computer configuration and requests a cost estimate from a vendor. If the vendor is asked to specify the configuration, the letter is called a **request for proposal (RFP).**

requirements definition   A detailed specification activity during which the design project team describes the outputs, data, inputs, and processing steps of the system.

service bureau   A company that owns and operates computer hardware and software and provides data processing services to other organizations.

source document   A form used in an accounting system to serve as the initial record of data for later processing.

subscription service   A newsletter published at regular intervals by companies that monitor and evaluate available computer hardware and software.

Questions

7–1. Which two major benefits accrue from performing a thorough system design?

7–2. How is the product of detailed specification different from that of preliminary system design? How are they similar?

7–3. Distinguish between the outputs of preliminary system design and the outputs of detailed specification when describing
    a. Outputs.

     b. Data.

     c. Inputs.

     d. Processes.

7–4. The following documents are produced during the system design phase. Which component of a computer-based system does each describe?

     a. Record layout.

     b. Procedures manual.

     c. Program narrative.

     d. Screen layout.

7–5. Application software may be either purchased or developed in-house. State three possible advantages and three possible disadvantages of purchasing software.

(CIA Adapted)

7–6. Which procedures should you follow when selecting a software package for acquisition?

7–7. What are the alternative ways of acquiring computer equipment?

7–8. Name and describe the three major activities that occur during detailed specification.

7–9. How can you use a subscription service during detailed specification? What advantages does one provide?

7–10. Should you always acquire the lowest-cost computer equipment? Which other factors affect the decision?

7–11. What does the auditor look for when conducting a specifications review during the system design phase?

7–12. It has been said that system design is a creative act and that creativity cannot be taught. To what extent do you agree with this statement? Why?

Exercises and Cases

7–13.   *DEFINITIONS*

Define each of the following terms:

a. Source document.

b. Ad hoc report.

c. RFQ.

d. RFP.

e. Hardware configuration.

f. Software standards.

g. Benchmark.

7–14.   *LEASE OR PURCHASE*

A study team at Oceanographic Enterprises has gathered the following information for a proposed information system:

Purchase price of computer equipment	$200,000
Annual rental of same equipment under a lease contract	$ 48,000
Initial cost:	
Installation	12,000
Programming	80,000
Training and conversion	40,000
Total	$132,000
Annual operating cost:	
MIS salaries	$115,200
Utilities and supplies	23,040
Facilities maintenance	15,000
Total	$153,240
Present annual operating costs	$260,000
Discount factor	20%
Estimated useful life of computer	5 years

Required:

Analyze the economic feasibility of the computerized system assuming the equipment is

a. Purchased.
b. Leased.

7–15.   SYSTEM DEVELOPMENT LIFE CYCLE

Curtis Company operates in a five-county industrial area. The company employs a manual system for all its recordkeeping except payroll; the payroll is processed by a local service bureau. Other applications have not been computerized because previously they could not be cost justified.

The company's sales have grown at an increasing rate over the past years. With this substantial growth rate, a computer-based system seemed more practical. Consequently, Curtis Company engaged the management consulting department of their public accounting firm to conduct a feasibility study for converting their recordkeeping systems to a computer-based system. The accounting firm reported that a computer-based system would improve the company's recordkeeping system and still provide material cost savings.

Therefore, Curtis Company decided to develop a computer-based system for their records. Curtis hired a person with experience in systems development as manager of systems and data processing. His responsibilities are to oversee the entire systems operations with special emphasis on the development of the new system.

Required:

Describe the major steps in developing and implementing Curtis Company's new computer-based system.

(CMA Adapted)

7–16.   BUDGET SYSTEM

Small Company wants to implement a budget system. A computer file containing budget data must contain, at a minimum, the following data items: an account number, an account description, and a budgeted amount. The actual amount in the account may be obtained from another computer file containing the general ledger. A computer program reads the budget data from the budget file, the actual data from the general ledger file, and prints a budget report.

Required:

a. Design a budget report that compares actual and budgeted amounts for each account.
b. Prepare a system flowchart for this budgeting system.
c. Draw a program flowchart for this computerized process.

7–17.   STRUCTURED METHODOLOGIES

For the budget system described in Exercise 7–16,

a. Design a budget report that compares actual and budgeted amounts for each account.
b. Prepare a data flow diagram.
c. Develop logic specifications using pseudocode.

7–18.   RETAIL INVENTORY SYSTEM

Megamarket Food Stores attempts to maintain its competitive position by keeping operating costs as low as possible. Megamarket managers are considering installing an optical character reader at each grocery checkout stand. The reader uses a laser beam to read the Universal Product Code printed in black ink on the label of each item that Megamarket sells.

When a customer brings an item to a checkout stand, the clerk scans its label with the reader. The reader notifies a computer elsewhere in the store that the item has been sold.

The store's computer maintains a computer file of all items sold during the day. At night, these data are transferred to a larger computer at corporate headquarters. The corporate computer deducts each sale from the quantities shown in the inventory records and places orders to replenish inventory levels at each store. Megamarket's management believes that this system can lower labor costs and minimize investment in inventory.

Required:

a. Suggest two daily reports and one monthly report that such a system would produce. What would be the purpose of each report?
b. Identify the data items that this system would use in the inventory records at
    1. Each store computer.
    2. The corporate computer.
c. Develop a system flowchart for this system.

7–19.   STRUCTURED METHODOLOGIES

For the inventory system described in Exercise 7–18:

a. Suggest two daily reports and one monthly report that such a system would produce. What would be the purpose of each report?
b. Identify the data items that this system would use in the inventory records at
    1. Each store computer.
    2. The corporate computer.
c. Develop a data flow diagram.

7–20.   PERSONNEL SYSTEM

Wagner Wagons, Inc., uses a computer-based personnel system in calculating payroll for hourly employees. The system maintains one entry for each hourly employee in a computerized personnel file. Each entry, a computer record, contains the following data items:

1. Social Security number (9 characters).
2. Employee last name (12 characters).
3. Employee first name (12 characters).
4. Employee middle initial (1 character).
5. Street address (15 characters).
6. City (12 characters).
7. State (2 characters).
8. Zip code (9 characters).
9. Department (4 characters).
10. Hourly pay rate (5 characters).
11. Job skill code (4 characters).
12. Job skill description (12 characters).

Required:

Develop a record layout for this personnel file.

7–21.   BILLING SYSTEM

Huge Lighting & Power Company (HL&P) is developing a computer-based billing system to improve its processing of accounts receivable. Once a month an employee reads the electric meter at each service location and enters the meter number and meter reading into a hand-held computer. At the end of the day the employee plugs the hand-held computer into the HL&P corporate mainframe computer.

The mainframe executes a data entry program that posts the reading at each meter to a computer file called the AR master file. The AR master file contains, for each meter number, the customer name, address, previous meter reading, the total amount owed from previous billing cycles, and a billing code. Residential, business, industrial, non-profit, and government customers all have different billing codes, allowing them to be charged for usage at different rates. The data entry program determines the quantity of electricity used at a meter by subtracting the previous reading from the current one.

The data entry program then calculates the charge for the electricity used. It looks up the customer's billing code in a computerized unit charge file. This file contains the cost in dollars per unit of electricity for each billing code. The data entry program then multiplies the unit charge by the quantity of electricity used to get the current amount owed.

Once this amount is known, the data entry program prints a statement that is mailed to the customer.

Required:

a. Identify the data items that should be disclosed on HL&P's monthly statement.
b. Identify the data items that are contained in each file processed by the data entry program.

c. Draw a system flowchart for this billing system. You may represent all computer files by the ON-LINE STORAGE symbol.

d. The system as designed has a major shortcoming. Although a monthly statement is produced for each customer, the system keeps no record either of the quantity of electricity used or of the amount that is invoiced on a statement. Describe how you would correct this design flaw in the system.

7–22.   SALES ANALYSIS SYSTEM

Universal Floor Covering is a manufacturer and distributor of carpet and vinyl floor coverings. The home office is located in Charlotte, North Carolina. Carpet mills are located in Dalton, Georgia, and Greenville, South Carolina; a floor covering manufacturing plant is in High Point, North Carolina. Total sales last year were just over $250 million.

The company manufactures more than 200 different varieties of carpet. The carpet is classified as commercial or residential and is sold under five brand names with up to five lines under each brand. The lines indicate different quality grades measured by type of tuft and number of tufts per square inch. Each line of carpet can have up to 15 different color styles.

Almost 200 varieties of vinyl floor covering are manufactured for either commercial or residential use. The four separate brand names are distinguished by type of finish, eight different patterns for each brand, and eight color styles for each pattern.

Ten different grades of padding are manufactured. The padding is usually differentiated by intended use, either commercial or residential, and by thickness and composition of materials.

Universal serves more than 2,000 regular wholesale customers. Retail showrooms are the primary customers. Many major corporations are direct buyers of Universal's products. Large construction companies have contracts with Universal to purchase carpet and floor covering at reduced rates for use in newly constructed homes and commercial buildings. In addition, Universal produces a line of residential carpet for a large national retail chain. Sales to these customers range from $10,000 to $1 million annually.

Company-owned retail outlets at each plant carry overruns, seconds, and discontinued items. This is Universal's only retail sales function.

The company has divided the sales market into seven territories. The majority of these are concentrated on the East Coast. The market segments are New England, New York, Mid-Atlantic, Carolinas, South, Midwest, and West. Each sales territory is divided into 5 to 10 districts, and a salesperson is assigned to each district.

The current accounting system has been adequate for monitoring sales by product. However, there are limitations to the system because specific information is sometimes not available. The accounting department has been asked to design a sales analysis system. The system should permit Universal to prepare sales analysis reports that would reflect the characteristics of the company's business. The first step in designing this system is to develop a method of coding sales transactions when they are recorded.

Required:

a. Identify and describe the factors that must be considered before a method of coding can be designed and implemented for an organization.

b. Develop a coding system for Universal Floor Covering that would assign sales analysis codes to sales transactions. This coding system should enable Universal to perform market analysis on past sales data. For each portion of the code,
1. Explain the meaning and purpose of the position.
2. Identify and justify the number of digits required.

(CMA Adapted)

7–23.   *SOFTWARE SELECTION*

AgriBank is a $14 billion financial institution that provides wholesale credit and services to 32 Farm Credit Service Associations in 11 midwestern states.[2] Currently it employs 3,200 people in 480 offices and serves about 200,000 customers. AgriBank never intended to become a cutting-edge computer user, but competitiveness in agriculture and excess capacity in the financial services industry forced it to update its technology.

The Needs

Most customers of the Farm Credit Service Associations live in agricultural communities. Through these associations, AgriBank provides loans for real estate and for farm production—seeds, fertilizer, livestock, and other supplies. The company also offers related services, including crop insurance, recordkeeping, business planning, and tax preparation. An essential element of these services is the ability of the associations' customer service representatives to answer customer questions promptly and accurately. The associations must also be able to process disbursements of loans and receipts of cash from customers. "For a financial institution, that's about as 'mission critical' as it gets," said Chief Information Officer Richard Spradling.

AgriBank chose to implement its applications with a central computer in its main office and a smaller file server in each association office. (A file server is a fast personal computer with large memory and a large attached hard disk. It provides data storage for other computers in a network.) Each customer service representative has a laptop personal computer. In an association office, the representative downloads components of the database from the file server to the laptop. Then the representative uses this information to answer questions and to originate loans at the customer's location. Other laptop applications help to identify and track prospective customers, provide on-line financial product comparisons, and tailor loan terms and conditions to a customer's particular requirements.

After returning to the association office, the representative updates the data in the file server from the laptop computer. The file servers daily update the data in AgriBank's central computer by telecommunication links. AgriBank needed to identify software that would efficiently maintain the data for its applications on each type of computer. The primary concern was finding software called a *database server* that would provide adequate service at reasonable costs. In this case, costs included license fees, installation, and support for the software at 480 different sites. The software had to be easy to use at each site and easy to administer from AgriBank's home office.

---

[2]Adapted from Lee The, "Big Isn't Always Better," *Datamation*, July 1, 1994, p. 66. © 1994 by Cahners Publishing Company. Used by permission.

The Process

The CIO appointed a study team to identify suitable software packages for evaluation. This team conducted a literature search to identify the industry-leading candidate packages. This search identified three articles in personal computer journals that provided evaluations of suitable software. The list of candidates from these articles was quickly narrowed to just a few. Packages intended for personal computers were inadequate, and those intended for larger computers were too expensive. Others could not easily support detached laptop computers. Ultimately, the study team chose to perform a detailed evaluation of two packages, product A and product B. The detailed evaluation looked primarily at six factors: (1) ease of installation, (2) data administration, (3) performance, (4) data access efficiency, (5) suitability for laptop use, and (6) cost.

Ease of installation refers to ease of defining the database and modifying its tables of data. Product A excelled in this category. Employees in the association offices did not have to be computer professionals to get the software running because product A's designers made assumptions, or defaults, about what the users wanted. Product B was much more flexible, but it required users to specify options for these defaults. This required more knowledge of the software than most employees in the association offices were likely to develop.

Data administration refers to ease of backup and recovery. These are the requirements for making extra copies of the data periodically, and for subsequently recreating the data from the extra copy when necessary. In this area, the study team decided that the products were about equal. Each could automatically perform backup and recovery functions.

Performance was evaluated based on the time it takes to read both small and large databases. Speed was not a primary concern for the package. However, the file servers had only four to five hours each day to transfer data to AgriBank's central computer, so the software had to be fast enough to meet this constraint. The study team ran benchmark tests to determine if the two candidate packages were capable of meeting the requirement. With a large database (about 3 million records), product B was about five times faster at reading records into the database. With smaller files, processing times for products A and B were essentially identical. Small databases, which were more typical, contained about 60 tables and 3,000 records.

Data access efficiency was measured by the time it takes for a complex query for information to pass through the database twice and establish totals and subtotals. With a large database, product B was about two and one-half times as fast at this task as product A. With a typical small database, however, there was no noticeable difference between efficiency of the two packages.

Cost was a concern since the package had to be licensed at 480 sites. Product A was priced per user, and product B was priced per site. AgriBank ranked prices assuming an average of nine users at a time at each site. On this basis, product A was somewhat better. However, the more important factor was product A's pricing method. With product A, price was unaffected by the number of copies of the software. This gave AgriBank the flexibility to add or move computers wherever needed without changing costs, as long as the total number of users did not change.

According to the CIO, product A seemed to excel at distributing data in the laptop computer environment. It more easily allowed the laptop to couple and decouple from

Exhibit 7–1

Case 7–23

Criteria	Product A	Product B
Ease of installation	B	D
Data administration	B	B
Performance	C	A
Data access efficiency	C	B
Cost	A	C
Laptop suitability	A	D
Overall GPA	3.6	2.3

the file server. This ease of use more than overcame the performance disadvantage of product A. "It seemed almost uniquely targeted at that environment," Spradling said.

Exhibit 7–1 shows a software evaluation report card produced by the study team at the close of this evaluation. The report card compares products A and B on each of the six criteria by assigning them letter grades.

Based on this evaluation, AgriBank chose to purchase product A. The contract with the package's vendor also provided the bank with access to a vendor support team permanently assigned to the account. Additionally, on recommendation of the vendor, Agribank selected a national accounting firm to help develop standards and procedures for these applications. The accounting firm has experience with this software and will provide implementation training for AgriBank personnel.

Required:

a. What factors do you think were most important to AgriBank in selecting a software package for this application?

b. Can you suggest what other steps the study team could have taken in the software selection process?

7–24.   MANUFACTURING CONTROL SYSTEM—PART II

Lockheed Austin Division (LAD) of Austin, Texas, designs and manufactures communications and surveillance systems for the military. Because of its haphazard growth through the early 1980s, it became a melting pot of people, projects, and systems. The lack of an integrated information system made it difficult for LAD to maintain its competitive position in the marketplace. To correct this problem, top management committed to the development of an operations support system (OSS) using structured techniques.

Starting the Project

Management assembled a project team representing the operational functions affected by the new system. Representatives from manufacturing, material, and product assurance were assigned the major responsibilities. These included creating detailed system specifications, developing user manuals, designing training programs, devising acceptance test procedures, and creating implementation schedules. Users from the data

EXHIBIT 7–2

Case 7–24

One-Time Costs	Recurring Costs
Hardware	Hardware maintenance
Software	Software maintenance
Software modification	Telecommunications
User interface construction	Support staff
Software package training	Training
Travel	
Internal staff time	
Consulting	
Telecommunications charges	
Facilities	
Cabling	

input area provided word processing and data entry services. Program controls personnel monitored the project activity and developed project reviews. The team member from information systems participated in developing acceptance test procedures, writing user manuals, providing data processing training, and creating requirement specifications. This person was also responsible for communications with vendors. The team maintained communications with representatives from logistics, finance, engineering, and human resources. Clearly, this was not just an MIS project.

Estimating Costs and Benefits

LAD began its cost–benefit analysis early in the project and refined its estimates as more accurate data became available. The project team developed cost estimates from preliminary discussions with vendors, information systems personnel, and consultants. Exhibit 7–2 shows the one-time and recurring costs they identified.

Hardware and software could be priced accurately early in the project, but estimating staff costs was more difficult. To make this easier, the team developed a detailed project plan. This allowed them to assign all tasks to individuals, estimate total hours required, and identify potential overloads. They could then correct these overloads before getting behind schedule. Preparing a range of costs for each cost component increased the probability of staying within budget and showed management the difficulty of preparing exact cost estimates.

Statement of Work

Once LAD management decided to proceed with the operations support system project, the project team prepared a statement of work. This outlined the tasks required of vendors in preparing quotations. It also contained an installation schedule and details of the manufacturing and financial interface requirements. For example, OSS would obtain data from other systems about work orders, budgets, work authorizations, employee status, job information, and configuration requirements. It would produce outputs used in payroll, inventory, purchasing, and general ledger systems.

The statement of work took three months to produce, consisted of about 75 pages of requirements for OSS, and about 90 pages of corporate interface requirements. It contained all the information that was sent to vendors as a Request for Proposal (RFP).

Software Selection

Often organizations first select a software package to meet their needs and then acquire the hardware that works with the package. However, LAD management decided to do the opposite.

They had been using computer hardware made by Tandem Corporation for data collection on the factory floor. Rather than incur costs of changing hardware manufacturers, management decided to continue with Tandem and select software that would execute on these machines. The software also had to interface with the IBM machines that were used for other systems. This narrowed the software selection process considerably.

The project team developed a complex scoring system for the hardware. They prepared selection criteria, evaluation criteria, and summary evaluation sheets for the software to be evaluated. This scoring procedure was performed "blind" so that no team member could be influenced by a vendor name. After visiting about 15 companies and examining 30 software packages, the team selected the software.

Required:

a. Who composed the project team for the LAD OSS project? What were each member's responsibilities? Do you think that this project had adequate user involvement?
b. Which components of cost were easiest to determine? Which were most difficult? What were the benefits of this project?
c. What was contained in the RFP for the OSS?

7–25.   *CORPORATE CONSOLIDATION SYSTEM—PART II*

R. J. Reynolds Industries, Inc., is a diversified worldwide corporation with consolidated net sales measured in billions of dollars. It serves as parent company for seven subsidiaries, each of which is a major line of business. These are R. J. Reynolds Tobacco Co.; Del Monte Corp. (processed foods and fresh fruits); R. J. Reynolds Tobacco International, Inc.; Aminoil USA, Inc. (energy); Sea-Land Service, Inc. (containerized shipping); RJR Foods, Inc. (convenience foods and beverages); and RJR Archer, Inc. (packaging).

As a result of corporate growth and of increased public reporting requirements, the corporate accounting group at R. J. Reynolds undertook a systems study during the mid-1970s. The study resulted in the selection and installation of a general ledger software package in corporate headquarters. The general ledger system, when installed, was named the corporate consolidation system (CCS). It processed the financial statements and selected account analysis of each of the reporting entities and consolidated them into the total corporate statements, with statements of earnings and balance sheets for each individual reporting company in a line of business. In addition, certain selected Form 10-K schedules were prepared using the statistical capabilities of the general ledger package.

Choosing the Software Package

When designing the system, the corporate accounting team examined in detail a number of alternatives and visited several companies that had installed this package, or other packages, to handle their consolidation accounting. The project team developed a set of criteria to evaluate each package on the market that possibly could meet the information requirements of RJR.

They categorized the criteria into "musts" and "desires." The musts were necessary before RJR would consider the system, and the desires included those elements the company hoped the system would have. The must criteria included

1. A report writer to easily design and implement required reports.
2. Account analysis for 10-K and 10-Q reporting.
3. Multiple consolidation paths to handle multiples of business consolidation accounting.
4. Intercompany account eliminations.
5. Package provided in COBOL source code.
6. The capability of extending the system to other companies and other operating computer facilities as a general ledger package.

The four desired criteria were

1. Five years of history.
2. Capability to provide a cash flow statement.
3. Ability to convert from one currency to another.
4. Terminal input and reporting capabilities.

After evaluating the various packages on the market, the corporate accounting team recommended a specific package that had been used at a large number of sites for several years. Additionally, it met all of the must criteria and most of the desired ones with slight modifications. In selecting the package, however, the team noted certain disadvantages:

1. Corporate accounting would have to write the 10-K report modules.
2. Corporate accounting would have to add any currency conversion routines.
3. The system was a generalized general ledger system and not a consolidation ledger system.

Why didn't RJR write the package in-house with its own MIS department? The answer was that the immediate purchase of proven experience tested by many companies in the software market was preferable to attempting to write a new consolidation accounting system in-house. It has been estimated that RJR saved a minimum of three calendar years of development effort by a project team by purchasing a package instead of attempting to write this application in-house.

Consolidation Accounting

In the consolidation process, corporate accounting is required to prepare financial statements and analyses on the individual reporting entities, to consolidate these entities by lines of business, and to prepare consolidated R. J. Reynolds Industries statements. Two major problems facing the team in the new system effort were the inflexibility of the old account code structure and the accurate and rapid elimination of intercompany accounts.

The old system would, for example, collect total property, plant, and equipment, and accumulate depreciation from each reporting entity. But the team wanted to collect the details behind such summary accounts so the analysis statements could be developed on the computer instead of by hand. By collecting the necessary level of detail and having the computer do the work, the accounting department would be able to devote more of its efforts to analyzing the financial information instead of just adding and footing worksheets. Also, the various operating companies have many intercompany relationships, such as intercompany sales, receivables, payables, and investments. These accounts must be handled quickly and accurately in the consolidation process to develop the financial statements quickly. Accounts have to be handled on an "intra" basis among companies within a line of business and on an "inter" basis between companies in different lines of business. In addition, the elimination process should be consistent from period to period and provide a good audit trail for review by both internal and external auditors.

Using the Package

After evaluating the old consolidation chart of accounts and the accounting systems used by the operating companies in light of the two major problems of consolidation, the team decided to develop a completely new set of accounts. Criteria for the new account structure required that it be as small as possible yet flexible enough to meet all anticipated accounting changes from the FASB and SEC and possible corporate acquisitions. As a result, the team chose a 13-position account code.

The first four positions are the identifier designators—the first position indicating the line of business and the next three positions indicating the company within that particular line of business. This four-position identifier provided enough flexibility so that the operating companies can be consolidated into entities other than the lines of business used for public reporting. For example, different reporting might be necessary for legal reasons or due to management's desires. The fifth position indicated the statement type—that is, statement of earnings, balance sheet, or 10-K account analysis. The sixth through the ninth are four-digit prime account codes. These use codes 0000–4999 for the balance sheet and codes 5000–9999 for the statement of earnings. Positions 10 through 13 are subaccount codes used in intercompany accounting and account analysis.

The designation "99" was chosen to indicate the consolidation of a group of similar reporting entities. Thus, the code 1199 indicated the consolidation of information for companies in line of business 11. The team took this consolidation point approach one step further by creating a complete company at each level of consolidation. Amounts posted at the operating company level automatically are combined with the other operating companies in that group's consolidation company. This system also provided an opportunity for possible adjustments at each account within a consolidation company. When requesting a specific amount, such as notes payable for a line of business, management addresses the notes payable account in the consolidation company. Because of the relationship between operating and consolidation companies, this account contains the sum of the notes payable for all companies in that line of business, plus any adjustments. In this way, the user does not have to add the amounts for each company in the line of business to determine the total.

One of the most difficult problems in consolidation accounting is the elimination of intercompany balances. The new account code and the operating consolidation company relationships provided the tools necessary to greatly speed up the intercompany accounting process. With the four position identifier in the new code, each individual reporting company within the corporation could be identified specifically with its own identifier code and line of business code. This code is used in handling intercompany relationships because it enables a particular company to report its intercompany balances with any other company. It does this by using that company's unique identifier in the subaccount positions in conjunction with the proper general ledger account. For example, company 0004's intercompany receivable from company 1135 should have a contra payable of company 1135 to company 0004.

By relating the intra-accounts receivable accounts to the intra-accounts payable accounts at a consolidation level, the intra-accounts within a line of business are eliminated at the consolidated line of business level. This eliminating relationship feature permits an accountant to use the report writer feature of the package to create a report showing how the intercompany accounts have been reported. The report developed is used as a working document by the accountant and makes it easy to determine whether or not the intercompany balances reconcile.

Required:

a. Why did RJR Industries choose to purchase and modify a software package, rather than develop a consolidation system in-house?
b. What procedure did the project team use in selecting a software package?
c. The package chosen was a general ledger package rather than a consolidation package. How did the project team adapt it to the problems of consolidation accounting?

7–26.   *CORPORATE CONSOLIDATION SYSTEM—PART III*

In developing the account structure for the CCS, **RJR**'s corporate accounting team used the statistical accounting capabilities of the package to develop certain critical information. The statistical account feature was used to develop a separate level of accounting information within the financial statements; such information is normally not available within a standard general ledger chart of accounts. This was accomplished by developing relationships to a given set of standard accounts designated as prime management information accounts. These accounts were established at each reporting entity as well as at each consolidation level. The profit and loss statement was established to contain 13 prime codes for all operating companies and consolidation levels. All of the sales and expense categories collected from each of the operating companies are eventually summarized into these standard 13 accounts. Exhibit 7–3 contains this standard profit and loss statement.

In addition, a three-way comparison is developed (current period compared to the same period last year, current year-to-date compared to last year-to-date, current period compared to previous period) using these standard accounts for evaluation during

EXHIBIT 7–3

Case 7–26

	Standard Profit and Loss Statement	Current Year	Prior Year
Sales and operating revenues	XXXX-A-5000-0000[b]		
Cost of products sold-OPR EXP	XXXX-A-6000-0000		
Selling, advertising, G&A	XXXX-A-7400-0000		
Earnings from operations[a]	XXXX-A-7500-0000		
Outside interest and debt	XXXX-A-8000-0000		
Intercompany interest expense	XXXX-A-8100-0000		
Intercompany interest (income)	XXXX-A-8200-0000		
Other financial (income)/expense	XXXX-A-8300-0000		
Realized foreign exchange	XXXX-A-8400-0000		
Unrealized foreign exchange	XXXX-A-8420-0000		
Earnings before income taxes[a]	XXXX-A-8500-0000		
Provision for income taxes	XXXX-A-8800-0000		
Net earnings/(loss)[a]	XXXX-A-9000-0000		
Net loss will print in brackets			

[a]The variable report writer calculates these amounts by totaling the accounts listed above. This total is compared with the statistical account on file, and an error message is printed if the two do not agree. The double-check ensures the accuracy of the reports.

[b]The four positions indicate a specific line of business and company within that line of business.

closings. Exhibit 7–4 shows how various accounts collected from the operating companies can be related to these standard accounts so that reports that are the same across company lines can be generated for management.

One requirement of consolidation accounting is to determine the changes in the balance sheet position from the end of last year to the current reporting period. This analysis forms the basis for certain schedules required in the annual 10-K report, such as the analysis of property, plant, and equipment. The data for developing the analysis are collected from the operating companies using statistical accounts within the general ledger system. For the statistical accounts, strict debit equals credit accounting procedures are not required. The prior year-end balance is already within the database from the prior year-end closing, and the current period balance has been input as part of the current closing activities.

Subaccount codes are recorded in the last four positions of the 13-digit account code. To collect the changes, a set of standard change codes is used in the subaccount positions. Each of the change codes on an account is related to a cross-check account that contains the sum of the changes to an account. The variable report writer program performs the analysis by first checking to see if the balance in the cross-check account equals the differences between the prior year-end balance and the current period balance. If the balances agree, then the program prints out the changes in an account. Again, through use of the consolidation company approach, changes posted for an operating company are automatically reflected in the appropriate consolidation level. Exhibit 7–5 illustrates how this occurs. By using the statistical account features and the report

EXHIBIT 7–4

Case 7–26

Standard Account Relationships*

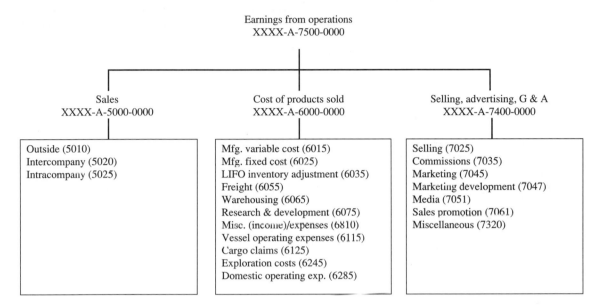

*Accounts are from different companies to show how different accounts could be related to the standard accounts.
There can be other posting accounts that relate to a particular account illustrated.

writer, the team was able to develop successfully an analysis on property, plant, and equipment, accumulated depreciation, and other long-term account analyses needed for both the 10-K and the 10-Q schedules.

Required:

a. The project team designed a 13-digit account code for RJR's chart of accounts. Identify the significance of each digit in this account code.

b. How did the project team modify the package to provide statistical information beyond that required for the basic financial statements?

c. CCS was designed by a project team containing members from the corporate accounting department. Do you think a team of nonaccountants could have designed this system?

7–27.   *YOUR COMPANY PROJECT—PART III*

For the company you selected in Exercise 5–26, perform the following:

a. Prepare a preliminary system design for your company.

b. Complete the detailed specifications for the system for your company.

c. Prepare a report to management containing the detailed specifications for your system.

Exhibit 7–5

Case 7–26

Variable Report Writer Program (dollars in thousands)

				Property, Plant, and Equipment Periods Ended Dec. 30, 1998			**Schedule X**
Run date 12/30/98	*Prior Year Ending Balance*	*Capital Expenditures*	*Retirements*	*Transfers out of CIP*	*Other Changes*	*Intercompany Transfers*	*Current Period Balance*
	(a)	0068	0058	0036	0032	0022	
Machinery and equipment							
004 [b]	$175,328	$18,201	(2,003)	331	(23)	(347)	$191,487
005	424	75	(1)	—	(18)	20	500
006	19	—	(19)	—	—	—	—
007	325,858	18,652	(205)	652	—	(454)	344,503
008	2,976	202	(50)	—	—	—	3,128
Total [c]	$504,605	$37,130	(2,278)	983	(41)	(781)	$539,618 [d]

[a]Standard change codes for this analysis of machinery and equipment.

[b]List of companies in this line-of-business report.

[c]Totals for this line-of-business report.

[d]The cross-check account does not print unless there is an error. Then the account and an error message will print.

8　SYSTEM IMPLEMENTATION AND OPERATION

Learning Objectives

1. To discover which activities take place during the third and fourth phases of the system development life cycle.
2. To know how auditors participate in system implementation.
3. To understand how to do a post-implementation review.
4. To learn how to properly account for the costs of an accounting information system.

Introduction

The previous chapters focused on the first two phases of the system development life cycle (SDLC). This chapter will present the last two phases of the SDLC, system implementation and system operation.

In the implementation phase, a project team creates a working system from the design specifications. The operations phase consists of the time period in which the system is used to process accounting data. It represents the objective of the system development process.

System Implementation

The implementation phase is the period of time during which a working system is produced and placed in operation. Implementation begins when the information systems steering committee accepts the detailed specifications produced during system design. It ends with the acceptance of the system by management as an operational success. The information systems steering committee appoints a project team to complete implementation. This project team consists of members of the design team, programmers, documentation specialists, and data entry clerks.

Five major activities take place during the implementation phase: equipment installation, coding, training, testing, and conversion. Unlike those in the system design phase, some of these activities may occur simultaneously. Auditors participate in

ILLUSTRATION 8–1

System Implementation and Operation

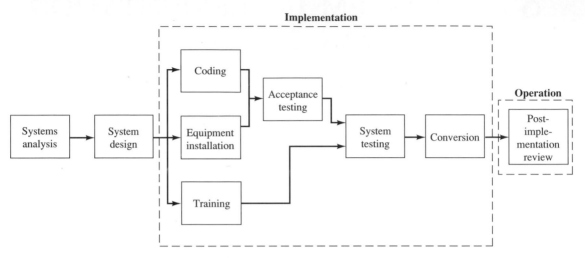

implementation by reviewing two of the activities. Illustration 8–1 shows the relationship between implementation and the other phases in the SDLC.

Equipment Installation

Frequently a new system requires the acquisition of additional computer equipment and software. The design team selects their sources during the system design phase and places orders for the equipment and software. The implementation project team then begins *equipment installation*, putting in place the equipment and software so that testing and conversion activities can occur. Sometimes the team must prepare a site for the equipment before installing it.

For a personal computer, *site preparation* may simply be clearing a desk, identifying a nearby electrical outlet, and installing a surge protector. For a mainframe computer, site preparation is much more extensive. For example, some computers are cooled by water, so plumbing must be installed at the site. Most computers require special wiring for electrical power, air conditioning for cooling, and cabling to connect the computer with other equipment. If the project team decides to run this cabling under the floor, special raised floors must be installed at the site. The team may also choose to install fireproof storage areas, a fire alarm and extinguishing system, and an emergency power supply. It must provide adequate space to locate all the additional equipment.

Next the project team installs any software packages that have been purchased. This allows programmers to verify that the equipment and packages work and to make any desired modifications. If the design team decided to develop programs in-house, the coding activity begins.

Coding

Coding is the process of producing programs containing instructions that the computer can execute. Computer code can be generated automatically by a computer, or it can be produced by human programmers.

ILLUSTRATION 8–2

Example Code Generated by a CASE Tool

Code Generated in COBOL Language

```
DATA DIVISION.
/
WORKING-STORAGE SECTION.
01 ACCRUED-INTEREST-REQUIRED            PIC x VALUE "Y".
01 ACCT-CONSULTANT-COMMISSION-ENT.
     05 ACC0UNT-CONSULTANT-NO            PIC 9(4) COMP.
     05 CALENDAR-YEAR         PIC X(3).
     05 ACCOUNT-COMMISSION-PCT           PIC 9(2)V99 COMP.
     05 ACCOUNT-COMMISSION-QUOTA               PIC 9(3) COMP.
01 AD-CAMPAIGN-ENTITY.
     05 ORDER-SOURCE          PIC X(3).
     05 ADVERTISING-JOB-NO                PIC X(4).
     05 START-AD-DATE         PIC X(6).
     05 END-AD-DATE                       PIC X(6).
     05 SERVICE-CODE          PIC X(3).
     05 MAILING-LIST          PIC X(3).
01 ALTERNATE-NAME.
     05 ALT-LAST-NAME         PIC X(15).
     05 ALT-FIRST-NAME        PIC X(15).
     05 ALT-MIDDLE-INITIAL    PIC X(1).
```

Code Generated in C Language

```
     struct acct_consultant_commission_entity_t
     {
       LONG INT account_consult_no;
       INT calendar_year;
       FLOAT account_commission_pct;
       INT account_commission_quota;
     };
     /*Derived from File 'Ad_Campaign'*/
     struct ad_campaign_t
     {
       RAW order_source;
       CHAR advertising_job_no[4];
       RAW service_code;
       DATE ad_start_date;
       DATE ad_end_date;
       CHAR mailing_list;
     };
```

Code Generation.   Many organizations use CASE tools to automate the process of developing new information systems. During the implementation phase, project teams use the CASE tool to generate computer code. The tool reads the design specifications that the team prepared (on the computer using the same CASE tool) during the design phase. From these, the CASE software produces the code in the computer language selected by the team. The tool also generates a description of how the data is stored, called the *database definition*. Using a CASE tool for code and database generation greatly speeds the development process. Illustration 8–2 shows examples of computer-generated code in two computer languages.

AIS in Practice

An implementation error, sometimes called the **Year 2000 Issue,** has information system managers worldwide concerned. Many computer programs, when processing dates, store only the last two digits of the year. Programmers assumed that the first two digits would always be "19." They never thought that their programs would still be in use 30 or 40 years later. These programs assume that dates after December 31, 1999, are dates 100 years earlier.

Why were only two digits used? In the early days of computers, storage was expensive. Furthermore, much data input occurred with punched cards containing only 80 columns. Using only the last two digits to record dates used half as much space and half as many keystrokes as using all four digits. In addition, some programmers used dates such as 01/01/99 and 12/31/99 not as dates but rather as triggers for certain systems functions.

The issue affects not only accounting, but also computers used to control appliances, manufacturing processes, air traffic, telephones, and climate control systems. Estimated maintenance costs to correct the programs range from $300 billion to $600 billion.

Programming.   If programs are coded by people, the project team devotes significant resources to *programming.* Whereas a CASE tool generates code and documentation for that code, human programmers must concentrate on producing code that not only executes correctly but also is self-documenting and easy to understand. This makes changes to the programs easier during the operations phase.

The project team performs four tasks during its programming activity. For each program identified during system design, the team develops its logic and then codes it, debugs it, and creates documentation for it.

Develop Program Logic.   The design team prepares specifications for each program during detailed specification. It identifies the purpose of the program, its internal controls, and the data records, inputs, and outputs it processes. In developing the logic of a program, members of the project team determine the code necessary for the program to accomplish these things.

Programmer Teams.   Many companies find that programmers work efficiently in teams of three to six members. The project manager assigns each program to a programmer team. The team leader then assigns each module to a member of the team. A *module* is a segment of the program that performs only one function within the program, such as printing the column headings for a report.

Sometimes the project manager uses the *chief programmer team* approach. With this approach, each programmer on the team has a special function such as documenting, editing, or testing modules. This type of team also includes a librarian, who organizes the program documentation.

Structured Programming.   When developing programs in-house, many organizations adopt standards requiring ***structured programming.*** Structured programming is a modular approach that provides a standardized way of coding a computer program. This approach calls for developing a program's logic prior to coding. Structured programs

ILLUSTRATION 8–3

Logic Constructs Used in Structured Programming

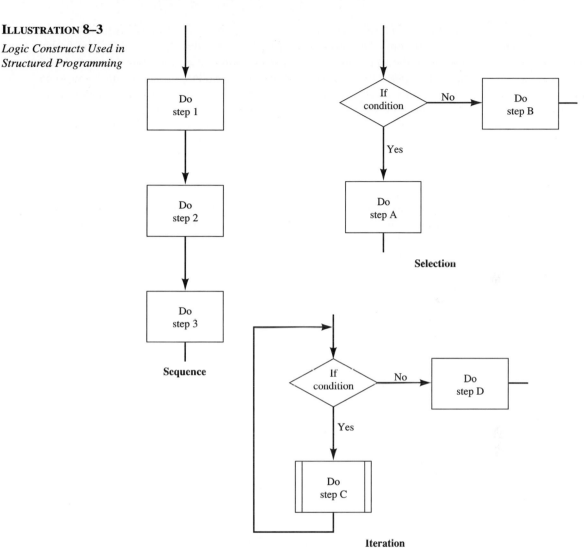

need less time to debug and test, and changes to these programs are easier to make during the operations phase.

Structured programming has two basic requirements. First, each module has only one entry point and one exit point. Second, only three logic constructs are allowed: the sequence, the selection, and the iteration constructs. Once a programmer learns how to code using these constructs, the programming task becomes easier. Illustration 8–3 presents these constructs using standard program flowchart symbols.

Code the Program.   Once the programmers on the team develop the logic for all the modules constituting a program, they begin to code the program. A *Programming Standards Manual* describes how this is done. In addition to structured programming, good standards require top-down coding and internal documentation.

Top-Down Coding.   The word *top-down* in this expression refers to the structure chart of the program. The programming team first codes the module at the highest level shown on the chart, normally called the *mainline module.* Once this module is functioning properly, the team proceeds to the second level, then the third, and so on.

In the example structure chart of Illustration 8–4, the mainline module is identified as "A-100-UPDATE-MASTER." This module causes execution of three second-level modules. One of these, "A-200-INITIALIZE," initiates execution of three third-level modules. Another second-level module initiates four modules, and the third initiates none. The entire program consists of 17 modules that the team codes in top-down sequence.

This approach is most useful when a team of programmers is coding a long program with many modules. It simplifies the process of locating errors in a program because it will be known in which module an error has occurred. In a programming course, top-down programming may not be as beneficial, because usually the programs written while a person is learning a computer language are relatively short.

Internal Documentation.   Good programming standards also require that programs contain internal documentation. These are verbal descriptions included in a program's code that describe what the program is doing. Internal documentation separates and identifies each module within a program and describes the data names or variables used in the module. Because another programmer can quickly ascertain what the module is doing, internal documentation facilitates debugging the program and making changes to it.

Debug the Program.   Program "bugs" are errors in the logic or syntax of the code that cause the program to malfunction.[1] Thus, when programmers "debug" a module, they are removing the errors from a module they have coded. Structured programming and top-down coding both make debugging easier. Structured walk-throughs are also commonly used for this purpose.

Structured Walk-Throughs.   These are useful in large projects that employ programming teams. A ***structured walk-through*** is a review of an individual programmer's work by the other programmers on the team. In conducting this review, the team examines the design of each module to ensure that it conforms to standards and satisfies the needs of users. It also reviews the adequacy of the documentation, the internal controls, and the testing procedures for the module. The team produces a list of defects and gives a copy to each team member. This process may be repeated several times during the development of a module. Frequently a programmer's coworkers spot problems the programmer would never see. It is easy for a programmer, engrossed in the complexity of the code, to lose sight of the forest for the trees. Structured walk-throughs prevent this.

Test the Program.   After all modules are complete, the programming team tests the program. When top-down coding is used, the team normally uses top-down testing.

---

[1]Grace Hopper, the developer of the COBOL computer language, first applied this term to program errors. She was working on an early model computer and kept having errors. The cause of the error was a dead moth caught in one of the components—a "bug" in the program.

ILLUSTRATION 8–4
Example of Top-Down Coding

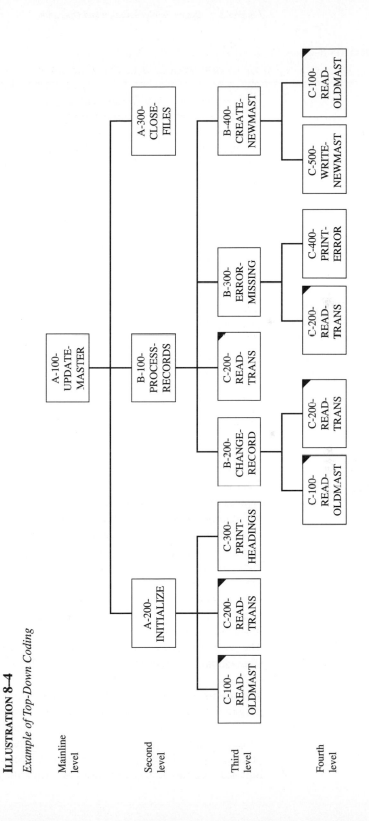

ILLUSTRATION 8–5

A Working Paper Showing the Design of Test Data and Analysis of Results

Test Transaction Number	Condition Tested	Description of Test Data	Expected Results			Actual Results		
			Description of Data Field Condition Before Test	Expected Data Field Condition After Test	Expected Error Type Out	Computer Output Number	Computer Output	Further Action Needed
1	...	...	...	...	...			
2	...	...	...	...	...			
3	Out of limit	Earnings for 3245 at $200	$5,200.35	$5,400.35	No			
4	Out of limit	Earnings for 3382 at $972	6,311.00	6,311.00	Yes			
.	.	.	.	.	.			
.	.	.	.	.	.			
.	.	.	.	.	.			
25	Illogical relation	Employee 3735 in Department 3 with earnings of $180	5,832.00	6,012.00	No			
26	Illogical relation	Employee 3862 in Department 5 with earnings of $200	6,431.00	6,431.00	Yes			
.	.	.	.	.	.			
.	.	.	.	.	.			
.	.	.	.	.	.			

A programmer tests each module as it is completed. After the last module is finished, the entire program should function according to design specifications. Later each program is tested in operation with the other programs in the system.

To test a program or a module, the programmer prepares test data. Sometimes programmers use computer software packages, called *test data generators,* for this purpose. Test data should be simple enough that the purpose of the test is evident, yet comprehensive enough to test all possible real occurrences of the data. The programmer includes in the program documentation a working paper summarizing the expected results for each test data item and the actual results produced by the program or module. The programmer team reviews this working paper during a structured walk-through. Illustration 8–5 presents an example of such a working paper.

Document the Program.   In the process of defining the logic of a program, the programming team creates several types of documentation. These include structure charts, pseudocode, memos produced during structured walk-throughs, and the working papers produced during testing. Once satisfied that the program works properly, the team also produces a listing of the program in its source language. The source language is the high-level computer language used in coding the program. Other methods of documen-

ILLUSTRATION 8–6

A Warnier-Orr Diagram

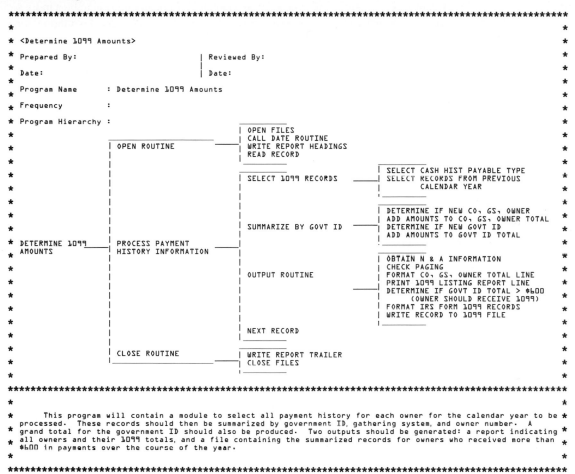

tation sometimes are used with structured programming. For example, many programmer teams use *Warnier-Orr diagrams* to describe how a module works. Such a diagram looks like a structure chart turned on its side containing pseudocode. Illustration 8–6 is an example.

At the conclusion of coding, the project team prepares a *Computer Operations Manual.* This document contains instructions for computer operators and describes the requirements for executing the programs in the system. For each program, the computer operations manual specifies the operating schedule, the data accessed, the equipment used, the kind of paper required on the printer, and internal control, security, and data retention requirements. It also describes any necessary procedures for stopping and restarting the program should erroneous conditions occur.

Importance of Documentation. In the early days of computerized accounting, programmers were primarily concerned with the size and efficiency of their programs. Today, most project teams consider the adequacy of documentation to be a more serious concern. A programming team is required to produce good documentation for three reasons.

First, documentation makes easier any changes to programs that may be required later. At some time in the operations phase, most programs require minor changes requested by system users or caused by errors in the original programs. Called ***program maintenance,*** these changes are usually made by a programmer who did not participate in the original programmer team. Good documentation is necessary for the maintenance programmer to make these changes efficiently.

Second, documentation facilitates the reviews of the programs by the project team and auditors. These reviews are needed to ensure that the system functions as intended. If the documentation is incomplete or not understandable, reviews may be difficult. This increases the costs of the development project during implementation and the costs of an audit during operations.

Third, programming and system documentation provide the basis for training personnel in the new system. Sometimes organizations use flowcharts, sample inputs and outputs, the *Procedures Manual,* and the *Computer Operations Manual* for this purpose. Some organizations develop other training materials from these forms of documentation. Training is difficult without accurate and complete documentation.

This chapter has covered the four tasks that occur during the development of a computer program and some of the preferred techniques for completing them. Illustration 8–7 summarizes the tasks performed during equipment installation and coding. Another activity during implementation is training, which often occurs at the same time.

Training

In some system development projects, ***training*** begins as soon as a preliminary system design is completed, and it may continue into the operations phase. Most training, however, occurs after the completion of the design phase and prior to testing of the system. The two groups of employees who benefit from training are the users and the computer operations personnel.

ILLUSTRATION 8–7

Equipment Installation and Coding Tasks

Equipment Installation
Site preparation. Complexity depends on equipment.
Equipment test. Find out if it works.

Coding
Code and database generation. With a CASE tool.
Programming. By human programmers. This includes:
1. Define program logic. Should be modular.
2. Write code. Use structured program constructs.
3. Debug. Use structured walk-throughs.
4. Test. Verify all logic paths.
5. Documents. Important for changes, reviews, training.

User Training.   Users include the managers, supervisors, and clerks who receive outputs from the system or provide inputs to it. Members of the system design team have primary responsibility for user training, although they may receive help from supervisors or outside consultants. User training relies heavily on the descriptions contained in the *Procedures Manual.* Members of the design team teach users the noncomputerized tasks required by the new system. They describe procedures for data entry and give instruction on the use of outputs from the system.

The design team sometimes provides training in a classroom, with lectures and discussion. At other times team members use computerized tutorials or training manuals that allow employees to work at their own pace. Developing training materials is often a major task for members of the design team during the implementation phase. In some projects, the team completes development of the *Procedures Manual* at this time. Many tasks, such as data entry at a terminal, cannot be described in detail until after programming is complete.

Operations Training.   The project manager provides operations training for employees directly involved with running the computer equipment. They include data entry clerks, computer operators, technical support personnel, and data control clerks. Data entry clerks are the people who convert accounting transactions into a magnetic form readable by the computer; computer operators work at a data center and physically operate the computer and its data storage devices; technical support personnel make repairs to equipment or software when it malfunctions; data control clerks distribute to users the reports produced. During operations training these employees learn how to use the equipment and software included in the system.

Members of the design team conduct operations training using classroom instruction, computerized tutorials, and training manuals. They use the *Computer Operations Manual* to train data entry clerks, computer operators, and data control clerks. Frequently, however, technical topics are taught by equipment and software vendors. Some vendors provide videotaped instruction courses; others offer regularly scheduled classes for their customers at which vendor personnel conduct operations training. Sometimes the best way to acquire adequate technical knowledge is through on-the-job training. Technical personnel study the documentation provided by vendors and learn by working with their software or hardware.

Testing

Another activity during the implementation phase is *testing.* This activity follows programming and must precede conversion, but it may proceed at the same time as some training tasks. Programmer teams test individual programs as a part of programming; during the testing activity two other tests occur: acceptance and system testing.

Acceptance Testing.   In many accounting applications, the output of one program provides an immediate input to another program. For example, one program may resequence a batch of accounting transactions. This sorted batch of transactions is then an input to another program that prints a report listing them. Next, another program posts each transaction to a ledger. In systems terminology, these programs are tightly coupled. It is not enough to know that each program works properly; the project team must also determine that the entire series of programs functions as intended.

During acceptance testing, the project team produces test data for the first of a series of programs. Team members then execute each program in the series and examine the validity of the last program's output. Acceptance testing ensures that the outputs produced by each program are consistent with the input requirements of the program that follows it. It is most important in those accounting systems that apply each computerized process to a batch of transactions before allowing the batch to proceed to the next process.

System Testing.   In contrast to acceptance testing, which evaluates only computerized procedures, system testing allows the project team to evaluate noncomputerized ones as well. System testing includes tests of procedures used to capture data, to convert data into computer-readable form, and to produce the outputs of the system. It concerns user and operations personnel involved in the system's routine operations.

The project team creates sample transactions representing a full range of both valid and invalid data. User and data entry personnel enter these transactions into the system. Computer operators execute on the actual equipment the computer programs to process the transactions. The project team then compares the outputs from processing with those expected.

During system testing, the project team's main concern is the system's capabilities. Team members determine whether the system has the capacity to process transactions correctly without creating backlogs. They also test to make sure that it does not produce excessive erroneous transactions or allow erroneous data to enter data records. System testing sometimes alerts the project team to errors made during system design. Such errors must be corrected before conversion, when the project team uses the system to process actual transactions.

Conversion

Conversion is the process of changing from the old system to the new one. During the conversion activity, the project team tests the new system under actual operating conditions. Conversion provides the team with the opportunity to make final modifications to the system before the organization relies on it for processing accounting transactions. The project team completes three tasks during conversion: data conversion, volume testing, and system changeover.

Data Conversion.   The first task in conversion is to change the way data are stored. The objective in data conversion is to maintain the accuracy and completeness of existing data while creating the new data entities required by the new system. The method for doing this depends on the technology used by the old system.

Sometimes, the project team converts from a noncomputerized system to a computerized one. In this case, the data used by the old system are recorded on paper in journals, ledgers, documents, and reports, which are stored in filing cabinets. The project team changes this data into a form that can be interpreted by the computer equipment. The method of organizing the data in the new system is consistent with the specifications created during system design.

This conversion process can be time consuming and expensive. Frequently, the project team hires temporary data entry clerks to complete the task. Because of the length of this type of conversion, the project team may decide to begin the process immediately after detailed specification, when the new data formats are known.

When the change is from one computerized system to another, the process of data conversion is usually quicker. The project team writes computer programs to change data from the old format to the new one. The team in this case verifies that the programs create the new data records without losing computer records or altering their contents.

From an internal control standpoint, data conversion is critical. Data contained in a new system may come from a variety of sources in the old system, and some may be computerized while others are not. Thus, the process may be a complex one. The project team concentrates on ensuring that all data are transcribed correctly. Even a seemingly insignificant error in data conversion can cause a new system to produce inaccurate reports. This can occur regardless of how carefully the system was designed, and the results of the error may be difficult to identify and eliminate. Data conversion requires thorough planning and careful attention to detail.

Volume Testing.   In a volume test, the project team executes the system using actual inputs for a typical processing period. This may be the number of transactions representing one day's, one week's, or one month's processing. These transactions are posted to copies of the actual data records created during data conversion. The test produces all outputs required by the system.

The purpose of volume testing is to determine how well the system works under an actual processing load. Often an inefficiency that appears minor during system testing may create serious problems when a new system attempts to handle a realistic number of transactions. During a volume test the project team discovers these inefficiencies and corrects them before the organization becomes dependent on the new system. A project team may repeat the volume test several times before all problems in the system are discovered and corrected.

Changeover.   After the new system has passed volume testing, the project team makes it operational. They call this task *system changeover.* The four alternative approaches to changeover are the direct approach, a pilot system, parallel operation, and system phase-in.

Direct Changeover.   Using this approach, the project team places the new system in operation and immediately ceases operating the old one. Direct changeover avoids the costs and inconvenience of the other approaches. It is a viable alternative for noncritical systems that involve simple processes and few people.

In most cases, however, unexpected problems surface during changeover. If this occurs with direct changeover, the old system is not available as a backup. The organization must function without any system until the problems with the new one are corrected. Because an organization cannot afford to do this for most accounting applications, the approach is seldom used.

Pilot System.   The project team may decide to implement the system first within a limited segment of the organization, such as a department, sales region, or a subsidiary. The team members correct the unexpected problems in this pilot system before introducing the system throughout the organization. In this way, the unexpected problems affect only a portion of the organization.

However, a system that works well in one department or region may not work as well in others. Furthermore, the high transaction volume of organizationwide implementation may produce problems that do not exist in the more limited pilot system. In some cases, a pilot system is a useful approach when used with parallel operation.

Parallel Operation.   Using ***parallel operation,*** the project team independently processes actual data on both the old system and the new one. Team members then compare the results from both systems and reconcile any differences. If differences arise because the new system functions improperly, they correct it before the organization becomes reliant on it. The old system continues to operate as a backup.

Because parallel operation is the safest approach to system changeover, it is also a common one. But this alternative requires that all operations be performed twice: once using the old documents, procedures, and programs, and once using the new ones. Often employees dread parallel operation because it doubles their workloads. If they are already working at near capacity, parallel operation may require extended overtime work. For this reason, the organization may choose to hire temporary workers to help the full-time employees.

Phase-in.   In some situations, the project team may choose to phase in the new system. With phase-in, team members implement portions of the new system one at a time until the entire new system is functioning properly. For example, they may decide to implement data entry procedures first. When all problems with data entry have been eliminated, they change to the new procedures for ad hoc reporting. Finally, after this works well, they use the procedures and programs for generating routine reports. This produces a working system acceptable to the users.

Phase-in limits the problems that can arise during changeover to those associated with the current portion of the system. This makes it easier to correct problems, and it helps control their impact. However, the characteristics of many systems do not allow phase-in. For example, the design of the system may dictate that data entry, ad hoc reporting, and routine reporting change simultaneously. In these cases, the design team must convert all procedures at the same time. Illustration 8–8 summarizes the advantages and disadvantages of each approach to changeover.

ILLUSTRATION 8–8

Approaches to System Changeover

Direct Changeover
Stop the old system and start the new one simultaneously.
  (A low-cost alternative, but it provides no backup system if implementation problems occur.)

Pilot System
Implement the new system first in only one department or division.
  (Any implementation problems affect only the division, but pilot may not disclose all such problems.)

Parallel Operation
Operate old and new systems simultaneously.
  (Provides a backup system but is more expensive.)

Phase-in
Implement new system one portion at a time.
  (Limits extent of implementation problems but may not be possible with some systems.)

User Sign-off

Of the four alternatives to system changeover, parallel operation is the most common. It may continue for several days with a personal computer system or for several months with a mainframe. The design team continues parallel operation until the two systems produce consistent outputs over a number of processing cycles. Once the design team and users are satisfied with the new system, a manager in the affected user department signs an agreement accepting the system. This agreement, called *user sign-off,* indicates that the users are satisfied with the system. It marks the end of the system development project. Illustration 8–9 summarizes the tasks performed during training, testing, and conversion.

Auditor Involvement in Implementation

Auditors devote more time to the implementation phase than to systems analysis, but less than to system design. They perform critical tasks during two implementation activities.

During *system testing,* auditors review the adequacy of the test data and the results of the tests. Their primary concern is that the test data adequately evaluate the internal controls in the system. If system test documentation does not show that control measures are functioning properly, auditors may produce their own test data to evaluate these controls. If the controls are not functioning, auditors insist on modifications to the system before proceeding with conversion.

In the *conversion* activity, auditors ensure the adequacy of data conversion procedures. They review the plans for conversion prior to its start, and they determine that these plans will maintain accurate data during changeover. After data conversion is complete, auditors satisfy themselves that data in the new records are complete and consistent with data contained in the old ones. Because accurate data conversion is so critical to the accuracy of accounting reports, the project team usually appreciates this independent check on their activities.

This review of the data conversion procedures and results does not terminate the auditors' involvement in a new system. Auditors are again involved during reviews that they make in the operations phase of the SDLC.

ILLUSTRATION 8–9

Training, Testing, and Conversion Tasks

Training
User training. Rely on written procedures.
Operations training. Operations manual and vendor training.

Testing
Acceptance testing. Execute a series of programs.
System testing. All computerized and noncomputerized procedures.

Conversion
Data conversion. Accuracy is critical.
Volume testing. With a normal processing volume.
Changeover. Safest approach is parallel operation.

System Operations

The operations phase is the period of time during which the system functions as a provider of accounting information. As the last phase in the SDLC, it is the objective of the system development process. A well-designed accounting system, requiring from six months to three years to develop, typically operates from 5 to 10 years before being replaced. Accountants are involved in three activities during the operations phase: post-implementation review, system maintenance, and accounting for systems costs.

Post-Implementation Review

The *post-implementation review* follows the completion of a system development project. This analysis and appraisal of the new system usually occurs about six months after conversion. Its purpose is to determine if the new system meets the objectives established for it during systems analysis.

Responsibility for the Review.   The information systems steering committee appoints a review team to conduct the post-implementation review. The review team normally consists of one or two systems analysts who participated in the development process from systems analysis through implementation. It should also include someone impartial, who did not work on the development project. Sometimes the committee appoints an internal auditor to the review team for this reason.

The systems analysts on the review team know the assumptions made when the system was designed and understand how the system was intended to work. Thus, during the review they center their attention on appraising the system rather than on learning about its design. The auditor brings expertise in auditability and controls to the review team. The review provides the auditor with an opportunity to learn about the system from analysts who designed it. This knowledge is valuable when the auditor conducts periodic operational audits throughout the operations phase.

Procedures in the Review.   In its review, the team evaluates the outcome of the system design project. Its members estimate the costs and benefits of the system and compare them to those predicted during development. They identify the source of differences between actual and predicted costs. They determine the adequacy of the documentation provided by the design team and the implementation project team. The review team also evaluates user satisfaction with the system, and the adequacy of its internal controls.

Evaluating Costs and Benefits.   The first step in the review is to estimate the costs and benefits of the system. The review team calculates the initial costs of developing the system. Because the system has operated for several months, it also develops accurate estimates of ongoing costs and savings. The review team calculates these and compares them to the costs and benefits projected during systems analysis. This provides the analysts on the team with feedback concerning the accuracy of the cost–benefit analysis that they performed when determining economic feasibility. This feedback aids them when performing another feasibility analysis for a later project. Illustration 8–10 contains such an evaluation of the cost–benefit analysis.

The review team then determines why actual costs differ from predicted costs. Differences sometimes arise from uncontrollable sources such as unexpected price

ILLUSTRATION 8–10

Evaluation of Cost–Benefit Analysis

	Estimated	*Actual*
Initial cost:		
Installation	$ 12,000	$ 20,000
Initial programming	72,000	85,800
Training and parallel systems cost	36,000	45,000
Total initial cost	$120,000	$150,800
Annual operating costs and savings:		
Salaries of computer personnel	$104,000	$120,000
Power and supplies	21,000	22,000
Computer rental	43,200	45,000
Total	$168,200	$187,000
Less: Salary savings	267,000	230,000
Net cost savings	$ 98,800	$ 43,000

changes, policy changes, or changes in the economic environment of the organization. In other cases, differences originate from controllable sources that include inaccurate estimates or inefficiencies in the development process. The review team learns by identifying these sources and is able to correct for them in future projects.

Evaluating Documentation.   During the post-implementation review, the review team evaluates the adequacy of the documentation for the new system. Preparing adequate documentation during a project is important because auditors review documentation as a part of operational and financial audits. Adequate documentation also aids systems analysts when they investigate future problems with the system. Furthermore, an examination of documentation is an efficient way to begin the other procedures in the post-implementation review.

In studying the phases of the SDLC, you have learned about three types of documentation: *Design documentation* includes the working papers produced by the design team when developing detailed specifications for the system; *user documentation* describes the features of the system that user personnel need to know to perform their jobs; *operations documentation* provides similar information for personnel in the MIS department. Illustration 8–11 describes the contents of an adequate documentation package.

Evaluating User Satisfaction.   The objective of a post-implementation review is to determine whether a new system meets its objectives. An effective way of doing this is to find out users' reactions to the system. In many cases, users initiated the development process. Such a system cannot be considered a success unless these users think that the objectives of the system have been met.

Commonly the review team determines user satisfaction by conducting interviews with key users or supervisors within the user departments. If there are many users, the team may develop questionnaires for this purpose.

ILLUSTRATION 8–11

A System Documentation Package

Development Documentation
Existing system description (from preliminary survey)
Cost–benefit analysis (from feasibility study)
System specifications, including:
    Sample outputs
    Sample input
    Data models
    Description of data storage methods
    Program documentation, including:
        Programming standards manual
        Program narratives
        Structure charts
        Pseudocode
        Test data and test runs
        Program listings
Acceptance test descriptions
Conversion results, including:
    File conversion procedures
    Volume testing results
    Changeover schedule
User sign-off agreement

User Documentation
Procedures manual
Training manuals

Operations Documentation
Operations manual, including a program operating schedule. For each program:
    Files accessed
    Equipment required
    Special requirements for printing, security, and file retention

---

Input from users during the review identifies shortcomings in the system design that are to be avoided in later projects. Additionally, the team may identify problems that can be corrected easily by changes to the system's programs or procedures.

Evaluating Internal Controls. Frequently, the review team includes an auditor to evaluate the effectiveness of internal control in the new system. Auditors evaluate controls as a part of their routine operational and financial audits. However, by examining them during the post-implementation review, an auditor identifies material control weaknesses before they have a widespread effect on the accuracy of the accounting records.

The review team pays special attention to the *error correction procedures* in the new system. Errors may be introduced into accounting data either on input, as transactions are recorded in computer-readable form, or during processing by computer programs. Many control measures, called *detective controls,* are included in accounting systems to identify these erroneous transactions before they are posted to a ledger. Error correction procedures provide a method of correcting these erroneous transactions and reentering them into computer processing.

In reviewing error correction procedures, the team looks for either of two possible occurrences. Sometimes these procedures may identify excessive erroneous transactions, which indicates to the auditor that additional *preventive controls* are needed in the system to stop these errors. On the other hand, the system may identify few errors, which may indicate that additional detective controls are needed. Error correction procedures provide the auditor with an accurate indicator of the adequacy of internal control.

Reasons for Performing the Review.   A post-implementation review may seem unnecessary. After all, at this time the system is completed, the project team has disbanded, and users have signed off indicating acceptance of the system. Nevertheless, there are four benefits from conducting a post-implementation review.

First, the review provides the design team with information that could improve future projects. It identifies shortcomings that can be avoided in future designs and improves the abilities of analysts to estimate costs and benefits. Second, the review occurs soon after conversion. If the system has serious shortcomings, these can be corrected promptly before excessive costs result. Third, the knowledge that a review will be performed motivates the members of the design and project teams. They are more thorough in their tasks knowing that a review team will later examine their work. Finally, the review provides another opportunity to evaluate the performance of MIS personnel. The success of future design projects depends on how effectively their skills are utilized.

Although the procedures of the post-implementation review consist of an examination of past actions, the focus of the review is on the future. A review is successful and worthwhile when it benefits future system development projects.

System Maintenance   An activity that takes place throughout the life of a system is the maintenance of both computer equipment and computer software.

Equipment maintenance is an ongoing activity performed by technical personnel. Usually the MIS department employs technical specialists for this purpose. Sometimes the organization enters into contracts with vendors to maintain selected pieces of equipment for a monthly fee. Accountants are only indirectly concerned with equipment maintenance.

Accountants and other users frequently initiate *program maintenance*. These are the inevitable minor changes to existing systems during the operations phase. Users submit requests for program maintenance whenever they identify improvements for the inputs, programs, or outputs of a system. Program maintenance also occurs when a malfunction in an accounting system requires unplanned changes.

Planned System Improvements.   Users' needs for information change rapidly, and accounting systems must adapt to new information needs. As users identify potential improvements, they submit program change requests to the chief information officer

(CIO), who refers the requests to the information systems steering committee. If they think a change has merit, they assign an analyst to conduct a preliminary survey. If the user's change is a minor one, however, the CIO assigns it to a maintenance programmer for implementation.

As you can see, the difference between a change that requires a new system and one that requires only system maintenance is a matter of degree. A major change requires a development project; a minor change requires maintenance. As a guideline, system maintenance changes are those small enough to be accomplished by one person rather than by a project team.

Unplanned Changes.   During the implementation phase the project team tests each individual program and then tests all the programs operating together. Ideally, they test every logic path in every program and every possible type of transaction. In reality, complete testing is difficult to achieve.

Sometimes the project team overlooks a possible combination of events or an unusual type of transaction, and the system is incapable of processing it. When this occurs, a program in the system terminates abnormally, and the system does not produce the desired output. Computer operators then call a maintenance programmer to modify the program. This unplanned maintenance is common in new systems; occasionally it is necessary even after a system has been operational for many years.

Controlling System Maintenance.   Because software maintenance is unavoidable, an organization must adopt measures to control it. Anytime a programmer changes an accounting program, there is a risk that the change may be improper or that the change will not be recorded in program documentation. For example, an unscrupulous programmer may make a program change that is intended to defraud the organization. Such a change would be difficult for anyone else to discover.

When changes are made, the maintenance programmer should enter them in a *program change record*. This record is usually a form included in the program documentation. It shows the date and nature of the change, the name of the programmer making it, and the approval of a supervisor. A supervisor signs the program change record indicating approval only after reviewing the change with the programmer and examining the updated program documentation. Auditors sometimes review the program change records for critical programs when studying internal control for a system.

Another good procedure is to refer all planned system improvements to the steering committee. The committee reviews the change and considers its impact on all users before they authorize a programmer or project team to implement it.

Unplanned changes are more difficult to control. Usually they occur in an emergency when there is insufficient time for review by the steering committee or CIO. Typically, all computer processing is halted while a maintenance programmer consults program documentation and attempts to isolate the cause of the problem. Once the cause is found, the programmer's main objective is to get the program working properly as quickly as possible. Unplanned maintenance presents the greatest risks and should always be reviewed later by the CIO and approved by the steering committee.

System maintenance consists of equipment maintenance, planned system improvements, and unplanned program changes. Accountants are involved in the last two forms. They often originate requests for system improvements, and auditors review approvals for program changes when studying internal control. Another activity in the operations phase that involves accountants is accounting for systems costs.

Accounting for Systems Costs

Developing and operating computerized information systems are costly activities; many organizations use responsibility accounting systems to control these costs. They trace the costs to a responsibility center and hold the manager of the center responsible for them. Accountants participate in deciding how this is done. The two kinds of systems costs are the initial costs of developing and implementing the system, and the ongoing costs of operating it. A responsibility accounting system charges each to responsibility centers.

Development Costs. Development costs include expenditures for supplies, equipment, and salaries of personnel working in a system development project. These costs may vary from a few thousand to a few million dollars, depending on the size of the project. In accounting for these costs, the organization must choose between two alternatives: allocating them to specific user departments or including them in general overhead. Each approach may be appropriate in certain circumstances.

Allocating Development Costs. A fair method of accounting for development costs recognizes that the departments benefiting from a system should bear its costs. Thus, many organizations choose to assign development costs to specific user departments. The most common approach is to allocate these costs to the responsibility center of the manager who submits the project proposal. This gives the manager a personal interest in the success of the project and motivates the manager to cooperate with the project team. The manager is more willing to assign personnel to it and wants to see the project completed on schedule. Furthermore, the manager cannot propose a project unless it produces enough benefits for the responsibility center to recover its costs.

This is a reasonable approach for those systems that clearly benefit a single department; however, in many cases this department may not be able to afford the system. Even though a proposed system is beneficial for the organization, a manager may reject it rather than absorb its costs in the department's budget. For this reason, some organizations simply include development costs as general overhead.

Development Costs as General Overhead. Advocates of this approach recognize that an improved system in any department or division benefits the entire organization. They argue that the costs of a new system should be included in general overhead.

With this approach, the costs of a new system are traced to a high-level responsibility center, such as at the organization or plant level. They are then allocated to all lower-level responsibility centers. In this way the costs are borne by all departments. This approach avoids the possibility that a manager might reject a beneficial system because of its effect on a departmental budget.

The disadvantage of including development costs in general overhead is that this approach offers individual managers no incentive to control development costs. Because the user department is not charged for these costs, its manager may propose projects that are unnecessary or unprofitable. Furthermore, the manager may not actively support the project because cost overruns do not adversely impact his or her performance reports.

Many organizations adopt a combination of these two methods of accounting for system development costs. Some allow the information systems steering committee to select a method for each individual project. Before selecting an accounting method, the committee evaluates the user managers' support for the project, the department's ability to pay for it, and its benefits to the entire organization. Other organizations establish a consistent policy in which all systems analysis costs are included in general overhead, and design and implementation costs are allocated to the proposing manager's responsibility center. This compromise approach provides the manager with incentives for cost control while not burdening the user department with all of the costs of development. It decreases, but does not eliminate, the disadvantages of each method.

Operational Costs.   Operational costs are the ongoing costs of using the system during the operations phase. These include expenditures for utilities, supplies, equipment repairs, software maintenance, and salaries for operations personnel.

Most organizations consider these costs a form of overhead and allocate them to user departments based on consumption of services. A computerized application system called a ***charge-out system*** measures the services provided to different departments. It multiplies these quantities of services by predetermined rates to assess the total charges. The organization adopts a *charging algorithm* for this purpose. The predetermined rates may be calculated as cost-based, market, or standard rates.

Cost-Based Rates.   When using cost-based rates, the charge-out system determines the actual expenditures for operating the MIS department. These actual costs are then allocated to user departments using the charging algorithm. User departments absorb these costs as part of their departmental overhead.

This method is an obvious one to most accountants, who are accustomed to recording and allocating other overhead costs. It requires the recovery of all MIS operating costs by revenue-producing departments. Each department absorbs its share of MIS expenditures based on its consumption of MIS services.

However, the use of cost-based rates may produce undesirable effects in user departments. The magnitude of the expenditures for MIS operations affects the costs allocated to each user department. The level of these expenditures may vary significantly from month to month or year to year. Because user managers have no control over these expenditures, they may react unfavorably to a responsibility accounting system that includes uncontrollable costs on their performance reports. They sometimes blame excessive overhead not on their department's consumption of MIS services but rather on the level of expenditures in the MIS department.

Adverse effects occur in the MIS department as well. Because all of its costs are recovered, the CIO has little incentive to minimize them. The use of market rates overcomes these shortcomings.

Market Rates.   In many cases, the services provided by an MIS department can also be provided by a service bureau or a timesharing service. When charging for their services, these businesses establish a market for MIS services. Some organizations choose to include these market rates in the charging algorithm for internally provided MIS services.

Market rates provide an objective measure of the value of MIS services. The costs allocated to a user department by the charging algorithm are approximately equal to the costs incurred if an external source were used. The manager of a user department cannot reasonably blame the MIS department for the magnitude of these costs. Furthermore, if the user department's manager has the authority to use a service bureau or timesharing service, the MIS department is motivated to limit its costs to compete with these external businesses.

This method is useful in many circumstances and is frequently adopted by companies who previously experimented unsuccessfully with cost-based rates. Many large organizations establish subsidiaries that provide MIS services not only within the organization but also to outside companies. However, the use of market rates may result in some MIS costs not being recovered. When user department managers purchase MIS services from outside, the organization's overall profitability is decreased. Services required by a user department may be unavailable from outside businesses, or a lack of competition may produce rates that are unreasonable. For these reasons, some organizations establish standard rates for MIS services.

Standard Rates.   Standard rates are set by negotiation between MIS and user department managers, who agree to rates that provide recovery of reasonable MIS operating costs averaged over an extended period. MIS costs should be approximately equal to market rates when the latter are available.

Organizations with highly developed standard costing and budgeting systems frequently adopt this method. Standard rates encourage CIOs to limit operating costs, so that actual expenditures are within those assumed in setting the charge-out rates. In this case, all MIS department costs are recovered by charges to user departments. With standard rates, charges to user departments are solely based on their consumption of services. Thus, any variation in a user department's MIS overhead charge results from changes in its activity, not from changes in expenditure level within the MIS department. These are controllable by the user department's manager.

Standard rates overcome the disadvantages of cost-based rates and are usable when market rates do not exist; however, setting them requires skill and effort. Managers with different objectives and perspectives must agree, and like standard costs for material, labor, and factory overhead, rates must be revised periodically.

The three methods for determining costs included in a charging algorithm are cost-based, market, or standard rates. The charging algorithm multiplies these rates by measures of system usage, such as time or computer memory used. These algorithms may become very complex; Illustration 8–12 shows the charging algorithm from an actual company. Illustration 8–13 summarizes the advantages and disadvantages of the methods of accounting for systems costs.

ILLUSTRATION 8–12

A Charging Algorithm

$$\text{Cost/Job} = A_0 + F_1\left[\sum_{n=1}^{n=n}[A_1(\theta_{CPU-X} + 1.5\,\theta_{CPU-Y})\right.$$

$$\left. + A_2\theta_{I/O} + A_3(\theta_{CPU-X} + 1.5\,\theta_{CPU-Y} + \theta_{I/O})\,(B)\,(.80 + .001B)]\right]$$

$$+ F_1\left[\sum_{n=1}^{n=n}(A_4T_{nr} + A_5D_{nr} + A_6C_{nr})\right]$$

$$\text{Cost/Month} = A_7D_r + A_8C_r$$

where

$A_0, A_1, A_2, A_3, A_4, A_5, A_6, A_7, A_8,$ and A_9 are charging rates

F_1	= Factor dependent on priority requested
n	= Job step number
θ_{CPU-X}	= CPU time in hours on Model X
θ_{CPU-Y}	= CPU time in hours on Model Y
$\theta_{I/O}$	= Input-output time
B	= Main storage requested in thousands of bytes
T_{nr}	= Number nonresident tape data sets used
D_{nr}	= Number nonresident disk data sets used
C_{nr}	= Number nonresident data cell data sets used
D_r	= Thousands of bytes of disk resident storage
C_r	= Thousands of bytes of data cell resident storage

Summary

This chapter describes the last two phases of the system development life cycle. During the implementation phase, a project team produces a working system from design specifications and places this system in operation. The operation phase is the period of time during which the system functions as a provider of accounting information; it may last for many years.

Five activities take place during the implementation phase: equipment installation, coding, training, testing, and conversion. During this phase, the project team completes a documentation package for the system. Good documentation facilitates later changes and reviews of the system and provides a source of training materials for users and operations personnel. Auditors participate in implementation by reviewing the project team's tests of internal control and its data conversion procedures. The end of this phase occurs when a user department manager signs off, indicating acceptance of the system.

This chapter describes three activities that involve accountants during the operations phase. They are the post-implementation review, system maintenance, and accounting for systems costs. System development costs may be allocated to the user department proposing the system, or they may be included in general overhead. System operating costs may be allocated to user departments based on cost-based rates, market rates, or standard rates. A later chapter describes a fourth activity during system operations—conducting reviews of the computerized system.

ILLUSTRATION 8–13

Accounting for Systems Costs

Development Costs. May choose to
1. *Allocate to user department proposing the system.*
   Provides incentive to limit development costs.
   Provides incentive to avoid unprofitable systems.
   May prevent development of beneficial systems.
2. *Include in general overhead.*
   Recognizes the system's benefits to entire organization.
   Provides little user department incentive to limit developmental costs.

Operational Costs. Allocate to user departments based on
1. *Cost-based rates.*
   All MIS expenditures are borne by those departments consuming MIS services.
   Allocated costs are uncontrollable in user departments.
2. *Market rates.*
   Allocated costs are objectively determined.
   Provides incentive to limit MIS expenditures.
   A market rate for equivalent services may not exist.
3. *Standard rates.*
   Provides recovery of MIS expenditures over long term.
   Provides incentive to limit MIS expenditures.
   May be difficult to set.

Key Terms

charge-out system   A system used to measure the information systems services provided to user departments and to allocate to them their share of ongoing operational costs.

conversion   The implementation phase process of changing from using the old system to using the new one.

equipment installation   The implementation phase process of putting in place the equipment and software required for a new system.

parallel operation   The most common form of system changeover, in which both old and new systems operate simultaneously for a period of time.

post-implementation review   An analysis and appraisal of a new system conducted by a review team several weeks after conversion to determine whether the new system meets its objectives.

program maintenance   The planned or unplanned changes to computer programs made during the operations phase.

programming   The implementation phase process of developing program logic, and of coding, debugging, testing, and documenting computer programs.

structured programming   A modular approach to writing computer programs. It allows only one entry and one exit point to each module and permits only three logic constructs.

structured walk-through   A review of an individual programmer's work by the others on a programming team.

testing   A system implementation activity that determines if modules, programs, and systems work properly.

training   A system implementation activity of training both user and operations personnel.

user sign-off   A written agreement between the managers of the project design team and the user department marking the end of the implementation phase and of the system development project.

Questions

8–1. Which actions begin and end the system implementation phase? Can you name five activities that occur between them?

8–2. Why is it important for programmers to produce code that is easy to understand? How do they accomplish this?

8–3. What is a computer operations manual? What are its contents?

8–4. When in the system development process does training occur? What is involved in training?

8–5. Identify four kinds of testing that occur prior to file conversion. Who performs each kind?

8–6. How is data conversion accomplished? Why is it important?

8–7. Distinguish between four approaches to system changeover. Which is the most common?

8–8. How is the auditor involved during the implementation phase of the system development life cycle?

8–9. Who performs the post-implementation review? Why? Which procedures are followed?

8–10. What is a program change record? How is it used?

8–11. Identify the ways of accounting for

a. System development costs.

b. Computer system operational costs.

8–12. It has been said that a system design is never completely finished. What are the reasons for this statement?

Exercises and Cases

8–13.   DEFINITIONS

Define each of the following terms:

a. Detective control.

b. Preventive control.

c. Pseudocode.

d. Acceptance test.

   e. Chief programmer team.
   f. Charge-out system.
   g. Volume testing.

8–14. PROJECT TEAMS

Project teams are used during all four phases of the system development life cycle. Which personnel are assigned to the project team during

   a. Systems analysis?
   b. System design?
   c. Implementation?
   d. Post-implementation review?

8–15. PERT DIAGRAM

Site preparation for a computer installation may consist of the following activities:

Activity	Time Estimate
a. Select site.	4 weeks
b. Prepare site plan.	2 weeks
c. Approve site plan.	1 week
d. Install electrical wiring.	2 weeks
e. Add false floor.	2 weeks
f. Install air conditioning (may be done after event *d* is completed).	1 week
g. Install air ducts and cooling water pipes.	3 weeks
h. Add overhead racks.	3 weeks
i. Complete building inspection (to be done after events *d, e, f, g,* and *h* are completed).	2 weeks
j. Clean site.	1 week

Required:

Prepare a PERT network diagram for the activities involved in site preparation.

8–16. GANTT CHART

Prepare a Gantt chart for the site preparation activities shown in Exercise 8–15.

8–17. PERT DIAGRAM

Equipment installation for a new computer system may be described by the following activities:

Activity	Time Estimate
a. Review site.	1 week
b. Select software package.	6 weeks
c. Receive equipment.	4 weeks
d. Inspect equipment.	1 week
e. Install equipment.	1 week
f. Test equipment (to be done after activities *b* and *e* are completed).	3 weeks
g. Accept equipment.	1 week

Required:

Prepare a PERT network diagram for the activities involved in equipment installation.

8–18.   GANTT CHART

Prepare a Gantt chart for the equipment installation activities shown in Exercise 8–17.

8–19.   DOCUMENTATION

Look at the two columns that follow. The left one lists 6 categories of documentation produced during system design and implementation. The right column lists 18 elements of documentation related to the categories.

Categories	*Elements*
a. System documentation.	1. Flowcharts showing the flow of information.
b. Program documentation.	2. Procedures needed to balance, reconcile, and maintain overall control.
c. Operations documentation.	3. Storage instructions.
d. User documentation.	4. Contents and format of data to be captured.
e. Library documentation.	5. Constants, codes, and tables.
f. Data entry documentation.	6. Verification procedures.
	7. Program flow diagrams and decision tables.
	8. Report distribution instructions.
	9. Messages and programmed halts.
	10. Procedures for backup files.
	11. Retention times.
	12. Source listings.
	13. Instructions to show proper use of each document.
	14. A complete history from planning through installation.
	15. Restart and recovery procedures.
	16. Rules for handling blank spaces.
	17. Instructions to ensure the proper completion of all input forms.
	18. List of programs in a system.

Required:

Match each of the elements of documentation with the category in which it should be found. Use every element only once.

(CIA Adapted)

8–20.   DOCUMENTATION

The documentation of data processing applications is an important step in the design and implementation of any computer-based system. Documentation provides a complete record of data processing applications. However, documentation is a phase of systems development that often is neglected. Even though documentation can be tedious and time-consuming, the lack of proper documentation can be very costly for an organization.

Required:

    a. Identify and explain briefly the purposes proper documentation can serve.

    b. Discuss briefly the basic types of information that should be included in the documentation of a data processing application.

(CMA Adapted)

8–21. POST-IMPLEMENTATION REVIEW

During a post-implementation review of a new system at Wilcox Corporation, a team member gathered the following data:

	Estimated	Actual
Computer rental	$ 42,000	$ 45,000
Programming	70,000	90,000
Installation	10,000	15,000
Power and supplies	20,000	21,000
Salaries of MIS personnel	100,000	120,000
Salaries of displaced workers	240,000	210,000
Training and parallel operations costs	35,000	44,000

Required:

Prepare a statement that computes the estimated and actual costs and cost savings.

8–22. YEAR 2000 ISSUE

Information systems professionals say that a computer or computer program that works properly after December 31, 1999, is "year 2000 compliant." A small industry focused on this problem has developed, and companies have spent millions of dollars to determine that their systems work properly. You can make the same determination for a personal computer that is available to you.

Required:

    a. Learn how to set the date and time in the operating system of your computer.

    b. Set the date to December 31, 1999, and the time to 12:56:00 P.M. Turn off the computer, and wait five minutes.

    c. Turn the computer on again, and check the time in the computer's clock. Is your operating system "year 2000 compliant"?

    d. Reset the computer's clock to the correct date and time.

8–23. YEAR 2000 ISSUE

Computer programs that store only two digits for the year may produce erroneous output after December 31, 1999. This occurs, for example, because they interpret the year 2001 as 1901.

Required:

Assume that computer programs in each of the following applications record the year as a two-digit field. For each, suggest an error that can occur.

a. A bank calculates interest on a $1,000 six-month certificate of deposit. The interest rate is 6 percent and is due on January 31, 2000.

b. An employee retires on December 31, 2004. The employee was hired on January 1, 1985. The employee's monthly pension is determined from his average salary and years of service.

c. A magazine publisher sells a three-year subscription that expires with the June 2001 issue.

d. A student attempts to use a credit card with an expiration date of August 2001. Before making the sale, the merchant contacts the card issuer to verify the card's validity.

8–24.   IMPLEMENTATION PROBLEMS[2]

De Efteling BV is an amusement park located in Kaatsheuvel, in the Netherlands. It entertains 3 million visitors annually from April through October, and generates revenues of $65 million per year.

Soon after the park opened in April 1996, De Efteling's new computer system began producing management reports with incorrect information. About two weeks later, the system "crashed"—that is, it abruptly and unexpectedly stopped executing. Managers identified two reasons for the occurrence. First, few users were adequately trained in using the new system, and they were inputting bad data. Second, the system lacked enough computer memory to handle the transaction volume. Correcting these problems caused a 50 percent increase in the system's implementation cost.

Required:

Describe how De Efteling could have avoided these implementation problems.

8–25.   CONVERSION

Since its inception one year ago, Instantware, Inc., a discount microcomputer software house, has used manual procedures to account for its receivables, payables, and inventory. The company receives most orders by telephone, billing customers' bank charge card accounts. Some customers order by mail, enclosing checks or money orders in payment. Instantware ships immediately on receiving certified checks or money orders but waits for personal checks to clear the bank before shipping software. Five sales representatives prepare order forms for telephone and walk-in customers, open mail orders, and complete those order forms as time permits.

Normally, a sales representative is preparing orders for several customers at the same time. The sales representatives give personal checks enclosed with mail orders to the accounting clerk. When personal checks clear, the accounting clerk tells the sales representative, who then prepares the order form. The sales representatives, all in their late twenties, are proud of their relationships with customers, many of whom place reorders with the same sales representatives.

The owner suspects that Instantware has outgrown its accounting and inventory procedures and also believes that using manual accounting and inventory procedures is a poor advertisement for a software house. Therefore, the owner has decided to install computer-based accounting and inventory systems.

---

[2]Adapted from "One Wild Ride," *Computerworld*, July 14, 1997, p. 53.

Required:

a. The owner intends to convert from a manual to a computer-based system. What should be done before the conversion activity begins?

b. Which steps should be taken to ensure that data are transcribed correctly from manual to computer-readable form?

c. How might the sales representatives' current level of autonomy affect the conversion?

(CIA Adapted)

8–26. AUDITOR INVOLVEMENT

A savings and loan association has decided to undertake the development of an in-house computer system to replace the processing it currently purchases from a timesharing service. The auditors have suggested that the system development process be planned in accordance with the system development life cycle concept.

The following nine items are major system development activities that must be undertaken:

1. System test.
2. User specifications.
3. Conversion.
4. Systems planning study.
5. Technical specifications.
6. Post-implementation review.
7. Implementation planning.
8. User procedures and training.
9. Programming.

Required:

a. Arrange these nine items in the sequence in which they should logically occur.

b. One major activity that occurs during system implementation is the conversion of data records from the old system to the new system. Indicate three types of documentation for a file conversion work plan that would be of particular interest to an auditor.

c. List the major steps taken by an auditor who participates in the system development process.

(CIA Adapted)

8–27. ALLOCATING MIS DEPARTMENT COSTS

The Independent Underwriters Insurance Co. (IUI) established an MIS department two years ago to implement and operate its own data processing systems. IUI believed that its own system would be more cost-effective than the service bureau it had been using.

IUI's three departments—claims, records, and finance—have different requirements for hardware, other capacity-related resources, and operating resources. The system was designed to recognize these differing requirements. In addition, the system was designed to meet IUI's long-term capacity needs. The excess capacity designed into the system would be sold to outside users until needed by IUI. The estimated resource requirements used to design and implement the system are shown in the following schedule:

	Hardware and Other Capacity-Related Resources	Operating Resources
Records	30%	60%
Claims	50	20
Finance	15	15
Expansion	5	5
Total	100%	100%

IUI currently sells the equivalent of its expansion capacity to a few outside clients.

At the time the system became operational, management decided to redistribute total expenses of the MIS department to the user departments based on actual computer time used. The actual costs for the first quarter of the current fiscal year were distributed to the user departments as follows:

Department	Percentage Utilization	Amount
Records	60%	$330,000
Claims	20	110,000
Finance	15	82,500
Outside	5	27,500
Total	100%	$550,000

The three departments have complained about the cost distribution method since the MIS department was established. The records department's monthly costs have been as much as three times the costs experienced with the service bureau. The finance department is concerned about the cost distributed to the outside user category because these allocated costs form the basis for fees billed to the outside clients.

James Dale, IUI's controller, decided to review the distribution method by which the MIS department's costs have been allocated for the past two years. The additional information he gathered for his review is reported in Exhibits 8–1, 8–2, and 8–3.

EXHIBIT 8–1

Systems Department Costs and Activity Levels

	Annual Budget		First Quarter			
			Budget		Actual	
	Hours	Dollars	Hours	Dollars	Hours	Dollars
Hardware and other capacity-related costs	—	$ 600,000	—	$150,000	—	$155,000
Software development	18,750	562,500	4,725	141,750	4,250	130,000
Operations						
Computer related	3,750	750,000	945	189,000	920	187,000
Input/output related	30,000	300,000	7,560	75,600	7,900	78,000
		$2,212,500		$556,350		$550,000

EXHIBIT 8–2
Historical Utilization by Users

	Hardware and Other Capacity Needs	Software Development		Operations			
				Computer		Input/Output	
		Range	Average	Range	Average	Range	Average
Records	30%	0–30%	12%	55–65%	60%	10–30%	20%
Claims	50	15–60	35	10–25	20	60–80	70
Finance	15	25–75	45	10–25	15	3–10	6
Outside	5	0–25	8	3–8	5	3–10	4
	100%		100%		100%		100%

Dale has concluded that the method of cost distribution should be changed to reflect more directly the actual benefits received by the departments. He believes that the hardware and capacity-related costs should be allocated to the user departments in proportion to the planned, long-term needs. Any difference between actual and budgeted hardware costs would not be allocated to the departments but would remain with the MIS department.

The remaining costs for software development and operations would be charged to the user departments based on actual hours used. A predetermined hourly rate based on the annual budget data would be used. The hourly rates for the current fiscal year are as follows:

Function	Hourly Rate
Software development	$ 30
Operations:	
Computer related	200
Input/output related	10

Dale plans to use first-quarter activity and cost data to illustrate his recommendations. The recommendations will be presented to the MIS department and the user departments for their comments and reactions. He then expects to present his recommendation to management for approval.

Required:

a. Calculate the amount of data processing costs that would be included in the claims department's first-quarter budget according to the method James Dale has recommended.

b. Prepare a schedule to show how the actual first-quarter costs of the MIS department would be charged to the users if James Dale's recommended method were adopted.

EXHIBIT 8–3

Utilization of Systems Department's Services in Hours (First Quarter)

| | Software Development | Operations | |
		Computer Related	Input/ Output
Records	425	552	1,580
Claims	1,700	184	5,530
Finance	1,700	138	395
Outside	425	46	395
Total	4,250	920	7,900

c. Explain whether James Dale's recommended system for charging costs to user departments will

1. Improve cost control in the MIS department.
2. Improve planning and cost control in the user departments.
3. Be a more equitable basis for charging costs to user departments.

(CMA Adapted)

8–28. MANUFACTURING CONTROL SYSTEM—PART III

Lockheed Austin Division (LAD) designs and manufactures communications and surveillance systems for the military. In the mid-1980s top management recognized the need for a new integrated information system for managing its manufacturing processes. It formed a system study team to analyze current information needs by business area. This team recommended a new manufacturing control system that would interface with LAD's budgeting, payroll, inventory, purchasing, and general ledger systems. Top management then formed a project team from all affected business areas to design a new system—the operational support system (OSS). The project team decided to implement the new system on existing hardware and identified a software package that best satisfied LAD's needs.

Implementation Experience

The system implementation process was scheduled to span 30 months from 1985 to 1988. It consisted of the seven steps described in Exhibit 8–4. During the process certain problems began to appear. These included incomplete software modules, differences in interpretation of requirements, timetable pressures, and technical problems. However, several factors enabled the project team to overcome these problems.

First was the effort devoted to communications. The project team met each day at 7:30 A.M., again near the end of the day, and during the day as necessary. The team operated outside the normal corporate bureaucracy and could reach decisions quickly.

Project reporting was extensive. Updates of project plans were made promptly, and there were weekly status reports and meetings for all participants. Monthly briefings or

Exhibit 8–4

Case 8–28

Step Number	Step Name	Procedures
1	Install software	The Lockheed IS group prepared detailed specifications for the software package. The LAD project team determined where existing modules could be modified to meet detailed requirements and identified required new modules. Lockheed IS personnel created the interfaces.
2	Pre-pilot test	The project team tested pieces of the software as it was delivered. They evaluated the results to see if modifications were necessary.
3	Live pilot test	After completing pre-pilot tests, the project team conducted a live pilot test on a small project in one work center. They gathered factory floor data, performed tests, and evaluated the results to see if modifications were necessary.
4	Initialize master files	Prior to stopping the old system, the project team loaded into the OSS the master files and other data needed to check shop orders. The old and new systems then ran concurrently for a period of time.
5	Volume test	The project team ran extensive tests using large numbers of transactions to evaluate performance under a realistic load. They studied in detail shop floor control, time and attendance, and material inventory control system results. Potential problem areas were identified and corrected before cutover to the new system.
6	Training	The project team held training sessions for all affected employees concurrent with implementation and testing. This included an overview of the entire package followed by hands-on instruction of individual modules.
7	Cutover	After implementation was complete, system responsibility was turned over to the operating staff.

reports to top executives identified accomplishments since the last monthly meeting, the schedule and budget status, and the top 10 problems facing the project. As a problem was resolved, it was dropped from the list and a new one added.

Another factor was the dedication of the team members. They were some of the most talented in the organization, were enthusiastic, and were totally committed to the project. About a third of the people initially assigned to the team were sent back to their departments because they lacked this commitment.

A third factor was the active involvement of management. When the project was started, the project team held a seminar for all managers, directors, and vice presidents at LAD to explain how the system would operate. Monthly briefings kept them involved for the life of the project. Personnel at corporate headquarters in Sunnyvale also kept informed on the progress of the project.

Members of the project team gave credit to the efforts devoted to education and training for the duration of the project. In all, about 500 people were trained on the system. This training ranged from a system overview lecture to daily classes for several weeks, including hands-on experience at the terminals.

Lockheed also relied heavily on its vendors. Both hardware and software vendors provided resources to the project team. Much assistance was in the form of on-site support and development in Austin, which greatly improved the team's responsiveness to problems.

Accomplishments

The finished product required more than four years in elapsed time and a $5 million expenditure for hardware and software. The project was large enough to be almost overwhelming, but LAD management says its business was doomed without the investment. LAD project team members enthusiastically identify the following improvements from the project.

The quality assurance function is now paperless. Electronic records replace hard copy documentation for product defects and rejects. Engineers, inspectors, production workers, and even customers can access up-to-the-minute information on their terminals. The government has approved electronic sign-off for payroll and payment processing. LAD can now meet delivery schedules 95 percent of the time. (This compares with 50 to 60 percent before the system was implemented.) LAD cut labor costs about 22 percent in manufacturing coordination and support, and productivity increased once employees learned the new system.

Although significant time and resources continue to be devoted to corporate financial reporting, the system provides division-level management with more information than was available before. OSS is a real-time integrated system that provides better operating control on a minute-by-minute basis. Whereas users used to rely on weekly or monthly reports, now they can check on a project at any time. This reporting capability makes Lockheed Austin Division able to react immediately to any opportunity or difficulty that arises.

Required:

a. How did the implementation procedures used by the LAD project team differ from those described in this chapter?

b. The project team considers this system development project successful. Do you agree? Why or why not?

c. To what factors did the project team attribute its success?

8–29.   *CORPORATE CONSOLIDATION SYSTEM—PART IV*

In response to corporate growth and to increased public reporting requirements, **R. J. Reynolds Industries, Inc.,** developed the corporate consolidation system (CCS), a computer-based system for consolidation accounting. A project team from the corporate accounting department created CCS from a general ledger package purchased from a software house. Using the package's report writer feature, the team modified its outputs to meet RJR's specific needs. Besides maintaining the corporate general ledger, CCS consolidates the financial statements of all the companies making up RJR's seven major lines of business. It also generates statistical data required for SEC reporting.

User Acceptance

Completing the new system was a high-priority project in the corporate accounting department. Nevertheless, during implementation all team members performed their normal departmental duties at the same time. In this way other members of the department could participate in the development of the system, and all had a vested interest in the system's success. Although the team relied heavily on the systems department for technical support, the team was responsible for the account structure and the reports generated by the system.

After CCS was completed three years ago, the corporate accounting department successfully completed a year-end closing the following year. The department established two criteria for the system's success. First, CCS had to generate detailed results that were consistent with summary results produced by the old system in two actual closings. Second, the system had to undergo a complete year-end audit by RJR's independent auditor.

To ensure the accuracy of the new system, a phased approach to system changeover was selected. This approach first developed the statement of earnings, then the balance sheet, and finally the statistical analysis for the SEC reports. Each phase had to be virtually complete before work could begin on the next phase. Although time consuming to implement, this approach provided accuracy and control and fostered the gradual acceptance of the new system by the staff. Their positive response was vital to the success of the project. Also, this phased approach minimized the impact of the new system on the reporting entities.

Extensions

After successful performance by CCS for two successive years, a decision was made to extend the system to the operating companies. The Winston-Salem–based companies use a common computer site, so they were chosen to be the first to adopt CCS. When completely installed, CCS allowed these companies' general ledgers to interface automatically with the consolidation system of the parent corporation. When this phase was completed, the system demonstrated the flexibility and capabilities necessary to handle multiple lines of business and the analysis needed by R. J. Reynolds Industries. However, because of new accounting pronouncements, reorganizations, and acquisitions, the system is constantly being modified to reflect changes in the environment.

Required:
a. Who constituted the project team for implementing the corporate consolidation system? Which benefits did this provide?
b. Which approach to system changeover did RJR use? What were the advantages and disadvantages of this approach?

8–30.   *YOUR COMPANY PROJECT—CONCLUSION*

The project began with Exercise 5–26 and continued with exercises in Chapters 6 and 7. It requires you to develop an accounting system for a small firm. You will now complete this system development project.

Required:
a. Complete the programming tasks for the accounting system for your company. (Be sure to apply appropriate debugging, testing, and documenting procedures.)
b. Create a general ledger master file for your firm as of November 30, 1998. This master file should contain the account balances shown in the partial trial balance

below. The file will also contain balances (determined by you) in accounts appropriate for a company in your industry.

YOUR COMPANY
Partial Trial Balance
November 30, 1998

Account	DR	CR
Cash	$ 1,200	
Prepaid Expenses	500	
Office Equipment	67,000	
Accumulated Dep—Off Eqpt		$18,700
Office Buildings	104,000	
Accumulated Dep—Off Bldgs		27,600
Accounts Payable		13,500
Wages & Salaries Payable		10,000
Common Stock		50,000
Retained Earnings		25,840
Revenue		40,000
Wages & Salaries Expense	19,000	
Office Supplies Expense	2,200	
Utilities Expense	4,000	
Depreciation Expense	6,700	

c. Obtain from your instructor a partial list of transactions for the month of December 1998. Using your company's accounting system, enter and post these transactions to your general ledger file. For realism, you may wish to post additional transactions to your file.

d. After your master file has been updated, prepare a balance sheet as of December 31, 1998, and an income statement for 1998. Also prepare any management reports called for in your system.

9   COMPUTER SOFTWARE AND CONFIGURATIONS

Learning Objectives

1. To review the components of a computer system.
2. To review the kinds of software used by a computer.
3. To understand the alternative configurations for a computer system.
4. To learn how computers are used in electronic commerce.

Introduction

In this part of the text you will learn about the technology used in computer-based accounting systems. This chapter discusses the software and hardware configurations that are the components of a computer system. Some of what you will read is a review, but there are also some new topics.

Any system consists of its component parts, a process that coordinates these parts in a defined way, and goals toward which the component parts are coordinated. For a computer system, a project team identifies goals during system design, identifies a hardware configuration, and creates software that determines the system's processes. Component parts include the computer software and hardware used by the system.

Computer Software

Computer software controls the activities of modern computers. However, computers have not always used software. Early computers were programmed by painstakingly wiring pegboards or setting scores of individual switches. This technology made computers difficult to adapt to varying applications.

In 1946 a mathematician, John von Neumann, proposed the idea of storing an entire set of instructions in the computer hardware. Thereafter, the operations of the hardware could be changed simply by changing these instructions. This concept, the *stored-program computer,* marked the beginning of computer systems as we know them today. For this reason, computer scientists refer to programmable computers as von Neumann computers.

Computers used for accounting purposes rely on two basic categories of software: systems and applications. Any organization with a computer-based information system uses many different programs in each category.

Systems Software

Systems software is a set of programs intended to execute on a specific kind of processor and is necessary for any application program to function properly. Systems software includes the operating system, utility programs, language translators, data management software, and communications software.

Operating System.   The *operating system* is a set of computer programs that direct the operations of the entire computer system. When starting a computer, an operator copies the operating system software from a secondary storage device into main storage. The operating system then takes control of the computer. Sometimes the operating system allows other programs to control the central processing unit (CPU) temporarily, but control always returns to the operating system. Illustration 9–1 summarizes the five basic functions of an operating system.

Utility Programs.   Computer manufacturers or program developers normally provide utility software. A utility program performs a specialized function such as sorting data, printing out the contents of main storage or of a computer file, or restoring data that has been deleted from a computer disk. A utility program may be useful in many different accounting applications.

Language Translation Programs.   Language translation programs convert application programs written in a form understood by humans into a form that the central processor can interpret.

Most people prefer computer languages that resemble either English sentences or mathematical equations. Procedural languages, such as COBOL or BASIC, have this characteristic. The CPU, however, requires instructions written in a binary form or *machine language*. These instructions are difficult for people to interpret, so we usually write them in a symbolic form called *assembly language*.

Programmers use software packages called *compilers* to translate a program from a procedural language into machine language. The procedural version of the program is the *source program;* the machine language version is the *object program.* Some

ILLUSTRATION 9–1

Functions of an Operating System

Job control. Keeping track of jobs submitted for processing.
Job scheduling. Assessing the priority of jobs awaiting processing and assigning them to a queue.
Library management. Making available various applications and systems programs needed in executing individual jobs.
Memory management. Keeping track of main memory usage and allocating it to individual jobs for storing their instructions and data.
Peripheral management. Keeping track of input and output devices in use and assigning output to them as it is produced by the CPU.

languages, such as BASIC, also have interpreters. An *interpreter* translates procedural language instructions one at a time, rather than translating the entire program at once. Although avoiding compilation makes it easier for users to debug a program, it slows the program's execution. For this reason, professional programmers normally use compilers rather than interpreters in developing systems.

In the early days of computers, programs were frequently written in assembly language. Today some programmers use assembly language whenever they develop programs for a new kind of computer or when they want the fastest possible execution speed. Software called an *assembler* translates from the symbolic assembly language into machine language.

Procedural languages require programmers to specify the procedures that are to be performed by a program. Other language translation programs, called *nonprocedural languages,* require only that the programmer specify *what* is to be performed. The software then figures out *how* to do it and makes it happen. Also called *fourth-generation languages,* this software makes it much easier to generate reports from accounting data files. A user of the package, such as a manager or a programmer, specifies in a nonprocedural language the data to be displayed or printed. The language translation package interprets these commands, formats the report, displays it at a terminal, and prints it on a printer. Illustration 9–2 shows how one such language translator, called FOCUS, works.

Data Management Software.   When learning a programming language, programmers learn to use input and output commands such as READ and WRITE. These commands identify to the computer system the procedure the user wants executed, and the system figures out how to do it. Programmers of early computers were required to specify in programs not only the desired procedure but also how the procedure was to be carried out. This made programming these machines complex and time consuming. Because computer systems use these procedures so frequently, computer manufacturers developed ***data management software***.

On large computers, data management software determines how to locate desired data when it is transferred from a peripheral device to the central processor. It also determines where to record data transferred from the central processor to a peripheral. This software allows a user to execute the foregoing simple commands without being concerned about the mechanics of input and output. This capability greatly eases the task of programming a new system. (On most personal computers, the operating system performs these functions.)

When designing a system, a project team selects for each set of data in the system a method of accessing the data. Each method requires that the system have a data management program to implement it. On large computers, these programs have names such as QSAM, VSAM, and ISAM. Many systems use another form of data management software called a *database management system* (DBMS). You will learn about these in the next chapters of this text.

Communications Software.   Computer networks use communications software to control the flow of data over the network. The functions of the software depend on the kind of network. Networks called *teleprocessing networks* consist of a single computer

ILLUSTRATION 9–2

FOCUS, a Fourth-Generation Language

Contents of a Computer File Containing Sales Data

Data Item	Meaning
REGION	Marketing region code
SITE	Store code
PONUM	Customer's purchase order number
DATE	Date of customer order
NAME	Customer's name
AMOUNT	Total amount of order
FILLCODE	Indicator of shipment status
PRODUCT	Product number of item ordered
UNITS	Quantity ordered

Nonprocedural Language Instructions
```
TABLE FILE SALES
PRINT NAME AND AMOUNT AND DATE
BY REGION BY SITE
IF AMOUNT GT 1000
ON REGION SKIP-LINE
END
```

Report Displayed and Printed

Page 1

Region	Site	Name	Amount	Date
MA	NEWK	ELIZABETH GAS	$2,877.30	90 JAN
	NEWY	KOCH CONSTRUCTION	$6,086.23	90 APR
		LASSITER STORES	$1,210.34	90 MAR
	PHIL	ROSS, INC.	$3,980.11	90 JAN
MW	CHIC	NORTHSHORE, INC.	$5,678.23	90 MAY
		ROPER BROTHERS	$2,879.43	90 JUN
	CLEV	BOXEY PARTS	$6,454.10	90 JUL
		ERIE TOOLS	$1,556.78	89 DEC
SE	ATL	RICH STORES, INC.	$1,345.18	90 FEB
	NASH	MUSIC CITY CO.	$1,195.23	89 DEC

FOCUS is a product of Information Builders, Inc., 1250 Broadway, New York, NY 10001.

with many attached external devices. These networks use *communication control programs* to communicate with these devices. Often such networks have terminals attached to the computer. If so, the system uses software called *terminal control programs* or *telecommunications monitors.* The network may use a small processor, called a *communications processor,* to execute these programs.

Other networks consist of many computers and external peripheral devices. Called *distributed systems,* these networks require software to properly route data from computer to computer. *Network control programs, LAN* (local area network) *managers,* and *communications routers* may be used for this purpose.

You will read more about teleprocessing networks and distributed systems later in this chapter.

ILLUSTRATION 9–3

Types of Systems Software

Operating System: directs the operations of the computer system.

    Examples: DOS
                      Windows
                      MVS
                      CMS

Utility Programs: perform specialized functions needed by many applications.

    Examples: copy
                      format
                      sort
                      file dump
                      main storage dump

Language Translation Programs: produce executable programs from source programs.

    Examples: compilers
                      interpreters
                      assemblers
                      fourth-generation languages

Data Management Software: determines how data are physically located on external storage devices.

    Examples: data base management systems
                      file management systems

Communications Software: controls the flow of data over a network.

    Examples: teleprocessing monitors
                      terminal control programs
                      network control programs
                      routers
                      LAN managers

Illustration 9–3 summarizes the five kinds of systems software. They are important because they make using computers much easier. However, the real purpose for having a computer system is to apply it to problems in accounting, management, or science. Applications software accomplishes this purpose.

Applications Software

In an earlier chapter, you learned that an accounting information system is composed of application systems such as the payroll and billing systems. In a computer-based system, these application systems rely on computerized processes to accomplish their goals. The computer programs used in these systems are examples of ***applications software***. There are three kinds of applications software: general purpose software (such as personal computer packages), transaction processing software (such as payroll and billing programs), and decision support software (such as computer models).

General Purpose Application Software.   Personal computer (PC) users become familiar with general purpose application software. They use word processing packages to prepare letters and documents, spreadsheet packages to manipulate numeric data, data management packages to handle large sets of data, and Internet browsers to access the

World Wide Web. Many other kinds of general purpose software exist. By learning the commands used by the package, PC users have powerful tools for creating and executing their personal applications.

Transaction Processing Software.   Most transaction processing software automates accounting procedures that have been performed manually for centuries. It is easy to identify the manual accounting procedures you learn in introductory accounting courses with those procedures performed in computerized systems. Although these procedures may vary from one organization to another—depending on the technology used and the preferences of management—the variations are predictable. For this reason, few organizations today choose to develop in-house programs for processing general ledger, accounts receivable, accounts payable, or payroll. They find it quicker and less costly to purchase this application software from software development companies. Frequently they modify these packages to suit the preferences of their management.

When an organization chooses to develop its own applications software, it may choose to do so using an *application generator,* which is a computer program that writes other programs. Members of the implementation project team specify to the application generator the data, inputs, and outputs of the application program. The software package then produces a source program in a procedural language that satisfies the specifications.

Because application generators are more difficult to use than fourth-generation languages, they are seldom used by managers to produce ad hoc reports. However, their use is quicker than programming in a procedural language. Furthermore, the programs generated operate more efficiently than those written in a fourth-generation language.

Decision Support Software.   A third classification of applications software consists of computer programs used in decision support systems. These programs are created to help managers make decisions. Decision support software includes computer models and most expert systems.

Managers use computer models to evaluate alternatives in both structured and unstructured decision making. *Optimization models,* such as linear programming formulations, are useful for making repetitive decisions in structured situations. You may, for example, have seen linear programming used in determining an optimal product mix. Managers frequently use *simulation models* in unstructured situations. These models rely on data estimates and require the evaluation of numerous "what if" scenarios.

Probably the most commonly used simulation model is the financial model, which is similar to a computerized budget. To create a financial model, a programmer describes in equations the relationships between income—a dependent variable—and several independent variables such as sales volume and costs. A manager executes the model to determine how net income would be affected by different decision alternatives. Several nonprocedural languages and spreadsheet packages make it easy for managers to create their own financial models. Some fourth-generation languages provide this modeling capability.

Computer models are useful in describing decisions that can be analyzed as algorithmic processes, whose relationships can be described by equations in a computer program. The inputs to the decision can be stated as inputs to the equations, and the results of the decision can be predicted by solving the equations. Many management decisions, however, do not have these characteristics and are better served by a form of decision support software known as the *expert system.*

Expert Systems.   *Expert systems* are a practical result of research in a branch of computer science called artificial intelligence. An expert system is an on-line, real-time system that uses computer programs and the knowledge of a human expert to mimic the expert's decision-making processes. It serves as an adviser to less-experienced managers who make decisions in the expert's field. Expert systems have applications in many areas, including medicine, computer system design, equipment maintenance, accounting, and auditing.

Expert systems can be written in procedural languages such as BASIC, Pascal, or LISP. However, implementing them is easier with an expert system *shell,* which is a software package designed for this purpose. An analyst, or *knowledge engineer,* customizes the shell to a specific decision-making application. The knowledge engineer uses the shell to create the components of the expert system: a knowledge base, an inference engine, a user interface, and an explanation facility. Illustration 9–4 summarizes these components.

The *knowledge base* consists of facts about a specific field and a set of rules for using those facts. These may describe objects, identify relationships, explain procedures, or encode rules of thumb that an expert has gained through experience. Typically each rule contains a condition and an action of the form "if X, then Y." This means that whenever condition X is true, then the expert concludes action Y. The knowledge engineer determines these facts and rules by interviewing the expert and encodes them as required by the expert system shell.

The *user interface* is a computer program that provides communication between the inference engine and the expert system user. Using the interface, the expert system conversationally asks the user for facts related to conditions in the knowledge base. The user interface also communicates the system's conclusions to the user. Some expert systems do not have a distinct user interface; instead, the inference engine performs that function.

The *inference engine* is a computer program that uses the data contained in the knowledge base. It first identifies information desired from the expert system user and

ILLUSTRATION 9–4

Components of an Expert System

Component	Description	Purpose
Knowledge base	Facts and rules encoded as data for the system	Provides a source for the knowledge obtained from a human expert
Inference engine	Computer program that processes data in the knowledge base	Creates a chain of inferences leading to a final conclusion
User interface	Computer program that handles on-line communication with system user	Requests information and displays explanations or conclusions
Explanation facility	Optional feature of the user interface	Explains why the expert system draws its conclusions

then combines this information with a rule from the knowledge base to develop a temporary conclusion. From this temporary conclusion, the inference engine formulates another question that is communicated to the user via the user interface. This process continues, forming a chain of rules that eventually lead to a final conclusion. Most inference engines are backward chaining—that is, they start with a final conclusion and look for rules that establish facts to support it. A forward-chaining inference engine starts with elementary data and develops a collection of facts leading to the final conclusion.

Not all expert systems have an *explanation facility,* but many of the most successful ones do. This component uses the user interface to explain to the user why the expert system reaches its conclusions. It increases the user's confidence in the system's conclusions and educates the user in how the expert approaches the decision. A similar situation occurs when an instructor returns an exam. You want to know why you received the grade you did. This explanation shows why your grade is a fair one and helps you to decide how to prepare for the next exam.

Many fields have used expert systems successfully. Because they replicate the decision-making processes of an expert, they enable less-experienced people to make better decisions than otherwise would occur. Often it is less expensive to create an expert system and distribute it throughout an organization than to hire as many experts. Whenever facts affecting decisions change, it may be easier to change the knowledge base of an expert system than to get individuals to change decision-making styles. Furthermore, decisions based on expert systems are made consistently and often more rapidly than those made when human experts are used. Finally, an expert system provides a good training vehicle for the user. By leading the user through the chaining process, the system educates the user in how the human expert makes similar decisions.

Nevertheless, most people agree that expert systems have yet to reach their potential. Creating an expert system is a skill relatively few people have mastered, so developing one is still difficult. Furthermore, many human experts have difficulty specifying how they make decisions, making identification of the rules difficult. Expert systems for complex decisions are time consuming and difficult to develop and may be expensive. Furthermore, the developer must anticipate every possible occurrence when creating the system and program the system to handle it. When a new or unforeseen situation develops, the expert system does not make good decisions.

Illustration 9–5 summarizes the benefits and problems from using expert systems.

Object-Oriented Systems

Newer kinds of translation programs, called *object-oriented programming system* (OOPS) languages, are more flexible than traditional languages. An **object-oriented system** can process very general data forms called objects. An *object* is a computer representation of a person, place, or thing. An object may include not only traditional data such as names, addresses, and account balances, but also binary data of any form. These include the visual images and audio sound tracks currently recorded on laser disks. They also include executable computer programs.

When storing visual images, organizations use a special kind of data management software called *imaging systems.* Imaging systems scan documents, convert them to binary form, and store them in computer memory or external storage devices. "Write once read memory" (WORM) systems record images on disks that are indestructible and can be read with a laser beam. This avoids the time-consuming data entry process using a keyboard.

ILLUSTRATION 9–5

Benefits and Problems with Expert Systems

Benefits

Users **benefit** from knowledge of a more-experienced person.
Less expensive than hiring many human experts.
Knowledge base **changes** as facts change.
Enables **consistent** decisions.
Enables **faster** decisions.
System **trains** the inexperienced decision maker.

Problems

Skill in developing them is rare.
Often **difficult** to develop.
Development is **expensive** for complex decisions.
Cannot handle **unforeseen situations** well.
Human experts have difficulty **specifying** how they make decisions.

OOPS make it possible to store the computer code for processing data along with the data itself. This feature, called *encapsulation*, is an important advantage of object-oriented systems. Illustration 9–6 describes this and other characteristics of object-oriented systems.[1]

Developing Object-Oriented Systems.   Traditional system development processes focus on identifying what the system does. Using them, development teams identify what people or machines do and figure out ways to do it better. Object-oriented development, in contrast, focuses on the objects, or elements of the system. Development teams identify the relevant objects, the knowledge associated with each element (its related data, call "attributes"), and the functions it must provide (its "methods" that must be programmed). In object-oriented systems, these are all stored together in the computer so that another person or program cannot obtain this knowledge without using the object's own methods.

This radically different approach requires the use of appropriate software developmental tools. It is intended to shorten developmental time, increase the reliability of the resulting systems, and make easier the maintenance of the system.

Computer System Configurations

Software and hardware components make up a computer system. Hardware consists of the central processing unit (CPU) and its peripheral devices. Software consists of the instructions that, when converted to machine language and stored in main storage, direct the activities of the hardware. All computer systems contain these components, but not all systems combine them in the same way. How they are combined depends on the

---

[1]For a synopsis of object-oriented systems, see M. Castelluccio, "Why All the Noise over OOP," *Management Accounting*, September 1997, pp. 53–55. For a technical description, see E. Bertino and L. Martino, "Object-Oriented Database Management Systems: Concepts and Issues," *Computer*, April 1991, pp. 33–47.

ILLUSTRATION 9–6

Object-Oriented Concepts

Concept	Description	Example
Object	A representation (in the computer) of a real-world entity of interest to the system	Bank customer Bank account
Attribute	The data that are relevant to a specific kind of object	Customer has a name and address. Account has a balance.
Methods	Actions that the object takes—that is, the behaviors that the object is permitted to use	Customer makes deposits and withdrawals. Account discloses its balance.
Class	A group of like objects	All checking account customers All savings accounts
Subclass	A subset of a larger group	All checking account customers with no minimum balance
Inheritance	The ability of objects in a class to pass attributes and methods to a subclass. (This allows the use of identical code on different subgroups.)	Checking account customers with no minimum balances have names and addresses.
Encapsulation	Each object is stored by the computer along with its attributes and methods. To know the attribute, you must use the object's methods. (This makes changes to the system easier since the code and data are stored in only one place.)	The name and address of a customer are stored along with the computer code required to read them.

configuration of the computer system. A project team determines system configuration during the system design process.

The ***configuration*** describes how a specific organization combines hardware devices to support the applications required by its computer system. A large number of different configurations are possible, and in the course of a career an accountant is exposed to many of them. In this section you will learn about some of the most popular ones.

Teleprocessing Networks

Teleprocessing networks connect peripheral devices at remote locations with a single central processor, usually a mainframe computer. They allow data entry at remote locations, such as in a different building or at a branch office in a different city. This data moves across a communication link to the central processor at a data center, where an application program processes it. Outputs from processing, such as CRT displays or reports for printing, may move from the CPU to the remote site. Outputs also may be printed or stored in secondary storage files at the data center.

Mainframes are also known as large-scale computers or general purpose computers. They are large, fast, powerful, and flexible in what they can do. Accountants often encounter mainframes in the data centers of large organizations. Mainframes are useful not only for accounting and management purposes but also for scientific and engineering applications. The cost of a mainframe system usually totals millions of dollars.

A configuration built around a mainframe may include dozens of tape and disk drives, hundreds of terminals, and several high-speed printers. A teleprocessing network also includes a *communications processor*. This smaller processor controls communication by the central processor with remote terminals.

ILLUSTRATION 9–7

Teleprocessing Configuration

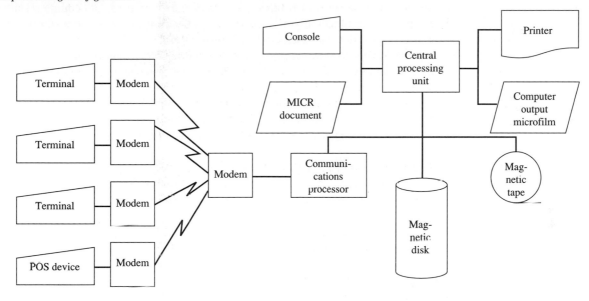

Many companies use the telephone lines intended for carrying voice signals as communication links in a teleprocessing network. When they do this, they must add modems to the network to translate digital signals coming from the remote device into an audible signal appropriate for the telephone line. They add another modem at the central processor to translate from the audible signal back to digital. Technical people say that the modem *mo*dulates and then *dem*odulates the signal at each end of the telephone line—thus the origin of the name.

Illustration 9–7 shows a typical teleprocessing configuration using a mainframe computer.

Distributed Systems

A *distributed system* contains two or more processors connected by data communications links. Thus, the processing done by the system is distributed between two or more remote locations. The communication links may utilize telephone lines, microwave radio relay towers, communications satellites, or a combination of these.

Some systems use a single large mainframe computer connected to several minicomputers or microcomputers. Others utilize several processors of approximately equal size and speed. Each processor may have its own peripheral equipment, or processors may share peripherals. A decentralized network in which users have hands-on access to processors and can develop their own applications is called *end-user computing*.

Advantages and Disadvantages.   Why have companies adopted distributed processing systems? The first and probably most significant reason is that distributed systems are so *adaptable* to the needs of users. Managers at remote sites control their own processing and do not have to rely on a distant centralized processor as in a teleprocessing system. Because each site has its own system, each site can customize or develop its own applications.

Second, in most cases distributed systems *decrease costs* of data communication. For example, local processing of accounting applications avoids the transfer of large numbers of transactions across the communication link.

A third advantage is *reliability.* A distributed system has multiple processors, each of which serves as a backup processor for the others; when one processor malfunctions, another can execute its applications.

And finally, another advantage is the *flexibility* of the distributed system. The processing capability of the network can be increased by expanding the number of its processors. This is much easier than upgrading a centralized system by replacing its processor with a larger one.

Distributed systems have disadvantages as well. *Control* of the system is more difficult because managers at remote locations can make unauthorized changes to their systems. Sometimes these managers decide that internal control measures are unnecessary and cease to implement them. This may introduce incorrect data into the network. Adequate *security* for the system is more difficult to achieve because security procedures must be implemented at numerous sites. *Technical support* is harder to provide if the distributed system employs varying brands of hardware or software. Nevertheless, companies that implement distributed networks conclude that their advantages outweigh the disadvantages.

Distributed Databases.   When a system design team decides to use distributed processing, it must select not only a configuration for the processing but also a way of distributing the data—either by replication or by partitioning.

When data is *replicated,* copies of all data are maintained at each processor location. This produces a system with faster response but increases the communication required between processors. Whenever a processor posts a journal entry to the general ledger, for example, that same entry must be posted at each processor. Otherwise, different processors in the system produce conflicting information.

With *partitioned* data, the design team assigns each data file to only one processor in the network. For example, the accounts receivable records may be stored at processor A. When a user at processor E wants to record a credit sale, the user enters the journal entry for the sale at processor E, which transfers it to processor A. This avoids the problem of conflicting data but may result in some processors being very busy while others are hardly used.

In most cases, organizations adopt a distributed database that is neither replicated nor partitioned but has some combination of the two. For example, the general ledger may be replicated at all processors that produce journal entries for it. Other data, such as those for accounts receivable, may be partitioned and kept only at those processors that use them frequently.

Local Area Networks   When distributed processing is applied within a limited geographic area, such as within a single building or office, the system is a ***local area network*** (LAN). LANs are frequently implemented with personal computers connected by a twisted pair of wires or by fiber-optic cables. A single LAN may have several processors and peripheral devices attached to it. A LAN may, in turn, be a part of a larger network called a *wide area network* (WAN).

A local area network usually contains five components: a hub, one or more workstations, a file server, a print server, and a communications server. The *network hub* is a central point for physically connecting the other components of the LAN. Each *workstation* may include a personal computer, a keyboard, a CRT display, a disk storage device, and a printer. A network user enters data, executes accounting application software, and receives output at a workstation. The LAN also contains a *file server.* This is a processor connected to a high-speed on-line form of secondary storage such as a magnetic disk drive. All workstations on the LAN may place files on the file server. A *print server* is a device that controls the high-speed printers connected to the network and can be used by all workstations. The *communications server*, sometimes called a *router* or *bridge,* is a processor in the LAN that handles communications with other systems or networks outside of the LAN. It provides an interface between the LAN and other processors in a distributed network. Small organizations that have only one LAN do not require a communications server.

Client/Server Computing

A popular development in computer networking is client/server computing. *Client/server technology* refers to the division of functions in a computer network between end-users ("clients") and processors that provide services to them ("servers"). Most computer professionals consider a client to be any workstation attached to the network. A server is another networked computer that provides specific services, such as managing data (called a "file server"), routing messages on the network (a "communications server"), or producing displays on the World Wide Web (a "Web server"). Sometimes the server is a mainframe computer.

A *client/server system* offers a number of advantages over traditional centralized networks. As client computers have become faster and more powerful, many functions have moved away from servers to their clients. This makes the systems more responsive to the needs of the users. It gives users control of their own applications at their own locations. Many organizations have significantly reduced the costs of executing routine accounting functions by moving these applications to clients while maintaining accounting data on a file server.[2]

Intranets

An *intranet* is a private network that is established by an organization and that behaves like an internal Internet. Many companies establish intranets for internal communication. Employees, customers, and suppliers access the company's intranet in the same way they access the World Wide Web on the Internet. The company establishes its own intranet server, which is very similar to a Web server on the World Wide Web. Users use a personal computer with Web browser software to read information provided on the intranet server. Users download data or send data to the intranet server just as they can on the World Wide Web. When users outside the company have access to an intranet, some people call it an "extranet."

---

[1]A more detailed overview of client/server computing is contained in A. Faye Borthick and Harold P. Roth, "Understanding Client/Server Computing," *Management Accounting,* August 1994, p. 36.

AIS in Practice

Heineken USA of White Plains, New York, a subsidiary of Heineken NV of the Netherlands, is the largest beer importer in the United States. It created Internet-based application software for real-time demand forecasting and order taking. Management named the system HOPS, which stands for Heineken Operational Planning System. HOPS enables Heineken USA to deliver customized sales forecasts to distributors by means of pages on the World Wide Web.

Distributors log onto HOPS by using an Internet browser. After entering their user ID and password, they can view their sales forecasts and enter orders. Once entered, orders are available in real time at the Heineken brewery in the Netherlands. This allows the brewery to adjust its brewing and shipping schedules.

Management believes that HOPS not only provides better information to marketers but also eliminates a lot of manual communication, lowers procurement costs, decreases inventories, and has shortened lead and cycle times. They believe that HOPS recovered their investment in it within one year.

The advantage of intranets is that companies can implement them inexpensively. They are a much less costly way of transferring data electronically than any of the other system configurations. In fact, someday they may become a primary means of communication within an organization.[3]

Intranets have disadvantages as well. Data transmitted over an intranet lacks the security features provided by other configurations. This means that unauthorized users gain access more easily to the information it contains. Furthermore, it is difficult for an intranet server to identify with certainty the user accessing it. This means that users normally are not allowed to make changes to the data that is stored on the server. Vendors currently are developing software intended to overcome these disadvantages.

The system configurations just described enable organizations to replace traditional forms of communications, such as mail, telephone, or courier, with electronic communications. Many organizations have found ways to use these computer networks in conducting business electronically.

Electronic Commerce

Conducting business electronically enables organizations to avoid the cost and time lags associated with mailing paper documents. *Electronic commerce* takes two forms, electronic data interchange (EDI) and commerce on the Internet. Most large companies use electronic data interchange. Many smaller companies that cannot afford EDI conduct business on the Internet.

Electronic Data Interchange

One way in which many companies use computer networks is through *electronic data interchange* (EDI). EDI is the computer-to-computer transmission of the data contained on standard business documents such as invoices or purchase orders. For example, when a company purchases materials from a supplier, the company normally sends the supplier a written request for materials on a document called a purchase order. The supplier

---

[3]The following article suggests some future implications for intranets: A. Kogan, E. F. Sudit, and M. A. Vasarhelyi, "Management Accounting in the Era of Electronic Commerce," *Management Accounting*, September 1997, p. 26.

responds by sending the customer a document called an order acknowledgment. If both companies use computers to process this transaction, they can transmit the purchasing and acknowledgment data over a computer network rather than printing it on paper and mailing it.

How EDI Works.   EDI requires appropriate computer hardware and software. A small company with one electronic trading partner can implement it with a microcomputer and a modem. A large company that expects a high volume of EDI transactions and many trading partners requires more powerful hardware and more sophisticated software.

There are two ways to implement EDI, by a value-added network or by private network. Either way, the company must acquire communication software that allows the computer to communicate over a communications link with another computer. It also must have translation software that converts data from the formats of the company's computer system to a standard EDI format.

Value-Added Networks.   A *value-added network* (VAN) is a computer network operated by a third company. Two companies implementing EDI each have an electronic "mailbox" on a computer owned by the VAN company. The VAN computer exchanges data between company electronic mailboxes in much the same way that a postal employee exchanges mail at a post office. People call these "value-added" networks because the VAN company usually provides other services as well.

Illustration 9–8 shows how a VAN works. Translation software changes the format of the data from that used by the sending company's computer to that used by the VAN.

ILLUSTRATION 9–8

EDI with a VAN

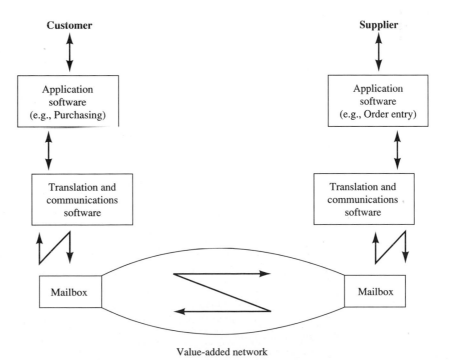

Value-added network

The receiving company has similar software that translates from the VAN's format into that used in its system.

VANs are used by small companies or by companies with several EDI trading partners. It is a relatively expensive alternative because the VAN company charges for its services. For this reason, a company with only one EDI trading partner may implement EDI by private network.

Private Networks.   With this approach, two companies desiring to exchange data electronically do not use a VAN but instead create their own private network. They agree on a data format to be used by both parties. Frequently, a smaller company will use translation software provided by the larger to make EDI transactions compatible with the larger one's computer system.

Some large companies, such as Sears and Wal-Mart, adopted EDI in order to cut costs and improve delivery times. As a part of the transition to the new system, they required that their suppliers become part of their own EDI networks. The supplier uses a personal computer, translation software running on that computer, and a telephone modem to communicate with the purchasing company's central computer. This approach is less flexible than a VAN because the supplier can communicate electronically with only one customer. But because there are no payments to a VAN company, it is less expensive to operate.

An Example.   Illustration 9–9 shows the flow of data in a private network when a customer places an order from a supplier. The customer's purchasing application system (a part of its expenditure transaction cycle) generates a purchasing transaction. Communications software sends the transaction over a communications link to the supplier's computer system.

The supplier's translation software decodes the transaction and sends it to the supplier's order entry system. This system generates an order acknowledgment transaction and sends it back to the customer the same way. The supplier's order entry system notifies the supplier's shipping system that a shipment is required.

The supplier's shipping system locates the merchandise and arranges for its shipment to the customer. When it is shipped, the shipping system generates a transaction called a *shipping notice* and forwards it via the network to the customer. The purpose of the shipping notice is to alert the customer that the merchandise is coming. The shipping system then notifies the supplier's billing system to send the customer an invoice for the shipment.

The supplier's billing system generates the EDI invoice transaction and sends it by the network to the customer, where the translation software forwards it to the customer's voucher application. The customer's voucher application notifies the cash disbursements application that a payment is necessary.

Although *electronic funds transfer* is not really a part of the EDI system, the customer and supplier may also agree to use it to make payments. This permits the customer's bank to transfer funds to the supplier's bank without using a traditional paper check. When this transfer occurs, the customer's cash disbursements application transfers payment electronically through the banking system to the supplier's cash receipts application.

ILLUSTRATION 9–9

An Example EDI Application

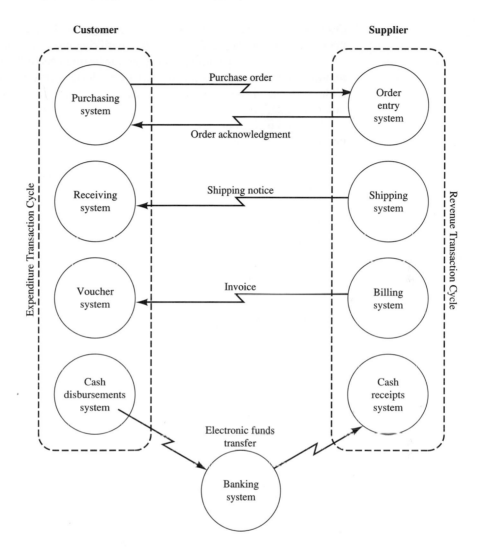

EDI Transactions.   An EDI transaction contains the same data found on a paper document in a traditional system. Companies using a traditional system produce paper purchase orders, order acknowledgments, shipping notices, invoices, and checks. The equivalent EDI transactions contain the same data as these paper documents but are encoded electronically. EDI is an alternative ways of recording transaction data.[4]

In EDI terminology, the EDI transaction is a *transaction set.* The transaction set contains not only the purchase data but also a *header* and a *trailer.* These are data fields marking the start and the end of the transaction. They show the type of transaction (for

---

[4]For a more thorough discussion of the technical details of electronic data interchange, see the following: A. Faye Borthick and Harold P. Roth, "EDI for Reengineering Business Processes," *Management Accounting,* October 1993, p. 32, and Ann B. Pushkin and Bonnie W. Morris, "Understanding Financial EDI," *Management Accounting*, November 1997, p. 42.

example, a purchase) and some control information (for example, the total amount of the purchase), and they assign a unique identifying number to the transaction set.

The EDI software combines several transaction sets of the same kind into a *functional group*. It assigns to the group its own header (marking the group's start) and trailer (marking the group's end). For example, a customer may initiate several purchase orders to a supplier at one time. The customer's EDI software combines them into a single functional group and sends it to the supplier. The supplier's software knows, when it reads the functional group header, how many transactions it is receiving and what type they are.

The software combines several functional groups intended for the same company into an EDI *envelope*. An EDI envelope may contain several functional groups of different kinds of transactions. The envelope also has its own header and trailer, which show the recipient and the sender of the envelope. For example, a supplier's translation software may combine order acknowledgment, shipping notice, and invoice transactions in an envelope addressed to a single customer.

Illustration 9–10 demonstrates the relationships between a transaction set, a functional group, and an envelope in an EDI system.

Difficulties.   The primary difficulties in implementing EDI relate to controlling the transactions and the lack of standard data formats.

Controls.   Control procedures ensure the accuracy and reliability of accounting data. Accountants understand these well and commonly implement them in systems that use paper documents. When exchanging data electronically, accountants must implement other control procedures that are appropriate for computer networks. EDI systems record control data in the headers and trailers used with transaction sets, functional groups, and envelopes. This control data enables the translation software to determine if data has been accidentally lost or altered on the communications link. You will read about other control procedures for computer networks in later chapters in this text.

ILLUSTRATION 9–10

EDI Transactions

A transaction set

A functional group

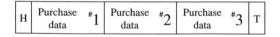

An envelope

H denotes a header.
T denotes a trailer.

Another control issue is the form of the audit trail. An audit trail provides the ability to trace a transaction from its initial record into the financial statements, and also in the reverse direction. With traditional systems, document numbers provide the audit trail. An EDI system also identifies electronic transactions with numbers. But it stores the data, and thus the audit trail, on magnetic media rather than paper. Although this makes the audit trail invisible to people, it becomes accessible much faster and more easily when a computer is used.

Some accountants are uneasy with EDI because these systems change the nature of the required control procedures. Yet when implemented properly, EDI maintains data accuracy and reliability at least as well as paper-based systems.

Standard Data Formats.   A purchasing company and a supplying company probably use different formats when storing data in their individual computers. If the companies have a direct EDI connection, translation software at either the purchasing company or the supplying company must change the data's format. If the companies connect through a value-added network, then each must convert to the VAN's data format. They could avoid translation, and speed up transfer of the transaction, if all companies used a standard data format.

In the United States, the American National Standards Institute developed standard data formats for many frequently used business documents. However, many companies and much EDI software were developed prior to adoption of this standard. Some industry associations also developed EDI standards that conflict with the national one. Thus, when adopting EDI, companies must ensure that all their trading partners have translation software that conforms to the same standard format.

Commerce on the Internet

Commerce on the Internet takes many forms. Most large companies have home pages on the World Wide Web. Many use them to sell products to the public. Small companies that cannot afford the expense of EDI systems conduct business on the Internet. By establishing a Web server and a home page on the World Wide Web, they can communicate with customers, potential customers, suppliers, and employees worldwide.

Internet Storefronts.   To the public, the most visible commerce on the Internet occurs through Internet storefronts. An *Internet storefront* is a retailer that uses a Web page rather than a store to sell its products. Many retailing companies open Internet storefronts *in addition to* stores. Some have been very successful selling *only* over the Internet. Because they do not display merchandise, Internet storefronts sell a wider variety of merchandise and incur lower operating costs than stores. This allows them often to provide better customer service at lower prices. Most Internet storefronts allow payment with credit cards, but some use other forms of cash payment over the Internet.[5]

EDI over the Internet.   Companies avoid the difficulties and expense of VANs and private EDI networks by using the Internet to transmit electronic transactions. Internet-based EDI is less reliable and less secure than private networks. But it is more interactive, easier to use, and available to more people.

---

[5]A short description of some Internet payment methods is contained in M. Castelluccio, "The Three-Cent Nickel Is Back," *Management Accounting*, September 1996, p. 45.

Companies use intranets with the Internet to conduct many forms of commerce. For example, some utilities make utility bills available to subscribers on their Web pages. A customer accesses the bill using the customer number and a personal identification number. The customer issues an instruction initiating an electronic funds transfer that pays the current charges.

Other companies use Web pages to communicate requests and receive bids from suppliers, to accept orders and send acknowledgments to customers, and to communicate sales forecasts and accept orders from distributors. As methods develop for verifying the identity of users and ensuring the security of transactions, companies will expand their use of Internet-based EDI.

Advantages and Disadvantages of Electronic Commerce

The most obvious benefit of electronic commerce is the savings in clerical costs it produces. Both buyers and sellers avoid the cost of processing paper documents and then converting them to computer-readable form. Both avoid the costs of correcting errors that occur with the processing of data on paper. For large companies that produce thousands of documents per day, the savings in clerical costs are substantial.

Other sources of cost savings are less obvious. Many manufacturing companies use electronic commerce to purchase raw materials. Because electronic commerce reduces the elapsed time required to receive the material, it also reduces the lead time and thus the inventory level necessary to maintain steady production or fill a customer order. A manufacturing company benefits from electronic commerce by avoiding the carrying costs of this additional inventory.

In merchandising companies, electronic commerce enables faster response to changes in customer demand. An order to replenish stock reaches its destination within a few seconds rather than in a few days as with a nonelectronic system. This quick response provides better customer service and increases sales.

Private EDI networks are expensive and difficult to establish. They are popular principally with large companies that have the resources to overcome these disadvantages. Internet-based commerce is easier to implement and more useful for small companies, but it is less secure, and currently it is difficult to reliably verify the user of these systems.

Summary

The components of a computer system are hardware and the software that controls it. Software can be systems software or applications software. Systems software is a set of programs controlling the activities of the hardware. Applications software programs accomplish specific business or scientific purposes. Transaction processing applications programs may be coded, purchased, or produced with an application generator. Decision support software includes computer models and expert systems.

The configuration of a computer system describes how its components are arranged. Many system configurations use a central mainframe computer in a teleprocessing network; the mainframe transfers data across communications links to devices at remote locations. Other configurations combine multiple processors in a distributed processing network, in a client/server system, or in an intranet. The selection of a configuration is an important decision in the design of a computer system. Electronic commerce provides businesses with the ability to conduct business without using paper documents. Instead, they transfer transaction data across computer networks.

Key Terms

applications software   Computer software used to achieve a specific accounting or managerial objective. When used to process accounting transactions, it is transaction processing software.

client/server system   A form of computer network that divides processing functions between clients (computers that use services) and servers (computers that provide services). Frequently clients are personal computers and servers are larger computers, such as mainframes.

configuration   A description of how a specific organization combines hardware devices to support the applications required by its computer system.

data management software   System software that determines the location on secondary storage of data transfers between secondary and main storage.

distributed system   A computer configuration in which two or more processors are connected by data communication links allowing the transfer of data between them.

electronic commerce   Conducting business electronically over computer networks. It allows organizations to replace paper documents with electronic data.

electronic data interchange   Called EDI, the computer-to-computer transmission of data contained on standard business documents.

expert system   Applications software that incorporates the knowledge of a human expert and can be used to mimic the expert's decision-making processes.

intranet   A private network within an organization that behaves like an internal Internet. Users access it with a Web browser. When users can access it from outside, it is an "extranet."

local area network   A distributed network usually composed of personal computers and used within a limited geographical area such as a building.

object-oriented system   An information system that can process not only traditional data such as names and balances but also data containing images and sound. It stores programs that process the data along with the data itself.

operating system   System software that controls the operations of the entire computer.

teleprocessing network   A computer configuration connecting peripheral devices at remote locations, such as terminals or printers, by communications links with a central computer.

Questions

9–1. What is meant by a "von Neumann" computer? Why is this type of computer significant?

9–2. What is the purpose of data management software? How is this function performed on a personal computer?

9–3. What are three kinds of applications software? Give an example of each.

9–4. Why is an operating system important to a computer system? What are its functions?

9–5. Computers use several kinds of language translation software. Distinguish between each of the following language translators:
   a. Compiler.
   b. Interpreter.
   c. Assembler.
   d. Fourth-generation language.
   e. Application generator.

9–6. What is the difference between a source program and an object program?

9–7. Name the components of an expert system, and explain what each component does.

9–8. What is an "object" in a computer system? How does an object-oriented system differ from a traditional accounting system?

9–9. Describe three ways in which companies use computer networks in electronic commerce.

9–10. Describe the differences among the three common configurations of distributed processing networks.

9–11. What are the components of a local area network?

Exercises and Cases

9–12.   SIGNIFICANT TERMS

For each of the following sets, distinguish between the terms listed:

a. System software and applications software.
b. Telecommunications monitor and communications router.
c. Value-added network and private network.
d. Attributes and methods.
e. Intranet and extranet.
f. Operating system and utility program.

9–13.   APPLICATION SOFTWARE

The administrator of Maddox Memorial Hospital would like to upgrade the hospital's information system. The current system, in place since 1989, consists of a telecommunications network with on-line terminals scattered throughout the hospital. Its software executes traditional accounting applications such as purchasing, receiving, and financial reporting. It also records services provided to patients and produces patient bills at the time of discharge.

The hospital relies on paper documents for its patients' medical records. These include diagnostic images (such as X rays), notes and drawings made by physicians and nurses regarding treatments and patient condition, and heart and brain wave patterns (EKGs and EEGs). As the hospital grows, these manual records become increasingly unwieldy and expensive to maintain. Furthermore, there is always a time lag between the patient's admission and the time the medical record is available to medical personnel. In the case of emergency admissions, this time lag can be fatal for the patient.

In upgrading the system, the hospital administrator would like to achieve two objectives. First, for each patient she wants a permanent electronic record that shows all relevant accounting and medical information concerning that patient. Second, she wants this information readily available to all authorized administrative and medical employees.

Required:

a. What kind of information system do you suggest for Maddox Memorial Hospital?
b. What characteristics would distinguish this system from the traditional one the hospital currently uses?

9–14.   LOCAL AREA NETWORK

Since the 1970s, many organizations' computing facilities have evolved from centralized mainframe computer environments to distributed networks. In recent years, one of the fastest growing forms of distributed network has been the local area network (LAN). LANs permit the transfer of information between microcomputers, word processors, data storage devices, printers, voice devices, and telecommunications devices. Many people argue that the flow of organizational communications has been enhanced by a transition from the traditional distributed network, which optimizes the use of computers, to the LAN environment, which optimizes human resources.

Required:

a. Describe the reasons why an organization would choose a distributed network over the traditional centralized computer environment.
b. Compare and contrast the characteristics of a traditional distributed computer network with those of a local area network as they relate to
   1. Utilization of computer hardware.
   2. User interaction and the sharing of electronic information.
c. Suggest three problems that can result from the use of local area networks.
d. Explain the hardware characteristics associated with a computer modem as it relates to distributed information processing.

(CMA Adapted)

9–15.   DISTRIBUTED PROCESSING

Megapolis Bank and Trust offers a wide range of financial services through a network of regional offices. The firm's present information system is highly concentrated: A large centralized mainframe computer provides services to individual offices through the use of remote data entry terminals.

Megapolis's information system steering committee proposes a major change in the configuration of the system. It recommends that each office be equipped with a personal computer that can communicate with the other personal computers and with the firm's mainframe.

Required:

a. What are the potential advantages of the system proposed by the steering committee?
b. Which system configuration would you recommend for Megapolis?

9–16.   ELECTRONIC COMMERCE

Mobil Corporation, the multinational petroleum company, has for several years used EDI in its dealings with its "lube" distributors. (These are the businesses that buy industrial oils and greases from Mobil and resell them to retailers.) Its traditional EDI system used a value-added network (VAN) to process electronic orders, shipping notices, and invoices.

Charges from the VAN totaled over $100,000 per year. Maintaining the system was difficult, because every change to Mobil's system required a change to the computer at each of the lube distributors. Furthermore, inventory information was updated only once a week. Communication with lube distributors was awkward; Mobil used a combination of phone calls, faxes, and e-mail.

Mobil replaced this traditional EDI system with a new one relying on the World Wide Web. They created an intranet that integrates Mobil's accounting and product information databases and connects them to its order entry system. Distributors access this intranet from personal computers at their own sites using a Web browser. They enter orders, modify them, review status orders, look at order history, or look up account balances. The system is simple enough that distributors can learn to use it in one day of training.

VAN charges have disappeared. When Mobil makes a change to its system, they put it on the Web server for distributors to download. Their next step is to integrate the intranet with the distributors' accounting programs that produce purchase orders.

Required:

a. What problems with its traditional EDI system caused Mobil to develop its intranet?
b. What shortcomings of intranets must companies overcome before implementing this form of electronic commerce?

9–17.   POINT-OF-SALE SYSTEMS

Pinta Company is a regional discount chain selling general merchandise in the Southwest. The company is considering acquiring a point-of-sale (POS) system for use in its stores.

Currently, three types of firms primarily use POS systems: large retailers, grocery stores, and fast-food chains. Pinta would probably employ cash registers that use light pens to read the universal product code (UPC) printed on the packages.

Cindy Brenski, president of Pinta, knows that the equipment is very expensive. She has asked her controller to prepare a report on POS systems including a survey describing the companies employing POS systems and why they have adopted them.

Required:

a. Explain briefly how a POS system operates.

b. Describe the potential advantages and disadvantages of a POS system for a company's operations and recordkeeping system.

c. Identify and explain the special control problems that a POS system could present to Pinta Company personnel.

(CMA Adapted)

9–18.   EXPERT SYSTEMS

You are a consultant with a major CPA firm and have been engaged by a client, Kindly Cat Kennels, Inc., to develop an expert system. You know that any expert system includes a knowledge base and that the knowledge base consists of a set of rules in the form IF *condition,* THEN *action.*

As the knowledge engineer on this engagement, you identify a set of questions. The expert system presents these questions one at a time to the system user. From the answers to these questions, the system determines which conditions are present. For each condition, you encode in the knowledge base the action to be taken next.

Your client wants the expert system to aid its employees in deciding if an animal is a cat.

Required:

a. Prepare a list of questions that, when answered, aid in determining if an animal is a cat.

b. Assuming a yes answer to each question in part *a,* identify the appropriate action. (*Hint:* Your actions are either [1] to ask another question, [2] to conclude that the animal is a cat, or [3] to conclude that the animal is not a cat.)

c. From your answers to parts *a* and *b,* formulate a set of rules for this knowledge base.

d. From these rules develop a chain that allows you to decide that an animal is a cat.

9–19.   SYSTEM CONFIGURATION

While attending college, Simple Simon studied finance and dabbled in the stock market. Since graduating, he has begun offering financial planning services to his friends and business associates. These are primarily small businesses and working people of modest means who rely on Simon for assistance in investment planning. He helps them in purchasing stocks and bonds and in setting up pension, profit-sharing, and retirement plans.

Simon attempts to track the performance of thousands of different stock and bond issues. He also tries to keep up-to-date on economic trends and investment opportunities to advise his clients effectively. In addition, he sometimes performs complex calculations when setting up profit-sharing and pension plans.

Simon has read about computerized databases that provide financial market and economic information on-line. He would like to get access to this information.

Required:

Configure a computer system that satisfies Simon's information processing needs.

9–20.   SYSTEM CONFIGURATION

Rex, Finney & Co. is a law firm specializing in personal injury litigation. The firm's five partners and eight associates are involved in litigating and settling claims regarding product liability, automobile accidents, and job-related injuries. As a result, they daily prepare and update legal briefs, pleadings, and correspondence with clients, litigants, and other attorneys.

At any time, Rex, Finney has dozens of cases pending. Law clerks research cases, prepare legal briefs, summarize points of law, and look up other documents. Partners review all of this material before it leaves the office. As a result, a document undergoes many changes and revisions before reaching its final form. The firm must be able to make changes to documents literally up to the final minute before an attorney leaves for a courtroom.

All these documents are prepared by a staff of legal secretaries using typewriters. Workloads for the secretarial staff change from periods of idleness to periods of continuous rush jobs. Frequently attorneys present to secretaries last-minute work requests that conflict with each other. Several attorneys have complained about being late for engagements and court appearances as a result.

Rex, Finney has a small computer that is used for accounts receivable and payroll. The partners wonder if it can be used in some way to correct some of their problems.

Required:

Configure a computer system that meets the information processing needs of Rex, Finney & Co.

9–21.   SYSTEM CONFIGURATION

Highsmith Auto Parts is an auto parts distributor headquartered in North Carolina. During the past 20 years the company has expanded to include 5 distribution centers and 48 retail outlets throughout the southeastern part of the country.

For many years Highsmith has relied on a centralized management information system. This includes two large centralized computers operating as multiprocessors and terminals in each store and distribution center. Terminals communicate with the central processors by means of high-speed data communication links provided by the telephone company. Using these terminals, employees at remote locations are able to access credit, sales, and inventory data stored on the mainframes. The mainframes also are used at company headquarters for executing general ledger, accounts payable, accounts receivable, and payroll applications.

Although the system works well, it is expensive to operate because it relies on expensive high-speed communications circuits. Recently Highsmith has begun to encounter problems with processor reliability. When the system goes down, it effectively halts data processing throughout the entire organization. Highsmith would like to find a way to eliminate these problems.

Required:

Configure a system to satisfy the information processing needs of Highsmith Auto Parts.

9–22.   IMAGING SYSTEMS

Kenwood USA Corp. is a $400 million consumer electronics company based in Long Beach, California.[6] In response to a top management edict to move toward a paperless

---

[6]Adapted from Caryn Gillooly, "Firm Goes Paperless with Imaging System," *Network World*, December 23, 1991, p. 13. Used by permission.

environment, the company implemented an imaging system that is expected to save more than $100,000 per year. The entire system cost about $350,000 and required about three months to implement.

The Application

Within the company, warranty claims is one of the most paper-intensive activities. Each day Kenwood receives about 100 warranty claims from its dealers. Since each form contains from eight to twelve pages, that amounts to about 1,000 pages each day.

With the old system, employees manually entered data from a warranty form into a mainframe system. They then stored the original forms in filing cabinets for three months. After that they boxed the forms and sent them to a warehouse. Later, questions about a form required employees to locate it either in an on-site filing cabinet or in the warehouse. Besides being time consuming, the system limited document sharing. If someone retrieved one of the copies, it was in that person's possession and no one else could use it. In addition, it was not unusual for a form to get misplaced or misfiled.

Handling invoices was also a problem. The old system printed invoices based on each day's shipments, and employees mailed them the following day. Document copies then went to a service bureau for copying to microfiche—a process that took three to five days. Twenty Kenwood employees had to share a single microfiche reader to look up invoices. If someone called with a question on an invoice, the employee had to take a name and number and call the customer back.

The New System

To solve both problems, Kenwood installed in its warranty claims and invoice processing departments a local area network. The LAN, using ethernet broadband technology, contains a file server connected to an optical jukebox, a server supporting a document scanner, several print servers, a separate server for downloading information from the mainframe, and about 30 workstations running imaging software. With the new system, an employee at the scanning station records claim forms on an optical disk in the jukebox. Later any of the 30 workstations can retrieve the image and display it on a screen or print a copy on paper.

Kenwood identifies three advantages to this system. These are the time savings in answering queries, the promptness with which they can respond to dealers and service centers, and the savings in warehouse storage space. The new system also eliminates Kenwood's reliance on microfiche. The imaging software provides automatic document indexing by selected fields such as order number, customer number, purchase order number, or date. This simplifies queries and makes it possible to answer questions while a customer is still on the telephone.

Future Plans

Kenwood plans to expand the network by connecting this LAN to the previously existing ones. This will extend the imaging capabilities to the rest of the company. They hope to have 100 workstations connected to the imaging system within five years.

Required:

a. What needs caused Kenwood to implement the imaging system?

b. Can you suggest other possible applications for this technology within the company?

9–23.   CLIENT/SERVER COMPUTING

Bank of America believes that its entry into client/server computing has been such a success that the San Francisco company is looking for other applications for the technology.[7] They call their new distributed system C*STAR, which stands for Customer Service Tracking and Reporting. They consider the system "mission critical," which means that it provides data that is central to the company's achieving its objectives.

The Problem

Bank of America (BOA) had a pair of mainframe systems that handled information important to a broad range of its customers. Although the systems were meeting their design goals, many departments complained that the complicated chargeback system for their usage made the systems too expensive. Departments incurred thousands of dollars per month in connect time, more than they were willing to pay in the long term. Furthermore, bottlenecks in the teleprocessing system caused performance to slow during peak usage hours. And users who wanted special reports had to request programming services from the information systems staff. Users already had desktop computers in their departments, and they felt that they could make better use of this technology.

The Solution

The solution to the problem was a local area network (LAN). The company had strict policies governing the acquisition of computing equipment, so the choice of hardware and software was straightforward. BOA purchased a file server and network control software and connected it with 10 workstations.

The company found quickly that it had substantially underestimated the application's processing and storage requirements. Furthermore, the bank's desktop database software package would not execute on the file server. After consulting with another company that had dealt with the problem, BOA identified database software for the file server. They also discovered a number of utility programs that would automate the exchange of data between different systems.

An automatic scheduling utility triggers the first stage of C*STAR execution. Each night, the file server receives a download of relevant customer data from the mainframe. Programs written by the bank's staff then transform the data into tables for the microcomputer database package. During the following day, workstation users read and update the customer data. At day's end, another utility program extracts the data from the workstations and transfers it to the file server database. That evening, the file server uploads new and updated records to the mainframe, and the process begins all over again.

---

[7]Adapted from Alicia LaPlante, "BofA Moves Cautiously into Client/Server Waters," *Infoworld,* June 7, 1993, p. 62. Used by permission.

The Result

Even though the file server database has grown substantially, users still get good response time from the LAN. When users request data, they use the workstation database package's menus and display screens. The movement of data through the LAN is invisible to them. Users familiar with the software package's nonprocedural language can reformat the downloaded data to satisfy their own needs.

Financial performance has also been better than expected. After considering the costs of additional hardware, software, and application development, the client/server system paid for itself within one year through savings on mainframe chargeback costs. Concerning the process, the project director said, "There's no magic bullet to getting all these different products to work together in a LAN environment. We had to put aside enough time and resources to go through a trial-and-error process."

Required:

a. What caused the bank to implement a client/server network? What type of configuration did the new system replace?
b. From the bank's perspective, do you believe that the new system was an operational success? Why or why not? Do you believe that it was a financial success? Why or why not?

9–24.   *EXPERT SYSTEMS*

Tax accrual involves calculating deferred income tax and explaining the difference between statutory and effective tax rates.[8] Audit staff accountants usually gather information needed for tax accrual by completing questionnaires. Frequently they give little attention to the significance of this information for tax planning, even though this may be important to the client.

Coopers & Lybrand has developed an expert system called ExperTAX[sm] to actively guide audit and tax staff accountants through the process of gathering information necessary for tax accrual and planning. At the same time, ExperTAX[sm] has the ability to point out the importance of the information being requested. It can be a very effective training and education tool, providing the professional with the experts' reasons for requesting specific information. Developed in a programming language called Common LISP, ExperTAX[sm] is intended to run on a microcomputer equipped with a hard disk and an attached printer. Coopers & Lybrand developed the system by encoding the expertise of more than 30 of its senior tax and audit professionals.

ExperTAX[sm] consists of three modules: the expert system shell (called QShell), the knowledge base, and the knowledge base maintenance system. The last module facilitates modification of the contents of the knowledge base as tax laws and experts' opinions change.

The Expert System Shell

QShell is rule based and designed specifically to accommodate the requirements of the tax accrual and planning process at Coopers & Lybrand. Although it was designed for

---

[8]Reprinted with permission from the *Journal of Accountancy,* copyright © 1987 by the American Institute of Certified Public Accountants, Inc. Opinions of the authors are their own and do not necessarily reflect policies of the AICPA.

ExperTAX^sm in particular, QShell has also been used as a flexible programming tool for other expert systems. Its two main components are the inference engine and the user interface.

The *inference engine* controls the logic search through the knowledge base by executing the appropriate rules, tracking the inference process, and communicating with the user through the user interface. The *user interface* controls the screen display and keyboard used to communicate with the user and issues printer commands to format and print reports.

The layout of a CRT display has three distinct horizontal portions. The top portion of the display shows information identifying the section being analyzed. The middle portion displays the questions being asked, the condition that caused the current question, and the possible valid answers. The lowest portion presents explanatory messages. It also allows the user to enter either notes desired by the user or information requested by the system. Exhibit 9–1 shows a sample display.

The user operates the user interface through a system of nested menus. The information it displays comes directly from the knowledge base. Responses to its questions direct its search processes and improve the intelligibility of its output. The printed reports generated by the user interface include lists of all issues identified by ExperTAX^sm, lists of all questions asked and answers received, notes entered during the session, and special forms. These forms are completed by the professional staff to provide additional documentation. Exhibit 9–2 is a sample report.

The Knowledge Base

The knowledge base contains several thousand frames, rules, and facts that constitute the system's expertise. It makes these available to the inference engine and to the user interface.

Exhibit 9–1

Case 9–24 ExperTAX^sm Display

ARTIFICIAL COMPANY   SEPTEMBER 3, 1997
Coopers & Lybrand—ExperTAX(sm)—
                    Tax Accrual & Planning Expert System Inventory

Any inventory: Yes

Does the client include any of the following items in inventory for TAX purposes?
  Real Estate
  Materials and supplies not held for sale (e.g., office supplies)
  Deferred cost under the Completed Contract method
  Consigned goods to which the client does not have title

Summary: Noninventory items
QB3   Answer one of: (Y N) Y
The items mentioned above may be treated as inventory items for BOOK purposes, but may not be treated as inventory items for TAX purposes (Ref. Atlantic Coast Realty v. Comm., Rev Rul 59–329, Reg. 1.471–1)

F1—Note F2—Skip F3—More WHY

Each frame in the knowledge base contains information on how and when it is used, what should happen next, and what to display or print. A frame can include several rules. The two kinds of frames are question and issue frames.

The *question frames* include the following:

1. Questions.
2. Conditions. These appear as antecedents and, if true, cause the questions to be asked.
3. Rules. These control the structure of the session and of the outputs.
4. Explanatory messages.

EXHIBIT 9–2

Case 9–24 ExperTAX^{sm} *Report*

Coopers & Lybrand

ExperTAX^{sm}
Planning Issues and Ideas

April 8, 1997

The practitioner should review the following planning ideas and issues to determine their applicability to the client.

Inventory

- Section 1.471–2(c) allows obsolete goods to be written down to bona fide selling price less direct cost of disposition. Such write-downs reduce taxable income. However, excess inventory does not come under this provision. See Thor Power v. Comm.*
- LIFO inventory may not be valued for tax purposes using the lower-of-cost-or-market method! The IRS may terminate the taxpayer's LIFO election if LIFO inventory is valued at the lower of cost or market. See Rev. Proc. 79–23. In limited situations, a taxpayer may be able to change to the cost method and preclude the IRS from terminating its LIFO election. See Rev. Proc. 84–74. Market write-downs are required to be included in income under the provisions of Sec. 472(d) when LIFO is elected.

---

*These issues require a change in accounting method for which IRS approval must be requested within 180 days of the beginning of the taxable year.

EXHIBIT 9–3

Case 9–24 ExperTAX^{sm}
Question Frame

Coopers & Lybrand—ExperTAX(sm)—Tax Accrual & Planning Expert System

Question:

What is client's bad-debt write-off method for TAX purposes?
        S—Specific charge-off
        R—Reserve method

Possible Answers:

        S—Specific charge-off
          (Clarifying explanation required)
        R—Reserve method
          Follow-up Questions:
          QA19—Bad-debt reserve method
          QA20—Difference between BOOK and TAX reserve
          QA21—Bad debt recoveries to reserve

WHY message:

In a typical environment, the Reserve method over time will result in larger tax deductions than the Specific charge-off method.

Exhibit 9–3 contains an example of a question frame.

The *issue frames* are simpler than the question frames. They include only a rule and a display. The inference engine tests the rule in the frame, and if it is true, the display appears on the CRT or in a printed report. Exhibit 9–4 is an example of an issue frame.

Required:

a. What motivated this large CPA firm to create this expert system? What financial justification can you suggest for their investment in it?

b. Which other possible applications can you suggest for expert systems in accounting and auditing?

9–25. *APPLICATION GENERATORS*

Hamilton Brothers Oil Company developed a comprehensive accounting and financial information system under an extremely difficult schedule.[9] A key ingredient in the success of this project was the use of an application generator to satisfy the programming requirements. An application generator is a software package that anticipates standard user requirements in a functional area such as accounting and finance. It provides data management facilities, automates common functions, and has a specialized language for coding.

Project Background

Hamilton Brothers senior management decided to terminate its service bureau computer support and to implement an in-house financial reporting system (FRS). This system

---

[9]Adapted from J. H. Waldrop, "Application Generators: A Case Study," *Proceedings of the 1982 National Computer Conference,* Houston, Texas, p. 363. Reprinted with the permission of the American Federation of Information Processing Societies, all rights reserved.

Exhibit 9–4

Case 9–24 ExperTAX^sm
Issue Frame

Coopers & Lybrand—ExperTAX(sm)—Tax Accrual & Planning Expert System
Rule:

(QB6 IS L): Inventory valuing IS Lower of cost or market
AND
(QB14 IS L): Method of accounting for inventory IS LIFO
OR
(QB14 IS B): Method of accounting for inventory IS Both LIFO and FIFO

Display:
LIFO inventory may not be valued for tax purposes using the lower-of-cost-or-market method!! The IRS may terminate the taxpayer's LIFO election if LIFO inventory is valued at the lower of cost or market. See Rev Proc 79–23. In limited situations, a taxpayer may be able to change to the Cost method and preclude the IRS from terminating its LIFO election. See Rev Proc 84–74. Market write-downs are required to be included in income under the provisions of SEC. 472(d) when LIFO is elected.

consists of five integrated subsystems: accounts payable, accounts receivable, general ledger, joint interest billing, and budget. After a thorough four-month evaluation of 19 vendors, management determined that Hamilton Brothers' requirements could best be met by making significant modifications to an existing software package. In addition to customizing the software, the company had to establish and staff a complete medium-size computer installation. The data in the new system would require a complex conversion effort from the previous service bureau environment. The target date for implementation of the new system was 20 months from the beginning of the project.

This project required completion of several phases. First, a project team issued requests for proposals (RFPs) to software package vendors. They evaluated the resulting proposals based on four criteria: (1) ability of the package to address user requirements, (2) its utilization of the most current software architecture, (3) maximum software flexibility, and (4) the financial and technical reputation of the vendor. After two months, a software package was selected. In the second phase, a system concept definition was performed to refine the general requirements presented in the RFP. This phase also required two months. Next, the project teams developed a general design for the system, requiring six months.

At this point, the project team had only 10 months remaining to accomplish detailed specification, programming, testing, and conversion. They began to examine techniques to maximize efficiency during programming, testing, and conversion. This led to their decision to use an application generator to perform the custom development work.

Project Goals

As with any new system, this project's ultimate goal was to provide a sound system meeting the user's requirements. The project team identified three ancillary goals in order to achieve this with FRS.

First, the new system must be user friendly. To accomplish this, the project team decided to provide on-line processing and user report development with minimal support from the data processing staff. They also wanted an architecture that provides flexible data modification by users. Second, the system must be capable of easy technical modification, thus providing a solid base for future expansion. This required a structured development methodology and self-documenting code. Third, the system development process must take advantage of development productivity tools. These required on-line program development, simple report writers, on-line screen generators, a data dictionary, and a project management plan.

The Completed System

The use of an application generator contributed to the achievement of the project's goals and its timely implementation. The following summary describes the completed system and provides insight into the magnitude of the project. The project entailed

- 1,300 pages of preliminary design narrative.
- 6,000 persondays to complete the entire project.
- 25 people assigned full-time at the peak of the project.
- 3,000 pages of automated technical documentation in a data dictionary.
- 1,320 data items.
- 285 programs, most of them developed using the application generator.
- 157 reports.
- 53 on-line screens.
- 132 data files.
- 48 input forms.

The project team both encountered problems and achieved benefits from the use of an application generator. All in all, the package was less flexible than a procedural language in how it accomplished specific tasks, and some adaptation by programmers accustomed to coding in COBOL was required. However, its structured architecture and selected keywords enforced programmer standardization. It also provided an excellent technique for developing common code used in many programs. The generator allowed the use of identical data names for multiple fields, thus minimizing unique data names. These characteristics reduced the amount of code that would have been required if a procedural language such as COBOL had been used.

A major benefit provided by this application generator is an automatic transaction suspense processing facility. On input, transactions reside in a holding file awaiting subsequent processing. After processing, transactions rejected because of invalid fields or account numbers are retained in this holding file until corrected. Valid transactions proceed through the remainder of the processing cycle. This feature eliminates the effort required to code programs to apply these procedures with transaction and master files.

The application generator supported several general housekeeping functions that directly contributed to improved programmer productivity both in the coding and in the testing stages. The use of selected application-unique keywords such as REJECT-BATCH or REJECT-DOCUMENT eliminated the need to code and test these types of routines. Other unique keywords such as POST or GENERATE offered no productivity gains but did relate the function (WRITE) to the application-oriented terminology (POST).

The on-line screen generation provided the greatest increase in programmer productivity. Fourteen of the 16 programmers on the project team had never developed a teleprocessing system and, therefore, had no experience in generating on-line screens. The application generator screen facility provided each programmer with an easy-to-learn tool to perform this function.

Perhaps the best measure of the productivity gains provided by this application generator was the relatively brief time required to develop the code through program testing. The elapsed time for this task was approximately three months, certainly a significant testimony to the potential value of an application generator.

Future Uses of Application Generators

The project team identified several factors that affect future decisions to use an application generator. Perhaps the most important is the size and complexity of the project. A complex system requiring unique access methods, specialized processing techniques, and sophisticated on-line requirements may not be suitable for development by means of an application generator. For less complex systems, the benefits from the time saved during coding and testing may make use of a generator worthwhile.

Whenever a project team decides to use an application generator, they should carefully evaluate its technical capabilities. Application generators are inherently oriented to specific functional areas. The selection of an appropriate generator for a given functional area is necessary for the success of the project. Furthermore, the design of the system must be consistent with the technical capabilities of the software. The project team must develop an understanding of the capabilities and constraints of the application generator and be willing to live within those constraints.

Conclusions

Hamilton Brothers' use of this application generator provided several key benefits. It did, however, introduce into the design process inefficiencies that could have been avoided with a COBOL-based system. How effective was the project team in meeting the goals of FRS as outlined earlier?

The user friendliness is superior to that of the old system. The application generator provides extremely flexible data file modifications, allowing users to change most edit criteria without programmer intervention. With the report development facility, selected users can create simple reports with minimal MIS support. However, more complex reporting requires direct programmer help.

Future modifications can easily be made to FRS if the new code is developed with the same application generator. The benefits of the generator's structured coding requirements were somewhat offset by the limitations in its flexibility.

The benefits of development productivity tools such as on-line program development, report writers, screen generators, a data dictionary, and project management planning exceeded original expectations. They were critical factors in the success achieved by the project team.

In conclusion, the use of application generators is a technique for improving the quality of a system and the timeliness of its development. The package used at Hamilton Brothers offers a good tool for accounting applications. Its potential for use in other application areas is, by design, limited.

Required:

a. Which source for computing services did Hamilton Brothers use prior to developing the new financial reporting system?

b. How long did the project team require to develop FRS? How much time was needed to create the code? How do you think this would have changed had the team used a procedural language such as COBOL?

c. What are the key considerations in the decision to use an application generator?

9–26.   DISTRIBUTED PROCESSING

Dial Corporation is a wholly owned subsidiary of The Dial Corp., which manufactures and markets Dial soap, Armour Star canned meats, Purex detergents and bleaches, and other personal care, canned food, and household and laundry products.[10] The product lines not only are diverse but are growing rapidly; revenues from new products increased from $20 million to $133 million within a recent two-year period. Exhibit 9–5 shows Dial's manufacturing plants, sales offices, distribution centers, and accounting centers, which are scattered throughout the United States.

When Dial Corporation developed plans to expand into the international market, top management recognized that the company's highly centralized management structure no longer met the needs of the organization. It undertook a seven-month organizational study that reduced the number of management levels and dramatically decentralized decision-making authority and accountability. The new strategy of decentralization led to a comprehensive assessment of Dial's management information system (MIS). This assessment led management to change the company's MIS from a centralized mainframe environment to a system of minicomputers and networked microprocessors distributed among the various operating locations.

The Centralized System

Prior to the change, the primary computer was a mainframe located at Dial's Phoenix headquarters. All major applications affecting more than one operating location were designed to run on this machine. The company deployed 27 midrange computers, mainly at manufacturing plants and distribution centers, and more than 100 personal computers (PCs) at sales offices and other locations. These minicomputers and micros were used primarily for data collection to feed mainframe batch processing, although the minis also were used for some purely local applications. The mainframe needed a major and expensive capacity upgrade. All hardware, from mainframe through micros, was a generation behind the latest equipment.

On the mainframe, the applications programs were heavily oriented toward finance, cost accounting, and other corporate staff functions. Most application systems were batch oriented, and there was no overall corporate database. Output was geared to after-the-fact reporting of transactions or summary reporting for analysis purposes. On-line access to operational data generally was inadequate. Also, many applications were more

---

[10]Adapted from Michael A. Robinson, "Dial's Approach to MIS Improvement," *Management Accounting,* September 1991, p. 27. Copyright by National Association of Accountants (1991), Montvale, N.J. 07645.

EXHIBIT 9–5

Case 9–26 Dial Corporation Facilities

▲ Distribution centers
● Sales offices
■ Manufacturing plants
★ Accounting centers
✖ Corporate offices

than 10 years old. Several key systems supporting the sales and marketing, manufacturing, transportation, and distribution functions needed extensive modification to serve Dial effectively in the future.

Company personnel had little flexibility in selecting applications to run on their mini- and microcomputers. Because they used different programming languages, applications could not be shared without separate programming efforts on each type of machine. Application system interfaces were numerous and complex, and the process of modifying applications to respond to changing business requirements was costly and slow.

The Phoenix headquarters had a staff of 78 experienced professionals, 38 of whom worked on applications programs. These application programmers were not assigned to business functional areas (manufacturing, sales, accounting, etc.) but were organized by application development and application support responsibility. These technicians spent the majority of their time modifying existing mainframe programs. In general, they lacked mini- and microcomputer skills and were not trained in state-of-the-art application design and development tools.

Problems with the Existing System

Dial's business-unit managers experienced several problems that were typical for end-users in highly centralized mainframe environments. With Dial's traditional application system development process, the results of software design efforts were unseen until the implementation stage, which was too late to make major adjustments. The managers had little interaction with MIS professionals. This led to "us vs. them" feelings between the two groups. With their limited system development tools, the MIS staff was unable to respond quickly to users' application development and modification requests. There was a long backlog of requests involving major systems.

Furthermore, end-users had little input regarding priorities assigned to their requests. Because the bulk of existing applications were financial and historical in nature, maintenance work on financial reporting systems of no strategic importance to Dial frequently took precedence over work that might have been initiated on strategic business applications. With mainframe capacity shared by all business units, end-users had difficulty understanding the MIS costs charged to their departments and could not relate them to benefits received. After documenting these shortcomings, management decided to change the MIS environment so that it would better meet the strategic business needs of operating-unit managers.

Alternatives

Dial's management, working with outside consultants, identified two alternatives for its new MIS environment. The first alternative was to upgrade the mainframe substantially, install a database management system (DBMS), acquire additional data management software for accessing older data files, add several newer model minicomputers, and purchase CASE tools to aid in developing mainframe applications. The second alternative was to implement a distributed system of minicomputers and networked PCs. Development activity would shift from mainframe-based applications to distributed applications, and the mainframe would remain in place until major applications could be moved to the distributed processors.

Dial's management rejected the mainframe alternative in order to gain the benefits of distributed processing. Distributed systems put more control into the hands of users, complementing Dial's strategy of pushing accountability outward geographically and downward organizationally. With these systems, management felt, users "own" their hardware and applications. This encourages them to search for creative ways to use their resources and improves their ability to compete.

In a distributed environment, MIS staff can be assigned to business functional units. This improves dialogue between them and business-unit managers, reduces feelings of distrust, and increases the emphasis on developing strategic business application systems. Interaction also increases the probability that internally developed applications meet the needs of their users.

Management also felt that the distributed system would be more flexible than a mainframe-based one. They could make capacity additions in smaller, less expensive increments. They expected to see processing completed faster because computing would be shared with fewer users. Finally, control over their systems and responsibility for their budgets should enable business-unit managers to understand what they are getting for their MIS charges.

Dial's managers projected savings of approximately $3 million in avoidable mainframe costs over the five-year decision period. They expected this savings, however, to be offset to a large extent by additional costs of distributed processors, software, training, and other network-related items. Management expects that the new Dial system will be substantially more functional than the one it replaces. Any net savings from distributed processing will depend on the totality of features demanded by operating-unit managers and decisions made by MIS managers as they gain experience with the new environment.

Outsourcing Mainframe Operations

When Dial's managers adopted the distributed processing strategy, they realized that the three-to-five-year implementation period would be a time of uncertainty and risk. Rather than maintain and operate the existing applications on the mainframe, they contracted with an independent company to "outsource" the mainframe operations during the period of transition. Outsourcing is an emerging trend in which an outside organization performs some portion of a company's data-processing function, either at the company's facilities or at a remote location. The terms of such relationships vary greatly but are specified in a contract between the two companies.

Under the terms of Dial's outsourcing contract, Dial personnel perform all software maintenance, perform data input over remote computer terminals, and determine the processing schedule. The outsourcing provider operates a mainframe computer at the provider's own site, maintains computer and telecommunications equipment, executes batch processing to meet Dial's schedule, assumes Dial's financial obligations under existing lease and maintenance contracts, and purchases Dial's mainframe computer and certain related peripherals.

Dial pays for these services at a set rate per hour of processing time and a rate per gigabyte per month of disk storage. Dial also pays on a "cost plus" basis for telecommunications charges and for systems software acquired after the effective date of the contract. This arrangement converts the structure of MIS costs from primarily fixed to variable. Dial management felt that the decision to outsource would reduce overall costs substantially during the transition period and allow MIS personnel to focus on implementing the corporation's distributed processing strategy.

The Future

When the outsourcing agreement was reached, Dial management expected to transfer gradually all applications from the mainframe to Dial's own minicomputers. These included both strategic applications such as Dial's Consumer Information System, with which the company differentiates itself from its competitors, and the transaction processing applications, which are common to all businesses and represent no strategic advantage.

Management now believes that it may be desirable to retain indefinitely some large applications, including Accounts Payable and General Ledger, on the mainframe. They question whether they should devote scarce resources to applications that are not specific to Dial's businesses and can be maintained by outside organizations. For example, Dial would have to purchase a large minicomputer, construct a larger computer room, and hire and maintain a staff of operators to support all accounting applications.

Outsourcing gives them the freedom to focus their attention initially on transferring to minicomputers those strategic applications that represent the greatest potential increase in functionality. Later they may choose to transfer those accounting applications that provide in-house cost savings.

When evaluating the decision to move to distributed computing, Dial management concluded that considerations of strategy and operational effectiveness outweigh the quantifiable financial factors of traditional cost–benefit analysis. They feel that this is especially true when the cost and benefits of new systems are difficult to predict.

Required:

a. What initially motivated Dial to consider a change to a distributed processing system?
b. What was the quantitative advantage of a distributed system at Dial? What were the qualitative advantages?
c. Does Dial management expect to have an MIS environment totally free of mainframe computers? Explain why.

10 DATA STORAGE AND PROCESSING METHODS

Learning Objectives

1. To review how a computer stores data in electronic devices.
2. To compare two alternative approaches to organizing accounting data in computer systems.
3. To understand four approaches to processing data stored in an accounting information system.

Introduction

The previous chapter examined the components of a computer system, including secondary storage devices. A computer system stores accounting records on secondary storage devices until needed. Then system software transfers accounting data into main storage for processing by application software.

This chapter explains how secondary storage devices store accounting information. The last part of the chapter describes four ways of implementing procedures to process this data.

Data Representation

The devices in a computer system record data by changing the *state* of the circuits and magnetic devices constituting the peripherals. A circuit or magnetic component can be in either of two states: either magnetized or energized one way or the opposite way. When data is transferred across a data communication link, an electronic pulse is either present or absent. Technicians use *binary notation* to describe the state of a circuit, a magnetic device, or a communication link.

Binary Encoding

In writing, the binary numbering system denotes the state of the component. This system uses the digit 1 to represent the existence of a pulse on a data communication link, or one way of energizing a circuit or device. The digit 0 represents the other way. In this manner, technicians can describe the contents of the computer system without concern for the specific device or circuit in use. The most elementary amount of information in a pulse or circuit utilizes one *bi*nary digi*t* when written; thus, these devices transfer or store information in *bits*.

Information stored in pure binary form is awkward and difficult to interpret. Consequently, computer manufacturers developed easier ways of encoding information using the digits 1 and 0. The two methods for encoding information are called EBCDIC and ASCII. Illustration 10–1 shows how each method encodes numbers. They encode letters of the alphabet, punctuation marks, and other characters similarly.

Computers use ASCII codes for transferring data over communications links. Most computer manufacturers also use ASCII to store data internally on devices. However, mainframe computers that use IBM operating systems employ EBCDIC.

Data Hierarchy

A data hierarchy describes how binary codes combine to provide meaningful information. Furthermore, there are two views of this hierarchy. One is the viewpoint of the computer hardware, and the other is that of the human user.

From the Viewpoint of the Computer.   When designing computer hardware, manufacturers select either EBCDIC or ASCII as a way of digitally encoding data. The circuit required to store one human-readable character in each method is called one *byte* of storage. A storage device that contains 1 million bytes can store 1 million characters readable by a human. Large storage capacity indicates a powerful computer that can execute large programs and store large amounts of data.

Another measure of the processing power of a computer is its word length. A computer *word* is the minimum amount of storage that can be addressed, or specifically identified as to location, by the CPU. Depending on the computer, the length of a word may be 1, 2, 4, 8, or 16 bytes. A modern computer with a large word length can store and process larger numbers, and it can store small numbers more accurately than can an older computer with a smaller word length. It can also execute larger programs.

From the Viewpoint of the User.   Although computers process data in the form of bits, bytes, and computer words, we as humans have difficulty thinking in these terms. To us, the most elemental form of data is the character. Usually this is either a number, a letter, or a punctuation mark. When we process data, we combine these characters to form data fields.

ILLUSTRATION 10–1

Methods of Binary Encoding

Decimal:	941		
Binary:	1110101101		
EBCDIC:	11111001	11110100	11110001
	9	4	1
ASCII:	01011001	01010100	01010001
	9	4	1

A *field* represents a single item of data needed by an accounting application, and it contains one or more characters. Unlike byte or word lengths fixed by computer manufacturers, the length of a field is determined by the designer of the application software. The designer also decides which characters compose the field and selects a *data name* to uniquely identify the field. Illustration 10–2 contains some accounting data fields.

Most accounting systems initially record data on documents. One type of document contains all the data needed to record a sales order from a customer; another type records data showing an obligation to pay a supplier for goods received. Data recorded on these documents constitute a logically related set of data items. When an accounting system converts all the data from a document into computer-readable form, it stores this set of data fields in a *logical record*. The application software designer decides not only how to store each data item in a data field but also how to combine these in the logical record.

For example, application software in an inventory system maintains perpetual inventory data. A logical record for an inventory application might contain the following seven fields:

INVENTORY-NUMBER	REORDER-QUANTITY
INVENTORY-DESCRIPTION	VENDOR-CODE
STANDARD-COST	QUANTITY-ON-HAND
REORDER-POINT	

In this example, the INVENTORY-NUMBER field is the primary key field for the record. The record's *primary key field* is a data field that uniquely identifies it. In an inventory application, the primary key contains a number that uniquely identifies the product or inventory item described by the contents of the record. In an accounts receivable record, the primary key is a customer number that uniquely identifies the customer with a receivables balance.

Some records also contain secondary (or generic) keys. A *secondary key field* is a field that identifies groups of records with a common attribute. For example, VENDOR-CODE in the preceding record is an attribute that identifies the supplier for the inventory item. The same vendor may supply numerous items; thus a vendor code may appear in numerous inventory records.

You have seen how characters combine to form data fields, and how fields combine to form records. A collection of similar data records forms a *data file*. Humans commonly maintain data files in filing cabinets; these collections of similar documents may be a

ILLUSTRATION 10–2

Fields and Their Data Names

Data Name	Length	Contents	Example
DEPARTMENT	10	Alphanumeric	ASSEMBLY-1
SOCIAL-SECURITY-NUMBER	9	Numeric	361267091
HOURS-WORKED	2	Numeric	40

file of old credit card bills, a file of old accounting exams, or the like. Each old document is a record in these manually processed files.

A computer file is a collection of similar computer records. Computers maintain their files on secondary storage devices. For example, a computerized inventory file might contain thousands of computer records, one for each item in inventory. Each record contains the data items identified earlier.

All the data used by an organization and stored on secondary storage devices constitute the organization's *database*. In older systems, the database is simply a collection of computer data files. Illustration 10–3 shows the data hierarchy in such a system. In many newer systems, data records are maintained in the database by a system software package, the database management system (DBMS). In all systems, the computer and its human users have two alternative views of how data are stored in a computer. Illustration 10–4 summarizes these.

Whenever a DBMS is used, the application software designer is unconcerned with how the data fields are arranged on secondary storage. The DBMS allows the computer application to access the data items it needs regardless of how they are stored.

Approaches to Data Organization

Two approaches exist for organizing data in a database. The first represents a modification of early manual procedures. The second was developed to overcome deficiencies with the first. However, both are common in today's business environment. In this text, we refer to them as the traditional data file approach and the database management

ILLUSTRATION 10–3

Data Hierarchy

A. Bit

1   A bit showing a yes-state.

B. Byte

11010011   An 8-bit byte representing an L in EBCDIC.

C. Field

CUSTOMER-NAME

A 15-byte field with the data name of CUSTOMER-NAME.

D. Record

CUSTOMER-
    NUMBER   CUSTOMER-NAME

A record with CUSTOMER-NUMBER as its key and CUSTOMER-NAME as one of its fields.

E. File

RECORD   RECORD   RECORD   RECORD

A segment of a file, on magnetic tape, showing four records. The title strip between records is known as interrecord gap.

F. Database

All files or records in the system.

approach. Accountants encounter both approaches as they develop and audit computer systems.

Traditional Data File Organization

From the perspective of a computer user, accounting data are stored in groups of logically related fields called *records.* In noncomputerized systems, these records are documents. Accountants collect groups of similar documents in files and store them in filing cabinets.

When businesses first computerized the accounting process, they created a computer file for each manual file and a computer record for each document. Computerized procedures replaced manual procedures when processing these records and files. In this way a computer application created and maintained its own data files independent of other applications. Even though these applications have expanded and improved over the years, many businesses still use this traditional approach to organizing data.

Characteristics.   With *traditional data file organization,* each application maintains its own accounting files. Each file consists of a collection of data records. Other applications may process records containing similar data items, but those applications store these records in different files. Thus the company's database contains many different data files and each is processed independently.

The three common methods of arranging records within a data file use sequential, direct access, and indexed sequential files.

Sequential.   A *sequential* file contains records that are physically arranged in sequence by the key field of the record. Thus, in a sequential customer file, the record containing the balance for customer number 12034 is located immediately prior to that for customer number 12035.

A computer program locates a record in a sequential file by searching through the entire file, record by record, from the first one until it finds the desired key field. All magnetic tape files are sequential, but magnetic disks allow this method as well.

ILLUSTRATION 10–4

Alternative Views of Data Storage

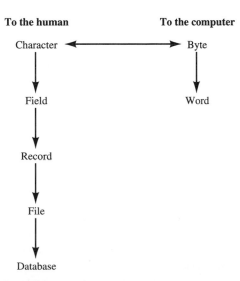

Direct Access.   With ***direct access,*** data management software accesses a record directly; it computes a physical location on a secondary storage device from the key field of a record. The software then stores the record at that location. Whenever a program must use the record, the data management software again computes the location and copies it from the device into main storage. The most common device used for direct access files is a magnetic disk, an example of a *direct access storage device.* Magnetic tapes cannot be used with this method.

Indexed Sequential.   ***Indexed sequential*** files are so named because they contain an index to records in the file. The index shows the key field and the location of the record for some (but not all) records. The records themselves are physically located in sequence by key field.

A program reads a record from an indexed sequential file by either simply searching sequentially through the file until it finds the desired key, or looking up the key field in the index. If the key field is not there, it finds the next lowest key field in the index and locates this record on the secondary storage device. The software then searches sequentially from the location of this record until the record containing the desired key field is found. Indexed sequential files must be stored on direct access devices, such as magnetic disks.

The way data management software uses a file index is similar to the way a reader uses an index to a book. The reader looks up a topic in the book's index and then reads sequentially from the page number shown until he or she finds the information needed.

Example Manual Procedures.   Consider, for example, the manual accounts receivable procedures for Acme Company. When Acme sells on account to customers, a clerk records these transactions in the general ledger by making debit entries in the Accounts Receivable account and credit entries in the Sales Revenue account. An accounts receivable clerk receives copies of sales invoices that show the amounts each customer owes. The clerk records these in the accounts receivable subsidiary ledger with entries to the customers' accounts. Each account consists of a ledger card arranged in alphabetical sequence. The clerk then stores the sales invoice copies by invoice number sequence in a filing cabinet. The accounts receivable clerk uses one document and two files when processing each transaction. The document is the sales invoice copy; the files are the sales invoice file and the accounts receivable subsidiary ledger, a card file.

Example Computerized Procedures.   After Acme computerizes this procedure, a computer program in the general ledger application posts the sale to the general ledger accounts. Another program in the accounts receivable application posts the sale to the customer's account. In processing this transaction, the accounts receivable program uses two computer records and two computer files. They are the sales invoice record, the customer master record, the sales invoice file, and the customer master file. The sales invoice file is organized sequentially by invoice number. The customer master file is organized sequentially by customer number. Illustration 10–5 shows the similarities between manual and traditional file processing in this example.

This accounts receivable application maintains two files. No other application uses them; thus many people say that the accounts receivable application "owns" the sales invoice and customer master files.

ILLUSTRATION 10–5

*Accounts Receivable
Procedures*

A. Manual Process

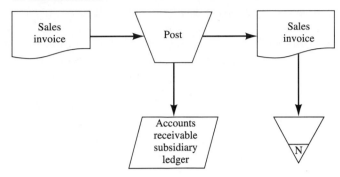

B. Computerized Process

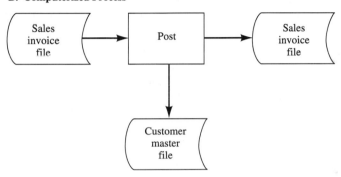

Deficiencies.   Companies adopted traditional data file organization as their manual systems evolved to computer-based ones. After using traditional methods for several years, however, they recognized deficiencies with this way of structuring their data-bases. These deficiencies exist because of *data redundancy.* Different computer files, maintained by several applications in the same computer-based system, store records containing the same data items. Three deficiencies result from data redundancy: inefficient use of storage, conflicting data, and the difficulty of making changes to the applications software.

Inefficient Use of Storage.   When a computer system stores the same data item in multiple locations on a secondary storage device, the system wastes storage capacity. The system requires less storage capacity if it records each data item only once.

For example, both billing and inventory systems maintain files containing data on quantities of products sold. Billing systems use this data to calculate amounts due from customers. Inventory systems subtract quantities sold from the QUANTITY-ON-HAND data item in the file containing perpetual inventory records. A record in a file of billing transactions and a record in a file of inventory transactions contain the same data item.

Although this is possibly the most obvious deficiency of traditional file processing, it is the least serious. Most computer systems have adequate secondary storage capacity, and this usually can be increased by adding devices. The storage capacity inefficiencies introduced by duplicate data fields are small.

Conflicting Data.   A more serious problem arising from duplicate data fields is the possibility of conflicting data. When the same data item exists in two or more files, the contents of these data fields may differ. Reports printed from these files show conflicting information and cause managers to question the validity of all reports produced by the system. Conflicting data may indicate errors. Or a conflict may occur simply because different applications may follow different processing schedules.

Consider again the preceding example. Suppose that the billing system executes daily but the inventory system executes only once a week, on Friday. And suppose that each system produces on Wednesday a report showing quantities sold by inventory item. These two reports will contain conflicting information: The report produced by the inventory system contains data three days older than that of the billing system.

When conflicting data occur in systems using traditional file organization, as in this example, there is usually a valid explanation. Furthermore, by careful system design a project team can avoid producing reports that contain conflicting information. In this example, both the billing and the inventory systems can produce reports using the most current data item, that from the billing system. However, this solution to the problem of conflicting data creates another deficiency of traditional data file organization.

Difficulty of System Change.   Many organizations corrected the problems arising from duplicate and conflicting data by allowing different application systems to share data files. With shared files, each data item is recorded only once in a file. This file is used by several different programs in different applications. Accountants call such a system an *integrated information system.*

Because they avoid many data inconsistencies, integrated information systems provide better accounting information. However, their use creates an even more serious deficiency—they make it difficult to change the applications.

Each program accessing a shared data file contains code describing the data processed by the program. Any change to one program that requires a change in data format also requires changes to all other programs that access the file. Thus, what seems to be a relatively small change may become far reaching and expensive. Furthermore, changes to existing programs may produce unintended consequences.

As an example, in 1981 the U.S. Social Security Administration decided to change its programs to allow benefit checks to be printed in excess of $999.99. Superficially, this was a simple change, requiring an increase in an amount field from five to six characters. However, this change was required in over 600 programs and cost about $500,000 to make. Furthermore, the altered systems then produced unexpected errors, such as issuing checks for incorrect amounts. In a large system like this one, a systems analyst or programmer cannot anticipate every possible effect of such a change.

Illustration 10–6 summarizes these deficiencies. How can they be avoided? By separating two processes performed by most accounting programs. Using the ***database management organization***, modern systems separate the process of accessing data from the process of using data to produce outputs. They accomplish this using a form of system software called a *database management system.*

AIS in Practice

Global Marine, Inc., is a $350 million oil and gas drilling company headquartered in Houston, Texas. In 1995 Global Marine shut down its mainframe computer after a four-year transition period. In its place, they implemented a network of 11 file and application servers in Houston and about 500 PCs at remote locations. Many of these are on off-shore oil drilling platforms.

The mainframe had run VSAM data management software, CICS telecommunications software, and application software written in FOCUS and COBOL. These were replaced by a relational database management system and accounting and personnel software packages purchased from vendors. The company expected savings of about $1 million per year from the change. This included a reduction in MIS staff from 35 to 22 employees.

The CIO believed that the new system would be ten times harder to manage and maintain. But, he observed, users love the freedom of the new system and will never go back to the old one.

Database Management Organization

This approach to structuring a database relies on system software to manage the data. This software, a ***database management system*** (DBMS), is a set of computer programs that maintain centralized control of the database. Whenever an application program or a user wants data from the database, it requests the data from the DBMS. The DBMS locates the data on a secondary storage device and transfers it into main storage in a form that can be used by the application. A DBMS uses on-line secondary storage devices.

Illustration 10–7 contrasts the two methods of data organization. The top portion shows how individual applications maintain their own files with traditional data file organization. In this illustration, the files are recorded on magnetic tape. The bottom portion shows that, with the database management organization, all applications access data using a DBMS. In it, the data are on a magnetic disk.

By eliminating redundancy, a DBMS overcomes the deficiencies of traditional data file organization. The DBMS stores data for use by all applications, so they are not required to maintain their own data files.

ILLUSTRATION 10–6

Deficiencies of Traditional Data File Organization

Inefficient
Duplicate storage on peripheral devices
The least serious problem

Conflicting Data
May occur due to different operating schedules
Can be avoided by using shared data files

Difficult Changes
A result of shared data files
Can be avoided by separating data storage from the use of the data

---

ILLUSTRATION 10–7

*Data File Versus
Database Management
Organization*

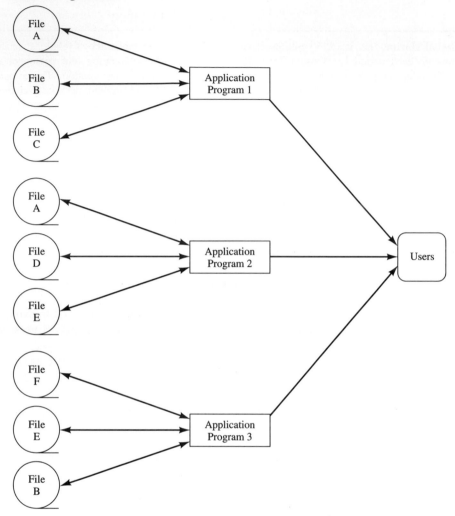

Data File Organization

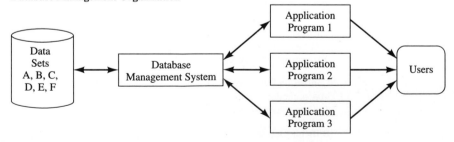

Database Management Organization

Characteristics.   Computer systems using database management systems store data in ways unknown to users of the computer. When application programs request data from DBMS software, system software determines data locations on secondary storage and makes this data accessible to the applications. This illustrates one of the major advantages of the database management approach—data independence.

Data Independence.   With a DBMS, the method of storing and organizing the data is independent of the computer programs that use it. Application programs requesting data neither specify its location nor describe its structure. Rather they identify it to the DBMS using a request such as that in Illustration 10–8. This is an example of a command in a *data manipulation language* (DML). A DML consists of a small set of commands included in the procedural language of the application program. The actual structure of the database, the location of the data, or how the fields combine to form records in the database are irrelevant to the application program.

When changes to a system occur that require altering the format of a data item, these changes affect only application programs using this data item. A traditional file system would require changes to all programs using the entire data record. This entails many more changes.

A simple example illustrates this characteristic. With a DBMS, if management decides to add another field to a record because of a new application, no previously existing programs require changes. Naturally, the data records in the database change, but only the DBMS software is concerned with this.

How does the DBMS achieve this data independence? It provides a different view of the data to each application program. Each view is called a *subschema.*

The Database Administrator.   Organizations using a database management system employ a database administrator (DBA). Illustration 10–9 shows this person's major responsibilities, one of which is to identify the data items needed by each application using the database. The DBA then specifies to the database software a label for each set of data items. The application programs use these labels when requesting the data.

The DBA specifies to the project team developing the application a ***subschema*** for the data. This is a restricted view of the data that describes how it looks when the DBMS provides it to the application program. In this way, the application program knows the

ILLUSTRATION 10–8

A Data Manipulation Language Statement

A COBOL request for data using IBM's DL/I:

CALL 'CBLTDLI' USING call function, pcb-name, i-o-area, label.

where

> *Call function* identifies what is to be done with the data record. This includes INSERT data,
>   DELETE data, or GET NEXT data.
> *Pcb-name* and *i-o-area* provide parameters needed by the operating system.
> *Label* identifies the desired subschema of the database.

ILLUSTRATION 10–9

Responsibilities of the Database Administrator

1. Define the schema, the data to be included in the database, and the logical manner in which it will be stored.
2. Define the subschemas, the subsets of data to be made available to users and application programs.
3. Maintain the data dictionary. Assign unique data names to all data items in the database.
4. Assign passwords and user access codes to control access to the database.
5. Monitor usage of the database to:
   • Eliminate inefficiencies.
   • Identify possible improvements.
   • Uncover unauthorized access to data.
6. Educate users and publish procedures for accessing the database.
7. Reorganize the database when necessary.

size and type of the data fields it will process. The subschema is usually different for each application. A billing system, for example, uses a different subschema from that used by an inventory system.

The database administrator also determines a ***schema*** for the database. This is a logical view of data records as they are stored by the DBMS software. The DBA communicates this to the database software using the software's *data definition language* (DDL). Each subschema defines a subset of the data fields contained in the schema.

Illustration 10–10 shows the DDL for a data record in a popular language called SQL. Can you figure out what this data is?

ILLUSTRATION 10–10

Example Data Definition Language

```
CREATE TABLE BOOK
(
    CALL_NUMBER                 CHAR(16)NOT NULL,
    USER_ID                     CHAR(8),
    ISBN                        CHAR(16),
    BOOK-TITLE                  CHAR(60),
    PUBLISHER                   CHAR(60),
    DATE_PUBLISHED              DATE,
    DATE_OUT                    DATE,
    DATE_DUE_BACK               DATE,

    PRIMARY KEY (CALL_NUMBER),
    FOREIGN KEY BORROWS
    (
     USER_ID
    )REFERENCES USER
);
CREATE UNIQUE INDEX PKBOOK ON BOOK
(
CALL_NUMBER
);
```

ILLUSTRATION 10–11

Example Schema and Subschema

Schema for a Customer Record
ACCOUNT-NUMBER
CUSTOMER-NAME
CUSTOMER-ADDRESS
SALES-DIVISION
CREDIT-LIMIT
BALANCE
CREDIT-TERMS
TOT-YEARS-SALE
DATE-RECENT-SALE

Subschema for a Sales Order Entry Application
ACCOUNT-NUMBER
CUSTOMER-NAME
CUSTOMER-ADDRESS
CREDIT-LIMIT
BALANCE
CREDIT-TERMS

Subschema for a Sales Analysis Application
ACCOUNT-NUMBER
CUSTOMER-NAME
CUSTOMER-ADDRESS
SALES-DIVISION
TOT-YEARS-SALES

Illustration 10–11 shows examples of schema and subschema for a simple customer database. Two applications use the customer records in it. An order entry application requires data necessary to check a customer's credit limit and send an order acknowledgment to the customer. A sales analysis application requires data to report periodically total sales by customer and by sales division. The two subschemas shown provide this data.

Using subschema, the DBMS separates the way application programs use the database from the way it is actually structured. This greatly eases the way application programmers use the data. Most database management systems also provide easy access to data for nonprogrammer users of the computer system. They obtain this access using a query language.

Query Languages.   A data *query language* (DQL) is a nonprocedural language similar to a fourth-generation language. It is composed of high-level commands that the DBMS software interprets and executes. Managers enter commands into a terminal identifying the data they wish to see. In response, the DBMS retrieves the data from the database and displays it at the terminal.

Query languages allow managers to access information in the database independently of application programs. Managers see ad hoc reports showing only the data they want to see, at the time they want to see it. This kind of easy access to data is difficult to obtain with traditional data file organization.

ILLUSTRATION 10–12

Entry in a Data Dictionary

Description	Entry
Data name	CUSTOMER-NAME
Meaning of data name	Customer name
Format	25 alphanumeric characters
Date originated	10-13-1997
Programs in which the data names are used	ORDER-ENTRY, SALES-ANALYSIS

A database management system provides a single source for all the accounting data of a company. This eliminates the problems of data duplication and conflicting data in traditional file systems. To do this, DBMSs use a data dictionary.

Data Dictionary.   A data dictionary is a computer file containing standardized names and formats for all data items included in the database. It ensures that applications programmers and managers use the correct name to identify any data item required by a program or a query language inquiry. The database administrator uses data dictionary software to keep this file up-to-date. Illustration 10–12 contains a data dictionary entry for a CUSTOMER-NAME data field.

In Illustration 10–12, CUSTOMER-NAME is a 25-character alphanumeric data field containing the name of a customer. Two programs, ORDER-ENTRY and SALES-ANALYSIS, use this data field. Because the data dictionary identifies all programs using each data item, the database administrator knows immediately which programs must be changed if the format of the data field changes. This simplifies making changes to systems when the schema of the database changes.

Because database management software always requires the use of a data dictionary, it includes the software to maintain the dictionary. However, use of a data dictionary eliminates conflicting data names and formats in a traditional file system as well. For this reason, many companies implement a data dictionary in that environment also.

Logical Data Structures.   Database management systems separate the way users view the data from the way the data is actually stored on the device. In addition, they distinguish between its physical arrangement and its logical arrangement.

The *physical* arrangement of data, which describes how data are recorded on the device, is determined by data management software. The *logical* arrangement, called the **logical data structure,** describes how the DBMS searches through the database to identify and retrieve a desired record. Different DBMS packages use different data structures; the choice is important because each has its strengths and weaknesses. Three data structures common among accounting systems are tree, network, and relational. Illustration 10–13 contrasts these structures.

Tree.   The first widely adopted DBMS packages utilized a tree structure, also called a *hierarchical data structure*. With this approach, the database consists of a set of "trees," each of which is a collection of data records associated in some way. A record in

ILLUSTRATION 10–13

Examples of Logical Data Structures

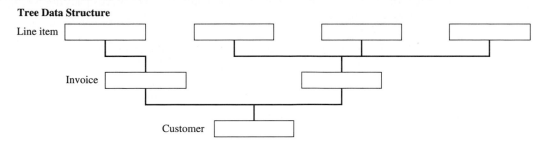

Tree Data Structure

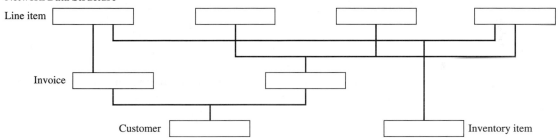

Network Data Structure

Relational Data Structure

Invoice	Line item	Customer

the tree can be located only through a single record, the "root" of the tree. A user must specify the key field of the root to locate any information in the tree.

For example, in Illustration 10–13 an individual customer's record is the root of a tree consisting of two other records representing invoices outstanding with the customer. The customer purchased four products and has been billed for one on the first invoice and three on the second. The system prints each product on a single line of the invoice, so we call it a *line item*. To find out if the customer has paid a specific invoice, give the DBMS the customer account number and the invoice number. The DBMS locates the root (with the customer number) and then searches the tree for the record containing the invoice number specified.

Tree structures were popular because they executed rapidly in transaction processing applications. However, because data is only accessible through the root, trees were less flexible than other structures in the reports they produced. They are inefficient for producing ad hoc reports.

Network.   Software companies developed network-structured packages to overcome the inflexibility of the tree structure. The database consists of sets of related data similar to trees. In the network structure, however, each set of data has multiple entry points. So the network structure is similar to a tree structure with multiple roots.

In the example in Illustration 10–13, the data set has two entry points: the customer record (discussed earlier) and the inventory item record. Users can find out the amount of a specific invoice if they know either the customer number or the number of the inventory item that was purchased.

Network structures make it easier to develop ad hoc reports because they are much more flexible than hierarchical ones. However, they are more difficult to create, and they execute more slowly in transaction processing applications.

Relational.   A DBMS using the relational data structure views the data as if they were organized in tables. Each table contains a set of identically structured rows. In Illustration 10–13, each row in the table identifies an invoice, a line item, and the customer who purchased the product and received the invoice.

It is easiest to view a relational database as if it were equivalent to a file. One row in the table contains all the data in the record of a file, and a column in the table shows the same data field for all records. However, with a relational DBMS these records may not actually exist; this is just the human way of viewing the data. The DBMS software determines how the data are actually stored on the secondary storage device.

Why is a relational DBMS better than a file system if a file is equivalent to a table? A relational DBMS is better because it allows operations on the data that cannot be performed either in a traditional file system or by using another kind of DBMS. With either approach to organizing data, users can identify specific records in a file (e.g., by customer and invoice number) and look at specific fields (such as an amount) within these records. However, with a relational DBMS, users can also (with one command) combine two or more tables. This creates a new table containing only those data fields they want to see. In a traditional data file system, this is equivalent to creating a totally new file—a complex and time-consuming operation. The chapter on database management systems, Chapter 12, covers relational operations.

Relational DBMSs are much more flexible than traditional file systems or tree and network-structured DBMSs. They make it easier for managers to produce ad hoc reports that are virtually impossible with other methods of data organization.

A database management system is a software package that separates managers, clerks, and applications programs from the actual physical structure of the database. These users always access data by requesting it from the DBMS. In this way, a DBMS avoids the problems of storage inefficiency and conflicting data inherent in a traditional file system. It also lessens the difficulty of change that accompanies integrated systems.

Illustration 10–14 shows graphically the function of a database management system. The DBMS software provides an interface between the DBA, human users,

ILLUSTRATION 10–14

Function of a Database Management System

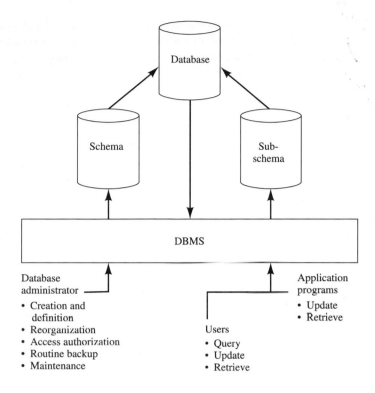

application programs, and the database. Application programs may update or retrieve data. In addition, managers may use the query language to produce ad hoc reports. When users and applications programs access data, they do so using the subschema. When the DBA defines the data in the database, the DBA creates the schema. The DBMS provides users and applications programs with data from the database.

This chapter has discussed two approaches to organizing the data in an accounting system. When an organization uses traditional data file organization, its applications process sequential files, direct access files, or indexed sequential files. When the organization uses a database management system, users and applications are unconcerned with how the data are physically stored. The choice of an approach affects the method they use in processing the data.

Approaches to Data Processing

There are four approaches to processing the data stored in an accounting system. Although some approaches use older forms of technology, many companies still use them for certain applications. Most organizations have accounting systems using all of them. The four approaches to data processing are manual systems, batch systems, batch systems with on-line inquiry, and on-line real-time systems.

Manual Systems

Manual systems do not use a computer in processing the accounting database. Several decades ago, all systems were manual; today, most accounting systems are a combination of manual and computerized processes.

Humans execute the processes performed in manual systems. In large manual systems of the 1930s and 1940s, hundreds of clerks recorded transactions on documents, transferred documents between departments, and recorded these transactions in human-readable journals and ledgers. Mechanical punched-card processing equipment sometimes aided in this process. Accountants stored these documents, punched cards, and accounting records sequentially in filing cabinets and books.

Today companies sometimes process transactions manually using *one-write systems.* A one-write system uses a pegboard with specially printed documents, pages, and ledger cards treated with a layer of black ink on one side. When a clerk records a transaction on a document by hand, the layer of ink transfers the information onto other pages or cards aligned behind it on the pegboard. The clerk writes the information only once, rather than copying it several times onto each document.

Illustration 10–15 shows how a one-write system records a sales transaction. The accounts receivable clerk receives a copy of an invoice. The clerk aligns a sales journal page (with a layer of ink on its back) above the customer's ledger card from the accounts receivable subsidiary ledger. In this way the clerk simultaneously records the data in both the sales journal and the accounts receivable subsidiary ledger.

Batch Sequential Processing Systems

The earliest computer-based systems used batch processing methods. Early systems relied on punched-card data entry; batch processing was an efficient way to control the keypunch process. After companies quit using punched cards, they recorded transac-

ILLUSTRATION 10–15

A Manual System

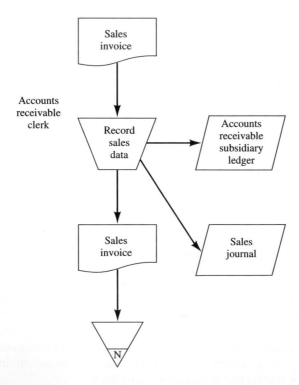

tions directly in magnetic form with on-line data entry. However, because of its efficiency, many companies continued to use the batch processing computer programs they had developed. Many still use the approach for accounting transaction processing. For example, there is little reason to process a payroll application in any other way.

With a *batch sequential processing system*, clerks write down the data necessary for recording accounting transactions. They then accumulate data in batches of, for example, 50 documents per batch and deliver these batches to data entry clerks who convert them into computer-readable form. With older punched-card systems, each batch of documents resulted in a deck of computer cards. In modern systems with on-line data entry, each batch becomes a computer transaction file. After data entry, computer programs process the transactions an entire batch at a time. Data control clerks in the MIS department monitor this processing to ensure that each batch stays intact. No transactions should be lost or added to any batch.

Illustration 10–16 contains a flowchart of a typical application. It shows how the manual accounts receivable process of Illustration 10–15 might be performed with batch processing. This system consists of four computer programs. The *validation* program examines each transaction in a batch for obvious recording or data conversion errors. It also verifies that the total of the debit entries equals the total of the credit entries in the batch. (Sometimes these programs are called *edit* programs.) The *sort* program, normally a utility program, resequences the batch of transactions into ascending customer number order. The *print* program produces a list of the transactions called the *sales journal*. And finally, the *update* program posts each sales transaction to the computer file containing the accounts receivable subsidiary ledger.

Batch sequential processing systems are conceptually simple, and it is relatively easy to convert to this form of processing from a manual system. Although Illustration 10–16 shows that all computer files are on magnetic tape, this is seldom the case. Most files in batch sequential systems are recorded in on-line devices.

Batch sequential processing systems also have disadvantages. First, the information they produce may not be current. Usually transactions are gathered into batches for a day, a week, or a month at a time. The system then posts many batches at once, either daily, weekly, or monthly. This means that the contents of a computerized data file are usually out-of-date in a batch system. Contents are current only when no transactions have occurred after the last execution of the update program. Second, batch sequential systems are inflexible. They are unable to produce ad hoc reports or provide information in any form other than that coded into the system's print programs. Other processing methods overcome these disadvantages.

Batch Systems with On-Line Inquiry

When many companies replaced magnetic tape files with on-line devices in batch processing systems, they made significant improvements in them without replacing the systems. They did this by providing *on-line inquiry* capability. This capability means that a user at a terminal can retrieve data from an accounting data file located in an on-line device. For example, a sales clerk may want to know if a customer has exceeded a credit limit. In a *batch system with on-line inquiry*, the clerk accesses the computerized accounts receivable subsidiary ledger using a query program to find the customer's balance. The clerk then decides whether or not to sell on credit to the customer. If the

ILLUSTRATION 10–16

*A Batch Processing
System Using Sequential
Files*

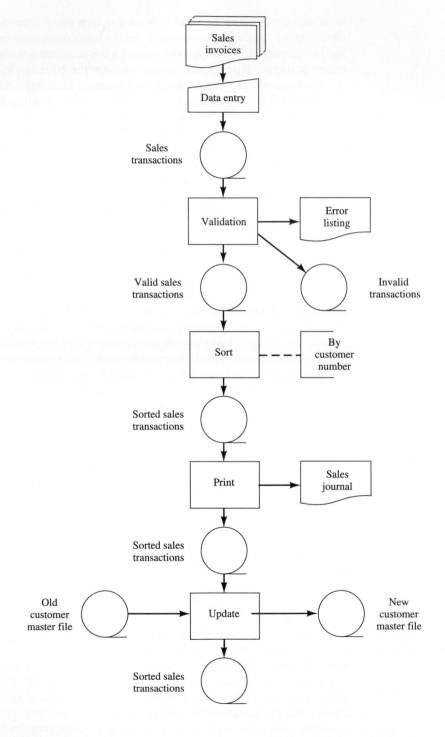

sale is made, the system posts the transaction to the computerized ledger using batch processing procedures.

Illustration 10–17 contains a batch processing system with on-line inquiry. It shows how the accounts receivable system in Illustration 10–16 could provide ad hoc information for credit-granting purposes. In systems of this kind, all data files are on-line.

Batch systems with on-line inquiry are popular in accounting applications using *indexed sequential* files. They achieve the efficiencies of batch sequential processing but are more flexible in how they produce their outputs. In a batch sequential system, a sales clerk wanting to check a customer's credit limit must consult a computer printed report. With on-line inquiry, this information is available at a terminal. However, in each of these systems the information may not be current, because the data in the file was updated at the last posting, which may have been yesterday, last week, or last month. On-line real-time systems overcome this disadvantage.

On-Line Real-Time Systems

When it is important that clerks and managers have access to data that is current, companies implement *on-line real-time systems.* A batch system applies a single processing step, such as validate, sort, print, or update, to an entire batch of transactions before proceeding to the next step. An on-line real-time system applies all processes to a single transaction before proceeding to the next transaction. This means that the results of processing are immediately available to the clerk or manager entering the data into the system.

On-line systems are invaluable for management purposes such as recording airline reservations. Many companies use them in accounting systems as well. An on-line accounts receivable system allows a sales clerk to determine a customer's current balance; an on-line inventory system allows the same clerk to determine if the product requested by the customer is currently in stock.

Illustration 10–18 shows an on-line real-time accounts receivable system. A single program validates and updates each transaction as it is entered. This program also guides the user in entering the data. It may prompt the user with questions, provide a menu, or display on the terminal a replica of the source document. Because the CPU interacts with the user in one of these ways, this is an example of an *interactive system.*

On-line real-time systems frequently provide no printed record of transactions. For this reason they make magnetic records of them on a *transaction log.* This allows reconstruction of the computer file containing the receivables records should the file accidentally be erased or destroyed.

On-line real-time systems provide current data because the results of processing are immediately available. They are frequently used with database management systems so users can easily produce ad hoc reports from the database. They are more complex to develop and maintain than the other approaches, however, and more expensive to implement. They use direct access files that are frequently less efficient for processing accounting transactions. Because they have no visible audit trail, an erroneous transaction entered into an on-line real-time system may create incorrect account balances that are difficult to detect and correct.

ILLUSTRATION 10–17

A Batch System with On-Line Inquiry Using Indexed Sequential Files

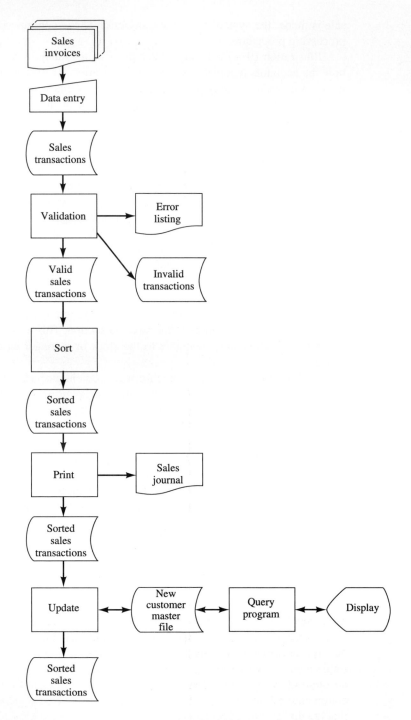

ILLUSTRATION 10–18

An On-Line Real-Time System Using Direct Access Files

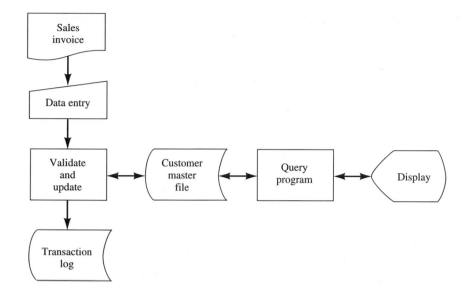

Summary

This chapter has discussed how accounting data are stored and processed in computer-based systems. As humans, we think of data as consisting of characters, fields, records, files, and the database. Some accounting systems do not use files; instead they use a database management system to store and locate data records. The chapter covered some advantages and disadvantages of each approach.

There are four approaches to processing data. Many accounting systems contain elements of all four. They are manual systems, batch sequential processing systems, batch systems with on-line inquiry, and on-line real-time systems. The chapter explained how each works and which advantages each provides.

Key Terms

batch sequential processing system   An approach to processing accounting data. Transactions are accumulated in batches, and a processing step is completed on the entire batch before another processing step begins.

batch system with on-line inquiry   An approach to processing accounting data. Transactions are accumulated in batches when changes are made to the database. However, the data in individual data records can be read one at a time.

database management organization   An approach to organizing data in which a set of computer programs, the database management system, maintains data for all applications.

database management system   A set of computer programs that maintains a database independent of the application programs using it.

direct access   An approach to organizing traditional data files. Data management software computes from the key field of a record the storage location for it on a secondary storage device.

indexed sequential   An approach to organizing traditional data files. The records are physically located in sequence by key field. An index shows the locations on secondary storage of some of the records in the file.

logical data structure   A logical view of how data is organized by a database management system. It describes how the software searches through a database to locate a data item.

on-line real-time system   An approach to processing accounting data. All processes are applied to one transaction before proceeding to the next transaction.

query language   A nonprocedural language that enables accountants and managers to easily retrieve data that are stored by a database management system.

schema   A logical view of data records as they are stored by a database management system.

sequential   An approach to organizing traditional data files in which records are physically arranged in sequence by primary key field.

subschema   A restricted view of data records maintained by a database management system. Each application program has its own subschema.

traditional data file organization   An approach to organizing data in which application software maintains data files independent of those maintained by other applications.

Questions

10–1. Why did computer manufacturers develop ways to encode numbers, letters, and punctuation marks in binary form?

10–2. How are accounting data stored in a computer from the viewpoint of the computer? Of the human user?

10–3. What is the difference between a logical record and a physical record?

10–4. What is the difference between a primary key and a generic key?

10–5. A customer master file contains one record for each customer. A field in the record shows the amount that the customer owes. How does a computer program locate the amount owed by customer number 43056 if the file is
   a. Sequential?
   b. Direct access?
   c. Indexed sequential?

10–6. What are the deficiencies of the traditional data file organization? Which deficiency is the least serious? Which is the most serious? How does a database management organization overcome them?

10–7. What is a database management system?

10–8. How does a subschema differ from a schema?

10–9. What do each of the following have in common? How do they differ?
   a. Data definition language.
   b. Data manipulation language.
   c. Query language.

10–10. Describe the purpose of a data dictionary.

10–11. A database consists of a set of related records. What is the difference between the physical arrangement of those records and their logical arrangement?

10–12. For which reporting situations is each of the following data structures best suited?
   a. Tree.
   b. Network.
   c. Relational.

10–13. What is a one-write system? When would one be most useful?

10–14. A batch processing system is so named because it processes transactions in batches. Which forms can these batches of transactions take?

10–15. How do batch processing systems that provide on-line inquiry differ from those that do not?

10–16. What distinguishes an on-line real-time system from other data processing systems?

10–17. In which system do you find a transaction log? What does it look like? What is its purpose?

Exercises and Cases

10–18.   PROCESSING METHODS

For each of the following application systems, suggest which kind of processing method is best.

a. Airline reservations.
b. Sales order entry.
c. Cash disbursements.
d. Inventory.
e. Cash receipts.

10–19.   PROCESSING METHODS

Why do you think that most payroll applications use batch processing?

10–20.   DATA STORAGE

Following are seven components of data as they are stored in a computer. For each component, identify the other component(s) of which it is a part.

a. Record.
b. Database.
c. Field.
d. Word.

e. Bit.

f. Byte.

g. File.

10–21.   DATA STORAGE

Exhibit 10–1 contains three different record layouts. After examining them, answer each of the following questions.

a. How many characters are in the VENDOR NAME field?

b. What is the primary key of record type 3, the transaction file expense detail record?

c. What is the primary key of record type 2, the master file vendor address record?

d. Identify one generic key in this system.

e. How many digits are in a purchase order number?

f. What is the largest quantity that this system can process? The largest amount?

10–22.   SHARED DATA ITEMS

The records in Exhibit 10–1 are from an accounts payable application. Identify four data items in these records that would be used in other applications. For each, suggest an application that would use it.

10–23.   STORAGE AND PROCESSING METHODS

A sales analysis application can be valuable for decision makers in a marketing department. Such a system generates reports allowing a sales manager to analyze the results of sales promotions, evaluate salespersons' performance, and identify successful products or important customers.

Often, data for sales analysis reports come from the billing system in an organization. This system uses an invoice transaction file that includes as a minimum the following fields: customer number, sales division code, shipment date, customer purchase order number, product number, quantity shipped, and unit price.

Required:

a. Of the four methods of processing, which would be most appropriate for a sales analysis application?

b. Assume that you are designing a sales analysis system using the traditional data file approach. Which routine reports would you want this system to provide?

c. Assume that you are a divisional sales manager and that the system uses the database management approach. Which ad hoc reports would you want to produce using a query language?

10–24.   DATABASE MANAGEMENT SYSTEMS

Progress in the design and development of computer-based management information systems has been impressive. Traditionally, computer-based data processing systems were arranged by departments and applications. Computers were applied to single, large-volume applications such as inventory control or customer billing. Other applications were added once the first applications were operating smoothly.

As more applications were added, problems in data management developed. Businesses looked for ways to integrate the data processing systems to make them more

EXHIBIT 10-1

Exercises 10–21 and 10–22

Record Type 1: Master File Vendor Name Record

Vendor Code	Recd. Type	Space	Blank	Vendor Name	Blank	Card Code 100

Record Type 2: Master File Vendor Address Record

Vendor Code	Recd. Type	Space	Blank	Address-Line 1	Address-Line 2	Address-Line 3	Blank	Card Code 120

Record Type 3: Transaction File Expense Detail Record

Vendor Code	Recd. Type	Voucher Number	Blank	Batch	Voucher Number	Voucher Date	Vendor Code	Invoice Date	Due Date	Invoice Number	Purchase Order Number	Debit Account	Prd. Type	Product Code	Blank	Amount	Quantity	Card Code 160

comprehensive and to have shorter response times. As a consequence, the database systems composed of the database itself, the database management system, and the individual application programs were developed.

Required:

a. Explain the differences between the traditional approach to data processing and the use of database management systems in
   1. File structure.
   2. Processing of data.

b. Identify and discuss the unfavorable issues that a company should consider before implementing a database management system.

10–25.   ON-LINE REAL-TIME SYSTEMS

Executive management of Continental Incorporated, a rapidly expanding manufacturing company, has been reviewing a proposal prepared by the manager of the data processing department to update the computer equipment now in use. The present equipment includes a central processing unit, tape drives, a card reader, and a printer. The chief information officer suggests that new equipment should be acquired to provide on-line real-time capability for inventory control and more efficient operations.

Required:

a. Briefly describe the function of each item of equipment now in use.

b. Identify two types of equipment not mentioned that would be required for the proposed on-line real-time application.

(CIA Adapted)

10–26.   DATABASE MANAGEMENT SYSTEMS

Mariposa Products, a textile and apparel manufacturer, acquired its own computer in 1978. The first application to be developed and implemented was production and inventory control. Other applications that were added in succession were payroll, accounts receivable, and accounts payable.

The applications were not integrated due to the piecemeal manner in which they were developed and implemented. Nevertheless, the system proved satisfactory for several years. Generally, reports were prepared on time, and information was readily accessible.

Mariposa operates in a very competitive industry. A combination of increased operating costs and the competitive nature of the industry have had an adverse effect on profit margins and operating profits. Ed Wilde, Mariposa's president, requested that some special analyses be prepared in an attempt to provide information that would help management improve operations. Unfortunately, some of the data were not consistent among the reports. In addition, there were no data by product line or by department. These problems were attributable to the fact that Mariposa's applications were developed piecemeal and, as a consequence, duplicate data that were not necessarily consistent existed on Mariposa's computer system.

Wilde was concerned that Mariposa's computer system was not able to generate the information his managers needed to make decisions. He called a meeting of his top management and certain data processing personnel to discuss potential solutions to

Mariposa's problems. At this meeting, Wilde concluded that a new information system was needed that would integrate Mariposa's applications.

Mariposa's controller suggested that the company consider a database management system (DBMS) that would be accessible by all departments. As a first step, the controller proposed hiring a database administrator on a consulting basis to determine the feasibility of converting to a DBMS.

Required:

a. Identify the components of a DBMS.
b. Discuss the advantages and disadvantages of a DBMS for Mariposa Products.
c. List the factors that Mariposa Products should consider before converting to a DBMS.
d. Describe the duties of a database administrator.

(CMA Adapted)

10–27.   *STORAGE AND PROCESSING METHODS*

The controller of Kensler Company has been working with the MIS department to revise part of the company's financial reporting system. A study is under way on how to develop and implement a data entry and data retention system for key computer files used by various departments responsible to the controller. The departments involved and details on their data processing activities are as follows:

General Accounting

- Daily processing of journal entries submitted by various departments.
- Weekly updating of file balances with subsystem data from areas such as payroll, accounts receivable, and accounts payable.
- Sporadic requests for account balances during the month with increased activity at month-end.

Accounts Receivable

- Daily processing of receipts for payments on account.
- Daily processing of sales to customers.
- Daily checks to be sure that the maximum credit limit of $200,000 per customer is not exceeded and to identify orders in excess of $20,000 per customer.
- Daily requests for customer credit status regarding payments and account balances.
- Weekly reporting to general accounting file.

Accounts Payable

- Processing of payments to vendors three times a week.
- Weekly expense distribution reporting to general accounting file.

Budget Planning and Control

- Updating of flexible budgets on a monthly basis.
- Quarterly rebudgeting based on sales forecast and production schedule changes.
- Monthly inquiry requests for budget balances.

The chief information officer has explained the concepts of the following processing techniques to the controller's staff and the appropriate members of the affected departments:

Batch processing.
On-line real-time processing.
Batch processing with on-line inquiry.

The chief information officer has indicated to the controller that batch processing is the least expensive processing technique and that a rough estimate of the cost of the other techniques would be as follows:

Technique	Cost in Relation to Batch Processing
On-line real-time processing	2.5 times
Batch with on-line inquiry	1.5 times

Required:

a. Define and discuss the major differences between the input options of the following processing techniques:
   1. Batch processing.
   2. Batch processing with on-line inquiry.
   3. On-line real-time processing.

b. Identify and explain the input technique and the file inquiry that probably should be employed by Kensler Company for each of the four departments responsible to the controller. Assume that the volume of transactions is not a key variable in these decisions.
   1. General accounting.
   2. Accounts receivable.
   3. Accounts payable.
   4. Budget planning and control.

(CMA Adapted)

10–28.   PROCESSING METHODS

Weekender Corporation owns and operates 15 large departmentalized retail hardware stores in major metropolitan areas of the southwest United States. The stores carry a wide variety of merchandise, but their major thrust is toward the weekend do-it-yourselfer. The company has been successful in this field, and the number of stores in the chain has almost doubled in the past 10 years.

Each retail store acquires its merchandise from the company's centrally located warehouse. Consequently, the warehouse must maintain an up-to-date and well-stocked inventory ready to meet the demands of the individual stores.

The company wishes to hold its competitive position with similar stores of other companies in its marketing area. Therefore, Weekender Corporation must improve its purchasing and inventory procedures. The company's stores must have the proper goods to meet customer demand, and the warehouse in turn must have the goods available. The number of company stores, the number of inventory items carried, and the volume of business all are providing pressure to change from basically manual data processing routines to mechanized data processing procedures. Recently, the company has been investigating two different approaches to computerization: batch processing and real-time processing. No decision has been reached on the approach to be followed.

Top management has determined that the following items should have high priority in the new system procedures:

1. Rapid ordering to replenish warehouse inventory stocks with as little delay as possible.
2. Quick filling and shipping of merchandise to the stores (this involves determining if sufficient stock exists).
3. Some indication of inventory activity.
4. Perpetual records to determine quickly inventory level by item number.

A description of the current warehousing and purchasing procedures follows:

Warehouse Procedures

Stock is stored in bins and located by an inventory number. The numbers are listed sequentially on the bins to facilitate locating items for shipment; frequently this system is not followed, and, as a result, some items are difficult to locate.

Whenever a retail store needs merchandise, it completes a three-part merchandise request form. One copy is kept by the store, and two copies are mailed to the warehouse the next day. If the merchandise requested is on hand, the goods are delivered to the store accompanied by the third copy of the request. The second copy is filed at the warehouse.

If the quantity of goods on hand is not sufficient to fill the order, the warehouse sends the quantity available and notes the quantity shipped on the request form. Then a purchase memorandum for the shortage is prepared by the warehouse. At the end of each day, all three memos are sent to the purchasing department.

When ordered goods are received, they are checked at the receiving area, and a receiving report is prepared. One copy of the receiving report is retained at the receiving area, one is forwarded to accounts payable, and one is filed at the warehouse with the purchase memorandum.

Purchasing Department Procedures

When the purchase memoranda are received from the warehouse, purchase orders are prepared. Vendor catalogs are used to select the best source for the requested goods, and the purchase order is prepared and mailed. Copies of the order are sent to accounts payable and the receiving area; one copy is retained in the purchasing department.

When the receiving report arrives in the purchasing department, it is compared with the purchase order on file. The receiving report is also checked with the invoice before the invoice is forwarded to accounts payable for payment.

The purchasing department strives periodically to evaluate the vendors for financial soundness, reliability, and trade relationships. However, because the volume of requests received from the warehouse is so great, currently this activity does not have a high priority.

Each week a report of the open purchase orders is prepared to determine if any action should be taken on overdue deliveries. This report is prepared manually from scanning the file of outstanding purchase orders.

Required:

a. Of the possible methods of processing, which one would best meet the needs of Weekender?

b. To implement the system you recommend in your answer to part *a,* which computer hardware must Weekender acquire?

(CMA Adapted)

10–29.   *REMOTE PROCESSING*

Champion Products, Inc., a subsidiary of Sara Lee Corp., is a Rochester, New York manufacturer of silk-screened T-shirts, jerseys, and sweatshirts.[1] Champion sells to retail outlets across the United States as well as to athletic and institutional customers such as the Notre Dame Fighting Irish football team. The company recently replaced its manual order entry system for retail sales with a computerized system relying on laptop personal computers.

The Old System

Champion produces for retail distribution approximately 42,000 designs, including variations in style, size, and color. The large number of ordering options made errors commonplace, and many were expensive to correct.

Previously, sales personnel had to write retail orders by hand on an order form. They then mailed the forms to a central office, dubbed the "black hole," where they would wait for up to three weeks. Ultimately, data entry personnel would key the order information into the mainframe. To find out what was currently on hand, sales representatives relied on inventory status reports that were two weeks old by the time they arrived in the mail. The process was time consuming and prone to errors, and it lacked the level of customer service that Champion wanted to achieve.

The New System

The new order entry system equips each member of Champion's 60-person sales force with a laptop personal computer containing a 40-megabyte hard drive. To fill an order, each sales representative merely responds to choices on a menu. This decreases errors because reps do not have to enter obscure codes or words at a keyboard. The chief information officer believes that the decrease in order errors will pay for the system in less than three years.

---

[1]Adapted from "T-Shirt Company Champions Automated Ordering Process," *Computerworld,* January 28, 1991. Used by permission.

The sales reps access the headquarters computer by using a 24-hour, toll-free telephone line. They use it to inquire about an earlier order or determine the status of current and projected inventories. The headquarters mainframe accumulates orders in a file and enters them nightly in the mainframe-based order entry application. This reduces order lead time to 24 hours, provides quicker reaction to changes in customer demand, and aids in inventory planning.

The mainframe holds the customer and product databases and can download to the laptops data such as design changes, customer address changes, and locations of new customers. An electronic mail system alerts sales reps to the existence of these changes.

User Involvement

The system design and implementation was a team effort. The MIS department recommended the hardware and determined the size of the hard drive required to store the retail product database. MIS personnel also provide in-house training in the system and maintain a sales support hot line to answer questions about the software.

A team of sales representatives developed the specifications for the software. Because the resulting design did not originate from MIS, all complaints are directed to sales reps who helped set the specifications.

Future Plans

Because of the success of the system, Champion is already planning its expansion. Future purchases of laptops will contain 100-megabyte hard drives in order to hold the 500,000-item database of their athletic and institutional product line. The MIS department is evaluating installing a minicomputer at headquarters to act as a bridge between the laptops and the mainframe. The new machine would process all file transfers and inquiries, thereby reducing contention for the mainframe, which already supports more than 500 users.

Required:

a. What processing method does Champion's new order processing system use? What data storage method?
b. What were the financial factors that justified the new system? What were the qualitative factors?

11   FILE PROCESSING METHODS

Learning Objectives

1. To understand how accounting data files are processed with the traditional data file approach.
2. To recognize the types of files used in accounting information systems.
3. To identify the operations that accounting information systems use when processing files.
4. To discover how batch processing systems use sequential files.
5. To find out how batch systems with on-line inquiry use indexed sequential files.
6. To learn how on-line real-time systems use direct access files.

Introduction

Organizations use two approaches when organizing the data in their databases: the traditional data file approach and the database management approach. This chapter deals with traditional data file organization. The chapter discusses the different forms that files can take and explains the three methods used for organizing data files. It details how these methods work and the advantages and disadvantages of each.

Types of Files

A *file* is a collection of information stored so that it can be retrieved for later use. Computer-based accounting systems use files in many forms. Most accounting records are contained in one type of file, the data file. However, other forms are employed as a system processes data files. To understand how systems retrieve information from data files, knowledge about the file types is useful. All files are classified by the technology used and by their content.

Classifying Files by Technology

When classified by technology, files are either manual files or computer files. A *manual* file stores information that can be retrieved, read, and used by people. A *computer* file stores information for retrieval by the systems software of the computer. It cannot be read by humans without additional computer processing.

Manual Files.   Companies have used manual files for hundreds of years. The procedures for manual files have much in common with those used in computerized files. Reviewing some examples of manual files makes it easier to understand how the computer processes its files.

Manual Storage Devices.   Most manual files in accounting systems use filing cabinets as the storage device. Clerks frequently combine similar documents in file folders within the cabinets. A label on the outside of each cabinet drawer identifies the file folders in that drawer. Within a filing cabinet, a clerk may sequence folders alphabetically, for example, by customer name, or numerically by invoice number. Documents within a file folder may also follow alphabetical, date, or numerical sequence.

Other storage devices used for manual files include a box to hold a card file or a bound volume containing a ledger or journal. For example, a perpetual inventory system may be kept in a card file with one card for each item in inventory. The inventory clerk files cards either alphabetically by description or numerically by item number. Early accounting systems used bound ledgers. One page in the ledger summarized transactions for one account. The bookkeeper creating the ledger sequenced the pages alphabetically by account name within the volume.

Manual Storage and Retrieval.   Regardless of the storage device, these manual systems use the same method of arranging the records they contain. Each system arranges the records sequentially by some key field. The key field is the customer name, invoice number, item description, item number, or account name used in determining the filing sequence. These manual systems, then, are all examples of *sequential* files.

How do clerks retrieve information from files in a manual system? Different clerks do this in different ways, even when working with the same system. An inexperienced clerk may start with the first filing cabinet and look in sequence at the label on each file drawer until finding the desired one. An experienced clerk, knowing that the customers whose names begin with the letter *C* start in the second drawer of the second cabinet, would begin a sequential search there. A large file room may have a map posted at its door showing the locations of various files within the room. Illustration 11–1 shows how information storage and retrieval may occur in such a manual system.

Manual systems are flexible in how a user retrieves information from them. Different clerks may use various methods, and their preferences may change as the amount of data grows. In this case, the method of information retrieval may change without changing the system's method of storage.

Computer systems do not have this advantage. The system design team determines the method of information retrieval for a computer file when the system is created. Changes to this method require changes to the system itself.

Computer Files.   Most modern accounting systems use both manual and computer files. Although each uses different recording techniques, they share similar methods for organizing data.

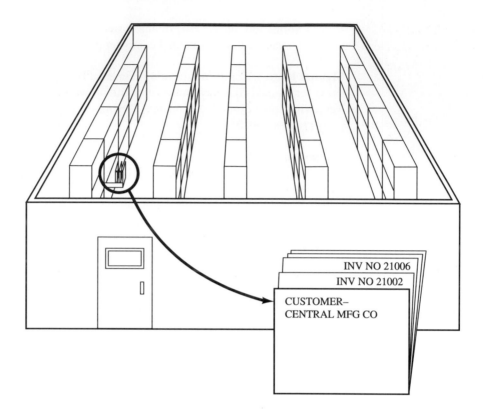

Computer Storage Devices.   The most common storage devices for computer files are magnetic disks, magnetic tapes, and floppy disks (or diskettes). Peripheral devices magnetically encode characters, fields, and records on these devices. Data management software places records on the device at locations it can identify. When a computer program requires a specific record, the software determines the location of the record on the device and retrieves the record for the program.

Computer Storage and Retrieval.   Just as a file room contains a fixed number of filing cabinet drawers, a magnetic storage device contains a fixed number of storage locations. On a diskette, for example, locations exist for each combination of a sector and a track. A *sector* is a segment of the disk radiating outward from its center at a specified angle from a reference point on the diskette. A *track* is an imaginary ring at a constant radius from the center. Data management software assigns to each sector–track combination an *address* that uniquely identifies it. Illustration 11–2 shows how a sector and a track identify an addressable location on a diskette. Other direct access storage devices work similarly.

Each direct access storage device also contains a *directory* written magnetically on it. This directory is equivalent to the file room map in Illustration 11–1, because it guides the data management software to the locations of specific data on the device. For example, a diskette contains a directory track about halfway outward from its center.

ILLUSTRATION 11–2

Record Storage and Retrieval on Direct Access Devices

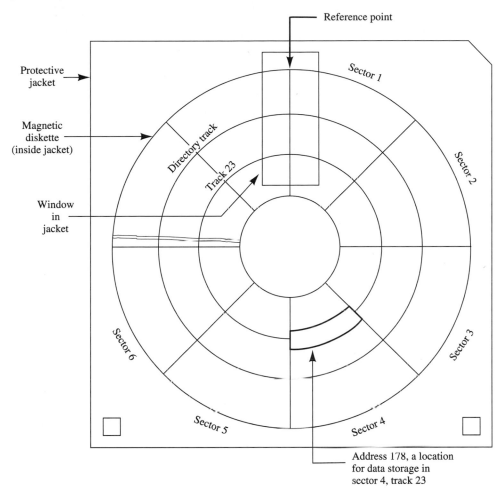

Whenever a user saves a new file on the diskette, data management software records the name of the file and the location of its first data record (along with other information) on this directory track.

A magnetic tape lacks addressable locations on its recording surface. For this reason, data management software always stores and retrieves records sequentially when using this device. A *header record* precedes the first data in the file and marks the beginning of the file; a *trailer record* after the last data marks its end. To locate a specific record in a tape file, a computer program first locates the header record for the file. It then reads each data record until it finds the desired one. This is similar to the way in which a clerk locates a specific invoice copy in a file folder of invoices. Illustration 11–3 shows how data are stored on and retrieved from magnetic tape.

ILLUSTRATION 11–3

Data Storage on Magnetic Tape

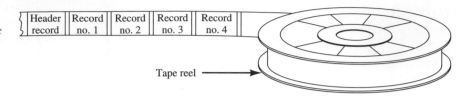

Tape reel ⟶

Sometimes, for efficiency, data management software locates multiple records together at the same location on a storage device. It transfers this group of records to and from main storage together, even when the application requires only one of them. Such a group of records is a *block*. The number of records stored in the group is the *blocking factor* of the data file.

Assume, for example, that a single record contains all the data relevant to one customer. Data management software writes the data for four different customers at a single location on a storage device. Then a block contains four records, and the blocking factor is four. When a user wants data about any one of the four customers, the data management software must transfer all four customer records from the device to main storage. Although it increases the complexity of processing, blocking records decreases the amount of time required to retrieve data from an external storage device. Computer systems commonly use blocking on magnetic tapes and frequently use it on other devices as well.

It should not come as a surprise, given how records are stored in both manual and computer files, that accountants use similar methods. After all, when accountants first began to use computers, they did so by simply converting existing methods to a new recording medium. A later section of this chapter points out similarities in file processing; however, the next section explains how to classify files by their content.

Classifying Files by Content

All files used in a computer system are either program files or data files. The operating system deals with each type of file in a different way.

A *program file* contains instructions that are executable by the computer. Program files include not only application programs but also system programs such as utilities. Most program files seldom change during the routine operation of an accounting system.

A *data file* contains records that are nonexecutable. These records are used for some purpose by program files and may be changed many times during the operation of a system. Data files include text files used by word processing software, index files used by data management software, and parameter files used by many kinds of system software. However, the data files of most concern to accountants are those containing accounting data. The five types of accounting data files are master, transaction, backup, archive, and scratch files. Illustration 11–4 summarizes these types of files.

Master Files.   All accounting systems use master files. A *master file* is the computer-readable equivalent of a ledger in a manual system. Each record in a master file typically contains a collection of data fields relating to a specific account. Although contents of these fields may change, the records are added or deleted from the file infrequently. Master file records consist of data fields containing both reference and balance data.

ILLUSTRATION 11–4

Accounting Data Files

Master file. Contains relatively permanent records that are added and deleted infrequently during file maintenance; balance data are changed during file update.

Transaction file. Records are removed from the file after posting; balance data change a master record during file update.

Backup file. A duplicate copy of another file that enables re-creating the original file if lost or destroyed.

Archive file. A file kept for many years as a record for historical or reference purposes.

Scratch file. A file used temporarily by computer programs.

For example, a general ledger master file contains one record for each account in the chart of accounts. **Reference data** in a record include those fields that seldom change, such as account numbers and account titles. Each record also contains **balance data,** the amounts or quantities that change each time a transaction is posted to the account. Other common master files include the inventory master file, containing one record for each item maintained in inventory, and the customer master file, with one record for each approved customer. Illustration 11–5 shows typical reference and balance data for these and some other master files.

Transaction Files.   Batch processing systems use *transaction files.* In these systems, clerks accumulate source documents—each representing one accounting transaction of a certain type—into batches prior to processing. Data entry clerks then convert each document into computer-readable form, producing a transaction file. The file thus

ILLUSTRATION 11–5

Reference and Balance Data in Master Files

Example	Reference Data	Balance Data
General ledger master file	Account number Account description	Account balance
Inventory master file	Item number Item description Reorder point Order quantity	Quantity on hand Quantity on order
Customer master file	Customer number Name and address Credit limit	Balance owed
Vendor master file	Vendor number Name and address Discount policy	Year-to-date purchases

Payroll master file	Employee number
	Name and address
	Personal data
	Deductions code
	Withholding code
		Year-to-date
		    earnings and
		    withholdings
		    amounts

contains one record for each transaction. The system applies each processing step to all transactions in the transaction file before proceeding to the next step. One process in many systems is posting the transactions in the transaction file to a master file.

For example, a computerized payroll system collects employees' timecards prior to payday on Friday. A payroll clerk sorts these cards into batches, one for each department. The clerk then enters the data from the timecards at a terminal, creating a file of payroll transactions. This file contains one record for each employee for whom a weekly paycheck is due. The system applies each processing step first to all the transaction records in a batch, and then to all batches in the transaction file, before proceeding to the next step. During a posting step, the system adds the gross pay for each employee to the year-to-date earnings field in that employee's payroll master file record.

A transaction record contains both reference and balance data. At a minimum, each record contains two fields: the primary key field identifying the master record affected by the transaction and an amount or quantity. Illustration 11–6 summarizes the data typically contained in three types of transaction file: a journal voucher transaction file, a payroll transaction file, and a sales order transaction file.

Accountants use transaction files because they are an efficient way to process a large number of transactions of the same type. However, on-line real-time systems process transaction records individually. They post a transaction record to a master record without first creating a file of transaction records.

Backup Files.   A *backup file* is a duplicate copy of another file. Computer operators make backup copies of files for use in case the original is accidentally damaged or erased. Mainframe system users commonly record the backup copies on magnetic tape. Those with personal computers may use tape or disks.

ILLUSTRATION 11–6

Data in Typical Transaction File Records

Example	Data Field	Type
Journal voucher transaction file	Account number	Reference
	Date	Reference
	Debit or credit code	Reference
	Description	Reference
	Amount	Balance
	Source number	Reference
Payroll transaction file	Employee number	Reference
	Regular hours	Balance
	Overtime hours	Balance
	Vacation time	Balance
	Sick time	Balance
Sales order transaction file	Customer number	Reference
	Salesperson number	Reference
	Purchase order number	Reference
	Item number	Reference
	Quantity	Balance
	Price	Reference

Most organizations make backup copies of all program files and store them away from the processing facility. If a fire, flood, or other disaster damages the facility, the organization avoids loss of its computer programs. They also make periodic backup copies of all master files. This allows re-creation of the file as of the last backup date. Backups of certain master files, such as a customer master file, are very important. The records in this file show the balances owed by customers. Many of these balances would never be collected if the organization lost its record of them.

Organizations frequently do not make backups of transaction files. Instead, they keep the original documents on hand for a reasonable period of time. They use these to re-create the transaction file when this is necessary.

If you have a personal computer, it is important that you learn to make routine backup copies of all your files. Many business files created on personal computers are irreplaceable. People never appreciate the importance of this backup procedure until they accidentally lose a file containing hours of hard work!

Archive Files.   An *archive file* is a copy of a master file and transactions maintained for historical or reference purposes. In the United States, tax laws require maintenance of documentation supporting taxable income for a specified period of time. Auditors are frequently concerned with account balances up to five years in the past. They may consult archive files as part of their audits.

Scratch Files.   A scratch file contains the computer-readable equivalent of a piece of scratch paper. Some utility programs require that the computer operator make a scratch file available to the program. The program then records data records in the scratch file temporarily while executing. At the conclusion of execution, the scratch file is no longer needed.

In summary, there are five types of files used in both manual and computer systems. Similarities exist between these two recording methods in how data are stored and retrieved from files. The next section discusses some operations performed on computer files when data are stored and retrieved.

File Operations

Computerized accounting systems routinely use certain procedures when processing computer files. Conceptually they are similar to the operations used in manual systems. However, the terminology describing them may be new. Knowing these concepts before learning how files are processed is important. Four common operations performed on computer files are updating, maintenance, sorting, and merging.

File Update

A *file update* is an operation in which a computer program changes the balance data in a master file record. This is the computerized equivalent of posting to a ledger in a manual system. The term *posting* with a computer system has already come up in this text, so the concept is familiar. When a system posts transactions, it also updates a master file. Both terms identify one of the procedures that the computer system applies to a transaction when processing it.

In a batch processing system, the update process uses an old master file and a transaction file containing batches of transactions for posting. For each record in the transaction file, a computer program adds the balance data to the record having the same key field in the master file. This creates a new master file with updated balance data. The accounting system may then apply other processes to the new master file. Illustration 4–6 contains a program flowchart of the update process in a batch processing system.

An on-line real-time system applies all processes to an individual transaction before it begins processing the next transaction. A computer user enters the transaction at a terminal. The data entry program examines the transaction for obvious errors. If there are none, the program updates an on-line master file with the balance data from the transaction. The program then copies the transaction onto the transaction log, and the user enters the next transaction. Illustration 11–7 contains system flowcharts contrasting the update process in batch processing and on-line real-time systems.

File Maintenance

File maintenance is an operation in which a computer program changes the reference data in a master file, adds records to the master file, or deletes them. In this way, the computer program maintains the reference data in the file.

For example, the reference data in a customer master file includes fields containing the customer's address. A file maintenance program changes the contents of this field whenever the address changes. When the company acquires a new customer, the file maintenance program adds a new record to the master file.

In batch processing systems, file maintenance routinely occurs prior to a file update. This avoids attempting to update a new master record that is awaiting addition to the master file.

In an on-line real-time system, a clerk executes the file maintenance program at an on-line terminal. The clerk makes changes one at a time to the master file.

Sort

A *sort* is an operation in which a computer program resequences the records in a data file. This produces a file in which all records are physically arranged on a secondary

ILLUSTRATION 11–7

File Update Processes

A. In a batch processing system

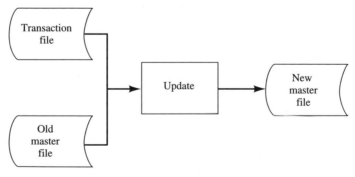

B. In an on-line real-time system

storage device in a sequence determined by one of the fields in each record. In accounting applications, this is frequently the primary key field.

Batch processing systems routinely apply a sort operation to transaction files prior to performing an update. The update procedure flowcharted in Illustration 4–6 requires that both transaction and master files occur in the same sequence. The master file ordinarily stays in sequence by primary key field. However, the records in a transaction file are in random order. This is why the system sorts this file into order of ascending primary key prior to executing the update program.

Illustration 11–8 contains a flowchart of a batch system requiring a sort operation. In this example, a program sorts the transaction file of sales orders into customer number order before updating a customer master file.

A utility program usually executes the sort operation. On-line real-time systems require sorts less often because they process individual transactions rather than transaction files.

Merge

A *merge* is an operation in which two sequential files are combined into a third file of the same sequence. The program performing this operation therefore merges two files into one. Some batch processing systems routinely merge two transaction files into a third one prior to updating. Merging is efficient whenever two conditions occur: (1) Transactions are entered into a transaction file more frequently than the update occurs, and (2) the transaction files are large.

To understand why the merge operation is useful, consider the example shown in the sales order entry system of Illustration 11–9. In this system, a clerk enters sales into the computer daily, creating a daily sales transaction file. The system sorts the daily transactions and merges them with those entered and sorted earlier in the week. It posts the sorted sales transaction file to the customer master file on Friday evening.

Why did the clerk use a merge operation rather than sort all the transactions each day? If only a few transactions are involved, the clerk can simply add the daily transactions to those recorded earlier in the week and then sort them. However, if there are a large number of transactions, the sort would be much slower than using a merge. Merging two sorted files daily occupies the central processor for much less time than would sorting an entire week's transactions.

So far this chapter has covered the different types of files in a computer system and the major operations applied to them. Next follows a discussion of how these files are organized and processed in a system using traditional data file organization.

File Organization Methods

Traditional data file systems use three forms of *file organization.* One form, sequential data organization, computerizes methods used in previous manual systems. Though more expensive to implement, the other approaches—direct access and indexed sequential file organization—overcome some of the disadvantages of sequential files.

Sequential Files

Sequential files contain data records physically located in primary key field sequence. Thus, records with successively higher keys are stored at successively higher addresses on a device. A program processing a sequential file writes and retrieves records in this physical sequence. Each time this type of file is processed, the records are retrieved in

ILLUSTRATION 11–8

Sort Operation in Batch Processing

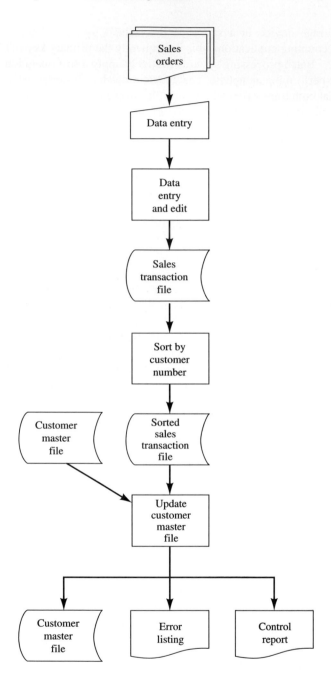

ILLUSTRATION 11–9

Merge Operation in Batch Processing

Daily

Sales orders

↓

Data entry

↓

Data entry and edit

↓

Daily sales transactions

↓

Sort by customer number

↓

Sorted daily sales transactions

↓

Weekly sales transactions (old) → Merge

↓

Weekly sales transactions (new)

↓

Weekly

Customer master file → Update customer master file

↓

Customer master file   Error listing   Control report sequence starting with the first one. Sequential data organization is useful for data files in which most of the records are updated each time the file is used.

Processing Sequential Files.   Companies developed sequential file processing techniques for mechanical systems using card sorters. They later adapted them to electronic computers using tape storage. Now they apply similar procedures to processing sequential files on direct access storage devices such as disks. This approach requires three separate sequential files: a transaction file, an old master file, and a new master file. Illustration 4–6 diagrams the update process. A file update program reads records in sequence from the transaction and master files and compares key fields of the records. If the keys are equal, the program adds amounts or quantities to the equivalent fields in the master record. If the transaction key is greater than the master key, the program reads additional master records in sequence until it finds matching keys. If the transaction key is less than the master key, the program prints an error message on a report. This alerts accounting personnel to add the proper master record by performing file maintenance.

The file update program creates the new master file, record by record, as it retrieves the records in the old master file. Changes to the master file are complete when the program reaches the end of the transaction file. It then copies all remaining records from the old master file to the new one. Usually the old master file is retained as a backup file.

Occasionally this is described as father–son sequential processing.[1] The term applies because the process uses the old master file, the *father,* to create the new master file, the *son.* Because the transactions in the transaction file are usually batched, people also call them *batch sequential* systems.

Illustration 11–10 shows how a central processing unit (CPU) processes sequential files when executing an application program. It reads transactions in sequence from the transaction and old master files. It compares their key fields (shown by the numbers in the boxes), takes the proper action, and writes the master record to the new master file. In this illustration, the CPU has copied the transaction record with a key field of 11 into main storage. It also has copied the master record with a key field of 11 into main storage and is changing the contents of this record. After the change is complete, it copies the changed master record to the new master file. It next processes the transaction and old master records with key fields containing the number 15.

Sequential processing requires that the application program search through every record in the file. In a manual system, this is like having a clerk search in sequence through every file in a file room. It is inefficient if the clerk needs only one document, but if the clerk must process a high percentage of the documents, it is an appropriate approach. This illustrates the major advantage of sequential files.

Advantages and Disadvantages.   Sequential processing is efficient for applications in which a relatively high percentage of master file records change during one pass through the file. The storage device requires only a short time to locate the next record in the file because the next record is physically located next to the last one processed.

---

[1]Some people prefer to call this *parent–child processing.*

ILLUSTRATION 11–10

Sequential File Processing

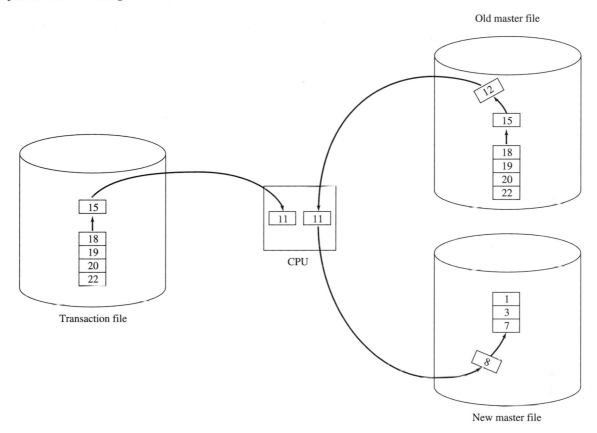

When a report printed from the files requires a listing in key field order, printing is faster because the files are already in the desired sequence. If the master file is massive, it can be processed without the entire file being on-line. This saves hardware costs. Sequential processing allows the use of magnetic tape files that are ordinarily less expensive.

When a relatively low percentage of master file records is required, however, sequential processing is inefficient. This is because the update program must copy all records in the old master file to the new one even if they are not used. For this reason, sequential processing is not used when on-line inquiry is desired. Furthermore, all files must be sorted in the same sequence prior to file update or file maintenance.

Direct Access Files

Direct access files are used on ***direct access storage devices,*** such as a magnetic disk. Rather than storing data physically in sequence, direct access files contain records stored at randomly chosen addresses throughout the device.

To store a record, data management software reads the primary key and with a *hashing algorithm* computes an address. (A hashing algorithm is a complex equation that distributes records evenly throughout the external storage device.) Later, when an application program wants to change the contents of the record, it recomputes this address to locate the record. If the hashing algorithm works properly, it always calculates the same address from any specific key field.

Designers for this data management software would like to develop algorithms that produce a unique storage address for each record in a file. This is practically impossible, so instead they develop routines that minimize the number of times more than one record receives the same address. These duplicate addresses, called *synonyms,* are difficult to avoid. Designers provide for synonyms by using either buckets or overflow areas.

A *bucket* is an area on the device, defined in size by a programmer, containing one or more records. When key fields of two different records produce the same device address, the software places both records, in no particular order, in the bucket at that address. To retrieve a record, the software again executes the algorithm originally used to store the data. It then searches the bucket at the resulting address to find the record with the proper key.

An *overflow area* is a section on the direct access device where data management software places all synonyms. When retrieving a synonym, it must search the overflow area sequentially.

Processing Direct Access Files.   An application system using direct access files processes transactions in any order. The application program provides the primary key of the desired record to the data management software. This software locates the record and transfers it into main storage.

Illustration 11–11 shows this process. Note that both the transactions and the master file contents are in no specified sequence. The CPU examines the key field of a transaction, currently the number 11. From this, it computes the address on secondary storage of the master record with the number 11 as its key field. It then transfers record number 11 from the device into main storage. After processing master record number 11, the

ILLUSTRATION 11–11

Direct Access File Processing

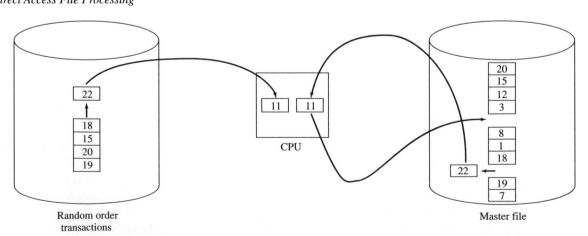

CPU rewrites it in its original location on the device. Then it processes the next transaction record, which has a key field of 22.

Direct access file processing is equivalent to a manual system in which a clerk reads a customer's name on an invoice. Knowing that this customer's file is in the third drawer of the fifth filing cabinet, the clerk goes directly there to file the invoice.

Advantages and Disadvantages.   Direct access files require retrieval of only the desired record. This gives them the fastest response of any file organization method to on-line inquiries. In fact, they are an efficient way to structure data in any low-activity file because direct access processing requires no sorting of files. This explains the usefulness of this organization method in on-line real-time systems.

If the address calculation algorithm is inadequate, data records are distributed unevenly throughout the direct access device. This causes inefficient use of file storage area and may result in excessive equipment costs. Furthermore, the system must sort the direct access file when printing reports requiring a certain sequence. In applications where a relatively high percentage of master file records is retrieved during a single execution, processing direct access files is slower than processing sequential ones.

Indexed Sequential Files   Indexed sequential files utilize an index that permits both rapid direct access of individual records and rapid sequential processing of all records in a file. This method physically stores each master file record in primary key field sequence. It also requires a reserved storage area either in memory or on the device for the index. Each entry in the index consists of two elements: the primary key of the indexed record and its address on the device. The index allows file processing as if it were a direct access file without reading the entire file as in a sequential process.

Ideally the index is stored in main storage; reading from it is much faster than from secondary storage. However, this is usually impractical, so the index is normally located on a direct access storage device. Some kinds of data management software use two indexes, a small one in main storage and a more precise one on the device.

The index can be as detailed as the applications using the file require. It need not contain an entry for each record, but fewer entries increase the time required to retrieve a record. Periodically a programmer redefines the index to develop a level of detail appropriate for the contents of the file.

Processing Indexed Sequential Files.   The usefulness of indexed sequential files is due to the flexibility allowed in processing them. Application programs may process them either sequentially or using direct access. Either way utilizes the index to locate records on a direct access device.

An application program provides the primary key to data management software. While searching in the index, if the software is unable to find the key, it selects the next lower key and locates the associated address on the direct access device. The data management software examines the record at this address and all records at successively higher addresses, until it finds the record containing the desired key field. It transfers this record into main storage. After the application program changes the record, data management software writes it at its original address on the device. (In a manual system, this is equivalent to a clerk consulting the map on a file room door to locate the desired filing cabinet.)

Sequential Processing.   With sequential updating of an indexed sequential master file, the transaction file is first sorted in the same sequence as the master file. Data management software finds a desired record quickly because the next master record it seeks is always near the previous one. Illustration 11–12 depicts sequential processing of an indexed sequential file.

With sequential processing of indexed sequential files, both the transaction file and the master file are in ascending key field sequence. The CPU executing an application program reads the key field of a transaction and identifies the key field to the data management software. It finds the key in the index, which gives the location of the master record. The CPU then retrieves the master record, changes its amounts or quantities, and copies it onto the secondary storage device.

In Illustration 11–12, the CPU has copied the transaction record with the key field containing the number 11 into main storage from the transaction file. It has looked up the location of the master record containing this key field in the index and transferred this record into main storage. After processing master record number 11, it again looks up its location in the index and copies the changed record into that location. Next it processes transaction and master records with key fields containing the number 12.

As mentioned earlier, a program updating a sequential file reads each master record into main storage, regardless of whether a transaction existed for the master record. If only a few master records in a file require changing, this process wastes processor time and is inefficient. A program sequentially updating an indexed sequential file avoids this problem. It reads into main storage only those master records for which there are transactions.

Direct Access Processing.   With direct access processing of an indexed sequential master file, transactions are not sorted. Because data management software processes them in the random order in which they occur, this approach requires more time to

ILLUSTRATION 11–12

Sequential Processing of Indexed Sequential Files

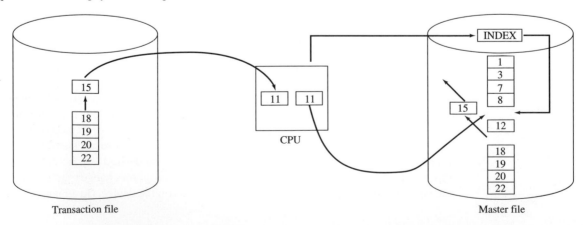

locate a set of transactions than does sequential processing. Illustration 11–13 shows how this works. Data management software has copied transaction record number 11 into main storage. It has also looked up key field number 11 in the index and retrieved the master record with this key. After processing these records, it again determines the address of master record number 11 in the index and copies it into that location. Next it looks up the address of record number 22 and copies it into main storage.

As Illustrations 11–12 and 11–13 show, direct access processing of an indexed sequential file differs from sequential processing only by the sequence in which transactions are processed.

Because it is slower than sequential processing, you may wonder why systems use direct access processing of this kind of file. In many applications, sorting transactions in advance is impractical. For example, a sales clerk may wish to check if a customer has exceeded a credit limit before charging a sale to a credit card. The clerk uses a terminal to interrogate an indexed sequential customer master file. The sales clerk queries the file as customers arrive. This occurs in random order and requires direct access processing.

Once the sale has been authorized and the clerk records it on a credit card charge slip, the system may exploit the efficiency of sequential processing. The clerk batches the charge slips, a data entry clerk creates a transaction file from them, and the system sorts the file and posts these transactions sequentially to the customer master file.

Advantages and Disadvantages.   The major advantage of indexed sequential file organization is the flexibility it provides. These files achieve the efficiency of sequential processing when there are a large number of transactions, while providing prompt responses to on-line queries. Only the desired master records are retrieved by the data management software, rather than all of them as with sequential files. Because the master file is sorted in key field sequence, printing many kinds of reports from this file is quicker than with a direct access file.

Each of these files, however, requires an index. When an application program accesses a record, the data management software conducts two searches of the direct

ILLUSTRATION 11–13

Direct Access Processing of Indexed Sequential Files

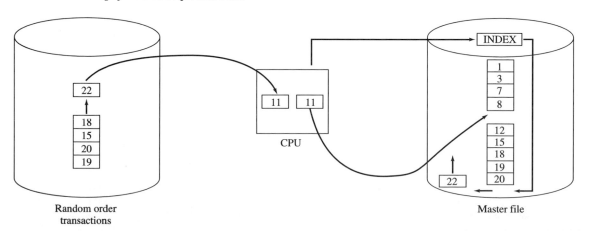

Random order
transactions

CPU

Master file

ILLUSTRATION 11–14

Summary of File Organization Methods

| | File Organization Method | | | |
Characteristic	Sequential	Direct Access	Indexed Sequential	Indexed Sequential
Processing method	Sequential	Direct	Sequential	Direct
Transaction input	Sorted file	Random transaction	Sorted file	Random transaction
Master file	Sorted order	Random order	Sorted order	Sorted order
Record location technique	Physical search	Hashing algorithm	Search an index	Search an index
Master record retrieval	Retrieve every record	Retrieve affected records	Retrieve affected records	Retrieve affected records

access device, first for the index and then for the data record. In contrast, direct access files only require one search of the device. Thus, accessing an indexed sequential file is almost always slower than accessing a direct access file. In applications where most of the master records are updated, processing an indexed sequential file is slower than processing a sequential one.

As this discussion shows, no one file organization method is best for all applications. The system design team selects a method based on its appraisal of the needs at the time an application is developed. Sequential files are best when capacity on direct access devices is limited, when most records are changed at each update of the file, or when no need exists to retrieve individual data records. Direct access files are best when the quickest possible response is required. To some extent, indexed sequential files provide the advantages of each of the other methods. Illustration 11–14 summarizes the major characteristics of the sequential, direct access, and indexed sequential file organization methods.

Organization Method and the Physical Device

The early part of this chapter identified several types of computer storage devices. These include magnetic tapes, magnetic disks, and diskettes. Technological constraints require that data files stored on magnetic tape use sequential data organization. Files on magnetic disks and floppy diskettes may use either sequential, direct access, or indexed sequential data organization.

The advantages of magnetic disks as physical storage devices are due to their ability to use direct access processing. For this reason, information systems professionals call them *direct access storage devices.* However, many organizations use them with sequential files. This is efficient whenever the application software was developed for use with tape files and later adapted to use with disks.

Summary

This chapter explains how accounting data are structured when organizations use the traditional data file approach. Early accounting systems used manual files. When computers were adapted to accounting, procedures for processing older manual files were applied to computer files. The chapter points out that computer files are actually structured in a way similar to those manual files.

Computers process program files and data files. Accounting application programs are stored in program files; accounting records are stored in data files. An accounting data file may be a master, transaction, backup, archive, or scratch file.

Accounting systems commonly perform four file operations. A file update is equivalent to posting in a manual system and refers to changing the balance data in a master file. File maintenance refers to changes to the reference data in a master file. Batch sequential processing systems also rely on file sorts and merges.

Three common methods of file organization are sequential, direct access, and indexed sequential. Each has advantages over the others in certain kinds of accounting applications.

Key Terms

archive file   A copy of a data file kept for historical or reference purposes.

backup file   A duplicate copy of a file kept in case the original is lost or destroyed.

balance data   The data items in a record that represent amounts or quantities.

data file   A file containing data records that are not executable by the computer.

direct access storage device   A form of secondary storage capable of recording direct access files, such as a magnetic disk.

file   A collection of information stored so that it can be retrieved for later use.

file maintenance   A file operation in which a computer program changes the reference data in a master file.

file organization   The way in which records are physically arranged in a data file. It may be sequential, direct access, or indexed sequential.

file update   A file operation in which a computer program changes the balance data in a master file.

master file   A data file whose records contain data relating to a specific account.

merge   A file operation in which a computer program combines two sequential files to produce a third file in the same sequence.

program file   A file containing instructions executable by the computer.

reference data   The data items in a record that identify or describe the record.

sort   A file operation in which a computer program resequences the records in a data file.

transaction file   A data file in which each record represents an accounting transaction.

Questions

11–1. Do you think a system that processes manual files is more flexible than one processing computerized files? Explain your answer.

11–2. How does data management software identify addresses on a magnetic disk?

11–3. How does data management software identify the beginning of a magnetic tape file? The end?

11–4. What is the distinction between a program file and a data file? How does an accountant use each type?

11–5. Name and describe five types of accounting data files.

11–6. What distinguishes a transaction file from a master file? Which file organization methods use transaction files?

11–7. What is the distinction between an archive file and a backup file?

11–8. Distinguish between the file update operation and the file maintenance operation. In any system, which operation should be performed first?

11–9. In which systems are the sort and merge operations used?

11–10. What is meant by father–son processing? What is the father in this approach? The son?

11–11. When is sequential data organization the most efficient method? When is direct access organization most efficient?

11–12. Describe two ways in which indexed sequential files are processed.

11–13. What advantages and disadvantages do indexed sequential files have in comparison to the other two methods?

Exercises and Cases

11–14.   TYPES OF DATA

The following are data fields commonly processed by accounting systems. Determine whether each field contains balance or reference data.

a. General ledger master file posting reference.
b. Sales order transaction file date of sale.
c. Inventory master file economic order quantity.
d. Customer master file year-to-date sales to the customer.
e. Payroll master file employee pay rate.
f. Payroll transaction file gross pay.

11–15.   MANUAL FILES

The following files are human-readable and may be processed manually. For each file, identify its key field and its method of organizing data. The method may be sequential, indexed sequential, or direct access.

a. A general ledger used by a bookkeeping machine. Each account is recorded on a ledger card stored in a rack, and arranged by account number.
b. A card catalog in a library.
c. An address book containing the addresses of your friends alphabetically by last name.

d. A filing cabinet. A label on each file drawer identifies the contents of the drawer. File folders in a drawer contain documents arranged by date.

e. An unabridged dictionary.

11–16.   SEQUENTIAL FILE UPDATE

The first of the following tables contains a customer master file with 11 records. The second contains 6 records representing sales transactions for the week of June 28, 1998. The key field for each record is the four-digit customer number.

Customer Master File		
1047	Gimlet Corp.	1,006.00
2110	ABC Manufacturing Co.	812.00
2132	Wixson Widgets, Inc.	45.00
2448	J. B. Sampson	18.00
2919	Bach Music Co.	219.00
3042	College Bookstores, Inc.	2,120.00
3166	Alpha Retail Co.	781.00
3529	Ma & Pa Grocery Co.	186.00
3584	J. Smith, CPA	7.00
4262	Expert TV Repair	68.00
4375	Big Donut Co.	333.00

Sales Transaction File—Week of June 28		
3584	June 28, 1998	10.00
2132	June 29, 1998	35.00
3166	June 29, 1998	21.00
3148	June 30, 1998	4.00
2132	July 1, 1998	8.00
4262	July 2, 1998	20.00

Required:

a. Sort the transactions in the sales transaction file into the correct order.

b. Following the flowchart in Illustration 4–6, post each transaction to the master file. Show the updated balance in each master file record.

c. What is the nature of the error message referred to in the flowchart of Illustration 4–6?

11–17.   SEQUENTIAL FILE UPDATE

The following table shows the content of the sales transaction file produced during the week of July 5, 1998. Use these transactions, together with the files provided in Exercise 11–16, to complete the requirements.

Sales Transaction File—Week of July		
4375	July 5, 1998	16.00
2132	July 5, 1998	37.00
3584	July 7, 1998	14.00
1047	July 8, 1998	11.00
2919	July 8, 1998	26.00
3166	July 9, 1998	8.00

Required:

a. Sort the records in the transaction file for the week of July 5 into the correct order.

b. Sort the records in the transaction file for the week of June 28 (given in 11–16) into the correct order.

c. Merge the two sorted transaction files (from parts *a* and *b*) into another transaction file in the correct order.

d. Post sales transactions for these two weeks to the customer master file given in Exercise 11–16. (Disregard any answer you may have obtained to Exercise 11–16.)

11–18.   DIRECT ACCESS FILES

One possible algorithm for computing an address on a direct access device is

$$address = [25 * Key]_{mod\ 1000}$$

Using this algorithm, data management software reads the key field of a record. It multiplies this key value by 25, thus obtaining a product. The last three digits of the product are the address where the record is stored.

The following five numbers represent key fields in the records of a vendor master file:

1. 10018

2. 10060

3. 10093

4. 10140

5. 10178

Required:

a. Using the preceding algorithm, calculate the address of the location for each vendor master record.

b. Identify the records in the list that produce synonyms.

c. Suggest how the algorithm could be changed to produce fewer synonyms.

11–19.   INDEXED SEQUENTIAL FILE MAINTENANCE

Whirlwind Corp. maintains its employee records in an indexed sequential file. Employees are identified to the personnel benefits system by four-digit employee numbers. The following index for the employee master file contains personnel and payroll data.

Index to Employee	Master File
1006	860
1014	246
1017	119
1018	201
1124	747
1129	831
1146	226
1183	661
1201	483
1222	780

During June 1998, the following changes took place in the workforce:

1. Employees terminated: 1124
                          1201
2. Employees added: 1019
                    1136
                    1211
3. Employees acquiring additional dependents: 1017
4. Employees receiving pay increases: 1006
                                      1017
                                      1129

Required:

Show how the index changes in response to the file maintenance required for the preceding workforce changes.

11–20.   *FILE ORGANIZATION METHODS*

Each of the following identifies a master file that is updated by an information system. In each case, describe the contents of a record, and identify the most appropriate file organization method.

Required:

a. A university student file. The file is used to produce fee statements at the beginning of each semester and for on-line registration.
b. A file used by a hotel chain for its reservation system.
c. A file of retirees. A pension fund uses this file to produce retirement checks at the beginning of each month.
d. The customer file of a retail chain.
e. The customer file of an electric utility.
f. A file containing perpetual inventory records of a wholesaler.

11–21.   DATA FILES FOR THE REVENUE CYCLE

Ivy Real Estate Company owns four apartment complexes in a college town. Because these complexes cater to the students at the college, tenant turnover is relatively high. In the spring students generally want to select apartments for the following fall from those Ivy has to offer. Occasionally Ivy encounters undesirable students who move out without paying all the rent that is due.

Ivy is developing a computerized system to maintain records regarding its rentals. It would like the system to show which apartments are available, which are rented, how much each rents for, and whether or not a tenant is behind in rent.

Required:

a. Describe the contents of a master file, and suggest a file organization method for this application.
b. For your master file, which events initiate
   1. File updates?
   2. File maintenance?
c. Which routine management reports should be produced from this file? Suggest an appropriate sequence for printing the items in each report you identify.

11–22.   DATA FILES FOR THE REVENUE CYCLE

Metropolis Life Insurance Company (Metro) is considering a computer-based system for maintaining data about its policyholders and for processing premium payments from them. Metro currently has about 15,000 life insurance policies in force. Policyholders may pay premiums annually, semiannually, or monthly. Although all payments are due on the first day of each month, experience shows that Metro can expect to receive premiums throughout the month. Because cash should be deposited quickly, the computerized cash receipts system must process premium payments promptly regardless of when they are received.

Each month Metro makes numerous changes to the data regarding policyholders. These include new policies, policy lapses, name and address changes for the policyholders, and beneficiary changes. The proposed system must be able to process these as well.

Required:

a. Identify the fields Metro needs for its
   1. Policyholder master file.
   2. Cash receipts transaction file.
b. Which file organization and file processing methods do you recommend for this application?
c. Draw a system flowchart describing this process assuming that
   1. The policyholder master file is updated daily.
   2. A merge operation is used and the master file is updated monthly.

11–23.   DATA FILES FOR THE CONVERSION CYCLE

Finley Foundry has used a manual cost accounting system for decades. However, business volume has increased to the point where Finley is now computerizing this system. A cost accountant working in the factory office operates the present manual system.

The cost accountant maintains three files in a filing cabinet: a file folder of job cost sheets, another of time reporting sheets, and a third folder of materials requisitions. When the factory begins a new job, the cost accountant prepares a job cost sheet for it. The job cost sheet summarizes the total costs incurred on the job through its completion.

At the end of each day supervisors turn in time reporting sheets that the cost accountant uses to record labor costs on the appropriate job cost sheets. Also daily the warehouse foreman turns in materials requisitions, from which the accountant determines and records the costs of materials used in each job. The cost accountant allocates factory overhead to jobs daily based on labor used the previous day. When the job is completed, the cost accountant computes the total costs of the job and sends the completed job cost sheet to the chief accountant.

Required:

a. Describe the master file for this computerized cost accounting system. For the file, identify
   1. Data fields.
   2. File organization method.
   3. File processing method.
b. Identify the transaction data used by this system. Suggest a preferred method for entering this transaction data into the system so it can be posted to the master file.
c. What file maintenance does this system require?

11–24.   DATA FILES FOR DECISION SUPPORT

Superway Grocery Stores, Inc., is a local grocery chain in a midwestern city. To compete with the national chains, they advertise special discounts on selected inventory items. The items selected for discount change each week based on expected competition and the overall budgeted profit margin. Discounted items are selected by a pricing specialist at company headquarters.

From estimates of sales volumes, the pricing specialist develops a weekly markdown plan that identifies the items for discount. First, the specialist computes the normal selling price for each item in inventory. This is the item's cost plus the normal markup, currently 20 percent. The specialist then identifies candidate items for discount and proposes a discount on them. Using sales volume estimates based on previous weeks' data, the specialist projects total sales revenue and gross profit on sales for the week. The specialist then adds or eliminates discounts to achieve weekly budgeted profit goals.

For example, the specialist may propose a special discount of 10 percent on a loaf of bread. If the cost of a loaf is $1.00 and the normal markup is 20 percent, the normal selling price for a loaf is $1.20. A 10 percent discount reduces the selling price to a markdown value of $1.08. If sales of 1,000 loaves are expected, then projected sales revenue from this item is $1,080 for the week. To reflect the discounted price, the pricing specialist normally adjusts the previous week's sales volume upward when projecting new volume.

Currently Superway has a computerized inventory system. Inventory quantities are updated nightly from sales volumes recorded for each item during the day at computerized checkout stands. The pricing specialist determines the markdown plan manually using reports from this inventory system. Superway would like to develop a computerized system to aid the pricing specialist.

Required:

a. Describe the inventory master file for the existing system. Identify
  1. Data fields in each record.
  2. File organization method.
  3. Method of file processing.
b. Describe the reports from this file needed by the pricing specialist to develop a markdown plan manually.
c. Assuming that a computerized system is developed to aid the pricing specialist, identify the following for this new system:
  1. Additional data fields required for records in the inventory master file.
  2. Master file organization method.
  3. Method of processing the master file.
  4. Additional reports that the new system can produce to aid the pricing specialist.

11–25. FILE OPERATIONS

Guaranty Bank of Lafayette, Louisiana, with assets in excess of $600 million, ranks in the 10 largest banks in the state. Faced with rapid growth and a competitive environment, its management decided to establish an in-house data processing department to provide accurate, timely information.[2]

The system Guaranty developed processes over 100,000 accounts and an average of 95,000 transactions during a single nightly production run. Each day's processing requires about 14 hours; this is expected to increase as the bank grows and adds new systems.

The Problem

Computerized systems automate the majority of Guaranty's deposit, loan, and financial departments. Application systems used by these departments include demand deposits, savings, commercial loans, mortgage loans, installment loans, and payroll. Each is a purchased software package maintained through maintenance agreements with vendors. Additionally, Guaranty uses a general ledger software package obtained from a different vendor.

Because each application system is a separate package and most are from different vendors, data files produced by them are incompatible. For most applications, this is not a serious operational problem. However, the general ledger system requires inputs from most of the other applications. After acquisition of the general ledger package, management realized the need to interface it with the others. They appointed a project team

---

[2]Adapted from Bobby L. Doxey and Jean Chambers, *"Making the Most of Bank Information Systems,"* Management Accounting, February 1983, pp. 58–61. Copyright by National Association of Accountants (1983), Montvale, N.J. 07645.

to develop a computerized system to extract data from the other applications and to provide them as inputs to the general ledger system.

Objectives of the General Ledger Interface

The project team identified four objectives for the general ledger/application system interface. They were to

1. Provide data from the application systems using account codes consistent with the general ledger chart of accounts. This creates greater flexibility in reporting and allows daily balancing procedures between application system totals and general ledger totals.

2. Provide the general ledger system with access to nonfinancial as well as financial information. This increases flexibility in producing reports for management. Internal management reports utilize nonfinancial data such as the number of IRA accounts, the number of personnel by department and by function, aging reports of loans and of certificates of deposit, and maturity schedules of loans and of certificates of deposit.

3. Provide the ability to reverse incorrectly run application data that have been posted to the general ledger without reprocessing the general ledger system.

4. Allow the data processing manager to bypass the processing of an application system one day, followed by processing multiple runs of the application the following day.

5. Establish controls that guarantee data integrity without creating excessive processing overhead. These include backup copies of all disk files made on magnetic tape at strategic points in processing. They also include control reports that allow manual comparison of information generated by application systems with totals submitted to the general ledger system.

Extract Procedures

Each day an extract program accesses each application system file and extracts data to build an interface data file. The data in this file are taken from the application systems' daily transactions and accruals and changed into the format required by the general ledger system. The interface data file then provides inputs to the general ledger system; the application data files produce reports for the application. Used in this way, interface data extraction provides consistent data for all systems.

After all application system extracts are completed, the computer operator makes backup copies of all interface data files. Each backup file contains one day's transactions for one application and provides protection against loss of the original data file before processing is completed. Exhibit 11–1 shows a system flowchart of these extract procedures.

Multiple-Run Processing

Multiple-run processing provides the ability to combine two days' data from an application system into a single interface data file. The previous day's extracted data are first copied into the multiple-run interface data file. Then the current day's application

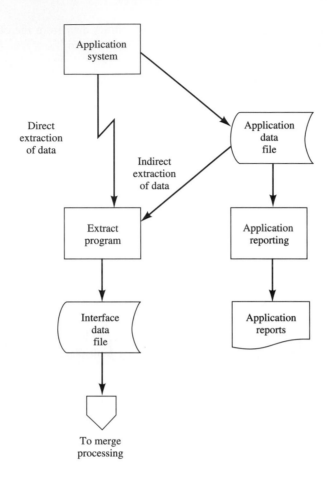

extracts are handled normally. This allows the receipt of multiple-run data and normal application data as a single input to the general ledger system.

The system generates a control listing of multiple-run data. This provides the accounting department with a list of erroneous transactions for correction. A copy also goes to the data control group in the data processing department. They compare the count of the records in the application data files with those in the interface data files to ensure that no transactions are lost in processing.

Reversal Processing

The computer operator executes a reversal program when the accounting department determines that an application system's data have significant errors after posting them to the general ledger. This program reverses all entries produced from the application data. Inputs to the program come from the merged interface data backup tape produced during the previous general ledger file update. Outputs are contained in a reversal data file that becomes an input to the current day's processing. These reversal entries contain the same data as the original entry but are distinguished within the general ledger system by a special code.

EXHIBIT 11–2

*Case 11–25 General
Ledger Interface System
Reversal Procedures*

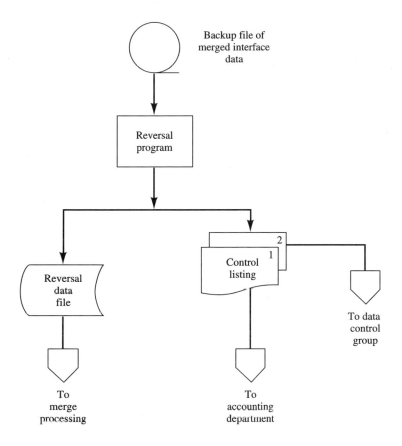

The reversal program produces a control listing used as in multiple-run processing. Use of the reversal program allows the accounting department to avoid making manual adjustments to the general ledger. It is followed by multiple-run processing to introduce the corrected data into the system. The computer operator makes a backup copy of the reversal data file. Exhibit 11–2 contains a system flowchart of these reversal procedures.

Merge Processing

Merge processing takes place after multiple-run and reversal backup files have been made. A merge program consolidates data from the application interface data file, the multiple-run data file, and the reversal data file into a merged interface data file. This is the input file to the general ledger system. This program has several control checks coded into it. If it detects an erroneous condition, it halts processing for corrective action. The computer operator can enter commands to exclude application data if this is necessary to complete processing.

The merge program produces two reports. The control listing provides an error report for the accounting department and a record count for the data control group. The invalid and unpostable transactions report is sent to the accounting department for correction and reentry of these transactions. The backup tape of the merged interface data is used for system backup and, when required, as an input to reversal processing.

Exhibit 11–3

Case 11–25 General Ledger Interface System Merge Procedures

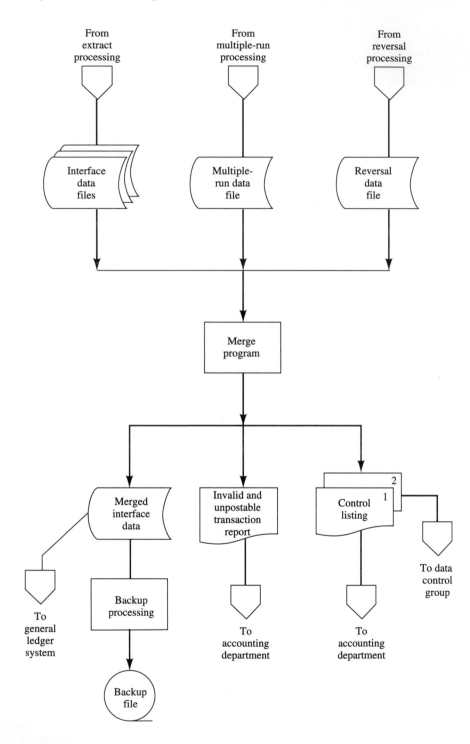

After merge processing has been completed, the application interface data files, multiple-run data files, and reversal data files are cleared of data in preparation for the next day's processing. Exhibit 11–3 shows the procedures used in merge processing.

Implementation of the general ledger system interface has been a success at Guaranty Bank. Besides producing accurate and consistent data for accounting reports, it supplies management with information on market conditions so it can make short-term decisions and plan for the future.

Required:

a. In this system, which manual procedures are performed by
   1. The accounting department?
   2. The data control group of the data processing department?
b. What is the purpose of the merge operation in Guaranty's general ledger interface system?
c. The case does not describe the methods of file organization used in this system. Based on the descriptions given, which method do you think is used for the general ledger master file? The master files in the other application systems? Why?
d. Guaranty created this system because its applications systems produce files containing records incompatible with the general ledger system. Based on what you learned in the previous chapter, can you suggest another way of correcting this problem?

12 IMPLEMENTING DATABASE MANAGEMENT SYSTEMS

Learning Objectives

1. To discover how a database management system maintains relationships between data.
2. To understand the structural models for data.
3. To learn how a project team designs relational databases.

Introduction

Chapter 10 describes two ways of organizing data in computer-based systems: traditional data files and database management systems (DBMSs). In that chapter, you learned the advantages and disadvantages of each approach. In Chapter 11, you learned the details of organizing and processing accounting data using traditional data files. This chapter describes how database management systems work and shows you how to design the most common type of DBMS.

A DBMS is a set of computer programs that maintain an organization's database. The method of storing data in the database is independent of the application programs using it. Users of the data are unconcerned with how data are physically organized on secondary storage devices. A DBMS stores data more efficiently, eliminates conflicting data, and allows easier changes to applications than does a traditional data file system. A database management system works most efficiently when it implements a data structure recognizing the logical relationships in the database.

Role of the Project Team

In implementing a database management system, the project team performs three functions. First, the project team identifies an appropriate structural model for the data. Second, it selects a DBMS software package to implement the structural model. Third, it determines the content of the database. This includes defining the data elements and the relationships between them.

Defining the Database

During systems design, systems analysts identify reports and displays produced by the system. The contents of these outputs summarize the *data elements* maintained in the database. A data element is equivalent to a data field in a traditional data file system. For example, a report disclosing customers' current unpaid balances contains information from three data elements: the customer's account number, name, and unpaid balance.

The relationships between data elements are as important as the elements themselves. For example, knowing an unpaid balance is useless unless you know which customer has the balance. A system not only records the customer name, number, and unpaid balance but also links them in some way to maintain their relationships. The developer of a DBMS writes the software to maintain not only the data elements but also the relationships between them.

Types of Relationships

The four possible relationships between data elements are

One-to-one.

One-to-many.

Many-to-one.

Many-to-many.

The terms *one* and *many* in these descriptions refer to the number of related data elements. If a data element is related to only one occurrence of another element, the relationship is one-to-one. If an element is related to many occurrences, the relationship is one-to-many. Systems analysts describe the type of relationship—either one-to-one, one-to-many, many-to-one, or many-to-many—as the ***cardinality*** of the relationship.

In the previous accounts receivable example, there is only one occurrence of an unpaid balance for a customer. Thus, there is a one-to-one relationship between the data element *customer name* and the data element *unpaid balance*. However, an unpaid balance may represent many sales transactions to the customer. Some accounts receivable systems record not only the total unpaid balance but also the individual sales amounts making up the balance. In this case, there is a one-to-many relationship between the customer name and the sales amount. There are many occurrences of the sales amount element for each occurrence of the unpaid balance element.

In accounting application systems, one-to-one and one-to-many relationships are common. Other types of relationships are frequently needed for producing management reports. To see how they may be used, consider the list of employees in Illustration 12–1. It contains the portion of an employee database applicable to Factory 3. In this example, Factory 3 consists of two departments, employs people in four jobs, and has four different pay rates. This list contains eight occurrences of seven data fields. Illustration 12–2 shows examples of the four kinds of relationships in it.

The payroll system prints a paycheck for each name listed in Illustration 12–1, so there is a one-to-one relationship. Each department may have four kinds of jobs, so there is a one-to-many relationship between these data elements. Because many employees work in each department, the data elements Employee Name and Department have a many-to-one relationship. A many-to-many relationship exists between the data elements Jobs and Pay Rates because employees in each job may receive one of two pay rates. A manager who wishes to know which employees work in the assembly

ILLUSTRATION 12–1

A List of Factory Employees

Employee Number	Employee Name	Factory Number	Department Number	Job Code	Employ Date	Pay Rate
11	Smith, A.	3	2	4	1999	10.00
14	Garcia, B.	3	2	2	1998	20.00
27	Wong, C.	3	1	3	1999	30.00
29	Riley, D.	3	2	4	1998	10.00
33	O'Hara, E.	3	1	1	1999	20.00
36	Weiss, F.	3	1	1	1998	10.00
41	Abbott, G.	3	1	3	1999	30.00
45	Powski, H.	3	2	4	1998	10.00

Departments	*Jobs*	*Pay Rates*
1—Factory office	1—Clerk	Clerk—$10 or $20
2—Assembly	2—Machinist	Machinist—$20 or $30
	3—Accountant	Accountant—$20 or $30
	4—Laborer	Laborer—$10

department must use the many-to-one relationship inherent in the data. A payroll clerk who uses a laborer's employee number to encode a payroll transaction utilizes the one-to-one relationship between Employee and Paycheck.

Logical versus Physical Structure

As you can see from these examples, relationships are inherent in the data. If a system is to produce meaningful outputs, it must record not only the data but also the relevant relationships. When system designers identify relationships, they determine the "logical structure" of the data. This is different from the physical arrangement of data on a storage device, called the "physical structure."

A traditional data file system maintains relationships by physically recording related data fields adjacent to each other. Programmers code application programs to recognize this relationship. With a DBMS, the physical location of the data is independent of the application programs. A DBMS achieves this independence by separating the physical structure of the data from the logical structure. The DBMS records relationships by linking logically related data using a method other than physical location.

ILLUSTRATION 12–2

Data Relationships

Relationship	Example
One-to-one	Paycheck to Employee
One-to many	Department to Employee
Many-to-one	Employee to Department
Many-to-many	Job to Department

The way a DBMS physically stores data differs from the way application programs use it. The DBMS's *schema* describes the physical structure of the data in the database. An application program uses only a portion of this data, defined by the application's *subschema*. A database may have many such subschemas; each is a description of a logical structure for the data. When designing the database, MIS professionals use special terminology to describe how the DBMS stores data.

DBMS Terminology.   When creating a schema, system designers combine two or more related data elements to form a ***data segment***. A segment is a set of elements stored together on a secondary storage device. Multiple occurrences of one type of segment form a ***data set.*** The DBMS combines many different data sets to form the database.

Illustration 12–3 shows the analogy between the physical structure in a traditional data file system and the schema of a DBMS. Data fields are analogous to data elements, data records are analogous to segments, and data files are analogous to data sets. You may also hear people refer to fields and records when using DBMSs. In this case, they describe the application's logical view of the data rather than how the data are physically stored.

With a DBMS, application programs process records formed from a restricted view of the data, the application's subschema. The data contained in a subschema may be stored within different segments of the database. The application program is unaware of this; the DBMS locates the appropriate data elements and makes them available to the program in the way defined by the subschema.

Illustration 12–4 shows data dictionary descriptions for a data set formed from the list of employees in Illustration 12–1. It demonstrates how the DBMS logically

ILLUSTRATION 12–3

Similarities in Data Storage

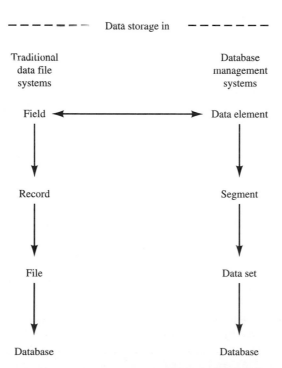

ILLUSTRATION 12–4

Schema and Subschema

Schema for the Employee Data Set

Data Attribute	Data Name	Data Format
Employee number	EMP NO	2 bytes numeric
Employee name	EMP NAME	15 bytes character
Factory code	FAC	1 byte numeric
Department code	DEPT	1 byte numeric
Job code	JOB	1 byte numeric
Employment date	EMP DATE	6 bytes numeric
Pay rate	PAY RATE	6 bytes numeric

Subschema for the Human Resources Application System

Data Attribute	Data Name	Data Format
Employee number	EMP NO	2 bytes numeric
Employee name	EMP NAME	15 bytes character
Job code	JOB	1 byte numeric
Employment date	EMP DATE	6 bytes numeric

Subschema for the Payroll Application System

Data Attribute	Data Name	Data Format
Employee number	EMP NO	2 bytes numeric
Employee name	EMP NAME	15 bytes character
Factory code	FAC	1 byte numeric
Department code	DEPT	1 byte numeric
Pay rate	PAY RATE	6 bytes numeric

eliminates and rearranges elements from a schema to form subschemas for human resources and payroll application systems.

When an organization uses a DBMS, its database consists of many different data sets. Each segment in a data set is one occurrence of a group of logically related data elements. A data set may contain many such related data elements that are physically located at different addresses on the device. The DBMS must record data relationships in some way other than physical location. Most DBMSs use pointers and chains to link related data segments.

Pointers and Chains.   A *pointer* is a data element added to a segment by the DBMS. The DBMS inserts information into this element that identifies another segment containing related data. Sometimes a DBMS copies the location of another segment into the pointer. Other DBMS packages copy the primary key of the other segment instead, and data management software computes its location from this key. In either case, this element points to another related record. Pointers create the links that maintain data relationships in a DBMS. When pointers connect several related segments in succession, the segments form a *chain*. Chains provide the physical capability of associating many data elements in a data set. The way the DBMS does this depends on the structural data model employed by the software.

Structural Models for Data

In implementing a database management system, the project team performs three functions. It identifies an appropriate structural model for the data and selects a DBMS software package to implement it. Next, it determines the content of the database. People call this process *database design*.

Most accounting systems use DBMS software that implements one of three structural models for data: the tree, the network, or the relational structure. Each model maintains certain relationships more efficiently than the others. Each offers some advantages over the others in certain kinds of accounting applications.

Tree and Network Structures

The earliest structural models used in database management systems are the *tree* and *network* structures. Many companies still use DBMS software using these structures, so you may encounter them on older systems.

How They Work.   DBMS software using the tree structure links segments in a data set so that they form a hierarchy resembling an inverted tree. At the top of the hierarchy is the root segment of the tree. The database administrator defines the root when creating the data set. A user or an application program accesses any data attribute in the set by identifying the root segment to the DBMS.

A network DBMS works as if it contains multiple trees within the same data set. Thus it has multiple roots, and a user or application program can use any of them to access data in the data set.

Advantages and Disadvantages.   Tree structures are useful for organizing data in which one-to-one or one-to-many relationships are important. Because many accounting applications process data of this type, organizations have used DBMSs based on tree structures for many years in processing accounting transactions. They are more efficient than other structures for many such systems. However, tree structures are less flexible than the other structures. They cannot describe many-to-one or many-to-many relationships.

Network structures offer greater flexibility because they are able to maintain all four relationships that may occur within a data set. They allow multiple entry points into the data, and when organized properly, they can be efficient both in processing accounting transactions and in providing information in response to managerial requests.

However, the database administrator (DBA) must anticipate all the desired relationships when creating the schema. The DBA then creates the required entry segments for the data and causes the DBMS to establish pointers and chains that allow retrieval of the data. If the DBA does not do this in advance, a manager or application program cannot access the data in the desired way. Furthermore, as the complexity of a network structure increases, the speed, responsiveness, and efficiency of the network DBMS decrease.

The relational structure overcomes many of the disadvantages of both tree and network structures.

Relational Structures

The structural model that provides the greatest flexibility to users is the *relational structure.* A DBMS using this structure does not organize data in trees or networks; rather it views *data attributes* as if they were organized in tables. Each table contains a

---

AIS in Practice

Kaiser Permanente Health Plan of the Mid-Atlantic States is a health maintenance organization (HMO) that employs 700 physicians. It serves over 500,000 people in 25 medical and mental health centers in Maryland, Virginia, and the District of Columbia. Budgeting and financial reporting for this company is a complex task, estimating and tracking expenses for physicians, clinics, hospitalizations, and referrals to specialists outside the organization. Its old system was a traditional one that required several weeks to produce a report showing operating income.

Management replaced the old system with a new one that utilizes a relational database management system. Implementation was phased in, first with expense budgeting and reporting and later with revenue and payroll. In addition to being a timesaver for the company, the new system provides complete flexibility in financial modeling and reporting. It allows user-defined consolidations and nearly unlimited freedom in report layout. Its primary user had the ability to create the same statement of operating income in minutes after a few days of training in the DBMS.

---

set of data attributes that are related to each other in some way. For this reason, MIS professionals refer to each table as a *relation.* Similar to a table, a relation contains rows (called *tuples*) and columns (one for each attribute). A row in a table represents an occurrence of two or more logically related data attributes. Illustration 12–5 shows the data set of Illustration 12–1 in the form of a relation.

Comparison to Data Files.   Logically, the content of a relation is no different from the content of a file in a traditional data file system. A row is equivalent to a record, and a column is equivalent to a data field. Thus one tuple in a relation contains two or more attributes, just as one record in a file contains two or more fields. A relation is a collection of similar tuples just as a file is a collection of similar records. Illustration 12–6 summarizes these similarities.

You may wonder why a relational DBMS is advantageous if its contents are equivalent to a traditional file. Its advantage arises because relations, like trees and networks, describe *logical* views of the data. Even though users may view a relation as a data set arranged in a table, the DBMS stores data differently on a direct access device. The DBMS software separates the physical arrangement of the data from the user's view. In other words, it separates the logical structure of the data from the physical structure. A file description in a traditional data file system, on the other hand, identifies both the

ILLUSTRATION 12–5

A Relation

——————————————— Attributes ———————————————

11	Smith, A.	3	2	4	1999	10.00
14	Garcia, B.	3	2	2	1998	20.00
27	Wong, C.	3	1	3	1999	30.00
29	Riley, D.	3	2	4	1998	10.00
33	O'Hara, E.	3	1	1	1999	20.00
36	Weiss, F.	3	1	1	1998	10.00
41	Abbott, G.	3	1	3	1999	30.00
45	Powski, H.	3	2	4	1998	10.00

Tuples

ILLUSTRATION 12–6

Similarities Between Relational DBMSs and Traditional Files

Relational DBMS	Traditional File
Relation (a table)	Data file
Tuple (a row)	Data record
Attribute (a column)	Data field
Key attribute	Key field

user's view of the data and how the data are physically arranged on the device.

Relational Operations.   A relational DBMS allows users to perform operations on data that are unavailable in a traditional data file system. These operations allow a manager to examine specific rows or columns in a table, or to combine two or more tables and produce another one. They provide the flexibility that makes relational DBMSs popular for producing ad hoc reports and answering unusual queries. Illustration 12–7 summarizes the major relational operations. It also gives examples showing how each operation is implemented in a common relational DBMS language called SQL. Managers use SQL as a query language (in fact, the letters stand for "Structured Query Language"). In addition, project teams use it to create databases

ILLUSTRATION 12–7

Data Operations in a Relational DBMS

SELECT. Extract one or more tuples (rows) from a relation (table).

SQL Implementation:

SELECT EMP-NAME, JOB FROM EMPLOYEE
WHERE NAME = Abbott, G.

PROJECT. Extract one or more domains (columns) from a relation (table).

SQL Implementation:

SELECT EMP-NO, PAY-RATE FROM EMPLOYEE
ORDER BY EMP-NO ASCENDING

JOIN. Combine two or more separate relations (tables) producing a new relation (table). The new relation (table) contains only specified attributes (columns) from the original ones.

SQL Implementation:

SELECT DEPT-NAME FROM EMPLOYEE, JOB-DEPT
ORDER BY NAME ASCENDING

during system implementation. (Looking carefully, you will notice that the SQL "SELECT" command is different from the relational "SELECT" operation.)

An Example of Relational Operations. Assume that the project team wishes to use a relational DBMS to maintain the employee data set of Illustration 12–1. The team identifies four important attributes: (1) the department of an employee, (2) the pay rate of an employee, (3) the job of an employee, and (4) the jobs assigned to a department. The team then establishes data sets containing the three tables shown in Illustration 12–8. The *Employee* table identifies the job of each employee. The *Pay-Rate* table identifies an employee's pay rate, and the *Job/Department* table shows which jobs are assigned to a department.

Why did the project team not establish a fourth table showing the department for each employee? Using relational operations, a manager can obtain this information from the other relations.

Illustration 12–9 shows how users employ the SELECT relational operation to obtain data from this database. Suppose, for example, a manager wishes to know the job performed by employee G. Abbott. The manager uses a query language command applying the SELECT operation to the Employee table. This selects the row of the table for this employee and displays it at the manager's terminal. The illustration shows a command and the results of the operation.

ILLUSTRATION 12–8

Relations in the Employee Database

An Employee Table

EMP NO	NAME	JOB
11	Smith, A.	4
14	Garcia, B.	2
27	Wong, C.	3
29	Riley, D.	4
33	O'Hara, E.	1
36	Weiss, F.	1
41	Abbott, G.	3
45	Powski, H.	4

A Job/Department Table

JOB	DEPT
1	1
2	2
3	1
4	2

A Pay-Rate Table

EMP NO	EMP DATE	PAY RATE
11	1999	10.00
14	1998	20.00
27	1999	30.00
29	1998	10.00
33	1999	20.00
36	1998	10.00
41	1999	30.00
45	1998	10.00

ILLUSTRATION 12–9

The SELECT Operation

Relational command: SELECT ABBOTT OF EMPLOYEE
DISPLAY EMP NAME AND JOB

11	Smith, A.	4
14	Garcia, B.	2
27	Wong, C.	3
29	Riley, D.	4
33	O'Hara, E.	1
36	Weiss, F.	1
41	Abbott, G.	3
45	Powski, H.	4

SELECT ⟶ points to row 41

CRT display:

NAME	JOB
Abbott,G.	3

In Illustration 12–10, you see the results of a PROJECT operation. A payroll clerk issues this command to obtain a list of the pay rates of all employees in the factory. The DBMS produces the list from the Pay-Rate relation.

What if the manager wishes to know the departments to which all employees are assigned? To find the answer, the manager uses the JOIN operation. The DBMS combines the Employee table and the Job/Department table into another table. A query language command selects from this table only the information of interest to the manager. Illustration 12–11 shows this.

ILLUSTRATION 12–10

The PROJECT Operation

Relational command: PROJECT EMP NO AND PAY RATE
OF PAY-RATE

PROJECT

11	1999	10.00
14	1998	20.00
27	1999	30.00
29	1998	10.00
33	1999	20.00
36	1998	10.00
41	1999	30.00
45	1998	10.00

CRT display:

EMP NO	PAY RATE
11	10.00
14	20.00
27	30.00
29	10.00
33	20.00
36	10.00
41	30.00
45	10.00

ILLUSTRATION 12–11

The JOIN Operation

Relational command: JOIN EMPLOYEE WITH JOB/DEPT
DISPLAY DEPT AND NAME

11	Smith, A.	4
14	Garcia, B.	2
27	Wong, C.	3
29	Riley, D.	4
33	O'Hara, E.	1
36	Weiss, F.	1
41	Abbott, G.	3
45	Powski, H.	4

1	1
2	2
3	1
4	2

JOIN

11	Smith, A.	4	2
14	Garcia, B.	2	2
27	Wong, C.	3	1
29	Riley, D.	4	2
33	O'Hara, E.	1	1
36	Weiss, F.	1	1
41	Abbott, G.	3	1
45	Powski, H.	4	2

CRT display:

DEPT	NAME
1	Abbott, G.
2	Garcia, B.
1	O'Hara, E.
2	Powski, H.
2	Riley, D.
2	Smith, A.
1	Weiss, F.
1	Wong, C.

Relational DBMS Requirements. The project team establishes the relations used by a relational DBMS. To work properly, the relations should possess certain characteristics:

1. Each primary key field should have associated with it only one value of each attribute in the relation. This would be violated in Illustration 12–5, for example, if employee A. Smith works both in Department 1 and Department 2.

2. All attributes in the relation should be dependent on the primary key field. In Illustration 12–5, the attributes identify the name, factory department, job, employ date, and pay rate of the person designated by the employee number. Thus they are all dependent on, or "related" to, the employee number. Any nondependent attributes should be put in a separate relation.

3. Each attribute in the relation should depend *only* on the primary key field. This means that any attribute is independent of all others in the relation except the primary key. The relation in Illustration 12–5 violates this rule. The job code depends both on the

employee number (the primary key) and on the department number (accountants and clerks only work in the office; machinists and laborers only work in assembly). Since they are not independent, they should be put in separate relations.

MIS professionals say that when a data set has these characteristics, it is *normalized.* Having normalized data is important for performing relational operations. During these operations, users create from the schema their own tables of data showing only the columns ("attributes") of interest to them. When the rules listed above are violated, the new tables may lose relationships or may imply relationships that do not exist. This produces tables with incorrect or misleading data.

Advantages and Disadvantages.   A relational DBMS is much more flexible than DBMSs using tree and network structures. With a relational structure, a user or application program accesses data from the database using the key attribute of a relation. Using query language commands, users can find answers to specific questions without help from MIS personnel. Accountants are accustomed to using data in tabular form, so the relational view of data is a more natural one than that provided by the other structures. Accountants readily learn relational operations and query language commands. This enables them to exploit the flexibility of the DBMS software package.

In transaction processing applications, a relational DBMS may perform more slowly than DBMSs using tree and network structures. Transaction processing applications use only one point of entry into the database—the key field of the application's data records. With tree and network structures, the DBA logically arranges the data to process specific transactions efficiently. A relational DBMS, structured for flexibility rather than efficiency, may require more time to process data. Yet in modern systems, a relational system's ability to summarize data in any form desired by a user overcomes these disadvantages. For that reason, most new information systems implement relational systems. As an accountant, you can expect to participate in project teams that design relational databases and implement relational database management systems.

Designing Relational Databases

When a project team decides to use a relational DBMS for a new information system, this decision affects the design and development process. The team not only determines the reports and displays produced by the system but also decides on the logical structure of the data. With a relational DBMS, all accounting and many nonaccounting applications share the data. Thus decisions made during design impact the entire organization.

When designing a relational DBMS, the project team identifies the tables ("relations") that the database will contain. The team determines the key fields ("attributes") that users will employ to retrieve data from the tables. After this is done, the team will be able to create the database and implement the system. When the project team identifies tables and key fields, they use a process called data modeling.

Data Modeling

Data modeling is a technique for organizing and documenting a system's data. The most common system tool for data modeling is the entity-relationship (E-R) diagram. Many MIS professionals consider that using E-R diagrams to model an organization's data is crucial for the development of a successful system. The following section suggests several reasons why this is the case.

Why Use E-R Diagrams? Organizations using a DBMS view data as a resource, just like cash, equipment, or a qualified workforce. Like those resources, data should be used efficiently for the benefit of the entire organization. To achieve this, data must be organized in a way that is flexible and adaptable to unanticipated future business events. Constructing E-R diagrams during system design helps the project team achieve this goal.

Second, because the contents of the database are shared by many applications, its structure is likely to be relatively permanent. Business processes change with changes in technology, and data is added to the database as new reporting requirements emerge. Yet the need for currently existing data does not go away, and its underlying structure seldom changes. Thus decisions about the content of tables and key fields often are long-term decisions.

In addition, data models using E-R diagrams are smaller than process modeling tools such as flowcharts and data flow diagrams. Thus they can be constructed more quickly and enable the project team to make a system operational earlier. And not only are they quicker to create, but the process of developing them helps the project team standardize terminology and rules regarding the data. For example, analysts modeling data for the Coca-Cola Company discovered that its systems had been using 16 different names for water. They were able to standardize on one data name for use worldwide.

Illustration 12–12 summarizes the benefits of creating data models during system development.

Entity Types, Occurrences, and Relationships. Entity-relationship (E-R) diagrams are an effective and popular tool for data modeling. Analysts create them from the information they gather during the systems analysis process. During this phase of systems development, analysts conduct interviews and study existing system documentation. This enables them to identify the types of entities that exist in the organization and the relationships between those entities. Then they construct E-R diagrams.

An *entity* is a fundamental thing of relevance to the organization, about which it needs to record data. An *entity type* is a collection of entities that share a common definition. Thus an entity is a single occurrence of an entity type. An entity type has associated with it *attributes*, or characteristics, used by the system to describe the entity. (In practice, people use the terms *entity type* and *entity* interchangeably.)

For example, the entity type *employee* may have the following occurrences: A. Smith, B. Garcia, and C. Wong. Each of these employees is an occurrence about which the organization needs to record data. Another entity type, *department*, may include the entities Department 1 and Department 2. Attributes of *employee* include employee

ILLUSTRATION 12–12

Benefits of Data Modeling

Efficiency: Flexible databases allow efficient use of the data resource.

Permanence: The contents and structure of databases will be used for a long time.

Ease of implementation: Data modeling is easy to learn and use.

Standardization: Data models enable standardization of data names and of the computerized processes that use them.

---

number, employment date, and pay rate. Attributes of *department* include the factory in which it is located.

Illustration 12–1 contains a table showing these entity types and their attributes. There are eight occurrences of the *employee* entity and two of the *department* entity. The table also contains a *job* entity that has four occurrences. Other entity types commonly encountered in business include customer, customer order, vendor, vendor invoice, and employee paycheck.

A *relationship* is a reason for associating two entities that is relevant to the organization. In the example of Illustration 12–1, if employee A. Smith (an occurrence of the entity *employee*) works in Department 2 (an occurrence of the entity *department*), then there is a reason for the organization to associate them. So an analyst identifies the relationship between A. Smith and Department 2 as *is employed in*. The opposite relationship also exists: Since A. Smith *is employed in* Department 2, the analyst also knows that Department 2 *employs* A. Smith. Among other common relationships encountered in business are these: Customer *places* customer order. Vendor *mails* vendor invoice. Employee *receives* paycheck.

Those examples show that all relationships are bidirectional—that is, every relationship connects two entities but is slightly different, depending on the perspective of the entity. E-R diagrams provide a convenient way of showing the entities and the directions of their relationships.

Constructing E-R Diagrams.   An E-R diagram represents an entity type by a rectangle containing the entity type's name. A line connecting two rectangles represents a relationship between two entity types. A small symbol at each end of the line shows the nature of the relationship: A bar perpendicular to the line means "only one." A crow's foot means "one or more." Some modeling conventions use a small circle next to the other symbol to indicate the possibility of no occurrence. A perpendicular bar with a small circle next to it means "zero or only one"; a crow's foot with a small circle next to it means "zero, one or more."

Above the line to the left, the analyst concisely describes in words the relationship that the left entity has with the right entity. Below the line to the right, the analyst describes the relationship that the right entity has to the left entity. The relative locations of the entities on the E-R diagram have no significance, so the one to the left may be exchanged with the one to the right. Of course, this reverses the small symbol and the relationship description.

Illustration 12–13 uses the examples in Illustration 12–2 to show these diagramming conventions. Since the relative locations of entities have no significance, the analyst models a "one-to-many" relationship in the same way as a "many-to-one" relationship.

Illustration 12–14 shows a complete E-R diagram for the data set of Illustration 12–1. In this diagram, the Job-Pay entity type has a one-to-many relationship with the Employee entity type. The small circle on this relationship's crow's foot shows that a pay rate may exist that applies to no employee.

Types of Data Models.   A project team first creates E-R diagrams during the systems analysis process. Ordinarily these are at a high level of detail. Later, during detailed specification, it refines these high-level models prior to determining the physical structure of the database.

ILLUSTRATION 12–13

*E-R Diagramming
Conventions*

A One-to-One Relationship

One-to-Many and Many-to-One Relationships

A Many-to-Many Relationship

The Enterprise Data Model.   Chapter 5 describes how system development processes occur within the context of a long-range system master plan. The master plan coordinates the organization's new information system development projects with its strategic plans. When the organization uses a DBMS, the master plan often includes a very high-level E-R diagram, the *enterprise data model.*

An enterprise data model typically identifies the fundamental entity types of the organization. It possibly contains a description of relationships between them, although it ordinarily omits identification of attributes. (The amount of detail contained in the

ILLUSTRATION 12–14

*A Detailed E-R Diagram
Produced During System
Design*

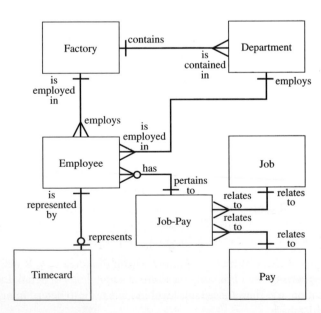

enterprise data model depends on the preferences of management.) It may evolve as the information systems of the organization evolve.

The enterprise data model provides a guideline, a starting point, for other more specific data models created during system design. The project team uses it as a basis for creating more detailed data models during system development.

The Application Data Model.   An *application data model* is the data model for a single application system. It is constructed early in the system development life cycle (SDLC), is refined as development progresses, and is included in the final documentation package for the system.

The project team creates a high-level version of the application data model during its feasibility study in the systems analysis phase of the SDLC. Called a *context data model*, this high-level model identifies entity types and relationships but not attributes. It is intended to clarify the project team's understanding of the data used by the system without requiring the team to delve into detail.

Later, during the preliminary design component of the system design phase, the project team creates the *key-based data model*. In it, the project team adds to the context data model descriptions of key fields for each entity. (Key fields are attributes that identify specific occurrences of an entity type.) This data model also specifies the cardinality of the relationships.

Finally, during detailed specification of the system design phase, the project team creates a *fully attributed data model*. It identifies the other attributes needed for each entity type. This includes descriptions of the form the data takes in storage (numeric, alphabetic, binary, etc.), the range of values the attribute can have (analysts call this the attribute's *domain*), and default values for the attribute. The project team includes the fully attributed data model in the documentation package for the new system. Illustration 12–15 summarizes these stages of data model development.

ILLUSTRATION 12–15

Stages of Data Model Development

Stage	Purpose	When Developed
Enterprise data model	A starting point for system development projects.	System planning
Application data model	Describes the data structure for an application system. It is made more specific as development proceeds.	Systems analysis and design
Context data model	Defines the scope of the design effort.	Feasibility study
Key-based data model	Shows key attributes for each entity type.	Preliminary system design
Fully attributed data model	Describes entity types, their relationships, and their attributes.	Detailed specification

Application data models developed with E-R diagrams provide documentation for a completed application system. Once you understand how to draw them, you are prepared to understand the process of database design.

Database Design

To fully benefit from the advantages of a DBMS, an organization must have a properly designed database. The database design process translates context data models produced during systems analysis into fully attributed data models during system design. The project team translates these models into tables containing logical views of the data. They then produce computer code (frequently in SQL) that translates the tables into the database schema, the physical representation of the data. You may view this process as consisting of three steps: identifying entities and relationships, performing data analysis, and creating the schema.

Identify Entities and Relationships.   The first step in database design is to identify the entities about which the organization needs to collect data. If the organization already has data models, such as an enterprise data model or older application data models, they provide a starting point. As the project team conducts interviews with system users, team members listen for evidence of entities about which users currently collect data. Existing forms and files often indicate data entities that are currently in use. For example, order forms, requisition forms, and vouchers are forms used in accounting that represent entities. Often users suggest other entities about which they need data.

Many accountants suggest using the REA accounting model as a useful way of identifying entities. According to this model, entities for an accounting system include *r*esources (cash, inventory, equipment, etc.), *e*vents (customer orders, cash receipts, equipment acquisitions, etc.), and *a*gents (customers, vendors, employees, etc.). Advocates believe that the REA approach makes the design process easier. It also enables accountants to integrate the database for accounting into the more extensive database required for managing the organization.

Once the project team identifies entities, it begins to construct context data models that show the relationships between them. The team refines and specifies relationships more completely as the design process proceeds.

Perform Data Analysis.   The second step in database design is ***data analysis***. Data analysis is the process that prepares a data model for implementation in a stable, flexible, and adaptable form. For a relational database, this means that the data tables are normalized.

When the tables are normalized, each nonkey field in a table depends on, and only on, the ***primary key*** of that table. Developing normalized tables is easy once you understand the process. Following a logical procedure and working through a few examples will help you gain that understanding. Illustration 12–16 contains a suggested procedure. A later section of this chapter contains an example.

During data analysis, the project team creates new tables that eliminate repeating fields and data dependencies. These new tables contain new primary keys. When an analyst forms a new key field by combining the key fields of other tables, the result is a ***concatenated key***. Sometimes an analyst establishes a relationship between tables by

ILLUSTRATION 12–16

A Suggested Data Analysis Procedure

---

1. Designate a table for each entity type that was identified in the context data model. For each table, determine a primary key field—an attribute that uniquely identifies each occurrence of the entity type. Identify any desired nonkey fields for each table. Include each nonkey attribute in only one table.

2. Examine the contents of each table, looking for repeating nonkey attributes. (An attribute is *repeating* if multiple values of it may exist for a single primary key field.) Create a new table for each type of repeating nonkey field. Create a new primary key for the new table. Update your data model to show these new tables.

3. Examine the contents of each table, looking for dependencies among the attributes. (An attribute is *dependent* if its value depends on another field.) How you treat it depends on the kind of dependency.

    3a. A *derivative* dependency exists if a field can be calculated from other fields in the row of the table. Simply eliminate any field containing a derivative dependency.

    3b. A *transitive* dependency exists if two fields are related for some other reason. Remove one of them, and place it in a new table with a new primary key. Include this new key field as a foreign key in the original table.

Update your data model to show these new tables.

---

using the primary key field in one table as a nonkey field in a second table. This becomes a ***foreign key*** in the second table. Concatenated keys and foreign keys are important because they maintain the relationships between data in the tables.

Once you have properly completed data analysis, you have a normalized data set. Then you are ready to create the physical representation of the data, the database schema.

Create the Database Schema.   Creating the schema usually involves the database administrator (DBA) and the DBA's staff. They are trained in the specific software that will be used to implement the DBMS. They are more qualified than most project team members to handle the technical details and write the code that creates the actual data set.

In Chapter 5, you learned about computer aided software engineering (CASE) tools. These are software packages that computerize system development activities. Many CASE tools automate the processes of data modeling and data analysis. Analysts use them to prepare E-R diagrams and document entities, relationships, and attributes. Some CASE tools aid in identifying data that requires normalization, and some can produce SQL code from E-R diagrams. Although they do not replace the judgment of competent humans, CASE tools greatly ease the process of database design.

Data Analysis—an Example

As an example illustrating data analysis, consider the list of factory employees in Illustration 12–1. You would like to prepare a data set for this factory that will contain two subschemas. The human relations department would like to access it to learn personal information about individual employees. The payroll department would like to be able to access it to prepare weekly paychecks. Thus this data set will maintain data for two applications.

ILLUSTRATION 12–17

A Context Data Model

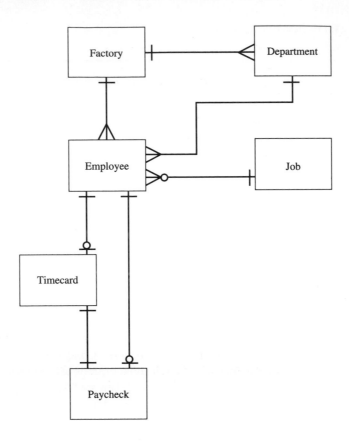

You study the documentation for the current systems, talk to their users, consider possible future applications for the data set, and determine that six entities are of interest: Employee, Factory, Department, Job, Paycheck, and Timecard. Each entity will become a table in the database. You then determine the cardinalities and create the context data model shown in Illustration 12–17.

Your next task is to select a primary key attribute for each entity. The primary key is used to distinguish individual occurrences of an entity type. From existing documentation (contained in Illustration 12–1) you designate the following key attributes: Employee Number (with the data name EMP-NO), Factory Number (data name FACT-NO), Department Number (DEPT-NO), and Job Code (JOB-CODE). Since you have only one timecard per employee, and expect to produce only one paycheck per employee during each pay period, you decide to use EMP-NO as the primary key for the Paycheck and Timecard entities. After updating your application data model to show these primary key fields, you have the key-based data model shown in Illustration 12–18. The letters (PK) next to the data names identify these attributes as primary keys.

Next you identify the attributes of interest to the users of the applications. Consulting your notes from interviews with users, you develop a list of the data elements they require. You assign each to the *one* entity to which it most directly relates.

ILLUSTRATION 12–18

A Key-Based Data Model

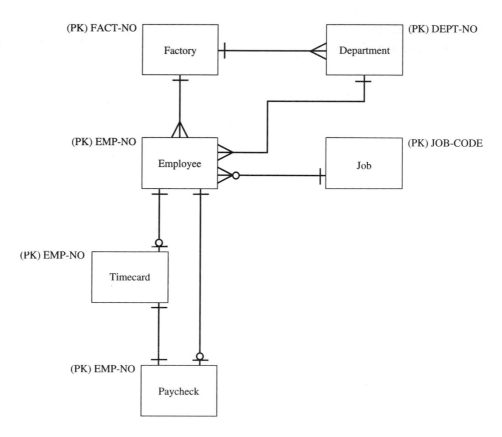

(Assigning each attribute to only one entity helps to ensure a normalized data set.) Then you update your documentation by adding data names for these nonkey attributes. This produces the partially attributed data model shown in Illustration 12–19.

This illustration shows the table names (entities) and the column names (attributes) for each table. The column names identify the data fields for a row representing one occurrence of an entity type. When the primary key of a table is included in another table as a nonkey field, analysts call it a "foreign key." In these illustrations, we identify foreign keys by the letters "FK."

In reality, the Factory, Department, and Job entities will contain several attributes beyond those shown here. These may include locations, managers in charge, qualifications, and information necessary for producing performance reports. But for the purposes of illustrating the database design process, we can omit them.

You next examine the data model in Illustration 12–19, looking for repeating fields within a table. You see that the Job table contains two pay rates, PAY-RATE-1 and PAY-RATE-2. (This occurred because Illustration 12–1 showed a maximum of two approved pay rates per job.) Repeating fields are undesirable in a database because they make the database difficult to maintain. For example, if the factory decides to add a third pay scale for a job, it must change the length of that job's logical record; then it must change all the computer programs that process that record.

ILLUSTRATION 12–19

A Partially Attributed Data Model

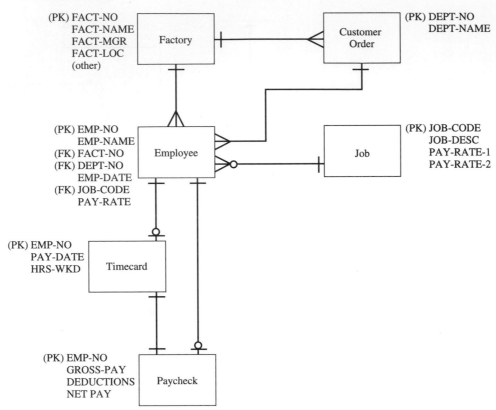

To eliminate a repeating field, create a new table. You decide to call this table Pay, define its primary key PAY-CODE as a one-digit numeric field, and include for each PAY-CODE one value of a nonkey attribute called PAY-RATE. You assign the PAY-CODE attribute a domain (takes on the values) of 1, 2, and 3. From Illustration 12–1, the PAY-RATE attribute has a domain of 10, 20, and 30. If the factory decides to add another pay rate, they simply add to this table another line containing a new pay code and pay rate.

After adding this table, you determine that there are no more repeating fields. Illustration 12–20 shows the application data model after this change. There is now a many-to-many relationship between the Job entity and the Pay entity.

Next you examine each table for dependencies. A dependency occurs when a nonkey attribute depends on a second nonkey attribute for its value. In the design of Illustration 12–20, the Employee entity contains both PAY-RATE and JOB-CODE. These attributes are related because, as you can see in Illustration 12–1, management restricts each job to certain pay rates.

This is an example of a transitive dependency. Transitive dependencies are undesirable because they make the database less adaptable to change. For example, if the

ILLUSTRATION 12–20

The Data Model After Repeating Fields Are Eliminated

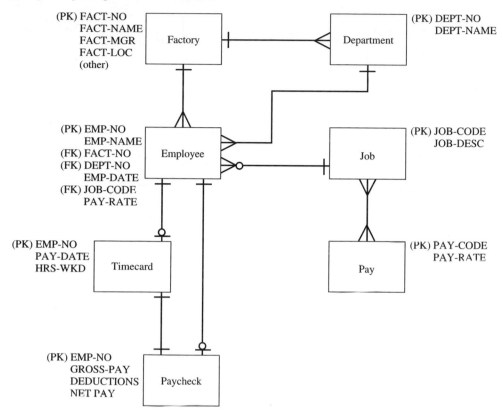

factory decides to increase the pay rate for laborers, they can do this by changing the PAY-RATE entry in the Pay table for PAY-CODE equal to 1. But they must also locate every occurrence for the laborer JOB-CODE in the Employee table and change its PAY-RATE also.

To correct the transitive dependency in Illustration 12–20, you create a new table from the Job and Pay tables. The new table has a primary key formed by combining ("concatenating") the keys from the Job and Pay tables. Call the new table by a name that is a combination of the original tables, Job-Pay, and give its primary key the data name JOB-PAY-CODE. This is an example of a concatenated key. JOB-PAY-CODE then replaces JOB-CODE and PAY-CODE as a foreign key in the Employee table.

Illustration 12–21 shows the updated data model after these changes are made. You see that the new model replaces the many-to-many relationship of the previous data model with two one-to-many relationships. Many analysts advocate replacing *all* many-to-many relationships in this way in order to ensure normalized data sets.

When examining the tables of Illustration 12–21, you see other dependencies. For the Paycheck entity, nonkey attributes NET-PAY and DEDUCTIONS are related to GROSS-PAY. In fact, they are each calculated from GROSS-PAY and are examples of

ILLUSTRATION 12–21

The Data Model After Transitive Dependencies Are Eliminated

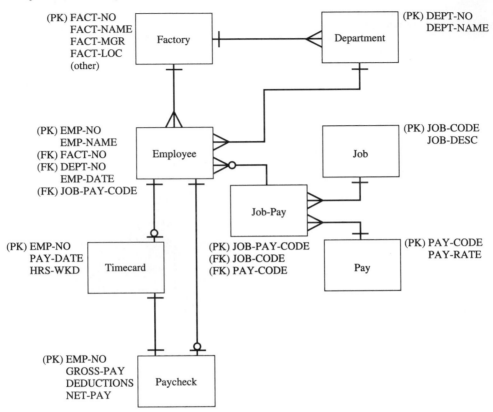

derived dependencies. Derived dependencies are undesirable because they are inefficient and may produce inconsistent data. If, for example, you change the DEDUCTIONS field for an occurrence of Paycheck, you must also change the NET-PAY field. If you don't, application systems using the Paycheck table may report inconsistent values for NET-PAY.

Eliminate these dependencies by eliminating the derived attributes. NET-PAY is unnecessary in the Paycheck table because the DBMS calculates it from GROSS-PAY and DEDUCTIONS. In fact, if you move DEDUCTIONS to the Employee table, you make the Paycheck table unnecessary because its only nonkey attribute, GROSS-PAY, can be calculated from PAY-RATE and HRS-WKD. Removing GROSS-PAY and the Paycheck table eliminates all derived dependencies from the data set.

Illustration 12–22 contains the result of the task. Since this data model contains no repeating fields or dependencies, we use it as our fully attributed data model. It provides a blueprint for the database administrator (or a CASE tool) to write the code that produces the schema.

ILLUSTRATION 12–22

A Fully Attributed Data Model After Derived Dependencies Are Eliminated

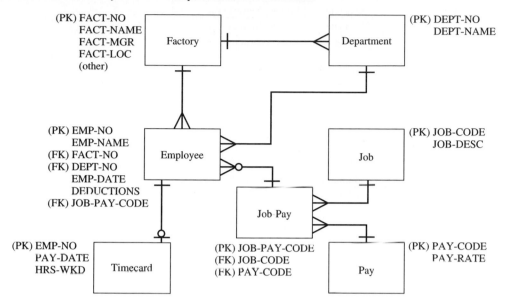

Illustration 12–23 shows the contents of the tables for this model. It is flexible because the factory can add additional occurrences of any entity by simply adding lines to a table. It is adaptable because the factory can add tables whenever other applications arise for the data in the data set. And it is stable because a change to a table does not produce unintended changes that can result in inconsistent data.

Summary

A database management system (DBMS) is a set of computer programs that control access to the database by users and by applications programs. This separates the way data are physically stored on a secondary storage device (its physical structure) from the way users and applications view the data (its logical structure). The DBMS maintains not only the data itself but also the relationships between the data.

Each DBMS software package assumes a structural model for the data. The DBA creates data sets on secondary storage devices that are consistent with this structural model. Three common logical structural models for data are the tree, network, and relational structures. Each has advantages over the others. The flexibility and tabular format of the relational structure makes it currently the most popular one for new systems.

When designing a relational database, analysts on the design team first identify the entities of interest and the relationships between them. They then perform data analysis,

ILLUSTRATION 12–23

Data Tables in the Fully Attributed Data Model

Factory Table

1	Automobile	Smith	Tampa	...
2	Electronic	Brown	Newark	...
3	Example	Chang	Lincoln	...
4	Textile	Jones	Seattle	...

Department Table

1	Factory Office
2	Assembly

Job Table

1	Clerk
2	Machinist
3	Accountant
4	Laborer

Pay Table

1	10
2	20
3	30

Job-Pay Table

11	1	1
12	1	2
13	1	3
21	2	1
22	2	2
23	2	3
31	3	1
32	3	2
33	3	3
41	4	1
42	4	2
43	4	3

Employee Table

11	Smith, A.	3	2	1999	1	41
14	Garcia, B.	3	2	1998	2	22
27	Wong, C.	3	1	1999	3	33
29	Riley, D.	3	2	1998	1	41
33	O'Hara, E.	3	1	1999	2	12
36	Weiss, F.	3	1	1998	3	11
41	Abbott, G.	3	1	1999	1	33
45	Powski, H.	3	2	1998	2	41

using E-R diagrams to produce a normalized set of tables. The DBA uses these tables to create the physical structure of the data. A well-designed database is stable, flexible, and adaptable to changes in the organization using it.

Key Terms

cardinality   A way of categorizing the relationship between two entities. It may be one-to-one (1:1), one-to-many (1:M), many-to-one (M:1), or many-to-many (M:M).

concatenated key   A key field formed by joining the primary keys of two tables.

data analysis   The process that prepares a data model for implementation in a stable, flexible, and adaptable form. For a relational database, the data tables are normalized.

data attribute   A descriptive characteristic of an entity that is recorded in a database.

database design   The process, performed by a project team, of developing logical data models that can be implemented in a physical structure, or schema.

data segment   Two or more related data elements stored together on a direct access device, equivalent to a record in a traditional data file system.

data set   Multiple occurrences of a data segment. For example, payroll records for all employees stored in multiple data segments constitute a payroll data set.

entity   A fundamental thing of relevance to the organization, about which it needs to record data.

foreign key   An attribute in a relation (column in a table) that serves as a primary key in another relation (table).

pointer   A data field added to a segment by the DBMS; it physically links the segment to other related segments.

primary key   A field that uniquely identifies a segment of a data set. In a relational DBMS, it uniquely identifies one occurrence of an entity type (row in a table).

relational structure   A structural model for data that considers a data set as a table. A row in the table contains one data segment, and a column represents one data attribute.

relationship   A reason relevant to the organization for associating two data entities.

Questions

12–1. What advantages does a database management system (DBMS) offer over a traditional file processing system? What disadvantages?

12–2. What four types of relationships exist among data?

12–3. When used by a DBMS, how does a data segment differ from a data record?

12–4. Explain the contents of a data dictionary description of a segment.

12–5. What is a pointer? What information is contained in a pointer?

12–6. A DBMS stores relationships explicitly using pointers. Why is this not required in a traditional data file system?

12–7. Identify three structural models for data. Which is most frequently used for new accounting systems?

12–8. In a relational DBMS, how is a relation similar to a file? In what way is it different?

12–9. What characteristics should relations have if a relational DBMS is to work efficiently?

12–10. Which operations are available to the user of a relational DBMS? Describe each.

12–11. What are the steps in designing a relational database? When in the system development process do they occur?

12–12. What problems can arise when a relational database is not properly normalized?

Exercises and Cases

12–13.   DEFINITIONS

Define each of the following terms:

a. Data attribute.
b. Data entity.
c. Data set.
d. Pointer.
e. Foreign key.
f. Concatenated key.

12–14.   RELATIONSHIPS

In the following list of comparisons between two items identify the relationship between each pair. It may be one-to-one (1:1), one-to-many (1:M), many-to-one (M:1), or many-to-many (M:M).

a. County to state.
b. Composer to musical work.
c. Orchestra to musical instrument.
d. Chapter number to chapter title.
e. Chapter number to book.
f. Chapter number to chapter subheading.

12–15.   DATA MODELS

Each of the following is a type of data model. Distinguish between each, and identify when it is created.

a. Enterprise data model.
b. Application data model.
c. Context data model.
d. Key-based data model.
e. Fully attributed data model.

12–16.   E-R DIAGRAM

Draw entity-relationship diagrams for each of the pairs of entities identified in items *a* through *f* of Exercise 12–14.

12–17.   ENTITIES AND RELATIONSHIPS—FINANCIAL CYCLE

Exercise 20–19 in Chapter 20 describes a property system used by an auto parts manufacturer.

Required:

a. Identify the entities in this application that are of interest to the company. For each entity, suggest relevant attributes.
b. Determine the relationships between these entities, stating the cardinality of each relationship.

12–18.   ENTITIES AND RELATIONSHIPS

Describe the nature of the relationships between each of the following pairs of entities:

a. Customer and customer order.
b. Customer order and customer.
c. Department and job.
d. Vendor invoice and vendor.
e. Check and vendor.
f. Employee and paycheck.

12–19.   E-R DIAGRAM

Examine the entity-relationship diagram below. For each pair of entities on the diagram, describe the relationships between them.

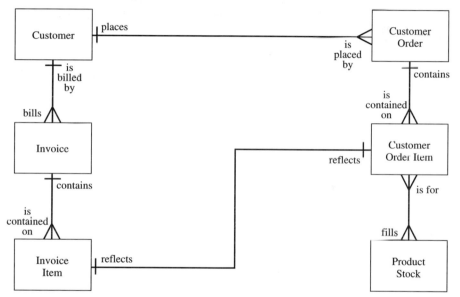

12–20.   PHYSICAL STRUCTURE

Wrigley Manufacturing Co. uses a job cost system. Workers obtain component parts required for manufacturing by listing them on a materials requisition and submitting the requisition to an inventory clerk. Wrigley uses a network DBMS to maintain its production cost records. The database contains segments representing jobs, material requisitions, and component parts issued for each job.

The diagram on the next page shows the data sets for Job No. 101 and Job No. 102. In this diagram, the number circled at the beginning of each segment is the physical address of that segment on a disk. The numbers in squares at the end of a segment are pointers to another location. There are three pointers, each maintaining relationships in a separate list.

Required:

Referring to the diagram, answer each of the following questions.

a. Which material requisitions were issued for Job No. 102?
b. List the parts issued for Material Requisition No. 34.
c. Which job(s) required Part No. 205?

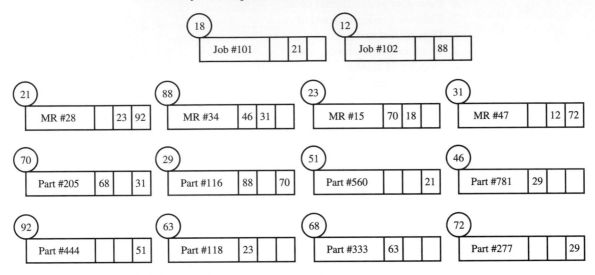

12–21.   *RELATIONAL STRUCTURE*

Ample Assets Co. uses a relational DBMS to maintain its accounting records. The following four tables are from its accounting database. Using the information in the tables, answer the questions listed below.

Customer Table

Customer No.	Name	Address
12	Able	Tulsa, OK
15	Baker	Seattle, WA
23	Charlie	Boston, MA
28	Delta	Chicago, IL
36	Easy	Cleveland, OH

Product Table

Product No.	Description	Unit Price
123	Widget	3.00
456	Bearing	10.00
789	Sleeve	7.00
432	Lubricant	4.00
765	Cleaner	5.00

Invoice Table

Invoice No.	Customer No.
A1111	12
A2222	15
B3333	36
D4444	12
E5555	28

Line Item Table

Invoice No.	Line Item No.	Product No.	Quantity
A1111	1	765	10
A2222	1	456	2
A2222	2	765	5
B3333	1	123	7
D4444	1	123	1
D4444	2	789	3

Required:

a. What products were billed to the customer on Invoice No. B3333?

b. What is the total amount due from Invoice No. A2222?

c. Which invoice(s) represent(s) sales to customer Baker in Seattle?

d. How much is owed to Ample Assets by customer Able in Tulsa? (Assume that the invoice table contains only unpaid invoices.)

12–22.   RELATIONAL OPERATIONS

Pixel Products is a job shop manufacturing company. The following three tables are from its database. The Job Table identifies each job currently in work-in-process inventory. The Product Table shows, for each product in Pixel's product line, the standard quantity of each material required. The Material Table contains the standard cost for each kind of material in raw material inventory.

Job Table

Job No.	Customer No.	Product No.	Quantity	Due Date
101	1234	216	10	12/12/98
102	2345	218	30	10/31/98
103	3456	217	5	11/30/98

Product Table

Product No.	Raw Material	Standard Quantity
216	A	1
216	R	2
216	Q	1
217	B	4
218	R	3
218	X	2

Material Table

Raw Material	Standard Cost per Unit
A	5.00
B	11.00
Q	2.00
R	4.00
X	10.00

Required:

a. Show the result of performing the JOIN operation on the Product and Material tables. Call the result Prod/Matl.

b. Show the result of performing the JOIN operation on the Job and Prod/Matl tables. (The latter is your result from part *a.*) Call the result from this JOIN operation Jobcost.

c. Show the result of performing the SELECT operation on Jobcost for Job No. 101.

d. From your answer to part *c,* determine the total standard material cost for Job No. 101.

e. Which operation can you use to simplify the display resulting from part *c* and yet enable an answer to part *d?*

12–23.   *EXTENDED EXAMPLE—PAYROLL*

Illustration 12–22 shows a fully attributed data model for the data analysis example given in the chapter. In this data model, the Employee entity has an attribute with the data name Deductions. For an employee, Deductions are subtracted from Gross Pay to determine Net Pay. The example in the chapter does not describe how the system determines the amount of the deductions.

Assume that, in the factory, only three types of deductions are allowed. Some workers have deductions for income tax (equaling 20 percent of gross pay), for social security (equaling 8 percent of gross pay), and for union dues (equaling $10 per pay period). Others do not pay union dues, so they have deductions only for income tax and social security.

Required:

a. Establish a data table containing these deductions. Determine a primary key that uniquely identifies each deduction type. (Hint: Each row in the table represents one value in the domain of the primary key.)
b. Modify the data model of Illustration 12–22 to incorporate the use of your Deductions table. Show the contents of any new tables you create. (Be sure your design meets the requirements for normalization.)
c. Describe how your design accommodates the addition of new, optional deductions (such as a weekly voluntary contribution to the United Way).

12–24.   EXTENDED EXAMPLE—RESPONSIBILITY ACCOUNTING

Illustration 12–22 shows a fully attributed data model for the data analysis example given in the chapter. In this data model, there is an entity called Factory that has four attributes. There is another entity called Department that has two attributes. This database design does not provide for responsibility reporting, and management would like to modify the design of the example system to improve on this shortcoming. They would like the system to produce responsibility reports for each factory and department. These reports show the labor costs for employees within a responsibility center as its only controllable costs.

Required:

a. Replace the entities Factory and Department in Illustration 12–22 with a new entity, Resp-Center. Identify the attributes for this entity that will be required for periodic performance reporting.
b. Determine the changes to the Employee attribute that are necessary to satisfy the desires of management. Draw a new entity-relationship diagram showing your changes.
c. Describe, in general terms, how you would design a database that could provide performance reports showing *all* costs and revenues (not just labor costs as above).

12–25.   DATABASE DESIGN—EXPENDITURE CYCLE

The case in Exercise 18-24 describes a manual purchasing system for an office in a university. The function of this office is to administer research grants and research funds obtained by professors, researchers, and students.

Required:

a. Identify the data entities that are relevant to this objective. Determine the attributes associated with each.
b. Describe the relevant relationships, including cardinalities.
c. Draw an entity-relationship diagram describing a database for this office.

12–26.   DATABASE DESIGN—CONVERSION CYCLE

The case in Exercise 19-21 describes a manual inventory system for a retailer, a discount tire dealer. This system maintains perpetual inventory records.

Required:

a. Identify the data entities that are relevant to this objective. Determine the attributes associated with each.

b. Describe the relevant relationships, including cardinalities.

c. Draw an entity-relationship diagram describing a database for this retailer.

12–27.   DATABASE DESIGN—REVENUE CYCLE

Franklin Flooring is a manufacturer and distributor of carpet and vinyl floor coverings. The company's home office is located in Springfield, Illinois, and its mills and manufacturing plants are spread throughout the Midwest. Franklin's total sales last year exceeded $300 million.

Retail showrooms are Franklin's primary customers. However, many major corporations buy Franklin's products directly, and large construction companies purchase carpet and floor covering on contract with Franklin at reduced rates for use in newly constructed homes and commercial buildings. In addition, there is a company-owned retail outlet at each plant where overruns, seconds, and discontinued items are sold; these are Franklin's only retail sales. The company has divided the sales market into seven territories—New England, Mid-Atlantic, Southeast, Great Lakes, South Central, Southwest, and Northwest. Each sales territory is divided into from 5 to 10 districts, and a salesperson is assigned to each district.

Franklin manufactures over 200 different varieties of carpet. The carpet is classified as commercial or residential and is sold under four brand names with up to five subproduct lines under each brand. The subproduct lines indicate the different grades of quality; grades are measured by type of tuft and number of tufts per square inch. Each subproduct line of carpet can have up to 15 different colors.

Approximately 180 varieties of vinyl floor covering are produced; they also are classified according to commercial or residential use. There are four separate brand names (largely distinguished by the type of finish), up to eight different patterns for each brand, and up to eight colors for each pattern.

Franklin's current accounting system is adequate for monitoring the sales by product; however, in-depth analysis of more specific market factors is limited because the information is not available. In order to improve the planning process and overall decision making, the accounting systems department has been asked to design a sales database that would make this information easily accessible. It should permit Franklin to prepare a sales analysis that reflects all or any of the company's operating characteristics.

Required:

As an analyst in the accounting systems department, you have been asked to design a database to assist Franklin Flooring in product analysis. For purposes of this assignment, you should ignore other applications that may use this database. As a part of your design process, complete the following.

a. Identify the data entities that are relevant to the product analysis objective. Determine the attributes associated with each.

b. Describe the relevant relationships, including cardinalities.

c. Draw an entity-relationship diagram describing a database for this manufacturing company.

(CMA Adapted)

12–28.   *ON-LINE REAL-TIME DBMS*[1]

American Airlines anticipated a lot of disasters that could disrupt its Sabre Passenger Services System, but it did not foresee the glitch that brought the reservation system down for 13 hours one weekend. Located in an underground storeroom, Sabre computers are protected from tornadoes, plane crashes, and power outages. But they were not isolated from an internal error that erased internal labels on 1,080 disk drives. This forced reservations clerks and travel agents to rely on printed flight schedules and to write out tickets by hand.

"Our reaction was one of absolute horror, it was our worst nightmare," said Jim Jackson, vice president of systems engineering for American's Sabre Computer Services Division. He had learned of the problem after being awakened by an emergency telephone call on Friday night. "Even if we had intended to do this damage, it would have been extremely difficult to duplicate."

The massive computer crash started just before midnight on Friday. It happened while Sabre technicians were reformatting the disk drives during an expansion project. This would have extended support from Sabre's operating system to a total of 1,260 disk drives.

"We had a program that was changed erroneously and did something that we never intended for it to do," said Jackson. The erroneous program stripped away the digital labels on each disk volume, making it impossible for the operating system to address any of Sabre's disk drives. Although only about 2,500 records were destroyed, this made it impossible to access about 1 million bytes of data.

"The field that was changed was a control field in the formatter utility," he explained. "The operating system, overwhelmed by its inability to address the disk drives, collapsed nearly instantaneously." Sabre technicians had to restart the crashed system, relabel each disk drive, and reset the pointers that indicate where passenger data is located. The pointers are critical because the information on just one ticket is scattered across multiple disk drives. This process took 100 programmers and systems engineers more than 10 hours.

The system was restarted just before 7:00 A.M. on Saturday, and reformatting was complete by 11:00 A.M. Then, due to pent-up demand, American's technicians had to gradually restart Sabre, slowly admitting more traffic from 27 front-end communications processors. American Airlines officials would not comment on the amount of revenue lost because of the problem.

Said one travel agent, "We could have booked the American flights on a competing reservations system, but we could not be certain the space was available. Without Sabre, the seats and the discounted fares could not be confirmed until flight time." Their 35 employees had to handwrite most tickets until 2:30 P.M. on Saturday. "We were picking

---

[1]Adapted from "Runaway Program Gores Sabre," *Computerworld*, May 22, 1989, p. 1. Used by permission.

up the phone and calling like in the old days," he said. "We really didn't catch up with the paperwork until Monday morning."

Required:

a. How were pointers used to link the data in this on-line real-time applications system?
b. Which procedures, implemented routinely at the data center, could have prevented this error?
c. Which routine procedures could have made recovery of the database easier?

12–29.   DATABASE DESIGN

The case in Exercise 17–30 describes manual procedures for the revenue cycle in the office of a physician, Dr. Pat Clark. Since her practice is new, Dr. Clark anticipates significant growth over the next few years as measured by the number of patients. If the patient load becomes large enough, she may have to take a partner—another physician who will share in the workload and the profits.

Required:

Design a relational database that will satisfy the current and future needs of this physician's practice.

13   INTERNAL CONTROL

Learning Objectives

1. To understand the components of an organization's internal control structure.
2. To know the objectives and limitations of internal control.
3. To discover which characteristics of a control environment promote an effective accounting system.
4. To learn how an accounting system aids in communicating information.
5. To describe effective control activities.

Introduction

Accounting systems provide information for people both internal and external to an organization. The users of this information rely on the accuracy of the system's reports and displays. Organizations adopt *internal control* policies and procedures to maintain accurate information and reliable operations. In this chapter you will learn about the components of an organization's internal control, its limitations, and some basic policies and procedures.

Features of Internal Control

An organization's internal control is intended to achieve certain organizational objectives. Since different people in an organization have different objectives, each has his or her own perspective on internal control. A widely accepted definition states that

> Internal control is a process, effected by an entity's board of directors, management and other personnel, designed to provide reasonable assurance regarding the achievement of objectives in the following categories:
>
> • Effectiveness and efficiency of operations.
> • Reliability of financial reporting.
> • Compliance with applicable laws and regulations.[1]

---

[1]Committee of Sponsoring Organizations of the Treadway Commission, *Internal Control—Integrated Framework,* p. 9 and p. 14. Adopted in Statement on Auditing Standards No. 78, *Consideration of Internal Control in a Financial Statement Audit,* AICPA, 1995, Paragraph 6.

Differing perspectives may produce different, more specific definitions based on this core definition, but each definition recognizes that internal control is a *process* effected by *people* to provide *reasonable assurance* that *objectives* are achieved.

Process

Internal control is not a single process but rather a combination of many processes that occur as a part of the organization's activities. As a tool for management, it is inherent in how management runs the organization. Internal control is effective when the processes achieve their objectives, ineffective when they do not. Because internal control is intermixed with the organization's operating activities, it is most effective when it is built into the organization's structure during system design.

Traditionally accountants have defined internal control as the plan of organization and the methods and measures used to achieve certain objectives of interest to accountants. From an accounting perspective, those may be the most important objectives. From a management perspective, internal control includes many other objectives as well.

People

People implement the processes of any organization—they make internal control work. Management determines *how* it works by approving the design of the organization's systems. Because the board of directors has oversight authority and approves certain transactions and policies, it also is an important element in internal control.

Accountants execute many of the internal control processes. By participating in system design, they help to create the system of internal control. Accountants who serve as auditors have access to the board of directors through its audit committee.

Objectives

Every organization has a mission, and management identifies organizational objectives that are consistent with that mission—objectives for the organization as a whole and for specific activities within it. Most organizational objectives relate to one of three categories: operations (the effective and efficient use of resources), financial reporting (preparing reliable financial statements), and compliance (abiding by applicable laws and regulations). Most organizations also have other, more specific objectives that internal control systems help to achieve.

Accountants traditionally have defined internal control as the measures taken to achieve four objectives: (1) safeguarding assets, (2) ensuring accurate and reliable accounting data, (3) promoting operational efficiency, and (4) encouraging employees to follow management's policies. Of these, the first two are of more significance to accountants and were called *accounting controls.* The second two, called *administrative controls,* are more important to management. Each of these traditional objectives is related to one of the three broad categories listed in the definition presented above.

Reasonable Assurance

Internal controls cannot guarantee that management's objectives will be attained. They can only provide **reasonable assurance** of attaining them. Any organization's internal controls have limitations that make absolute assurance impossible.

Limitations of Internal Control.   When creating internal control policies and procedures, most managers consider it unreasonable to try to establish ones that absolutely prevent errors, collusion, and management override—the three major limitations of internal control.

Errors.   Errors arise when employees exercise poor judgment or have a breakdown in their attention to the job. Poor judgment produces bad decisions and results from poor training, lack of experience, or lack of knowledge. Breakdowns in attention arise from carelessness, which may occur because of fatigue, outside interruptions, or overwork.

For example, an error from carelessness occurs when a sales clerk unintentionally hits the wrong key and enters an incorrect amount into a cash register. Lack of knowledge causes an error when a clerk unknowingly codes a transaction incorrectly as a cash sale rather than a credit sale. Appropriate control procedures detect these errors when they occur. Most cash registers display the sales amount to the customer, and most retailers daily compare total cash in a register to its recorded cash sales.

Even though well-trained and conscientious employees make few errors, most managers recognize that even the best employees sometimes make mistakes. But they consider it unreasonable to try to develop internal controls that would prevent or detect every error. Rather, they attempt to hire good employees and to devise processes that prevent or detect the most likely or most serious errors.

Collusion.   *Collusion* occurs when two or more employees conspire to commit a theft from their employer. For example, a sales clerk and a sales supervisor may agree to steal cash from a cash register and to cover the theft by falsifying the daily reconciliation for that register. By colluding in this way, they may succeed in perpetrating a theft of assets.

Although it is possible to adopt policies and procedures that detect theft where collusion occurs, most managers consider that effort unreasonable and instead try to hire honest employees and to keep them satisfied with their jobs. This minimizes the desire to steal and makes collusion unlikely. Accountants and managers recognize, however, that if collusion occurs, existing control will be ineffective in preventing it.

Management Override.   Because managers in an organization have more authority than production or clerical personnel, control processes that are effective at lower levels in an organization become ineffective at higher levels. For example, a store manager may steal cash from the day's receipts after the daily cash reconciliation at each register is complete. The manager can then simply misstate the amount of cash received in reports to superiors in the organization. The reconciliation procedure, though effective at the sales clerk level, is ineffective in preventing or detecting these irregularities at a higher level. The store manager overrides this control procedure.

Management override, like collusion, cannot be prevented by reasonable means. Instead organizations try to employ honest managers and to compensate them adequately for good performance. The possibility of management override is a limitation to any well-designed internal control policies and procedures.

It is unreasonable to try to select controls that are absolutely effective in detecting errors from carelessness or in preventing collusion between employees. And even if management established them, no internal control could prevent management from violating its own policies and procedures. Illustration 13–1 summarizes these limitations of internal control and provides examples.

Costs and Benefits.   The concept of reasonable assurance implies that the costs of internal control should not exceed the benefits to be derived from it. Reasonable controls are those for which the benefits exceed the costs.

ILLUSTRATION 13–1

Limitations of Internal Control

Limitation	Example
Errors	Clerk unintentionally hits the wrong key during data entry
Collusion	Sales clerk and sales supervisor agree to steal cash from a cash register and falsify the daily cash reconciliation
Management override	Store manager steals from cash receipts after daily cash reconciliation is complete

For example, a sales clerk may steal cash from a cash register and immediately leave the country. A supervisor may not discover this theft until the cash in the register is reconciled at the end of the day. One way to prevent such a theft is to hire an employee to constantly watch the sales clerk. However, because this threat is unlikely, most managers think the cost of hiring the second employee will exceed the benefits. Managers require a daily reconciliation of the cash in the register because it is a cost-effective way to detect and prevent the most likely problems involving cash sales.

Threats to Accounting Data

Inaccurate accounting data hampers the efficiency and effectiveness of the organization, produces unreliable financial reports, and, if material, violates laws. Traditionally accountants have identified two sources of threats to accounting data: errors and irregularities. Errors are accidental. Irregularities are intentional. Top management creates internal control policies and procedures to detect or prevent both errors and irregularities.

As you saw earlier, errors arise from two sources. Poor judgment results from lack of knowledge, and lack of attention produces carelessness. *Irregularities* also arise from two sources. *Management fraud* occurs when a manager intentionally misstates financial information. Managers sometimes do this to overstate earnings. In this way they may increase the size of their bonuses or increase the selling price of stock they own. A *defalcation* is a theft of assets from the organization. For example, a sales clerk may remove cash from a cash register and use the cash for personal purposes. Because this theft is unrecorded in the accounting records, the theft causes them to overstate the balance in the cash account.

Internal controls prevent or detect defalcations. A retailer who reconciles cash in the register with recorded sales at the end of each day can detect theft by sales clerks. Illustration 13–2 summarizes these threats to the accuracy of accounting information.

The next section discusses the elements, or components, of internal control.

Components of Internal Control

An organization's five *internal control components* are the control environment, risk assessment, control activities, information and communication, and monitoring.

The Control Environment

The *control environment* sets the tone of the organization. Providing discipline and structure, it is a foundation for the other components of internal control. It is influenced by the organization's history and culture and has a pervasive influence on how the

ILLUSTRATION 13–2

Threats to the Accuracy of Accounting Information

Errors	Accidental misstatements.
	Errors from *carelessness*—due to inattention or fatigue.
	Errors in *judgement*—due to lack of knowledge or inadequate training.
Irregularities	Intentional misstatements.
	Defalcation—theft of an asset.
	Management fraud—management's deliberate distortion of financial information.

organization achieves its objectives. The following discussion identifies some of the factors that affect the control environment.

Integrity and Ethical Values.   The organization's objectives and how they are achieved are based on preferences and value judgments that, when translated into standards of behavior, reflect management's integrity and commitment to ethical values. Because management creates, administers, and monitors the system of internal control, its effectiveness is limited by management attitudes toward integrity and ethical values. A strong organizationwide ethical climate at all levels is vital. It is affected by the incentives and temptations that management provides. It is also affected by the guidance that management communicates, both formally and informally, to employees.

Ethical behavior and management integrity are products of the organization's culture. Official policies specify what management wants to happen, but organizational culture determines what actually happens—which rules are followed, bent, or ignored. Top management, by its own actions and choices, demonstrates its commitment to integrity and ethical behavior and thus creates an ethical culture for the entire organization. If employees see top management engaging in unethical behavior, they are more likely to commit irregularities themselves.

Establishing ethical values is difficult because different parties have conflicting interests. Top management must balance its own interests with those of the organization, its owners, employees, suppliers, customers, competitors, and the public. When these conflict, determining an ethical course of behavior may become complex and frustrating. For example, the production of certain products creates environmental problems. Solving those problems requires sacrifices by management, owners, and employees. Adequate solutions, which fairly address the concerns of all parties, are difficult to determine.

Commitment to Competence.   Competence means that employees have the knowledge and skills they need to perform their tasks. Management decides how well these tasks need to be performed and whether obtaining competent performance is worth the costs of hiring people with the necessary skills. Management must also evaluate the trade-off between employee skill levels and the amount of supervision required. But when management has a commitment to competence, the system of internal control is more likely to achieve its objectives. In an organization lacking a climate characterized by competence, both errors and irregularities are more likely to occur.

Board of Directors and Audit Committee Participation.   An audit committee consists of several of the organization's outside directors—that is, directors who are not employed by the organization in another capacity. If the audit committee takes an active role in overseeing policies and practices, the internal control system is more effective in achieving the organization's objectives. The audit committee can alert the entire board of directors to problems before they become serious.

An active and involved board of directors who have an appropriate amount of technical and management knowledge is critical to effective internal control. The board should contain enough outside directors that it is able to question management's activities and act in the event of management wrongdoing.

Management Philosophy and Operating Style.   These include management's approach to taking business risks, attitudes toward the accuracy of accounting data, and emphasis on meeting budget and operating goals. They have a significant influence on the effectiveness of the organization's control activities. A management inclined to take risks is less likely to be concerned with measures taken to maintain internal control. This lack of inclination increases the likelihood of errors and irregularities. When top management insists that managerial employees show continued improvement at all costs, managers are more likely to attempt management fraud to meet budget goals.

Organizational Structure.   The organizational structure provides an overall framework for the planning, executing, controlling, and monitoring activities performed by management. Objectives are more easily achieved in an organization whose structure reflects its management functions and that assigns authority and responsibility appropriately.

Assignment of Authority and Responsibility.   Management assigns authority and responsibility for operating activities and establishes reporting relationships and methods of authorization. Often management wants to push authority downward in the organization and give decision-making authority to lower-level personnel. This decentralization is intended to encourage creativity, initiative, and the ability to react quickly to competition. Management's critical challenge is to align authority with accountability and to delegate only to the extent required to achieve objectives. The control environment is influenced by the extent to which employees recognize that they will be held accountable.

Human Resource Policies and Practices.   Human resource policies and practices send messages to employees about what the organization expects in the way of integrity, ethical behavior, and competence. These policies describe how the organization hires, trains, evaluates, promotes, and compensates employees.

Well-organized recruiting practices show that the organization is committed to its people. Hiring practices demonstrate the organization's commitment to hiring competent and trustworthy employees. Training practices communicate expected levels of performance and behavior. Periodic performance appraisals demonstrate the organization's commitment to the advancement of its employees. Bonus incentives and disciplinary actions send messages about desirable and undesirable behavior.

ILLUSTRATION 13–3

Good Human Resource Policies and Practices

Training. Employees who understand their jobs are less likely to make errors.
Recognition for work well done. Encourages employees to prevent errors and irregularities.
Adequate pay. Fairly compensated employees are less likely to steal.
Investigate employees before hiring. A potential employee may have a history of carelessness or dishonesty.
Job rotation. Require employees to change jobs periodically. Then an employee cannot continue to conceal an error or irregularity that occurred in the past.
Required vacations. An employee filling in for an employee on vacation may discover an error or irregularity that occurred in the past.
Bonding. A bond is a contract whereby a surety company agrees to reimburse the employer for loss if an employee commits theft. The surety company thoroughly investigates the background of the bonded employee before issuing the bond.

Ultimately, the effectiveness of any internal control structure relies on the honesty and the abilities of the employees. Honest employees are less likely to commit defalcations, and capable ones are less likely to make errors. Adequate personnel policies and practices ensure that the organization hires capable people, trains them properly, treats them fairly, and compensates them adequately. Such policies and practices make errors and irregularities less likely. Illustration 13–3 describes some internal control practices that encourage a workforce of honest and capable employees. Illustration 13–4 summarizes the factors affecting the control environment.

Risk Assessment

Risk assessment, the second component of internal control, is management's process of identifying and analyzing the risks that might prevent the organization from achieving its objectives. Risks arise from both external and internal factors. Risks from external factors affect the organization as a whole. They include risks from competition, economic or technological change, government regulation, and natural catastrophes. Risks from internal factors relate to specific activities of the organization. They include disruption of the information system, errors due to untrained or unmotivated employees or to changes in management responsibilities, and the result of an ineffective board of directors or audit committee.

Change is a source of risk for all organizations. Economic, industry, and regulatory environments change, and any organization's activities evolve in response. A system of

ILLUSTRATION 13–4

Factors Affecting the Control Environment

Integrity and ethical values
Commitment to competence
Board of directors or audit committee participation
Management philosophy and operating style
Organizational structure
Assignment of authority and responsibility
Human resource policies and practices

AIS in Practice

Peregrine Investments Holdings, located in Hong Kong, was once the largest investment bank in Asia outside Japan. Peregrine's willingness to make risky investments contributed to its 1996 operating profit of $132 million. It had pioneered the junk bond market in Asia and had handled securities issues for companies in China, Vietnam, and Myanmar (Burma). But its failure to impose controls over credit risk contributed to its bankruptcy in early 1998.

Peregrine's problems arose because of loans it made to PT Steady Safe, an Indonesian taxi cab operator. These loans, totaling about a quarter of Peregrine's equity capital, were intended to help Steady Safe expand into rail, ferries, and toll roads. When Steady Safe was unable to repay, Peregrine was forced to liquidate.

The loans were made without the knowledge of the head of Peregrine's credit risk management. Bond traders advanced the money by purchasing securities over a long period of time and passing them off as normal securities purchases. When top management realized the extent of its exposure to the Indonesian economy, it was too late.

internal control that is effective under one set of conditions may be ineffective under another. As part of its risk assessment, an organization needs a process to identify changed conditions that can significantly affect the organization's ability to achieve its objectives.

Management's responsibility is to identify risks to the organization's objectives, estimate the significance of each risk, assess its likelihood, and identify actions that should be taken to reduce its significance or likelihood. In response to perceived risks, management may for example identify alternative supply sources, expand product lines, obtain more relevant operating reports, or improve training programs.

Control Activities

Control activities, the third internal control component, are the policies and procedures that management adopts to provide reasonable assurance that management directives are carried out. They help ensure that actions are taken to address risks to the achievement of the organization's objectives.

Accountants recognize many different types of control activities. One method of classifying them identifies four categories: (1) procedures for authorizing transactions, (2) security for assets and records, (3) segregation of duties, and (4) adequate documents and records.

Authorizing Transactions.   Management implements procedures for authorizing transactions and prescribes activities for processing them. The proper way to process transactions differs for each class of accounting transaction. For example, good procedures for processing cash disbursements transactions in the expenditure cycle differ from procedures for processing cash receipts in the revenue cycle. Yet good procedures in different transaction cycles have many characteristics in common. Illustration 13–5 summarizes some of these. Employees should record all transactions promptly and examine their records for obvious inaccuracies. Batch controls and balancing procedures help to discover errors.

Proper procedures for authorizing transactions likewise depend on the kind of transaction. Management authorizes transactions in two ways, using general and specific authorizations.

ILLUSTRATION 13–5

Good Procedures for Processing Transactions

Prompt recording. Employees record transactions immediately as they occur. This decreases opportunities for errors and irregularities regarding the transactions.

Visual checking. An employee recording the transaction confirms visually that all data are complete and correct.

Balancing. An employee determines that the total debit entries equal the total credit entries for the transaction.

Batch controls. Employees accumulate transactions into batches. They total the amount of the transactions in each batch and attach this total to the batch. In each later processing step, this total is recalculated and compared to the original batch total. This verifies that no transactions are lost from the batch.

General Authorization.   Management's ***general authorization*** relates to a whole class of transactions. A general authorization describes conditions under which employees may initiate, record, and process one kind of transaction. When these conditions are met, an employee is authorized to carry out these actions without further consultation with management. For example, management of a retail store approves a sales price for certain merchandise. Whenever a customer arrives who wants that merchandise and has the cash to pay for it, employees are authorized to initiate, record, and process the sales transaction.

Specific Authorization.   Management's ***specific authorization*** applies only to a single, specific transaction. Management normally requires specific authorization for large dollar amount transactions or those that represent high potential for fraud. Before an employee initiates a transaction of this kind, the employee consults with management and obtains approval specifically for it.

Transactions for larger amounts require specific authorization at higher organizational levels than do smaller transactions. For example, if a customer wishes to purchase merchandise but wants to pay by check rather than currency, management may require that a sales clerk obtain specific approval of the transaction from a supervisor. If a manager wishes to initiate a transaction to purchase a new factory building, the manager obtains specific authorization for this transaction from the board of directors.

Security for Assets and Records.   The second category of control activities concerns security for assets and records. Management should implement adequate safeguards to protect assets and records. Safeguards include providing physical security and fixing responsibility for the assets.

Physical Security.   Management implements procedures to provide physical security for inventory, cash, property, plant and equipment, and for the records of these assets. Inventory and cash are easily stolen and should be locked up; access should be limited to authorized employees. Thieves are sometimes able to steal other property and equipment, so these require safeguards as well. Many organizations attach nonremovable labels to each item of equipment. The label assigns an identifying number to the item. A property master file—a subsidiary ledger for the property account in the general ledger—lists each item by identifying number.

In a computer-based system, records include documents, filing cabinets, and computer data. When an employee steals an asset, the accounting records concerning the asset are overstated. To cover up a theft of assets, the thief must alter the accounting records for the asset. Adequate security over records prevents this and allows detection of the theft. For example, if a clerk steals something from the inventory warehouse, the inventory records show more on hand than actually exists. If the thief cannot gain access to inventory records, a supervisor or internal auditor may discover the theft by comparing the inventory records to the quantity on hand. Adequate physical security prevents unauthorized access to inventory records as well as to inventory itself. Physical security, however, is effective only when management fixes responsibility for it with specific individuals.

Fixed Responsibility.   Management assigns responsibility for specific assets and records to specific job positions. Then if an error or irregularity occurs, management holds the individual in that job position responsible. For example, management appoints an employee to the position of inventory clerk and gives that employee responsibility for physical security of inventory. If inventory is stolen, the inventory clerk is held responsible. Even if the inventory clerk did not commit the theft, the clerk was responsible for protecting the inventory and failed in that responsibility.

Internal control is best when management summarizes and communicates responsibilities in writing. During system implementation, a project team creates a procedures manual for this purpose. When it clearly fixes responsibility in this way, management encourages employees to do their jobs accurately and honestly.

Segregation of Duties.   The third category of control activities concerns separation of responsibilities, or *segregation of duties*. Management should assign responsibility in order to attain adequate segregation of duties. This means that no employees have the opportunity both to commit and to conceal errors and irregularities in the normal course of their duties. Management assigns duties so that different people perform three duties affecting an asset. Different employees are responsible for *authorizing* transactions in an asset, for *recording* transactions in an asset, and for *maintaining custody* of the asset.

For example, inventory is an asset that is easily stolen. In applying the principle of segregation of duties to inventory, management assigns responsibility for the custody of the inventory to an inventory clerk. When the records indicate that inventory is missing, management holds the inventory clerk responsible. An accounting clerk maintains the inventory records, and a shop supervisor authorizes issuance of inventory by signing a materials requisition. These individuals do not have access to the inventory warehouse. Thus neither the inventory clerk, the accounting clerk, nor the shop supervisor is in a position to steal inventory and then conceal the theft by altering the inventory records. At least two of these employees must collude to commit and successfully hide a theft of inventory.

Accountants say that having custody of an asset, authorizing transactions in the same asset, and keeping the records regarding the asset are *incompatible functions*. Management should design the organization's structure and assign responsibilities so that no employee performs functions that are incompatible. Although this is often difficult to do in a small organization, in such firms management can more closely monitor the actions of employees.

Adequate Documents and Records.   The fourth category of control activities concerns the kinds of documents and records used in the accounting system. Management should require the use of accounting documents and records that ensure proper recording of transactions and events. A double-entry accounting system helps achieve this objective. Controlling blank forms and prenumbering documents do so as well.

Forms Control.   When filled out, the forms used in an organization provide authorization for transactions or for the transfer of assets. An employee can cover up a theft of assets by stealing a document and falsifying it to alter the accounting records. For this reason, an individual employee should be assigned responsibility for each type of blank form. This employee maintains custody of the form and ensures its physical security.

For example, an unscrupulous employee may steal a materials requisition form from a shop supervisor. The employee fills out the form, forges the supervisor's signature, receives the inventory from the inventory clerk, and sells the inventory to a nonemployee. Nothing in the accounting records discloses this theft because the records agree with the quantity of inventory on hand. When checking for missing requisitions, the supervisor will discover the theft.

Management should review each form periodically and change it if necessary. A review may disclose that the form collects data no longer used or that it could easily collect data useful for management purposes if other lines were added. Management may also decide to change the number of copies produced or their distribution. Many organizations establish a policy of reviewing each form every few years. A form has the date of its last review printed in small letters somewhere on it, so management can easily see when it is time for another review.

Numbered Documents.   Adequate forms control is much easier when a unique identifying number is printed on each copy of a form. Then a supervisor can periodically check the quantity on hand of each prenumbered document and verify that none are missing. If one is missing, the supervisor can determine its number, halt its processing, and thus prevent a thief from using it to falsify a transaction. Documents that should be numbered and controlled include blank checks, check requests, purchase orders, receiving reports, invoices, materials and purchase requisitions, journal vouchers, and credit memos. Any of these, when stolen, can be falsified and used to cover the theft of an asset.

Once a form has been filled out, it becomes a completed document. Completed documents must be controlled just like blank forms, because thieves use them to falsify transactions as well. For example, an unscrupulous employee may steal a completed materials requisition—documenting an issue of material earlier in the year—from the filing cabinet in the factory office. The employee alters the requisition by changing its date, submits the requisition, receives the inventory from the inventory clerk, and sells the inventory to a nonemployee. Again the accounting records agree with the inventory on hand, so reconciling them does not disclose the theft. However, while periodically checking the sequence of the completed requisitions stored in the filing cabinet, the supervisor will discover the theft of one of them. The supervisor can then search for the missing requisition and, perhaps, catch the thief.

ILLUSTRATION 13–6

Control Activity Categories

1. **Procedures for authorizing and processing transactions**
   General authorization
   Specific authorization
2. **Security for assets and records**
   Physical activity
   Fixed responsibility
3. **Segregation of duties**
   Different employees (*a*) authorize transactions in an asset, (*b*) record those transactions, and (*c*) have
   custody of the asset.
4. **Adequate documents and records**
   Numbered documents
   Control of blank forms and completed documents

Many organizations prevent defalcations of this kind by defacing documents once they have been used. They may punch small holes in the document forming the word "paid," or they may ink-stamp it with the word "canceled." This control procedure indicates to all employees that the document should not be used again.

The four categories of control activities concern proper procedures for authorizing transactions, security for assets and records, segregation of duties, and adequate documents and records. Illustration 13–6 summarizes these categories of control activities.

Information and Communication

The fourth component of internal control is information and communication. Information is needed at all levels of the organization for making operating decisions, for financial reporting, and for compliance. It is identified, captured, processed, and reported by information systems.

Communication is inherent in information systems. However, communication extends beyond the processing of financial data to encompass other internal and external forms. Communication takes such forms as policy manuals, accounting manuals, and memoranda. It also can be made orally and through the actions of management. It should send a clear message from top management that personnel should take internal control responsibilities seriously. Each individual should understand the relevance of the internal control system and his or her role in it.

Information systems communicate both internal and external information. Traditionally, accountants recognize the accounting system as one means of internal communication. The accounting system consists of the methods and records used to identify accounting transactions, assemble them, and analyze, classify, and report them. The accounting system also maintains accountability for the organization's assets and liabilities.

Modern accounting systems implement double-entry accounting methods. A double-entry system includes several features that prevent and detect errors and irregularities: debit and credit analysis, a chart of accounts, standard journal vouchers, a trial balance, and control accounts.

ILLUSTRATION 13–7

Characteristics of a Well-Designed Chart of Accounts

Responds to organization's needs. Accounts included in a chart of accounts should meet management's needs for control of operations and financial accounting requirements for external reporting.

Facilitates report preparation. Accounts in the chart of accounts should be listed in their order of appearance in the financial statements and should be compatible with the organizational structure.

Provides adequate description. A description of each account and its contents should be provided. This guidance to the accounting staff enables consistent use of the accounts.

Account titles provide clear distinctions. Account titles should be chosen to minimize ambiguities concerning the contents of an account.

Control accounts. When cost-effective, the chart of accounts should incorporate control accounts.

Debit and Credit Analysis.   When an accounting system records a transaction, it records the effects of that transaction in at least two accounts. Half of the journal entry is a debit, and the other half is a credit. And, as you learned in your first accounting course, the total of the accounts debited must equal the total of the accounts credited. This simple feature detects many errors and detects or prevents many irregularities.

How does the double-entry accounting system detect errors? Any accounting transaction contains entries in two or more accounts. An incorrect entry in one account must be compensated for by an equal error in another account. Otherwise, the entry does not balance, and a clerk easily detects the error. For example, when an organization purchases inventory, the system records a debit to the Inventory account and a credit to the Accounts Payable account. To go undetected, an error must be repeated twice, once in Inventory and again in Accounts Payable. Two equal errors are more unlikely and much easier to detect than a single error would be if debit and credit analysis were not required.

The double-entry system also makes detecting defalcations easier. If an employee steals inventory, then the inventory on hand does not equal the recorded balance in the accounting records. An auditor or supervisor can easily detect the theft by counting the inventory. An employee wishing to cover the theft must make fraudulent entries in two accounts rather than one. This doubles the chance of detection.

Chart of Accounts.   The chart of accounts is a list of all the account names and account codes used by the organization. An employee may use only those accounts listed when making debit and credit entries. This restricts the opportunity for employees to make errors or commit irregularities when recording transactions. For example, when an employee steals cash, the employee may attempt to cover the theft by crediting the Cash account and debiting an expense account. If there are only a limited number of expense accounts in the chart of accounts, any prolonged use of this scheme produces excessive expense account balances. Management would question the cause of these excessive expenses and discover the defalcation.

A properly designed chart of accounts also minimizes errors. Illustration 13–7 shows some characteristics of a well-designed chart of accounts.

ILLUSTRATION 13–8

*A Standard
Journal Voucher*

SUNLIGHT MANUFACTURING COMPANY			JV No. 4 -29
105 Red Hot Road			
Dallas TX 75248			

STANDARD JOURNAL VOUCHER

For the month of April 19 98

	Account Title	Debit	Credit
106	Allowance for Doubtful Accounts	255.15	
105	Accounts Receivable/RST Company		255.15

EXPLANATION

To write off accounts receivable from RST
Company, declared bankruptcy; see attached documents.

Prepared by	Approved by	Reviewed by	Entered by
D. Li			
Date 4/28/98	Date_____	Date_____	Date_____

Standard Journal Vouchers.   A *standard journal voucher* is a document on which an accountant makes a standard journal entry. Accountants repeat many adjusting entries each time the closing process occurs in the accounting cycle. Fewer errors occur if a project team, when designing the system, creates a *standard journal entry* for each of these repeated adjustments. Then during closing, the accountant records the standard journal entry on a standard journal voucher printed to show the proper accounts to debit and credit. An accountant determines the appropriate amounts and records them on the standard journal voucher. In this way the accountant does not make entries in incorrect accounts.

For example, at each closing an accountant makes an adjusting entry accruing unpaid wages as of the closing date. If the design project team creates a standard journal voucher for this adjustment, it contains a debit to Wages Expense and a credit to Wages Payable. A set of standard journal vouchers for this entry is printed. At closing, the accountant determines the amount of the accrual, fills in the amount on a standard journal voucher form, obtains proper approvals, and enters the adjustment in the records.

Illustration 13–8 shows an example of a standard journal voucher. For this company, Journal Voucher No. 4-29 is used to write off the accounts receivable balance of a customer. A credit manager initiates this document after reviewing an aged trial balance of accounts receivable. The treasurer initials approval of it after verifying that the debt is uncollectible. The chief accountant or controller reviews it for correctness before an accounting clerk enters it in the computer system.

Trial Balance.   Accountants prepare a trial balance as one step in the accounting cycle. Preparation of the trial balance provides an opportunity to determine if the system has recorded transactions erroneously. Because each transaction is recorded as a combination of equal debits and credits, the total of the debits must equal the total of the credits on the trial balance. An inequality is evidence of an error in recording transactions.

Common errors disclosed on the trial balance include transposition and misfooting. A transposition error occurs when a clerk records the amount of an entry but interchanges two of its digits. For example, the clerk may intend to write 456 but instead writes 465. Misfooting occurs when the clerk adds numbers incorrectly.

Accountants also review the trial balance for abnormal account balances. An abnormal account balance may indicate errors either in posting or during debit and credit analysis. Asset and expense accounts normally have debit balances. Liability, Capital, and Revenue accounts normally have credit balances. If a different balance is noted during review of the trial balance, the accountant investigates to determine its cause.

Control Accounts.   A control account in the general ledger summarizes the contents of many accounts in a subsidiary ledger. Organizations commonly use control accounts when recording accounts receivable, inventory, fixed assets, and common stock. An accounts receivable control account, for example, summarizes the amounts owed by those customers with outstanding balances in the accounts receivable subsidiary ledger. In a computerized system, this subsidiary ledger is the customer master file.

When a transaction produces an entry in a control account, the accounting system also records the transaction in the proper account in the subsidiary ledger. At the end of a reporting period, the total of the debits (or credits) in the control account should equal the total of the debits (or credits) in the subsidiary ledger. An inequality alerts an accountant to the existence of a recording error.

To summarize, the fourth component of an organization's internal control is information and communication. The information system communicates both internal and external information to personnel, and the accounting system is a part of that information system.

Monitoring

Monitoring, the fifth and final component of internal control, is a process that assesses the quality of internal control performance over time. Organizations change, and the ways in which controls are applied in them evolve. Monitoring helps management determine what modifications to the system are needed as conditions change. It involves assessing the design and operation of controls and taking corrective actions. Monitoring can be done in two ways: through ongoing activities or by separate evaluations.

Ongoing Monitoring Activities.   Many activities serve to monitor the effectiveness of internal control in the ordinary course of operations. These include clerical checks, reconciliations, comparing assets on hand with the accounting records, control procedures carried out by computer programs, management review of summaries of changes in

ILLUSTRATION 13–9

Monitoring Activities

Check	Example
Clerical checks	A shop worker fills out a materials requisition. The shop supervisor reviews it before signing it.
Reconciliations	A shop supervisor examines the sequence of completed materials requisitions to ensure that none are missing.
Comparison of assets with records	An internal auditor and an inventory clerk count the physical inventory. The auditor compares the count totals with quantities shown in accounting records.
Computer-programmed controls	A computer program checks calculations on a materials requisition after the data is entered into the computer.
Management review of accounts	A factory manager investigates the cause of an excessive materials quantity variance.
User review of computer reports	An inventory clerk reviews a list of materials requisitions to look for duplicate processing of the same requisition.

account balances, and review by users of computer reports. Illustration 13–9 contains examples of each of these.

Separate Evaluations.   From time to time management may decide to perform a separate evaluation of the effectiveness of the organization's system of internal control. These evaluations may vary in scope and in frequency, depending on the risks being controlled and the importance of the controls being evaluated. Management may choose to evaluate all internal control processes or to assess specific controls. The evaluation may be a self-assessment performed by managers over the controls in their areas of responsibility. Or it may be an independent check performed by outsiders such as internal or independent auditors. Auditors provide an objective form of monitoring because they have no superior–subordinate relationship with employees. Both independent auditors and internal auditors perform evaluation procedures.

Independent Auditors.   Independent auditors are employees of a firm of certified public accountants. They may perform monitoring procedures as part of their annual audits of the financial statements. Because they are not employees of the organization being audited, their examination provides the most objective form of monitoring.

Independent auditors examine only those control activities important for the independent audit. Standards for independent auditing require them to obtain an understanding of the internal control structure sufficient to plan the audit. Yet they ordinarily do not examine control procedures related to each account or each class of transaction. They may omit monitoring procedures that are not relevant to their objectives. Management relies on internal auditors to verify performance in these areas.

Internal Auditors.   Internal auditors are staff people employed by the organization. Frequently they have backgrounds in accounting, although they may come from other disciplines such as management information systems. As a service to management, the internal audit staff reviews the operations of the organization and makes recommendations for improving them.

Internal auditors make periodic reviews, called *operational audits,* of each department in the organization. A part of these reviews is to carry out monitoring procedures appropriate for the department. For example, as part of a review of inventory procedures, an internal auditor may supervise the count of physical inventory in the warehouse. The internal auditor then reconciles the inventory on hand with the accounting records for inventory. This evaluates the performance of those employees involved in authorizing and recording transactions in inventory and those who have custody of it.

Operational audits are most effective when internal auditors are completely independent of the department being audited. An internal audit staff that reports to the controller would be independent of the inventory function in a production department. It would not be independent of the accounting department, however, because the controller has a superior–subordinate relationship with both accounting and internal audit. For maximum independence, the internal audit staff should report as high in the organizational hierarchy as possible. The internal audit staff should always have direct access to the audit committee of the board of directors.

You have learned the five components of internal control: control environment, risk assessment, control activities, information and communication, and monitoring. Management creates internal controls in order to ensure that the organization's goals are met. In the United States, federal law also requires management attention to internal control.

The Foreign Corrupt Practices Act

In 1977 the Congress enacted the Foreign Corrupt Practices Act (FCPA) in response to scandals during the early 1970s involving bribery of foreign officials. Congress was concerned that such activities could occur without the knowledge of top management and without detection by auditors. The law has two main provisions, one relating to illegal foreign payments and another to internal control.

Illegal Foreign Payments

It is a criminal offense for any U.S. business to make a payment to a foreign official to expedite the performance of a routine governmental action. A business violating this provision may be fined up to $2 million, and its managers may be fined up to $100,000, imprisoned up to five years, or both.[2] This provision of the FCPA is an effective deterrent against bribes by businesses in the United States. The provision of most interest to accountants, however, concerns internal control.

Internal Control Provisions

These provisions apply only to companies required to file reports with the U.S. Securities and Exchange Commission (SEC). The provisions require that these companies maintain books, records, and accounts accurately recording their transactions. The FCPA also requires these companies to

---

[2]The provisions of the law were amended by the Omnibus Trade and Competitiveness Act of 1988. For a specific discussion of the amended bribery provisions, see J. W. Morehead and S .G. Gustavson, "Complying with the Amended Foreign Corrupt Practices Act," *Risk Management*, April 1990, pp. 76–82.

devise and maintain a system of internal accounting controls sufficient to provide reasonable assurance that

    (i)   transactions are executed in accordance with management's general and specific authorization;

    (ii) transactions are recorded as necessary (I) to permit preparation of financial statements, and (II) to maintain accountability for assets;

    (iii) access to assets is permitted only in accordance with management's general or specific authorization; and

    (iv) the recorded accountability for assets is compared with the existing assets at reasonable intervals and appropriate action is taken with respect to any differences.[3]

The SEC has responsibility for monitoring compliance with these provisions.

Thus, management must establish adequate internal control not only to fulfill its obligations to owners of the business but also to comply with the FCPA. Because accountants are the experts in internal control, in most organizations top management relies heavily on them to satisfy these provisions.

Summary

An organization's internal controls consist of the policies and procedures established by management to achieve the organization's objectives. There are three categories of objectives. *Operations objectives* pertain to the effectiveness and efficiency of the organization's operations. *Financial reporting objectives* concern the preparation of reliable published financial statements. And *compliance objectives* relate to laws and regulations that affect the organization.

The threats to accurate accounting data include accidental errors and intentional irregularities. Internal controls provide reasonable but not absolute assurance that the objectives will be obtained. As a result, any organization's internal control is limited by the possibilities of errors from carelessness, collusion, or management override.

The components of internal control are the control environment, risk assessment, control activities, information and communication, and monitoring. The control environment sets the tone of the organization and is the foundation for the other components. Risk assessment is the identification and analysis of risks that might prevent the organization from achieving objectives. Control activities are the actions that are taken to address these risks. There are four categories of control activities: authorization procedures, security for assets and records, segregation of duties, and adequate documents and records. Information and communication are required for making operational decisions, for financial reporting, and for compliance with laws. Monitoring is the process of assessing the quality of a system's performance over time. It may focus on ongoing activities or take the form of special evaluations.

---

[3]Sec. 102 of the Foreign Corrupt Practices Act of 1977 (PL 95-213).

Key Terms

accounting system   The methods and records used to identify, assemble, analyze, classify, and report accounting transactions.

collusion   Conspiracy by two or more people to steal from an organization.

control activities   Procedures adopted by management to provide reasonable assurance that the organization achieves its objectives.

control environment   Those circumstances surrounding an organization's accounting system that either improve or limit the effectiveness of control procedures.

defalcation   The theft of assets from an organization.

general authorization   Management's authorization in advance for a class of transactions.

internal control components   An organization's control environment, risk assessment procedures, control activities, information and communication methods, and monitoring activities.

internal controls   Policies and procedures established by management to achieve the organization's objectives.

irregularity   An intentional act, such as defalcation or management fraud, that may misstate accounting data.

management override   The ability of managers to overcome control policies or procedures that are effective with operations-level employees.

reasonable assurance   A concept applied to internal controls stating that the costs of a control policy or procedure should not exceed its benefits.

segregation of duties   The assignment of responsibility so that no individual performs any two of these three functions affecting an asset: authorizing transactions in the asset, recording transactions in the asset, and maintaining custody of the asset.

specific authorization   Management's authorization for a single, specific transaction.

standard journal voucher   A document used to record a standard journal entry. It shows the proper accounting entry for a common transaction and minimizes the likelihood of recording the transaction incorrectly.

Questions

13–1. Which three categories of objectives do accountants recognize for internal control?

13–2. What is internal control?

13–3. What are the two threats to accurate and reliable accounting data? Describe and distinguish between them.

13–4. What is meant by the following statement: "Internal control policies and procedures are intended to provide reasonable but not absolute assurance that management's objectives are attained"?

13–5. Which kinds of errors and irregularities can occur even in an organization having good internal control?

13–6. What are the components of internal control?

13–7. Identify seven factors that affect an organization's control environment.

13–8. Which features of a double-entry accounting system prevent and detect errors and irregularities?

13–9. How does debit and credit analysis aid in preventing and detecting errors? Irregularities?

13–10. What is a standard journal voucher? Why is it a good control practice?

13–11. What are four categories of control activities?

13–12. Describe the difference between general authorization and specific authorization.

Exercises and Cases

13–13. *Control Procedures*

The following is a list of control procedures discussed in this chapter. Identify to which of the four categories of control activity each belongs.

a. Separating custody from recordkeeping.
b. Merchandise price tags.
c. Prenumbered documents.
d. Prompt recording.
e. Locks.
f. Fixing responsibility to avoid incompatible functions.

13–14. *Control Procedures*

Describe how each control policy, practice, or procedure in the following list either prevents or detects errors and irregularities:

a. Training.
b. Locking up blank forms.
c. Bonding.
d. Chart of accounts.
e. Job rotation.
f. Batch controls.

13–15. *Incompatible Functions*

The following list contains pairs of job functions. From this list identify the pairs that are incompatible. Explain your answer.

a. Inventory clerk and shop supervisor.
b. Inventory clerk and payroll clerk.
c. Shop supervisor and payroll clerk.
d. Factory superintendent and shop supervisor.
e. Chief accountant and controller.
f. Treasurer and controller.

13–16.   Chart Of Accounts

The following chart of accounts is that of Summertime Patio Furniture, a small retail store that rents space in a shopping center:

Current Assets (100—199)
101 Cash in Bank
102 Prepaid Rent
105 Petty Cash

Other Assets (200—299)
200 Delivery Truck
201 Accumulated Depreciation—Delivery Truck
210 Office Equipment
211 Accumulated Depreciation—Office Equipment
220 Merchandise Inventory

Liabilities and Equity (300—499)
310 Accounts Payable
320 Loan from Bank
400 Pat Summertime, Capital
410 Pat Summertime, Drawings

Revenue and Expenses (500—999)
501 Cash Sales
502 Sales on Account
610 Salaries Expense
620 Supplies Expense
699 Other Expenses
999 Income and Expense Summary

Required:

a. Suggest five account titles that should be added to make Summertime's chart of accounts internally consistent.
b. Renumber two accounts so that the account title sequence makes the preparation of accounting reports easier.

13–17.   Chart of Accounts

The chart of accounts of Dobson Distributors, Inc., a manufacturers' representative, follows:

Current Assets (10—19)
10 Cash in Bank
11 Petty Cash
12 Inventories
15 Supplies
17 Prepaid Rent

Property (20—25)

20 Land

25 Office Machines

Other Assets (26—29)

28 Organizational Costs

Liabilities and Equity (30—59)

31 Accounts Payable

33 Notes Payable

40 Bonds Payable

50 Capital Stock

51 Retained Earnings

Revenue (60—69)

60 Sales from Showroom Displays

61 Sales from Direct Shipments

Expenses (70—89)

71 Salaries

72 Power

73 Supplies

75 Rent

Other Revenue and Expenses (90—99)

99 Income and Expense Summary

Required:

a. Suggest five account titles that should be added to make Dobson's chart of accounts internally consistent.

b. Identify account titles that are not needed in Dobson's chart of accounts.

13–18.   *Standard Journal Vouchers*

The following entries are routinely recorded by accounting systems. Identify those appropriate for standard journal vouchers. Explain your choices.

a. Record wages payable.

b. Record cash sales.

c. Record purchase of inventory.

d. Record prepaid insurance.

e. Record supplies expense.

f. Record depreciation expense.

13–19.   *Incompatible Functions*

The Mid-Cities Company has three clerical employees who must perform the following functions:

a. Maintain general ledger.
b. Maintain accounts payable ledger.
c. Maintain accounts receivable ledger.
d. Prepare checks for signature.
e. Maintain disbursements journal.
f. Issue credits on returns and allowances.
g. Handle and deposit cash receipts.
h. Reconcile the bank account.

Of the eight functions, items *f* and *h* take a negligible amount of time; all other functions require an equal amount of time. All three employees are equally capable; they perform no accounting functions other than those listed. Accounting functions not listed are performed by others.

Required:

a. Distribute the functions among the three employees in a way that provides the best internal control.
b. List four possible unsatisfactory combinations of these functions.

(AICPA Adapted)

13–20.   *Incompatible Functions*

The following list contains functions to be performed by personnel of the Metroplex Paint Company, a small wholesaler. Each function marked by an asterisk (*) takes about the same amount of time. These should be assigned equally to employees A and B, who have the same training and competence. The president of the company, C, is unwilling to perform any function marked with an asterisk but is willing to assume two of the other functions.

*a. Assemble supporting documents for disbursements and prepare checks for signature.
*b. Sign general disbursement checks.
*c. Record checks written in the cash disbursements and payroll journal.
 d. Mail disbursement checks to suppliers.
 e. Cancel supporting documents to prevent their reuse.
*f. Approve credit for customers.
*g. Bill customers and record the invoices in the sales journal and subsidiary ledger.
*h. Open the mail and prepare a prelisting of cash receipts.
*i. Record cash receipts in the cash journal and subsidiary ledger.
*j. Prepare daily cash deposits.
*k. Deliver daily cash deposits to the bank.
*l. Assemble the payroll timecards and prepare the paychecks.
*m. Sign paychecks.
 n. Post the journals to the general ledger.
 o. Reconcile the accounts receivable subsidiary ledger with the control account.
 p. Prepare monthly statements for customers by copying the subsidiary ledger accounts.
 q. Reconcile the monthly statements from vendors with the subsidiary accounts payable accounts.

r. Reconcile the bank account.

Required:

Divide the above duties among A, B, and C.

(AICPA Adapted)

13–21.   Reasonable Assurance

Sally Jones, CPA, has been engaged to examine the financial statement of Ajax, Inc. Jones is about to undertake a study of Ajax's internal control and is aware of the inherent limitations that should be considered.

a. Which objectives do accountants recognize for internal control?
b. What is meant by the concept of reasonable assurance?
c. When the potential effectiveness of internal control is considered, which inherent limitations should be recognized?

(AICPA Adapted)

13–22.   Control Environment and Activities

Management is responsible for establishing and maintaining an organization's internal control. This consists of a set of five components whose overall purpose is to ensure that the organization's objectives are attained. The control environment and activities of an internal control include the following features:

a. Assignment of responsibility.
b. Segregation of duties.
c. Use of appropriate forms, documents, and procedures.
d. Qualified personnel.
e. Review and comparison of records.

Required:

a. Define each feature listed above.
b. Identify one specific control for the characteristic.
c. Describe how the identified control for the characteristic contributes to the objectives of internal control.

(CMA Adapted)

13–23.   Segregation of Duties

As the internal auditor for a large savings and loan association, you are concerned about segregation of duties for a wholly owned real estate investment subsidiary. The subsidiary, despite its $10 million in assets, operates out of the main office of the parent. The parent company administers all purchasing, payroll, and personnel functions. The subsidiary's board of directors consists entirely of selected officers of the parent.

The real estate investment subsidiary's activities consist primarily of buying, developing, and selling real estate; some development projects involve joint ventures with contractors. Day-to-day operations are handled by the president and two vice presidents. The president also acts as liaison with the parent; each vice president has additional projects to manage.

All invoices and itemized statements requiring direct payment or reimbursement to contractors or vendors are delivered to one of the two vice presidents for review and approval. After approval, the staff accountant prepares checks and then obtains the signature of one of the vice presidents on the checks. After being signed, the checks are returned to the staff accountant for mailing, and supporting documents are filed. All blank checks are kept by the staff accountant.

All customer payments on notes and accounts receivable originating from the sale of real estate are sent to one of the two vice presidents and then forwarded to the staff accountant who records the payment and prepares the deposit slip. The deposit may be given to the parent's accounting department or to a teller of the parent.

If the subsidiary experiences a cash shortage, a promissory note is prepared by the staff accountant and signed by the president or one of the vice presidents. The staff accountant submits the promissory note to the parent and awaits receipt of the funds. The staff accountant is responsible for billing customers and advising management when payments are due. The staff accountant reconciles the bank statement once a month on receipt.

The staff accountant prepares monthly financial statements, including the accrual of interest receivable and the capitalization of certain interest charges. These financial statements are prepared to reflect the substance of both joint ventures and subsidiary operations. The board of directors reviews the financial statements.

Required:

Identify specific areas in which segregation of duties is inadequate.

(CIA Adapted)

13–24.   *Foreign Corrupt Practices Act*

The home office of GHP Insurance Company has a formal statement on policies and procedures for the expense reimbursement of agents. A description of these policies and procedures follows.

Agents are to obtain an expense report form at the beginning of each week. The completed forms are submitted to the branch manager at the end of each week. The branch manager looks over the expense report to determine if (1) the expenses qualify for reimbursement under the company's expense reimbursement policy statement; and (2) the amounts are reasonable. Agents are asked to explain any questionable expense item and to show documentation supporting the amounts. Any single expenditure that is expected to exceed $100 should be approved by the branch manager in advance.

The branch manager approves each expense report by signing it and forwards the report to the accounting department at the home office. The accounting department makes the appropriate journal entries and posts to the general ledger accounts and agent subsidiary records. A check is prepared by the cash disbursements office to each agent to whom an amount is owed. These expense reimbursement checks are sent to the branch manager, who then distributes them to the agents.

Agents may receive cash advances for expenses by completing a cash advance approval form. The branch manager reviews these forms and gives approval by signing the forms. One copy of the form goes to the accounting department at the home office for recording in the general ledger accounts and agent subsidiary records. A second copy of the form is given to the agent, who submits it to the branch office cashier and obtains the cash.

At the end of the month, the internal auditing department at the home office adds the total dollar amounts on the expense reports from each branch, subtracts the sum of the dollar totals on each branch's cash advance approval form, and compares the net amount to the sum of the expense reimbursement checks issued to agents. Any differences are investigated.

The Foreign Corrupt Practices Act of 1977 identifies five general control objectives related to transactions or accounts: authorization, recording, safeguarding, reconciliation, and valuation. To evaluate internal control effectively, these general objectives must be related to specific internal control procedures for each aspect of a system.

Required:

a. Define and discuss each of the five internal control objectives identified in the Foreign Corrupt Practices Act of 1977 (FCPA).

b. Discuss whether GHP Insurance Company's internal control system for the reimbursement of agent expenses satisfies the first four objectives—authorization, recording, safeguarding, and reconciliation—identified in the FCPA.

(CMA Adapted)

13–25.   Risk Assessment

Bertly Company was organized in 1935. Management has always recognized that a well-designed accounting system provides many benefits, including reliable financial records for decision making and a control system that increases the probability of preventing or detecting errors or irregularities. Thus Bertly has developed adequate internal control.

Bertly's internal audit department periodically reviews the company's accounting records to determine if the internal accounting control system is functioning effectively. The internal audit director believes such reviews are important because inconsistencies or discrepancies can serve as a warning that something is amiss. The following seven conditions were detected by Bertly's internal audit staff during a routine examination of accounting records:

1. Daily bank deposits do not always correspond with cash receipts.

2. Bad checks from customers are consistently approved by the same employee.

3. Physical inventory counts sometimes differ from perpetual inventory records, and there have been alterations to physical counts and perpetual records.

4. There is a high percentage of customer refunds and credits.

5. There is an excessive use of substitute documents because originals are lost or missing.

6. An unexplained and unexpected decrease in gross profit percentage has occurred.

7. Many documents are not countersigned.

Required:

For each of the seven conditions detected by Bertly Company's internal audit staff,

a. Identify a risk that may have caused the condition.
b. Recommend actions to be taken and/or controls to be implemented that would correct the condition.

(CMA Adapted)

13–26.   Double-Entry System

On November 9, Leslie Young, president of the High Sierra Development Company, received a letter from the Redwood Lumber Company saying that a check for $1,500 issued to Redwood in payment of lumber purchased was returned by the bank marked "insufficient funds." Redwood asked whether an error had been made and whether the check could be redeposited. Young was surprised at this; according to its records, High Sierra had an ample cash balance at the bank to cover the check.

Young was a ski enthusiast and a frequent visitor to Mamouth, California, a well-known ski resort. On the way home during one of many trips, Young had noted a ranch for sale. Young persuaded several friends to join in acquiring the property, and the High Sierra Development Company was organized. It was agreed that the amount of initial capital contribution should be at a minimum. Accordingly, the capitalization of the company was set initially at $20,000. Payment for this amount was received on November 1.

In acquiring the property valued at $80,000 for the land and $20,000 for the building, the company paid a cash down payment of only $18,000; the balance was financed by a noninterest-bearing note, payable in five equal annual installments, beginning a year from November 2, the date at which the transaction took place.

Young made a careful review of the records of High Sierra Development Company. No error could be found. To further ensure correctness, Young prepared a trial balance as of November 9; it was in balance. Puzzled, Young came to you for assistance. The journal on which analyses are made is shown in Exhibit 13–1. The ledger accounts are in Exhibit 13–2, and the trial balance is in Exhibit 13–3.

Required:

a. What comments do you have about the records kept by Leslie Young?
b. What is the proper cash balance as of November 9?
c. Why is the trial balance unable to disclose the errors you have located?

13–27.   Internal Control

Days Inns of America, Inc., is the sixth largest lodging company in the United States, with a total revenue of $306 million during a recent year. Being privately owned, Days Inns is not subject to regulations of the Securities and Exchange Commission concerning financial activities or the adequacy of internal controls. Nevertheless, corporate management believes that sound internal control is a prerequisite to sound managerial accountability. As a result, it launched an improved managerial control (IMC) project in July after a presentation by its independent auditors on management's responsibility for internal control.

EXHIBIT 13–1

Case 13–26

GENERAL JOURNAL			Page 1

Date		Accounts and Explanation	Ref.	Debit	Credit
Nov.	1	Cash	1	20,000	
		Capital Stock	9		20,000
		Issued capital stock for cash.			
	2	Land	3	80,000	
		Building	4	20,000	
		Cash	1		18,000
		Notes Payable	8		82,000
		Purchased ranch as investment. Note is payable			
		in five annual installments and bears no interest.			
	3	Building	4	1,500	
		Accounts Payable	7		1,500
		Purchased lumber for building renovation.			
		Amount is to be paid in 10 days.			
	4	Prepaid Insurance	2	600	
		Accounts Payable	7		600
		Purchased one-year insurance policy, paying cash.			
	5	Building	4	400	
		Accounts Payable	7		400
		Purchased paint for building renovation, paying			
		cash.			
	6	Accounts Payable	7	1,500	
		Cash	1		1,500
		Paid lumber purchased on account.			

Task Force

In approving the IMC project, the company's president appointed a task force composed of senior executive vice presidents for finance, operations, and administration—the three top officials below the company's chief executive. Their participation underlined executive support for the project and its broad coverage of all areas of corporate activity. Others named to the task force were the senior vice president for human relations, the director of internal audit, and the director of systems, standards, and procedures.

The executive vice president for finance was designated task force leader, with responsibility for calling meetings and presiding and approving the agenda. The director of systems, standards, and procedures was named project coordinator, responsible for planning, organizing, directing, and controlling staff activities, and for periodically reporting results. The director of internal audit was made responsible for conducting specific internal control reviews and for eventual systematic monitoring of internal control, and served as the task force's secretary.

Objective and Action Plan

The task force agreed on an action plan, shown as Exhibit 13–4, and immediately initiated the project. The plan set forth the following as the project's primary objective:

EXHIBIT 13–2

Case 13–26   Ledger Accounts

Cash			1
Nov. 1 (1)	30,000	Nov. 2 (1)	18,000
		6 (1)	1,500

Prepaid Insurance			2
Nov. 4 (1)	600		

Land			3
Nov. 2 (1)	80,000		
5 (1)	400		

Building			4
Nov. 2 (1)	20,000		
3 (1)	1,500		

Accounts Payable			7
Nov. 6 (1)	1,500	Nov. 3 (1)	1,500
		4 (1)	600
		5 (1)	400

Notes Payable			8
		Nov. 2 (1)	82,000

Capital Stock			9
		Nov. 1 (1)	30,000

To establish and maintain a control environment and internal managerial and accounting controls adequate to safeguard the company's resources and ensure their efficient and effective utilization.

EXHIBIT 13–3

Case 13–26

HIGH SIERRA DEVELOPMENT COMPANY
Trial balance
November 9, 1998

Cash	$ 10,500	
Prepaid insurance	600	
Land	80,400	
Building	21,500	
Accounts payable		$ 1,000
Notes payable		82,000
Capital stock		30,000
	$113,000	$113,000

EXHIBIT 13–4

Case 13–27   Phases of the IMC Action Plan

Phase 1.   Strengthening the Management Control Environment

Objective: To evaluate, strengthen, and maintain a control environment within the company to stimulate honesty, integrity, ethical behavior, accountability, self-discipline, supervisory review, and adherence to corporate policies, standards, and procedures among all personnel.

Time frame: August 1997 to March 1998.

Focus: Developing, documenting, and communicating most important corporate policies and organizational responsibilities, stimulating control consciousness, and evaluating employees' integrity and potential risks.

Responsibility: Systems, standards, and procedures department in collaboration with executive management.

Phase 2.   Strengthening Internal Accounting Controls

Objective: To permit management to reach a conclusion about the overall effectiveness of the total structure in achieving the broad objectives of internal accounting control *at fiscal year-end* in order to make a public statement of management's unqualified opinion in its annual report.

Time frame: October 1997 to September 1998 (corporate fiscal year).

Focus: Developing and evaluating achievement of control objectives, identifying high risks, and improving specific internal accounting controls.

Responsibility: Systems, standards, and procedures department and internal audit department in cooperation with all management levels.

Phase 3.   Monitoring and Reporting on Internal Accounting Control with Auditor's Opinion

Objective: To annually and systematically reach a conclusion about the overall effectiveness of the total structure in achieving the broad objectives of internal accounting control *during the entire fiscal year*, to include a statement of management's unqualified opinion in each annual report, and to obtain and publish the unqualified opinion of the company's independent auditors regarding management's representations.

Time frame: Annually for each fiscal year after September 30, 1998.

Focus: Correcting immediately any material weaknesses reported by the independent auditors, continuous monitoring by internal auditors, and eliminating control weaknesses based on informal risk or cost-benefit analysis.

Responsibility: Internal audit department in collaboration with all levels of management.

Preliminary Assessment

In preparing the action plan, the task force made a preliminary assessment of the company's control environment. This did not involve an in-depth review because management was already aware of the need for many improvements; indeed, several improvements in the control environment were already in progress. Instead, the assessment consolidated reports of the internal and independent auditors into a brief analysis of basic needs. The assessment resulted in including "strengthening the management control environment" as phase one of the action plan.

To simplify departmental contacts, one person in each of the company's 20 departments was appointed to serve as internal control coordinator. The role of these coordinators was to assist the project in obtaining information and documenting policies and procedures.

Other important actions taken at the beginning of the project included determining documentation requirements and defining the role of the company's independent auditors.

Actions During Phase One

The first step during phase one was to draft and issue three basic corporate policy statements:

- Statement No. 1, *General Corporate Policy,* contains many policies covering corporate responsibilities to customers, employees, franchisees, management, and stockholders; these had been observed but never committed to writing.
- Statement No. 2, *Standards of Corporate and Personal Conduct,* provides guidance to officers and employees about legal areas, accounting and internal control requirements, conflicts of interest, and so on. Possible violations are to be reported to the director of internal audit who sets procedures for appropriate review and for reporting to responsible corporate officers.
- Statement No. 3, *Internal Audit,* prescribes responsibilities for the internal audit function and for taking corrective actions based on internal audit findings.

A high-quality brochure presenting these policy statements was printed for distribution to all Days Inns employees and franchisees.

Other activities in phase one included developing the internal audit follow-up procedures under the new policies, completing the internal managerial policy framework, ensuring adequate policy communication, publishing an organization manual, improving employee integrity and risk evaluation, and evaluating forms and reports in current use.

Actions During Phase Two

At the outset, the task force decided to use the transaction cycle approach to monitor internal accounting control. Cycles were defined according to the nature of the company's business, and control objectives tailored to these cycles were then developed.

During phase two, achievement of each objective was evaluated; results were documented and included in working papers. The work in this phase was done primarily by staff members in the systems, standards, and procedures department. They were responsible for following through from the initial interview to installing new procedures, controls, and even systems. They were assigned this task because the implementation responsibility might impair the independence of internal auditors.

During this phase, standard procedures to be followed in the review of functions were also developed. These are shown in Exhibit 13–5. The flowchart for reviewing internal accounting controls within a specific function is shown in Exhibit 13–6.

Required:

a. How would you characterize the control environment in this company? Why?
b. What observations do you have concerning the company's approach to studying its internal controls?

EXHIBIT 13–5

Case 13–27   Procedures for Organizing and Controlling Implementation of the IMC Project

IMC Phase 2—Review of Functions

1. Obtain all readily available information relative to the function. Prepare a preliminary review program and/or control evaluation questionnaire indicating procedures and scope of the review to conduct. Contact the department head responsible for the function in advance of a request for an initial appointment.

2. Meet with the department head and briefly discuss the objectives, scope, and nature of the review. Inquire about improvements under consideration and about actual or anticipated problems. Arrange to meet with the supervisor of (or individual primarily responsible for) the function.

   The time length and depth of discussion depend on the department head's interest and availability. Care must be taken to avoid tying up top executives with minute details. Where appropriate, steps 1 and 2 may be combined into a single interview with both department head and supervisor.

3. Meet with the supervisor and

   a. Indicate review objectives, scope, and nature.

   b. Determine the objective(s) of the function and related existing policies. If policies are not in writing, note the principal existing policies and practices.

   c. Ask what other specific persons or units are involved directly with the function or interface with it.

   d. Discuss current procedures, making notes on the logical sequence of tasks.

4. Observe the tasks being performed and make sufficient inquiries to have a general understanding of the function and its tasks. Obtain copies of all forms and reports, determining origin, number of copies, recipients, and so on.

   This work varies depending on the complexity of the function and number of persons involved. It is essential to note existing controls as well as opportunities for improvements. Under no circumstances should the preliminary review interfere with the normal work process, especially if the work provides key services to others. You may find it necessary to conduct one- or two-hour interviews separated by periods for performing regular duties.

5. (Optional) After the preliminary review (steps 1–4), the department head may ask for a conference to discuss the work completed. Take care to discuss only the conditions observed without giving conclusions or recommendations at this time. Alternate actions may be discussed without making any commitment regarding a final position.

6. Review all notes and documents and prepare either a brief general narrative description of the work flow or a high-level flowchart that includes only highlights and leaves out such details as copies and files.

7. Assess the effectiveness of the general corporate control environment as it relates to the specific function.

8. Develop specific control objectives applicable to the function and consistent with the overall cycle control objectives. Furnish copies of the first draft to persons interviewed for their comments and suggestions. Obtain their acceptance of the final objectives. Identify "material," "high-risk," or significant "potential-saving" areas within the function by considering

   a. Areas in which errors or irregularities could involve large dollar amounts because of volume or significance of transactions.

   b. Areas where there are significant changes in circumstances.

   c. Areas that management recognizes as having poor controls or a history of "surprises."

   d. Areas pointed out by internal or external auditors in reports or management letters.

9. Document all control techniques applied in the function, especially those related to step 8.

10. Determine whether the specific control objectives are being met through the control techniques in step 9 by evaluating the specific control environment, potential risks, and the internal accounting controls surrounding each area.

11. Identify and evaluate any specific internal accounting control objectives not achieved due to weaknesses. Discuss their significance with the internal and external auditors. Identify those functional components where policies and procedures are lacking, inadequate, or obsolete. (Some of these may not bear directly on internal accounting control but should be identified to eventually perfect the full structure of company policies and procedures.)

EXHIBIT 13–5 (*continued*)

Case 13–27

IMC Phase 2–Review of Functions

12. (Optional) Confirm the evaluation in step 11 by preparing and executing a program to test compliance with controls considered most likely to achieve the internal accounting control objectives. (These tests, which show whether the internal control system is actually functioning as intended, may be unnecessary at this point if weaknesses are significant, obvious, or admitted.)

13. Tentatively formulate conclusions regarding control weaknesses, developing one or more alternative control technique proposals for overcoming them.

14. Draft those tentative policies and procedures considered necessary to properly operate and document the function:

    a. Furnish advanced copies or drafts to the supervisor.

    b. Discuss the proposed alternate control techniques and drafts of policies and procedures with the supervisor. Obtain suggestions and, if possible, acceptance of any modifications.

    c. Finalize the proposals and discuss them with the department head. Obtain suggestions and, if possible, acceptance of any modifications. (Steps *b* and *c* may be combined, but subordinates are sometimes reluctant to speak up in the presence of a superior. Discussions with higher-echelon executives should be limited to policy decisions and a general outline of procedural controls without great detail to save time.)

15. When all matters and actions to take are agreed on, prepare a summary to include in the monthly progress report to the task force. Include review results, recommendations, actions taken, and decisions not to act. (The latter should be a normal situation).

16. (Optional) If you have failed to reach agreement on specific actions, it may be appropriate to apply informal cost-benefit analysis with a relatively nontechnical approach to obtain a more concrete estimate of the risks involved. By weighing the benefits against the costs of introducing new control techniques and then comparing these with the risks of not introducing new techniques, a convincing argument in their favor is possible. Conversely, a decision to withdraw or modify proposed control techniques may be justified. (This step may be applied as an option after step 11, step 14 *b or c,* or at the request of the task force after step 17. The decision whether and when to apply it should be based on the importance of the proposed control techniques and the degree of resistance encountered.)

17. In cases of a department head's rejection, resistance, or reluctance to accept suggested control techniques and/or significant policy content, refer the matter to the next higher managerial level. If acceptance is still not forthcoming and the matter is considered significant, present it to the IMC task force in a brief, specific report outlining results of the review, proposed alternatives, and why the department head disagrees. At this point, further action rests with the task force, which will likely discuss the matter directly with the department head.

18. Once a final decision is made, issue or modify the related policies and/or procedures.

Exhibit 13–6

Case 13–27 Flowchart for Review of Internal Accounting Control Within a Specific Function

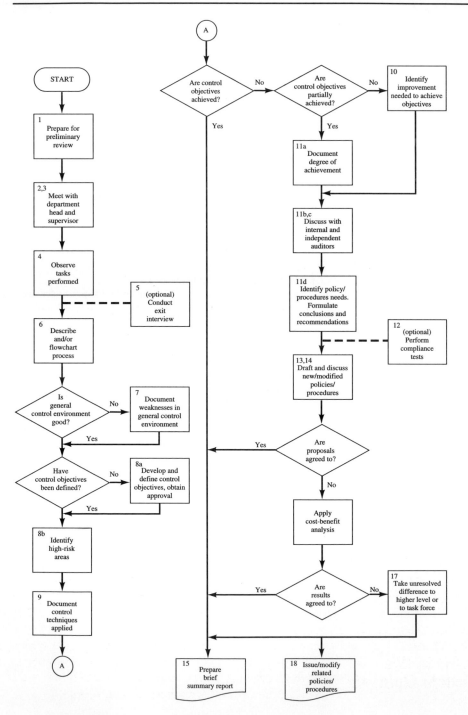

14 INFORMATION SYSTEM CONTROLS

Learning Objectives

1. To understand the control policies, practices, and procedures that are important in computer-based accounting systems.
2. To learn the three functions for internal controls in information systems.
3. To categorize control policies, practices, and procedures by their scope.
4. To describe practices that control the input, processing, and output of application systems.

Introduction

An organization's internal control includes the measures adopted by management to achieve the organization's objectives. These relate to the effectiveness and efficiency of operations, the reliability of financial reporting, and compliance with laws and regulations. Accountants call the policies, practices, and procedures directed toward these objectives *internal controls*. Those internal controls implemented in a computer-based accounting system are *information system controls*. This chapter describes many important ones. Management selects from these and implements them to provide reasonable assurance that objectives are achieved.

Because accountants are responsible for providing accounting information, they have a professional interest in maintaining adequate system controls. As auditors, accountants evaluate these controls to determine their effects on the accuracy of accounting information. An understanding of information system controls is vital for any competent accountant.

Views of Information System Controls

Accountants may view an organization's information system controls in different ways. Some prefer to categorize them by function; others categorize them by scope. Each view is correct; each represents a different perspective on the same set of policies, practices, and procedures. This chapter presents both views.

Categorizing Controls by Function

Management implements internal controls either to prevent or to detect errors and irregularities. An error is an accidental misstatement of accounting information; an irregularity is an intentional misstatement.

Procedures adopted to achieve the first function, preventing errors and irregularities, are *preventive controls.* These procedures are valuable because they do not allow certain errors and irregularities to occur. The use of standard journal vouchers in a double-entry accounting system is a preventive control. They prevent bookkeepers from making entries to improper accounts.

Procedures adopted to achieve the second function, detecting errors and irregularities, are *detective controls.* These procedures identify errors and irregularities after they have occurred. For example, a double-entry accounting system summarizes account balances in a trial balance. Bookkeepers detect the existence of errors in the general ledger whenever the debit and credit totals on the trial balance are unequal. The trial balance provides a detective control.

Usually management prescribes procedures to correct errors and irregularities after detection. These are *corrective controls.* As a corrective control, management may establish a policy requiring an adjusting journal entry to correct an error found on the trial balance. Because a detective control is always accompanied by a corrective one, some accountants do not distinguish between them. These accountants classify as detective controls those procedures used both to find and to correct errors and irregularities.

One way of classifying controls in a system is by function. Using this method, accountants describe control policies, practices, and procedures as either preventive, detective, or corrective controls.

Categorizing Controls by Scope

Other accountants prefer to classify controls by the scope of the systems they affect. Policies, practices, and procedures that prevent or detect errors and irregularities for all accounting systems are *general controls.* They affect all transaction cycles and all application systems in each transaction cycle. For example, locking the rooms that contain workstations affects all applications of the computer and is a general control.

Other policies, practices, and procedures affect only a specific application system, such as the cash receipts system or the inventory system. Accountants call these *applications controls.* For example, many companies use an application system to process charges to credit cards. A sales clerk inserts the credit card into a terminal and connects the terminal to a computer by a telephone line. Then a computer program verifies the account number on the card before authorizing a charge to it. If the program determines that the account number is invalid, the system rejects the sales transaction. This system uses an application control called a check digit to verify the account number.

Applications systems frequently differ in the quality of the information system controls they contain. One on-line system with very good controls may be reliable and produce accurate information. Another on-line system using the same hardware and system software may lack adequate controls and produce erroneous information. Inadequate application controls in a system are frequently a justification for initiating the system development process.

Within any transaction cycle, the combination of general controls and applications controls determines whether or not information system controls are effective. Both categories

ILLUSTRATION 14–1

Categories of General Controls

Data center operations controls
System software acquisition and maintenance controls
Access security controls
Applications system development and maintenance controls

---

affect the ability of the applications systems to prevent or detect errors and irregularities. A strength in applications controls may compensate for a weakness in general controls.

For example, a credit card charge system may have terminals in thousands of locations in retail stores all over the country. Security for these terminals may be quite weak, allowing easy access to them by unauthorized users. Yet an application control that verifies the validity of an account number effectively compensates for this weakness in general controls. It prevents charges to fraudulent credit card accounts.

Accountants view information system controls in different ways. The remaining discussion in this chapter is structured around the second view, which categorizes them by scope. As you read about specific information system controls, you can determine if they are preventive, detective, or corrective controls. The chapter describes the four types of general controls next, giving the most important examples of them.

General Controls

General controls are the information system controls that affect all applications of the computer in the organization. Illustration 14–1 lists the four types of general controls. The first type discussed here is data center operations controls.

Data Center Operations Controls

The data center is the segment of the organization that provides computer services to other segments. In a large company, the data center may be a subsidiary or a division headed by a vice president. In a medium-size company, it is frequently a separate department headed by a manager of MIS reporting to the controller. In a small company, it may be a few employees who operate a personal computer in addition to performing other accounting duties. Some large companies have several data centers, located in operating divisions or subsidiaries.

Data center operations controls include data backup procedures, contingency plans, and segregation of duties.

Data Backup Procedures.   Information systems process many data sets each day. Occasionally, when an event occurs that destroys one or more of them, data backup procedures can prevent the loss of data.

Using Data Backups.   A power fluctuation sometimes causes a disk drive to malfunction, destroying the disk and making the information on the disk inaccessible. Floods, lightning, temperature extremes, vandalism, or mistakes by a computer operator may also destroy data. For these reasons, computer operators routinely make *backup copies* of all computer data. The backup copy is a duplicate of the original that is stored at a different location. If an unusual occurrence destroys the original, the computer operator re-creates it from the backup copy.

Management establishes control policies that describe data backup procedures. These policies describe routine procedures for making copies of the data, for storing them separately from the original, and for reconstructing them if they are destroyed. The nature of these procedures depends on the processing method and on the technology used by the accounting system.

In manual systems, backup files are human-readable records and documents that require no special procedures. Good backup procedures for systems using batch processing are the same as those used for batch processing with on-line inquiry. Good backup procedures for on-line real-time systems or local area networks differ significantly from these.

Data Backup in Batch Processing Systems.   A batch processing system applies all processing steps to batches of transactions. A data entry program converts each transaction in a batch to computer-readable form. Another program then examines each transaction in the batch, looking for obvious errors. An update program then posts each transaction in the batch to a master file. When processing of a batch is complete, then processing of the next batch begins.

The standard method for backing up data in a batch processing system, or a batch system with on-line update, uses the ***grandfather–father–son technique***.[1] It requires the data center to have available at all times three "generations" of each master file. The most recent version of the master file is the "son." Employees use this generation in daily processing, and it requires a backup copy. The previous generation master file, the "father," is the version that was updated to produce the current one. If the current file is destroyed, computer operators can re-create it from the father. The "grandfather" is the version that was updated to produce the father. Computer operators can use it to re-create both the father and the son.

In the application of the grandfather–father–son technique in Illustration 14–2, a computer program daily updates a master file with a transaction file. (Although this illustration shows tape files, the method works equally well with direct access devices.) In this example, the computer operators maintain three generations of the master file after Wednesday's file update: (1) the master file from Wednesday (the current file, or son), (2) the master file from Tuesday (the father), and (3) the master file from Monday (the grandfather). On Thursday the system updates Wednesday's master file with Thursday's transaction file, producing Thursday's master file. The operators use Thursday's master file (the son) for current processing. They save as backups Wednesday's master file (now the father) and Tuesday's master file (now the grandfather). Monday's master file is no longer needed, and the operators do not save it. After Friday's file update, Tuesday's master file is no longer required.

Most managers do not consider it cost-effective to require backups of transaction files. When they are maintained, however, they can be used to re-create a current master file. An alternative is to keep for a specified period of time copies of the original documents recording the transactions. If a transaction file is destroyed, the data center re-creates it from these documents.

---

[1]Some people prefer to call this the *grandparent–parent–child technique.*

ILLUSTRATION 14–2

The Grandfather–Father–Son Technique

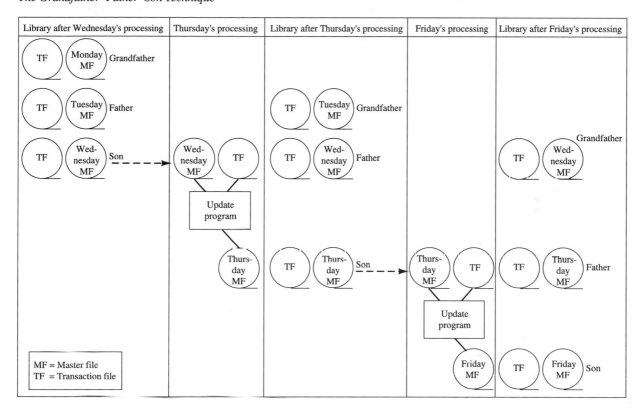

The grandfather–father–son technique works well in batch processing systems because these systems update master files daily, weekly, or monthly. An on-line real-time system, on the other hand, updates its master files continually. For them, the technique is not cost-effective.

Data Backup in On-Line Real-Time Systems.   In an on-line real-time system, users at terminals or workstations enter transactions as they occur. A computer program controls entry of the data fields in a transaction, examines them for obvious errors, posts the transaction to a master file, and then proceeds to the next transaction. All processing of a transaction occurs at once, and the results of processing immediately change the master file. The standard method of file backup in on-line real-time systems uses a transaction log with periodic master file dumps.

A ***file dump*** occurs when the computer operator copies the contents of an on-line data set to a removable device. This serves as a backup of the data set in case the original on-line copy is destroyed. Management establishes policies that determine how frequently file dumps should occur, but commonly they are done once or twice each day. The file dump provides a backup data set as of the time of the dump. But

ILLUSTRATION 14–3

File Backup Procedures in On-Line Real-Time Systems

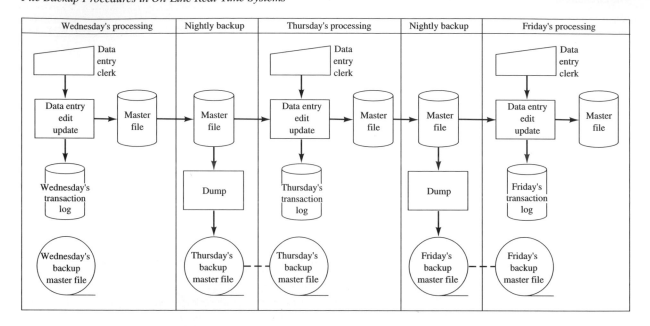

because transactions occur continually in an on-line real-time system, the backup copy quickly becomes out-of-date. As a result, the computer operator also maintains a ***transaction log.*** This contains a copy of all transactions posted to the data set since the last file dump. While posting a transaction to the data set, the system also copies it to the transaction log. If the on-line data set is accidentally destroyed, the operator re-creates it from the transaction log and the most recent file dump.

   Illustration 14–3 shows how file backups work in on-line real-time systems. In this example, the master files are on a magnetic disk, and the backup files and transaction logs are on magnetic tapes. During Wednesday's processing, data entry clerks continuously enter transactions. The system posts these transactions to the master file and copies them to the transaction log. On Wednesday night at midnight the computer operator dumps the master file to magnetic tape. This produces the backup master file for use on Thursday. During Thursday's processing, the system again creates a transaction log as file updates occur. If the master file is accidentally destroyed sometime Thursday, the operator can re-create it as of the moment of destruction. The operator does this by updating Thursday's backup master file with Thursday's transaction log.

Data Backup in Local Area Networks.   Local area networks (LANs) store data on workstations and on file servers. The computers in a LAN employ devices such as magnetic disks, magnetic diskettes, or optical disks for storing data. Making regular backups is important in these systems because these data devices are less protected than those in a data center.

The Headingley Library

Item(s) borrowed on:

08/11/05
01:03 pm

Accounting information systems:
transaction processing andcontrols
1703951124

Due Date: 22/11/2005,23:59

For renewals, telephone (0113) 283 6161

Please retain this receipt

ILLUSTRATION 14–4

File Backup Tips for Workstations and Personal Computers

- **Make full backups**. Most backup systems can, if the user wishes, back up only files that have changed since the last backup. However, backing up *all* files (including those that have not changed) makes the process of restoring damaged files much easier.
- **Back up applications programs**. This avoids having to reinstall and customize a program from its original diskettes.
- **Use the verify option**. Most backup systems can copy the file and then read it to verify that the copy is correct. This verifies that the backup file is identical to the original.
- **Back up every day**. Most backup systems can do this automatically.
- **Test the backups**. The only way to be sure the backup system works properly is to periodically restore the backups and test the restored files.
- **Store backup copies off-site**. This protects from loss of data due to catastrophe at the user location.
- **Maintain a boot disk**. This is a copy of the computer's startup configuration and operating system made by a utility program. Use it to re-create the hardware settings in case of a complete hard drive failure.
- **Save some tapes or disks permanently**. A common practice is to save all data each month. This is useful if someone wants to re-create a file that was erased several months before.
- **Rotate new tapes and disks**. Tapes and disks have a limited life. By constantly introducing new ones, you reduce the chance of tape or disk failure.

Source: Adapted from Larry Wolfe, "Computer Backups Checklist," *Journal of Accountancy,* January 1994, p. 16.

A file server frequently has attached to it a backup disk or tape drive. The LAN administrator periodically (perhaps each evening) copies the contents of all files to a magnetic disk or tape mounted in this drive. The same drive may contain another disk or tape used as a transaction log while the LAN is in operation. Procedures for routine backups at the file server are important because users of individual workstations frequently neglect to make backup copies.

Workstation users, like operators of all personal computers, should make regular backup copies of files stored at their locations. Many use magnetic diskettes for this purpose, although individual workstations may also include backup drives. Illustration 14–4 summarizes good procedures for making data backups with workstations and personal computer systems.

File backup procedures are a form of general control that prevent the loss of data. Another data and procedural control involves contingency plans.

Contingency Plans.   A *contingency plan* is a formal document that describes procedures to be used should a catastrophe occur at the data center. Catastrophes such as fires, explosions, floods, or tornadoes are unlikely, yet when one occurs, it can completely destroy a facility. If all accounting records are destroyed as well, it will be difficult to collect receivables and determine how much the organization owes to vendors and employees. The contingency plan should provide adequate insurance coverage, designate alternative locations for processing and data storage, identify vital applications, and assign responsibility for recovery procedures.

Provide Adequate Insurance Coverage.   Periodically, management should review the insurance coverage for the data center. Insurance should be adequate to replace equipment and software destroyed by a catastrophe. Management should also purchase business loss insurance. This compensates the organization for the costs of reconstructing the database and for any revenues lost due to computer downtime.

Designate an Alternative Processing Location.   If a data center is destroyed, the MIS activity may require many months to place it in operation again. Because some applications are vital for its continued existence, the organization should identify another computer that it can use during reconstruction. As an alternative processing site, many companies designate another of their data centers at a different location. Smaller organizations may reach a reciprocal alternative processing agreement with others that have similar equipment. Or they may arrange to use a service bureau or time-sharing service. The alternative site must have enough unused processing capacity to process all vital applications.

Identify Vital Applications.   Vital applications are those the organization requires to continue operating. If a data center is destroyed, the MIS activity must implement these applications first at an alternative processing location. Management must identify vital applications and ensure that they can be implemented quickly at the alternative site.

Accounts receivable, accounts payable, and payroll are vital applications to most organizations. Other applications are vital in specific industries. For example, an airline reservations system is vital to an airline, and a computerized typesetting system is vital to a newspaper. These companies cannot function if management fails to reimplement them promptly. Vital applications require an off-site storage location.

Designate an Off-Site Storage Location.   Management should designate a place, away from the data center, to store items necessary to continue operating the vital applications. These include copies of system software, programs, backup data files, documentation, and operating instructions. Management should establish policies ensuring that these items are current. Some organizations use the alternative processing site for this purpose. Others use a warehouse that is convenient, secure, and safe from environmental hazards, and has controlled access.

Assign Responsibility.   Management should assign responsibility to an individual for maintaining and implementing an up-to-date contingency plan. This includes acquiring an adequate alternative processing site, selecting a satisfactory off-site storage location, keeping current backup files at that location, and testing the plan. Someone should be designated in advance as responsible for beginning recovery procedures if a catastrophe occurs. The plan should also identify and assign other responsibilities necessary to begin operation at the alternative site. Assigning responsibility in advance minimizes delays at a time when top management is preoccupied with things other than the information system.

A contingency plan prevents the sizable financial losses an organization could incur if an information system were destroyed. Illustration 14–5 summarizes its contents. Because a contingency plan affects several vital accounting applications, it is a general control. A third kind of control concerns segregation of duties at the data center.

Segregation of Duties.   Proper segregation of duties requires that critical functions performed at the data center be separated. These functions are systems analysis and programming, machine operations, and data maintenance.

ILLUSTRATION 14–5

Contents of a Contingency Plan

1. *Adequate insurance coverage.* For lost equipment, software, and business.
2. *Location of the alternative processing site.* Another organization or data center with similar equipment.
3. *Vital applications.* The applications necessary for the organization to function.
4. *Location of off-site storage.* The alternative processing site or a warehouse; maintain current records necessary to begin operation at the alternative site.
5. *Responsibility assignments.* Person responsible for beginning recovery procedures; other responsibilities necessary to resume operation at the alternative site; person responsible for maintaining a current contingency plan.

Systems Analysis and Programming.   Systems analysts and programmers participate in the projects that develop accounting systems. Some organizations also assign to certain programmers the duty of program maintenance. Rather than working on new systems, maintenance programmers correct coding errors or make minor changes to existing programs.

Systems analysts and programmers are more knowledgeable than anyone else about how information systems work. If given access to the production program files (those actually used in processing accounting transactions), they could easily alter them to carry out and conceal thefts of assets. For this reason, organizations with good general controls ensure that systems analysts and developmental programmers never gain access to production program files. When changes to existing programs are needed, maintenance programmers make them after authorization from the chief information officer.

Machine Operations.   Machine operators physically operate the computer equipment. They communicate with the operating system at the computer keyboard and respond to malfunctions of hardware. These personnel have the opportunity to enter fraudulent transactions into an accounting system. Because they have access to computer hardware while it executes production programs, machine operators can make unauthorized changes to them.

Organizations with good general controls ensure that machine operators have no access to program documentation, including source code. This information would give them the knowledge they need to both carry out and conceal a theft. Many accountants believe that the most important segregation of duties in the data center should be between systems development and machine operations. No individual should have job responsibilities in both areas, even if one of the jobs is part-time.

Data Maintenance.   In a traditional data file system, a file librarian has custody of computer files. When files are stored on magnetic tape, the librarian may be a person who maintains the tape library and issues tapes to operators when needed by a program. With on-line files, the librarian may be a computer program that keeps records of every attempted file access and prevents access by unauthorized personnel or programs. An employee monitors the actions of this computer program to detect unauthorized attempts to access records.

When an organization uses a database management system (DBMS), the DBMS software maintains custody of the accounting records and prevents unauthorized changes to them. The database administrator (DBA) determines which users gain access to accounting records and monitors the database to detect attempts at unauthorized access. The librarian or DBA has access to records regarding assets. An organization with good general controls prevents their access to the computer while it executes production programs. This minimizes their opportunities to commit irregularities.

You have learned about those general controls relating to data center operations. They include data backup procedures, contingency plans, and segregation of duties. A second category of general controls concerns those over system software acquisition and maintenance.

System Software Acquisition and Maintenance Controls

Controls over system software and maintenance affect all applications and thus are general controls. These activities require highly specialized knowledge, and usually people assigned to the data center perform them. Management should assign responsibilities for system software acquisition and maintenance and should implement appropriate policies and procedures over these activities.

Responsibilities.   Responsibilities for system software acquisition and maintenance include network administration, personal computer (PC) technical support, database administration, and web administration.

A *network administrator* is a person who is responsible for maintaining the software that controls a computer network. This person installs updated versions of software when it becomes available, answers complaints regarding malfunctions of the network, and supervises technicians who correct malfunctions. The network administrator may also be responsible for updating operating system software on a network server and for supervising hardware maintenance on the network. If the network is a local area network (LAN), the LAN administrator may physically be located in proximity to the users of the LAN. When the organization uses electronic data interchange (EDI), the network administrator must install updates to EDI software and maintain the security and integrity of EDI transactions.

Many data centers have a means of providing technical help to PC users in the organization. This often is in the form of a *PC help center* that users may contact with questions about how to use their PCs. The help center may be responsible for scheduling the work of technicians who provide hardware and software maintenance to personal computers.

The *database administrator* (DBA) is usually located at the data center as well. Chapter 10 describes the responsibilities of the DBA. They include defining schemas and subschemas, assigning passwords, maintaining the data dictionary, monitoring usage of the database, and reorganizing it when necessary. Chapter 15 discusses in detail the risks associated with database management systems, and how the DBA helps to minimize them.

Companies that use intranets or extranets, or are involved in electronic commerce on the World Wide Web employ *web administrators*. A web administrator is responsible for updating content on the organization's web site, for implementing new uses for the World Wide Web in electronic commerce, and for implementing appropriate security features for web-based electronic commerce.

ILLUSTRATION 14–6

Systems Software Acquisition and Maintenance Controls

Fixed Responsibility

Network administration. Selecting and updating network communication software.
PC help center. Answers user questions about personal computers, schedule maintenance.
Database administration. Selecting and updating software, limiting access to data, maintaining efficiency.
Web administrator. Determines content of web site, implements security in electronic commerce.

Policies and Procedures

Screen applicants. Technical knowledge becomes outdated quickly.
Information systems steering committee. Reviews software acquisition decisions.
Standard PC configurations. Software and hardware that the organization agrees to support.

Control Policies and Procedures.   You see how organizations typically fix responsibility for system software maintenance activities. Other policies and procedures involve screening personnel for these jobs, reviewing the acquisition of new system software, and establishing software standards.

Highly technical jobs such as those involved in network, PC, database, or web administration require people with adequate technical training. The manager of the data center should *screen applicants* to ensure that they have the intellectual capabilities and technical knowledge required. The manager should also budget time and money to allow these people, once employed, to update their skills. Knowledge in these areas becomes dated very quickly.

The *information systems steering committee* (ISSC) should review and approve all acquisitions of system software. Prior to approval, proposals for new acquisitions should also be reviewed by someone who has adequate technical knowledge. This person may be either an employee or an outside consultant. The ISSC, as a representative group of users, may not understand the technical implications of system software changes. However, since the consequences of these decisions affect their work, they should have final approval authority over them.

The ISSC should establish standard configurations for PCs or workstations supported within the organization. The *standard configuration* identifies the types of system software and associated hardware that personnel at the data center maintain. A data center cannot employ people with the technical knowledge required to maintain and provide support to *all* software and hardware available to users. By restricting support to certain operating systems and brands of hardware, they encourage users to make purchases consistent with the organization's policies.

Illustration 14–6 summarizes these system software acquisition and maintenance controls. A third category of general controls includes those limiting access to computer equipment and files.

Controls over Access Security

Access controls restrict a person's ability to retrieve or modify data and to gain unauthorized use of computer equipment. They ensure that all changes to data are properly authorized. Management implements access controls by establishing segregation of duties, by requiring identification and authentication procedures, and by providing physical security for computer equipment.

Segregation of Duties.   By properly assigning duties in the data center, management minimizes the opportunities for employees to alter computer programs or records to cover the theft of an asset. This requires segregation of duties between system development, machine operations, and data maintenance.

For example, the librarian or DBA controls access to data and to the computer files containing production programs. They allow machine operators access to these files only on a predetermined operating schedule. Machine operators have no access to program documentation. This prevents them from making changes to production programs or files, because they lack knowledge of them. System development personnel who have adequate knowledge have no access to production programs and are prevented from making unauthorized changes.

Maintenance programmers have access to production programs and data files and are able to make unauthorized changes. However, a chief information officer who reviews all program maintenance after it occurs can detect any inappropriate changes to program or data files.

Identification and Authentication Procedures.   System software implements identification and authentication procedures. This system software may be the operating system software, or it may be a computer security software package used in conjunction with the operating system.

System Access.   Before allowing people to use a computer system, the software requires users to identify themselves to the system. Management assigns them account numbers or user IDs for this purpose. The software then consults an authorization file containing authentication information for that individual. After requesting authentication information, the system compares the information provided by the user with that recorded in the computer file. For example, the system may ask the user to provide a password for access to the system. The software then looks up in the authorization file that user's password. If the password and the authorization file agree, the user is logged on the system. If they differ, the software does not allow the user access to the system.

Some systems that allow dial-up access by telephone use an automatic callback procedure. A user calls the telephone number of the computer's automatic switchboard. The computer answers the call, accepts the user's password, and then disconnects. The computer looks up in a file the telephone number of the user listed for this password, and calls the user back at that number. This makes unauthorized access by telephone more difficult.

Passwords are effective in preventing unauthorized system access only if used properly. All passwords should be changed periodically and selected from a random combination of letters and digits. Too often, employees select as a password a familiar name that is easy for an unauthorized user to guess. Some people even write down their passwords and tape them to desks or PCs. These actions make passwords less effective as control procedures.

User IDS and passwords known by the user are common forms of identification and authentication. Some systems use other forms, such as badges, keys, fingerprints, or

ILLUSTRATION 14–7

Using an Authorization File to Control Data Access

User ID	System Name	System Password	File Name	File Password	Permission
1122	J. Thomas	9898	all	1776	R/W
2233	I. Watts	steam	inv	vapor	R
			sales	water	W
			credit	ice	R
3232	T. Edison	wizard	product	87654	R/W
			inv	light	R
4321	L. Pasteur	germ	vendor	germ	R
			voucher	wheat	W
			Purchase	virus	R
			Gen Led	vaccine	R/W
5112	L. Pacioli	quill	Gen Led	ink	W

voiceprints. Software uses all of these as methods of identification and authentication to prevent unauthorized system access.

Data Access. The authorization file identifies not only system passwords but also passwords for individual files stored by the system. It shows all the files a user is authorized to access, a password for each file, and a file permission.

The *file permission* shows the kind of access authorized for the user. It tells whether the user can only see the contents of the file (read permission), can change its contents (write permission), or can both read and change the file (read/write permission). Illustration 14–7 shows how an authorization file stores this information.

Many organizations employ a data security officer to maintain the authorization file. When properly used, this file prevents many unauthorized changes to data and program files. The data security officer assigns write permission only to those employees and applications that must update or maintain files. Employees and applications that need only to see the information contained in files receive read permission.

For example, an accounts receivable clerk may have both read and write permission in a customer master file. This allows the clerk to perform file maintenance, such as changing customer names and addresses. A salesperson may have only read permission, allowing the salesperson to see the balance of the customer's account but not to change it. Application programs in the cash receipts system, which record cash payments from customers, require only write permission.

Physical Security. Another way in which management limits access to data and equipment is by providing physical security. Management implements policies and procedures to secure the organization's data center and its remote computer devices.

Security for the Data Center. A data center is the location of a mainframe computer and its peripherals in a teleprocessing system, or of servers in a network. Management should restrict routine access to the data center to those employees whose jobs require such access. Entry by others, such as auditors, systems development personnel, or visitors, should require special authorization. Entrances should be locked at all times.

Security for Remote Devices.   Remote devices include terminals and personal computers. Such devices create two threats: the improper use of the device and theft of the device.

When connected to a server or mainframe by a communication link, remote devices allow access to data files. Employees can use them to gain unauthorized access to accounting records. Many of these devices are small enough to be easily stolen. And because remote devices are located in user areas throughout the organization, limiting physical access to them is more difficult than restricting access to devices at a data center.

Data security software packages on the server or mainframe can help control access to it from remote devices. Such a package monitors communication between them and restricts the access that is made available. A security package may allow access from specific devices only to specific data files or schemas, or it may allow access only during specified hours of the day. For example, company policy may specify that all cash receipts are to be processed from 9:00 A.M. to 12:00 noon each day. The accounts receivable department uses a workstation for this purpose. Data security software restricts access from this workstation to accounts receivable files from 9:00 A.M. to 12:00 noon. During these hours, supervisors monitor physical access to it.

Often, sensitive data are stored on personal computers not connected to a server. Management must assign to individual employees responsibility for these computers and for the accuracy of the data on them. Computers should be physically attached to the desk and locked when not in use. If a computer is stolen, or if unauthorized people gain access to data stored in a personal computer, the individual is responsible.

Access controls prevent unauthorized access to data and prevent theft of remote devices. A fourth category of general controls includes those that affect applications system development and maintenance.

Applications System Development and Maintenance Controls

Adequate procedures for system and program changes are preventive controls. They minimize errors and irregularities introduced by new systems or changes to existing systems. An organization should have procedures requiring *formal review and authorization* for any new system before implementing it. This prevents implementation of many systems that are inefficient, ineffective, or unable to meet the organization's needs. Many organizations use the information systems steering committee (ISSC) to review and recommend information system project proposals for this purpose.

All manual and computerized procedures should have *adequate documentation* enabling programmers and analysts to understand existing procedures before changing them. This may prevent changes that have an unforeseen effect or that may produce inaccurate or unreliable data. Documentation also provides auditors with the information needed to perform an effective review of controls in the system.

A project team or programmer should adequately test each new system or change to an existing system before implementing it. This prevents many systems from creating inaccurate data. It also enables the project team or programmer to detect inefficiencies in processing or to select areas for improving the design. During the system development life

ILLUSTRATION 14–8

Applications System Development and Maintenance Controls

Formal review and authorization for each new system (as by an information systems steering committee).
Adequate documentation for manual and programmed procedures.
A plan for adequately testing each new system.
Authorization and documentation for changes to existing systems.

---

cycle, a project team that correctly uses program or module testing, acceptance testing, and system testing has tested the system adequately.

The organization should have *required procedures for authorizing and documenting changes* to existing programs and systems. Many organizations require the inclusion of a program change record in the documentation package for a computer program. Whenever a programmer makes a change to the production version of a program (the version used during routine processing), the chief information officer requires the programmer to list the change in the program change record. The programmer includes a more thorough description of the change elsewhere in the documentation. The chief information officer then reviews the change and its documentation. This procedure prevents a change that would cause errors or irregularities.

You have seen some desirable procedures for controlling and documenting changes to systems and programs. Illustration 14–8 summarizes these. Other policies, practices, and procedures may affect only one application. Accountants call these *applications controls*.

Applications Controls

Applications controls affect an individual application, such as the sales order entry, cash receipts, or payroll application. A project team develops them during design and implementation of the application system. Traditionally, accountants identified three ways in which applications controls prevent or detect errors and irregularities. Input controls prevent or detect errors when the system converts data from human-readable to computer-readable form. Processing controls detect errors during computer processing, and output controls detect them after processing is complete. In on-line real-time systems, where a user may perform input, processing, and output functions during a single session, an application may use the same control procedure in all three ways.

Input Controls

Input controls are concerned with converting data into computer-readable form and with preventing or detecting errors while inputting data. Four forms of input controls common in accounting systems are check digits, data validation, control totals, and direct data entry procedures.

Check Digits.   A *check digit* is a digit added to an account number. An algorithm determines how to calculate the correct value of the check digit from the other digits in the account number. A computer program uses the algorithm to verify the account number of a transaction. If, using the algorithm, it calculates a check digit that is different from the one in the transaction's account number, the system knows that the

ILLUSTRATION 14–9

Calculating a Check Digit

1. Take a customer number.	6 7 3 5 5
2. Multiply each digit by a weight equaling its position plus 1 (here, the number has 5 digits; the most significant digit is thus multiplied by 6; the next one, by 5; and so on).	6 5 4 3 2
3. Add the product.	$36 + 35 + 12 + 15 + 10 = 108$
4. Subtract the total from the next higher multiple of 11 to get the self-checking digit.	$110 - 108 = 2$
5. Include the self-checking digit as the last digit of the customer's account.	673552

account number is invalid. In this way, it detects data entry errors. Almost all major credit card companies use check digits in their credit card account numbers. When an account number contains a check digit, it is referred to as a *self-checking number.*

Illustration 14–9 shows one way to calculate a check digit. Known as the modulus 11 method, it is both simple and effective in detecting errors and preventing irregularities. Companies use a method similar to this one to calculate the check digit when assigning account numbers.

Illustration 14–10 shows how an application system verifies an account number that contains a check digit. It again uses the modulus 11 method. However, for verifying the account number, the procedures are slightly different from those used to compute the check digit.

In practice, people seldom calculate check digits as shown in these illustrations. Programs in applications systems calculate them to assign account numbers and also to verify a transaction's account number before posting the transaction. The project team selects an algorithm during system design, and a programmer codes it into a program during system implementation.

Check digits are a common method of verifying account numbers before posting transactions. Applications systems also use data validation procedures to identify invalid transactions before posting.

ILLUSTRATION 14–10

Using a Check Digit to Verify an Account Number

	Example A	Example B
1. Take the customer's number.	6 7 3 5 5 2	6 3 7 5 5 2
2. Multiply each digit by a weight equaling its position.		
3. Add the product.	6 5 4 3 2 1 $36 + 35 + 12 + 15 + 10 + 2 = 110$	6 5 4 3 2 1 $36 + 15 + 28 + 15 + 10 + 2 = 106$
4. Divide the total by 11 and establish the remainder.	$110 \div 11 = 10$ remainder 0	$106 \div 11 = 9$ remainder 7
5. Accept the number if the remainder is 0; reject it if it is not.	Valid	Invalid

AIS in Practice

NationsBank Corp. is a bank holding company headquartered in Charlotte, North Carolina. It has annual revenues of about $200 billion and owns banks primarily in the southeastern and mid-Atlantic states and Texas.

A U.S. Bankruptcy Court judge in Miami, Florida, recently held a NationsBank computer in contempt of court. The computer had repeatedly sent letters to a Miami couple requesting payment for a debt that had been excused by the court. Although the letters showed that no balance was due, the couple complained to the bankruptcy judge and threatened to take the problem to a higher court. This, said the bankruptcy judge, "established beyond all reasonable doubt, that [the couple has] no sense of humor."

The bankruptcy judge fined the computer 50 megabytes of hard drive memory and 10 megabytes of random access memory. NationsBank attorneys complied by sending the court a hard disk and memory chips that exceeded the amount of the fine. The unwanted letters had been generated by a corrupt database.

Data Validation. *Data validation* consists of procedures to detect erroneous data as it enters an application system and prevent the system from posting the invalid data. It also provides for the data's correction and reentry. You may see different forms of data validation, depending on the approach to data processing.

Data Validation in Batch Processing Systems. In batch processing systems, and in batch systems with on-line inquiry, a separate computer program performs data validation. This program, an *input edit* program, examines data fields in each transaction record and identifies those transactions that have fields containing obvious errors. The program prints a listing of transactions containing errors and removes these transactions from the transaction file. In this way, the application system does not post these erroneous transactions to a master file.

Many application systems add erroneous transactions to a computer file called a *suspense file.* The system suspends further processing of each of these transactions until someone reviews the error listing, corrects the error in the transaction, removes it from the suspense file, and reenters it in the system. The project team determines these error correction procedures during design of the application.

The project team also determines the actions of the edit program during system design. They select the fields in a transaction record for examination and decide which kinds of errors should be detected. An input edit program would not find all possible errors in transactions, but a well-designed program could find most of the common ones. Illustration 14–11 shows some common data validation procedures (sometimes called *edit checks*) performed by edit programs.

Data Validation in On-Line Real-Time Systems. On-line real-time applications apply all processes to a transaction before beginning to process the next transaction. Usually a single program converts data into computer-readable form, performs validation checks on certain fields in the transaction, copies it to the transaction log, and then posts the transaction to a master file. The program may also add the transaction to a file. The system later prints the contents of this file in the form of a journal.

ILLUSTRATION 14–11

Common Data Validation Procedures

1. *Field check.* Verify that fields that should contain only numeric data contain no nonnumeric characters. Also verify that fields that should contain only alphabetic data contain no nonalphabetic characters.
2. *Validity check.* Determine that a field that should contain only characters from a limited set contains no improper characters. For example, assume a transaction contains a RECORD TYPE field and there are only two record types, Record Type 1 and Record Type 2. A transaction with a Record Type of 3 is invalid.
3. *Sign check.* Determine if a field contains data of the proper sign, either positive or negative.
4. *Limit (reasonableness) check.* Determine that a field does not contain an excessive amount. For example, an HOURS WORKED field in a weekly payroll program should not contain numbers greater than 168.
5. *Sequence check.* The key field of the current transaction should be greater than that of the transaction previously processed.
6. *Self-checking account number.* Use the modulus 11 method (or some other method) to verify that a check digit is correct.
7. *Completeness check.* Determine that a critical field in a record has not been left blank. If the field is blank, the record is not processed.
8. *Default values.* Determine if a field in a record is blank. If it is blank, the program assumes a value; this is the default value.

Many on-line real-time systems use data entry clerks to enter transactions at terminals. Data entry programs apply validation procedures, such as those in Illustration 14–11, to data fields as the clerk enters them. If the validation procedure identifies a field as erroneous, the program does not accept the transaction until the clerk corrects it. In this way these systems avoid suspense files, error listings, and delayed reentry of many transactions.

Validation procedures enable the computer to prevent or detect erroneous data before it affects a master file. Another source of errors for a master file is lost or added data. Control totals are useful in detecting errors from this source.

Control Totals. A *control total* is the sum, taken from all transactions in a batch, of a numeric data field that exists in each transaction. For example, a clerk may form a batch of sales transactions from all the sales orders accepted on Wednesday. The clerk calculates a control total by summing the gross sales amounts from each sales order. When a control total is taken on a batch of documents such as this, accountants also call it a *batch total.* In an on-line real-time system, where transactions are not batched, it is simply a control total.

Control totals ensure that no transactions are lost or added during processing. For example, assume you are entering cash receipts transactions in a batch order entry system. After inputting Wednesday's receipts, you enter the control total. At the conclusion of each succeeding processing step, a computer program recalculates the control total. It compares the most recent calculation with the control total you entered at data entry. If these differ, the program has detected an error in processing. If you are using an on-line real-time system, a computer program compares your control total with the total changes in the balances of the cash and accounts receivable accounts.

Control totals are most useful in detecting lost or added transactions; they include amount or quantity totals and hash totals. Another similar device is the record count.

Amount or Quantity Totals.   A control total taken on amount fields produces an amount control total. The total of all gross sales amounts from a batch of sales transactions, as described above, is an example. The total of all quantities issued from inventory of an item is an example of a quantity total.

Amount or quantity totals have significance for decision making as well as for control purposes. A sales manager may wish to know the total gross sales for Wednesday to evaluate the performance of sales personnel. When a performance report discloses this amount, the manager uses it for decision making. Clerks may also use this control total to detect errors in the report.

Hash Totals.   A hash total is a form of control total that has no significance for decision making. It is useful only for control purposes. For example, rather than summing the gross sales amounts for all sales orders accepted on Wednesday, the clerk may sum the customer account numbers. This produces a total that has no significance for decision making. The clerk enters this hash total in the system during data entry, and computer programs may recalculate it during later processing steps. Clerks compare hash totals at the conclusion of each processing step to ensure that no transactions are lost or added. For control purposes, the hash total functions like an amount control total. Yet it serves no other purpose.

Record Counts.   A record count is simply a total of the number of transactions in a batch. Similar to a hash total, it is useful only for control purposes. For example, a clerk may count the number of sales orders accepted on Wednesday. After entering the data from these transactions into the computer-based system, the clerk enters the number of transactions. During each subsequent processing step, a computer program counts the number of transaction records and compares it to that entered during data entry. If they differ, a transaction has been lost or added.

Because a record count is not obtained from a field in each transaction, it is not really a control total. Yet record counts are used like control totals, so most accountants consider them to be equivalent. In fact, many batch processing systems detect lost or added data using both a control total and a record count.

Illustration 14–12 summarizes the forms a control total can take. Another input control utilizes procedures for direct data entry.

Direct Data Entry Procedures.   Many application systems prevent errors by using direct data entry. With this kind of procedure, data enters a file in a computer-based system directly from its source. Human intervention is not required to convert the data from human-readable to computer-readable form. These systems avoid errors originating from human fatigue, inattention, or mistakes in judgment during data entry.

For example, many sales order entry systems require that salespersons complete written sales orders. They send the sales orders to a data entry clerk, who enters the data from the orders in the system at a workstation. The data entry clerk occasionally makes errors that are not detected by the validation procedures of the system. If the salesperson completes the written sales order on a document that can be read directly by a computer, the system avoids these errors.

ILLUSTRATION 14–12

Control Totals

Distinguishing Characteristic	Example
Batch Total A control total of a batch in a batch processing system	Total of gross sales from the documents in a batch of written sales orders
Amount or Quantity Total A control total useful for decision making as well as for control purposes	Total of gross sales from the transactions in a file of sales transactions
Hash Total A control total that has no significance for decision making	Total of customer account numbers from the transactions in a file of sales transactions
Record Count The total number of transactions to be processed	The number of sales transaction records processed in one day by a sales order entry system

There are many forms of direct data entry. These include source input documents, turnaround documents, and point-of-sale data entry.

Source Input Documents.   When a salesperson records sales data on a form that a computer input device can read, that form is a source input document. An *optical character reader* scans the form and creates a transaction record from the data it contains.

Students use one form of source input document when they take standardized college entrance examinations. They mark their answers on the form in the appropriate places using a pencil. When grading each exam, the optical character reader senses these marks, and a computer program interprets the answers according to where the marks are on the form.

Source input documents provide fast and accurate ways to enter data into an application system. However, because they require special equipment, they may be more expensive to develop than systems using workstations.

Turnaround Documents.   A turnaround document is an output from a computerized process that later becomes an input to another process. When producing the document, a computer program records data on it needed by another application. By recording data that an input device can read, it avoids human input errors.

For example, many utility bills contain turnaround documents. The utility's billing application produces a remittance advice that is mailed to the customer. Recorded on the remittance advice in magnetic ink is the customer's account number and amount owed. The customer returns the remittance advice with the payment, and it becomes an input to the cash receipts application. An input device called a magnetic ink character reader reads the account number and amount owed and records it in a transaction record. This prevents erroneous account numbers, because people do not enter them in the system.

Point-of-Sale Data Entry.   Retailers use this form of direct data entry when recording sales. In point-of-sale systems, the cash register is also a computer terminal. When a sales clerk punches buttons to record the addition of cash to the register, the clerk also produces a sales transaction record for a transaction file. Later, perhaps at night after the store closes, a computer posts these transactions. Because it does not use written sales tickets or data entered at a terminal, this system prevents many errors.

Bar codes provide a convenient method of point-of-sale data entry for retailers. Store personnel tag merchandise with labels containing bar codes printed in black ink. A light-emitting source, such as a handheld wand connected to the cash register, reads the bar code. The register then deducts the item from inventory and records the sale. When using bar codes, the store clerk must guard against substituted, tampered with, or fraudulent labels.

Source input documents, turnaround documents, and point-of-sale data entry are input controls because they prevent errors during data input. Other applications controls are processing controls.

Processing Controls

Processing controls monitor the accuracy of accounting data during computer processing. If an application system is tested adequately during system development, errors due to its hardware or software are rare. Errors arising from human intervention during processing are more common. Certain control procedures used during processing detect errors arising from these sources.

Sequence Checks.   Batch processing systems require records in data files to be in the proper sequence. If they are not, the system does not function properly. Sequence checks verify that records are in the proper sequence.

For example, batch processing file update programs require two input files, a transaction file, and a master file. The records in these files must be sorted in the same sequence. If a transaction is out of sequence, the update program produces an error message rather than posting it to the master file. To prevent this, a programmer codes a program to check the sequence of records in data files prior to posting. Rather than posting it, the program adds to a suspense file any record that is out of sequence.

System designers also include sequence checks in programs that print reports. Many reports contain listings of data in a desired sequence. Sequence checks ensure that these are printed properly. For example, a payroll register is a list of all paychecks issued for a pay period. When printed, these checks should be sequenced by employee.

Control Totals as Run-to-Run Controls.   Accountants use control totals to detect lost or added records. With a batch processing system, they become processing controls called *run-to-run controls*. In these systems, a computer program applies a processing step to all transactions before beginning the next step. In information systems terminology, a processing step is a *run*. In each run, the computer prints a report disclosing control totals. A clerk compares control totals from successive runs. If the totals are identical, the clerk knows that no transactions were lost or added during processing. Sometimes the program adds control totals to a report containing other data, such as a list of transactions. In other cases, the program prints a special *control report* that discloses only the control totals.

ILLUSTRATION 14–13

Control Totals as Run-to-Run Controls

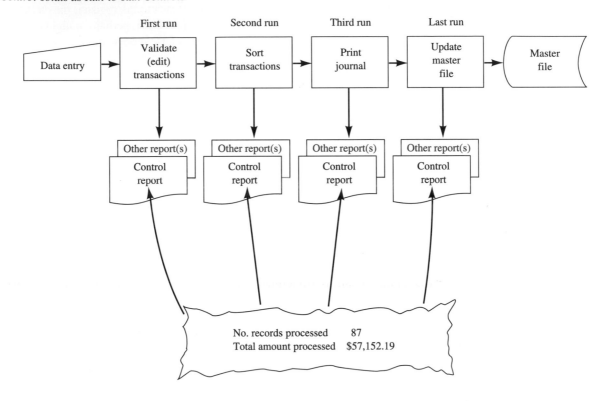

Illustration 14–13 shows how a batch processing system uses control totals as run-to-run controls. A data entry clerk enters transactions at a keyboard. An edit program validates each transaction as it is entered, and creates from the transactions a transaction file. Subsequent processing steps in this example consist of a program that sorts the transactions, one that prints a listing of them, and one that posts them to a master file. Each step produces a report containing amount totals and a record count. These are control reports because they disclose only control totals.

Physical File Identification.   Sometimes during processing computer operators erroneously mount the incorrect tape, disk pack, or diskette. This applies a processing step to the incorrect file and produces incorrect data. Physical file identification prevents this occurrence.

Physical file identification comes in two forms. The computer operator attaches *external file labels* to identify the proper tape, disk pack, or diskette to insert on the equipment. Devices also contain *internal file labels* read by the computer's operating system. Internal file labels include header and trailer records on magnetic tape and volume labels on magnetic disks and diskettes. If a mainframe operating system encounters a file with an improper internal label, it displays a message alerting the operator.

ILLUSTRATION 14–14

Summary of Applications Controls

Input Controls
Check digits
Data validation
Control totals
Direct data entry

Processing Controls
Sequence checks
Control totals as run-to-run controls
Physical file identification
Programmed controls

Output Controls
Data control group reviews and distributes reports

Programmed Controls.   During system design, the project team determines the computerized processing steps for the application system. In accounting applications, they identify control procedures, or *programmed controls,* to be performed by computer programs.

Programmed controls sometimes duplicate the error detection procedures performed by a bookkeeper in a manual system. For example, a bookkeeper may foot and crossfoot the columns of numbers on a schedule to detect arithmetic errors. A programmer may code a computer program to do the same thing. This is a *crossfooting check.* A bookkeeper looks at numbers in manual accounting records and verifies that they are of reasonable magnitude, or of the proper sign. Computer programs use limit checks and sign checks to accomplish these objectives.

Output Controls

Output controls apply to the output of a computer-based accounting system. They include those policies, practices, and procedures that ensure the accuracy of the results of processing. These controls also ensure that only authorized personnel receive the reports produced by an application system.

In batch processing systems, implementing output controls is a major responsibility of the *data control group.* These clerks scan reports produced by this system. When a report is clearly erroneous or illegible, they alert the machine operator to the problem. They reconcile control totals on reports with those totals established at the beginning of processing. In this way, they detect the loss or addition of data. The data control group distributes reports to authorized users, which prevents exposure of sensitive information against company policy. They maintain an output distribution log, which is a record of the reports produced and the disposition of those reports.

You have seen many control procedures that accountants include in computerized application systems. These prevent or detect errors and irregularities at the input of data, during its processing, and at its output. Accountants devote the most attention to data input. Input controls prevent and detect the most common errors—those concerned with transcription into computer-readable form. Processing controls detect errors primarily when people intervene in processing. Output controls are a final check on the accuracy of accounting information. Illustration 14–14 summarizes these applications controls.

Summary

Policies, practices, and procedures adopted to prevent or detect errors and irregularities in a computer-based system are information system controls. Those that affect all applications in a computer-based system are general controls. Management establishes policies and adopts procedures to implement them. Information system controls that affect only a specific application are applications controls. They help ensure that transactions are valid, properly authorized, and completely and accurately processed. A project team identifies applications controls during the design of the application system.

There are four categories of general controls and three categories of applications controls. General controls include controls over data center operations, system software acquisition and maintenance, access security, and applications system software development and maintenance. Applications controls may be input, processing, or output controls. A strength in applications controls may compensate for a weakness in general controls. Management selects combinations of general and applications controls to provide reasonable assurance that assets are safeguarded and accounting records are accurate.

Key Terms

applications controls   Policies, practices, and procedures that prevent or detect errors and irregularities within a specific application system, such as payroll.

check digit   A digit in an account number that is calculated from the other digits in the number. It is used to detect erroneous account numbers.

contingency plan   A formal document that describes procedures for processing data should a catastrophe occur to the data center.

control total   The sum, taken from all transactions in a batch, of a numeric data field in each transaction. It may be an amount total, a quantity total, a hash total, or a record count.

corrective controls   Procedures adopted by management to correct misstated records after an error or irregularity has occurred.

data validation   The examining of accounting transactions for erroneous data. Also called data editing, data validation is frequently performed by a computer program.

detective controls   Procedures adopted by management to identify errors and irregularities after they have occurred.

file dump   The process of copying the contents of a master file onto a removable device. This creates a backup copy.

general controls   Policies, practices, and procedures that prevent or detect errors and irregularities for all application systems.

grandfather–father–son technique   The standard file backup policy in batch processing systems using sequential files. It maintains three generations of each master file.

preventive controls   Procedures adopted by management to prevent errors and irregularities.

transaction log   In an on-line real-time system, a computer file containing copies of all transactions posted to a master file since the last master file dump. It serves as a backup copy of the transactions.

Questions

14–1. How are information system controls categorized by
   a. Function?
   b. Scope?

14–2. A basic principle of internal control is fixed responsibility. How does fixed responsibility aid in controlling system software acquisition and maintenance?

14–3. What is the objective of providing adequate segregation of duties? How is this done with a computer-based system?

14–4. How is custody of accounting records maintained in a
   a. Traditional date file system?
   b. Data base management system?

14–5. What are appropriate procedures for authorizing and approving
   a. Implementation of a new accounting system?
   b. Changes to an existing computer program?

14–6. How does segregation of duties in the data center control access to accounting records?

14–7. Why are file backup procedures needed? How do these differ between batch processing and on-line real-time systems?

14–8. What are the contents of a contingency plan?

14–9. What is the purpose of data validation procedures? How do they differ between batch processing and on-line real-time systems?

14–10. Which system control procedures are classified as both input and processing controls?

14–11. Distinguish between three kinds of control totals.

14–12. How do direct data entry procedures prevent errors?

14–13. Who in the data center is primarily responsible for output controls? Which functions do they perform?

Exercises and Cases

14–14.   *CHECK DIGITS*

Calculate a check digit for each of the following account numbers using the modulus 11 method:

a. 666335.
b. 62779.
c. 1234.
d. 10102.

14–15.   SELF-CHECKING NUMBERS

Each of the following is an account number. The last digit is a check digit calculated using the modulus 11 method. Identify the invalid account number(s).

a. 66635.
b. 6661.
c. 666774.
d. 770701.

14–16.   SYSTEM CONTROL FUNCTIONS

Controls over system activities can be classified as either preventive or detective controls.

Required:
a. Briefly define these classifications of controls, and give two examples of each.
b. Cite two examples of controls that may be used either as a preventive control or as a detective control.

(CIA Adapted)

14–17.   CATEGORIES OF CONTROLS

For items *a* through *g* below, identify each control as a *general* control or an *applications* control:

a. Parity check.
b. Password.
c. Turnaround document.
d. Daily file dump.
e. Edit check.
f. Software librarian.
g. Sequence check.

14–18.   ACCESS TO DATA

The Ultimate Life Insurance Company recently established a database management system. The company is now planning to provide its branch offices with terminals that have on-line access to the central computer facility.

Required:
a. Briefly discuss three security steps to safeguard the database from improper access through terminals.

b. Briefly describe four steps to control the completeness and accuracy of data transmitted through terminals to the database.

(CIA Adapted)

14–19.   ACCESS TO DOCUMENTATION

The documentation of data processing applications is an important step in the design and implementation of any computer-based system. Documentation provides a complete record of data processing applications.

Required:

Describe policies to regulate access to documentation data for each of the following groups of company employees:

a. Computer operators.
b. Internal auditors.
c. Production planning analysts.
d. Systems analysts.

(CMA Adapted)

14–20.   SEGREGATION OF DUTIES

The following questions are often asked on internal control questionnaires:

a. Is there controlled access to computerized data files?
b. Are computer programmers and computer operators prohibited from correcting errors and reconciling control totals appearing on computer-generated reports?

Required:

For each of these questions, identify two risks or exposures that could exist if the related internal control procedure is not followed.

(CIA Adapted)

14–21.   INPUT VALIDATION PROCEDURES

Illustration 12–1 shows a list of employees in a factory. This factory employs people in the departments and jobs listed below.

Department Code	Department	Job Code	Job
1	Factory office	1	Clerk
2	Assembly	2	Machinist
		3	Accountant
		4	Laborer

Clerks and accountants are employed in the factory office, and machinists and laborers work in assembly. The payroll department has received the following payroll transactions from this factory for the third week in June.

Employee Number	Name	Department	Job Code	Hours Worked
11	Smith, A.	2	4	40
14	Garc9a, B.	2	2	37
27	Wong, C.	1	3	47
33	O'Hara, E.	1	1	40
36	Weiss, F.	3	1	20
45	Powski, H.	2	4	42
41	Abbott, G.	1	3	74

Required:

a. Compute a hash total and a quantity total for these transactions.

b. Identify the errors in the transactions. Determine a control procedure that would detect each error.

14–22.   APPLICATIONS CONTROLS

The left column in the table below lists 6 procedural controls often found in accounting information systems. The right column lists 10 explanations of various types of procedural controls.

Procedural Controls	Explanation
1. Default option	A. Rekeying incorrect data detected on a CRT display.
2. Hash total	B. A test of specified amount fields against stipulated high or low limits of acceptability.
3. Completeness check	C. A test of characters in a coded field against an acceptable set of values, patterns, formats, subcodes, or character values.
4. Visual verification	D. A test to determine that data entries are made in fields that cannot be processed in a blank state.
5. Validity check	E. The automatic utilization of a predetermined value in situations where input transactions having certain values are left blank.
6. Limit check	F. Internally initiated processing in a predetermined manner unless specific input transactions are received that specify processing with different values or in a different manner.
	G. The immediate return of input information to the sender for comparison and approval.
	H. Provides a control total for comparison with accumulated counts or values of records processed.
	I. A meaningless but useful value developed from the accumulated numerical amounts of nonmonetary information.
	J. Any type of control total or count applied to a specific number of transactions documents or to the transactions documents that arrive within a specified period of time.

Required:

Identify the explanation that best applies to each procedural control. (Each procedural control has only one explanation.)

(CIA Adapted)

14–23.   CONTINGENCY PLAN

The headquarters of Gleicken Corporation, a private company with $3.5 million in annual sales, is located in California. Gleicken provides for its 150 clients an on-line legal software service that includes data storage and administrative activities for law offices. The company has grown rapidly since its inception three years ago, and its MIS department has mushroomed to accommodate this growth. Because Gleicken's president and sales personnel spend a great deal of time out of the office soliciting new clients, the planning of the computer facilities has been left to MIS professionals.

Gleicken recently moved its headquarters facility into a remodeled warehouse on the outskirts of the city. While remodeling the warehouse, the architects retained much of the original structure, including the wooden-shingled exterior and exposed wooden beams throughout the interior. The data center, containing a minicomputer and data communication equipment, is located in a large open area with high ceilings and skylights. This openness makes the MIS area accessible to the rest of the staff and encourages a team approach to problem solving. Before Gleicken occupied the new facility, city inspectors declared the building safe, with sufficient fire extinguishers and exits.

In an effort to provide further protection for its large database of client information, Gleicken has instituted a tape backup procedure. It is on a time-delay mechanism and automatically backs up the database weekly, every Sunday evening, thus avoiding interruption to the daily operations and procedures. All the tapes are then labeled and carefully stored on shelves reserved for this purpose in the data center. The computer operator's manual has instructions on how to use these tapes to restore the database should the need arise. In the event of an emergency, there is a home phone list of the individuals in the MIS department. Gleicken has recently increased its liability insurance for data loss from $50,000 to the current $100,000.

This past Saturday, the Gleicken headquarters building was completely ruined by fire, and the company must now inform its clients that all their information has been destroyed.

Required:

a. Describe the control weaknesses present at Gleicken Corporation that made it possible for a disastrous data loss to occur.
b. List the components that should have been included in the contingency plan in order to ensure computer recovery within 72 hours.
c. What factors, other than those included in the plan itself, should a company consider when formulating a contingency plan?

(CMA Adapted)

14–24.   SYSTEM CONTROLS

A small local bakery has expanded its operations into a regional area. Expansion has increased the business information needs in all areas including distribution (truck routes), fixed assets (including tracking mobile equipment), inventory, order processing, and accounting (general ledger, accounts payable, payroll, etc.). These factors have required a change from a manual to a computerized environment.

Required:

Identify control procedures that the internal auditor, as a member of the system design project team, should suggest for the following activities:

a. Transaction origination.
b. Data communication.
c. Computer processing.
d. Data storage and retrieval.
e. Output processing.

(CIA Adapted)

14–25. GENERAL CONTROLS

As an auditor, you conducted a review of a client's computer-based information system and observed the following:

1. The chief information officer reports to the director of accounting, who in turn reports to the controller. The controller reports to the treasurer, who is one of several vice presidents of the company. The chief information officer has made several unsuccessful requests to the director of accounting for another printer.

2. There is no written charter for the MIS function, but the chief information officer tells you that the primary objective is to get the accounting reports out on time.

3. Transaction tapes are used daily to update the master file and then are retired to the scratch tape area.

4. A new computer with large disk capacity was installed three years ago. The MIS activity previously used an older computer, and many of the programs written for that computer are used on the present equipment by means of an emulator. (The emulator is a computer program that translates code from the form required by the old computer to that required by the new one.)

5. You observe that the output from the computer runs is written on tape for printing at a later time. Some output tapes from several days' runs are waiting to be printed.

6. The chief information officer states that the central processing unit could handle at least twice the work currently being processed.

Required:

a. Identify the defect inherent in each of the six preceding conditions.
b. Briefly describe the probable effect if the condition is permitted to continue.

(CIA Adapted)

14–26. DATA VALIDATION

Talbert Corporation hired an independent computer programmer to develop a simplified payroll application for its computer. The programmer developed an on-line, DBMS-based computer system that minimized the level of knowledge required by the operator. It required a user to type answers to input cues that appeared on the terminal's viewing screen. Examples of these cues follow:

Access Routine

1. Operator access number to payroll file?

2. Are there new employees?

New Employees Routine

1. Employee name?

2. Employee number?

3. Social Security number?

4. Rate per hour?

5. Single or married?

6. Number of dependents?

7. Account distribution?

Current Payroll Routine

1. Employee number?

2. Regular hours worked?

3. Overtime hours worked?

4. Total employees this payroll period?

The auditor is attempting to verify that certain input validation (edit) checks exist to ensure that errors resulting from omissions, invalid entries, or other inaccuracies would be detected during the typing of answers to the input cues.

Required:

Identify the various types of input validation (edit) checks the auditor would expect to find in the system. Describe the assurances provided by each validation check you identify.

(AICPA Adapted)

14–27. CONTROL PROCEDURES

Carrie Welsh's mother got a little defensive when she received her phone bill for three weeks' service—$8.7 million.[2] "She says, 'I only called my sister,'" said Welsh, who handles her elderly mother's bills. The bill from Illinois Bell should have read $87.98, not $8,709,800.33.

"At first, I didn't really notice it," said Welsh. "Then, I looked again, and I couldn't stop laughing." Welsh said that she had a hard time explaining the mistake to the telephone company. "They said, 'Why do you want a new bill?'" she recalled. "I said, 'Well, it's rather high.' Then they pulled it up on the computer and said, 'Yes, I see what you mean.'"

"The error occurred when someone incorrectly typed a 'correction' into the computer system," said Lawrence Curry, a Bell spokesman. "We apologized, of course," Curry said. "Something like this rarely happens."

---

[2]Adapted from "The Bell Tolls for Woman—$8.7 Million," *Houston Chronicle,* September 21, 1990. Copyright 1990 by Associated Press. Used by permission.

Required:

Which control procedure(s) could have prevented this error?

14–28.   DISASTER RECOVERY

At the **Federal Reserve Bank of New York**, the week of September 29, 1987, will be remembered forever as a nightmare come to life.[3] That week, the computer that runs the Fedwire funds transfer system crashed twice in two days. Not only did this bank's funds transfers cease, but all the banks with which it did business found themselves ignorant of their exact financial positions. Said James Smith, executive vice president of the bank, "On a scale of 1 to 10, this event was a minus 2. Hordes of vendor technicians were at the bank, the database was corrupted, and after the second crash we ended the night at 3:45 A.M."

Background

Fedwire is the United States' primary mechanism through which commercial and other banks transfer funds and securities. As one of a dozen reserve banks in the country, the New York Fed moves about $1 trillion each day over its portion of the nationwide Fedwire network. This is about 30 percent of Fedwire's total funds volume, about 75 percent of the total securities volume, and requires 150,000 transactions each minute.

Fedwire runs on one of the New York Fed's three mainframe computers in the bank's New York data center. The second mainframe is used for all non-Fedwire bank business, and the third resides at the bank's alternative processing location in Pearl River, New York.

Preventive Measures

The bank never fully recovered from those crashes, but the experience caused management to reexamine their approach to providing backup. Some argued that the bank should start over, re-creating the Fedwire system on fault-tolerant hardware. (A fault-tolerant computer contains duplicate circuits, such as multiple CPUs and memory storage devices. When one circuit ceases to function, the operating system automatically replaces it with an identical standby circuit so the machine continues to operate.) But according to Smith, "We did not need fault-tolerant hardware, because hardware is the component that crashes least often. We needed a fault-tolerant system, and this includes everything—environment, software, people, procedures, and utilities." The philosophy that prevailed was to build fault-tolerant capabilities throughout the entire network.

This approach apparently worked. The New York Fed improved its funds transfer rate of availability from 97.2 percent in 1987 to the current 99.98 percent. To get to this point, the bank focused on educating both management and users, identifying the single points of failure, and buying backups of items most prone to failure.

Many past crashes were caused because the bank had not been improving software with updates provided by vendors, especially those to the operating system and the database management system. Now the bank's policy is to convert to the most recent

---

[3]Adapted from "Planning Is Key at Reserve Bank," *Computerworld,* April 22, 1991. Used by permission.

version of software within six months of its availability. Maintenance changes and updates are made only once per month and tested both individually and as a group before being put on-line. The bank also purchased and implemented a utility program that automatically switches applications in one mainframe to a connected mainframe in the event of a failure. The New York Fed also reduced the amount of time required to recover at its alternative processing location from six hours to one. The Fedwire database is copied and sent four times each day to the Pearl River facility.

These preventive measures paid off last August when one of the bank's electrical generators failed. After getting proper approvals, the responsible people had everything running in about 40 minutes. "After the 1987 experience, I was very grateful that things worked like we said they would," Smith said.

Required:

What changes did the New York Fed make to improve its disaster recovery procedures?

14–29.   SYSTEM CONTROL OBJECTIVES

A bank provides services such as money transfers, letters of credit, and foreign exchange for its customers who maintain minimum balances in demand deposit accounts (DDAs). Earnings on DDA balances compensate the bank for the services and contribute to income. The amount of income earned by DDA balances, however, is a function of variable interest rates. These are beyond the bank's control, and the bank cannot continually change minimum balance requirements as interest rates fluctuate.

The bank uses a spreadsheet model on a desktop computer to help it plan changes in minimum balances. The spreadsheet model projects operating results for different minimum balances. As interest rates fall, larger balances are required to produce the same income. The costs of the services include fixed costs and variable costs that are linear functions of volume.

Required:

For this application, identify three preventive controls, three detective controls, and three corrective controls. For each one, indicate the risk of errors or irregularities it is intended to control.

(CIA Adapted)

14–30.   SYSTEM CONTROLS

The state department of taxation is developing a new computer system for processing state income tax returns. The new system features on-line input and inquiry capability. Identification of taxpayers is provided by the Social Security number for individuals and federal identification number for corporations. The new system should be fully implemented in time for the next tax season. The new system will serve the following three primary purposes:

1. Data entry clerks will input data from tax returns using cathode ray tube (CRT) terminals at the department's central headquarters.

2. The returns will be processed using the main computer facilities at headquarters. Processing includes

    a. Verification of mathematical accuracy.

    b. Auditing the reasonableness of deductions and tax due through the use of edit routines. These routines also include a comparison of the current year's data with the prior year's data.

    c. Identification of returns that should be considered for audit by revenue agents of the department.

3. Inquiry service will be provided to taxpayers on request through the assistance of tax department personnel at five regional offices. A total of 50 CRT terminals will be placed at the regional offices. Taxpayers will be allowed to determine the status of their returns or get information from the last three years' returns by calling or visiting one of the department's regional offices.

The state commissioner of taxation is concerned about data security during input and processing. This includes both protection against the loss or damage of data during input or processing and the improper input or processing of data. In addition, the tax commissioner and the state attorney general have discussed the general problem of data confidentiality that may arise from the nature and operation of the new system. Both individuals want to have all potential problems identified before the system is fully developed and implemented so that the proper controls can be incorporated into the new system.

Required:

a. Describe the potential risks that could arise in each of the following three areas of processing. Recommend corrective action(s) to minimize the risks.
    1. Data input.
    2. Processing of returns.
    3. Data inquiry.

b. The state tax commission wants to incorporate controls to provide security against the loss, damage, or improper input or use of data during data input and processing. Identify the potential problems (other than natural hazards such as fire or floods) for which the state department of taxation should develop controls, and recommend the possible controls for each problem identified.

(CMA Adapted)

14–31. SEGREGATION OF DUTIES

Robinson Industries is a loosely knit conglomerate that offers centralized data processing services to its affiliated companies.[4] To improve the attractiveness of its services, this past year the data processing department introduced on-line service. Several affiliates have become, or are becoming, users of this service. It has resulted in a reorganization of the department, although a new organization chart for it has yet to be prepared.

The data processing department now consists of 25 persons reporting to the president through the director of data processing. In addition to these data employees, key committees perform important roles as do the internal and independent auditors for the company.

---

[4]Adapted from a case prepared by Professors Frederick L. Neumann and Richard L. Boland, University of Illinois, through a grant by the Touche Ross Foundation.

Committees

Selected functions of key committees important to the management and control of the data processing department are as follows:

Data Processing Committee.   The data processing committee, composed of three members of the board of directors, meets as required to review and evaluate major changes in the data processing area and to review approval of all pricing of services offered. Their responsibilities also include a review of major agreements with hardware and software vendors.

Audit Committee.   In its oversight of the audit function, this committee of the board of directors is directly concerned with the quality of the records and reports processed by the department and the controls employed.

Users' Groups.   Users' groups consist of representatives from on-line users within a specific geographical area. They meet periodically throughout the year to discuss common areas of interest, possible enhancements, and current problems related to the on-line system. The results of these group meetings are reported directly to the data processing committee through a user advisory committee.

Data Processing Department

Data processing department management consists of five managers who report to the director through an assistant director. The department management meets weekly to review the status of projects, customer service levels, and any problems. Weekly status reports are then prepared and distributed to each level of line management. Formal meetings with Robinson's president are held quarterly, or more often if required, to review future plans and past performance.

Each of the following five sections in the department is under the direction of a manager:

1. *On-Line Services*
   a. *On-line technical staff.* The on-line technical staff conducts all user training, conversions, and parameter definitions necessary to set up a new user. Training classes are conducted at the data processing center. Conversion assistance is provided to the user prior to the initiation of on-line services. If conversion programs are required, these are defined by the on-line services section to the on-line analyst programmers for program preparation. During the first month after conversion of a new user, calls are directed to on-line services; thereafter, user calls are directed to the user liaison section.
   b. *Applications coordinator.* The applications coordinator is responsible for coordinating the approval of user and data processing department project requests, assisting in the requirements definition of a systems maintenance project, monitoring ongoing projects, and approving project test results.
2. *Operations*
   a. *Data communications coordinator.* The coordinator of data communications monitors all service levels and response time related to the communications network and terminals. The coordinator receives all user calls regarding

communications problems, logs these calls, identifies the nature of the problem, and reports the status of the problems until they are corrected.

b. *Computer operators.* Operators, supervisors, and librarians in this section execute, review, and service the daily computer production runs, special computer runs, and program compilations and tests. The operations are scheduled on a 24-hour basis for six days a week. Shift supervisors review all on-line operations and prepare written documentation of each problem encountered.

c. *Scheduler.* The scheduler is responsible for setting up the computer job runs and adjusting them for one-time special requests.

d. *User liaison.* User liaison staff consists of four persons who receive, log, and report all questions or potential problems, other than communications problems, by on-line users. User input is obtained through telephone calls, letters, and on-line messages over the communications network and notes from users' group meetings.

e. *On-line reports control.* The on-line reports control staff is responsible for the distribution of all hardcopy output to all users. Microfiche are sent directly to users from the outside processing vendor. Logs are maintained where appropriate to control distribution and to reconcile items such as check numbers and dividend totals.

3. *Systems and Programming*

a. *On-line analyst programmers.* On-line analyst programmers are responsible for all of the applications and system software programming required for the on-line system. Systems analysis and programming consists primarily of maintenance to existing computer programs, correction of problems, and enhancements to the current applications.

b. *In-house analyst programmers.* In-house analyst programmers are responsible for all applications and system software programming not on-line.

4. *Research and Development*

The research and development staff evaluates and conducts preliminary investigations into new applications.

5. *Marketing*

The marketing staff responds to requests for information regarding the services provided by the data processing department. Once a new user signs an on-line service agreement, that member is turned over to on-line services for training and conversion.

Required:

a. Prepare an organization chart of the data processing department and of its relationship to the rest of the organization.

b. From a controls standpoint, how could organizational independence be improved?

15   DATA SECURITY AND INTEGRITY

Learning Objectives

1. To distinguish between data security and data integrity in computer-based accounting systems.
2. To understand data security risks and their sources.
3. To learn methods of detecting fraud.
4. To discover how auditors evaluate data security and integrity in computer-based accounting systems.

Introduction

Management adopts an organization's internal control structure. It selects control policies, practices, and procedures for its accounting systems to provide reasonable assurance of preventing or detecting errors and irregularities. These help to safeguard assets and to ensure accurate and reliable accounting data.

Those control policies, practices, and procedures that ensure accurate and reliable data provide *data integrity.* Because computers contain records and authorize transactions regarding assets, the controls that safeguard computer files also safeguard assets. These controls provide *data security.*

This chapter discusses the risks associated with data security and integrity, the sources of those risks, and an approach to detecting fraud. It also explains how auditors evaluate security and integrity in a computer- based system.

Security in Computer-Based Systems

Criminals who gain unauthorized access to computerized accounting records may alter data to defraud the organization. Security features prevent unauthorized access and thereby safeguard the organization's assets. A computer-based system that safeguards its data from risk is one that provides adequate data security.

Sources of Security Risk

Weaknesses in data security allow risks from three sources: internal, external, and collusive.

Internal Sources.   Internal sources of risk are employees who might exploit weaknesses in data security. They include managers and operations-level employees.

Operations-Level Employees.   Operations-level employees include accounting clerks, sales clerks, and factory workers. Because these employees have routine access to the assets of the organization, they have opportunities to steal these assets. They have, however, only limited access to computerized records concerning assets.

When the organization implements good segregation of duties, no one has both custody of an asset and access to the records concerning that asset. This separation restricts the ability of operations-level employees to both steal an asset and conceal the theft by altering computerized records.

Managers.   Managerial and supervisory employees have greater access to records but fewer opportunities to steal assets. Although they can more easily falsify records to cover a theft, it is difficult for managers to steal an asset without the knowledge of others in the organization. They may, however, bypass restrictions by threatening to dismiss operations-level employees who know of their thefts.

External Sources.   External sources of risk include business contacts and potential criminals who have opportunities to steal the organization's assets.

Business Contacts.   Several kinds of business contacts have the opportunity to commit a computer-related crime. Two major sources of risk are customers and vendors. Because they process transactions with the organization, the employees of customers and vendors have indirect access to assets and to records. The greatest risk occurs when their employees act in conjunction with one of the organization's employees. Acting together, they may commit a theft and conceal it by entering fraudulent transactions in the computer-based system.

Former employees also constitute a risk to an accounting system. Frequently they have intimate knowledge of the system and its control weaknesses. If they hold a grudge against their former employer, they may attempt to exploit weaknesses to commit computer-related crimes.

Another source of risk is business competitors who may seek competitive advantage by gaining access to confidential data stored in computer files.

Unknown Criminals.   Other criminals may also become sources of risk to computerized records. Hackers attempt to bypass system security features using access by telephone. Other unknown criminals write programs (called viruses) that maliciously destroy data, erase programs, or use up system resources. Usually the challenge, rather than theft, is the motive for these criminals. Nevertheless, they can do extensive damage to an organization's database. Organized crime may also exploit weaknesses in data security to defraud an organization of its assets.

Collusive Sources.   Collusive sources of risk exist when two or more individuals conspire to defraud an organization and to conceal the theft by altering computerized records. All organizations, even those with adequate segregation of duties, are subject to

ILLUSTRATION 15–1

Sources of Data Security Risks

Internal

Operations employees. They have direct access to assets but limited access to records.
Managers and supervisors. They may bypass control policies, practices, and procedures.

External

Business contacts. Includes competitors, employees of customers, and employees of vendors.
Unknown criminals. Includes hackers, virus programmers, and organized crime.

Collusive

Internal collusion. Two or more employees. This source is not prevented by most control practices and
   procedures.
External collusion. An employee and a nonemployee. This source is difficult to detect.

frauds from this source. For this reason, accountants must be aware of these sources and adopt procedures to prevent or detect them. Collusive sources exist in two forms: internal collusion and external collusion.

Internal Collusion.   Internal collusion occurs when two or more employees of the organization cooperate to bypass its control policies, practices, or procedures. For example, internal collusion occurs when an operations employee steals an asset and a manager or another employee conceals the theft by falsifying records. Effective segregation of duties may not prevent frauds of this kind.

External Collusion.   External collusion exists when an employee acts with a nonemployee to defraud the organization. The nonemployee may simply be an acquaintance or an employee of one of the organization's business contacts. For example, a vendor's employee mails a fraudulent invoice to the organization. A clerk in the accounts payable department uses it to support issuing a check to the vendor. The vendor's employee intercepts the check, cashes it, and shares the proceeds with the accounts payable clerk. Good cash disbursements procedures prevent this form of external collusion; however, other forms are more difficult to prevent or detect.

In organizations with sound control policies, practices, and procedures, managers and collusive sources are the primary sources of risk. Without good internal control, risks exist from all sources. Illustration 15–1 summarizes the sources of risk arising from weaknesses in data security.

Risks

Just as you must know the sources of risk due to weaknesses in data security, you must also understand the four risks: destruction, espionage, invasion of privacy, and fraud.

Destruction of Data or Programs.   All accounting data are important, but certain data and program files are vital to the operation of any organization. These, including accounts receivable and accounts payable detail records, are difficult to reconstruct accurately if destroyed.

Destruction of data or programs may be accidental or it may be intentional. The data center minimizes the risk of accidental destruction by employing trained computer

ILLUSTRATION 15–2

An Example of Data Destruction

A Texas jury convicted Jean Burley, a former employee of an insurance and brokerage firm, on a felony charge of harmful access to a computer. Burley faced up to 10 years in prison.

Burley had been fired on September 18. Three days later, at about 3 A.M., she broke into her old office and sat down at her old workstation. She signed on with a password that allowed her to perform her old job, that of data security officer. She then erased 168,000 records in the company's payroll system. Burley also activated a "time bomb" program intended to erase these records on a monthly basis.

"She was having continual conflict with the company and anticipated being fired," said the district attorney. "Burley created the time bomb in a new program beginning with the letter Q. This is the same letter that begins program names provided in the operating system software, so the program would go undetected. Burley then tied this program, which was intended to erase data, to legitimate data and put in it a time switch." The company made a cursory check of the accounts after Burley was fired but did not find the hidden program file.

Saturday morning, after Burley's break-in, a programmer came to the office to figure out how a new bonus system would affect the company's payroll. Every time the programmer executed the system, the payroll came up with zeros. This led the company to shut down the computer for two days to cleanse the system, and allowed discovery of the time bomb.

Damages were about $12,000, including computer downtime and the cost to fix the payroll accounts. "In the scheme of things, it was not a large loss. but 550 people did not get their checks for a week or two. And if the program had gone off as planned, it would have created havoc," said the district attorney.

Source: Adapted from "Computer Time Bomb Defused; Felon Nailed," *Computerworld,* September 26, 1988. Used by permission.

operators, by having a computer operations manual that describes procedures for safeguarding data, and by following standard data backup policies. They prevent intentional destruction by having security procedures that eliminate the possibility of unauthorized access to data files. Computer viruses enter the system on data obtained from outside the organization. Companies minimize the risk of damage from viruses by obtaining data only from safe, reliable sources. They routinely use virus detection software to ensure that viruses have not infected personal computers.

Intentional data or program destruction usually arises from one of two sources. Disgruntled employees or former employees may gain unauthorized access to the employer's system and destroy files as a form of revenge. Hackers and virus programmers destroy files as a form of sport, to demonstrate their ability to bypass the security features of the system.

Illustration 15–2 describes a computer-related crime that details the risk of data destruction. In this example, a former employee was able to commit a crime because of inadequate controls over access to the system.

Espionage.   Managers are continually concerned about the actions and plans of competing companies. They can acquire much useful information about competitors by gaining access to computerized data. For example, lists of customers from accounts receivable records are useful to a competitor's sales force. Competitors can learn proprietary manufacturing processes by accessing certain production data. They may learn pricing strategies by accessing sales or cost accounting records. Budget data disclose plans for future operations and capital expenditures. Payroll data reveal information on pay rates a competitor may use to lure away key employees.

ILLUSTRATION 15–3

An Example of Data Espionage

A Florida news reporter was arrested and charged with 14 felony counts of breaking into a computer system. Each count carries a maximum sentence of 15 years and a $10,000 fine.

Michelle Shaffer, an assistant news director at WTSP-TV (Channel 10), allegedly broke into a rival station's system on at least six occasions to steal sensitive news information. The missing data contained information about news stories in progress or being planned, rundowns of how stories were to be handled during midday and evening news broadcasts, and planned format changes and special projects.

The accused news director was formerly employed by WTVT-TV (Channel 13) as an assignment manager. There she had participated in the installation of a system about six months earlier and had been made responsible for administering it. Shaffer had recently left Channel 13 for its crosstown rival. Although computer users and system administrators at the station routinely change computer system access codes and passwords when employees leave, a few "slipped through" when Shaffer left, according to a Channel 13 official.

The first theft was discovered on January 12 when the morning producer came to work and discovered a number of confidential and sensitive files missing. Channel 13 managers contacted the Florida Department of Law Enforcement, which began investigating and tracing calls to the station's computers. Phone records showed that Shaffer was making calls from her residence and from a personal computer in her office. A search warrant was obtained, and law enforcement officials seized a personal computer, 200 floppy disks, and operating manuals for the system. Shaffer was subsequently fired from her job at Channel 10.

Source: Adapted from "Newsman Faces Tamper Charge," *Computerworld*, February 13, 1989, p. 4; and from "TV News Execs Ousted After Hacking Charges from Rival," *Computerworld*, March 20, 1989, p. 16. Used by permission.

Espionage is primarily an external threat. However, a competitor may also gain access to sensitive data by collusion with an employee. Illustration 15–3 contains a description of how a company used data gained from espionage for competitive advantage. In this case, inadequate access controls allowed the crime to occur.

Invasion of Privacy.   Computerized data files contain much personal information about individuals. Disclosure of this information is an invasion of privacy. For example, many employees object to release of data concerning their pay rates, ages, pension records, or home addresses. Customers expect confidentiality concerning current balances, credit ratings, and payment histories. In the United States, laws protect individuals from release of personal information contained in data files. These laws require organizations to maintain adequate security for personal data.[1]

Threats to privacy come from hackers and from employees. Hackers enjoy examining the contents of computer files simply to learn about other people or to demonstrate their ability to bypass data security. Employees may gain unauthorized access to pay rates, for example, when dissatisfied with their own pay.

Employee Fraud.   Fraud is the risk that affects the accuracy of the accounting records. Frauds result in misstatements of assets and expenses in the financial statements. Major frauds also endanger the ability of an organization to continue its operations. Many

---

[1]In the United States, the Privacy Act of 1974 and several state statutes establish these requirements for federal, state, and local governments and for regulated industries. For a discussion of their provisions, see W. Thomas Porter and William E. Perry, *EDP Controls and Auditing*, 5th ed. (Boston: Kent Publishing Co., 1987), p. 188.

ILLUSTRATION 15–4

An Example of Fraud

Samuel Stanford didn't worry too much about getting caught by his fellow employees. "Most people just don't want to know much about computers," he said in a deposition to investigators. "When they saw that I was doing something, they would just turn and leave. They would say 'That turkey, that technician, all he ever does is talk his buzz words . . .we can't talk to him.'" So Stanford was left alone to steal from the State of Washington.

Stanford was the employee who developed the software through which Washington's Division of Vocational Rehabilitation authorized payments to injured loggers and others requiring retraining. One-armed since a childhood accident, he was an expert programmer and was trusted even more because of his handicap. He used the system to authorize payments of nearly $17,000 to himself and two friends. Using the computer he prepared records that the state required to issue the payments. Following their issue, he erased the records. He also capitalized on people's tendency to ignore small computer errors—he had the computer make out checks to Samuel Tanford. No bank ever questioned the missing S in his last name.

He was arrested after the daughter of one of his friends tipped police to the crime. A search of the paper records turned up the name Tanford, and the searcher recognized Stanford's address. He eventually pleaded guilty.

Stanford claimed he never kept a dime for himself, but rather gave the money to friends who were down on their luck. He called himself the "one-armed bandit" and liked to think of himself as Robin Hood. The judge didn't accept this view of the crime and sentenced Stanford to 10 years in prison.

Source: Adapted from "Computers Turn Out to Be Valuable Aid in Employee Crime." Reprinted by permission of *The Wall Street Journal*, Dow Jones & Company, Inc., 1985. All rights reserved.

control policies and procedures protect against fraud by lower-level employees. Employees at a managerial level, however, may be in a position to override these controls. And when employees collude with other people, either internal or external to the organization, controls may fail to prevent or detect fraud.

The case history in Illustration 15–4 shows how an employee bypassed controls to commit fraud. Illustration 15–5 summarizes the most common types of employee fraud.

The Fraud Triangle
Perpetrators of the biggest frauds are usually highly trusted employees in their companies. These are the people who have the opportunity to commit long-running crimes without detection. The circumstances that motivate a person to commit fraud against an employer are known as the ***fraud triangle.*** It consists of pressure, rationalization, and opportunity. Illustration 15–6 shows the circumstances that make up the fraud triangle.

Pressure.   Usually individuals commit fraud as a result of some form of pressure. Most often the pressure is financial—the criminal wants the money for personal purposes. Frequently employees need the money to support illegal drug or gambling habits or use it to compensate for outside business or investment losses. Sometimes the pressure may be job related. Often managers feel pressure to produce improved financial results in order to earn bonuses, increase stock prices, or keep their jobs. This motivates them to report fraudulent accounting information.

Rationalization.   The second factor in the fraud triangle is rationalization. Individuals who perceive themselves as honest may engage in criminal behavior because they rationalize their actions. They convince themselves that they are justified in committing the fraud.

ILLUSTRATION 15–5

The Most Common Employee Frauds

Type of Fraud	Examples
Theft of cash	Stealing checks, cash receipts, petty cash Altering bank deposits Forgery Using company checks to pay personal bills
Billing fraud	Sending fictitious or overstated invoices and intercepting the resulting payments Lapping of accounts receivable
Theft of inventory	Stealing goods in transit or those in poorly controlled conditions
Purchasing fraud	Kickbacks from suppliers Purchases from nonexistent suppliers Paying excessive prices Fixing competitive bids
Kiting of funds	Using cash transfers between banks to conceal a shortage of cash
Misuse of company resources	Using company credit cards or purchase orders for personal purchases Using company equipment for personal purposes Unauthorized sale of assets
Payroll crimes	Cashing unused paychecks Overstating hours worked Issuing paychecks to fictitious employees

Source: Adapted from W. Steve Albrecht, Gerald W. Wernz, and Timothy L. Williams, *Fraud Bringing Light to the Dark Side of Business* (Burr Ridge, Ill.: Irwin Professional Publishing, 1995), p. 13.

Employees who steal cash commonly rationalize their actions by intending to repay the money later. Thus they insist that they are not really stealing but only borrowing. Sometimes they believe that they have been wronged in some way by the employer and fraud is a way of getting even. Employees sometimes justify thefts by rationalizing that

ILLUSTRATION 15–6

The Fraud Triangle

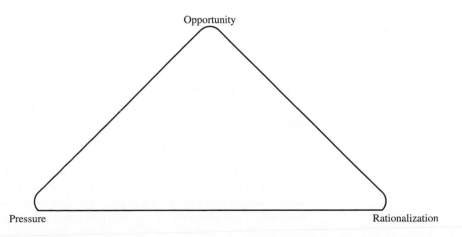

"everyone else does it, so why shouldn't I." A manager may rationalize reporting fraudulent accounting information by saying that the action is in the best interests of the company and its employees.

Opportunity.   An employee who commits fraud must be in a position that provides the opportunity. Usually the employee has custody of an asset or has authority to initiate transactions in an asset. For example, to steal inventory or equipment, one must have access to them; to issue a fraudulent check, one must have authority to begin check preparation procedures. If a manager wants to issue fraudulent accounting reports, the manager must have authority to make fraudulent entries in the general ledger.

A good system of internal control limits the opportunities to commit fraud. When an organization has proper segregation of duties, it separates custody, recordkeeping, and authorization of transactions in an asset. Thus, if an employee commits a fraud, another employee is in a position to discover it. However, even good systems are limited by the possibilities of collusion or management override of controls.

Whenever employee fraud occurs, the three circumstances of the fraud triangle are present. The employee must have an opportunity, must feel pressure from some source to commit the crime, and must be able to rationalize the behavior. Management can prevent many employee frauds by recognizing when these circumstances occur for its employees.

Just as recognizing the fraud triangle aids in *preventing* frauds, knowing the components of any fraud aids in *detecting* them.

Components of a Fraud

The most common employee frauds consist of three acts: theft of assets, conversion of those assets, and concealment of the theft.

Theft.   An organization entrusts its employees with its assets so they can perform their duties. A fraud begins when someone steals assets. This causes the overstatement of asset accounts in the accounting records.

Because of its liquidity, the most desirable asset to a thief is currency. Most organizations implement controls making a theft of currency difficult to commit and conceal. Therefore, most frauds involve stealing other assets such as checks, inventory, or equipment. These require a second fraudulent act, conversion of the assets.

Conversion.   When a criminal steals an asset other than currency, usually the asset itself is not valuable to the criminal. So the criminal attempts to convert the asset into currency. This occurs, for example, when a thief sells stolen inventory or equipment or cashes a stolen check.

Conversion does not affect the accuracy of the accounting records, but it does provide opportunities to detect a theft. Furthermore, making conversion difficult is an effective way to discourage theft.

Concealment.   A thief who has an ongoing relationship with an organization, such as an employee or business contact, usually attempts to conceal the theft. This either prevents or delays recognition of it or prevents identification of the thief. Concealment provides additional opportunities to steal and can result in an ongoing fraud.

To conceal a theft, the criminal must alter the records concerning the stolen asset. For example, if inventory is stolen, the thief must alter the inventory records. Otherwise, an auditor or supervisor could discover the theft when performing a routine inventory count. Alterations to the records require fraudulent accounting entries that produce misstated account balances. They require that the thief bypass those system controls limiting access to data.

One well-known type of fraud is a ***lapping fraud.*** It occurs in companies lacking adequate segregation of duties over accounts receivable. In a lapping fraud, an accounts receivable clerk intercepts and steals a check mailed by a customer in payment of the customer's account. Conversion occurs when the clerk endorses the check and cashes it. Because the customer's account is not credited for the payment, the customer would eventually complain, causing a supervisor to discover the theft. So to conceal the theft, the clerk intercepts a later check from a second customer and credits it to the first customer's account. To conceal the second theft, the clerk must intercept a third check and credit it to the second customer's account. This requires a third false credit, followed by a fourth one, and so on. The clerk must continue to intercept payments and make false entries to conceal the theft.

Lapping may be prevented by separating responsibilities for handling cash receipts from those for maintaining accounts receivable records. Firms that mail monthly statements enable their customers to detect lapping.

Fraud Detection

Any fraud requires three acts: theft, conversion, and concealment. Each act provides an opportunity to detect the fraud. Accountants may detect one when performing their routine duties, or auditors may detect fraud while conducting an audit.

Detecting Theft.   Accountants detect thefts by periodically reconciling asset records with assets on hand. If records indicate that assets are missing, the accountant alerts management at least one level higher than the employee responsible for the assets. For example, accountants and auditors routinely reconcile bank accounts, count the physical inventory, and verify property and equipment records to detect theft.

Detecting Conversion.   *Conversion* occurs when a thief converts a stolen asset into currency. Many forms of asset conversion are difficult to detect from within the organization. The sale of stolen inventory or equipment, for example, is more likely to be detected by the police than by accountants. In their audits of cash disbursements, however, auditors perform procedures to uncover fraudulent check endorsements. These disclose the conversion of stolen or fraudulent checks into currency.

Detecting Concealment.   Accountants and auditors use their understanding of the accounting system to detect the ***concealment*** of a theft. To conceal a theft, the criminal must record an entry that keeps the recorded assets equal to the actual assets on hand. Because assets have been taken, the thief must make a fraudulent credit entry to an asset account. For example, to conceal a theft of inventory, an employee must make a credit entry to an inventory account.

At the same time, a double-entry accounting system requires that the thief falsify a debit entry. Commonly thieves conceal a theft by debiting an expense account such as bad debts expense or miscellaneous expense. As an alternative, they may debit an asset account that is less carefully controlled than that of the asset stolen. For example, the thief may make a debit entry in a goodwill or prepaid asset account. Accountants or auditors discover the theft by identifying the fraudulent debit entry.

Experienced accountants learn the most likely ways to commit and conceal frauds in transaction processing applications, and they establish control procedures to detect these schemes. Auditors develop audit procedures to detect material frauds. If accountants and auditors lack this experience, management may engage a *forensic accountant* as a consultant. This accountant's specialty is detecting fraud.[2] Many organizations also hire a *data security officer*, whose primary responsibility is maintaining adequate data security and integrity.

The next section discusses security and integrity risks associated with database management systems.

Security and Integrity with a DBMS

A database management system (DBMS) is a systems software package that maintains centralized control over an organization's database. When a DBMS is used, effectiveness of procedures to ensure data security and integrity depends primarily on database controls implemented by the database administrator (DBA).

Risks with a DBMS

Because data administration is centralized with the DBA, use of a DBMS ordinarily results in greater reliability of data than in a traditional data file system. This centralized control reduces the risk of fraud and error. Inconsistencies in data are eliminated because each data item occurs only once with a DBMS, whereas in a traditional data file system it may occur in several different files. Also, DBMS packages normally incorporate many features that protect data from improper access or corruption. These include routing procedures for backup, recovery, data validation, and password verification. DBMS report generation features aid in creating control reports, and DBMS query languages enable users to identify and correct errors in the data.

However, if the DBA fails to implement properly the control features of the DBMS, then risk of fraud or error may be increased. In a traditional data file system, strengths in application controls may compensate for weaknesses in general controls. With an inadequately controlled DBMS, this may not be the case. For example, the controls in an accounts receivable application will not safeguard accounts receivable data if other applications are allowed to modify the data in the database.

Controls with a DBMS

A DBMS improves data security and integrity when the DBA properly implements its control features. Critical control features in DBMS are in four areas: segregation of duties, database access, procedures for system and program changes, and data ownership.

Organization of the Data Center.   Good segregation of duties requires that the chief information officer structure the data center to separate the design, implementation, and

---

[2]Many forensic accountants earn a professional designation as a *certified fraud examiner.* Students may obtain information about the CFE program from the National Association of Certified Fraud Examiners, 716 West Avenue, Austin, Texas 78701.

ILLUSTRATION 15–7

Tips for Using Passwords

Password Don'ts
- Don't write down or tell others your password.
- Don't select a commonly used password.
  Examples: Two of the most common passwords are PASSWORD and FOOTBALL.
- Don't use your name or the name of someone close to you.
  Examples: Avoid using the name of a relative, a close friend, or a pet.
- Don't use a word related to your occupation or field of study.
  Examples: Avoid using ACCOUNTANT, UNIVERSITY, LAW.
- Don't use a date that can easily be associated with you.
  Examples: Avoid using your birthday, wedding anniversary, or a date such as DEC25.

Password Dos
- Do change your password often.
- Do use an acronym for an easy-to-remember phrase.
  Example: ASITS9 stands for "A stitch in time saves nine."
- Do combine two or more words to form a password.
  Examples: NICEGIRL or BIGDUDE.
- Do add a punctuation mark or number to a password.
  Examples: WE-WON! or I'MNO1!.

operation functions. To maintain adequate security and integrity, responsibility for maintaining programs must be separate from responsibility for accessing and updating the database. Normally, user personnel have ability to read and modify data, and MIS personnel lack this ability. Sometimes a DBA creates a separate test database for the use of MIS personnel when developing computer programs. MIS personnel have access to application source programs, and user personnel lack such access. This organization implements segregation of duties over the data with a DBMS.

Database Access.   Passwords limit database access to persons authorized by the DBA. With a DBMS, separate passwords should be required to access the system through a terminal, to execute a program, and to access specific records in the database. The DBA must implement adequate procedures for assigning and changing passwords, maintaining their secrecy, and investigating repeated attempts to guess passwords and gain unauthorized access to data. Users must assume responsibility for proper control of passwords. Illustration 15–7 summarizes some good and bad procedures for using passwords.

Procedures for System and Program Changes.   With a DBMS, the same data are used by many users. This increases the significance of the need to have standard procedures for changing programs and application systems. Consistently applying appropriate procedures may prevent changes to an application or program that may create fraudulent or erroneous data. In a traditional data file system, such a change affects only one application. With a DBMS, it may affect the users of many different applications.

Data Ownership.   With a traditional data file system, where the data of an application system are typically modified by one or a few employees of the organization, these users become "owners" of the data. With a DBMS, where many users access and modify data, the DBA must assign data ownership for each data item. The owner of a data item is responsible for deciding who can use the data and what kind of functions they can perform on it. This fixes responsibility for the security and integrity of the data item. For example, the DBA designates a credit manager as the "owner" of each customer's credit limit. The credit manager may give sales personnel the authority to read a customer's credit limit but not to change it.

Security and Integrity in Computer Networks

In a computer network, computers transfer data and instructions across data communications links. The links may be wire, cable, or satellites. The network configuration may be a teleprocessing system with on-line terminals and workstations or a distributed system such as a local area network or wide area network. Each creates risks for data security and integrity.

Risks in Teleprocessing Systems

Organizations frequently use teleprocessing networks as a way of implementing on-line real-time (OLRT) systems. Users at terminals and workstations enter data, and a computer at another location processes that data. OLRT processing improves data integrity over batch processing but creates risks for data security.

The risk of errors decreases whenever on-line data entry occurs at or near the point where the transaction originates. With OLRT data entry, the person entering the data is more likely to understand the purpose of the transaction and is thus less likely to make an error. Furthermore, the transaction is more likely to be recorded in the proper accounting period. These characteristics improve the integrity of data.

For example, errors are less likely in a point-of-sale data entry system than in a batch processing one. In a typical batch system, a sales clerk writes data on a sales order form that is later keyed into the computer by a data entry clerk. This makes possible four errors: The data may be recorded incorrectly twice, the transaction may be incorrectly entered in a later accounting period, and the form itself may be lost.

In a well-designed OLRT system the entry of incorrect data is detected immediately by the data entry program, and the user entering the data must correct the data before it is accepted. In a batch system, the entry of incorrect data is detected later by a validation program that is processing an entire batch of transactions, and there is a greater risk that the error won't be corrected, or that it will be corrected in a later accounting period.

OLRT systems increase security risks when compared to batch processing systems. When many on-line terminals are scattered throughout the organization, the opportunity is greater for unauthorized access to the system. This increases the risks of improper modifications to data and programs. Interruptions to telecommunications may result in lost transactions that cannot be recovered. Because many OLRT systems produce highly summarized totals without paper documentation for transactions, a poorer audit trail may exist than in a batch environment.

Risks in Distributed Systems

A distributed system transfers data in much larger quantities and at much higher rates than a teleprocessing network. Thus the potential magnitude of the risks is much greater. Distributed systems contain four major distinguishing risks.

First, unauthorized users may use a connected processor to circumvent the access controls of a networked computer. Hackers, unauthorized users who exploit the telephone dial-up capabilities of many computers, receive much attention in the press. But authorized users also have the ability to attempt unauthorized access using permanent communication links. Second, unauthorized users may attempt to intercept data during its transmission across a communications link. Encryption of that data before transmission deters this kind of crime. Third, the network may lose data during transfer due to damage or a loss of connection in the link. Backup copies of data allow recovery from this risk. And fourth, remote processors may lack the integrity safeguards, such as validation procedures, associated with a centralized system. Data from such a remote computer could harm data integrity on a well-controlled computer in the same network.

General controls over the network should ensure that all changes to computer records are from authorized sources that maintain data integrity themselves.

General Controls in a Computer Network

Any network control procedure normally affects many applications, so accountants usually consider such procedures general controls. Useful network control procedures include encryption, firewalls, a network control log, automatic disconnect, automatic callback, and the use of change control software.

Data Encryption.   When the contents of data records are especially sensitive, management may conclude that data encryption is worthwhile. With *encryption*, a computer program encodes, or "encrypts" data—that is, it translates data into a code from its original form in a language such as English. To read the data, a user must know how to use the encryption program in order to decode the data.

Encryption may be appropriate, for example, with data subject to privacy restrictions, such as salaries, criminal records, and personnel evaluations. Or it may be desirable for data that might be the object of espionage, such as competitive or military data. Some organizations also encrypt the source language versions of computer programs in order to prevent their theft.

When management decides to use encryption, it chooses from either private key or public key methods.

Private Key Encryption.   This approach uses a single specified data field, the *encryption key*. To encode data, a user must provide the encryption program with this code. The program uses the encryption key to translate from plain text into encoded text. If at a later time other users wish to read the data in plain text form, they again input the key to the program. The encryption program uses this key to decode the data before making it available.

Private key encryption requires that all users of the data, both those modifying it and those reading it, know the key. Because knowing the key provides access to the data, users must keep private their knowledge of the key. For this reason, those who use this method call it "private key encryption."

Public Key Encryption.   This form of encryption uses two types of encryption keys, one to encode the data and another type to decode it. The data security officer selects an encryption key and distributes its contents to all potential users of the data. Because it is known to all users, it is the "public key." When a user wishes to encode data, the user provides the public key to the encryption program.

The data security officer also assigns to each user a unique encryption key, the "private key." The private key is known only to the officer and to that user. That user must input this secret code to the encryption program when decoding encrypted data.

Public key encryption methods provide better security over data in two ways. First, with them, the computer program identifies the specific user from the user's private key and then uses other techniques (such as a password) to verify this user's identity. Such a verification procedure is impossible with private key encryption. Second, public key methods require less stringent controls over the public key. Even if unauthorized users gain access to the public key, they cannot use it to decode encrypted data. With private key encryption, if the key becomes known to an unauthorized user, this person can decode the data, and the key must be changed. This requires notifying all users of the new key while keeping it secret, which is time consuming and difficult.

Illustration 15–8 shows how the two encryption methods work when used across a communications link.

Firewalls.   A *firewall* is a combination of hardware and software that restricts access to an organization's computer network. Managers implement a firewall whenever they want to prevent access by unauthorized people, such as hackers. Often the firewall controls access to the network by outsiders—for example, by telephone dial-up or via the Internet. It prevents hackers and other intruders from entering the system by one of these routes in order to steal, alter, or destroy data.

Sometimes organizations use firewalls *within* a network to restrict access to certain applications. For example, a company that considers its research and development (R&D) database especially valuable may use a firewall to prevent access to this database (and the applications using it) by non-R&D personnel within the company.

Network Control Log.   A network control log is a computer file used to list all messages transferred to or from a computer. It contains the time, date, initiating party, and receiving party of any message. The network control log provides an audit trail of all network activity and is useful in identifying sources of errors or unauthorized access to the computer's operating system.

Automatic Disconnect.   Many networked computers rely on security software that implements an automatic disconnect feature. Whenever a remote user attempts to access the system or a data file, whether through telephone lines or a permanent connection, the software allows only a limited number of attempts. Frequently this software is configured so that after three unsuccessful attempts to provide a valid password, the software automatically disconnects the connection with the user. Thus, unauthorized users have difficulty programming computers to guess passwords.

Automatic Callback.   Some system software implements a feature known as automatic callback. When a remote user gains access to the computer, the software immediately disconnects the connection. It then determines the location where that user should be from its system files, calls the user back at that location, and reconnects with the user. This prevents an unauthorized person from exploiting an authorized user's identification

ILLUSTRATION 15–8

Private Key and Public Key Encryption

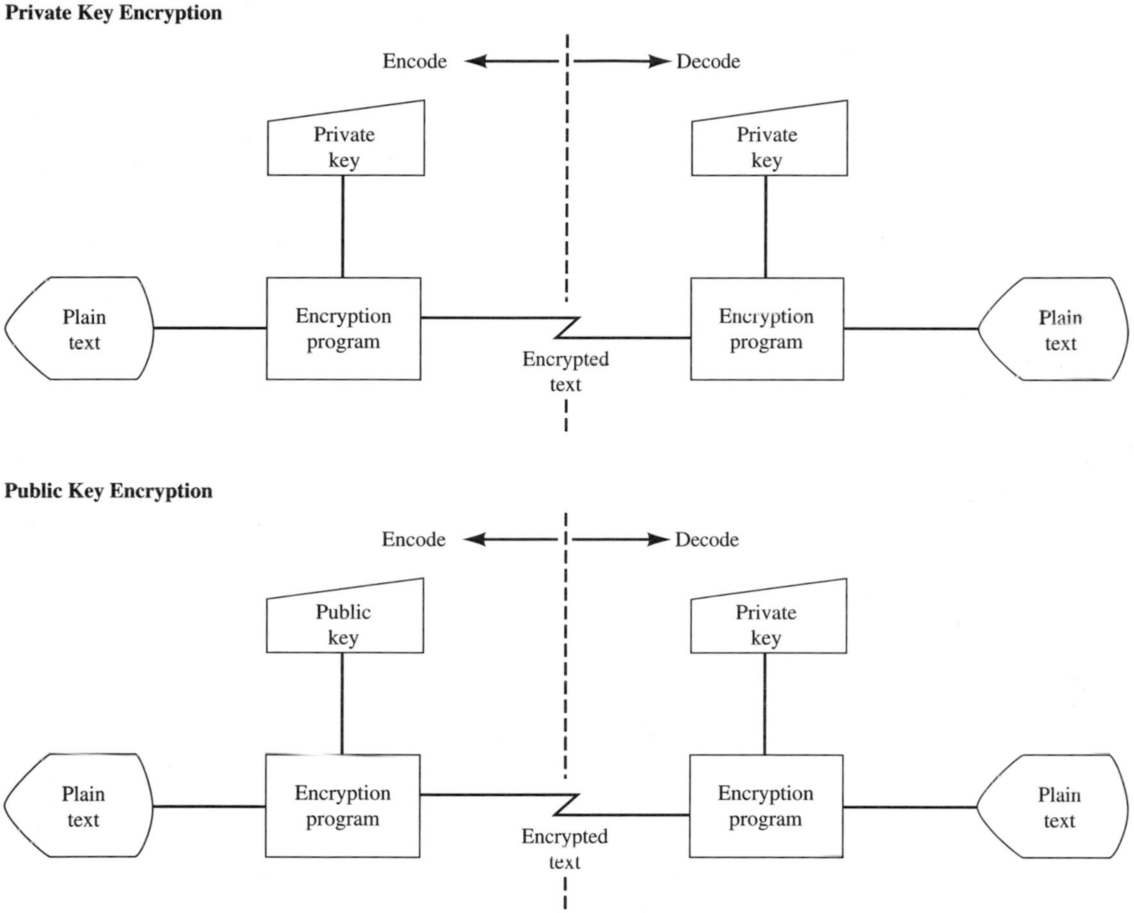

Private Key Encryption

Encode ← | → Decode

Private key — Encryption program — Private key

Plain text — Encryption program — Encrypted text — Encryption program — Plain text

Public Key Encryption

Encode ← | → Decode

Public key — Encryption program — Private key

Plain text — Encryption program — Encrypted text — Encryption program — Plain text

and password. Automatic callback is an effective way to prevent unauthorized telephone access by hackers.

Change Control Software.   This type of system software makes a record in a special change control file whenever users access data or programs. It prints periodic reports from the file showing which data or programs were accessed and by whom. The report provides an audit trail showing the source of changes. The data security officer is responsible for periodically reviewing this report to verify that access was proper and that changes to data or programs are from authorized sources.

The preceding section discusses general controls in computer networks. Certain controls are also important for network applications in order to maintain data security and integrity.

Applications Controls in Computer Networks

Procedures should be implemented in each application to ensure that persons initiating a transaction are authorized to do so, and that the proper master record data will be accessed. A program controlling data entry should perform edit checks on the data before posting it to a master record. This program requires users to correct obvious errors.

Data update procedures change balance data (such as amounts and quantities); data maintenance procedures change reference data (e.g., changes to customer names, adding or deleting records). The procedures for maintaining data records should be different from those for updating the records. Incorrect file or database maintenance changes may result in errors that are difficult to correct, so these changes require more stringent applications control procedures.

Frequently file maintenance utilizes *closed-loop verification*. With these procedures, the data entry program accepts input from the workstation operator, displays the input, and requires that the operator verify its validity. This provides additional assurance that data are entered correctly.

On-line data entry programs should maintain control totals over transactions entered at each workstation during a preselected time period. A computer program or individual should compare these totals to the total changes made to the balance data over the same period.

Automatic teller machines (ATMs) used by the banking industry illustrate effective use of these applications controls. ATMs require that a user both have a card and know a secret code to authorize a transaction and to access a customer's account data. If the customer enters the secret code incorrectly, the ATM allows only a limited number of repeated attempts. Many ATM terminals are designed to allow the entry of only numeric data, preventing the erroneous entry of alphabetic characters. During normal operation the machine calculates a control total of each type of transaction, which a bank clerk reconciles with total changes to the bank's cash balance whenever the ATM is replenished with currency. A customer cannot create an account or make changes to the customer's name, address, or account number through the ATM. The customer does these separately with the help of a bank employee.

Controlling Electronic Data Interchange

In networks using electronic data interchange (EDI), most of the control procedures described above are appropriate. However, because of the elimination of paper documents with EDI, additional procedures may be cost-effective.

With EDI, many traditional control procedures become obsolete. Prenumbering and accounting for documents no longer prevent and detect unauthorized transactions, as in older systems. Procedures to ensure prompt processing of incoming documents have no affect on EDI transactions. Different control procedures must accomplish these objectives.

EDI systems rely on access controls to ensure that all transactions are properly authorized. A data security officer assigns passwords so that only those employees authorized to initiate a specific type of EDI transaction can execute the required software. For example, only purchasing agents know the passwords that allow execution of EDI programs that generate electronic requests for purchases.

To ensure prompt processing of transactions, EDI systems collect incoming electronic transactions in computer files. Authorized users, using proper passwords, access

AIS in Practice

Experian Corporation, formerly known as TRW Credit Systems, disconnected its extranet on Friday, August 15, after two days of use. Experian had decided to let consumers access its Internet Web site to check their credit ratings. Unfortunately, it showed each consumer's credit report to a different consumer. The report of a man in California went to a man in Massachusetts, his went to a man in New York, that one to Maryland, and so on.

Experian had established a firewall to keep out hackers, extra verification to prevent a person from ordering some-

one else's credit report, and encryption to keep data communication secure. As far as Experian could determine, these controls worked properly. But network technicians did not anticipate the heavy demand for information—over 2,000 requests in the first few hours. That quantity was much greater than that for which the system had been tested, and it failed under actual operating conditions.

Fortunately, Experian personnel were monitoring the site. They shut it down after only 213 reports were misdirected.

these files and initiate processing of EDI transactions using accounting application system software. To provide an audit trail, software produces listings of EDI transactions for review by accounting personnel.

EDI software records control data, such as control totals and record counts, in the header and trailer records used when transferring EDI transactions. These control data enable the EDI translation software to determine if data have been accidentally lost or altered on the communications link.

Controlling Intranets and Extranets

An intranet is a private network established by an organization that behaves like an internal Internet. Many companies establish intranets as a means of internal communication. People use a personal computer with Web browser software to read information provided on an intranet web server. Users download data or send data to the intranet server just as they can on the World Wide Web. When users outside the company have access to an intranet by using the Internet, the network is an *extranet.*

Risks with an Extranet.   Intranets and extranets use Internet technology for communication. Their ease of use also creates risks that do not exist with other forms of computer networks.

First, messages using this technology lack reliable assurance about their origin. When you receive a message over the Internet, you rely on the sender's identification within the message. If the sender chooses to falsify identity, you have no way of detecting the deception.

Second, an unknown or incorrectly identified sender may falsify the contents of a message without detection. If applications on your intranet use these contents, you have incorrect data on your intranet. Because this is so easy to do, most people assume that data stored on an intranet have a low level of integrity.

Third, most Internet communication is easy to intercept by unauthorized persons. Internet communications occur when information is passed from one computer to another. At any computer along the route, someone may intercept and read the message. Thus intranets and extranets also provide a low level of security.

ILLUSTRATION 15–9

Summary of Controls with DBMSs and Computer Networks

Database Management Systems

Separate access to database from access to programs.
Effectively use passwords.
Have standard procedures for program and system changes.
Designate ownership of each data item.
Use encryption when appropriate.

Computer Networks

Design effective controls into applications.
Use firewalls as appropriate.
Keep a network control log.
Use automatic disconnect and automatic callback software.
Use change control software.
Use encryption when appropriate.
Use tunneling software and digital certificates to limit Internet access.

Controls with an Extranet.   Procedures exist for controlling the risks associated with intranets and extranets. However, these procedures make these networks more difficult to use.

Using software to encrypt Internet messages before transferring them to another computer improves their security. A good encryption method, using a long encryption key, makes it difficult for an unauthorized person to interpret a message intercepted on the Internet.

Some intranet servers require passwords before allowing user access. This improves data security and integrity by limiting access to only those users who know the password. Some companies secure their intranets from outsiders by using *tunneling software*, which consists of combinations of passwords and public key encryption.

Some companies also use *digital certificates* to authenticate users and protect intranet data. Users apply to a "certificate authority," a company in the business of issuing them, for a digital certificate. The authority sends the user a digital certificate and a public key. When the user wants to access a Web server, the server reads the user's certificate and public key (these are encoded in the browser) and checks with the certificate authority to verify the user. When approved, the server uses the public key to encrypt messages before sending them to the user.

Encryption, tunneling software, and digital certificates enable secure communication over the Internet. However, they require advance planning that makes browser software more difficult to use. Thus they eliminate a major advantage of using Internet technology for data communications.

You have seen the risks to data security and integrity in DBMSs and in computer networks, and how general and applications controls help to reduce those risks. Illustration 15–9 summarizes these controls. Auditors must evaluate controls in these systems as a part of their audits. You will now learn ways in which they can do this.

Evaluating Security and Integrity

Management relies on auditors to evaluate the security and integrity of a computer-based system. They hire internal auditors whose objectives are to review and appraise operations as a service to management. They also engage independent auditors to evaluate the fairness of the financial statements. Each auditor is responsible for evaluating data security and integrity and reporting weaknesses to management. Auditors sometimes refer to these activities as *information system auditing* or *EDP auditing* (a term used when information systems were still called *electronic data processing systems*).

Auditors' Responsibilities

Management is responsible for establishing policies, practices, and procedures that provide adequate data security. Auditors review these policies, practices, and procedures in conjunction with the evaluation of other internal controls.

Internal Auditors.   Internal auditors evaluate computer security during their reviews of operating departments. They identify security risks and report them to management in the reports containing their recommendations. They may also recommend methods of improving data security; however, whether or not management implements these recommendations depends on management's evaluation of their costs and benefits. Internal auditors fulfill their responsibility to management by communicating risks to them.

Independent Auditors.   Independent auditors also evaluate computer security while studying and evaluating internal control. They provide recommendations to management in the form of a management letter. In this letter they describe, as a service to management, security and other control weaknesses observed during the audit. The responsibility of independent auditors extends beyond this advisory one, however; they use their evaluation of internal control as a basis for determining which procedures are necessary in their audit.

Weaknesses in data security increase the risk that errors and irregularities may cause material misstatements in the financial statements. Generally accepted auditing standards require that independent auditors assess the risk of material misstatement of financial statements due to fraud and consider altering audit procedures when fraud is found. They must also document in their working papers the actions they take. By creating additional risks, weaknesses in data security affect the scope of the independent audit.

The methods used by auditors to evaluate security and integrity include reviews and tests of controls. When testing controls, auditors frequently implement computer-assisted audit techniques.

System Reviews

Auditors conduct periodic reviews of computer-based accounting systems to gain an understanding of the accounting system prior to conducting tests of controls. These reviews also allow auditors to evaluate certain controls, such as segregation of duties, that are not documented by the system's records. Independent auditors conduct reviews as a part of their annual audit. Internal auditors review systems when they examine the data center, or as a part of examinations of departments that use the information system.

Methods of Conducting Reviews.   A system *review* is a survey of those activities in a department that the auditors consider important. The accounting system and internal controls primarily concern the independent auditors. In addition to these, internal auditors evaluate the efficiency and effectiveness of the department. They use three methods in conducting reviews: interviews, walk-throughs, and questionnaires.

Interviews.   An auditor begins the review of a department by first interviewing the manager of the department. The purpose of this interview is to meet the manager, gain an overview of the functions of the department, and gain the manager's support for the auditor's other activities during the review. An auditor then interviews other employees to understand their functions in the department. While conducting interviews, the auditor takes notes on the discussions. Later the auditor may refer to these notes when developing flowcharts of the system.

Interviews are valuable during a review because they allow the auditor to request the specific information needed. They also provide an opportunity for the auditor to gain the confidence of client personnel. This helps to establish a good working relationship and may make later audit tests easier. Interviews are difficult to conduct, however, and require practice. Another method sometimes used in conjunction with interviews is the walk-through.

Walk-Throughs.   In a walk-through, an auditor traces a transaction through the department from the time it enters until the time it leaves or is recorded in a journal or ledger. This gives the auditor an understanding of the sequence of activities performed in the department.

Many auditors prefer to conduct interviews during the walk-through. When the auditor identifies the next step in the sequence of activities, a person supervising or performing that step becomes the next person to interview. At the conclusion of a walk-through, the auditor draws flowcharts documenting the flow of transactions.

Walk-throughs are beneficial in small departments or with small clients where they can be conducted in a reasonable length of time. They allow the auditor to obtain evidence by direct observation of how the client functions. The operations of large clients may be so widespread or diverse that a walk-through for certain kinds of transactions is impractical. Also, in highly computerized systems there may be no visible evidence of how transactions are processed. In these situations, walk-throughs are impossible.

When a purpose of the review is to evaluate internal control, auditors use questionnaires to guide them in conducting interviews and walk-throughs.

Questionnaires.   An internal control questionnaire is a set of questions developed from a list of desirable control practices, policies, and procedures. Auditors use such a questionnaire in reviews of both general controls and application controls.

An experienced auditor develops the questionnaire to ensure that it contains all important controls. A less experienced auditor then determines answers to each question during the review. Questions are worded so that a *no* answer indicates a weakness in internal control. In this way, the questionnaire clearly identifies control weaknesses.

Use of an internal control questionnaire guides the auditor in conducting the review, ensures that a complete review is performed, and documents its results. It allows a less

ILLUSTRATION 15–10

Summary of Methods Used in Reviews

Interviews. To acquaint employees with the purpose of the review and to learn the function of each job
    position.
Walk-throughs. To learn the sequence of the activities performed in the department.
Questionnaires. To identify internal control weaknesses in the department.

experienced auditor to benefit from the knowledge of a more experienced one. In this
way, a less experienced auditor can perform the review. However, a thorough questionnaire is difficult to develop. If it is developed inadequately, the reviews performed using
it will be inadequate. Furthermore, some users may learn that *yes* answers are more
desirable and may answer affirmatively without seriously considering the question.
Illustration 15–10 summarizes the methods used in conducting reviews.

Reviews of General Controls.   General controls are those practices, policies, and procedures that affect all application systems. A review of general controls emphasizes the
organization and operation of the data center. Auditors examine evidence for proper segregation of duties, adequate access controls over data files and equipment, routine
backup of data files, and the existence of a contingency plan.

 Weaknesses in general controls, considered alone, may not concern the auditor. A
strength in applications controls may, in certain circumstances, compensate for a general
controls weakness. For this reason, auditors also review applications controls.

Reviews of Applications Controls.   Applications controls are the control practices,
policies, and procedures included in specific application systems during their design.
They include input, processing, and output controls.

 Auditors conduct applications controls reviews for specific applications that are of
interest to the auditor. As examples, internal auditors may be interested in applications
that are most susceptible to fraud. Independent auditors may review those applications
that may have a material affect on the financial statements. In conducting these reviews,
they look for controls that compensate for general controls weaknesses and document
them in their working papers. They later use ***tests of controls*** to determine if these
function as intended.

 During system reviews, auditors hold interviews, conduct walk-throughs, and complete questionnaires. From these procedures, auditors document how internal control
should function within the department. However, auditors obtain little assurance from
a review that control policies are being followed or that control practices and procedures
are implemented properly. To determine these things, auditors conduct tests of controls.

Tests of Controls   Auditors perform tests of controls to determine that employees routinely follow control
policies, practices, and procedures. In the past accountants called these tests *compliance
tests,* because they show whether employees are complying with the policies, practices,
and procedures established by management. Because auditors cannot read computer
data or see computerized processes, they cannot determine whether many computerized

ILLUSTRATION 15–11

Auditors' Use of Test Data

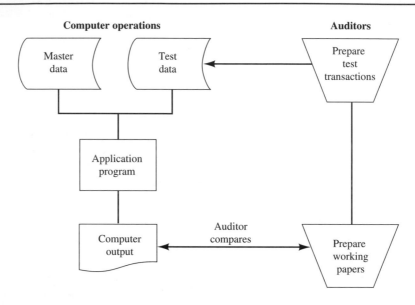

controls function properly by observing them. As a result, they use computer-assisted techniques to evaluate controls.

Auditors employ computer-assisted audit techniques (CAATs) whenever they examine on-line real-time systems. They also may use them when auditing batch processing systems because they are an efficient way to obtain reliable evidence. There are many kinds of CAATs; four that auditors use to evaluate data integrity are test data, parallel simulation, an integrated test facility, and embedded audit modules.

Test Data.   The use of ***test data*** in auditing is similar to its use in program and system testing. Auditors develop a file of simulated input transactions for the program to be tested. They also prepare working papers showing how each transaction should be processed if the program functions properly.

Auditors execute the program using these test data and examine the output. If actual output differs from that expected, auditors identify the source of the difference. This may occur because of program logic errors or because a programmed control is ineffective.

The file of test data contains both valid and invalid transactions. Auditors create an invalid transaction to test each application control procedure of interest. Such transactions should be detected by input or processing controls; if they are, auditors know that these controls function as intended. Using valid test transactions shows that the program produces desired reports accurately. Illustration 15–11 shows how the auditor uses test data.

Auditors encounter two problems when using test data. First, they must ensure that the application program they test is the one used during normal processing of accounting

ILLUSTRATION 15–12

Auditors' Use of Parallel Simulation

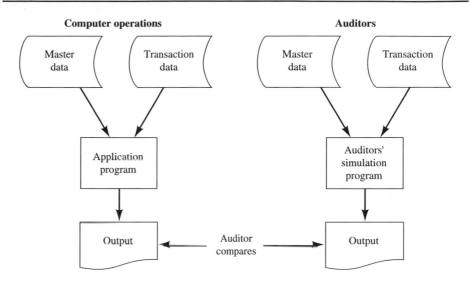

transactions. Second, the auditors must take steps to avoid recording the test transactions in the actual accounting records. Parallel simulation is a technique that lacks these problems.

Parallel Simulation.   Using *parallel simulation,* auditors write a computer program that performs the major functions of a client's application program. The auditors execute this simulation program for a representative time period using the client's data. The auditors then compare the output of the simulation program with the output produced by the client's application program during the same time period. Differences may indicate that the application program processes data erroneously.

Illustration 15–12 shows how this technique got its name. The auditor's simulation program executes in parallel to the client's application program because each uses identical transaction and master file data.

Parallel simulation allows auditors to avoid the limitations of test data; however, developing an adequate simulation program requires significant computer skills. The auditors must understand the application program and be proficient enough in a computer language to program a simulation of it. Because the auditors never test the application program directly, they obtain no assurance about how it processes erroneous or unusual transactions.

A technique that overcomes the latter disadvantage is the integrated test facility.

Integrated Test Facility.   The *integrated test facility* (ITF) is an effective technique. Although it takes other forms, most commonly it is a dummy cost center created for use by auditors. To use it, auditors first create test transactions for the controls they wish to test. They create working papers showing the expected results of processing with these test transactions; then they enter the test transactions in the application program. The program processes these transactions along with actual ones during a routine reporting period. Auditors examine the results of processing the test transactions, comparing them to the expected results. This allows the auditors to verify that the application program functions properly.

Because test transactions are processed along with real ones, auditors know that they are testing the client's production programs. And because the auditors create test transactions, they can develop both valid and invalid ones and thoroughly test application controls. If left in the data files, the test transactions would produce inaccurate information; therefore, auditors must either take steps to prevent their posting to master files, or post adjusting journal entries to eliminate them.

Because ITF entities are integrated into master files, auditors create them most efficiently during the development of the application system. Once they are developed, auditors use them routinely to provide assurance that controls function as desired. Illustration 15–13 shows how an ITF works. Auditors call the ITF a *concurrent auditing technique* because the audit test is performed at the same time as (or concurrent with) the processing of real transactions.

In large companies, the dummy cost center may be coded as a subsidiary company. In these circumstances, auditors call this the *minicompany approach.*

Embedded Audit Modules.   Using an integrated test facility requires changes to the client's master files. In contrast, embedded audit modules require changes to the client's application programs. Auditors sometimes create small programs, or modules, and include them in an application program. As the application program executes, a module performs functions of interest to the auditors. ***Embedded audit modules*** allow auditors to monitor the actions of the application program as actual transactions are processed.

Auditors use embedded audit modules for many purposes. With a technique known as *real-time notification,* the module identifies transactions of special interest and displays them at an auditor's terminal. The module may, for example, identify cash disbursements transactions intended for a vendor suspected of fraud.

In another technique, called *tagging,* the module marks a specified data field for certain transaction records. This tag identifies the transaction as one of special interest to the auditor. For example, the auditor may tag all transactions for very large amounts, or transactions in accounts subject to fraud. An audit module copies tagged transactions to a computer file or prints a report listing them for later examination by auditors.

Sometimes tagging is used in conjunction with the *snapshot* technique. The snapshot is a report showing the contents of main storage. An audit module produces this report immediately before processing a tagged transaction (called a *beforeimage*) and immediately after (producing an *afterimage*). The auditors then compare the changes produced with those expected. Auditors sometimes use the snapshot technique to identify logic errors that produce erroneous data in master files. An application program may use several snapshots; the example in Illustration 15–14 produces three of them.

ILLUSTRATION 15–13

Auditors' Use of an Integrated Test Facility

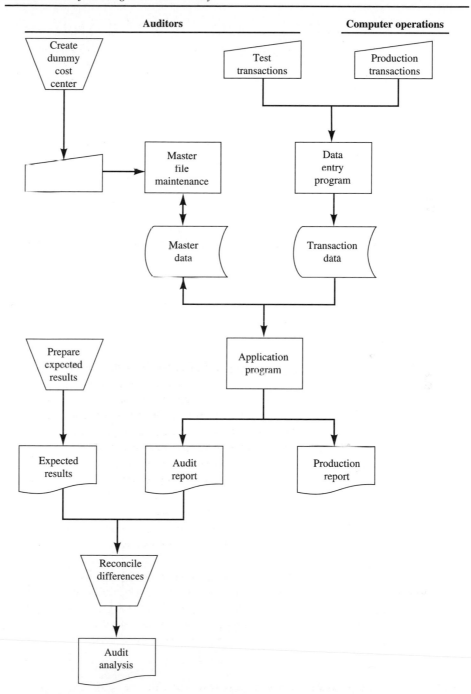

ILLUSTRATION 15–14

Auditors' Use of Snapshots

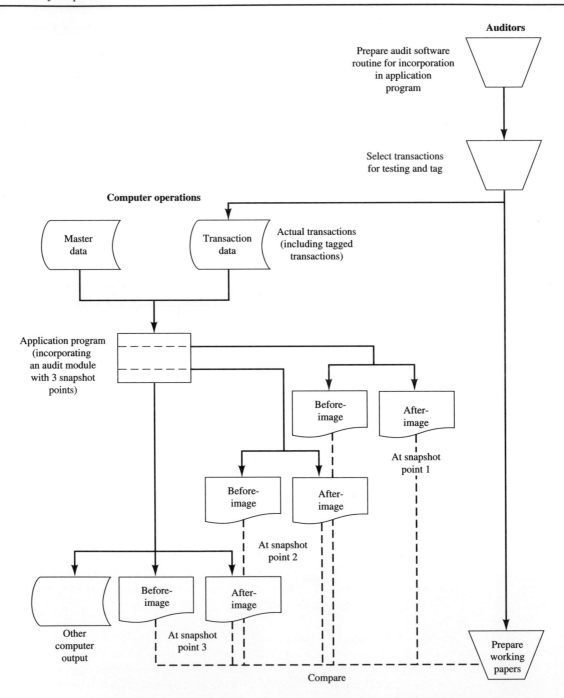

ILLUSTRATION 15–15

Applications of Computer-Assisted Audit Techniques

Technique	Audit Objective	Application Audit Test	Auditor Concludes
Test data	Auditor wants to determine if a validation program correctly calculates a check digit.	Auditor creates several transactions containing both valid and invalid account numbers, and enters them in the validation program.	Auditor concludes that the program does (or does not) calculate the check digit correctly.
Parallel simulation	Auditor wants to determine if a validation program properly performs completeness tests.	Auditor codes a program to perform the test and executes it using a client transaction file containing errors.	Auditor concludes that the program does (or does not) correctly perform the completeness test.
Integrated test facility	Auditor wants to determine if all expenditures are recorded in proper expense accounts.	Auditor creates test expenditure transactions for a dummy cost center. A data entry clerk enters them along with real transactions.	Auditor concludes that the expenditures are (or are not) recorded in the proper accounts.
Embedded audit module	Auditor wants to determine that all large dollar value paychecks are not fraudulent.	Auditor creates a module to tag all payroll transactions for more than $5,000. The module copies all such transactions into a file.	Auditor examines payroll transactions in the file and identifies questionable ones for further investigation.

Another technique sometimes used with tagged transactions is *tracing*. A trace is a computer report that describes the path followed by a transaction through the logic of an application program during execution. Utility software and some computer languages provide the ability to produce traces. Auditors use this software to record execution steps for specific transactions tagged for the purpose. This allows the auditor to identify the logic errors that produce erroneous data in an application program.

As you can see, embedded audit modules can be complex and difficult to develop. Because they require changes to application programs, auditors create them most easily during the development of the application system. When auditors attempt to detect fraud or to correct problems with existing systems, they may add audit modules to existing programs. Developing and using audit modules is expensive, and auditors require significant computer skills to use them successfully. Embedded audit modules, like integrated test facilities, are examples of concurrent auditing techniques.

Illustration 15–15 gives applications for the four computer-assisted audit techniques just discussed. Each requires auditor proficiency in computer technology and computer programming. Achieving adequate programming proficiency is easier when the auditor uses a generalized audit software package.

Generalized Audit Software

Most auditors use **generalized audit software** (GAS) during their evaluations of computer-based systems. GAS is a software package developed to aid in performing common audit tasks. GAS can be purchased from software development companies, and some large CPA firms have their own. GAS packages are different from the computer-assisted audit techniques described earlier. Auditors seldom use GAS programs to test

ILLUSTRATION 15–16

A Generalized Audit Software Specification Sheet

PARAM CODE (1)	TAG B = NONE (XXX) (2–4)	INPUT – DATA NAME FROM L: FIELD SIZE (5–7)	AREA CODE (8)	FIELD LOCATION FILL = FORMULA DERIVED FIELD (9–12)	DECIMALS (13)	DATA TYPE (14)	PRINTED OUTPUT: PRINT FIELD SIZE (NNN) B = USE I/P OR EDIT SIZE (15–17)	FIXED LOCATION: AREA (18)	PRINT POSITION B = COMPOSE TAG = ALIGN (nnn) = FIXED POS (19–22)	DECIMALS (N) (23)	EDIT CODE (24)	ROUND X = YES (25)	JUSTIFY ② (26)	CAUSE BREAK ① (27)	TOTAL FIELD (28)	DETAIL (29)	PRINT CONTROL – PRINT AT CONTROL BREAK MINOR → MAJOR (B = NO PRINT, X = PRINT, P = PRINT PRIOR, S = PRINT IF CHG): 1 (30)	2 (31)	3 (32)	4 (33)	5 (34)	6 (35)	7 (36)	MULTI-LINE CONTROL: LINE NO B = 1 (37–38)	SPACE AFT PRINT B = 1 ③ (39–40)	CONTROL (41)	COLUMN HEADINGS, LITERAL, FORMULAS & COMMENTS (42–71)	(72)	SEQUENCE NUMBER (73–80)
P	A	2	A	1										2		S		X									'REGION		REPT2Ø31
P		2	A	3										1		S	X										'WHSE		2
P		3	A	5	Ø	P				Ø	Z					X											PRODUCT'CODE		3
P		25	A	16												X											'PRODUCT DESCRIPTION		4
P	B	5	A	77	Ø	P				Ø	E					X											'QUANTITY		5
P		3	A	13												X											UNIT OF MEASURE		6
P		4	A	82	Ø	P	12			Ø	E				X	X	X	X	X								ENDING'INVENTORY		7
P		23							B								X									V	WHSE ENDING INVENTORY		8
P		23							B									X								V	REGION ENDING INVENTORY		9
P		23							B										X							V	TOTAL ENDING INVENTORY		4Ø
P		29							A										X							V	NUMBER OF ITEMS PROCESSED		1
P			U	1	Ø	N			A+3Ø	Ø	E				X		X	X	X							*	ITEM COUNT		2
P		8	U	EDT				1	1Ø																	*	RUN DATE		
P		13	U	LPG				1	11Ø																	*	PAGE		
P																													
P																													
P																													
P																													
P																													
P																													

EXAMPLES:

FORMULA — 41 42: F A = B + 3 2/6 – Determine Field A by adding 32 to field B and divide the result by 6

COULUMN HEADING — 41 42: B GROSS AMOUNT – PRINTED GROSS AMOUNT

NOTE COLUMN HEADINGS ARE SEPARATED BY ( )

AREA CODES (I/P)
Ø = A INPUT
B, C, D = INPUT AREAS
J, K, L, M = WORK AREAS
U = USER AREA
R = REFORMAT AREA

DATA TYPE
Ø = CHAR
P = PACKED
B = BINARY
N = NUMERIC ZONED

AREA CODES
Ø = NORMAL PRINT LINE AREA
1–9 = TITLE LINE AREA

EDIT CODES
Ø = NONE OR UNPACK DATA IF PACKED
E = FULL EDIT
Z = ZERO SUPRESS
D = DATE EDIT (MM/DD/YY)
S = SOC SEC

TOTAL THIS FIELD
Ø = NO TOTAL
X = TOTAL THIS FIELD
(N) =1–7 ACCUM TOTAL THRU LEVEL GIVEN

CONTROL
D = FIELD NOT PRINTED–BREAK FIELD OR USED IN FORMULA
F = COLUMNS 42–71 CONTAIN FORMULA
L =PRINTED FIELD WITH LEFT JUSTIFIED COLUMN HEADINGS
R = PRINTED FIELD WITH RIGHT JUSTIFIED COLUMN HEADINGS
Ø = PRINTED FIELD WITH NO COLUMN HEADINGS OR CENTER JUSTIFY COLUMN HEADINGS IF COLUMNS 42–71 NON-BLANK
P = PRINTED FIELD WITH COLUMNS 42–71 CONTAINING COMMENTS NOT COLUMN HEADINGS
V = PRINTED FIELD IS LITERAL CONTAINED IN COLUMNS 42–71

① BREAK
Ø = FIELD DOESN'T CAUSE CONTROL BREAK
(N) = 1–6 BREAK AT LEVEL GIVEN
LINE SPACING ON BREAKS GIVEN IN COLS 16–29 OF R PARAM

② JUSTIFY
Ø = CENTER
L = LEFT
R = RIGHT

③ SPACE AFTER CONTROLS
FOR LINES 2 & UP
01–99 = SPACE LINES
EJ = EJECT

controls; instead, they use them to mechanize the gathering of evidence. The use of GAS replaces manual operations performed by auditors with computerized operations controlled by the GAS programs.

How GAS Works. Each GAS package has its own programming language that auditors use to write programs. The software package interprets the program and from it produces instructions that are executable by the CPU. Auditors can perform most operations in the GAS language that are possible in general purpose languages.

Auditors program in the language by entering parameters on specification sheets. Each line in a specification sheet becomes one instruction in the GAS program. In this way, the specification sheet makes it easy for the auditor to encode correctly the commands required by the GAS language. An auditor then enters the instructions into a computer file that becomes an input to the GAS package. Illustration 15–16 contains a GAS specification sheet that causes the computer to print a heading for a report.

ILLUSTRATION 15–17

Functions Performed by Generalized Audit Software Programs

1. Scan computer data to
   a. Count records.
   b. Verify contents for
       Completeness.
       Arithmetic accuracy.
       Consistency.
   c. Retrieve records of significance to auditors.
   d. Summarize contents.
2. Print contents of data.
3. Select samples from data.
4. Perform arithmetic operations.
5. Compare contents of two files.
6. Sort and merge files.
7. Print reports, such as
       Aging schedules.
       Audit sample listings.
8. Print confirmations.
9. Calculate parameters for statistical samples.

What Can GAS Do?   GAS packages make it easy for auditors to perform commonly used audit functions. GAS programs access data in computer files, manipulate the data, perform calculations and comparisons, and print reports. Illustration 15–17 shows some common applications of GAS in an audit. GAS also provides an efficient way to write programs used in parallel simulation.

Advantages of GAS.   Auditors use GAS to perform many audit procedures that would be performed manually without the package. Using GAS, the computer performs the procedure faster, more thoroughly, and with greater accuracy than a person would be able to perform it. In this way, GAS increases both the efficiency and the effectiveness of the audit.

GAS also improves the auditor's independence. It allows the auditor to examine the contents of a client's data files without using the client's software. Whenever the auditor uses client programs, there is a possibility that an employee has modified them in a way unknown to the auditors. This modification could misstate accounting data or conceal a theft.

Coding in the GAS language is much quicker than writing a program in a general purpose language. Auditors can execute in 20 lines of GAS code a program that would require hundreds of lines of code in COBOL. This ease of programming allows auditors to use the computer to perform audit tests that would be too costly if done in a general purpose language.

A GAS language is also easier to learn than a general purpose language. As an auditor, you learn how to complete the dozen or so types of specification sheets used by a GAS language. Specification sheets replace rules of syntax so there are few rules to master. It is possible to learn the GAS language and how to use it during an audit in two or three weeks.

ILLUSTRATION 15–18

Advantages and Disadvantages of Using Generalized Audit Software

Advantages

1. *Speed.* With GAS, a computer performs audit procedures that would otherwise be done manually. A computer is much faster.
2. *Accuracy.* A computer performing audit procedures directed by GAS makes fewer mistakes than people performing the same procedures.
3. *Thoroughness.* Because of the speed of a computer using GAS, many more records can be examined than could be done by a person.
4. *Ease of use.* An auditor can code a program in a GAS language faster than in a general purpose language.
5. *Ease of learning.* An auditor can learn how to code in a GAS language faster than in a general purpose language.

Disadvantages

1. *Execution efficiency.* Programs written in a GAS language require more main storage and more time when executing than those in a general purpose language.
2. *Flexibility.* GAS packages are intended to perform audit procedures. Using them for other procedures, such as calculations, is awkward.
3. *Transportability.* A GAS package is intended for use on specific makes of hardware and software. For some computers, GAS is unavailable.

Disadvantages of GAS.   If GAS is quicker and easier than general purpose languages, why not always use it rather than, say, COBOL? In most cases, GAS is less efficient than a general purpose language. GAS programs require more main storage and execute more slowly, so they are not used for routine transaction processing. In most cases these limitations are unimportant to auditors.

GAS is also less flexible. Auditors have designed GAS commands to make it easy to perform common audit tasks. However, the limited variety of commands makes GAS awkward for complex procedures.

Its developers design a GAS package to execute on a specific brand of computer using a limited set of operating systems. A specific GAS package does not work on all brands of computers, and for some brands no GAS packages are available. Additionally, most GAS packages are awkward to use with database management systems.

Generalized audit software packages enable auditors to perform audit tests rapidly and thoroughly and to utilize audit techniques that would be impractical without the assistance of a computer. Modern accounting systems require the use of a computer in an audit, so you will probably encounter one of these packages sometime in your career. Illustration 15–18 summarizes the advantages and disadvantages of using generalized audit software.

Summary

An accounting system that implements good control policies, practices, and procedures maintains data security and integrity. Data security procedures safeguard assets. Data integrity procedures provide accurate and reliable accounting data.

Data security risks come from three sources and take four forms. Sources may be internal, external, or collusive. Risks include data destruction, espionage, invasion of privacy, and fraud. Fraud is the threat that both deprives the organization of assets and misstates its accounting records. Accountants must understand the sources of fraud and develop procedures to detect or prevent it.

System controls must be adapted for use with advanced technologies, such as database management systems and computer networks. Encryption may be worthwhile with very sensitive data.

Auditors use reviews and tests of controls to evaluate the data security and integrity of a computer-based system. Reviews rely on interviews, walk-throughs, and questionnaires. Tests of controls allow auditors to see how well computerized processes maintain the integrity of data. Computer-assisted audit techniques and generalized audit software aid the auditor in examining computerized processes.

Key Terms

concealment   Hiding a theft by falsifying accounting records. This causes the recorded assets to be consistent with the assets on hand and allows a fraud to continue.

conversion   Changing into cash the proceeds from the theft of inventory, checks, or equipment.

data integrity   An objective of internal control. Data have integrity when data are accurate, reliable, and safe from improper changes.

data security   An objective of internal control. Data are secure when data are safeguarded from theft or unauthorized access.

embedded audit modules   As part of client application programs, these small programs perform tasks of interest to the auditor, including real-time notification, tagging, tracing, and snapshots.

encryption   Using a secret code to translate computer records from plain text into a form that cannot be read without the code.

fraud triangle   Three circumstances that, when combined with weak integrity, lead to employee fraud. They are opportunity, pressure, and rationalization.

generalized audit software   A software package that makes it easy for auditors to perform common audit tasks on data stored in computer files.

integrated test facility   A computer-assisted audit technique. The auditor enters simulated and actual transactions for processing by client programs and verifies that these are processed properly.

lapping fraud   A fraud in which an employee steals and cashes a customer's check. To conceal the theft, the employee falsifies a credit to the customer's account by applying a subsequent payment from another customer. The clerk must continue this process to conceal the crime.

parallel simulation   A computer-assisted audit technique. The auditor processes actual client data with an auditor-written program and compares the outputs with those produced by client programs.

review   A survey in which an auditor evaluates a department's data security and integrity.

test data   A computer-assisted audit technique. The auditor creates a file of simulated data, processes it with client accounting programs, and verifies that the programs work properly.

tests of controls   Audit procedures to determine whether or not employees are complying with the control policies, practices, and procedures established by management. They are used to evaluate data security and integrity.

Questions

15–1. What are the primary sources of risks to security in organizations with
    a. Good internal control?
    b. Poor internal control?

15–2. Can you name four data security risks? Who are the sources of each of these risks?

15–3. What are three ways in which auditors detect frauds involving a computer-based system? Can you give an example of each?

15–4. What are the circumstances that make up the fraud triangle? Give an example of each.

15–5. What is the difference between data integrity and data security?

15–6. Which methods do auditors use in conducting a review? Distinguish between each.

15–7. Why do auditors use computer-assisted audit techniques when conducting tests of controls?

15–8. What are the limitations of the following computer-assisted audit techniques for auditing a computer-based accounting system?
    a. Test data.
    b. Parallel simulation.
    c. Integrated test facility.
    d. Embedded audit modules.

15–9. When are auditors likely to use embedded audit modules?

15–10. How does generalized audit software improve the effectiveness and efficiency of an audit?

15–11. Why does an auditor use generalized audit software rather than writing programs in a general purpose computer language?

15–12. What are the auditors' responsibilities for evaluating computer security?

Exercises and Cases

15–13.   *Computer-Assisted Audit Techniques*

Management has requested a special audit of the recently established electronic controls system division because the last three quarterly profit reports seem to be inconsistent with the division's cash flow. The division sells customized control systems on a contract basis. A work-in-process record is established for each contract on the work-in-process master file, a sequential file on a magnetic disk. Contract charges for material, labor, and overhead are entered in batches by terminal and processed by the work-in-process computer program to maintain the work-in-process master file and to provide billing information.

An audit review revealed that not all costs have been charged against the work-in-process records. Thus when contracts are closed, reported profits have been overstated. It is now necessary to determine the reasons for this loss of data integrity.

Required:

a. What computer-assisted audit technique would be most appropriate to evaluate the accuracy of the computer program posting transactions to the work-in-process master file?
b. How could the auditor most efficiently determine the contents of the work-in-process master file?
c. How could the auditor most effectively evaluate the overall business and systems environment of this computerized work-in-process system?

(CIA Adapted)

15–14. Threats From Employees

Federal agents recently arrested a disgruntled programmer for allegedly planting a logic bomb designed to wipe out programs and data related to the U.S. government's billion-dollar Atlas missile program.[3] Michael Laffer, 31, was arrested after a co-worker accidentally discovered the program, disarmed it, and alerted authorities.

Laffer was the principal developer of a database program used to track the availability and cost of parts used in building the missile. Allegedly he created another program, called Cleanup, that would have deleted the database program and then deleted itself without a trace. This program was set to execute at 6 P.M. on Friday of the Memorial Day weekend.

According to agents, the programmer hoped to be rehired by General Dynamics Corp., his former employer and builder of the missile, as a high-priced consultant to repair the damage. Instead, he is charged with unauthorized access to a federal-interest computer and attempted computer fraud. If convicted, he could be imprisoned for up to 10 years and fined $500,000.

Required:

What control procedures could have prevented this crime?

15–15. Computer-Assisted Audit Techniques

The following flowchart was drawn by an auditor and included in the audit working papers.

---

[3]Adapted from "Feds Arrest 'Logic Bomber,'" *Computerworld,* July 1, 1991. Used by permission.

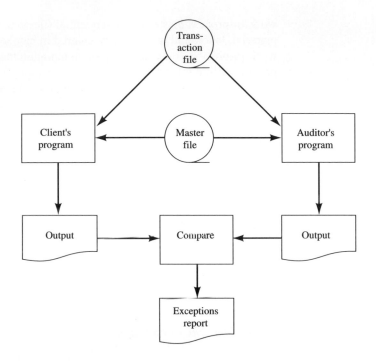

Required:

Which computer-assisted audit technique does this flowchart represent? Explain how the technique is used.

(AICPA Adapted)

15–16.   *Types of Fraud*

It is estimated that several hundred million dollars are lost annually through computer crime. Most experts maintain, however, that the number of computer crimes publicly revealed represent only the tip of the iceberg. Many companies that have been victims of crimes have not acknowledged them in order to avoid adverse publicity and not advertise their vulnerability.

Although the threat to security is seen as external, through outside penetration, the more dangerous threats are of internal origin. Management must recognize these problems and develop and enforce security programs to deal with the many types of fraud to which computer systems are susceptible.

The primary types of computer fraud include (1) input manipulation, (2) program alteration, (3) file alteration, (4) data theft, (5) sabotage, and (6) theft of computer time.

Required:

For each of the six types of fraud identified above,
a.   Explain how each is committed.
b.   Identify a different method of protecting against each type of fraud. Describe how each method operates.

(CMA Adapted)

15–17. *Test Data*

You are an auditor about to test controls in Bennett Company's computerized sales order entry system. In this system, outside salespersons take orders from customers and record them on a sales order form. Completed forms are returned to the district sales office, where data entry clerks enter each sales transaction into the system at a terminal.

From the data dictionary you obtain the following description of a sales transaction record:

Data Name	Length	Contents
Customer-number	9	Numeric
Customer-name	30	Alphanumeric
Customer-PO-number	12	Alphanumeric
Product-number	9	Numeric
Product-description	20	Alphanumeric
Quantity	5	Numeric
Unit-price	9	Numeric
Extended-amount	9	Numeric

By examining system documentation, you find that the data entry program should perform the following checks to validate the data:

1. Determines that the customer number is a valid one by calculating its check digit using the modulus 11 method (a validity test).
2. Determines that the quantity is a numeric and a positive number (a field test and a sign test).
3. Verifies that the extended amount does not exceed $10,000 (a limit or reasonableness test).
4. Verifies that the customer purchase order number is not omitted (a completeness test).

Required:

Develop a set of test data to determine if each of the preceding input controls works properly.

15–18. *Integrated Test Facility*

The internal audit department of Abacus Corp. has created an integrated test facility for evaluating certain of its accounting application systems. Abacus uses a responsibility accounting system that assigns a four-digit code to each responsibility center. The code for the internal audit department is 4210.

As an auditor, you wish to test the controls in Abacus's accounts payable system. In this system, payables clerks enter expenditure transactions in the system by creating voucher transaction records. Examining the documentation for this system, you determine that a transaction record contains the following fields:

Data Name	Length	Contents
Voucher-number	7	Numeric
Vendor-number	5	Numeric
Vendor-invoice-no	12	Alphanumeric
Vendor-invoice-date	6	Numeric
Vendor-due-date	6	Numeric
Gen-ledger-account	4	Numeric
Responsibility-code	4	Numeric
Amount	9	Numeric

A batch processing program performs the following validation procedures:

1. Determines that the voucher number is not omitted (a completeness test).
2. Determines that the vendor number is numeric (a field test).
3. Verifies that the amount of the voucher does not exceed $200,000 (a limit or reasonableness test).

Required:

a. Develop test transactions that enable you to evaluate these validation procedures using the integrated test facility.

b. Assume that the test is complete and that the validation procedures work satisfactorily. What must you do next?

15–19. *Generalized Audit Software*

Boos & Baumkirchner, Inc., is a medium-size manufacturer of products for the leisure-time activities market (camping equipment, scuba gear, bows and arrows, etc.). Boos maintains its inventory records in a sequential file stored on magnetic disk. Each record in the inventory master file contains the following information:

Item or part number.

Description.

Size.

Unit of measure code.

Quantity on hand.

Cost per unit.

Total value of inventory on hand, at cost.

Date of last sale or usage.

Quantity used or sold this year.

Economic order quantity.

Code number of major vendor.

Code number of secondary vendor.

In preparation for the year-end inventory count, Boos has prepared two identical sets of preprinted inventory count cards. One set is for Boos's counts, and the other is for the auditors' use in making audit test counts. The following information is printed on each card:

Item or part number.

Description.

Size.

Unit of measure code.

In taking the year-end inventory, Boos's personnel write the actual counted quantity on the face of each card. When all counts are completed, the counted quantity is entered into a computer program. This program processes the counted quantities against the inventory master file and adjusts the quantity-on-hand numbers to reflect the actual count. A computer listing shows any missing inventory count cards and all quantity adjustments of more than $100 in value.

These items can be investigated by client personnel, and all required adjustments can be made. When adjustments are complete, the final year-end balances are computed and posted to the general ledger. You, as the auditor, use generalized audit software that executes on Boos's computer.

Required:

List and describe at least five ways in which a generalized audit software package can assist in the audit of inventory at Boos & Baumkirchner, Inc.

(AICPA Adapted)

15–20.   *Generalized Audit Software*

You plan to use generalized audit software during your examination of the accounts payable system of Solt Manufacturing Company. Solt's EDP manager has agreed to prepare special tapes of data from company records for your use with generalized audit software programs. The following information is applicable to your examination:

1. The formats of the pertinent files are shown in Exhibit 15–1.
2. You wish to prepare the following audit reports using GAS:
   a. Cash disbursements by check number.
   b. Outstanding payables.
   c. Purchase transactions arranged by
      i. account debited.
      ii. vendor.
3. Vouchers and supporting invoices, receiving reports, and purchase order copies are filed by vendor code. Purchase orders and checks are filed numerically.
4. Company records are maintained in sequential files on a magnetic disk.

Required:

Prepare instructions for the chief information officer outlining the data that should be included on the special tape. These instructions should state

1. Client file from which the item should be extracted.
2. Name of the item of data.

(AICPA Adapted)

EXHIBIT 15–1

Exercise 15–20 File Formats

Master File — Vendor Name

Vendor Code	Recd. Type	Space	Blank	Vendor Name	Blank	Card Code 100

Master File — Vendor Address

Vendor Code	Recd. Type	Space	Blank	Address-Line 1	Address-Line 2	Address-Line 3	Blank	Card Code 120

Transaction File — Expense Detail

Vendor Code	Recd. Type	Voucher Number	Blank	Batch	Voucher Number	Voucher Date	Vendor Code	Invoice Date	Due Date	Invoice Number	Purchase Order Number	Debit Account	Prd. Type	Product Code	Blank	Amount	Quantity	Card Code 160

Transaction File — Payment Detail

Vendor Code	Recd. Type	Voucher Number	Blank	Batch	Voucher Number	Voucher Date	Vendor Code	Invoice Date	Due Date	Invoice Number	Purchase Order Number	Check Number	Check Date	Blank	Amount	Blank	Card Code 170

15–21.   Embedded Audit Modules

In December, Jack Brown was arrested and charged with theft, forgery, and tampering with records in connection with a fraud committed against his employer, Girard Bank in Philadelphia.[4] Brown's job was to examine computer printouts of transactions at automatic teller machines (ATMs), looking for suspicious withdrawals. Brown's department also received automatic teller cards returned as undeliverable by the U.S. Postal Service and issued the personal identification numbers that made these cards useful.

On December 6, Brown made a fake $5,000 deposit in the account of a man whose bank card had been returned. (Police and bank officials refused to reveal how he did it.) Because of this entry, the bank's files showed that this account contained more money than it actually did. Brown also used his terminal to raise the withdrawal limit on this ATM card from the usual $200 daily ceiling to $4,500 a day.

The card was then used to make 13 withdrawals totaling $2,500 from a teller machine. The following day Brown faked another deposit. The card was again used to withdraw money. Then, by computer, Brown returned the withdrawal limit to its proper level. Fortunately, an audit program was monitoring Brown's maneuvers and provided evidence for the discovery of his theft.

Required:

a. Which weaknesses in system controls allowed this fraud to occur?

b. How could an embedded audit module aid in detecting Brown's actions?

15–22.   Threats From Managers

After deliberating for two hours, a Florida jury found A. B. Crocker, former chief financial officer at Golden Eagle Group, Inc., guilty of extortion and denying computer access with intent to defraud.[5] These are second-degree felonies carrying up to 15 years in prison. Crocker was arrested on May 6.

During a three-day trial, Crocker testified that he created a secret password for a computer billing system that he developed and considered his. Crocker said that company officials failed to respond to his request for a $5,000 a year raise. In a letter of resignation, Crocker threatened to withhold the password if certain demands were not met.

He resigned on May 6, leaving the billing system inoperable because its files could not be accessed. On May 11 company employees succeeded in determining the password; however, the search had delayed a $400,000 monthly billing. According to Crocker, the password, "WGACA," stood for "What goes around comes around."

Required:

a. Which control procedures could have prevented this crime?

b. Would you consider these accounting data vital? Why or why not?

---

[4]Adapted from "Computers Turn Out to Be Valuable Aid in Employee Crime." Reprinted by permission of *The Wall Street Journal,* © Dow Jones & Company, Inc., 1985. All rights reserves.

[5]Adapted from "Man Convicted of Holding Firm's Computer Hostage," *Houston Chronicle,* October 24, 1987. Copyright 1987 by Associated Press. Used by permission.

15–23.   Threats From Hackers

Richard Marsh, a 24-year-old former computer science graduate student, was convicted by a jury of felony charges in a U.S. court in New York.[6] He had earlier been indicted by a federal grand jury on one count of violating the Computer Fraud and Abuse Act of 1986. He was charged with gaining access to university and military computers without authorization, preventing authorized access to those computers, and causing losses of $1,000 or more. He was sentenced to three years' probation, a $10,000 fine, and 400 hours of community service.

Marsh was the author of a "worm," a computer program that copied itself into processors connected to the Internet computer network. The program contained a list of 370 passwords, and according to sources, 90 percent of the computers it contacted had users that employed one of those passwords.

Once the program entered a processor, it continued to replicate itself uncontrollably until it clogged the memory of the computer and caused its shutdown. It caused substantial damage at many computer centers resulting from the loss of computer services and the expense of halting the program and correcting its effects. It entered as many as 6,200 computers, including those at the National Aeronautics and Space Administration's Ames Research Center, Wright-Patterson Air Force Base, the University of California at Berkeley, and Purdue University.

According to Marsh, the program was created to point out weaknesses in computer security on the Internet. It was intended, he said, to make a single copy of itself on every computer on the network. Instead, an error in the program caused it to multiply and spread uncontrollably.

Required:

a. What risk to security is posed by a hacker such as Marsh? Explain your answer.

b. Do you consider Marsh's actions unethical? Do you consider them criminal? Explain your answer.

15–24.   Destruction Of Data

Paul Louis, a 23-year-old former employee of a large Los Angeles accounting firm, was placed on three-year probation and given a five-month jail sentence after his conviction for computer fraud.[7] Louis pleaded no contest to charges that he illicitly used a San Francisco–based system belonging to U.S. Leasing International, Inc. He was also convicted of physically breaking into Pacific Telephone Company's local computing center and stealing sensitive documents, including password lists and computer manuals.

After swiping this material, Louis publicized the material through various electronic bulletin boards. From there other hackers used the information to change the phone company's billing data, enter fake stop orders, and otherwise wreak systems havoc.

---

[6]Adapted from articles in *Computerworld,* dated July 31, 1989; August 7, 1989; January 21, 1991; and October 14, 1991.

[7]Adapted from "'Phone Freak' Going to Jail for Two Schemes," *Computerworld,* June 28, 1982. Used by permission.

"From what I know, their ultimate goal was to shut down the entire phone system in Southern California," said the prosecuting attorney. "Phone freaks don't like Ma Bell, and they enjoy harassing the firm whenever they can."

Louis's crime spree began two years earlier when he and a woman companion used a terminal in her home to gain unauthorized access to U.S. Leasing's computer. After bypassing the processor's security safeguards, the two used the remote terminal to delete information from files belonging to one of the company's subsidiaries. The destruction occurred in the files that tell the subsidiary where its rented equipment is located and when it will become available for future leasing.

By destroying the files, Louis seriously impeded the company's business. "When U.S. Leasing was contacted by a customer and asked for a piece of equipment, the company was unable to say where it was located or when it would become available," said the attorney. Louis also used the terminal to create his own program files on the system. One was designed to inform him whenever U.S. Leasing changed its passwords. In addition, Louis peppered the company's data files with messages, including "some very foul language" according to the prosecuting attorney.

"In at least one of his inserts, Louis boasted openly of his sabotage and threatened to do further damage. He was very proud of being able to get into someone else's system and was eager to tell other people about his activities," the attorney said.

Required:

a. What did Louis gain from these activities? What did the victims lose?

b. Do you consider Louis a criminal? Why or why not?

15–25. *Computer-Related Fraud*

A Louisiana man was convicted of stealing more than $100,000 in money orders from a minicomputer system that he helped to develop.[8] Nowell Norris, 30, faces up to 10 years in prison and a $3,000 fine for the theft from National Bonded Money Orders Corp.

Norris was an employee of a systems development company that provided the packaged system to National. The systems development company fired Norris shortly after the applications programs were completed. Norris was then hired by Charles Carrs, National's office manager and a close personal friend, to "help work some of the remaining bugs out of the system."

National later began to notice excessively large losses of paper and engaged an auditor to investigate. During this investigation, National was burglarized and the computer printout records and money order code numbers were stolen. A probe of the investigation revealed that more than 1,000 money orders had been stolen throughout the preceding months and that the system was programmed not to reveal the losses.

The investigation led to Norris, who admitted his guilt. Norris had also altered programs so that money orders he wrote to fictitious people and cashed himself were ignored by the system after they were returned.

"We know that he was using some of the stolen money orders to pay off his VISA charge card, among other things," said the assistant district attorney. Those other things included gambling debts and an investment in a small business.

---

[8]Adapted from "CPU Programmed to Hide Theft," *Computerworld,* June 8, 1981. Used by permission.

Required:

a. In this fraud, identify the

    1. Theft.

    2. Conversion.

    3. Concealment.

b. How was this fraud detected?

c. Which control procedures could have prevented it?

15–26.   Computer-Related Fraud

A federal grand jury indicted three people for conspiracy, making and receiving false government securities, fraudulent use of a government computer, stealing money from the United States, and mail fraud in connection with the fraudulent issuance of a government check.[9]

Adell Adams, 31, was a customer relations clerk at the Defense Contract Administration Services (DCAS) region in Los Angeles. DCAS, a branch of the U.S. Department of Defense, administers ongoing U.S. defense contracts. Adams accessed the DCAS computer to alter the name and address of a legitimate contractor, Tasker Systems Division. She then submitted false paperwork, with Tasker's valid contract number, to another clerk showing a $9.5 million check was due. As a result a check was issued on February 19 to Fortress Indemnity. Adams then changed the computer files so that all later checks would be issued to Tasker as usual.

Fortress Indemnity was a fictitious company set up by Bob Baker, 31, of Los Angeles, and Cecil Carlson, 35, of Seattle. The check was mailed to a Los Angeles address provided by Carlson, who picked it up and mailed it to Baker in Seattle. Baker tried to deposit the check at Northwest Commercial Bank on February 23, but suspicious bank officials called federal agents. Baker was arrested on February 25 when he returned to the bank to collect the proceeds of the check. When confronted, Baker disclosed the identities of the other two defendants.

Required:

a. In this fraud, identify the

    1. Theft.

    2. Conversion.

    3. Concealment.

b. How was the fraud detected?

c. Which control procedures could have prevented it?

15–27.   Reviews

Mark Tick is an internal auditor employed by the Highlight Corp. Tick's supervisor has assigned him to perform a general controls review of Highlight's data center.[10]

---

[9]Adapted from "Three Indicted in Computer Contract Fraud," *Houston Chronicle,* October 25, 1987. Reprinted with permission of United Press International, Inc. Used by permission. Copyright 1988.

[10]Reprinted from *EDPACS* (New York: Auerbach Publishers). © 1974 Warren, Gorham & Lamont, Inc. Used with permission.

As Tick drove up, he was welcomed by a neon sign on the roof of the building indicating the data center's presence. The data center was in the basement of the corporate headquarters building on the river side, four inches below flood level.

Tick donned his dark glasses, combed his hair, checked his supply of red lead pencils, and entered the building. He approached the receptionist and asked for the data center manager. Without questioning Tick's identity or his reason for being there, she informed him that the manager was away from the data center for a few minutes and told him to wait in the computer room.

"We have all our visitors wait there. They seem to be infatuated with the twinkling little lights on the console," she said.

"What's a console?" asked Tick.

"It's the thing next to the 10-gallon gas-fired coffee urn," was her reply.

Tick walked toward the data center, down a hallway crowded with employees on their way to the cafeteria. On both sides of the hall he noticed, without interest, open racks of magnetic tapes labeled neatly with such titles as "accounts receivable master file," "YTD payroll master," "stockholder records," and "general ledger summary." He paused for a moment to watch a pickup game of ring toss, noting that the lunch crowd had obtained the rings from the sides of magnetic tape reels.

"Ingenious people," he thought, "finding use for those worthless little rings."

As Tick walked through the data entry room, he noticed employees drifting into the room and dumping loose source documents into a box labeled "Input." The data entry operators were taking out handfuls of the documents and entering them at terminals. Tick, ever alert, recognized the documents were selected in conformity with the generally accepted "random LIFO" method.

Entering the computer room, Tick waved to the sole occupant, a machine operator who was hastily punching up cards and inserting them in a deck labeled "payroll source code."

"Obviously a valuable employee," mused Tick. "It's good to see someone putting forth some extra effort."

Tick poured a cup of coffee, and as he started to count petty cash, placed it on top of the 4-foot-high stack of dust-covered disk packs. He wondered if the small amount of coffee he spilled would stain the floor as it drained through the disks.

Tick noticed that the machine operator, having run the unnumbered payroll checks through the check signer, was separating the carbons from the checks. The fourth copy of the checks passed neatly into the fiberboard wastebasket as the machine hummed smoothly, giving the operator a chance to have a smoke and discuss with two mailboys, who had just entered, how much the various vice presidents were being paid. Tick was impressed with the operator's concern for neatness—he even ran the console log sheets through the shredder as soon as he finished the payroll run. Tick drew an appreciative smile from the operator as he quipped, "Nobody could make anything out of the gobblygook the typewriter just printed, so better to destroy it than get buried under it."

Tick saw a box in the corner labeled "To Contingency File" and inquired, "What's this for?"

The operator explained that the maintenance department's foreman allowed the data center to store copies of important programs in the bottom of his locker.

"What type of programs?" asked Tick.

"Well, as far as I know, the only program over there is the one which causes the printer to use millions of little X's to form a cartoon character saying `Merry Christmas,'" was the reply.

Tick glanced at the bulletin board and immediately got an indication of how well organized the data center manager was and that he was nobody's fool. The three signs that impressed him most read:

Fairness is our motto. All input is processed on a first come, first served basis.

This is a data processing operation, not a delivery service. All output for the current week will be placed on the big table in the cafeteria before 4 p.m. each Friday. Help yourself!

To expedite processing and cut down on unnecessary paper shuffling, all documents rejected by the computer because of out-of-balance controls or invalid data will be immediately corrected and reentered by machine operators.

The data center manager came in, introduced himself to Tick, and apologized for being away so long. He explained that he had a difficult time finding a garden hose long enough to reach into the data center through a hole in the plywood partition separating it from the adjacent boiler room.

"Good idea," Tick said approvingly. "A lot cheaper than buying fire extinguishers for the data center."

"Well, how does the place look?" the manager asked, perspiring slightly in the heat.

"Great!" said Tick. "There will be only one item in my report. There is the serious matter of the 47-cent unexplained shortage in your $5.00 petty cash fund. Now, as soon as you buy me lunch, I can be off on my next assignment."

Required:

If you had conducted this review, what would you have included in your report?

15–28.   *Interviews*

Mike Kess, a senior auditor for the regional accounting firm Sanders and McDonald, was assigned to audit the Rayo Corporation.[11] He was to conduct a review of the general controls over systems and programming. Kess has already identified the current applications used in the accounting system (described in Exhibit 15–2) and is about to start on system maintenance.

Kess contacted Jim Stram, the manager of systems and programming in the MIS department, and requested an interview. A summary of their conversation follows:

Kess: How are system maintenance projects initiated and developed?
Stram: All potential projects are sent to a member of my staff, called an *application coordinator,* for analysis. We do all our systems and programming work in-house. If a programming change is required for a project, the application coordinator prepares a revision request form. These revision request forms must be approved by both the manager of operations and me. The director of data

---

[11]Adapted from a case prepared by Professors Frederick L. Neumann and Richard J. Boland of the University of Illinois, with a grant from the Touche-Ross Foundation.

EXHIBIT 15–2

Case 15–28

CLIENT <u>RAYO CORPORATION</u>   AUDIT DATE _____

GENERAL INFORMATION

	Yes	No	N/A
1. Provide a copy of the EDP department organization chart including names and titles of all personnel assigned to the department.	X		
2. Is there a written plan for this year's new applications and changes?		X	

    a. If yes, attach a copy of the plan or a summary.

    b. If no, list any changes in financial or accounting applications expected to be implemented prior to year-end.

      <u>None planned this year</u>

3. Indicate whether the following applications have been significantly modified since the prior audit. ("Significantly modified" means additions or deletions of reports, changes in the types of data input as stored on the files, modifications in calculations or decision criteria, etc.)

	Yes	No	N/A
a. <u>Payroll</u>		X	
b. <u>Accounts payable</u>		X	
c. <u>Accounts receivable</u>		X	
d. <u>General ledger</u>		X	

4. List below, or on a separate schedule, a summary of the significant financial and accounting applications now in use.

Application	Name or nature of principal reports or other output	Brief description of application, impact on other applications, comments, etc.
Payroll	Weekly batch run updating payroll and providing reports.	
Accounts payable	Batch system with on-line inquiry, providing daily status reports.	
Accounts receivable	Both on-line processing of A/R and batch reporting.	
General ledger	On-line system to post G/L and provide all cash flow, operating and statement of condition reports.	

EXHIBIT 15–2

Case 15–28 (continued)

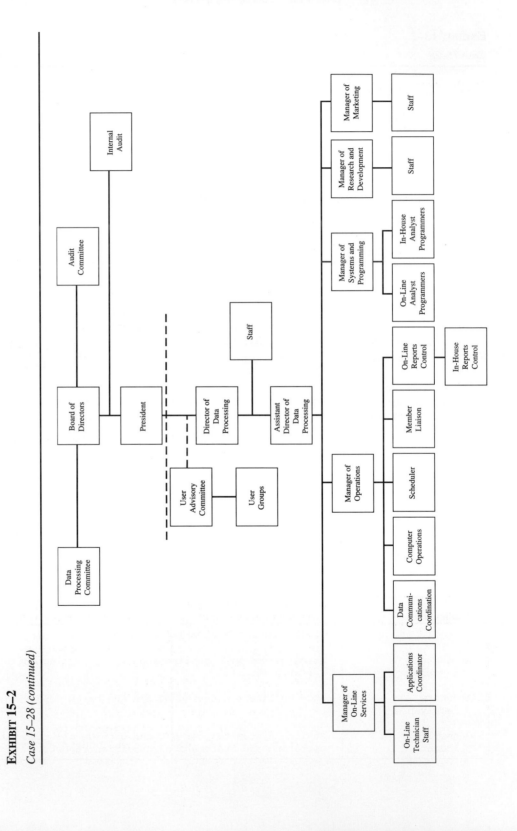

processing and the internal auditor receive copies of each revision request form for information purposes.

Kess: How does the application coordinator keep track of the revision request form and any change that might be made to it?

Stram: The revision request forms are numbered in different series depending on the nature of the change requested. The application coordinator assigns the next number in the sequence and records in a master log each request he prepares. Changes in revision requests, from whatever source, are prepared on request forms just as initial requests are. Each change request is given the same basic number with a suffix indicating it is an amendment, and there is a place for recording amendments in the master log.

Kess: What is the distribution of an approved request form?

Stram: It goes to one of my systems supervisors for design, programming, and testing. The primary effort is usually performed by a programmer who has responsibility over the area of the application or the specific programs to be changed.

Kess: But how are projects controlled?

Stram: At the beginning of each programming project, estimated start and completion dates are assigned and entered on the request form and the master log. The system supervisor keeps on top of the projects assigned to him, and the application coordinator also monitors the open requests. The system supervisor files written status reports with the applications coordinator twice a month and briefs me on any problems. However, I'm usually aware of any difficulties long before then.

During the programming and testing phase, I think we have good control over the project. None of the compiles made during this phase changes any production source code for the existing computer programs. Also, all test object programs are identified by a strictly enforced naming convention that clearly distinguishes them from production programs. So far this has been successful in inhibiting their use in processing production. If a programmer has specific questions or problems on a project, the systems supervisor is generally available to give advice.

Kess: Are there written guidelines to direct this activity? If so, how detailed are they?

Stram: Only informal procedures exist to provide any uniformity to the programs and the coding changes made to a program. Formal standards do exist to define which documentation should be present for a system and for the programs within a system. These apply to program changes as well and again are strictly enforced. There is a periodic management review to see that we comply. We just had one about a month ago and got a clean bill of health.

Kess: Are adequate tests and reviews made of changes before they are implemented?

Stram: The application coordinator, the systems supervisor, and the individual programmer informally discuss the necessary tests for a specific project. Sometimes I get involved, too, but our guidelines are pretty good in this area and provide a fairly thorough approach to test design. After the tests have been completed to the systems supervisor's satisfaction, the applications coordinator reviews and approves the test results. This must be done on all revision requests before they are implemented into production. I usually review the programmers' work to see that all authorized changes are made correctly and are adequately tested and documented.

Kess: How does implementation take place and which controls are exercised over it?

Stram: After the test results for a revision request have been approved by the applications coordinator, it is the responsibility of the programmer to implement the changes into production. Before putting a program change into production, a programmer must update the source code of the production program version. The programmer is required to give the program name and compile date for all changed programs to the system supervisor. The programmer also has the responsibility for updating the systems and programming documentation. The system supervisor is supposed to review this and certify completion to the applications coordinator who then completes the log entry.

Kess: Are post-implementation reviews undertaken on systems maintenance projects?

Stram: Once the project is implemented, the applications coordinator reviews the output from the first few production runs of the changed program. The coordinator also questions users to see if any problem areas can be identified. A documented audit trail is provided by the completed project file maintained by the application coordinator for each request number. This file contains all the required documentation, including test results. A copy of the final summary goes to the department that originally submitted the request. A table in the computer is updated to provide listings of the most current compile dates for each set of production object codes within the system. Before any program is implemented, it is checked against this table.

Kess: Well, that seems to be it. I think I have all that I need for now, but I'll probably be back to take a look at the files and records. I may have more questions for you then. Thanks very much for your time and thoughtful answers. I really appreciate your help.

Stram: That's quite all right. If I can be of any more help, just let me know.

Required:

a. Which additional questions would you have asked Jim Stram if you had been in Mike Kess's place?

b. What are some weaknesses in internal control that you identified from the interview?

c. Based on the interview, attempt to fill in the questionnaire contained in Exhibit 15–3.

EXHIBIT 15–3

Case 15–28

CLIENT <u>RAYO CORPORATION</u>   AUDIT DATE _____

SYSTEMS AND PROGRAMMING

	Yes	No	N/A
1. Are there systems and programming standards in the following areas:			
a. Applications design?	____	____	____
b. Programming conventions and procedures?	____	____	____
c. Systems and program documentation?	____	____	____
d. Applications control?	____	____	____
e. Project planning and management?	____	____	____
2. Does the normal documentation for an application include the following:			
Application documentation:			
a. Narrative description?	____	____	____
b. Systems flowchart?	____	____	____
c. Definition of input data and source format?	____	____	____
d. Description of expected output data and format?	____	____	____
e. A listing of all valid transactions and other codes and abbreviations and master file fields affected?	____	____	____
f. File definition or layouts?	____	____	____
g. Instructions for preparing input?	____	____	____
h. Instructions for correcting errors?	____	____	____
i. Backup requirements?	____	____	____
j. Description of test data?	____	____	____
Program documentation:			
a. Program narrative?	____	____	____
b. Flowchart of each program?	____	____	____
c. Current source listing of each program?	____	____	____
Operations documentation:			
a. Data entry instructions, including verification?	____	____	____
b. Instructions for control personnel, including batching?	____	____	____
c. Instructions for the tape librarian?	____	____	____
d. Operator's run manual?	____	____	____
e. Reconstruction procedure?	____	____	____
3. Is there a periodic management review of documentation to ensure that it is current and accurate?	____	____	____
If yes, when and by whom was it last performed? _____			
4. Is all systems and programming work done in-house?	____	____	____
If not, is it done			
a. By computer manufacturer's personnel?	____	____	____
b. By contract programming?	____	____	____
c. Other? Describe. _____	____	____	____
5. Are all changes programmed by persons other than those assigned to computer operations?	____	____	____
6. Are program changes documented in a manner that preserves an accurate chronological record of the applications?	____	____	____
If yes, describe _____			

EXHIBIT 15–3

Case 15–28 (continued)

	Yes	No	N/A
7. Do the users participate in the development of new applications or modifications of existing applications through frequent reviews of work performed?	——	——	——
If yes, are the results of reviews documented?	——	——	——
8. Are testing procedures and techniques standardized?	——	——	——
9. Are program revisions tested as stringently as new programs?	——	——	——
10. Are tests designed to uncover weaknesses in the links between programs, as well as within programs?	——	——	——
11. Are users involved in the testing process, i.e., do they use the application as it is intended during the testing process?	——	——	——
12. Do user departments perform the final review and signoff on projects before acceptance?	——	——	——

13. What departments and/or individuals have the authority to authorize an operator to put a new or modified program into production? _____

_____

_____

14. What supervisory or management approval is necessary for the conversion of files? _____

_____

_____

16   ACCOUNTING TRANSACTION CYCLES

Learning Objectives

1. To recognize those economic activities in which all organizations engage.

2. To understand how economic events are recorded as accounting transactions.

3. To find out the transaction cycles that make up an accounting transaction processing system.

4. To learn the application systems constituting each transaction cycle.

Introduction

The preceding chapters describe the technology that accounting information systems use and the information system controls that prevent and detect errors and threats to these systems. The last chapters of this book describe how this technology and these controls are used to process specific accounting transactions. To make it easier to understand these procedures, they are structured by accounting transaction cycle. This chapter explains four transaction cycles and provides an overview of the detailed descriptions of them presented in Chapters 17 through 20.

Different accountants describe transaction cycles in different ways. The cycles described in this chapter represent just one way of looking at them. As you work with information systems, you may encounter accountants who use five or even six transaction cycles. They are not incorrect; they are simply using different ways of viewing the economic events that make up an organization's activities.

Why learn about transaction cycles? How does understanding the cyclical nature of transaction processing help you as a student and as an accountant? There are several benefits from your study of transaction cycles.

Accounting Is Continuous

Transaction cycles emphasize the continuous nature of all business and accounting processes. You learned accounting by thinking of journals and ledgers, debits and credits, and their effect on accounts in a general ledger. Because of this, you may think of the accounting process as static, as something that happens at the end of a month or a year. In fact, accounting activities occur constantly, just as do the activities of the business in which the accounting system operates.

Cycles Emphasize Relationships

Transaction cycles demonstrate how events early in a transaction cycle affect events and records later in the cycle. A weakness in internal control affecting a transaction may mean that records created later in that same cycle are misstated. For example, a purchase from a fraudulent vendor is possible due to poor internal control in the purchasing system of the expenditure cycle. Although this might cause excessive expenses in the voucher system of the same cycle, transactions in the other cycles are not affected. These questions greatly concern auditors, who must evaluate the effects of internal control weaknesses in determining audit tests.

Cycles Make Your Task Easier

Modern organizations use highly computerized accounting systems with records maintained in a unified database. In these systems, it is often difficult to distinguish the processes applied to accounting transactions. Analyzing these processes by transaction cycle makes it easier to understand the effects on the accounting data of these systems.

Finally, accounting information systems process many kinds of accounting transactions and, in so doing, generate a variety of documents and reports. Many data are processed by both manual and computerized methods. Transaction cycles provide a framework for the study of these processing methods that emphasizes the similarities among them. Thus, the use of transaction cycles makes easier your study of accounting information systems.

Economic Events

We live in a complex society. It contains many organizations engaging in different activities for both profit and nonprofit objectives. Accounting systems are designed to record, summarize, and report the results of *economic events* for a wide range of organizations. How can you begin to understand or structure this variety of economic events? How could the designer of an accounting system hope to anticipate all the possible events that can occur? Designing such a system is easier than you think, if you first consider the basic activities of all businesses.

The Cycle of Business Activities

Even though businesses differ in their operations, all of them engage in a *cycle of business activities*. Each activity has certain economic events common to most; these economic events produce accounting transactions that must be processed by the accounting system. By examining these economic events, you can identify a small number of accounting processes appropriate for most organizations. Illustration 16–1 summarizes these basic business activities.

Capital Investment.   The cycle of business activities begins when capital is invested in a business. Generally accepted accounting principles (GAAP) require recognizing the business as an entity separate from the sources of this capital. These sources may be the owners of the business, or they may be creditors. If the source is the owners, the investment is owners' equity. If the source is creditors, the investment is either long-term debt or current liabilities. In many businesses, most of the capital is used to purchase long-term productive assets. The business uses the productive assets to increase its

ILLUSTRATION 16–1

The Cycle of Basic Business Activities

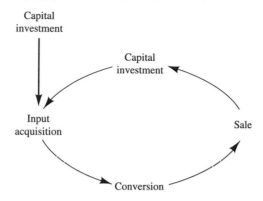

capital. Periodically, the business reports the results of its operations to the sources of its capital.

Capital investment comprises two significant economic events: raising capital and using capital to acquire productive assets. Another event that occurs during this activity is not economic in the sense of the other two: Periodically the business reports to its sources of capital. This is necessary to maintain those sources when additional capital is needed later. Chapter 20 describes how these events are recorded by the accounting system.

Input Acquisition.   The second component of the cycle of business activities is the acquisition of materials and overhead items such as supplies. These inputs are used to increase the capital of the business. The exact way in which they are used is not important at this point; they are used differently for different businesses.

Most organizations operate on credit—that is, when a business purchases inputs, it receives the inputs in return for a promise to pay for them. The business records an obligation to pay and pays for them at a later date. So, the activity of *input acquisition* has these four economic events: ordering of inputs, receiving them, recording an obligation to pay for them, and paying for them.

Conversion.   The next step in the cycle of activities is the *conversion* of inputs into goods or services. The business sells these to increase its capital. The conversion process is different for different businesses.

Manufacturing companies buy raw material inventories, apply labor and overhead to them, and produce an output different from the material purchased. Service companies convert inputs that are predominantly labor into outputs in the form of services. In contrast, the conversion process of merchandising companies (retailers and wholesalers) uses relatively little labor. These organizations purchase inventories of goods, repackage them, and then market them. All three businesses use inventories of supplies in their conversion processes.

ILLUSTRATION 16–2

Events in the Business Activity Cycle

Business Cycle Activity	Events
Capital investment	Raise capital
	Use capital to acquire property
	Periodic reporting
Input acquisition	Request inputs to the conversion process
	Receive inputs
	Record obligation to pay
	Pay for inputs
Conversion	Consume labor, material, and overhead
Sales	Receive request for goods or services
	Deliver to customer
	Request payment
	Receive payment

One economic event taking place during conversion is the consumption of labor, materials, and overhead to produce a salable product or service.

Sales.   The final component in the cycle of basic business activities is the *sale* of the goods or services that were outputs of the conversion process. When these are sold at a profit, the capital investment of the business increases. Additional cash is available for reinvestment, or for making payments to the sources of capital in the form of dividends and interest. By providing a source of additional capital, the sales component completes the cycle of business activities.

The sale of goods or services consists of four economic events: receiving a customer order, delivering goods to the customer, requesting payment for the goods, and receiving payment. Illustration 16–2 summarizes the economic events in the cycle of business activities.

Economic Events and Accounting Transactions

Normal business operation consists of a series of economic events. This series results from the cycle of business activities that describes how all accounting entities operate. An accounting system records economic events in the form of accounting transactions, summarizes those transactions, and reports them in some useful way. Thus, you can consider business activities as cycles of accounting transactions. In fact, the study of transaction cycles is a convenient way to understand how most accounting systems work.

Transaction Cycles

A *transaction cycle* is a set of accounting transactions that occur in a normal sequence. They record the economic events of a component in the cycle of business activities. For example, a sales transaction is normally followed by a shipping transaction, a billing transaction, and a cash receipts transaction. These constitute a cycle.

Illustration 16–2 shows the four basic business activities. From them you can identify four accounting transaction cycles: the financial cycle, the expenditure cycle,

ILLUSTRATION 16–3

The Financial Cycle

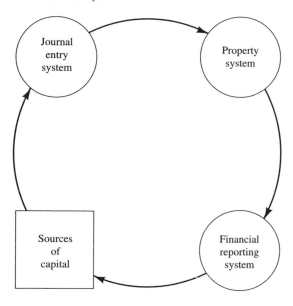

the conversion cycle, and the revenue cycle. Early in this text, you encountered these cycles as subsystems of the accounting transaction processing system. At that time you learned that the transaction cycles consist of subsystems called *application systems.* Now you can see in detail how these subsystems record common business economic events.

Financial Cycle.   The *financial cycle* consists of those accounting transactions that record the acquisition of capital from owners and creditors, the use of that capital to acquire productive assets, and the reporting to owners and creditors on how it is used. The two significant economic events in the financial cycle are raising capital and using that capital to acquire property, plant, and equipment. A third event—not really an economic one—is periodic reporting to the sources of capital.

The basic financial statements provide periodic reporting. These statements include the balance sheet, the income statement, and the statement of cash flows. The summaries in these statements come from the general ledger. Periodic reporting to the sources of capital enables a business to raise additional capital. For this reason, you can view the series of transactions as a cycle.

The three accounting application systems that record the events in the financial cycle are the property, the journal entry, and the financial reporting systems.[1] Illustration 16–3 depicts the relationships among these application systems and the sources of capital.

---

[1]Many accountants refer to the journal entry and financial reporting systems together as the *general ledger system.* However, it is easier to understand how they work if you learn them as separate systems.

ILLUSTRATION 16–4

The Expenditure Cycle

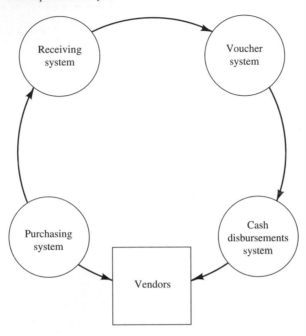

Expenditure Cycle.   The *expenditure cycle* consists of those transactions incurred to acquire material and overhead items for the conversion process of the business. This cycle processes transactions representing the following economic events: requesting the items, receiving the items, recording the obligation to pay for the items, and paying for them.

Most businesses use a purchasing department to acquire materials and supplies. A purchasing agent orders material from a vendor, who ships the material and mails an invoice. The business uses the invoice to record the payable and later pays the vendor. When the vendor is paid according to the terms of the sale, the vendor again sells items to the business. This causes the sequence of transactions to form a cycle.

The application systems in the expenditure cycle execute these transactions. They include the purchasing, receiving, voucher, and cash disbursements systems.[2] Illustration 16–4 shows the relationships among vendors and the systems in the expenditure cycle.

Revenue Cycle.   The *revenue cycle* includes the accounting transactions that record the generation of revenue from the outputs of the conversion process. As mentioned earlier, these four economic events generate revenue: receiving an order from a customer, delivering goods or services to the customer, requesting payment from the customer, and receiving the payment.

---

[2]Many accountants consider the voucher and cash disbursements systems as one, called the *accounts payable system*. It is easier to learn them as separate processes.

ILLUSTRATION 16–5

The Revenue Cycle

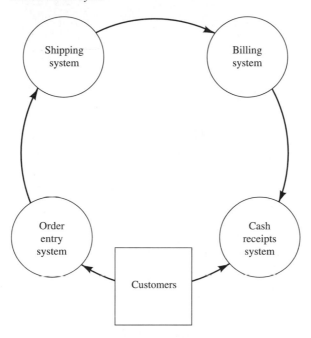

Whenever companies sell goods or services on credit, each of these events produces a transaction. Each transaction may occur at separate times. If the sale is a cash sale, then ordering, delivery, request, and payment occur at the same time. In this case, accounting systems ordinarily record these four events with one transaction. When a customer pays and the accounting system records the cash receipt, the business is willing to sell again to the customer. This causes the cycle of transactions to repeat.

Companies that sell on credit use four application systems in the revenue cycle. They are the order entry, shipping, billing, and the cash receipts systems.[3] Companies that sell on a cash basis frequently use a point-of-sale system that combines the four economic events in one transaction. Illustration 16–5 provides a graphic description of the transactions in the revenue cycle.

Conversion Cycle.   The *conversion cycle* contains those transactions incurred when inputs are converted into salable goods or services. One economic event exists in the conversion cycle. Materials, labor, and overhead are consumed in the conversion process.

In manufacturing and service companies, either actual or standard material and labor costs are recorded in a cost ledger as conversion occurs. Overhead costs are allocated in the cost ledger, usually based on the amount of labor used. These costs become associated with the products and are matched with revenue when the products are sold.

---

[3]The billing and cash receipts systems are called the *accounts receivable system*. As before, it is easier to learn them separately.

ILLUSTRATION 16–6

The Conversion Cycle in a Merchandising Company

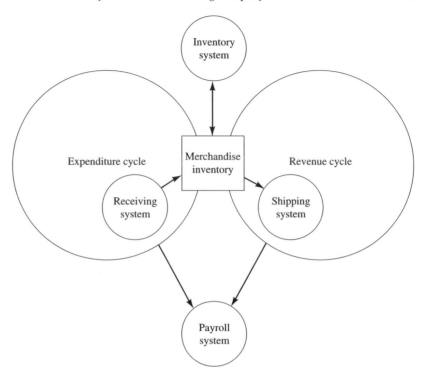

In merchandising companies, costs of conversion are recorded when incurred and matched against revenue in the same period.

Depending on the type of organization, the conversion cycle contains either two or three application systems. Manufacturing and service companies use the cost accounting system to record material, labor, and overhead costs. All types of organizations use the payroll system. It ensures that employees are paid for their labor. Manufacturing and merchandising companies use the inventory system to maintain records of inventory on hand.

In merchandising and manufacturing companies, the systems of the conversion cycle provide interfaces between the expenditure and revenue cycles. Because it contains only one event, the conversion cycle cannot be represented as a circle as can the other cycles.

For example, a merchandising company maintains a merchandise inventory for sale. The expenditure cycle adds to this inventory, and the revenue cycle takes from it. The inventory system records the associated transactions. The payroll system in a merchandising company compensates sales and administrative personnel for their work. Illustration 16–6 shows the interfaces between the expenditure and revenue cycles and the inventory and payroll systems in such a company.

A manufacturing company has raw materials, work in process, and finished goods inventories. The production process converts raw material into finished goods. Raw materials are acquired in the expenditure cycle, and finished goods are sold in the

ILLUSTRATION 16–7

The Conversion Cycle in a Manufacturing Company

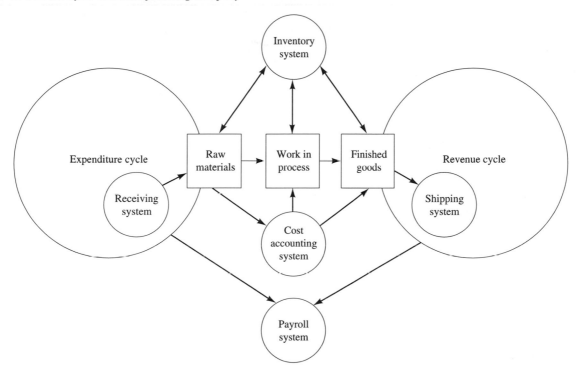

revenue cycle. In this way, these inventory accounts are a part of two cycles. The cost accounting, payroll, and inventory systems provide interfaces by recording transactions during the production process. Illustration 16–7 shows a graphic representation of the conversion cycle in a manufacturing company.

Cycles and Applications

Basic business activities were used to identify four transaction cycles common to all businesses. These transaction cycles differ in various businesses. In large corporations, the financial cycle is complex. In a small business, there are fewer sources and uses of capital, so the cycle is much simpler. In manufacturing companies, the conversion cycle may contain a highly developed cost accounting system that is unnecessary in a merchandising company. Service companies may also use inventory and cost accounting systems, but they are simpler because these companies do not have raw material inventories.

The diversity among companies is significant. Although they engage in basically the same activities and their accounting transactions record the same economic events, all companies cannot use identical application systems. Large companies have a greater number of computerized application systems, and these systems are more sophisticated than those in smaller companies. Older application systems are less complex than newer ones, even within the same company. Some applications are much more important in some industries than in others. Illustration 16–8 suggests the relative significance of various accounting applications in different industries.

ILLUSTRATION 16–8

Relative Significance of Accounting Applications, by Industry

Industry	Shipping	Purchasing	Receiving	Cost Accounting	Inventory
Agriculture	Maj	Maj	Maj		Min
Banking		Min	Min	Min	Min
Construction		Maj	Maj	Maj	Maj
Health care		Maj	Maj	Min	Maj
Insurance		Min	Min	Min	Min
Manufacturing	Maj	Maj	Maj	Maj	Maj
Merchandising	Maj	Maj	Maj		Maj
Mining	Maj	Maj	Maj		Min
Transportation		Min	Min		Min
Utility		Maj	Maj	Maj	Min

Legend: Maj indicates that the application is a major one in the industry.

   Min indicates that the application is a minor one in the industry.

   Blank indicates that the application is not used in the industry.

Note: The following applications are not shown because they are major ones in most industries: billing, cash receipts, voucher, cash disbursements, property, payroll, order entry, journal entry, and financial reporting.

While learning how accounting information systems process transactions, you are learning different ways of recording the same economic event. As a practicing accountant, you will be working with systems of varying complexity and technology. The systems described in this book are typical transaction processing methods with *good internal control;* however, these examples are not the only ways in which a business can operate.

Just as accounting transaction cycles were identified with basic business activities, accounting application systems can be identified with economic events, as shown in Illustration 16–9. This illustration identifies 14 application systems, which the following chapters describe.

ILLUSTRATION 16–9

Economic Events and Application Systems That Process Them

Transaction Cycle	Economic Event	Application System
Financial	Raise capital	Journal entry
	Consume capital	Property
	Periodic reporting	Financial reporting
Expenditure	Request inputs	Purchasing
	Receive inputs	Receiving
	Obligation to pay	Voucher
	Payment	Cash disbursements
Conversion	Consume labor, material, overhead	Cost accounting, payroll, and inventory
Revenue	Receive request	Order entry
	Deliver	Shipping
	Request payment	Billing
	Receive payment	Cash receipts

Summary

In this chapter you learned the structure that underlies the processing of accounting transactions. Analyzing the cycle of basic business activities reveals the origin of the transaction cycles that make up the accounting transaction processing system. They are the revenue, expenditure, conversion, and financial cycles. Each of the economic events that occur in each of the basic business activities has an accounting application system associated with it.

Key Terms

application systems   The components of a transaction cycle.

capital investment   The first component in the cycle of business activities. It concerns acquiring money to generate products and services and produce revenue.

conversion   The third component in the cycle of business activities. Inputs of labor, material, and overhead are converted into salable goods or services.

conversion cycle   Those transactions incurred when inputs to the conversion process are converted into salable goods or services.

cycle of business activities   A series of activities in which all businesses engage.

economic event   An action by a business affecting its assets, liabilities, and owners' equity; the accounting system records it as a transaction.

expenditure cycle   Those accounting transactions recording the acquisition of material and overhead items for the conversion process of the business.

financial cycle   Those accounting transactions recording the acquisition of capital from owners and/or creditors and reporting to them on how it is used.

input acquisition   The second component in the cycle of business activities. It is concerned with the acquisition of materials and overhead.

revenue cycle   The accounting transactions recording the generation of revenue from the outputs of the conversion process.

sales   The fourth component in the cycle of business activities. Goods or services are sold, producing revenue and income for the business.

transaction cycle   A set of accounting transactions occurring in a normal sequence and used to record economic events.

Questions

16–1. What are the components of the cycle of business activities?

16–2. Describe the conversion processes that take place in

    a. Manufacturing companies.

    b. Service companies.

    c. Merchandising companies.

16–3. Which economic events occur during each of the following components of the business cycle:
   a. Capital investment?
   b. Input acquisition?
   c. Conversion?
   d. Sales?

16–4. What is a transaction cycle?

16–5. What are the four transaction cycles?

16–6. How do the events in the financial cycle make it different from the other cycles?

16–7. Which application systems are in each of the following transaction cycles:
   a. Financial cycle?
   b. Expenditure cycle?
   c. Conversion cycle?
   d. Revenue cycle?

16–8. How can the same transaction cycle differ significantly between different businesses, even if they are in the same industry?

16–9. What are the major accounting applications in companies in the following industries:
   a. Agriculture?
   b. Construction?
   c. Health care?
   d. Transportation?

16–10. What are the advantages of using transaction cycles to understand how accounting information systems work?

Exercises and Cases

16–11.   APPLICATION SYSTEMS

The left column below contains transaction cycles, and the numbered columns list application systems.

a. Revenue.	1. Cost accounting.	7. Property.
b. Expenditure.	2. Order entry.	8. Voucher.
c. Conversion.	3. Cash disbursements.	9. Billing.
d. Financial.	4. Cash receipts.	10. Receiving.
	5. Shipping.	11. Payroll.
	6. Journal entry.	12. Inventory.

Required:

Match each application system with the transaction cycle to which it belongs.

16–12.   ECONOMIC EVENTS

The left column below contains transaction cycles. In the right column are economic events common in organizations.

a. Revenue.

b. Expenditure.

c. Conversion.

d. Financial.

1. Request inputs to production.
2. Deliver goods to customer.
3. Raise capital.
4. Use property in production.
5. Recognize obligation to pay.
6. Receive request from customer.
7. Consume material and labor.
8. Give periodic reports.
9. Receive inputs to production.
10. Receive payment from customers.

Required:

Match each economic event with the transaction cycle to which it belongs.

16–13.   ACCOUNTING ENTRIES

The following list contains economic events common in organizations:

a. Receive material for use in production.

b. Ship goods to customers.

c. Receive a loan from a bank.

d. Pay employees.

e. Receive cash from customers.

f. Consume equipment in production.

Required:

Show the accounting entries for each of these economic events.

16–14.   BUSINESS ACTIVITIES

Each of the activities in the following list is commonly performed by the employees of a business:

a. Mail an invoice to a customer.

b. Issue stock.

c. Manufacture a product.

d. Acquire equipment.

e. Provide a service for a customer.

f. Complete a timecard.

g. Fill out a receiving report.

Required:

Identify the transaction cycle in which the accounting system records each activity.

16–15.   DOCUMENTS

The economic events in the following list are common in organizations:

a. Receive material for use in production.

b. Ship goods to customers.

c. Receive a loan from a bank.

d. Pay employees.

e. Receive cash from customers.

f. Consume equipment in production.

Required:

Identify the documents used by an accounting system to record each economic event.

16–16.   DATA RECORDS

The data records in the following are maintained by accounting application systems:

a. Property master record.

b. General ledger master record.

c. Customer master record.

d. Vendor master record.

e. Open purchase order record.

f. Inventory master record.

Required:

Determine the transaction cycle or cycles that affect each record listed above.

16–17.   DOCUMENTS

The documents in the following list are commonly used by accounting applications:

a. Material requisition.

b. Sales order.

c. Timecard.

d. Job cost sheet.

e. Standard journal voucher.

f. Receiving report.

Required:

Identify the transaction cycle of each document in the preceding list.

16–18.   CONVERSION CYCLE

Mom's Cookie Company employs 17 people and produces 11 varieties of cookies for sale in local supermarkets. The firm purchases ingredients from a wholesale grocery company and stores them in a refrigerated storage area next to the bakery.

When a batch of cookies is started, an assistant baker blends into dough the appropriate ingredients for that particular cookie. A machine squirts dough onto oversize cookie sheets, which the assistant baker inserts into ovens for baking. When the cookies are done, a packing machine scrapes them, to be sold by weight rather than count, into bags. A packer then assembles them into cartons of 20 bags for delivery to supermarkets.

Required:

a. What are the inputs and outputs of this conversion process?

b. Which activities does the conversion process contain?

c. Which documents and records are needed to record the economic events in this conversion cycle?

16–19.   CONVERSION CYCLE

Tiny TV Repair Co. has been in existence for two years. The owner and sole employee, Jo Wizard, works out of a shop in a building adjacent to her home. In this shop she stores tools and test equipment, as well as any televisions requiring major service that cannot be performed in owners' homes.

Because of the size of her business, Jo operates on a cash basis. When she repairs a set, her terms are strictly cash on delivery. The charges include an hourly rate plus the cost of any repair parts required. She maintains a charge account at a local electronic parts supply house where she obtains repair supplies. Jo pays this account in full on a monthly basis.

Required:

a. What are the inputs and outputs of this conversion process?
b. Which activities does the conversion process contain?
c. Which documents and records are needed to record the economic events in this conversion cycle?

16–20.   CONVERSION CYCLE

Howell's Ready to Wear has been selling men's clothing in the same location for over 40 years. The founder, Henry Howell, has achieved stability and growth because of a reputation for service and fair dealing. The company now employs 12 sales personnel, an office administrator, and a bookkeeper. The business has a loyal clientele, in part because of Howell's record of community service and philanthropic activities.

Howell's avoids fashion fads, thereby minimizing the risk of obsolescence in the items it carries. As a result, sales are never held, and profit margins are adequate on all items. Howell's maintains a sizable inventory of traditional styles in a wide range of selections and sizes. Sales personnel provide personal service of a kind seldom found in the larger chain stores, which constitute Howell's primary competition.

Required:

a. What are the inputs and outputs of this conversion process?
b. Which activities does the conversion process contain?
c. Which documents and records are needed to record the economic events in this conversion cycle?

16–21.   TRANSACTION CYCLES

Abacus Manufacturing Company operates a job shop producing a variety of heavy exercise equipment, including stationary cycles, rowing machines, exercise machines, and barbell equipment. Customers are primarily chains of sporting goods stores scattered throughout the Midwest.

Abacus accepts orders for its products in lots of six or more items, producing to the specifications in the order. Prior to accepting an order from a customer, the sales manager prepares a quotation for the cost of the lot. He mails the quotation to the customer, who signs it and returns a copy to the sales manager indicating acceptance of the terms. The sales manager then forwards the customer's order to the shop foreman and the quotation to the invoicing clerk.

Raw materials include steel bars, sheets, tubing, and angles; plastic foam padding; and plastic sheets. Abacus purchases these items in bulk from warehouse distributors and fabricates them into finished products.

When the shop foreman receives the customer's order, he verbally notifies the purchasing agent of the material needed for the job. The purchasing agent prepares a purchase order for the material and mails it to the supplier. When the material arrives, the supervisor at the loading dock prepares a receiving report and carries it to the accounting office. As soon as the invoice arrives from the supplier, the bookkeeper in the accounting office prepares and mails a check to the supplier in payment.

When manufacture of the lot is complete, all items in it are transferred to the loading dock. The loading supervisor then calls a truck line and arranges for delivery to the customer. The loading supervisor prepares a bill of lading in duplicate. One copy goes to the truck line and the other to the invoicing clerk, indicating that shipment has taken place. From it and the original quotation, the invoicing clerk prepares an invoice and mails it to the customer.

Required:

a. Draw a flowchart showing the events and documents just described in the revenue cycle at Abacus Manufacturing Company.

b. Draw a flowchart showing the events and documents used in the expenditure cycle of Abacus.

16–22.   APPLICATIONS BY INDUSTRY

Tower Park Marina is located on the Delta, a series of rivers and sloughs containing about 1,000 miles of waterway in California's Central Valley.[4] A full-service marina, Tower Park contains a restaurant, retail store, gas sales, boat storage, and recreational vehicle (RV) campground. It also leases space for other businesses on the premises. During the busy season (May through September), Tower Park employs about 75 people including an accounting staff of three full-time and two part-time employees. During the off-season, it reduces staffing by about 40 percent. Combined annual sales for all its operations are about $3 million.

Customers who store boats in Tower Park's covered slips are mostly in their 40s and 50s and vary in occupation from professionals to small-business owners to blue-collar workers. Campground customers are generally families with teenage children or retired couples. Most come from the San Francisco Bay and Sacramento areas, although many also visit from Southern California.

Accounting Requirements

Tower Park Marina's accountants keep the general ledger, inventory, accounts receivable, and accounts payable records on four IBM-compatible personal computers.

---

[4]Adapted from Yvonne M. Mabee, "Accounting for a Marina/Resort," *Management Accounting,* May 1991, p. 50. Copyright by National Association of Accountants (1991), Montvale, N.J. 07645.

They purchased some of their software from vendors. However, because of the specific requirements of the marina business, much of the needed software is unavailable on the market. Furthermore, many of the available packages are overly simplified and designed for use by an owner/operator lacking an accounting background. For these reasons, the staff developed several custom accounting programs using PC spreadsheet and database management software.

Each month the accounting staff prepares computer reports of food costs, wholesale cost of store inventory sold, first-in first-out inventory for gasoline, rent deferrals, and items transferred from retail stock to maintenance use. For accounting purposes, they divided the enterprise into two operating entities. The store, restaurant, and rental businesses make up one; the other holds leases on the store and restaurant and contains the rental operations. Each month they prepare detailed financial statements for the two companies.

Inventory Transactions

The accounting staff make physical counts of restaurant and bar inventory on the last calendar day of each month. They input this data into a custom computer program developed for a database management software package. This program assigns all inventory items, from canned tomatoes to sirloin steaks to salt and pepper shakers, an identification number. They have arranged the items on the shelves in the same sequence as the numbers. This makes taking the inventory easier and lessens the chance of overlooking an item and thus overstating costs.

The fields used by the program include item number, description, unit of measure, quantity, price, and the date. An accounting clerk updates the computer with any price changes since the last inventory, and records the date of the last price update on the item. By sorting on the date field, the clerk can print a report of the items that have not been changed in the last few months.

At 7:00 A.M. each New Year's eve morning, the accounting staff join all the store personnel and count the store inventory. These items range from skis and wet suits to fishhooks and frozen anchovies. Accounting records identify five categories of store inventory items: grocery items, store taxable items, boating accessories, apparel, and gifts. Since the physical store inventory is taken only once a year, accountants estimate inventory using historical cost percentages.

Expenses

Every item from the store used in the marina's business is accounted for through the store transfer system. For example, if the outside crew needs a scrub brush for washing a boat, they purchase it from the store the same way a customer does. The store clerks ring the scrub brush on the cash register and charge sales tax on the item if it is taxable. The clerk describes on a cash receipt the inventory category of the item and where the items are to be used, and both parties sign it. This receipt becomes a transfer voucher and is returned to the cash drawer. When this voucher reaches the accounting department, a clerk uses the description to code the item with a correct expense account number.

At the end of the month, an accounting clerk enters all transfer vouchers into a custom-written database management program. The clerk enters the voucher number, the inventory category number, the amount, and the expense account number in the program. It produces two reports, one summarizing the information by inventory category and one by expense account. Because store inventory has a standard markup, this program calculates the cost of each item and the amount to be expensed because of it. The clerk then makes a journal entry to reverse the sale, record the sales tax (for taxable items), debit the expense account, and credit the inventory account.

Sales Transactions

The amount of clerical work required of the accounting staff decreased significantly when one accountant prepared a program to computerize the sales journal. This program was also written with a database management software package.

When a store clerk closes out a cash register, the clerk places the register readings, the currency, checks, and transfer vouchers in a "sales close envelope." These envelopes have preprinted on them the following information: sales categories and related general ledger account numbers, lines to record credit card receipts by type of card, extra lines for miscellaneous entries, the total bank deposit, and cash over or short.

Each envelope is numbered sequentially, and its contents are considered a batch. An alphabetic code in the batch number indicates whether the register came from the restaurant, the store, or the bar, or from gas sales. The code makes researching an item easier, and flags any items that may have been entered incorrectly. For example, if the clerk reviewing the general ledger account for gas sales spots a batch number in the listing that designates a store, the clerk knows that there has been an error.

At the end of the month, the program summarizes the sales transactions by account number and prints a report listing the detail that went into each account and the total. An accounting clerk then keys this report into the general ledger software package as the sales journal. When an error occurs, the clerk can always trace it back to a specific register close and review the documents in the envelope.

Accounts Receivable

Accounts receivable are processed by a software package obtained from an external vendor. Finding a suitable program was difficult because of the peculiarities of the marina business. For example, a marina receivables program must be able to keep track of customers by name *and* by slip or space number. It is also useful if the customer master record has fields for a boat registration number, the boat name, and the hull identification number.

So that the receivables clerk can issue just one bill per customer, the software package had to be able to handle several recurring charges to each customer's account. Recurring charges include a specific customer's expenditures for slip rent, electricity, maintenance, and gas. At the monthly billing time the program creates a statement listing the charges and the total amount owed.

An accountant developed another program because of a unique solution to a collection problem. Tower Park Marina rents its RV park spaces on a daily, weekly, monthly, or yearly basis. The longer the contracted rental period, the less expensive the rate. Because the yearly rate is about half the monthly rate, some tenants would rent a site on a yearly basis and then vacate prior to the end of the 12-month period. To prevent this, Tower Park began collecting the entire year's rent in the first six months. If a tenant vacates prior to the full year of occupancy, accounting recomputes the rent at the *monthly* rate (which is close to the amount they had been paying), and makes a refund for the difference.

The accountant created a program using a spreadsheet package to maintain data on the 126 sites rented on a yearly basis. The program includes a field for name, site number, lease date, lease amount, charges to date, amount of rent earned (computed by the program), and amount of rent deferred as of the date specified. A liability account, Deferred Rent, is simply increased or decreased according to the ending deferred balance. The accountant's program turned this accounting problem from a nightmare into an easy clerical function.

Management Reports

Tower Park Marina's computerized accounting system also produces certain programs that make the manager's job easier. A monthly vacancy report lists the number of vacant berths, the potential income from them, and the actual income. A weekly dockage checklist shows the boat slips in their actual order, so the manager can walk the docks and verify the boats in their slips against billings. When the manager spots an unauthorized vessel, he notes its registration number. With this number, the manager gets the owner's name and address from the Department of Motor Vehicles.

Because Tower Park Marina operates in a specialized industry, relatively few accounting software packages exist that satisfy its needs. Yet, by combining off-the-shelf software with custom programs developed in-house, the accounting staff has been able to automate many of its accounting processes. This has increased staff efficiency and reduced its overall costs.

Required:

a. What transaction cycles are described in this case?
b. Is Tower Park Marina involved in manufacturing, merchandising, or providing a service? What are the components of its conversion cycle?
c. What features distinguish the accounting requirements for a company in this industry?

16–23.   INTEGRATIVE CASE—PART I

Agee Company is a manufacturer of large diameter valves located in a major southwestern city. Management has engaged a local CPA firm to aid the company in updating its accounting systems, and you have been assigned to a design team responsible for developing the new processes. Members of the team include management accountants, Agee operating personnel, and representatives of the CPA firm's staff. The team leader is an experienced systems analyst from the CPA firm. In this and the following four chapters, you will complete assignments that allow you to participate in the design of Agee's new system.

The Company

Agee Company was established in the early 1970s by two entrepreneurs who became unhappy with their previous employer. John Albertson had been a production manager and Dave Green a salesperson for a large, publicly held company in the metal fabrication industry. As the story goes, Albertson and Green were at lunch one day discussing the frustrations of dealing with the bureaucracy of a large corporation. Green said, "You know, for two bits I'd quit this outfit and start my own." Albertson, who had skills that complemented those of Green, threw a quarter on the table, and the two men resigned to form Agee Company. Initially a closely held corporation, the company has since gone public, and its stock is traded in the over-the-counter market.

Agee is engaged in the design, manufacture, and marketing of conventional and special-purpose precision valves. Its approximately 100 customers are primarily in the petroleum, chemical, and natural gas transmission industries. In a recent year Agee had sales of $20 million and a net income of $1,600,000. Its return on stockholders' equity has averaged 15 percent over the past few years. The company has 200 employees, of which 150 are paid by the hour. Of these, 130 are utilized on the company's three production lines at its main plant. Agee is capable of manufacturing a wide variety of valves, but its current product line includes 25 basic sizes and types. Special purpose valves for certain customers can normally be fabricated from one of the standard types with very little additional production effort.

Agee has several competitors, primarily located in the Northeast and Midwest. Because of its location in a major petrochemical center, Agee enjoys a competitive advantage due to its proximity to a major part of the market. With the increasing nationwide emphasis on efficient energy generation and distribution, company management foresees a period of growth over the next decade. They are increasingly concerned that existing systems and procedures will become inadequate in providing the information necessary for management.

Existing company procedures for operational control are essentially those that were established in the first few years of the company. Increased volume has required more formalized procedures and has dispersed responsibility for tasks within the organization. Many operational personnel complain that the large volume of paperwork associated with existing manual systems prevents them from devoting sufficient attention to supervisory and management tasks. For several years, Agee has used a local service bureau for routine bookkeeping operations. But the services from this source are limited in scope and have been susceptible to system breakdowns. For these reasons, management decided to investigate the possibility of implementing a computer-based information system within the company.

Although management has recognized for some time the need for improvement in company operating systems, it has hesitated to implement a computerized system for several reasons. Management feels that the company's expertise is in valve manufacturing and marketing, not in information processing. Although employees use desktop computers for word processing and in some spreadsheet applications, they have no experience with computerized information processing and controls. The company would like to avoid the expense of hiring a large staff of analysts, programmers, and data entry personnel. Management takes pride in the extent to which it has delegated operational authority to key supervisors and wishes to avoid any change that will appear to lessen their autonomy or prestige. Any proposed system, to be acceptable to the company, should operate within these constraints.

Exhibit 16–1 summarizes the current transaction volume on the existing systems. All officers of the company agree that any new system should be capable of handling existing processing demands while providing for expected growth. They would also like

Exhibit 16–1

Case 16–23

AGEE COMPANY
Approximate Transaction Volume

Transaction Type	Average Volume	Frequency
Customer orders received	20	Day
Shipments to customers	20	Day
Cash payments received	20	Day
Purchase orders issued	30	Day
Shipments from suppliers	40	Day
Supplier invoices received	40	Day
Requests for materials from stores	50	Day
Checks issued to suppliers	40	Day

a new system that could be expanded to provide information for management decisions beyond those at the operational level.

Required:

a. What application systems would you expect to find in the transaction cycles at Agee Company?
b. Suggest a computer system configuration that you think would be appropriate for Agee.

17 REVENUE CYCLE APPLICATIONS

Learning Objectives:

1. To review the accounting entries recorded in the revenue cycle.
2. To learn which documents, reports, and records are used in the revenue cycle.
3. To understand how accounting transactions are processed by the application systems in the revenue cycle.
4. To see how control practices and procedures are applied in the revenue cycle.

Introduction

An accounting system records the activities of a business using four transaction cycles. In this chapter, you learn how accounting systems record those activities that generate revenue. These activities are a part of the revenue cycle.

In this transaction cycle, the accounting system records four economic events. First, the organization receives a request for goods or services. Computer-based systems use an order entry application system to record these requests. Second, the organization delivers the goods or services. When goods are involved, a shipping application system records this event. Third, the organization requests payment for the goods or services; this economic event is processed by the billing system. An organization uses a cash receipts application system to record the fourth economic event, the receipt of cash in payment from the customer. Sometimes the billing and cash receipts applications together are called the *accounts receivable system.*

Illustration 17–1 shows the relationships among the application systems in the revenue cycle. In this diagram, circles represent application systems, the large square depicts an external entity, and small squares stand for general ledger accounts. The interfaces between the systems contain accounting data and may take the form of documents or computer records. You will learn about them in this chapter.

ILLUSTRATION 17–1

Application Systems in the Revenue Cycle

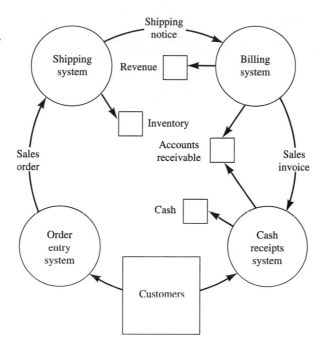

Documents, Records, and Reports

An accounting system records economic events in the form of accounting transactions. In an introductory accounting course, you described this process conceptually by making journal entries. Very few organizations actually record transactions that way today. This chapter explains how application systems record the entries that you learned earlier. An application system captures transaction data on source documents, enters these data in the subsidiary accounting records, and discloses the transactions in reports.

Revenue Cycle Transactions and Documents

This chapter discusses five transactions that occur routinely in the revenue cycle. Illustration 17–2 summarizes these transactions and shows the documents used by the accounting system in recording them.

Credit Sales.   Most businesses sell to their customers on credit. The general ledger entry recording such a sale is

        Dr.   Accounts Receivable xxx
        Cr.   Sales xxx

An accounting system records a credit sale in general and subsidiary ledgers using three documents. The sales department records the customer's request for merchandise or services on a *sales order.* The shipping department records shipment of merchandise on a *shipping notice.* (Sometimes a copy of the bill of lading, a document provided for the transportation company and completed by the shipping department, serves as a

ILLUSTRATION 17–2

Revenue Cycle Transactions and Related Documents

Type of Transaction	Related Documents
Credit sale	Sales order
	Shipping notice
	Sales invoice
Cash sale	Sales ticket
Cash receipt	Remittance advice
Sales return	Credit memo
Sales allowance	Credit memo
Bad debts write-off	Memo and aged accounts receivable trial balance
	Journal voucher

shipping notice. Other companies include a copy of the shipping notice with the goods as a packing slip.) The accounting department prepares a ***sales invoice*** and mails it to the customer, requesting payment for the merchandise. From the sales invoice, the system records these entries in both the general ledger and the accounts receivable subsidiary record.

Illustrations 17–3 and 17–4 contain examples of a sales order and an invoice. Although their forms look very similar, these documents represent very different things. The sales order shows items *to be shipped* to a customer; the invoice shows items *that have been billed* to the customer. A packing slip and a shipping notice look similar, but they represent items that have been packed and shipped.

The format and contents of these documents vary from company to company and from industry to industry. When designing the system, the design team ensures that they capture the data necessary to record properly the transaction in the accounting records and to produce management reports.

Usually when the customer is another business, the customer mails to the sales department a document called a *purchase order.* A salesclerk receives the purchase order and records its number and date on the sales order. This number then is recorded on all other records relating to that sales transaction, enabling the customer and seller to identify the order in later correspondence. The next chapter describes the use of purchase orders in more detail.

Some organizations record sales not only by customer but also by product, salesperson, or district. They do so by maintaining subsidiary records for each. In a computerized system, the coding structure allows salesclerks to code transactions by product, salesperson, and district. A nonaccounting application system, the *sales analysis system,* summarizes these transactions and produces sales analysis reports for use by marketing personnel.

Cash Receipts. Businesses receive cash in return for their goods or services from two sources: credit sales and cash sales.

Cash Receipts from Credit Sales. The accounting entry recording a customer's payment for a sale made on credit is

ILLUSTRATION 17–3

A Sales Order

```
                                      * * * * * * * * * * * * * * *
      W.D. Peachtree & Company        *                           *
      3900 Peachtree Street           *       O R D E R           *
      Atlanta, GA 30309               *                           *
                                      * * * * * * * * * * * * * * *

                               Document Number: 023549

                                 Document Date: 08/17/98

                                          Page:  1

      Sold   Christine Andrews          Ship   Christine Andrews
      To:    444 Elm Street             To:    444 Elm Street
             Duluth, GA                        Duluth, GA
             30234                             30234

                                        Cust I.D.....: ANDREC
      Ship Via.:                         P.O. Number..:
      Ship Date: 08/17/98                P.O. Date....: 08/10/98
      Due Date.: 09/17/98                Job/Order No.:
      Terms....: 2/10,NET 30             Salesperson..: GMC

      Item I.D./Desc.    Ordered     Shipped    Unit    Price        Net       TX
      ─────────────────────────────────────────────────────────────────────────
      APP10040TRA          1.00        1.00    EACH    149.9500     149.95   T
        SUPERTRASH COMPACTOR
      Discount On Above                                               7.50-




                                                        Subtotal:    142.45
                                                        Tax.....:      8.54
                                                        Total...:    150.99
```

Dr. Cash xxx
Cr.   Accounts Receivable xxx

Businesses ask customers to return a document called a ***remittance advice*** with their payments. The remittance advice shows the customer's account number and the amount paid and is the system's source of data for making the entry in the accounts receivable subsidiary record.

ILLUSTRATION 17–4

A Sales Invoice

```
                                        ***************
   W.D. Peachtree & Company             *             *
   3900 Peachtree Street                *  I N V O I C E  *
   Atlanta, GA 30309                    *             *
                                        ***************

                           Document Number: 023545

                           Document Date: 11/08/98

                                 Page:  1

   Sold  Gloria S. Cooper         Ship  Gloria S. Cooper
   To:   37 North Avenue          To:   37 North Avenue
         Atlanta, GA                    Atlanta, GA
         30333                          30333


                                 Cust I.D.....: COOPEG
   Ship Via.:                     P.O. Number..:
   Ship Date: 11/08/98            P.O. Date....: 11/08/98
   Due Date.: 12/08/98            Job/Order No.:
   Terms....: 10/10,NET30         Salesperson..: BBS


   Item I.D./Desc.      Ordered   Shipped   Unit    Price       Net      TX

   CLC463487G              3.00     3.00   EACH    11.9900      35.97    T
    GIRL'S PRINT DRESS. AVAILABLE IN A
    VARIETY OF COLORS AND PATTERNS
   Discount On Above                                            1.89-

   CLC463444               5.00     5.00   PAIR     1.7900       8.95    T
    ASSORTED COLORED TUBE SOCKS - BOY'S
    ASSORTED COLORED ANKLET SOCKS - GIRL'S

   CLC436781G              2.00     2.00   PAIR    12.5000      25.00    T
    GIRL'S BLUEJEANS


                                       Subtotal:      68.03
                                       Tax.....:       4.08
                                       Total...:      72.11
```

Illustration 17–5, a remittance advice, shows the amount due and identifies the customer's account number. Accounts receivable procedures credit the customer's account from this document. Whenever a customer mails a cash payment without including a remittance advice, a mail room employee must prepare one on a preprinted form prior to further processing.

Cash Receipts from Cash Sales   The required accounting entry to record a cash sale is

ILLUSTRATION 17–5
A Remittance Advice

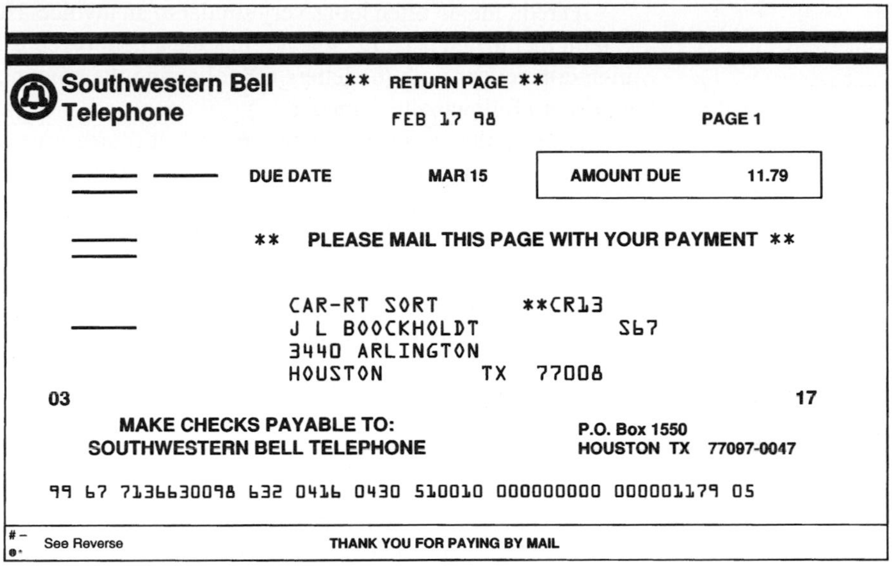
Southwestern Bell Telephone
** RETURN PAGE **
FEB 17 98
PAGE 1

DUE DATE MAR 15
AMOUNT DUE 11.79

** PLEASE MAIL THIS PAGE WITH YOUR PAYMENT **

CAR-RT SORT **CR13
J L BOOCKHOLDT S67
3440 ARLINGTON
HOUSTON TX 77008
03 17

MAKE CHECKS PAYABLE TO:
SOUTHWESTERN BELL TELEPHONE
P.O. Box 1550
HOUSTON TX 77097-0047

99 67 7136630098 632 0416 0430 510010 000000000 000001179 05

See Reverse
THANK YOU FOR PAYING BY MAIL

Courtesy of Southwestern Bell Telephone Company.

Dr.	Cash	xxx	
Cr.	Sales		xxx

When businesses make a cash sale, they safeguard the cash by placing it in a cash register. A salesclerk enters the amount of the sale either on a sales ticket or in an internal record maintained by the register. A sales supervisor reconciles these with the cash in the register at least once daily. The register also produces a receipt so the customer can verify that the transaction was recorded at the proper amount. This occurs each time you purchase from a retailer.

Sales Returns. A third transaction in the revenue cycle is the sales return. This occurs when a customer returns merchandise to the seller. Sometimes the customer is dissatisfied with the quality of the merchandise, or at other times the seller ships a quantity in excess of that desired. In either case, the seller usually subtracts the cost of the returned items from the balance owed by the customer. The entry recording a sales return is

Dr.	Sales Returns	xxx	
Cr.	Accounts Receivable		xxx

The accounting system documents a sales return with a ***credit memo.*** The credit memo shows the customer's name, account number, and the amount for the entry. The billing department attaches it to a memo from the customer and a receiving report from the receiving department showing the quantity of the items returned. These documents allow the treasurer to authorize the entry.

A credit memo often looks very similar to an invoice. However, it will be labeled as a credit memo and usually indicates that the amounts represent a credit balance. This is often done either with the letters *CR* following the amount, or with a minus (the negative sign) following the amount.

Because the credit memo also records a fourth transaction, the sales allowance, some companies call it a *sales return and allowance memo.*

Sales Allowances.   A sales allowance occurs when the sales department agrees to give the customer credit for items that were not returned. For example, if defective merchandise was shipped, the sales department may authorize a deduction from the customer's balance without requiring return of the merchandise. The entry for a sales allowance is

Dr.	Sales Allowances	xxx	
Cr.	Accounts Receivable		xxx

The sales department prepares a memo explaining why the credit to the customer's account is justified. This initiates the preparation of a credit memo by the billing system to record this entry in the accounts receivable subsidiary records.

Sometimes a thief attempts to make a fraudulent entry in the sales allowances account to cover the theft of merchandise. For this reason, all credit memos should be approved by a manager or supervisor who has no access to the merchandise.

Bad Debt Write-Offs.   When a business determines that the cash from a credit sale will never be received, management may choose to give up efforts at collecting it and assume that it is a bad debt. The entry to record a bad debt write-off is

Dr.	Allowance for Doubtful Accounts	xxx	
Cr.	Accounts Receivable		xxx

The credit department usually initiates a bad debts write-off after efforts to collect from the customer have failed. The credit manager documents the inability to collect the account in a memo. The treasurer authorizes the write-off by approving the memo, and the accounting department prepares a journal voucher to record it in the general ledger. The billing system removes the bad debt from the accounts receivable subsidiary records.

The documents in the revenue cycle generate the accounting entries produced from the data on these documents. Accounting systems enter these data in the accounting records and summarize the data to produce reports.

Revenue Cycle Reports

Application systems in the revenue cycle produce three kinds of reports: control reports, registers, and special purpose reports.

Control Reports.   Accounting systems produce control reports whenever they process multiple changes to a file. Control reports may disclose the transactions posted or the total number or amount of these transactions, or they may list changes made during file maintenance. In computer-based systems, control reports disclose record counts, control totals, and hash totals. Data control clerks review control reports, comparing these totals to verify that all changes were made properly.

ILLUSTRATION 17–6

A Control Report

```
RUN DATE: 11/30/98                       W.D. Peachtree & Company                          PAGE  1
RUN TIME:  1:48 PM                          Accounts Receivable
                                       Create G/L Transfers Control Report
─────────────────────────────────────────────────────────────────────────────────────────────────
All Entries

ACCOUNT    SC    REFERENCE     DATE     DESCRIPTION     TRANS. TYPE      DEBIT        CREDIT      NET AMOUNT
───────    ──    ─────────     ────                                     ─────        ──────      ──────────

 11000      R                11/30/98                                  4150.00                   4150.00

 12000      R                11/30/98                                                2548.46-    2548.46-

 23600      R                11/30/98                                                  78.49-      78.49-

 30512      R                11/30/98                                                 559.95-     559.95-

 30516      R                11/30/98                                                 289.95-     289.95-

 30531      R                11/30/98                                                 673.15-     673.15-

=======    ==    =========    ========  ============  ===============  ============  ============  ============

GRAND TOTALS - Transactions Processed  :      6                                      4150.00      4150.00-       0.00
               Transactions In New File:      6

Total Debits  :        4,150.00
Total Credits :        4,150.00-
                       ─────────
Difference    :            0.00

*** End Of - Create G/L Transfers Control Report ***
```

Copyright 1995 Peachtree Software, Inc. Reprinted by permission.

Illustration 17–6 contains a control report prepared by a billing application; it shows the entries produced by the system for posting to the general ledger. Most systems prepare a similar control report when entering the other changes.

Registers.   A register is a listing of all the transactions of a certain type that were processed during a single processing period. For example, if the accounting system processes billing and sales return transactions each day, then it produces a daily *document register* showing all sales invoices and credit memos prepared during that day. An example of this register is shown in Illustration 17–7.

The revenue cycle may produce other registers as well, such as a cash receipts register, an invoice register, or a credit memo register. In a manual system, the register is the journal in which transactions are initially recorded. In computerized systems, registers are frequently identified as "journals" for this reason.

Registers are important components in accounting systems because they provide an audit trail. They allow auditors to link the documents recording transactions with the general ledger account balance summarizing them. The design team determines which registers are needed during the system design process.

ILLUSTRATION 17–7

A Register

```
RUN DATE: 11/10/98                  W.D. Peachtree & Company                         PAGE  1
RUN TIME:  4:03 PM                    Invoicing/Order Entry
                                        Document Register

Current Invoices
```

DOC NUMBER	S	DOC DATE	CUST. ID	CUSTOMER NAME	TERMS	MERCHANDISE /SERVICES	OTHER CHARGES	FREIGHT	SALES TAX	DOCUMENT TOTAL
023545		11/08/98	COOPEG	Gloria S. Cooper	10/10,NET30	68.03	0.00	0.00	4.08	72.11
023546		11/08/98	HENDEK	Kathy Henderson	2/10,NET 30	413.10	0.00	0.00	24.78	437.88
023547		11/08/98	MILLEJ	Joel S. Miller	NET 30	149.95	0.00	0.00	9.00	158.95
023550		10/30/98	ANDERA	Anita S. Anderson	2/10,NET 30	0.00	8.73	0.00	0.00	8.73
023551		10/30/98	ANDREC	Christine Andrews	2/10,NET 30	0.00	23.79	0.00	0.00	23.79
023552		10/30/98	CANNOP	Paul P. Cannon	2/10,NET 30	0.00	10.59	0.00	0.00	10.59
023553		10/30/98	COOPEG	Gloria S. Cooper	10/10,NET30	0.00	15.45	0.00	0.00	15.45
023554		10/30/98	DURAND	Dorothy Durand	NET 30	0.00	35.94	0.00	0.00	35.94
023555		10/30/98	FIELDJ	Jonathan S. Fields	2/10,NET 30	0.00	48.34	0.00	0.00	48.34
023556		10/30/98	GRAYC	Charles A. Gray	2/10,NET 30	0.00	17.44	0.00	0.00	17.44
023557		10/30/98	HENDEK	Kathy Henderson	2/10,NET 30	0.00	6.16	0.00	0.00	6.16
023558		10/30/98	HOLLOJ	James R. Holloway	2/10,NET 30	0.00	15.50	0.00	0.00	15.50
023559		10/30/98	JOHNSM	Michael H. Johnson	2/10,NET 30	0.00	36.45	0.00	0.00	36.45
023560		10/30/98	JONESE	Elizabeth A. Jones	2/10,NET 30	0.00	27.56	0.00	0.00	27.56
023561		10/30/98	MARSHJ	Joanne Marshall	10/10,NET30	0.00	10.75	0.00	0.00	10.75
023562		10/30/98	MILLEJ	Joel S. Miller	NET 30	0.00	9.18	0.00	0.00	9.18
023563		10/30/98	MITCHT	Thomas C. Mitchell	2/10,NET 30	0.00	64.19	0.00	0.00	64.19
023564		10/30/98	PARKEB	Bill Parker	10/10,NET30	0.00	2.00	0.00	0.00	2.00
023565		10/30/98	SCOTTB	Benjamin S. Scott	2/10,NET 30	0.00	23.16	0.00	0.00	23.16
023566		10/30/98	SMITHR	Robert M. Smith	2/10,NET 30	0.00	26.12	0.00	0.00	26.12
023567		10/30/98	SMITHS	Susan S. Smith	2/10,NET 30	0.00	10.08	0.00	0.00	10.08
023568		10/30/98	THOMPS	Samuel L. Thompson	10/10,NET30	0.00	26.47	0.00	0.00	26.47
023569		10/30/98	TRACED	Darryl Tracer	NET 30	0.00	7.27	0.00	0.00	7.27
023570		10/30/98	TURNEC	Catherine M. Turner	2/10,NET 30	0.00	41.68	0.00	0.00	41.68
023571		10/30/98	WILLIL	Lisa R. Williams	2/10,NET 30	0.00	25.93	0.00	0.00	25.93

```
NO. OF ITEMS LISTED:    25              631.08     492.78      0.00     37.86    1161.72
```

Special Purpose Reports. Most systems require three special purpose accounting reports in the revenue cycle. They are the customer statement, the aged accounts receivable trial balance, and the remittance list. In addition, systems may produce sales analysis reports for evaluating management performance.

Customer Statement. A *customer statement* is a list of all transactions in a customer's account during a specified time period. Many businesses mail a monthly statement to each active customer. It shows the sales made to the customer since the last statement, the payments received, and the balance still owed by the customer.

Monthly statements are beneficial for two reasons: First, they enable the customers to monitor transactions in their accounts. This may disclose errors or irregularities undetected by the control procedures in the accounting system. Second, they remind customers about outstanding balances, which sometimes encourages customers to pay their accounts more promptly. Illustration 17–8 shows a monthly statement.

ILLUSTRATION 17–8

A Customer Statement

```
W.D. Peachtree & Company
3900 Peachtree Street
Atlanta, GA 30309


                          STATEMENT DATE:   11/26/98

                          ACCOUNT NUMBER:   DURAND



  Dorothy Durand
  908 Forest Drive
  Apt. 5
  Atlanta, GA                30303



  INVOICE    DATE     REFERENCE      CODE    DEBITS      CREDITS     BALANCE
  _____   _____  _____    _____  _____   _____   _____

                          BALANCE FORWARD                          $2,465.55

  0          10/29/98  CK            PMNT     $0.00     $223.66-    $223.66-
  021700     09/10/98                SALE    $223.66      $0.00     $223.66
  023510     10/30/98                SALE  $2,411.52      $0.00    $2,411.52
  023528     10/31/98                SALE     $18.09      $0.00      $18.09
  023554     01/30/99  Ser Charge    SALE     $35.94      $0.00      $35.94



    CURRENT            1 - 30
  _____         _____

    $35.94             $18.09                                    =============
                                             TOTAL DUE             $2,465.55
                                                                 =============
   31 - 60           OVER   60
  _____         _____

  $2,411.52            $0.00
```

Copyright 1995 Peachtree Software, Inc. Reprinted by permission.

Aged Accounts Receivable Trial Balance.   An accounts receivable trial balance is a list of all customers and the balances they owe at a specified date. When this trial balance is *aged,* each customer balance is categorized according to how long it has existed. Usually an aged accounts receivable trial balance discloses for each customer the amounts less than 31 days old, and those 31 to 60, 61 to 90, and more than 90 days past due. Illustration 17–9 contains an aged accounts receivable trial balance.

ILLUSTRATION 17–9

An Aged Accounts Receivable Trial Balance

```
RUN DATE: 12/05/98                    W.D. Peachtree & Company                        PAGE  1
RUN TIME:  3:05 PM                       Accounts Receivable
                                   Detailed Aged Receivables Report
```

Aging Date: 11/30/98

CUST. ID	CUSTOMER NAME	INVOICE NUMBER DUE DATE	CURRENT	1 - 30 PAST DUE	31 - 60 PAST DUE	OVER 60 PAST DUE	OPEN CR	TOTAL
ANDERA	Anita S. Anderson 404/555-1212	023513 11/25/98		590.19				590.19
ANDREC	Christine Andrews 404/555-1212	023111 11/01/98		95.73				95.73
		023489 11/04/98		603.30				603.30
		023515 11/29/98		365.18				365.18
		023549 09/08/98				3408.44		3408.44
				1064.21		3408.44		4472.65
CANNOP	Paul P. Cannon 404/555-1212	023345 11/02/98		238.36				238.36
		023517 11/30/98	1335.55					1335.55
		023548 12/05/98	15.00					15.00
			1350.55	238.36				1588.91
COOPEG	Gloria S. Cooper 404/555-1212	023105 10/31/98		410.00				410.00
		023490 11/04/98		61.40				61.40
		023519 11/30/98	953.95					953.95
			953.95	471.40				1425.35
DURAND	Dorothy Durand	— —		18.09	2411.52			2429.61
FIELDJ	Jonathan S. Fields 404/555-1212	— —		40.85	3226.71			3267.56
GRAYC	Charles A. Gray 404/555-1212	022969 10/23/98			463.04			463.04
		023488 11/04/98		1166.00				1166.00
		023514 11/29/98		1908.00				1908.00
				3074.00	463.04			3537.04
HENDEK	Kathy Henderson 404/555-1212	023500 11/25/98		1249.69				1249.69

Many businesses produce aged accounts receivable trial balances each month. Credit managers review them to identify customer accounts that are unpaid for excessive lengths of time. They also use these documents to determine when customers' accounts should be written off as uncollectible. Accountants use these trial balances to determine the adequacy of the Allowance for Doubtful Accounts.

Remittance List. A ***remittance list*** enumerates all currency and checks received during one day. It establishes a control total over cash receipts, prevents theft, and

ILLUSTRATION 17–10

A Remittance List

SUNLIGHT MANUFACTORY COMPANY 105 Red Hot Road Dallas, Texas 75248 Remittance list			No. _____ Date _____
Check no.	Customer name	Amount	Check here if remittance advice is attached
4123	ABC Company	123.29	✓
816	H. Jackson	19.56	✓
2803	Betty's Home Interiors	228.00	✓
666	I.M. Able	26.00	
	Total	4,012.20	

ensures that no receipts are lost before being credited to a customer's account. Illustration 17–10 shows a remittance list.

In many companies, customers' payments for credit sales arrive in the mail. These companies assign the responsibility for opening the mail to a mail room clerk who also prepares the remittance list. One copy accompanies the checks that go to the company cashier, and another goes with the remittance advices to the accounting department.

This procedure ensures adequate segregation of duties over cash receipts because the cashier and mail room clerk have custody of the checks while the accounting department has the records regarding them. The use of a remittance list allows an auditor or manager to determine that no remittance advice has been removed to cover the theft of a check.

Sales Analysis Reports.   From the accounting files maintained in the revenue cycle, the sales analysis application produces various management performance reports. These summarize sales revenue, costs, and profit margin by customer, product, salesperson, or sales district. They enable marketing management to evaluate the profitability of products, the performance of sales personnel, or the effects of special advertising campaigns or promotions. Illustration 17–11 shows an example of a sales analysis report.

To summarize, the revenue cycle produces three kinds of reports: Control reports ensure that changes are made correctly, registers provide an audit trail, and special purpose reports provide management information. Application systems in the other cycles produce these kinds of reports as well.

ILLUSTRATION 17–11

A Sales Analysis Report

```
RUN DATE: 11/30/98                          W.D. Peachtree & Company
RUN TIME: 10:48A                         SALES ANALYSIS BY SALESPERSON            PAGE NO:    1
                                   POSTED INVOICES FOR 10/01/98 THROUGH 12/01/98

          SALES-   INV/RET  CUST.   CUSTOMER              INV       GROSS                   TOTAL
  TYPE    PERSON   NUMBER   ID      NAME                  DATE      SALES     SALES TAX     SALES       PAYMENTS    NET DUE


  INVOICE   BBS    023488   GRAYC   Charles A. Gray       10/05/98  1,166.00     0.00     1,166.00        0.00     1,166.00
  INVOICE   BBS    023490   COOPEG  Gloria S. Cooper      10/05/98     61.40     0.00        61.40        0.00        61.40
  INVOICE   BBS    023493   HOLLOJ  James R. Holloway     10/05/98  1,612.32     0.00     1,612.32        0.00     1,612.32
  INVOICE   BBS    023498   WILLIL  Lisa R. Williams      10/15/98     92.54     0.00        92.54        0.00        92.54
  INVOICE   BBS    023499   ANDERA  Anita S. Anderson     10/15/98  1,122.54     0.00     1,122.54        0.00     1,122.54
  INVOICE   BBS    023545   COOPEG  Gloria S. Cooper      11/08/98     68.03     4.08        72.11        0.00        72.11

                                    Salesperson Total:            4,122.83     4.08     4,126.91        0.00     4,126.91

  INVOICE   GMC    023489   ANDREC  Christine Andrews     10/05/98  1,006.30     0.00     1,006.30        0.00     1,006.30
  INVOICE   GMC    023492   SMITHS  Susan S. Smith        10/05/98    275.45     0.00       275.45        0.00       275.45
  INVOICE   GMC    023495   JOHNSM  Michael H. Johnson    10/05/98  1,812.60     0.00     1,812.60        0.00     1,812.60
  INVOICE   GMC    023546   HENDEK  Kathy Henderson       11/08/98    413.10    24.78       437.88        0.00       437.88
  INVOICE   GMC    023547   MILLEJ  Joel S. Miller        11/08/98    149.95     9.00       158.95        0.00       158.95
  INVOICE   GMC    023572   ANDREC  Christine Andrews     11/13/98  5,927.92   355.68     6,283.60        0.00     6,283.60
  INVOICE   GMC    023573   JOHNSM  Michael H. Johnson    11/13/98  1,424.97    85.50     1,510.47        0.00     1,510.47

                                    Salesperson Total:           11,010.29   474.96    11,485.25        0.00    11,485.25


                                    Grand Totals:                15,133.12   479.04    15,612.16        0.00    15,612.16
```

Accounting systems capture transaction data in documents and disclose these data in reports. They produce these reports from data contained in the accounting records.

Revenue Cycle Accounting Records

Accounting systems maintain records in journals, ledgers, and filing cabinets for manual processes, and in computer files and databases for computerized ones. Although the forms of the records differ, their contents are similar.

Noncomputerized Records.   Manual journals and ledgers may be in the form of books or card files. In the revenue cycle, the accounting records consist of three special journals and one subsidiary ledger.

The subsidiary ledger is the accounts receivable subsidiary ledger. It contains one page or card for each customer. This page shows debit and credit postings from the journals to the account of that customer and the balance the customer owes.

The special journals are the sales journal, the credit memo journal, and the cash receipts journal. Accounting clerks enter transactions chronologically in these journals from documents. Then daily, weekly, or monthly totals from these journals are transferred to the general ledger and the accounts receivable subsidiary ledger. Illustration 17–12 shows how these records look.

ILLUSTRATION 17–12

Noncomputerized Accounting Records

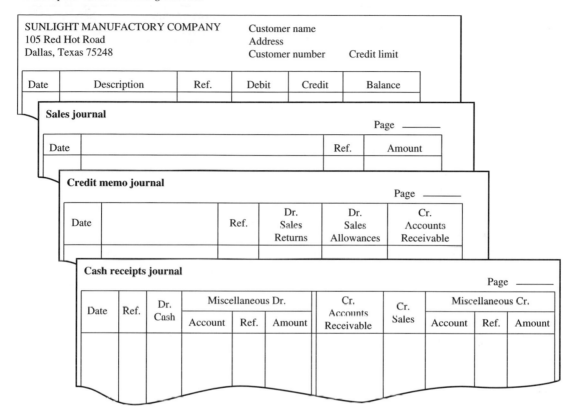

Computerized Records.   Accounting records kept by computerized processes are in the form of computer files and databases. In a traditional data file system, revenue cycle applications use two master files and as many as six transaction files.

If database management system (DBMS) software is used, the applications do not maintain separate files. Instead, they store data in the database, and each application has access to these data determined by the application's subschema. The subschema contains the same data fields provided by the files in a traditional data file system.

Master Files.   Applications in the revenue cycle routinely update the ***customer master record.*** This file has one record for each credit customer and contains data on the customer's address, credit limit, credit terms, and balance owed. During system design, the design team determines that this record contains data required to maintain the accounting records and produce management reports.

Illustration 17–13 shows the contents of a master record. By comparing these contents with Illustration 17–12, you can see that the customer master file is the computerized equivalent of the accounts receivable subsidiary ledger in a manual system. In the manual system, the customer name identifies the ledger page; in the

ILLUSTRATION 17–13

Contents of a Customer Master Record

1. CUSTOMER-NUMBER*	6. CREDIT-TERMS
2. CUSTOMER-NAME	7. STATEMENT-DATE
3. BILLING-ADDRESS	8. STATEMENT-BALANCE
4. SHIPPING-ADDRESS	9. CURRENT-BALANCE
5. CREDIT-LIMIT	

*Designates the primary key.

computerized system, the primary key field, CUSTOMER-NUMBER, uniquely identifies the record.

The shipping application also updates the *inventory master file,* which contains perpetual inventory records. It has one record for each item kept in the inventory warehouse. When merchandise is shipped, the billing application subtracts the quantity shipped from the quantity on hand in the inventory master file. A later chapter on conversion cycle applications describes its other contents.

Transaction Files.   Different companies process revenue cycle transactions in various ways. Businesses relying on noncomputerized processes use fewer transaction files than highly computerized firms. With noncomputerized processes, data flow between departments on documents rather than on computer records. Depending on the extent of computerization, a computer-based system may have as many as six transaction files.

The *invoice detail file* contains one record for each sales invoice mailed to a customer. The billing application adds a record to this file when a sales invoice is mailed, and the cash receipts application removes the record when the invoice is paid. Illustration 17–14 shows the contents of a record in this file; as you can see, it is the same data contained on a sales invoice.

The RESPONSIBILITY-CODE field identifies the salesperson and sales division producing the sale. The responsibility accounting system uses this field to summarize sales transactions by responsibility center on performance reports. The TRANS-ACTION-CODE field contains a code identifying this as a record representing a sales invoice. Illustration 17–15 contains an example set of transaction codes. The combination of INVOICE-NUMBER and TRANSACTION-CODE uniquely identifies any

ILLUSTRATION 17–14

Contents of an Invoice Detail Record

1. INVOICE-NUMBER*	7. SALES-TERMS
2. TRANSACTION-CODE*	8. RESPONSIBILITY-CODE
3. CUSTOMER-NUMBER†	9. PRODUCT-CODE
4. TRANSACTION-DATE	10. PRODUCT-PRICE
5. SALES-ORDER-NUMBER	11. PRODUCT-QUANTITY
6. SHIPPING-NOTICE-NUMBER	

*Designates the primary key.
†Designates a secondary key.

ILLUSTRATION 17–15

Transaction Codes

12	Cash collection from customers' payment on account
27	Sales on account
72	Sales return
82	Sales allowances
92	Write-off accounts receivable

transaction in the system. By multiplying the PRODUCT-QUANTITY by the PRODUCT-PRICE, a computer program derives the total amount of the transaction recorded by the invoice detail record. The secondary key field, CUSTOMER-NUMBER, identifies the customer producing the transaction. It is not unique, since a customer may have several transactions in the system at once.

Computerized systems may also have a sales order detail file and a shipments file. The *sales order detail file* contains one record for each customer sales order that has been accepted, and it contains the data shown on a customer sales order. It is created by the order entry application and provides inputs to the shipping application. The *shipments file* contains one record for each shipment made to a customer and contains the data shown on the shipping notice. After the shipping application creates it, the record is an input to the billing application.

The *cash receipts detail file* contains the transactions processed by the cash receipts application. A data entry clerk adds a transaction record to this file for each remittance advice received from a customer. The cash receipts application then identifies the transaction with an unpaid invoice record from the invoice detail file, deletes the invoice record, and posts the cash receipt to the customer master file. Illustration 17–16 shows the contents of a record in the cash receipts detail file.

The **accounts receivable change log file** provides an audit trail and allows preparation of monthly customer statements. It contains one record for each change to a customer's balance since the date of the last statement. The billing and cash receipts applications add a record to this file for each invoice detail record and cash receipts detail record they process. When customer statements are printed, a program in the billing application converts the accounts receivable change log file into an archival file.

ILLUSTRATION 17–16

Contents of a Cash Receipts Detail Record

1. INVOICE-NUMBER*
2. TRANSACTION-CODE*
3. CUSTOMER-NUMBER†
4. TRANSACTION-DATE
5. CUSTOMER-CHECK-NUMBER
6. DATE-RECEIVED
7. AMOUNT

*Designates the primary key.
†Designates a secondary key.

ILLUSTRATION 17–17

Contents of an Accounts Receivable Change Log Record

1. CUSTOMER-NUMBER*
2. DATE*
3. TRANSACTION-CODE*
4. TRANSACTION-AMOUNT
5. INVOICE/CM-NUMBER

*Designates the primary key.

The MIS department keeps this file on tape for use by the auditors. Illustration 17–17 shows the contents of a record.

Revenue cycle applications also provide inputs to another file, the ***general ledger batch summary file.*** After producing all records for the accounts receivable change log file, the billing application prepares a transaction record containing the general ledger entry summarizing the transactions. Similarly, the cash receipts application adds a transaction record to this file summarizing all cash receipts transactions. Throughout the month, these and other application systems add transaction records to the general ledger batch summary file. Then, during the monthly closing process, the general ledger application posts these records to the general ledger master file. The general ledger batch summary file is also discussed in the chapters describing the other transaction cycles.

Types of Accounts Receivable Systems.   A computerized system maintains accounts receivable records in the customer master file and the invoice detail file. Depending on how much data are kept in these files, they are categorized as balance only, balance forward, or open item systems.

Balance Only Systems.   In a ***balance only system,*** the customer master file contains only the current balance of the customer. The system uses no invoice detail file. Detailed data on customers' purchases and payments are available only from manual files containing copies of the original documents.

Some older credit card and department store credit sale applications use the balance only approach. Their monthly statements disclose only the current amount owed by the customer. They include copies of the documents with the monthly statement mailed to customers to support the balance due.

Balance Forward Systems.   In a ***balance forward system,*** the record in the customer master file shows both the customer's current balance and the balance as of the last statement date. The invoice detail file contains records for all invoices prepared since that date. The system routinely deletes old records for the customer from the invoice detail file when it prints the customer's monthly statement. This system uses prior customer statements to obtain detailed data supporting balances more than one month old.

Newer credit card and department store systems are of the balance forward type. Your credit card statements probably show your unpaid balance at the beginning of the billing cycle, the transactions in your account since then, and the resulting balance at the billing date.

Open Item Systems.   An open item system is similar to a balance forward one except that it has a larger invoice detail file. In an ***open item system,*** this file contains a record for each unpaid invoice. The system deletes records from the file when the invoice is paid.

When customers make payments, they may not identify specific invoices for them. Instead, they may pay either a fixed amount or the amount on their statements. An open item system must be able to accept such payments and treat them as partial payments on invoices. This is called an *automatic cash application* feature.

Businesses that sell to other businesses use open item systems. They frequently establish discounting policies that encourage customers to pay specific invoices promptly.

The revenue cycle can use both computerized and manual accounting records. As you can see, the contents of the records in the two recording media are similar. In many respects, the methods of processing them are also similar.

Transaction Processing

In an introductory accounting course, you studied the procedures for recording transactions in journals and ledgers. In a large company, these procedures may be performed by different people. A computer-based accounting system implements many of these procedures using computer programs. These computer programs, together with documents, reports, records, and manual procedures, constitute a computer application system.

Manual Processes

Before the development of computers, companies processed transactions manually; today, few have manual systems. Instead, most companies use a combination of computerized and manual procedures. For this reason, you should understand noncomputerized as well as computerized processes.

Credit Sales.   Illustration 17–18 shows manual procedures for processing credit sales transactions. The sales department initiates the transaction by completing a customer sales order. Once the credit department approves credit for this customer, the shipping department obtains the merchandise from the warehouse and ships it. The shipping department sends a shipping notice to the billing department, which initiates preparation of a sales invoice.

Illustration 17–19 depicts the manual procedures for processing sales returns, sales allowances, and bad debt write-offs. The sales department initiates returns and allowances, while the credit department initiates the write-off of an account as uncollectible. The treasurer approves each transaction before the accounting department enters it in the accounting records. The receiving department completes a receiving report to document the return of goods.

Cash Receipts.   Illustration 17–20 contains manual procedures for processing cash receipts. In this system, the mail room receives customers' payments from credit sales, while the sales department receives them from cash sales. All cash goes directly to the cashier for deposit in the bank, while remittance advices and sales tickets go to the accounting department for entry in the accounting records.

ILLUSTRATION 17–18

Manual Procedures for Credit Sales

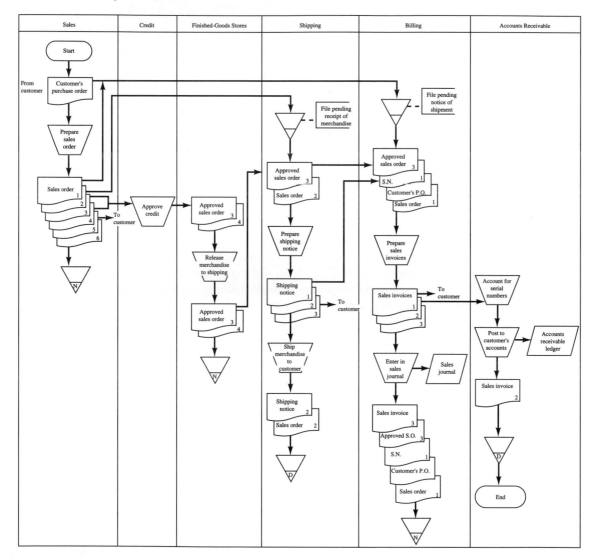

Rather than receive customer payments for credit sales in the mail room, many companies use a lockbox. A *lockbox* is a post office box to which only bank personnel have access. The company asks that its customers mail their payments to this special post office box. A representative from the bank removes all payments from the box daily and deposits them in the company's bank account. The bank then mails the remittance advices that accompany the payments to the company. A lockbox improves control over cash because the company's employees never have custody of customer payments.

ILLUSTRATION 17–19

Manual Procedures for Sales Returns, Allowances, and Bad Debt Write-Offs

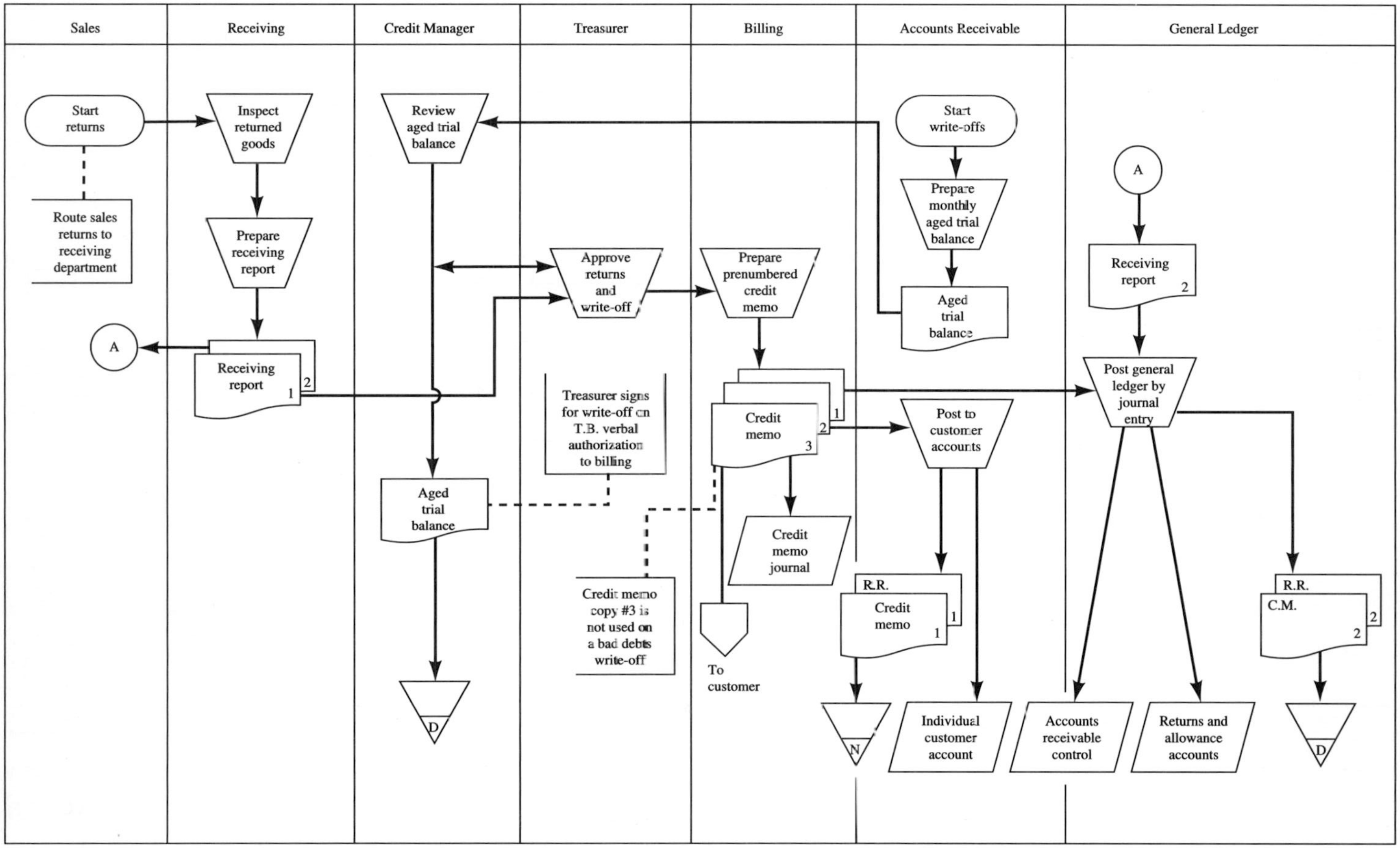

ILLUSTRATION 17–20

Manual Procedures for Cash Receipts

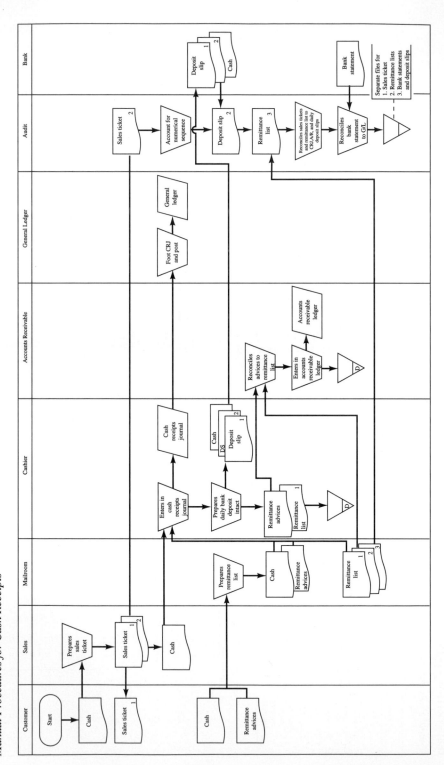

Control Activities.   Manual procedures for processing transactions should have adequate authorization procedures, maintain security for assets and records, ensure adequate segregation of duties, and provide adequate documents and records. The chapter on internal control structure describes these control activities. Segregation of duties requires separation of three functions: custody of the asset, recordkeeping for the asset, and authorizing transactions in the asset.

Credit Sales.   The sales order entry personnel and the credit department authorize credit sales transactions. Inventory warehouse and shipping personnel have physical custody of inventory prior to shipment. Accounts receivable and general ledger clerks keep the records regarding credit sales. Thus, segregation of duties requires that these functions are assigned to different individuals.

Most companies also assign duties so that order entry is separate from credit approval, inventory warehouse is separate from shipping, and maintaining accounts receivable detail records is separate from maintaining the general ledger. These divisions not only provide improved control by allowing employees to verify the actions of others but also improve efficiency by allowing specialization.

For example, the credit department verifies that sales personnel do not accept a sales order from a customer unable to pay for it. Because credit department employees work full-time evaluating the creditworthiness of customers, they become skilled at making these decisions.

Sales Returns and Allowances.   Usually a customer service department and a credit department authorize sales returns and allowances transactions. A receiving department and personnel in the inventory warehouse have custody of returned goods. Accounts receivable and general ledger clerks maintain records regarding these transactions. A company that maintains these distinctions implements adequate segregation of duties over sales returns and allowances.

As with credit sales transactions, companies frequently further divide responsibilities to improve control and efficiency.

Bad Debt Write-Offs.   Segregation of duties over a credit transaction prevents an employee from intercepting a payment from a customer, stealing the check, and then writing off the debt as uncollectible. Someone in the treasurer's department, such as a cashier, has custody of cash when it is received. Accounts receivable and general ledger personnel keep the records regarding cash and bad debts. In most companies, a credit manager authorizes a bad debt write-off and the treasurer approves it. With good segregation of duties, these positions are separate.

Illustration 17–21 shows good internal control measures for credit sales, sales returns, sales allowances, and bad debt write-off transactions. It provides detail on how the four kinds of control activities are applied when these transactions are processed.

Customer Payments on Account.   These transactions represent cash receipts received in the mail. Mail room personnel and the cashier have custody of these assets each day. These duties should be separate from those of people maintaining accounts receivable and general ledger records.

ILLUSTRATION 17–21

Control Activities for Billing Transactions

Activity	Credit Sales	Returns and Allowances	Bad Debt Write-Offs
Transaction authorization	Sales authorizes Credit approves	Customer service and credit authorize Treasurer approves	Credit manager authorizes Treasurer approves
Security for assets and records	Goods *a.* Order filled only with approved sales invoice *b.* Quantity independently counted *c.* Shipped to customer only on receipt of sales invoice from order entry	Returned goods *a.* Sales returns and allowance memo prepared only on receipt of goods *b.* Quantity independently counted	
Segregation of duties	*a.* Order entry and credit *b.* Warehouse and shipping *c.* Accounts receivable and general ledger	*a.* Customer service and credit *b.* Receiving and warehouse *c.* Accounts receivable and general ledger	*a.* Credit and treasurer *b.* Cashier *c.* Accounts receivable and general ledger
Adequate documents and records	Sales invoice *a.* Prepared only on receipt of customer purchase order *b.* Prenumbered *c.* Credit approved *d.* Checked against current price list *e.* Verified before sent to customer Accounts receivable *a.* Posted daily *b.* Control total established daily *c.* Customer statement sent monthly *d.* Aged accounts receivable trial balance prepared monthly General ledger *a.* Standard journal voucher used *b.* Control total compared daily *c.* Journal entry made daily	Sales returns and allowance memo *a.* Prepared only on receipt of goods and/or customer advice *b.* Prenumbered *c.* Return or allowance approved *d.* Price checked against sales invoice *e.* Verified before sent to customer Accounts receivable *a.* Posted daily *b.* Control total established daily General ledger *a.* Standard journal voucher used *b.* Control total compared daily *c.* Journal entry made daily	Write-off memorandum *a.* Prepared only with proper documentation *b.* Approved *c.* Approved by a second officer if amount is over certain limit Accounts receivable *a.* Control total established General ledger *a.* Standard journal voucher used *b.* Control total compared

Separating accounts receivable processing from that for the general ledger makes falsifying accounts receivable records more difficult. If an accounts receivable clerk creates a false entry, perhaps to cover the theft of a customer's payment, the clerk must also falsify a general ledger entry. This is examined by a general ledger clerk who may detect it as a fraudulent entry. Otherwise, a supervisor or auditor detects the theft when reconciling the accounts receivable detail records with the general ledger control account.

ILLUSTRATION 17–22

Control Activities for Cash Receipts Transactions

Activity	Cash Sales	Customer Payments on Account
Transaction authorization	Sales price as marked authorizes	Receipt of remittance advice authorizes
Security for assets and records	Cash receipts *a.* Deposited intact daily *b.* Authenticated deposit slip secured	Cash receipts *a.* Deposited intact daily *b.* Authenticated deposit slip secured
Segregation of duties	*a.* Counter sales and cashier *b.* Cashier and general ledger	*a.* Mail room and cashier *b.* Mail room and accounts receivable *c.* Cashier and accounts receivable *d.* Cashier and general ledger *e.* Accounts receivable and general ledger
Adequate documents	Initial documentation *a.* Prepared before asking customer to pay *b.* Prenumbered *c.* Tendered to customer as a matter of course *d.* Control total established for each shift Sales *a.* Control total established daily General ledger *a.* Standard journal voucher used *b.* Control total compared daily *c.* Journal entry made daily	Initial documentation *a.* Remittance list prepared by the mail room as soon as mail is opened *b.* Remittance list is prenumbered Accounts receivable *a.* Posted daily *b.* Control total established daily *c.* Customer statement sent monthly General ledger *a.* Standard journal voucher used *b.* Control total compared daily *c.* Journal entry made daily

Cash Sales.   Sales personnel and the cashier have custody of the assets arising from these transactions. Accountability for cash is established by recording each cash sale in a cash register or terminal and providing each customer with a receipt. Customers verify that the amount of the sale on the receipt and recorded in the register is correct. This creates records for the asset summarized in the general ledger. Illustration 17–22 provides detail concerning the four kinds of control activities for cash receipts transactions.

Computerized Processes

A computer-based accounting system uses both computerized and manual processes. In the revenue cycle, a computer-based system uses four application systems: the order entry, shipping, billing, and cash receipts applications.

Order Entry Application.   The purpose of the order entry application is to record a customer's request for goods or services, to obtain credit approval for the customer, and to ensure that the order is filled.

Procedures for credit approval usually require the credit department to establish a credit limit for each customer. This credit limit is the maximum unpaid balance the customer is allowed to have. Whenever an order is received from a customer, the order entry system determines if the order would cause the outstanding balance to exceed the credit limit. If so, the customer's order is disapproved.

AIS in Practice

Office Depot, the largest office products superstore chain in North America, has 575 stores and annual revenues of over $6.1 billion. Because of its rapid growth, Office Depot's old accounts receivable system was modified so many times that it became inefficient. They required a new system that would run on their mainframe computer using a relational database management system. It had to concurrently handle on-line and batch processing and be available 24 hours a day.

Office Depot purchased such a package and modified it to meet their needs. The new system allows the addition of new

customers at any time, and customers' records are immediately available to the credit authorization system. It allows payments not only by checks and cash but also from electronic bank transmissions. The new system applies payments to a customer's account by matching the payment amount with an outstanding invoice balance. These features allow the company to process 30 percent of its payments without manual intervention. The more efficient software has decreased the time required to print customer statements from 20 to 5 hours.

Illustration 17–23 contains a flowchart of an on-line real-time order entry system. A salesclerk enters data from a customer's purchase order. A computer program validates the data entered by the clerk, verifies that the order is within the customer's credit limit, and creates a sales order detail record. The program produces two documents. An *order acknowledgment* is mailed to the customer confirming acceptance of the order. The *sales register* provides a list of all sales orders entered by the clerk.

Older accounting systems used batch processing for this application. With such a system, a clerk prepared sales orders and accumulated them in batches. The clerk also created a control total, called a *batch total*, for each batch. The batch system then applied the processing steps described above to transactions a batch at a time. Clerks checked the batch total after each processing step to ensure that no transactions were lost.

ILLUSTRATION 17–23

An Order Entry Application

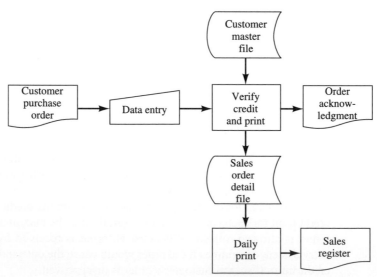

ILLUSTRATION 17–24

A Shipping Application

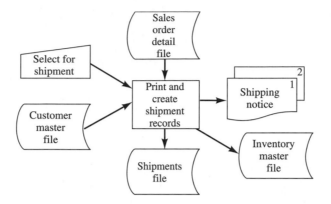

On-line real-time systems provide query capability, allowing users to examine the contents of specific records in the file. In this order entry application, a salesclerk may query the customer master file to determine a customer's balance, credit limit, or terms of sale. The clerk may also query the order entry detail file to determine the status of a past order.

Shipping Application.   The purposes of the shipping application are to ensure that merchandise is shipped prior to the date desired by the customer and that the customer is promptly billed for the merchandise. Illustration 17–24 shows an on-line real-time shipping system.

A shipping clerk examines the contents of the sales order detail file and identifies orders that are due for shipment. The program creates a record in the shipments file for each order that is due, and reduces the quantity on hand for that item in the inventory master file. It produces two copies of the shipping notice. One serves as a bill of lading, and another goes to the warehouse as a packing list.

Billing Application.   The purposes of the billing application are to prepare sales invoices for merchandise that has been shipped and to record the sale in the appropriate accounts. This application also produces credit memos to document sales returns and sales allowances. These credit memos, similar to sales invoices, are mailed to the affected customers.

The flowchart of the system in Illustration 17–25 shows these procedures. The program creates a sales invoice and an invoice detail record for each shipment record created in the billing application. It also allows a billing clerk to enter data creating credit memos. The program adds invoice detail records to the accounts receivable change log file and produces a record summarizing the transactions for the general ledger batch summary file. The clerk prints a daily document register from the contents of the invoice detail file. A clerk may query the invoice detail file to determine the status of a specific unpaid sales invoice.

ILLUSTRATION 17–25

A Billing Application

A. Daily processing

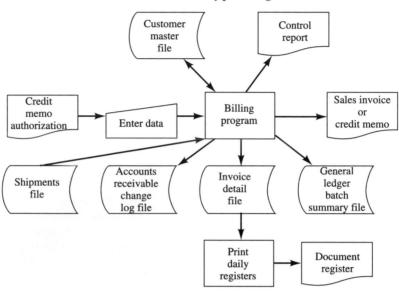

B. Monthly processing

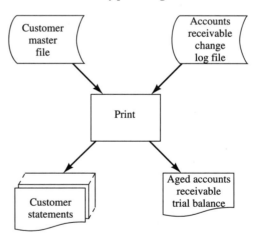

Monthly, the system prints customer statements and an aged trial balance. Many companies practice *cycle billing,* which means they print and mail statements to a different portion of their customers each day of the month. This avoids the difficulties of producing all customer statements at the month's end.

ILLUSTRATION 17–26

A Cash Receipts Application

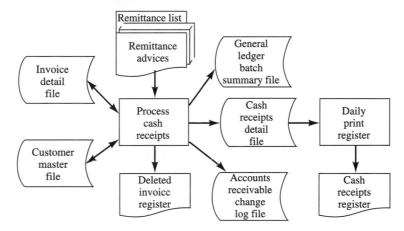

Cash Receipts Application.   The purpose of the cash receipts application is to record payments made by customers for credit sales. It also deletes paid invoice records from the invoice detail file. Illustration 17–26 shows these procedures.

A clerk enters data from remittance advices and creates a cash receipts detail record from each. The computer program matches each cash receipts detail record with its appropriate invoice detail record, deletes the invoice detail record, and prints a register of deleted invoices. It posts the cash receipt to the appropriate customer master record, adds a record for each cash receipt to the accounts receivable change log file, and produces a record summarizing these transactions for the general ledger batch summary file. The clerk executes another program that prints a daily cash receipts register from the cash receipts detail file.

File Maintenance.   During file maintenance, a computer application system adds or deletes a master record or makes changes to the reference data in an existing master record. In the revenue cycle, file maintenance is necessary when the organization obtains a new customer or loses an old customer, or when the name, address, credit limits, or credit terms of an existing customer change. These require changes to a customer master record.

The sales department initiates these changes by recording them on a file maintenance form. In an on-line real-time system, the clerk enters changes from these forms at a terminal. In a batch processing system, a clerk batches file maintenance changes, a data entry clerk converts them to computer-readable form, and a file maintenance program makes the changes prior to execution of the order entry application. This ensures that master records exist for all approved customers and that customer data are current prior to the processing of sales transactions. The credit department should approve any master record changes adding new customers or any changes to existing credit limits and credit terms.

ILLUSTRATION 17–27

Example Input Controls in the Revenue Cycle

System	Control Procedure
Order entry	**Validity test.** Program computes a check digit for the field CUSTOMER-NUMBER. **Completeness test.** Program verifies that each input record contains data in the following fields: TRANSACTION-CODE, TRANSACTION-DATE, SALES-ORDER-NUMBER, SALES-TERMS, PRODUCT-CODE, PRODUCT-PRICE, PRODUCT-QUANTITY, TRANSACTION-AMOUNT.
Shipping	**Validity test.** Program verifies that cutoff date is of the form AA-BB-CCCC, where AA < 13, BB < 32, and CCCC is numeric.
Billing	**Validity test.** Program computes a check digit for the field CUSTOMER-NUMBER. **Completeness test.** Program verifies that each input record contains data in the following fields: TRANSACTION-CODE, TRANSACTION-DATE, SALES-ORDER-NUMBER, SALES-TERMS, PRODUCT-CODE, PRODUCT-PRICE, PRODUCT-QUANTITY, TRANSACTION-AMOUNT.
Cash receipts	**Validity test.** Program computes a check digit for the field CUSTOMER-NUMBER. **Completeness test.** Program verifies that each input record contains all data fields.

Application Controls.   The designers of a computer-based system include application controls when an individual application is developed. Application controls may be input controls, processing controls, and output controls.

Input Controls.   Input controls prevent or detect errors on the input of data. They ensure that data entry clerks accurately convert data from the human-readable form on a document to a form readable by the computer. Most computer systems implement input controls using validation procedures. Validity tests, completeness tests, and control totals are examples of control procedures used for data validation. Illustration 17–27 shows examples of how to employ these procedures in the application systems of the revenue cycle.

Processing Controls.   Processing controls prevent or detect erroneous processing by computer programs. They are procedures coded into the programs during the development of the application system. Frequently programs reconcile the transactions read by the program with the number produced, or reconcile the total amounts on the input transactions with the amounts processed. Accountants call these *control totals* and *record counts;* other programs may use limit and reasonableness checks. Illustration 17–28 applies some of these control procedures in the application systems of the revenue cycle.

Output Controls.   Output controls prevent and detect erroneous outputs from computer processing. In many companies, the data control group implements them; other companies assign these responsibilities to clerks in user areas. Output controls compare record counts and control totals from successive computer runs to verify that all transactions were processed correctly. They also scan output documents and reports to

ILLUSTRATION 17–28

Example Processing Controls in the Revenue Cycle

System	Control Procedure
Order entry	**Limit test.** Program verifies that sale does cause customer to exceed credit limit.
Shipping	**Completeness test.** Program verifies that each record contains SHIPPING-NOTICE-NUMBER.
Billing	**Completeness test.** Program verifies that each record contains INVOICE-NUMBER.
	Reasonableness test. Program verifies that on a document, TRANSACTION-AMOUNT < $99,999.
	Control total. Program verifies that total postings to the customer master file = total amounts in the accounts receivable change log file = total debits and total credits in general ledger batch summary file.
Cash receipts	**Control total.** Program verifies that total postings to the customer master file = total amounts in the accounts receivable change log file = total debits and total credits in general ledger batch summary file.

identify obvious errors in their preparation. Illustration 17–29 shows examples of how output controls may be implemented in the revenue cycle.

You now see how a system design team includes application controls in the application systems of the revenue cycle. Perhaps you can identify some other control procedures that would be useful as well in these applications.

ILLUSTRATION 17–29

Example Output Controls in the Revenue Cycle

System	Control Procedure
Order entry	**Visual verification.** Data control group examines documents for proper preparation.
	Record count. Data control group verifies that number of order acknowledgments = the number of valid sales order transactions shown on the error listing.
Shipping	**Record count.** Data control group verifies that the number of shipping notices = number of records in shipments file shown on shipments register.
Billing	**Record count.** Data control group verifies that the number of credit memos and invoices printed are the numbers shown on the credit memo and invoice registers.
	Visual verification. Data control group examines invoices and credit memos for proper preparation.
Cash receipts	**Control total.** Data control group verifies that total amount of listings on deleted invoice register = total listings on cash receipts register.
All batch systems	**Run-to-run controls.** Data control group reconciles control totals and record counts on registers and control reports produced by each pair of programs executed in succession.

Summary

The revenue cycle processes accounting transactions that record four economic events: the request for goods or services by a customer, the delivery of those goods or services, the request for payment, and the receipt for payment.

Accounting systems in the revenue cycle must be able to process five types of transactions. The data for these transactions are recorded on documents, entered into accounting records, and summarized in reports. Documents in this transaction cycle are the sales order, the shipping notice, the sales invoice, the credit memo, and the remittance advice. Reports include control reports, registers, customer statements, the aged accounts receivable trial balance, and the remittance list.

Manual systems in this cycle process three special journals and the accounts receivable subsidiary ledger. Computer-based systems include the order entry, shipping, billing, and cash receipts applications. They post sales and cash receipts transactions to the customer master file and provide inputs to the general ledger system. When a database management system is used, these applications access the data using their sub-schemas.

Key Terms

accounts receivable change log file   A file containing one record for each transaction in a customer's account since the last statement. It is used to print a monthly statement.

accounts receivable system   A name sometimes applied to a combination of the billing and cash receipts applications.

balance forward system   An accounts receivable system that maintains records of transactions since the last statement date. Details on older transactions are deleted.

balance only system   A type of accounts receivable system that records only the current balance owed by a customer. Detail concerning that balance must be obtained from documents.

credit memo   A document that records a sales return or sales allowance.

customer master record   A record for each customer showing reference data, a credit limit, and balances owed.

customer statement   A list of all transactions in a customer's account during a specified time period, usually a month. It is mailed to the customer.

cycle billing   The practice of mailing customer statements to a different group of customers each day of the month.

general ledger batch summary file   A file containing records produced by revenue cycle applications that are to be posted to the general ledger master file.

open item system   An accounts receivable system that maintains records showing all transactions making up the customer's unpaid balance.

remittance advice   A document returned by customers with their payments.

remittance list   A list of all currency and checks received during one day.

sales invoice   A document mailed to customers informing them of the amount due from them because of shipments.

sales order   A document on which the sales department records an order from a customer.

shipping notice   A document completed by the shipping department to notify the billing department that a shipment has been made.

Questions

17–1. Which economic events produce transactions in the revenue cycle?

17–2. Which six types of transactions do accounting systems record in the revenue cycle?

17–3. What is the purpose of each of the following documents:
  a. Sales order?
  b. Shipping notice?
  c. Sales invoice?
  d. Credit memo?

17–4. When is a control report used? What is its function?

17–5. Which information is disclosed in a register? Why is it important to accountants?

17–6. Describe three special purpose reports produced in the revenue cycle.

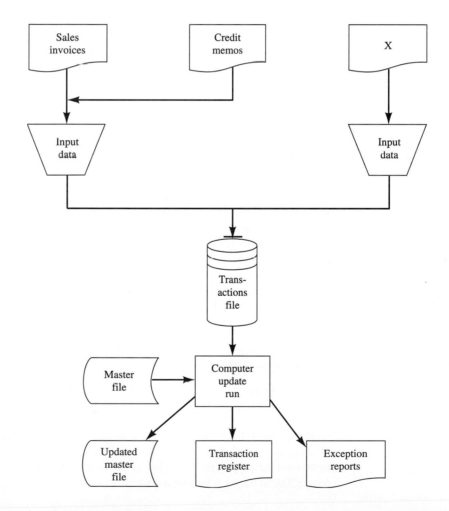

17–7. What form do noncomputerized records take in the revenue cycle?

17–8. In a computerized accounting system, which data files are used in the revenue cycle? Can you identify the purpose of each file?

17–9. Describe each of the three kinds of accounts receivable systems and distinguish among them.

17–10. In a computer-based accounting system, what are the applications in the revenue cycle? What is the purpose of each?

17–11. The system flowchart on page 569 illustrates a credit sales and cash receipts system. What does the symbol X represent?

(AICPA Adapted)

Exercises and Cases

17–12. TRANSACTIONS AND DOCUMENTS

The column on the left lists accounting transactions processed in the revenue cycle. In the right column is a list of documents and reports. Identify the document(s) and report(s) associated with each transaction.

Transaction	Document or report
a. Cash sale.	1. Sales invoice.
b. Credit sale.	2. Credit memo.
c. Bad debts write-off.	3. Remittance advice.
d. Sales return.	4. Aged trial balance.
e. Sales allowance.	5. Sales ticket.
f. Payment on account.	6. Sales order.

17–13. TRANSACTIONS AND APPLICATIONS

The column on the left lists accounting transactions. In the right column is a list of application systems used in the revenue cycle. Identify the application system that processes each transaction.

Transaction	Application System
a. Cash sale.	1. Order entry.
b. Credit sale.	2. Shipping.
c. Sales return.	3. Billing.
d. Sales allowance.	4. Cash receipts.
e. Payment on account.	

17–14. FRAUD

Consider the following situations involving fraud in the revenue cycle.

1. Cash receipts for discount sales to employees were misappropriated as a result of inadequate control over, and accounting for, special sales invoices used to document them. A clerk who knew of the lack of control over the invoices stole over $20,000 during a two-year period.

2. A company had given employees unlimited authority to issue customer cash sales adjustments under a specified dollar amount without a supervisor's approval. An employee made over $10,000 of false adjustments to cash sales and kept the money.

3. Substantial amounts were collected daily from cash sales. A single trusted employee recorded the cash receipts, made the bank deposits, reconciled the cash accounts, and posted accounts receivable. External auditors had previously noted inadequate segregation of duties even though extensive audit tests had revealed no shortages. Internal auditors then discovered that over an eight-year period, the trusted employee had embezzled over $100,000.

Required:

For each situation just described:
a. Which conditions allowed the fraud?
b. What could a manager or auditor have done to detect the fraud?

(CIA Adapted)

17–15.   CREDIT SALES

After a shipment is prepared, the shipping department completes a three-part shipping notice form. The first copy is included with the goods sent to the customer as a packing slip. The second copy is forwarded to the billing department. The third copy is sent to the accountant. When the billing department receives the second copy of the shipping order, it uses the information on it to prepare a two-part sales invoice. The second copy of the shipping order is then filed in the billing department. The first copy of the sales invoice is sent to the customer. The second copy of the sales invoice is forwarded to the accountant. Periodically, the accountant matches the copy of the shipping order with the copy of the sales invoice and files them alphabetically by customer name. Before doing so, however, the accountant uses the copy of the sales invoice to post the sales entry in the subsidiary accounts receivable ledger.

Required:

a. Prepare a document flowchart showing the preceding steps.
b. Identify the internal control deficiencies and omissions in the foregoing procedures.

(CIA Adapted)

17–16.   SALES RETURNS

Customers return goods—usually with a copy of the original sales invoice—to Wilson & Company's customer service department. Using the information on these original invoices, the department prepares a prenumbered, three-part sales return slip. In instances where the returned goods are not accompanied by an original invoice, the customer service department uses the company's current sales price lists to prepare sales return slips.

After mailing the customer the original sales return slip, the customer service department sends copies two and three to the inventory control department, along with the returned goods. After noting the quantity of goods returned on the slip, the inventory control department uses copy three to post to the perpetual inventory records. It then sends a control total, along with copy two of the sales return slip, to the accounts receivable department. Copy three is then filed by date.

On receipt of copy two of the sales return slip, the accounts receivable department posts to customers' accounts. At the end of posting, the accounts receivable department verifies the control total supplied by the inventory control department. Then accounts receivable forwards the total to the general ledger department, where a journal entry is made.

Required:

a. Prepare a document flowchart showing the steps just described.

b. Identify the internal control deficiencies and omissions in these procedures.

17–17.   DATA RECORD DESIGN

A department store, Sanger Harris, accepts all charges incurred on credit cards issued by that store. Exhibit 17-1 shows a copy of a monthly customer statement.

Required:

Assume that you are developing a system that produces the customer statement in Exhibit 17–1. Design record layouts for the following:

a. Customer master record.

b. Invoice detail record.

c. Cash receipts detail record.

d. Accounts receivable change log record.

17–18.   ON-LINE REAL-TIME CONTROLS

In Exhibit 17–2 a flowchart depicts a section of an open item accounts receivable system. The system is 1 of 10 computerized on-line real-time systems installed at a large manufacturing company. At 11 control points in the cash application segment of this system, control practices are applied.

Required:

a. Identify the 11 control points in Exhibit 17–2.

b. Explain how each control point aids in preventing or detecting errors and irregularities.

(CIA Adapted)

17–19.   CASH RECEIPTS FROM CREDIT SALES

Procedures for handling the cash receipts of the Alaska branch of the Far Distributing Company are as follows: The branch's substantial annual sales are billed and collected locally. Cash collections on over-the-counter sales and COD sales are received from the customer or delivery service by the cashier. On receipt of cash, the cashier stamps the sales ticket "paid" and files a copy for future reference. The only record of COD sales is the copy of the sales ticket the cashier holds until the cash is received from the delivery service.

Mail is opened by the credit manager's secretary, who gives remittances to the credit manager for her review. The credit manager then places the remittances in a tray

EXHIBIT 17–1

Exercise 17–17

Sanger Harris

66555310007350000073500

```
--  --   DR & MRS DAVID H LI
--  --   7707 QUEENSFERRY LANE
--  --   DALLAS, TX
         75248
```

PLEASE SHOW
AMOUNT PAID _____

ACCOUNT NUMBER	ACCOUNT TYPE	NEW BALANCE	PAYMENT NOW DUE
6-6555-3-1	30 DAY ACCOUNT	73.50	73.50

PLEASE DETACH AND RETURN THIS PORTION WITH YOUR PAYMENT
CHECK BOX FOR CREDIT CARD REQUEST(S) OR ADDRESS CHANGE AND COMPLETE OTHER SIDE ☐

DATE	STORE LOC* CODE	REFERENCE NUMBER	DEPT	DESCRIPTION	PURCHASES AND OTHER CHARGES	PAYMENTS, RETURNS AND OTHER CREDITS
06-19	09	9008001491	446	LINGERIE	15.75	
06-29	13	1344004270	171	HANDBAGS	57.75	
07-12		10217690		PAYMENT--THANK YOU		17.84

THIS MONTH'S BILL CLOSING DATE	SANGER HARRIS ACCOUNT NUMBER	NEXT MONTH'S BILL CLOSING DATE	PAYMENT NOW DUE*
JULY 16, 1998	6-6555-3-1	AUG. 16, 1998	73.50

PREVIOUS BALANCE		FINANCE CHARGE		PURCHASES AND OTHER CHARGES		PAYMENTS, RETURNS AND OTHER CREDITS		NEW BALANCE
17.84	+	NONE	+	73.50	–	17.84	=	73.50

To avoid a Finance Charge on your next statement we must receive the New Balance in full on or before your Next Month's Bill Closing Date

TERMS CHANGE DATE	OLD PREVIOUS BALANCE*	NEW PREVIOUS BALANCE*
N/A	N/A	N/A

*NOTICE: SEE REVERSE SIDE FOR IMPORTANT INFORMATION   CRBAL CREDIT BALANCE

on the cashier's desk. At the daily deposit cutoff time, the cashier delivers the checks and cash on hand to the assistant credit manager. He prepares remittance lists, makes up the bank deposit, and takes the deposit to the bank. The assistant credit manager also posts remittances to the accounts receivable ledger cards and verifies the cash discount allowable.

   To write off uncollectible accounts, the credit manager obtains approval from the executive office of Far Distributing Company in Chicago. The credit manager has

EXHIBIT 17–2

Exercise 17–18

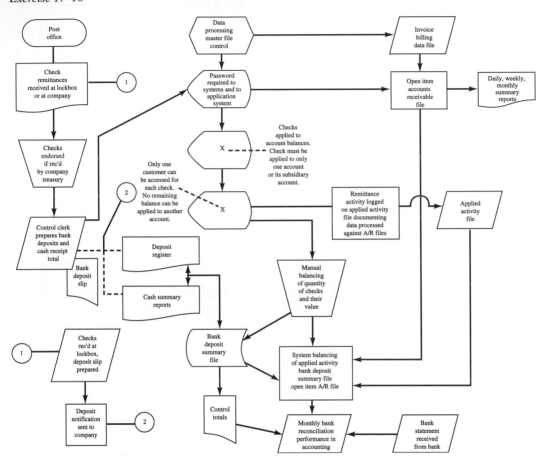

retained in her custody, as of the end of the fiscal year, some remittances that were received on various days during the month.

Required:

a. Describe the irregularities that might occur under the procedures now in effect for handling cash collections and remittances.

b. Identify procedures that you would recommend to improve internal control over cash collections and remittances.

(AICPA Adapted)

17–20. *REVENUE CYCLE PROCEDURES*

While auditing the Top Manufacturing Corporation, the auditor prepared the flowchart of credit sale activities shown in Exhibit 17–3. In this flowchart, the letter *A* represents CUSTOMER.

EXHIBIT 17-3
Exercise 17-20

TOP MANUFACTURING CORPORATION
Flowchart of Credit Sales Activities

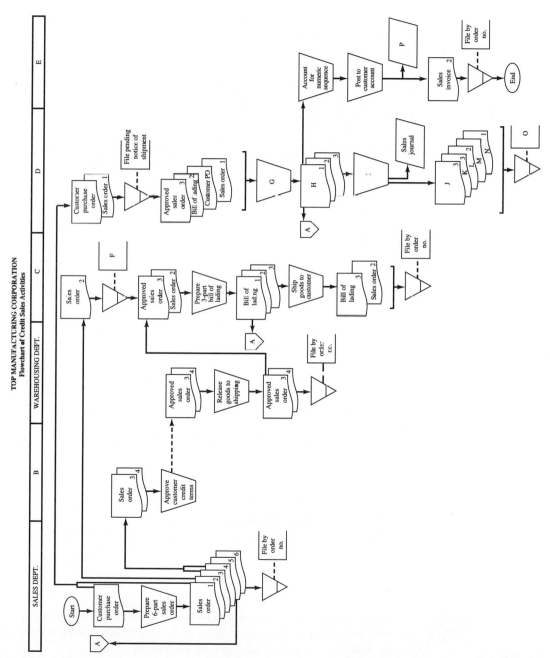

Required:

Identify what is represented by the letters *B* through *P*.

(AICPA Adapted)

17–21. CASH RECEIPTS

The town of Oaks Park operates a private parking lot near the railroad for the benefit of town residents. The guard on duty issues annual prenumbered parking stickers to residents who submit an application form and show evidence of residency. A sticker affixed to the auto allows a resident to park anywhere in the lot for 12 hours if four quarters are placed in the parking meter. Applications are maintained in the guard office on the lot. The guard checks to see that only residents are using the lot and that no resident has parked without paying the required meter fee.

Once a week the guard on duty, who has a master key for all meters, takes the coins from the meters and places them in a locked steel box. The guard delivers the box to the town storage building, where it is opened and the coins are manually counted by a storage department clerk, who records the total cash counted on a weekly cash report. This report is sent to the town accounting department. The storage clerk puts the cash in a safe; on the following day the cash is picked up by the town's treasurer, who manually recounts the cash, prepares the bank deposit slip, and delivers the deposit to the bank. The deposit slip, authenticated by the bank teller, is sent to the accounting department, where it is filed with the weekly cash report.

Required:

a. Describe internal control weaknesses in these procedures.

b. For each weakness, recommend at least one way to improve internal control over parking lot cash receipts.

(AICPA Adapted)

17–22. CONTROL PROCEDURES AND DOCUMENTS

A partially completed flowchart for credit sales appears in Exhibit 17–4. The flowchart depicts the activities of the Bottom Manufacturing Corporation.

When a customer's purchase order is received, a six-part sales order is prepared from it. The six copies are initially distributed as follows:

Copy 1—to billing department

Copy 2—to shipping department

Copy 3—to credit department

Copy 4—to credit department

Copy 5—to customer

Copy 6—file in sales order department

When a copy of the sales order reaches its destination, it initiates specific control procedures and related documents. Some of the procedures and documents are indicated on the flowchart. Others are labeled with letters *a* through *r*.

EXHIBIT 17–4

Exercise 17–22

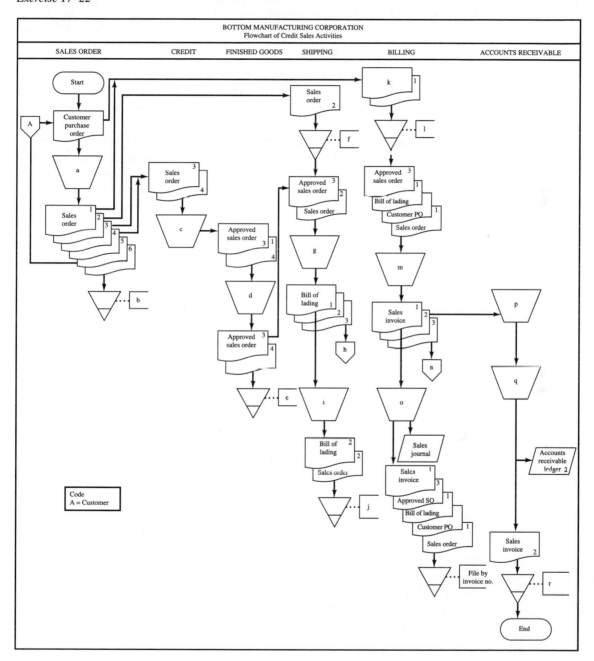

BOTTOM MANUFACTURING CORPORATION
Flowchart of Credit Sales Activities

Required:

List the control procedures and documents represented by letters *a* through *r* in the flow-chart of Bottom Manufacturing Corporation's credit sales system.

(AICPA Adapted)

17–23.   GENERAL AND APPLICATION CONTROLS

Ajax, Inc., recently installed a new computer-based system to process more efficiently the shipping, billing, and accounts receivable records. During a review, an auditor determined the following information concerning the new system.

Each major application—that is, shipping, billing, cash receipts, and so forth—is permanently assigned to a specific computer operator responsible for making program changes, running the program, and reconciling the computer log. Responsibility for the custody and control over tape files and system documentation is randomly rotated among the computer operators on a monthly basis to prevent any one person from having access to the tapes and documentation at all times. Each computer programmer and computer operator has access to the computer room via a magnetic card containing an individual digital code. The systems analyst and the supervisor of the computer operators do not have access to the computer room.

The system documentation consists of the following items: program listing, error listing, logs, and record layouts. To increase efficiency, batch totals and processing controls are omitted from the system.

Ajax ships its products directly from two warehouses, which forward shipping notices to general accounting. There, the billing clerk enters the price of the item and accounts for the numerical sequence of the shipping notices. The billing clerk also prepares daily adding machine tapes of the units shipped and the sales amounts. Shipping notices and adding machine tapes are forwarded to the computer department for processing. The computer output consists of

- A three-part sales invoice that is forwarded to the billing clerk.
- A daily sales register showing the aggregate totals of units shipped and sales amounts that the computer operator compares to the adding machine tapes.

The billing clerk mails two copies of each invoice to the customer and retains the third copy in an open invoice file that serves as a detail accounts receivable record.

Required:

Describe one specific recommendation for correcting each control weakness in the new system and for correcting each weakness or inefficiency in the procedures for processing and controlling shipping notices and sales invoices.

(AICPA Adapted)

17–24.   CONTROL WEAKNESSES

The document flowchart in Exhibit 17–5 depicts the revenue cycle activities of Smallco Lumber, Inc.

EXHIBIT 17-5

Exercise 17-24

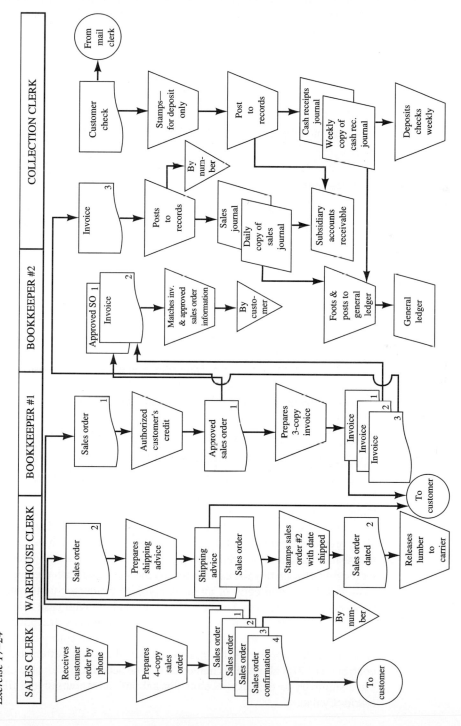

Required:

Identify the control weakness related to the activities of each of the following job functions:

a. Warehouse clerk.

b. Bookkeeper 1.

c. Bookkeeper 2.

d. Collection clerk.

(AICPA Adapted)

17–25.   CASH RECEIPTS AND SALES

Charting, Inc., processes its sales and cash receipts documents in the manner described below:

Cash Receipts

The mail is opened each morning by a mail clerk in the sales department. The mail clerk prepares a remittance advice (showing the customer and amount paid) if one is not received. The checks and remittance advices are then forwarded to the sales department supervisor, who reviews each check and forwards the checks and remittance advices to the accounting department supervisor. The accounting department supervisor, who also functions as the credit manager, reviews all checks for payments of past-due accounts and then forwards the checks and remittance advices to the accounts receivable clerk, who arranges the advices in alphabetical order. The remittance advices are posted directly to the accounts receivable ledger cards. The checks are endorsed by stamp and totaled. The total is posted to the cash receipts journal. The remittance advices are filed chronologically.

After receiving the cash from the preceding day's cash sales, the accounts receivable clerk prepares the daily deposit slip in triplicate. The third copy of the deposit slip is filed by date, and the second copy and the original accompany the bank deposit.

Sales

Salesclerks prepare the sales invoices in triplicate. The original and the second copy are presented to the cashier, while the third copy is retained by the salesclerk in the sales book. When the sale is for cash, the customer pays the salesclerk, who presents the money to the cashier with the invoice copies.

A credit sale is okayed by the cashier using an approved credit list after the salesclerk prepares the three-part invoice. After receiving the cash or approving the invoice, the cashier validates the original copy of the sales invoice and gives it to the customer. At the end of each day the cashier recaps the sales and cash received and forwards the cash and the second copy of all sales invoices to the accounts receivable clerk. The accounts receivable clerk balances the cash received with cash sales invoices and prepares a daily sales summary. The credit sales invoices are posted to the accounts receivable ledger, and then all invoices are sent to the inventory control clerk in the sales department for posting to the inventory control catalog. After posting, the inventory control clerk files all invoices numerically. The accounts receivable clerk posts the daily sales summary to the cash receipts journal and sales journal and files the sales summaries by date.

The cash from cash sales is combined with the cash received on account; this constitutes the daily bank deposit.

Bank Deposits

The bank validates the deposit slip and returns the second copy to the accounting department, where the accounts receivable clerk files it by date. Monthly bank statements are reconciled promptly by the accounting department supervisor and filed by date.

Required:

a. Prepare a document flowchart covering the preceding narrative.

b. Identify potential internal control weaknesses in the Charting, Inc., procedures.

(AICPA Adapted)

17–26. PROPOSED BATCH SYSTEM DESIGN

Tunefork, Inc., is a large wholesaler of sheet music, music books, musical instruments, and other music-related supplies. The company acquired a medium-size, batch processing computer system last year, and an inventory control system has been implemented already. Now the systems department is developing a new accounts receivable system.

The flowchart in Exhibit 17–6 is a diagram of the accounts receivable system proposed by the design project team. The objectives of the new system are to produce current and timely information that can be used to control bad debts, to provide information to the sales department regarding customers whose accounts are delinquent, to produce monthly statements for customers, and to produce notices to customers regarding a change in the status of their charge privileges.

Input data for the system are taken from four source documents: approved credit applications, sales invoices, cash payment remittances, and credit memoranda. The accounts receivable file is maintained on magnetic disk by customer account number. The record for each customer contains identification information, last month's balance, current month's transactions (detailed), and current balance. The following output items are some of those generated from the system:

> *Accounts receivable register (weekly).* A listing of all customers and account balances included in the accounts receivable file.
>
> *Aging schedule (monthly).* A schedule of all customers with outstanding balances detailing the amount owed by age classifications: 0–30 days, 31–60 days, 61–90 days, and more than 90 days old.
>
> *Delinquency and write-off registers (monthly).* Two reports, one listing those accounts that are delinquent and a second listing those customer accounts that have been closed and written off. Related notices are prepared and sent to these customers.

Required:

a. Which system controls should be instituted with the new system? When appropriate, describe the location in the flowchart where the control should be introduced.

EXHIBIT 17–6

Exercise 17–26

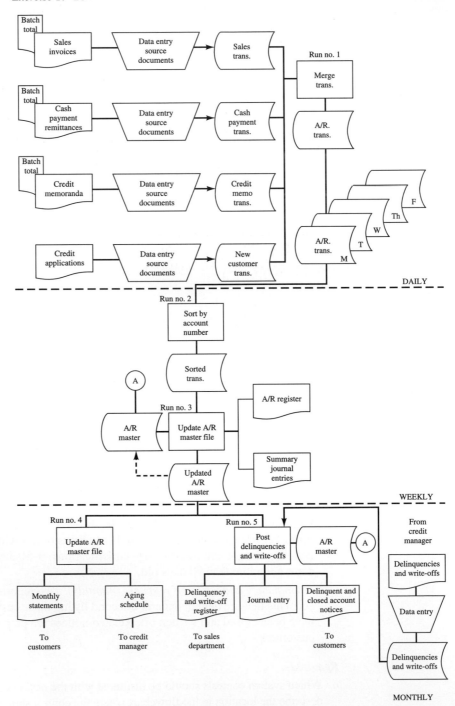

b. The credit manager has indicated that the department receives frequent telephone inquiries from customers regarding their accounts. The manager has asked if the department could have a cathode ray tube (CRT) terminal connected to the main computer. Can a CRT terminal be used with the new accounts receivable system as proposed to satisfy the needs of the credit manager?

(CMA Adapted)

17–27. DESIGNING FILES AND REPORTS

Value Clothing is a large distributor of all types of clothing acquired from buyouts, overstocks, and factory seconds. All sales are on account with terms of net 30 days from date of monthly statement. The number of delinquent accounts and uncollectible accounts has increased significantly during the last 12 months. Management has determined that the information generated from the present accounts receivable system is inadequate and untimely. In addition, customers frequently complain of errors in their accounts.

The current accounts receivable system has not been changed since Value Clothing started its operations. A new computer was acquired 18 months ago but no attempt has been made to revise the accounts receivable application because other applications were considered more important. Recently the IS Steering Committee has authorized the formation of a design project team to develop a new accounts receivable system. Top management has requested that the new system satisfy the following objectives:

1. Produce current and timely reports regarding customers; these reports would provide useful information to
   a. Aid in controlling bad debts.
   b. Notify the sales department of customer accounts that are delinquent (accounts that should lose charge privileges).
   c. Notify the sales department of customers whose accounts are considered uncollectible (accounts that should be closed and written off).

2. Produce timely notices to customers regarding
   a. Amounts owed to Value Clothing.
   b. A change of status of their accounts (loss of charge privileges, account closed).

3. Incorporate the necessary procedures and controls to minimize the chance for errors in customers' accounts.

Input data for the system would be taken from four source documents: credit applications, sales invoices, cash payment remittances, and credit memoranda. The accounts receivable master file would be maintained on a machine-readable file by customer account number. The preliminary design of the new accounts receivable system has been completed by the project team, who also put together this brief description of the proposed reports and other output generated by the system:

1. *Accounts Receivable Register.* A daily alphabetical listing of all customers' accounts showing balances as of the last statement, activity since the last statements, and current account balances.

2. *Customer Statements.* Monthly statements for customers showing activity since the last statements and the new account balances. The top portion of the statement is returned with the payment and serves as a remittance advice.

3. *Aging Schedule for All Customers.* A monthly schedule of all customers with outstanding balances displaying the total amounts owed with the amounts classified into age groups: 0–30 days, 31–60 days, 61–90 days, and more than 90 days. The schedule includes totals and percentages for each age category.

4. *Aging Schedule for Past-Due Customers.* A schedule prepared monthly of only those customers whose accounts are past due—that is, over 30 days outstanding, classified by age. The credit manager uses this schedule to decide which customers receive delinquent notices or temporary suspension of their charge privileges or have their accounts closed.

5. *Activity Reports.* Monthly reports that show
   a. Customers who have not purchased any merchandise for 90 days.
   b. Customers whose account balance exceeds their credit limit.
   c. Customers whose accounts are delinquent yet they have current sales on account.

6. *Delinquency and Write-Off Register.* A monthly alphabetical listing of customers' accounts that are (*a*) delinquent and (*b*) closed. The listings show names, account numbers, and balances; related notices are prepared and sent to these customers.

7. *Summary of Journal Entries.* Entries are prepared monthly to record write-offs to the accounts receivable file.

Required:

a. Identify the data that should be captured and stored in the computer records for each customer.

b. Review the proposed reports to be generated by the new accounts receivable system.
   1. Discuss whether the proposed reports would be adequate to satisfy the objectives listed.
   2. Recommend changes, if any, that should be made in the proposed reporting structure generated by the new accounts receivable system.

(CMA Adapted)

17–28. DESIGNING AN ON-LINE SYSTEM

Until recently, Consolidated Electricity Company employed a batch processing system for recording the receipt of customers' payments. The following narrative and the flow-chart of Exhibit 17–7 describe the procedures involved in this system.

The customer's payment and remittance advice (a turnaround document) are received in the treasurer's office. An accounts receivable clerk in the treasurer's office, using magnetic ink, encodes the cash receipt on the remittance advice and forwards the advice to the data center. The cash receipt is added to a control tape listing and then filed for deposit later in the day. When the deposit slips are received from the data

EXHIBIT 17–7

Case 17–28

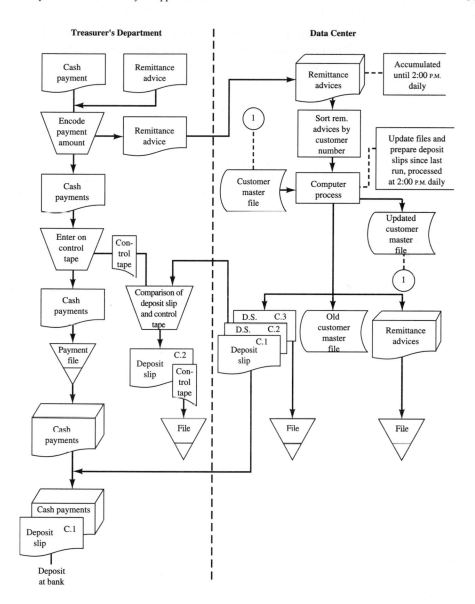

center at approximately 2:30 P.M. each day, the cash receipts are removed from the file and deposited with the original deposit slip. Before the deposit is made, the second copy of the deposit slip and the control tape are compared for accuracy and then filed together.

In the data center, the remittance advices received from the treasurer's office are held until 2:00 P.M. daily. At that time the customers' payments are processed to update the records and to prepare a deposit slip in triplicate. During the update process, data are read from the master accounts receivable records, processed, and then recorded on a new master file. The original and second copy of the deposit slip are forwarded to the treasurer's office. The old master file (yesterday's accounts receivable file) is retained, and the remittance advices (in customer number order), and the third copy of the deposit slip are stored in a secure place. The updated accounts receivable master file is maintained in the system for processing the next day.

Consolidated Electricity Company has redesigned its computer system so that it has on-line capabilities. The new cash receipts procedures, described next, are designed to take advantage of the new system.

The customer's payment and remittance advice are received in the treasurer's office as before. A desktop computer (connected to the data center) is located in the treasurer's office to enter the cash receipts. An operator keys in the customer's number and payment from the remittance advice and checks. The cash receipt is entered into the system once the operator has confirmed that the proper account and amount are displayed on the screen. The payment is then processed on-line against the accounts receivable file maintained on magnetic disk. The cash receipts are filed for deposit later in the day. The remittance advices are filed in the order they are processed. These documents are kept until the next working day and then destroyed. The computer prints out a deposit slip in duplicate at 2:00 P.M. for all cash receipts since the last deposit. The deposit slips are forwarded to the treasurer's office. The cash receipts are removed from the file and deposited with the original deposit slip; the duplicate deposit slip is filed for further reference. At the close of business hours (5:00 P.M.) each day, the data center prepares a record of the current day's cash receipts activity on a magnetic tape. This tape is then stored in a secure place in the event of a system malfunction; after 10 working days the tape is released for further use.

Required:

Prepare a system flowchart of the company's new on-line cash receipts system.

(CMA Adapted)

17–29.   SYSTEM CONVERSION

Delmo, Inc., is an automotive parts wholesale distributor serving customers east of the Mississippi River. The company has grown during the last 25 years from a small regional distributorship to its present size.

The states are divided into eight separate territories to service Delmo customers adequately. Delmo salespersons regularly call on current and prospective customers in each of the territories. Delmo customers are of four general types: automotive parts stores, hardware stores with an automotive parts section, independent garage owners, and buying groups for garages and filling stations.

Because Delmo must stock such a large variety and quantity of automotive parts to accommodate its customers, the company acquired its own computer system very early and implemented an inventory system first. Other applications such as cash receipts and disbursements, sales analysis, accounts receivable, payroll, and accounts payable have since been added.

Delmo's inventory system consists of an integrated purchase ordering and perpetual inventory system. Each item of inventory is identified by an inventory code number identifying both the product line and the item itself. When the quantity on hand for an item falls below the specified stock level, a purchase order is automatically generated by the computer. After approval by the purchasing manager, the purchase order is sent to the vendor. All receipts, issues, and returns are entered into the computer daily. A printout of all inventory items within product lines showing receipts, issues, and current balance is prepared weekly. However, current status for a particular item carried in the inventory can be obtained daily if it is desired.

Sales orders are filled within 48 hours of receipt. Sales invoices are prepared by the computer the same day that the merchandise is shipped. At the end of each month, several reports are produced that summarize the monthly sales. The current month's and year-to-date sales by product line, territory, and customer class are compared with the same figures from the previous year. In addition, reports showing only the monthly figures for product lines within each territory and customer class within each territory are prepared. In all cases, the reports provide summarized data—that is, detailed data, such as sales by individual customers or product, are not listed. Terms of 2/10, net 30 are standard for all of Delmo's customers.

Customers' accounts receivable are updated daily for sales, sales returns and allowances, and payments on account. Monthly statements are computer-prepared and mailed following completion of entries for the last day of the month. Each Friday a schedule is prepared showing the total amount of accounts receivable outstanding by age: current accounts (0–30 days), slightly past-due accounts (30–90 days), and long overdue accounts (more than 90 days).

Delmo, Inc., recently acquired Wenrock Company, a wholesale distributor of tools and light equipment. In addition to servicing the same type of customers as Delmo, Wenrock also sells to equipment rental shops. Wenrock's sales region is not as extensive as Delmo's, but the Delmo management has encouraged Wenrock to expand the distribution of its product to all of Delmo's sales territories.

Wenrock Company uses a computer service bureau to aid in its accounting functions. For example, certain inventory activities are recorded by the service bureau. Each item carried by Wenrock is assigned a product code number identifying the product and the product line. Data regarding shipments received from manufacturers, shipments to customers (sales), and any other physical inventory changes are delivered to the service bureau daily, and the service bureau updates Wenrock's inventory records. A weekly inventory listing showing beginning balance, receipts, issues, and ending balance for each item in the inventory is provided to Wenrock on Monday morning.

Wenrock furnishes the service bureau with information about each sale of merchandise to a customer. The service bureau prepares a five-part invoice and records the sales in its records. This processing is done at night, and all copies of each invoice are delivered to Wenrock the next morning. At the end of the month, the service bureau provides Wenrock with a sales report classified by product line showing the sales in units and dollars for each item sold. Wenrock's sales terms are 2/10, net 30.

The accounts receivable function is still handled by Wenrock's bookkeeper. Two copies of the invoice are mailed to each customer. Two of the remaining copies are filed, one numerically and the other alphabetically by customer. The alphabetic file represents the accounts receivable file. When a customer's payment is received, the invoice is marked "paid" and placed in a paid invoice file in alphabetical order. The bookkeeper mails monthly statements according to the following schedule:

> 10th of the month: A–G
>
> 20th of the month: H–O
>
> 30th of the month: P–Z.

The final copy of the invoice is included with the merchandise when it is shipped.

Wenrock has continued to use its present accounting system and supplies Delmo management with monthly financial information developed from this system. However, management is anxious to have Wenrock use Delmo's computer and its information system because that would reduce accounting and computer costs, increase Wenrock's financial reports' usefulness to Delmo management, and provide Wenrock personnel with better information to manage the company.

At the time Delmo acquired Wenrock, it also hired a new marketing manager with experience in both product areas. The new manager wants Wenrock to organize its sales force using the same territorial distribution as Delmo to facilitate the management of the two sales forces. The new manager also believes that more useful sales information should be provided to individual salespersons and to the department. Even though the monthly sales reports currently prepared provide adequate summary data, the manager would like additional details to aid the sales personnel.

The acquisition of Wenrock Company and expansion of its sales to a larger geographic area have created a cash strain on Delmo, Inc., particularly in the short run. Consequently, cash management has become much more important than in prior years. A weekly report that presents a reliable estimate of daily cash receipts is needed. The treasurer heard that a local company had improved its cash forecasting system by studying the timing of customers' payments on account to see if a discernible payment pattern existed. The model payment pattern was applied to outstanding invoices to estimate the daily cash receipts for the next week. The treasurer thinks this is a good approach and wonders if it can be done at Delmo.

Required:

a. Which additional data must Wenrock Company collect and furnish to use the Delmo data processing system? Which data currently accumulated by Wenrock would no longer be needed due to the conversion to the Delmo system?

b. Using only the data currently available from the Delmo data processing system, which additional reports could be prepared that would be useful to the marketing manager and to the individual salespersons? How would each report be useful to the sales personnel?

(CMA Adapted)

17–30. MANUAL SYSTEM

Pat Clark, an obstetrician/gynecologist, began her solo practice two years ago. Currently, she has a caseload of about 500 patients. An average of one new patient a day is being added to the caseload. She sees between 10 and 12 patients each day.

Organization

The physician employs a registered nurse, who provides clinical support to the practice. An office manager is also employed to handle most of the administrative responsibilities, including financial functions and maintenance of medical records.

As a result of this small staff, the majority of the tasks associated with billing and collections are performed by the office manager. No office functions are automated; a one-write pegboard accounting system is used.

Billing

Three main documents are used in the billing process: (1) a patient communication sheet is completed for each patient visit; (2) a daily business summary records all of the transactions for a two- or three-day period (when patient volume increases, it will be used daily); and (3) a patient ledger card is an ongoing record of each patient's individual account.

When a patient comes to the office for medical services, the office manager initiates a patient communication sheet (PCS), which is on three-part NCR paper. Using the one-write pegboard system, the patient's name, previous balance, and PCS serial number are entered on the PCS and on one line of the daily business summary. The PCS is then attached to the medical record and sent to the examination room. After providing services, the physician checks the appropriate boxes on the PCS indicating which procedures were performed.

The PCS is returned to the office manager, who enters the charges for each of the procedures performed. The patient ledger card is pulled. The procedure codes and total charges are entered on copy three of the PCS as well as on the patient ledger card and the daily business summary using the one-write pegboard. If the patient makes any payment, or if the physician authorizes any adjustments, the payments and/or adjustments are also written on the PCS, the ledger card, and the daily business summary. Finally, the new balance is entered.

At this point, the PCS contains this information: patient name, procedures performed, previous balance, charges, payments, adjustments, and current balance. Identical information has also been entered on one line of the daily business summary and on the patient ledger card.

Copy three of the PCS is given to the patient. Copy one is filed numerically by PCS serial number. Copy two is used for insurance claims. If any hospitalization has taken place, copy two is put in a folder for filing insurance claims. If no hospitalization occurred, it is given to the patient along with copy three. Each patient has to file her own insurance claim.

Cash Receipts

The cash receipts are received by the office manager, either at the time of the visit, during a later visit, or through the mail. If the payment is received at the time of a visit, it is entered as previously described on the PCS, the patient ledger card, and the daily business summary. If payment is received through the mail, the office manager enters the credit on the patient ledger card and the daily business summary.

Cash and checks are kept in a locked drawer until the end of each day, when they are put into a locked box in the office. The checks are endorsed immediately by the office manager using a rubber stamp indicating the bank account number and "For Deposit Only." Every few days deposit slips are prepared and deposits are made by the office manager.

Aging of Accounts Receivable

At the end of the day, the office manager reviews all ledger cards pulled that day and color-codes them according to the month in which the oldest unpaid charge was incurred. A colored tab is attached to the top of the ledger card indicating whether an account is 30, 60, 90, 120, or more than 120 days old. Accounts with zero balances have no tabs on the ledger card. The ledger cards are then filed in one of two alphabetical files, one for zero balances and one for patients owing money.

Balancing of the Daily Business Summary

Every two or three days, totals for the daily business summary are calculated. Control totals are run to do a proof of posting, an accounts receivable control, an accounts receivable proof, and a cash control. The proof of posting verifies that the total current balances on the daily business summary equal the total previous balances plus charges minus payments minus adjustments. The accounts receivable control takes the previous day's total accounts receivable, adds charges, subtracts payments and adjustments, and produces a current total for accounts receivable. The accounts receivable proof takes accounts receivable at the beginning of the month, adds month-to-date charges, subtracts month-to-date payments and adjustments, and compares the result to the current total for accounts receivable. The cash control provides a current total for cash on hand by taking the beginning cash on hand, adding receipts, subtracting cash paid out and bank deposits, and verifying that against an actual cash count. The daily business summary is then filed by date.

Monthly Accounts Receivable Statement

Once a month, all patient ledger cards with debit balances are pulled. For each patient who owes money, an entry is made on the monthly accounts receivable statement listing the date, name, present balance, aging of the account (30, 60, 90, 120, or more than 120 days), and a notation if an insurance claim has been filed. From this accounts receivable statement, the office manager prepares monthly statements and mails them to the patients. Accounts that are more than 120 days past due are reviewed by the physician and turned over to a collection agency.

The physician totals the balances on the ledger cards and compares this total with the total on the monthly accounts receivable statement and with the accounts receivable total on the daily business summary. The accounts receivable statement is then filed by date.

Required:

a. What observations do you have with regard to Dr. Clark's billing and collection system?

b. Prepare a flowchart covering the preceding narrative.

17–31.   *ELECTRONIC DATA INTERCHANGE*

In the mid-1980s, **Cummins Engine Company, Inc.,** decided to pursue the productivity benefits of electronic data interchange (EDI) as an element of its business strategy.[1] Over a 14-month period, its credit group went from "novice" to "expert" in receiving electronic remittance advices and payments from customers, distributors, and banks.

The Pilot Project

Cummins is a major producer of diesel engines, components, and power systems for heavy-duty trucks and industrial machinery. Its primary U.S. customers are truck and equipment manufacturers and a nationwide network of distributors. Companies in this industry recognize the need for cooperation in order to improve productivity and enhance the competitiveness of the North American trucking industry. This led Cummins to join with Freightliner Corporation, a major truck manufacturer, in a pilot project for implementing EDI in a broad range of manufacturing and financial applications.

Cummins had relatively few (100 or so) customers. A typical customer paid either daily (as does Freightliner) or weekly. A weekly payment may apply to as many as 500, or as few as 100, invoiced items. The accounts receivable system that Cummins installed in 1988 had the ability to receive detail on each of these invoiced items and to apply it to customer accounts.

In 1989, Cummins, Freightliner, and their banks (Chase Manhattan and First National Bank of Chicago) implemented the pilot project. Freightliner used EDI to transfer payments and provide remittance detail for its daily payment to Cummins. The success of the pilot allowed Cummins to implement the same procedures for other customers who requested it with minimal effort.

Expansion to Distributors

Its success with customers led Cummins in 1989 to begin implementation of the same procedures with its 32 distributors. The distributors already had direct access to Cummins's main computer and had been exchanging data with it using private formats. The new system would allow distributors to exchange data in the same standard format used by the customers. However, whereas customers exchanged data through banks and a mailbox at a value-added network (VAN) company, the distributors would transmit the detail directly to Cummins's accounts receivable system.

Because of the differences in procedures, Cummins management decided to implement them first with a pilot distributor. Once they became operational on a weekly basis, they gradually implemented them at the remaining distributors through 1990 and 1991.

Lockbox Payments

A third step in implementing EDI in Cummins's revenue cycle concerned lockbox payments. Those customers who were not using EDI would mail their checks and remittance

---

[1]Adapted from Martha M. Heidkamp, "Reaping the Benefits of Financial EDI," *Management Accounting,* May 1991, p. 39. Copyright by Institute of Management Accountants (1991), Montvale, N.J. 07645.

advices to a lockbox, a post office box accessed by one of Cummins's banks. The bank would then deposit the checks in a Cummins account and send the remittance advices to Cummins by mail or courier.

With the new system, the banks would transmit the data for the lockbox payments as EDI transactions in the same standard format used with customers and distributors. Parallel testing for the new system occurred for one bank in mid-1990 and was completed at the second in early 1991.

Exhibit 17–8 shows the data flow for the three types of EDI transactions.

The Benefits

The objective of using EDI was to improve productivity by replacing paper payment detail with computerized data. When Cummins's credit department began the project, its personnel knew little about the concepts, terminology, or requirements of EDI. There were many days of frustration and wondering whether benefits would ever materialize.

By 1990, when personnel discovered that they could initiate EDI with a new customer in a matter of hours, the benefits began to be apparent. Workers did not have to wait for paper copies of remittance advices to arrive by mail, and all routine matching of items was done by computer. An analyst started the day by reviewing accounts on-line after payments had been applied, rather than in searching in files for paper copies of payment detail. Credit analysts were required to analyze only unusual situations. The time saved was spent resolving specific problems, collecting old accounts, or taking on new responsibilities.

Why did the project succeed? Cummins attributes its success with EDI in the revenue cycle to the following:

- A commitment to work with trading partners to improve transaction flows.
- Leadership and involvement in the industry by key Cummins personnel.
- A commitment to spend the time needed to work through the pilot implementations fully.
- Adherence to standards, even when they created slowdowns initially.

Because of the benefits obtained in the credit department from using EDI, Cummins has extended its use to a variety of other financial and manufacturing applications.

Required:
a. Which transactions from the revenue cycle did Cummins implement using EDI?
b. If you were assigned to this project, what controls would you incorporate into the new system?

17–32.   INTEGRATIVE CASE—PART II

Agee Company is a manufacturer of large diameter valves located in a major southwestern city. Management has engaged a local CPA firm to aid the company in updating its accounting systems, and you have been assigned to a design team responsible for developing the new processes. Members of the team include management accountants, Agee operating personnel, and representatives of the CPA firm's staff. The team leader

Exhibit 17–8

Case 17–31   Cummins EDI Data Flows

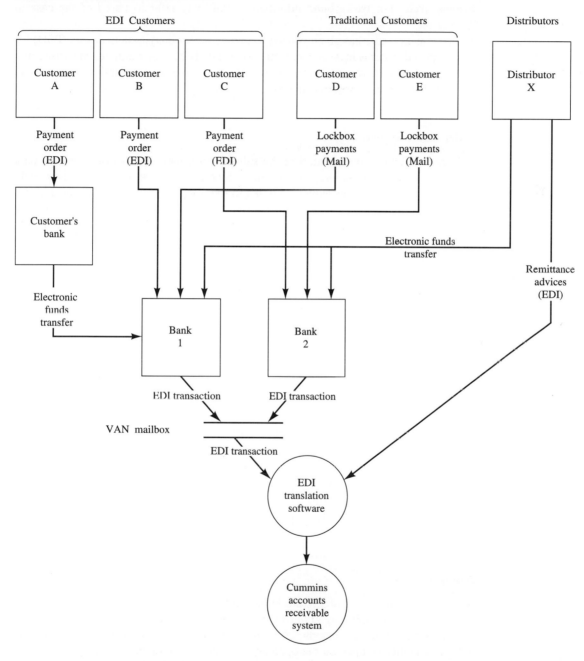

is an experienced systems analyst from the CPA firm. In this chapter, you will complete assignments that allow you to participate in the design of application systems in Agee's revenue cycle. For background information, you may refer to Part I of the case in Chapter 16.

Your team leader has given you the following preliminary system design (PSD) for four proposed systems in Agee's revenue cycle. The PSD is incomplete, consisting of a short narrative and a system flowchart for each one. Make any assumptions necessary to complete the requirements, but state your assumptions.

Order Entry System

Customer orders arrive by mail at the sales department. A sales clerk enters data from the customer order into the system, which performs an on-line credit check. The system then adds the requested items to the open order file and prints an order acknowledgment that is mailed to the customer. Once each day, after all orders have been entered, the system prints an open order listing and an updated master assembly schedule. The production department uses this to schedule the order for production.

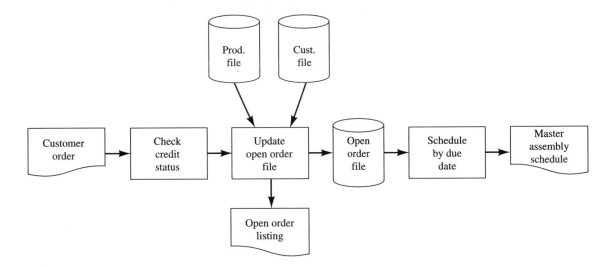

Billing System

Agee's policy is that all orders are billed on the day they are shipped. The shipping department sends a shipping notice to the billing department when they load the goods on a truck bound for the customer. A billing clerk uses data from the shipping notice to indicate quantity shipped on the open order record in the open order file. The system then deducts the goods from inventory and prints an invoice that the clerk mails to the customer. The system then updates the general ledger, the detailed accounts receivable records, and the sales history records.

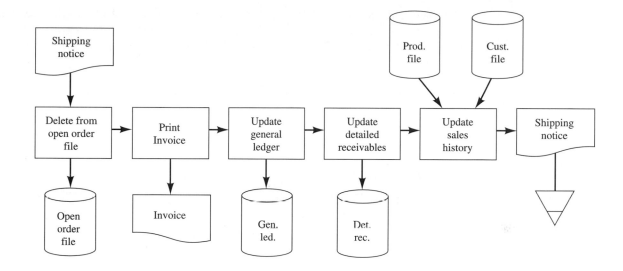

Cash Receipts System

Cash receipts arrive by mail. The receptionist opens the mail and separates the check from the remittance advice. The receptionist then prepares a remittance list in two copies. One copy is attached to the checks that go to the treasurer. The other copy is attached to the remittance advices that go to the accounts receivable clerk. The clerk uses data from the remittance advice to update the detailed accounts receivable records, the customer's credit status, and the general ledger.

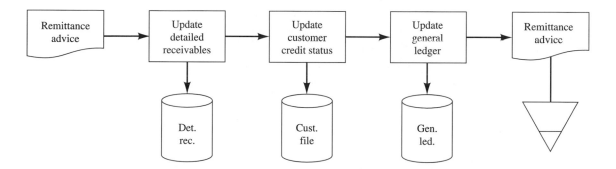

Sales Analysis System

The sales analysis system produces reports or displays that provide historical summaries of sales both by customer and by product. The sales department can produce these reports at any time, but normally this is done at the end of each month. To produce the summary, the operator enters a key date in the system. The system totals sales that have occurred since the key date and either prints or displays them, at the operator's option.

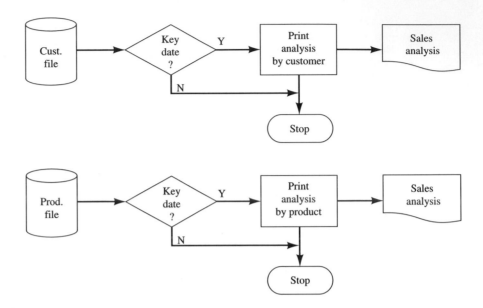

Required:

a. What observations do you have about this preliminary design? Do you think that modifications are needed?
b. Prepare a data flow diagram for the sales analysis system.
c. Design a control report for the cash receipts system.
d. Design a register for the billing system.
e. Develop a record layout for the open order file.
f. Design a data entry screen for the order entry system.
g. Design a remittance advice for the cash receipts system.
h. What control procedures should you incorporate in the applications of Agee's revenue cycle?

18 EXPENDITURE CYCLE APPLICATIONS

Learning Objectives

1. To review the accounting entries recorded in the expenditure cycle.
2. To learn which documents, reports, and records are used in the expenditure cycle.
3. To understand how accounting transactions are processed by the application systems in the expenditure cycle.
4. To see how control practices and procedures are applied in the expenditure cycle.

Introduction

An accounting system records the activities of a business using four transaction cycles. In this chapter, you will learn how accounting systems record those activities that acquire goods and services. These activities are part of the expenditure cycle.

In this transaction cycle, the accounting system records four economic events. First, organizations request goods or services. Computer-based systems use purchasing systems to record these requests. Second, organizations receive the goods or services. When goods are involved, a receiving system records this event. Third, organizations recognize an obligation to pay for the goods or services. This economic event is processed by the voucher system. Finally, organizations use cash disbursements systems to record the fourth economic event, payment for the goods or services. The voucher and cash disbursements systems together are called the *accounts payable system.*

Illustration 18–1 shows the relationships among the application systems in the expenditure cycle. The circles in this diagram represent application systems, the large square is the external entity, and the small squares stand for general ledger accounts. The accounts interface these systems with those in other transaction cycles. The interfaces shown between these systems may take the form of documents or data records.

ILLUSTRATION 18–1

Application Systems in the Expenditure Cycle

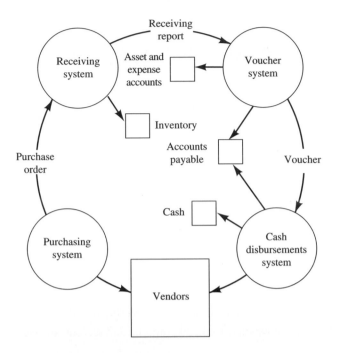

Documents, Reports, and Records

In an introductory accounting course you studied entries for recording transactions that provide a conceptual representation of how accounting systems work. Few organizations record transactions in that way now. However, this chapter reviews those entries so you can relate what you learned in introductory accounting to how modern organizations record transactions.

In practice, an accounting system records transaction data in documents, accumulates the data in accounting records, and discloses the data in reports. To understand the accounting system, you must know how manual and computerized procedures process these documents, records, and reports.

Expenditure Cycle Transactions and Documents

Three types of transactions occur routinely in the expenditure cycle: credit purchases, cash disbursements, and purchase returns. Illustration 18–2 summarizes these transactions and shows the documents used by the accounting system in recording them.

ILLUSTRATION 18–2

Expenditure Cycle Transactions and Related Documents

Type of Transaction	Related Documents
Credit purchase	Purchase requisition
	Purchase order
	Receiving report
	Voucher
Cash disbursement	Check
Purchase return	Debit memo

Credit Purchases.   An organization with a good credit rating makes most of its purchases on credit. To initiate a credit purchase, someone in the organization recognizes the need for goods or services. An authorized person such as a supervisor requests them on a ***purchase requisition.*** A copy of this document goes to the purchasing department, where a purchasing agent approves the purchase, selects a vendor, prepares a ***purchase order,*** and mails it to the vendor. The purchase order, when accepted by the vendor, becomes a legally binding contract.

When the vendor provides the goods or services, a ***receiving report*** documents their receipt in the receiving department. After receiving a copy of the receiving report, an invoice from the vendor, and a copy of the purchase order, the accounts payable department prepares a ***voucher*** showing which asset or expense account to debit. Accountants call this the *account distribution.* Accounts payable then attaches the invoice, receiving report, and purchase order to the voucher and submits it to the treasurer for approval.

The accounting entry recording a credit purchase in the general ledger is

Dr.   Asset or expense account   xxx
Cr.   Accounts Payable   xxx

Illustration 18–3 contains a purchase requisition. Illustration 18–4 shows a purchase order, and Illustration 18–5, a receiving report. During system design, the design team determines the contents and layouts of these documents. They must capture the

ILLUSTRATION 18–3

A Purchase Requisition

```
                                    ********************************
                                    * OFFICIAL TEXTBOOK REQUISITION *
                                    ********************************

  UNIV. OF HOUSTON BOOKSTORE                                          RETURN THIS FORM BY : 10/01/98
   CALL : 748-XXXX            TXT. MGR


                    SIGNATURE DEPT CHAIR
                    SIGNATURE INSTRUCTOR
                    PRINT OR TYPE INSTRUCTOR NAME                 INSTRUCTOR PHONE #


  INFORMATION FOR TERM : S89     CLASS :

  DEPARTMENT CONTACT :                  PHONE :                   _ _ _ _ _ _ _ _ _ _ _ _
                                                                 _ FILL  IN  DATA  BELOW : _
                                                                 _ _ _ _ _ _ _ _ _ _ _ _
      AUTHOR    :                                                REQUIRED      ? : YES / NO
      TITLE     :                                  EDITION :     ENROLLMENT     :
      PUBLISHER :              COVER :                           SECTION NUMBERS:
                               ISBN  :                           INSTRUCTOR     :

      AUTHOR    :                                                REQUIRED      ? : YES / NO
      TITLE     :                                  EDITION :     ENROLLMENT     :
      PUBLISHER :              COVER :                           SECTION NUMBERS:
                               ISBN  :                           INSTRUCTOR     :

      AUTHOR    :                                                REQUIRED      ? : YES / NO
      TITLE     :                                  EDITION :     ENROLLMENT     :
      PUBLISHER :              COVER :                           SECTION NUMBERS:
                               ISBN  :                           INSTRUCTOR     :


  REQUIRED SUPPLIES:
```

ILLUSTRATION 18–4

A Purchase Order

```
                                        ****************
W.D. Peachtree & Company                *              *
3900 Peachtree Street                   *  PURCHASE ORDER  *
Atlanta, GA 30309                       *              *
                                        ****************

                              Purchase Order Number:   2401

                              Purchase Order Date: 12/01/98

                                             Page:   1

   To:  BILL'S STEREO WAREHOUSE        Ship  W.D. Peachtree & Company
        167476 P'TREE IND BLVD.        To.:  3900 Peachtree Street
        ATLANTA, GEORGIA                     Atlanta, GA 30305
        30048


   Ship Via..: Surface          Confirm To: Jean Hightower
   Receive By: 12/15/98         Buyer.....: Wanda Dewberry
   Terms.....: Net 30           Phone.....: (404)-555-3432
   F.O.B.....: Shipping Point   Vendor....: ELE001


   Item ID      Description      Unit  Quantity  Unit Price    Total Price

   340TV        COLOR TELEVISION  EACH     6.00  345.0000000      2070.00




                                          Subtotal:           2070.00
                                          Total...:           2070.00

                       Authorized Signature: _____.
```

data required for the accounting and management reports produced by the systems in the expenditure cycle.

Vouchers exist in different forms. Sometimes the voucher is a large envelope containing the other documents and showing the expense distribution on the outside. Other companies use a rubber stamp applied to the vendor invoice. Regardless of its form, the voucher should show the general ledger accounts to be debited, the amounts, the name and address of the vendor, and the due date for payment. Illustration 18–6 shows a common approach. This voucher is a prenumbered form that is fastened to the other documents.

ILLUSTRATION 18–5

A Receiving Report

```
                                RECEIVING CHECK LIST                              Page:  1


    Purchase Order Number:   2401      Ship To:  W.D. Peachtree & Company    Vendor:   BILL'S STEREO WAREHOUSE
    Purchase Order Date..: 12/01/98              3900 Peachtree Street                 167476 P'TREE IND BLVD.
    Receive By Date......: 12/15/98              Atlanta, GA 30305
    Vendor ID...........: ELE001                                                       ATLANTA, GEORGIA
                                                                                       30048

 =====================================================================================================================
    Vendor         Our                                          Quantity   Already   Received   Partial   Qty. Received
    Item #      Inventory ID     Item Description      Stk       Ordered   Received   All Units  Receipt   (If Partial)
    _____      _____                                                          _____  _____   _____

  340TV         PELE810340TV     COLOR TELEVISION      Yes         6.00      6.00     _____  _____   _____

  123131        PELE810104SPK    SPEAKERS              Yes        15.00     15.00     _____  _____   _____

  45646         PELE810534BAT    BATTERIES             Yes       100.00    100.00     _____  _____   _____




    Number of items on this page:    3.00    Total number of items:    3.00          Signature:
```

Copyright 1995 Peachtree Software, Inc. Reprinted by permission.

Cash Disbursements. After a voucher is attached to the associated invoice, receiving report, and purchase order, these documents remain filed in the accounts payable department until the date payment is due. On the due date, this voucher package goes to the treasurer's department, where it is approved for payment. This department then mails a check in payment.

Some vendors offer discounts from the invoice price in return for prompt payment. For example, a common discount policy is 2/10, n/30, read as "two ten, net thirty." This means that a buyer paying the invoice within 10 days of its mailing is entitled to a 2 percent discount from the amount shown on the invoice. Otherwise, the buyer should pay the total, or net, amount within 30 days.

When an organization takes discounts of this kind, it records the amount of the discount in a special account. The accounting entry recording the cash disbursement transaction is

Dr. Accounts Payable xxx
Cr.   Cash xxx
Cr.   Purchase Discounts xxx

Illustration 18–7 contains a check with a check stub attached showing the specific invoices paid by the check. This allows the vendor to record the payment properly in the

ILLUSTRATION 18–6

A Voucher

SUNLIGHT MANUFACTORY COMPANY					Voucher No.	175324
105 Red Hot Road						
Dallas, Texas 75248					Date _____	

Vendor invoice date	Vendor invoice number	Amount	Discount	Return and allowance	Net	Account distribution

Detach Here

SUNLIGHT MANUFACTORY COMPANY   Check No. _____
105 Red Hot Road
Dallas, Texas 75248   Date _____
Pay to the order of   _____ $ _____

_____

First National Bank of
Far North Dallas
Box 7707   _____
Dallas, Texas 75248   _____

Prepared by	Verified by	Entered by	Filed	Due date

vendor's accounts receivable records. It also shows the dates of these invoices and any discounts claimed by the buyer.

Purchase Returns. This transaction occurs when an organization returns to the vendor an item purchased on credit. This may occur because the purchaser received unrequested items, an excessive number of items, or items of inferior quality. Along with the returned goods, the purchaser sends a request that the vendor credit the purchaser's account (containing a debit balance in the vendor's accounting records) for the cost of the return. The document used by the purchaser to make this request is a *debit memo*. Purchasers use this name because of the accounts payable entry recording the purchase return:

Dr.	Accounts payable	xxx	
Cr.	Asset or expense account		xxx

ILLUSTRATION 18–7

A Check

W.D. Peachtree & Company

BRATCHWORTH CLOTHES 4867 MITCHELL BOULEVARD	Invoice No	Date	Amount	Discount	Net Amount
LOS ANGELES, CALIFORNIA	BB46399765	11/24	2113.11	0.00	2113.11
95860		11/24	812.00	0.00	812.00-
DATE			TOTAL=		$1,301.11
11/30/98					

CHECK NUMBER
1000011

Negative Amounts Are Credits Applied On This Payment

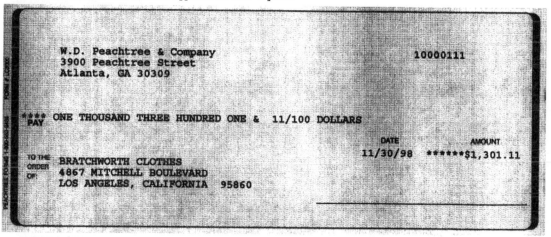

W.D. Peachtree & Company
3900 Peachtree Street
Atlanta, GA 30309

10000111

**** ONE THOUSAND THREE HUNDRED ONE & 11/100 DOLLARS
PAY

DATE   AMOUNT
11/30/98 ******$1,301.11

TO THE BRATCHWORTH CLOTHES
ORDER 4867 MITCHELL BOULEVARD
OF LOS ANGELES, CALIFORNIA 95860

W.D. Peachtree & Company

BRATCHWORTH CLOTHES 4867 MITCHELL BOULEVARD	Invoice No	Date	Amount	Discount	Net Amount
LOS ANGELES, CALIFORNIA	BB46399765	11/24	2113.11	0.00	2113.11
95860		11/24	812.00	0.00	812.00-
DATE			TOTAL=		$1,301.11
11/30/98					

CHECK NUMBER
1000011

Negative Amounts Are Credits Applied On This Payment

You are now familiar with the documents used in the expenditure cycle and with the accounting entries produced from the data on these documents. Next you will see the reports produced in this transaction cycle.

Expenditure Cycle Reports

Just as in the revenue cycle, application systems in the expenditure cycle produce three kinds of reports: control reports, registers, and special purpose reports. However, these disclose different data from those in the other cycle.

Control Reports. A control report summarizes the changes made to a file. Accountants use a control report to determine when changes were made improperly or to ensure that no transactions were omitted during processing. With a computer-based system, data control clerks examine control reports. They compare control totals, hash totals, and record counts to detect improper processing.

Illustration 18–8 contains a control report that lists the vendor invoices received and added to a file of pending vendor invoices by an on-line real-time system. It allows the data entry clerk to ensure that all invoices were properly added by the system.

Registers. A register contains a list of transactions of a certain type recorded during a processing period, such as a day, a week, or a month. Registers contain detailed data supporting summary entries in accounting ledgers, so they provide an audit trail for account balances.

A register in a manual system is a special purpose journal. For this reason, a register in a computer-based system is sometimes identified as a journal.

Illustration 18–9 contains a check register that shows a list of checks issued in payment of vendor invoices. Other registers produced in the expenditure cycle include purchase order, receipts, and voucher registers.

Special Purpose Reports. Special purpose reports in the expenditure cycle help managers schedule payments to vendors. They include the open invoices report, the voucher aging report, and the cash requirements report. An on-line real-time system may also produce a query vendor report.

Open Invoices Report. An open invoices report lists unpaid vendor invoices as of the date of the report. It lists the invoices received from each vendor and the amounts owed on each invoice, as shown in Illustration 18–10.

Voucher Aging Report. A voucher aging report summarizes vouchers by how long they have existed. Vendor invoices that remain unpaid for an excessive length of time may damage a firm's business relationship with the vendor. They may also harm the firm's credit rating, making it difficult to purchase on credit. Frequently, old unpaid invoices are a result of disagreements with the vendor. The voucher aging report, as shown in Illustration 18–11, alerts the accounts payable department to the existence of such problems.

Cash Requirements Report. A cash requirements report lists vouchers by the date they are due to be paid. It aids the accounts payable department in planning cash

ILLUSTRATION 18–8

A Control Report

```
RUN DATE: 11/30/98                      W.D. Peachtree & Company                          PAGE  1
RUN TIME:  3:26 PM                          Accounts Payable
                                      Enter Invoices Control Report
```

VENDOR ID	VENDOR NAME/ INVOICE NO.	INVOICE DATE	DUE AMOUNT/DATE	DISCOUNT AMOUNT/DATE	DISTRIBUTION ACCOUNT	AMOUNT	PRE-PAID	ACCOUNT C/AP	COMMENT
ELE012	STEREO CITY								
	4564613	11/01/98	300.00 12/01/98	6.00 11/11/98	13500	300.00	N	0/1	
	7987	11/15/98	464.00 12/15/98	9.28 11/25/98	13500	464.00	N	0/1	
	15949	11/20/98	8,797.00 12/20/98	175.94 11/30/98	13500	8,797.00	N	0/1	
	37665	11/20/98	456.00 12/20/98	9.12 11/30/98	13500	456.00	N	0/1	
	213313	11/23/98	789.00 12/23/98	15.78 12/03/98	13500	789.00	N	0/1	
	3265	11/23/98	564.00 12/23/98	11.28 12/03/98	13500	564.00	N	0/1	
	384957	11/25/98	930.00 12/25/98	18.60 12/05/98	13500	930.00	N	0/1	
	03540	11/25/98	233.00 12/25/98	4.66 12/05/98	13500	233.00	N	0/1	
ELE873	JACKSON ELECTRONICS								
	23732947	11/25/98	780.00 12/25/98	15.60 12/05/98	13500	780.00	N	0/1	
ELE006	JVP COMPUTERS & STEREOS								
	39147	11/15/98	45.00 12/15/98	0.90 11/25/98	13500	45.00	N	0/1	

JOB NUMBER	PHASE CODE	COST CODE	AMOUNT		JOB NUMBER	PHASE CODE	COST CODE	AMOUNT
000123	01	ALL	45.00					

```
    TOTAL INVOICES ADDED:    10           13,358.00        267.16
```

flows and in identifying which invoices should be paid promptly to receive discounts and maintain good relations with vendors. This report also shows the effect of paying these invoices on the cash balance. Illustration 18–12 contains a cash requirements report.

Query Vendor Report. An on-line real-time system allows users to query the database for current information. In the expenditure cycle, accounts payable clerks often need to know the status of a specific vendor's account. They obtain this information from a

ILLUSTRATION 18–9

A Register

```
RUN DATE: 11/30/98                    W.D. Peachtree & Company                      PAGE  1
RUN TIME:  3:45 PM                        Accounts Payable
                                           Check Register

** CASH ACCOUNT:  1 11000
———CHECK———  ——————VENDOR——————              INVOICE        DISCOUNT
                                             INVOICE    ——————————————
NUMBER  DATE     ID     NAME        INVOICE NUMBER  DATE    AMOUNT    AMOUNT   AMOUNT PAID

10000112 11/30/98 AUTFNC THIRD NATIONAL BANK OF GA 1 Auto Inv. - 12/30/98  12/30/98  5,000.00   10.00    4,990.00

10000113 11/30/98 BBBANK Barstow Bailey Bank      3241              10/30/98    500.00    0.00      500.00

10000114 11/30/98 BRATCH BRATCHWORTH CLOTHES      BB46399765        11/24/98    812.00    0.00      812.00

10000115 11/30/98 ELE006 JVP COMPUTERS & STEREOS  39147             11/15/98     45.00    0.00       45.00

10000116 11/30/98 ELE022 BRECKER'S ELECTRONICS    810945R20         11/15/98  1,176.55    0.00    1,176.55
                                                  811965R20         12/05/98  1,100.00    0.00    1,100.00
                                                                      Total Check Amount:    2,276.55

10000117 11/30/98 ELE032 HARRIS ELECTRONICS       810999A20         11/14/98  1,234.55    0.00    1,234.55

10000118 11/30/98 ELE084 STEREO CITY DISTRIBUTORS 811888R30         12/05/98  1,234.55    0.00    1,234.55

10000119 11/30/98 ELE873 JACKSON ELECTRONICS      23732947          11/25/98    780.00   15.60      764.40

10000120 11/30/98 ELE923 GLASS DISTRIBUTORS       810999C20         11/15/98  1,234.44    0.00    1,234.44
                                                  811555C20         11/23/98  1,987.56    0.00    1,987.56
                                                                      Total Check Amount:    3,222.00

10000121 11/30/98 FRIGID FRIGID-AIRE DISTRIBUTORS 900911-2          11/17/98  5,786.76    0.00    5,786.76
                                                  910987-2          11/29/98  4,211.33    0.00    4,211.33
                                                                      Total Check Amount:    9,998.09

10000122 11/30/98 GLENNS GLENN'S SPORTS & HARDWARE B29865B27        11/27/98  2,991.54    0.00    2,991.54
                                                  B31456B27         12/05/98  1,113.40    0.00    1,113.40
                                                                      Total Check Amount:    4,104.94

10000123 11/30/98 MAYTAB MAYTAB APPLIANCES        093567-004        11/15/98  6,098.76    0.00    6,098.76
                                                  0946789-004       11/25/98  3,877.99    0.00    3,877.99
                                                                      Total Check Amount:    9,976.75

10000124 11/30/98 NUMCO  NUMCO CLOTHING, LTD.     463487G20         10/31/98    105.00    0.00      105.00
                                                  81960813          10/31/98     71.50    0.00       71.50
                                                  81961999          11/17/98  1,237.66    0.00    1,237.66
                                                  81962345          11/29/98  1,009.55    0.00    1,009.55
                                                  81963114          12/05/98    667.98    0.00      667.98
                                                                      Total Check Amount:    3,091.69
```

query vendor report, shown in Illustration 18–13. Many systems allow users the option of printing the report or displaying it on a CRT.

Four special purpose reports are produced by the applications in the expenditure cycle. The application systems in this cycle use registers and control reports to summarize the information from data maintained in the accounting records.

ILLUSTRATION 18–10

An Open Invoices Report

```
RUN DATE: 11/30/98                        W.D. Peachtree & Company                         PAGE  1
RUN TIME: 11:29 AM                           Accounts Payable
                                            Open Invoices Report


** A/P ACCOUNT:  ALL

VENDOR    VENDOR NAME/        ENTRY  ------INVOICE------  ----DISCOUNT----
  ID      INVOICE NUMBER      DATE   INVOICE AMOUNT  DATE  DUE DATE  DISC. AMOUNT   DATE     PAYMENTS    NET INVOICE   PAY

BLASS   P. BLASS MEN'S CLOTHING
        9453BB08             11/05/98    1,432.66 11/05/98 12/05/98      0.00   01/01/00      0.00       1,432.66  YES
        9687BB08             11/05/98    1,113.44 11/25/98 12/25/98      0.00   01/01/00      0.00       1,113.44  NO

                                         2,546.10                       0.00                 0.00       2,546.10

        BRATCH  BRATCHWORTH CLOTHES
        BB42530807           10/31/98       62.16 10/31/98 11/30/98      0.00   01/01/00      0.00          62.16  YES
        BB46378999           11/05/98    5,432.65 11/10/98 12/10/98      0.00   01/01/00      0.00       5,432.65  NO
        BB46399765           11/05/98    2,113.11 11/24/98 12/24/98      0.00   01/01/00      0.00       2,113.11  NO

                                         7,607.92                       0.00                 0.00       7,607.92

CANNON  CANNON LINEN SUPPLIES
        810987B50            11/05/98    2,334.54 11/19/98 12/19/98      0.00   01/01/00      0.00       2,334.54  NO
        811899B50            12/15/98      775.88 12/05/98 01/04/99      0.00   01/01/00      0.00         775.88  NO

                                         3,110.42                       0.00                 0.00       3,110.42

        CURTIS  CURTIS APPLIANCES
        10060P10             10/31/98    1,100.00 10/31/98 11/30/98      0.00   01/01/00      0.00       1,100.00  YES
        10287P11             12/15/98    1,555.78 12/05/98 01/04/99      0.00   01/01/00      0.00       1,555.78  NO

                                         2,655.78                       0.00                 0.00       2,655.78

DIOR    CHRISTOPHER DIOR APPARELS
        D91013222            11/05/98    2,311.55 11/26/98 12/26/98      0.00   01/01/00      0.00       2,311.55  NO

                                         2,311.55                       0.00                 0.00       2,311.55

ELE001  BILL'S STEREO WAREHOUSE
        810534B100           10/31/98       55.56 10/31/98 11/30/98      0.00   01/01/00      0.00          55.56  YES
        810765B100           11/05/98    2,322.54 11/11/98 12/11/98      0.00   01/01/00      0.00       2,322.54  NO
        811564B100           11/05/98    1,917.77 11/12/98 12/12/98      0.00   01/01/00      0.00       1,917.77  NO

                                         4,295.87                       0.00                 0.00       4,295.87

ELE003  STEREO WAREHOUSE SUPPLIES
        811688C20            11/05/98    3,112.22 11/29/98 12/29/98      0.00   01/01/00      0.00       3,112.22  NO
                                                  11/2 /98 12/29/98
                                         3,112.22                       0.00                 0.00       3,112.22

ELE006  JVP COMPUTERS & STEREOS
        811654E07            11/05/98    1,221.33 11/10/98 12/10/98      0.00   01/01/00      0.00       1,221.33  NO
        812433E07            11/05/98    2,333.66 11/24/98 12/24/98      0.00   01/01/00      0.00       2,333.66  NO

                                         3,554.99                       0.00                 0.00       3,554.99
```

Copyright 1995 Peachtree Software, Inc. Reprinted by permission.

Expenditure Cycle Accounting Records

Accounting systems maintain records for manual processes on paper journals, in ledgers, and in filing cabinets. For computerized processes, journals and ledgers are in computer-readable form and contain master records and transaction records. Although their forms differ, their contents are similar.

Noncomputerized Records.   Manual systems maintain accounting records in the form of books, cards, and filing cabinets. The expenditure cycle uses two special journals and several manual files.

ILLUSTRATION 18–11

A Voucher Aging Report

```
RUN DATE: 12/30/98                        W.D. Peachtree & Company                      PAGE  1
RUN TIME: 12:36 PM                           Accounts Payable
                                               Aging Report
```

** A/P ACCOUNT: ALL

VENDOR ID	VENDOR NAME/ INVOICE NUMBER	CURRENT	1 TO 30	31 TO 60	61 TO 90	OVER 90	CREDITS	TOTAL DUE
BLASS	PHIL BLASS MEN'S CLOTHING							
	9453BB08		1,432.66					1,432.66
	9687BB08		1,113.44					1,113.44
	Vendor Totals:	0.00	2,546.10	0.00	0.00	0.00	0.00	2,546.10
BRATCH	BRATCHWORTH CLOTHES							
	12323					500.00		500.00
	BB42530807		62.16					62.16
	BB46378999		5,432.65					5,432.65
	BB46399765		2,113.11					2,113.11
	Vendor Totals:	0.00	7,607.92	0.00	0.00	500.00	0.00	8,107.92
CANNON	CANNON LINEN SUPPLIES							
	12312321					75.00		75.00
	13200					5,000.00		5,000.00
	810987B50		2,334.54					2,334.54
	811899B50	775.88						775.88
	Vendor Totals:	775.88	2,334.54	0.00	0.00	5,075.00	0.00	8,185.42
CURTIS	CURTIS APPLIANCES							
	10060P10		1,100.00					1,100.00
	10287P11	1,555.78						1,555.78
	Vendor Totals:	1,555.78	1,100.00	0.00	0.00	0.00	0.00	2,655.78
DIOR	CHRISTOPHER DIOR APPARELS							
	D91013222		2,311.55					2,311.55
	Vendor Totals:	0.00	2,311.55	0.00	0.00	0.00	0.00	2,311.55
ELE001	BILL'S STEREO WAREHOUSE							
	810534B100		55.56					55.56

In a manual system, the voucher register and the check register are special journals. Accounts payable clerks record vouchers in the voucher register as they prepare vendor invoices for payment. Cash disbursements clerks record checks in the check register as they prepare them. These, similar to all registers, provide an audit trail by showing the sources of entries in the general and subsidiary ledgers. Additionally, they serve as methods of initially recording the transactions creating the entries. Illustration 18–14 shows the contents of these journals.

ILLUSTRATION 8–12

A Cash Requirements Report

```
RUN DATE: 12/22/98                      W.D. Peachtree & Company                          PAGE  1
RUN TIME: 11:11 AM                         Accounts Payable
                                        Cash Requirements Report

**DATA SORTED BY DUE DATE
DUE DATE/
VENDOR       VENDOR NAME       INVOICE NUMBER    INV.DATE   AMOUNT   DISCOUNT      NET    DAILY TOTAL   REQ. TO DATE
____

11/30/98
BRATCH  BRATCHWORTH CLOTHES BB42530807           10/31/98     62.16    0.00       62.16
CURTIS  CURTIS APPLIANCES    10060P10            10/31/98  1,100.00    0.00    1,100.00
ELE001  BILL'S STEREO WAREH  810534B100          10/31/98     55.56    0.00       55.56
NUMCO   NUMCO CLOTHING, LTD  463487G20           10/31/98    105.00    0.00      105.00
                             81960813            10/31/98     71.50    0.00       71.50
SACKS   SACKS 6TH AVENUE DI  46344475            10/31/98     51.75    0.00       51.75
SCULLY  SCULLY HAIR PRODUCT  SC3SP7024           10/31/98     45.12    0.00       45.12
SPEAR   SPEAR'S BEAUTY SUPP  SP7010              10/31/98     22.50    0.00       22.50
STEWRT  STEWART'S APPARELS   FP398308            10/31/98     71.11    0.00       71.11
WILSON  WILSON, INC.         H02099765           10/31/98     19.50    0.00       19.50
                             H02099925           10/31/98     47.00    0.00       47.00
                             S006B08             10/31/98    124.40    0.00      124.40
                             S0100M20            10/31/98     71.11    0.00       71.11
                             S0500P11            10/31/98    220.00    0.00      220.00
                             TNT98400615         10/31/98    360.00    0.00      360.00    2,426.71      2,426.71

12/05/98
BLASS   PHIL BLASS MEN'S CL 9453BB08             11/05/98  1,432.66    0.00    1,432.66    1,432.66      3,859.37

12/10/98
BRATCH  BRATCHWORTH CLOTHES BB46378999           11/10/98  5,432.65    0.00    5,432.65
ELE006  JVP COMPUTERS & STE 811654E07            11/10/98  1,221.33    0.00    1,221.33    6,653.98     10,513.35

12/11/98
ELE001  BILL'S STEREO WAREH 810765B100           11/11/98  2,322.54    0.00    2,322.54
ELE010  TONY'S STEREO/ELECT JVP9385433           11/11/98  2,114.65    0.00    2,114.65    4,437.19     14,950.54

12/12/98
ELE001  BILL'S STEREO WAREH 811564B100           11/12/98  1,917.77    0.00    1,917.77    1,917.77     16,868.31

12/14/98
ELE032  HARRIS ELECTRONICS  810999A20            11/14/98  1,234.55    0.00    1,234.55    1,234.55     18,102.86

12/15/98
ELE022  BRECKER'S ELECTRONI 810945R20            11/15/98  1,176.55    0.00    1,176.55
ELE873  JACKSON ELECTRONICS 810899E15            11/15/98  2,212.34    0.00    2,212.34
ELE923  GLASS DISTRIBUTORS  810999C20            11/15/98  1,234.44    0.00    1,234.44
GLENNS  GLENN'S SPORTS & HA 52345B27             11/15/98  3,119.77    0.00    3,119.77
MAYTAB  MAYTAB APPLIANCES   093567-004           11/15/98  6,098.76    0.00    6,098.76
SACKS   SACKS 6TH AVENUE DI 46344988             11/15/98  3,221.44    0.00    3,221.44
```

Computerized Records.   In computerized systems, accounting records are kept in computer files and databases. In a traditional data file system, applications in the expenditure cycle use one master file and seven transaction files.

A database management system (DBMS) stores data in a database rather than in files. The difference between how traditional data file systems and how DBMSs store data has no effect on how application systems process the data. The difference only affects how the system retrieves the data from the secondary storage device.

ILLUSTRATION 18–13

A Query Vendor Report

```
RUN DATE: 12/22/98                    W.D. Peachtree & Company                      PAGE  1
RUN TIME: 11:00 AM                       Accounts Payable
                                           Query Vendor
───────────────────────────────────────────────────────────────────────────────────────────
VENDOR
  ID       NAME / ADDRESS       PHONES        AMOUNTS    CALENDAR    FISCAL          LAST CHECK

BRATCH   BRATCHWORTH CLOTHES                YTD Purch:  10,246.75   10,246.75    No. :   10000086
         4867 MITCHELL BOULEVARD           YTD Paymt:   2,138.83    2,138.83    Amt.:     106.56
         LOS ANGELES, CALIFORNIA           Curr. Bal:   8,107.92                Date:  12/07/98
                                           Net Pending:     0.00
         95860

         USR1 (          ) -
         USR2 (          ) -
         USR3 (          ) -
         USR4 (          ) -
         USR5 (          ) -

    INVOICE      AMOUNT DUE    DISCOUNT                                                     DISC.
  NUMBER / DATE  / DATE DUE  AMOUNT / DATE  ACCOUNT - AMOUNT   ACCOUNT - AMOUNT  ACCOUNT - AMOUNT  TAKEN PAY

12323             500.00        0.00      13500    500.00   0     0.00    0     0.00     No  SS
  08/03/98       09/02/98     08/13/98        0      0.00   0     0.00    0     0.00
                                          A/P ACCOUNT 1  20500
BB42520812        106.56        0.00      13500    106.56   0     0.00    0     0.00     No  PD
  10/31/98       11/30/98     01/01/00        0      0.00   0     0.00    0     0.00
                                          A/P ACCOUNT 1  20500
BB42530807         62.16        0.00      13500     62.16   0     0.00    0     0.00     No  NN
  10/31/98       11/30/98     01/01/00        0      0.00   0     0.00    0     0.00
                                          A/P ACCOUNT 1  20500
BB46378999       5,432.65       0.00      13500   5,432.65  0     0.00    0     0.00     No  NN
  11/10/98       12/10/98     01/01/00        0      0.00   0     0.00    0     0.00
                                          A/P ACCOUNT 1  20500
BB46399765       2,113.11       0.00      13500   2,113.11  0     0.00    0     0.00     No  NN
  11/24/98       12/24/98     01/01/00        0      0.00   0     0.00    0     0.00
                                          A/P ACCOUNT 1  20500
Ck 01-10000086    106.56-       0.00          0      0.00   0     0.00    0     0.00     No  CK
  12/07/98       12/07/98     12/07/98        0      0.00   0     0.00    0     0.00
                                          CASH ACCOUNT  1  11000

*** End of Query Vendor ***
```

This means that if you learn how a traditional file system arranges data in files, you will understand how the DBMS software maintains relationships in the database. The record layout for an application in a traditional file system identifies the subschema required by that application with a DBMS.

Master Files.   The ***vendor master file*** contains one record for each approved supplier of goods and services. The primary key field for this record is the vendor number. The record contains the vendor's name, address, discount terms, and payment terms. In some systems the vendor master record also contains data summarizing past transactions with the supplier. This file constitutes the list of suppliers from whom employees are authorized to purchase goods and services.

ILLUSTRATION 18–14

Noncomputerized Records in the Expenditure Cycle

A voucher register

Date	Voucher Number	Date Paid	Check Number	Cr. Vouchers Payable	Miscellaneous Cr.			Dr. Inventory	Dr. Accounts Payable	Expense Ledger Dr.			Miscellaneous Dr.			Page ____
					Account	Ref.	Amount			Account	Ref.	Amount	Account	Ref.	Amount	

A check register

Date	Check No.	Voucher No.	Name of Payee	Amount	Page ____

Good internal control requires that a manager screen and approve all additions to the vendor master file. This prevents employees from creating a nonexistent vendor and then creating false documentation to cause issue of payments to that vendor. Purchasing agents should be allowed to acquire goods or services from other suppliers only with special approval.

Transaction Files.   Depending on the design of the system, applications in the expenditure cycle use as many as seven transaction files. On-line real-time systems, because they process transactions one at a time rather than in batches, require fewer computerized transaction files.

Some systems create a *requisitions file* containing one record for each item that requires purchasing. This file is an input to the purchasing application. Other systems enter data into the purchasing system directly from a manual file containing purchase requisitions. From the data in the requisitions file, a purchasing agent creates files containing the data required for printing purchase orders. Two files, the open purchase order file and the purchase order detail file, contain this data.

The *open purchase order file* has one record for each purchase order that has been mailed; its primary key field is the purchase order number. Most purchase orders authorize the vendor to ship several different products. The purchase order shows each one on a separate line, and each is called a *line item.* The purchasing application uses a *purchase order detail file* to show the data that are printed on one line of a purchase order. Its primary key field, which uniquely identifies that line item, is the purchase order number and line item number combined. A computer program derives the cost of a line item by multiplying its quantity by its unit price. Illustration 18–15 shows the contents of the two purchasing files.

Some systems create a computerized *receipts file* containing one record for each item received from vendors. This record shows the purchase order and line item numbers authorizing receipt, the date, and the quantity received. The receiving system produces this file as an input to the voucher system. Other systems use a manual file of receiving reports for this purpose.

ILLUSTRATION 18–15

Contents of Purchasing Records

Open Purchase Order File	*Purchase Order Detail File*
PURCHASE-ORDER-NUMBER*	PURCHASE-ORDER-NUMBER*
VENDOR-NUMBER†	LINE-ITEM-NUMBER*
PURCHASE-ORDER-DATE	REQUISITION-NUMBER
DELIVERY-DUE-DATE	REQUISITION-DATE
PURCHASING-AGENT-NAME	INVENTORY-ITEM-NUMBER
	VENDOR-PRODUCT-NUMBER
	ITEM-DESCRIPTION
	ITEM-QUANTITY
	ITEM-UNIT-PRICE

*Designates a primary key.
†Designates a secondary key.

A similar transaction file is the *pending invoice file*. Its records contain data on vendor invoices that have arrived in the mail prior to receipt of the goods. The voucher system matches a pending invoice record with one or more receipts records before producing a record for the voucher file. Some systems replace the pending invoice file with a manual file of vendor invoices.

The *voucher file* contains one record for each unpaid voucher. A fully computerized voucher system creates a voucher record when it finds matching purchase order, pending invoice, and receipts records in those files. In other systems, an accounts payable clerk matches the purchase order, vendor invoice, and receiving report. The clerk then prepares the voucher documents and enters data from the document in the voucher system. Each voucher produces a record in the voucher file whose primary key is the voucher number. The cash disbursements application removes the record from the voucher file when the invoice is paid.

Illustration 18–16 shows the contents of a voucher record in a traditional data file system. It shows two fields, GENERAL-LEDGER-ACCOUNT and GENERAL-LEDGER-AMOUNT, repeating six times. This allows each voucher record to represent debit entries in up to six accounts. As an example, three debits are required when a single vendor's invoice requests payment for raw materials inventory, supplies inventory, and freight. When a relational DBMS is used, each debit account requires a separate voucher record. The primary key field for the record is a combination of two fields, VOUCHER-NUMBER and GENERAL-LEDGER-ACCOUNT. In such a system, a single vendor invoice may produce multiple voucher records.

The voucher system adds records to the *general ledger batch summary file* summarizing the transactions processed by these systems. These record a credit entry in

ILLUSTRATION 18–16

Contents of a Voucher Record

VOUCHER-NUMBER*
VOUCHER-DATE
PURCHASE-ORDER-NUMBER
REQUISITION-NUMBER
RESPONSIBILITY-CODE
VENDOR-NUMBER†
VENDOR-INVOICE-NUMBER
VENDOR-INVOICE-DATE
GROSS-AMOUNT
DISCOUNT-DATE
PAYMENT-DUE-DATE
GENERAL-LEDGER-ACCOUNT } repeats
GENERAL-LEDGER-AMOUNT } six
   •   times
   •
   •
   •

---

*Designates a primary key.
†Designates a secondary key.

Accounts Payable, and debit entries to several asset and expense accounts. Each record also shows the responsibility code of the department that requested the expenditure. The general ledger batch summary file accumulates summary records from many application systems. The general ledger system posts the records in this file to the general ledger and produces performance reports.

As you can see, the expenditure cycle records maintained in a computerized system are similar to those maintained in a manual system. Most systems combine both computerized and noncomputerized processing. The next section describes another way in which applications in this cycle vary between organizations.

Types of Accounts Payable Systems.   Applications in the revenue cycle, described in the previous chapter, maintain a computerized subsidiary ledger for the general ledger Accounts Receivable account. The computer files just described have no equivalent subsidiary ledger for the Accounts Payable account because the system described in this chapter is a pure voucher system. Other systems use a subsidiary ledger instead of vouchers, while still others use both vouchers and an accounts payable subsidiary ledger.

Voucher Systems.   A *voucher system* assigns a unique identifying number to each invoice received from a vendor. The system accounts for all vouchers and voucher numbers. In this way, it prevents lost vendor invoices and omitted payments. Once a check is issued in payment of the voucher, an accounts payable clerk stamps the voucher and all supporting documents as paid. This prevents a dishonest employee from using the documents to cause the issue of a second check and then stealing and cashing the check.

Many companies use voucher systems because they provide good control over vendor invoices. However, these systems require the preparation of voucher documentation for each cash payment, which may be inconvenient or difficult. For example, receiving reports that document the receipt of services may not exist. Special documentation must be prepared showing receipt of the services.

Furthermore, pure voucher systems make it difficult to determine the total amount owed to a vendor. To produce the vendor query report, for example, a person or a computer program must search the entire voucher file for invoices from the desired vendor. Locating this information is easier when the system maintains a subsidiary ledger for the Accounts Payable account.

Systems with a Subsidiary Ledger.   In a manual system, an accounts payable subsidiary ledger is a book or card file containing one page or card for each approved vendor. In a computerized system, the subsidiary data is kept in the vendor master file.

With this system, a vendor's record in the vendor master file contains a field showing the balance owed to that vendor. When a vendor invoice and a receiving report are received, the system adds the amount of the invoice to this balance and adds a record to the pending invoice file. When a check is issued to the vendor, the amount of the check (including the discount) is deducted and the pending invoice record removed. With database management system software, the vendor master record is linked with its invoice records.

An accounts payable subsidiary ledger enables the system to determine the balance owed to a vendor more easily. However, it requires more recordkeeping. With a manual system, management may consider the costs of a subsidiary ledger excessive. In a computerized system, where the added recordkeeping is performed by computer programs, management often considers it worthwhile to use both vouchers and vendor master records containing payable totals.

You have seen the documents and records used in the expenditure cycle by both manual and computerized systems. These records can take a variety of forms. A similar variety exists in the way systems process these documents and records.

Transaction Processing

Most organizations today use a combination of computerized and manual processes to keep their records. The way these processes combine differs from one organization to the next. Because many combinations are possible, few companies process an accounting transaction in exactly the same way. This is why you should understand both manual and computerized processes. Fortunately, the concepts underlying the procedures are the same regardless of the method of implementation.

Manual Processes

Illustrations 18–17 and 18–18 contain document flowcharts showing manual procedures for purchasing and cash disbursement transactions. With these procedures, the purchasing department receives a purchase requisition, identifies a vendor, and mails a copy of the purchase order. A second purchase order copy alerts the receiving department to expect a shipment of goods, and a third goes to accounts payable. When the vendor invoice arrives in accounts payable, the clerk files it until a receiving report indicates that the goods have arrived. Then accounts payable prepares the voucher that supports approval and issue of a check by the treasurer's department.

Control Procedures. The accounting system includes control procedures in the systems that process purchase transactions. Some practices, such as segregation of duties, are appropriate regardless of whether the system uses computerized or manual processes. Other control procedures, called *application controls,* relate specifically to computerized processes.

Illustration 18–19 summarizes appropriate control procedures for purchase transactions. It shows the procedures appropriate for the documents, for the goods or services, and for the voucher package itself. Effective segregation of duties requires the separation of asset custody (in the warehouse and receiving departments) from records custody (in inventory records and accounts payable). The receiving department should be separate from the inventory warehouse. The purchasing function that authorizes transactions in the asset should also be separate from accounts payable.

Illustration 18–20 shows the four types of control activities applied to cash disbursement transactions. The most important segregation of duties is between accounts payable personnel, who maintain records, and cash disbursements personnel, who prepare checks and thus have access to the asset. These should be separate from the general ledger personnel who maintain the control accounts for cash and accounts payable. A later section in this chapter describes example application controls in these systems.

ILLUSTRATION 18–17

*Manual Purchasing
Procedures*

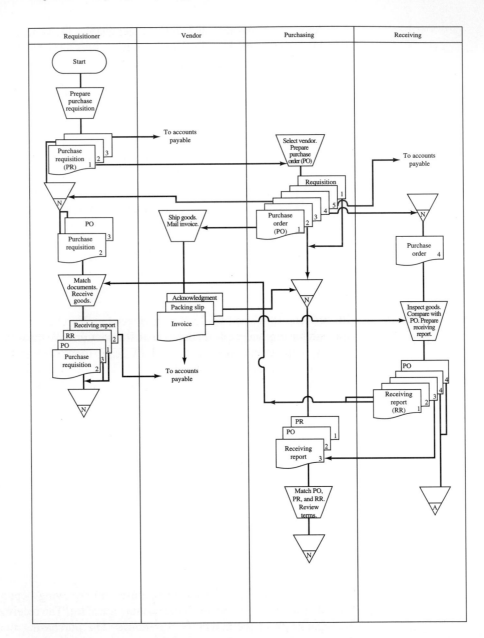

ILLUSTRATION 18–18

*Manual Cash
Disbursement Procedures*

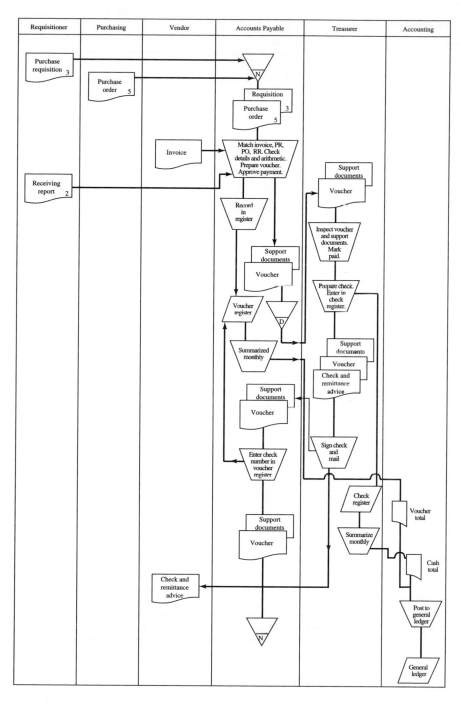

ILLUSTRATION 18–19

Control Activities for Purchase Transactions

Activity	Purchase of Inventories	Purchase of Services	Purchase Returns
Transaction authorization	a. Requisitioning manager authorizes, purchasing manager approves	a. Requisitioning manager authorizes, purchasing manager approves	a. Requisitioning manager authorizes, purchasing manager approves
Security for assets and records	Goods a. Receiving report prepared as goods are received b. Receiving report is prenumbered c. Quantity counted at time of receipt d. Quantity independently counted		Return of goods a. Released only on receipt of copy of debit memo b. Shipped only on receipt of copy of debit memo c. Quantity returned is independently counted
Segregation of duties	a. Purchasing and accounts payable b. Inventory records and warehouse c. Receiving and warehouse	a. Purchasing and accounts payable	a. Purchasing and accounts payable b. Inventory records and warehouse c. Receiving and warehouse
Adequate documents and records	Purchase requisition a. Based on reorder point and reorder quantity b. Approved if a special order	Purchase requisition a. Initiated by user department b. Approved	Debit memo a. Prepared only by purchasing department b. Prenumbered
	Purchase order a. Prepared only on receipt of purchase requisition b. Prenumbered c. Vendor selected from approved vendor list d. Checked for vendor price, terms	Purchase order a. Prepared only on receipt of purchase requisition b. Prenumbered c. Vendor selected from approved vendor list d. Checked for vendor price, terms e. Note receipt of services on a copy of purchase order	New voucher package a. Debit memo sent to accounts payable b. Prenumbered c. Supported by original voucher package and debit memo d. Verified
	Voucher package a. Invoice sent directly to accounts payable b. Prenumbered c. Supported by purchase requisition, purchase order, receiving report, and original invoice d. Verified	Voucher package a. Invoice sent directly to accounts payable b. Prenumbered c. Supported by purchase requisition, purchase order, acknowledged copy of purchase order, and original invoice d. Verified	

ILLUSTRATION 18–20

Control Activities for Cash Disbursements Transactions

Activity	Cash Disbursements
Transaction authorization	Authorized by accounts payable, approved by treasurer
Security for assets and records	Checks a. Prepared only based on properly prepared voucher package b. Prenumbered c. Signed only if properly prepared d. Signed by two officials when amount reaches a predetermined figure e. Mailed out by persons other than check preparer f. Voided checks kept
Segregation of duties	a. Accounts payable and cash disbursements b. Cash disbursements and general ledger c. Accounts payable and general ledger
Adequate documents and records	Initial documentation a. Reviewed for completeness of voucher package, particularly original invoice b. Canceled immediately after check is signed Accounts payable a. Posted daily General ledger a. Journal entry made daily

Computerized Processes

In the expenditure cycle, a computer-based accounting system uses four applications: the purchasing, receiving, voucher, and cash disbursements systems.

Purchasing Application. The purposes of the purchasing application are to identify materials, supplies, and equipment for acquisition; to select a supplier for these items; and to ensure that the items are requested and received.

A purchase requisition initiates a purchases transaction in a manual system. Computerized systems use this document as well; however, inputs to a computerized purchasing system may also come from computerized applications in other transaction cycles.

A computerized inventory system maintains an inventory master file, which contains one record for each item held in inventory and shows the quantity of that item on hand. Many such systems also identify a *reorder point* and an *order quantity* for the item. Whenever the quantity on hand drops below the reorder point, the inventory system generates a computer record requesting the issue of a purchase order to replenish inventory. This record is an input to the purchasing system, and the quantity shown in the record is the item's order quantity.

Other inputs to the purchasing system may come from a computerized production control system. Some such systems, called *material requirements planning* (MRP) systems, compute the quantities of raw materials needed for production from a production schedule for finished products. An MRP system then generates computer

AIS in Practice

General Electric Corporation, one of the world's largest companies, spends about $30 billion a year on supplies. It communicates with about 1,400 of its suppliers through its Internet Web site known as the Trading Process Network (TPN). Purchasing agents at GE use TPN to announce requests for bids, and suppliers use TPN to enter their bids. TPN software performs an initial screening of bids, shortens processing time, and has increased the number of bids that can be solicited. Accessing TPN requires only a PC and an Internet connection, so very small suppliers can enter bids. Furthermore, GE suppliers can create their own Web pages on the TPN server. As a result, they get requests for bids from GE divisions that are unknown to them. GE's long-term objective is to expand use of TPN to more suppliers, to make it more interactive, and to allow suppliers to use it for negotiations among themselves.

records requesting the purchase of this material. This record is another input to the purchasing application.

Some mail order merchandising companies stock little inventory. Instead, when a customer requests an item, they promptly acquire the item from a supplier. If such a company has a computerized order entry system, it may generate a record as input to the purchasing application. This record requests the purchase of the item needed for resale.

Illustration 18–21 shows these sources for inputs to an on-line real-time computerized purchasing system. Purchase requisitions and computer record inputs from other applications initiate transactions. Purchasing agents review them, assign vendors, and adjust order quantities based on their knowledge of the business. The system prints a purchase order register and the purchase orders and adds records to the open purchase order and purchase order detail files. These files are inputs to the voucher application.

Receiving Application.   The purposes of the receiving application are to ensure that all receipts of material, supplies, and equipment are authorized, and to record their receipt in the accounting records. A system flowchart of an on-line real-time receiving system is shown in Illustration 18–22.

ILLUSTRATION 18–21

A Purchasing Application

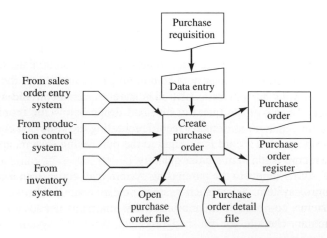

ILLUSTRATION 18–22

A Receiving Application

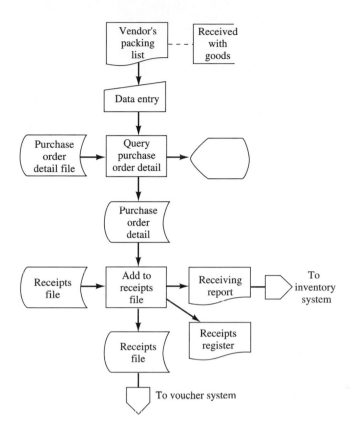

When a transportation company brings items to the receiving department, a clerk first locates the purchase order authorizing the shipment in the purchase order detail file. A computer program prints the receiving report and creates a record for the receipts file. The system prints a receipts register to provide an audit trail and provides the receipts file as an input to the voucher system.

Voucher Application.   The purpose of the voucher application is to record the obligation to pay a supplier. Inputs to this system are vendor invoices and records from the receipts, open purchase order, and purchase order detail files. Illustration 18–23 shows the procedures in a voucher system.

In a batch system, a mail clerk batches vendor invoices and a data entry clerk enters them in the system. In an on-line real-time system, the clerk enters invoices one at a time. The system adds a new invoice record to the pending invoice file for each invoice received. It then matches records in this file with those in the receipts and purchasing files. When it locates a receipts record and a purchase order record for the invoice, it creates a record in the voucher file and assigns it a voucher number. This program prints a voucher register and provides the voucher file as input to the cash disbursements application. It also generates summary records for the general ledger batch summary file.

ILLUSTRATION 18–23

A Voucher Application

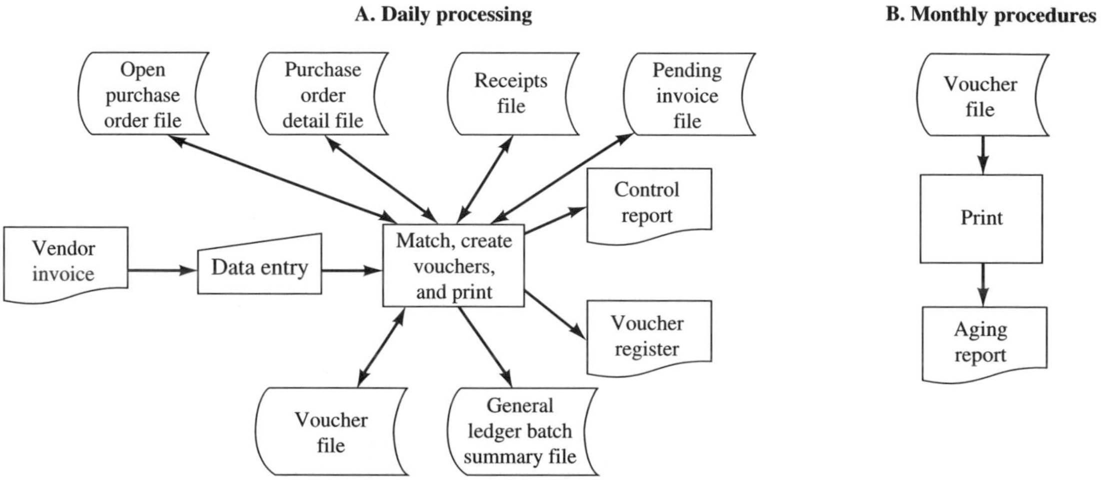

A. Daily processing

B. Monthly procedures

Cash Disbursements Application.   The purpose of this application system is to ensure that payments are made to vendors in the proper amount and at the proper time. Illustration 18–24 shows a flowchart for this system. The inputs to this system are records from the voucher file.

This system first sorts the voucher file by due date and then prints the cash requirements report. A cash manager or clerk in the treasurer's department identifies the vouchers to be paid and enters the cutoff date. From this point, the remainder of the processing is done in batch mode. The system establishes control totals for the vouchers to be paid and maintains those totals until the checks are mailed. This prevents a dishonest employee from concealing the theft of a check during later processing.

The system removes all vouchers due prior to the cutoff date from the voucher file and creates from them a file of cash disbursements transactions. From these, computer programs print the check register and checks and create records for the general ledger batch summary file.

Application Controls.   The system design team creates application controls when developing the application systems of the expenditure cycle. They may be input, processing, or output controls.

Input Controls.   Input controls prevent or detect errors as data are converted from human-readable to computer-readable form. Most computer systems implement input controls using validation procedures. Validity tests, completeness tests, and control totals are examples of control procedures that can be used for data validation. Illustration 18–25 shows how these procedures are used in the application systems of the expenditure cycle. The system design team may implement these procedures when designing the system.

ILLUSTRATION 18–24

*A Cash Disbursements
Application*

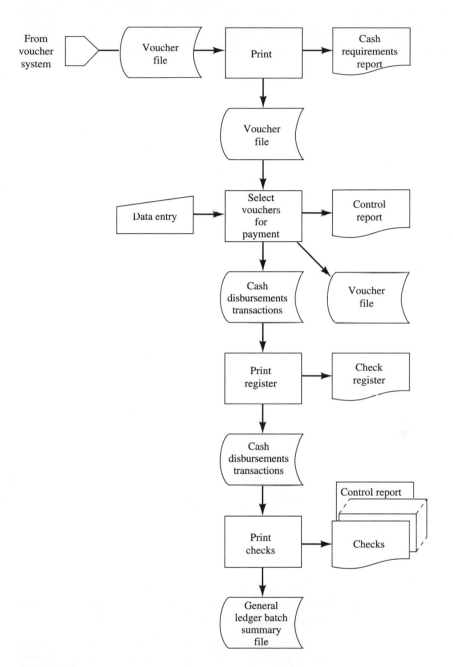

Processing Controls.   Processing controls prevent or detect erroneous processing by computer programs. These controls are coded into the programs during the development of the application system. Batch processing systems make extensive use of record counts and control or hash totals. Sometimes these totals are useful in on-line real-time systems as well. Illustration 18–26 shows how processing controls are applied to the applications in the expenditure cycle.

ILLUSTRATION 18–25

Example Input Controls in the Expenditure Cycle

System	Control Procedure
Purchasing	**Completeness test.** Program verifies existence of REQUISITION-NUMBER, INVENTORY-ITEM-NUMBER, ITEM-DESCRIPTION, ITEM-QUANTITY, DELIVERY-DUE-DATE. **Completeness test.** Purchasing agent enters VENDOR-NUMBER, PURCHASING-AGENT-NAME, VENDOR-PRODUCT-NUMBER, ITEM-UNIT-PRICE. **Validity test.** Program computes check digit on VENDOR-NUMBER.
Receiving	**Completeness test.** Program verifies existence of PURCHASE-ORDER-NUMBER, RECEIVED-QUANTITY, ITEM-NUMBER, ITEM-DESCRIPTION, VENDOR-NAME.
Voucher	**Consistency test.** Program verifies that total of GENERAL-LEDGER-AMOUNT fields equals NET-AMOUNT field. **Validity test.** Program verifies that dates are of the form AA-BB-CCCC, where AA<13, BB<32, and CCCC is numeric.

Output Controls. Output controls prevent and detect erroneous outputs from computer processing. In many companies, a data control group implements these controls. In batch processing systems, these clerks compare record counts and control totals from successive computer runs to verify that all transactions were processed correctly. Accountants call these *run-to-run controls.* The data control group also scans output documents and reports to identify obvious errors in their preparation. Illustration 18–27 shows example output controls that are performed in the expenditure cycle.

ILLUSTRATION 18–26

Example Processing Controls in the Expenditure Cycle

System	Control Procedure
Purchasing	**Record count.** Program verifies that the number of new purchase numbers = the number of purchase requisitions + the number of records from order entry, production control, and inventory systems.
Voucher	**Record count.** Program verifies that the decrease in the number of open purchase order records = the increase in the number of pending invoice records. **Record count.** Program verifies that the decrease in the number of receipts records = the increase in the number of pending invoice records. **Record count.** Program verifies that the number of records in the old pending invoice file = the number of records in the new pending invoice file + the number of new voucher records.
Cash disbursements	**Record count.** Program verifies that the number of records in the old voucher file = the number of records in the new voucher file + the number of cash disbursement transaction records.

ILLUSTRATION 18–27

Example Output Controls in the Expenditure Cycle

System	Control Procedure
Purchasing	**Record count.** Program verifies that the number of new records in the purchase order detail file = the number of line items on purchase orders.
Receiving	**Record count.** Program verifies that the number of lines on the report = the number of receipts in transaction records.
Voucher	**Record count.** Program verifies that the number of lines on the voucher register = the number of records added to the voucher file.
Cash disbursements	**Record count.** Program verifies that the number of lines on check register = the number of cash disbursement transaction records.
	Limit test. Program flags for review by data control group those transactions with amounts > $100,000.
	Run-to-run controls. Data control group verifies that total amount of checks = total amounts of vouchers disclosed on control reports and check register.

Summary

The expenditure cycle processes accounting transactions that record four economic events. These events are the request for goods or services from a supplier, their delivery, recognition of the obligation to pay for them, and payment.

Accounting systems in the expenditure cycle must be able to process three transactions: credit purchases, purchase returns, and cash disbursements. The documents that record these transactions are the purchase requisition, the purchase order, the receiving report, the voucher, and the check. Reports that disclose the results of processing include control reports, registers, the open voucher report, the accounts payable aging report, the cash requirements report, and the query vendor report.

Manual systems in this cycle utilize two special journals and files containing documents. Computer-based systems include the purchasing, receiving, voucher, and cash disbursements applications. They make changes to the open purchase order, the purchase order detail, the voucher, and the vendor master files. If database management software is used, these applications access the database using their subschema.

Key Terms

accounts payable system   A name sometimes applied to a combination of the voucher and cash disbursements applications.

debit memo   A document sent by a purchaser to a vendor that documents a purchase return.

purchase order   A document prepared in the purchasing department and mailed to a vendor requesting that the vendor sell goods or services on credit.

purchase requisition   A document prepared by someone in an organization requesting that the purchasing department acquire goods or services.

receiving report   A document prepared in the receiving department to record the receipt of goods from a vendor.

vendor master record   A record that contains data concerning an approved vendor, from which a purchasing agent is authorized to acquire goods or services.

voucher   A document prepared in the accounts payable department to record accounts payable and show the proper account to debit.

voucher system   An accounts payable system that assigns a unique identifying number to each vendor invoice.

Questions

18–1. Which economic events produce transactions in the expenditure cycle?

18–2. Which three types of transactions do accounting systems record in the expenditure cycle?

18–3. What is the purpose of each of the following documents:
  a. Purchase order?
  b. Vendor invoice?
  c. Voucher?
  d. Debit memo?

18–4. When is a control report used? What is its function?

18–5. Which information is disclosed in a register? Why is it important to accountants?

18–6. Describe three special purpose reports produced in the expenditure cycle.

18–7. What form do noncomputerized records take in the expenditure cycle?

18–8. In a computerized accounting system, which data files are used in the expenditure cycle? Identify the purpose of each file.

18–9. Describe two types of accounts payable systems and distinguish between them.

18–10. In a computer-based accounting system, what are the applications in the expenditure cycle? What is the purpose of each?

18–11. How does use of a database management system affect the way application systems process accounting records?

Exercises and Cases

18–12.   *TRANSACTIONS AND DOCUMENTS*

The column on the left lists accounting transactions processed in the expenditure cycle. The right column lists documents and reports. Identify the document(s) and report(s) associated with each transaction.

Transaction	Document or Report
a. Credit purchase.	1. Vendor invoice.
b. Cash payment.	2. Debit memo.
c. Purchase return.	3. Receiving report.
	4. Purchase order.
	5. Check.

18–13.   TRANSACTIONS AND APPLICATIONS

The column on the left lists accounting transactions. The right column lists application systems used in the expenditure cycle. Identify the application system that processes each transaction.

Transaction	Application System
a. Credit purchase.	1. Voucher.
b. Cash payment.	2. Receiving.
c. Purchase return.	3. Cash disbursements.

18–14.   RECEIVING PROCEDURES

To strengthen internal control, some have suggested that information on quantity should be omitted from the copy of a purchase order going to the receiving department.

Required:

a. What are some advantages of omitting quantity information from this copy?
b. What are some disadvantages?
c. Considering your answers to *a* and *b,* which approach do you favor?

18–15.   CREDIT PURCHASE PROCEDURES

The Witt Company is engaged in manufacturing. When materials are ordered, a duplicate of the purchase order is sent to the receiving department. When the materials are received, the receiving clerk records the receipt on the copy of the order, which is then sent to the accounting department to support the entry to accounts payable and material purchases. The materials are then taken to stores, where the quantity is entered on bin records.

Required:

a. Identify any control deficiencies in these procedures.
b. Explain which errors or manipulations might occur as a result of each weakness.
c. Recommend changes in procedures that could be made to correct each weakness.

(AICPA Adapted)

18–16.   PURCHASING PROCEDURES

Wooster Company is a beauty and barber supply and equipment distributorship servicing a five-state area. Management generally has been pleased with the overall operations to date. However, the present purchasing system, which evolved through practice rather than having been formally designed, is inadequate and needs to be redesigned. A description of the present purchasing system is as follows.

Whenever the quantity of an item is low, the inventory supervisor phones the purchasing department with the item description and quantity to be ordered. A purchase order is prepared in duplicate in the purchasing department. The original is sent to the vendor, and the copy is retained in the purchasing department and filed in numerical order. When the shipment arrives, the inventory supervisor sees that each item received is checked off on the packing slip that accompanies the shipment. The packing slip is then forwarded to the accounts payable department. When the invoice arrives, the packing slip is compared with the invoice in the accounts payable department. Once any differences between the packing slip and the invoice are reconciled, a check is drawn for the appropriate amount and is mailed to the vendor with a copy of the invoice. The packing slip is attached to the invoice and filed alphabetically in the paid invoice file.

Required:

Wooster Company intends to redesign its purchasing system from the point when an item needs to be ordered until payment is made. The system should be designed to ensure that all of the proper controls are incorporated into the system.

a. Identify the internally and externally generated documents that would satisfy the minimum requirements of a basic system, and indicate how many copies of each document would be needed.
b. Explain how all of these documents should interrelate and flow among Wooster's various departments, including the final destination or file for each copy.

(CMA Adapted)

18–17.   CONTROLS AND FRAUD

In each of the following situations, companies suffered the loss of assets as a consequence of employee fraud.

Situation No. 1. Although most bills are sent to the corporate office for payment, each manufacturing plant maintains a petty cash fund to pay small, routine purchases. While reviewing the accounts payable at one of the plants, an auditor discovered that a trusted employee had embezzled $152,000 during the past 10 years. Using the petty cash fund, the employee had processed and paid fictitious freight bills by using copies of authentic shipments for support. The employee had pocketed the duplicate payments.

Situation No. 2. While examining a random sample of employee expense reports, an auditor found that altered receipts and duplicate receipts were being routinely submitted for reimbursement by members of the sales force.

Situation No. 3. The company had a contract with a tire manufacturer to supply tires for company vehicles at favorable discounts. As a courtesy, company employees were allowed to purchase tires at discounted prices by placing an order with the office manager, who ordered the tires in the company name. When the bill arrived, the office manager asked employees to make checks payable to him. The invoices were processed for payment through the company's accounts payable system. As a consequence, 37 tires were billed to the company, and the office manager deposited the employees' checks to his own account.

Required:

For each of the three situations,

a. Identify the concept of internal control that was violated.

b. Recommend a specific control that would prevent or detect future occurrences.

(CIA Adapted)

18–18.   SYSTEM FLOWCHART

Flowcharts are frequently used to represent an activity graphically. These flowcharts allow identification of the physical flow of documents through the accounting system.

Required:

Given the flowchart in Exhibit 18–1,

a. Identify the activity taking place and the document(s) involved at each numbered symbol when applicable.

b. Describe control procedures you would expect to find in practice at symbols 1, 6, 7, and 10.

(CIA Adapted)

18–19.   RECEIVING PROCEDURES

Dunbar Camera Manufacturing, Inc., is a manufacturer of high-priced precision motion picture cameras in which the specifications of component parts are vital to the manufacturing process. Dunbar buys valuable camera lenses and large quantities of sheet metal and screws. The screws and lenses ordered by Dunbar are billed by the vendors on a unit basis. Sheet metal ordered by Dunbar is billed by the vendors on the basis of weight. The receiving clerk is responsible for documenting the quality and quantity of merchandise received. A review indicates that these internal control procedures are being followed:

> *Receiving report.* Properly approved purchase orders, which are prenumbered, are filed numerically. The copy sent to the receiving clerk is an exact duplicate of the copy sent to the vendor. Receipts of merchandise are recorded on the duplicate copy by the receiving clerk.
>
> *Sheet metal.* The company receives sheet metal by railroad. The railroad independently weighs the sheet metal and records the weight and date of receipt on a bill of lading (waybill) that accompanies all deliveries. The receiving clerk only compares the weight on the waybill to the purchase order.
>
> *Screws.* The receiving clerk opens cartons containing screws, then inspects and weighs the contents. The weight is converted to the number of units by means of conversion charts. The receiving clerk then checks the computed quantity against the purchase order.
>
> *Camera lens.* Each camera lens is delivered in a separate corrugated carton. Cartons are counted by the receiving clerk when they arrive; the total is checked against purchase orders.

EXHIBIT 18–1

Exercise 18–18

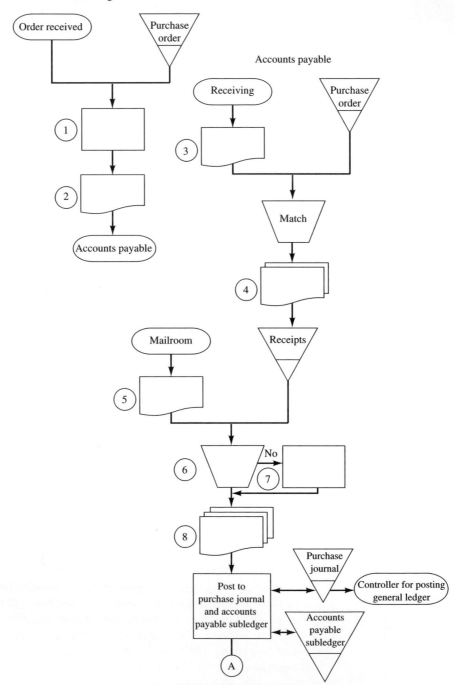

EXHIBIT 18–1

Exercise 18–18 (concluded)

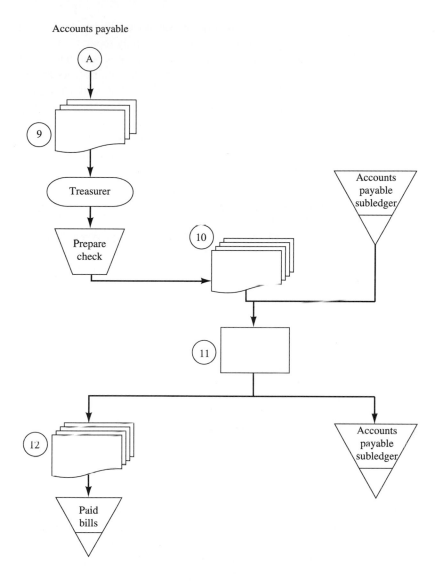

Accounts payable

Required:

Explain why the control procedures applying to receiving reports and to receipts of sheet metal, screws, and camera lenses are adequate or inadequate.

(AICPA Adapted)

18–20. COMPUTERIZED PURCHASING PROCEDURES

Peabock Company is a wholesaler of soft goods. The inventory is composed of approximately 3,500 different items. The company employs a computerized batch processing system to maintain its perpetual inventory records. The system is run each weekend so that the inventory reports are available on Monday morning for management use. The system has been functioning satisfactorily for the past 15 months, providing the company with accurate records and timely reports.

The preparation of purchase orders has been automatic as a part of the inventory system to ensure that the company maintains enough inventory to meet customer demand. When an inventory item falls below a predetermined level, a record of the item is written. This record is used in conjunction with the vendor file to prepare purchase orders.

Exception reports are prepared during the update of the inventory and the preparation of the purchase orders. These reports identify any errors or exceptions found during the processing. In addition, the system provides for management approval of all purchase orders exceeding a specified amount. Any exceptions or items requiring management approval are handled by supplemental runs on Monday morning and combined with the weekend results.

A system flowchart of Peabock Company's inventory and purchase order procedures appears in Exhibit 18–2. The flowchart was prepared before the system was fully operational. Several steps important to the successful operation of the system were inadvertently omitted from the chart. Now that the system is operating effectively, management wants the system documentation to be complete and would like the flowchart corrected.

Required:

a. Describe the steps that have been omitted and indicate where the omissions occurred. The flowchart does not need to be redrawn.

b. Describe the type of control procedures Peabock Company would use in its system and indicate where these procedures should be placed.

c. Design the contents of each master record required by the system flowchart in Exhibit 18–2.

(CMA Adapted)

18–21.   *PURCHASING FRAUD*

A dead child, a love triangle, and a computer scheme all contributed to the swindling of some $155,000 from Magnum Products, Inc. (MPI), a subsidiary of Consolidated Corp. in Chicago.[1]

According to the district attorney assigned to the case, in May Betty X. Tipps was transferred into MPI's accounts payable department. After the transfer, she discussed with her boyfriend, Robert Katz, the possibility of stealing money from MPI using a bogus company set up for the purpose.

Tipps and Katz went to a local graveyard and learned the name of a child who had died shortly after birth. They then obtained the birth certificate of the deceased child, Larry Robert Gandalf, from the Cook County Government Center. With the birth certificate, they opened a bank account, obtained picture identification for Katz, and established an address for L. R. Gandalf Co. at an answering and mailing service.

---

[1]Adapted from "Love and Death Figure in $155,000 DP Scam," *Computerworld,* May 3, 1982, p. 20. Used by permission.

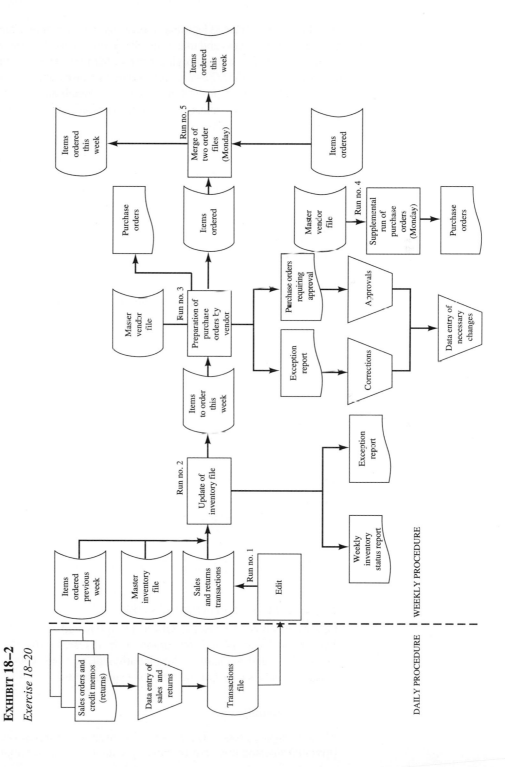

EXHIBIT 18–2
Exercise 18–20

Tipps then obtained legitimate receiving documents that came from companies supplying MPI with parts and materials. She altered these documents to make it appear that L. R. Gandalf Co. was supplying parts to MPI for which payment was required. Five checks totaling $155,000 were received by the false company in August and September. These checks were deposited into the L. R. Gandalf savings account, from which both Tipps and Katz could make withdrawals. Around the time the last check was received, Tipps terminated her employment with MPI.

According to investigators, the couple traveled to Costa Rica, Panama, Florida, California, and Arizona, invested in gold coins, and bought three cars—one each for Tipps and Katz and one for his former wife. While the couple was in Florida, they had a bad fight, and the police were called.

How was the crime discovered? "He assaulted her," the district attorney said. "He had a three-way love triangle going with Tipps and his ex-wife. Tipps just turned herself in. I guess she just had enough." The couple is awaiting sentencing, and each faces up to 10 years in prison and a $10,000 fine.

Required:

Which control procedures would have prevented this crime?

18–22. RECORD LAYOUTS

Exhibit 18–3 contains layouts for two master file and two transaction file records used by applications in the expenditure cycle.

Required:
a. Identify the files that contain these records.
b. Based on the information contained in these record layouts, identify reports
   obtained from these files that would be useful to company management.

(AICPA Adapted)

18–23. PURCHASES AND CASH DISBURSEMENTS

Exhibit 18–4 contains a document flowchart describing manual procedures for processing purchases and cash disbursements transactions.

Required:

Indicate what each of the letters *A* through *L* in Exhibit 18–4 represents.

(AICPA Adapted)

18–24. MANUAL PURCHASES SYSTEM

One of the functions of the Office of Sponsored Research at the Southwest State University is to administer grants and research funds obtained by professors, researchers, and students. Administration of purchases to be paid from grants and research funds is a part of the office's responsibilities.

Purchase Requisitions

The purchasing process begins with the initiation of a purchase requisition by either a principal investigator or a research assistant. The office maintains a list of persons

EXHIBIT 18-3

Exercise 18–22

Master File — Vendor Name

| Recd. Type | Vendor Code | Space | Blank | Vendor Name | Blank | Card Code 100 |

Master File — Vendor Address

| Recd. Type | Vendor Code | Space | Blank | Address—Line 1 | Address—Line 2 | Address—Line 3 | Blank | Card Code 120 |

Transaction File — Expense Detail

| Recd. Type | Blank | Vendor Code | Batch | Voucher Number | Voucher Date | Vendor Code | Invoice Date | Due Date | Invoice Number | Purchase Order Number | Debit Account | Prd. Type | Product Code | Blank | Amount | Quantity | Card Code 160 |

Transaction File — Payment Detail

| Recd. Type | Blank | Vendor Code | Batch | Voucher Number | Voucher Date | Vendor Code | Invoice Date | Due Date | Invoice Number | Purchase Order Number | Check Number | Check Date | Blank | Amount | Blank | Card Code 170 |

635

Exhibit 18–4
Exercise 18–23

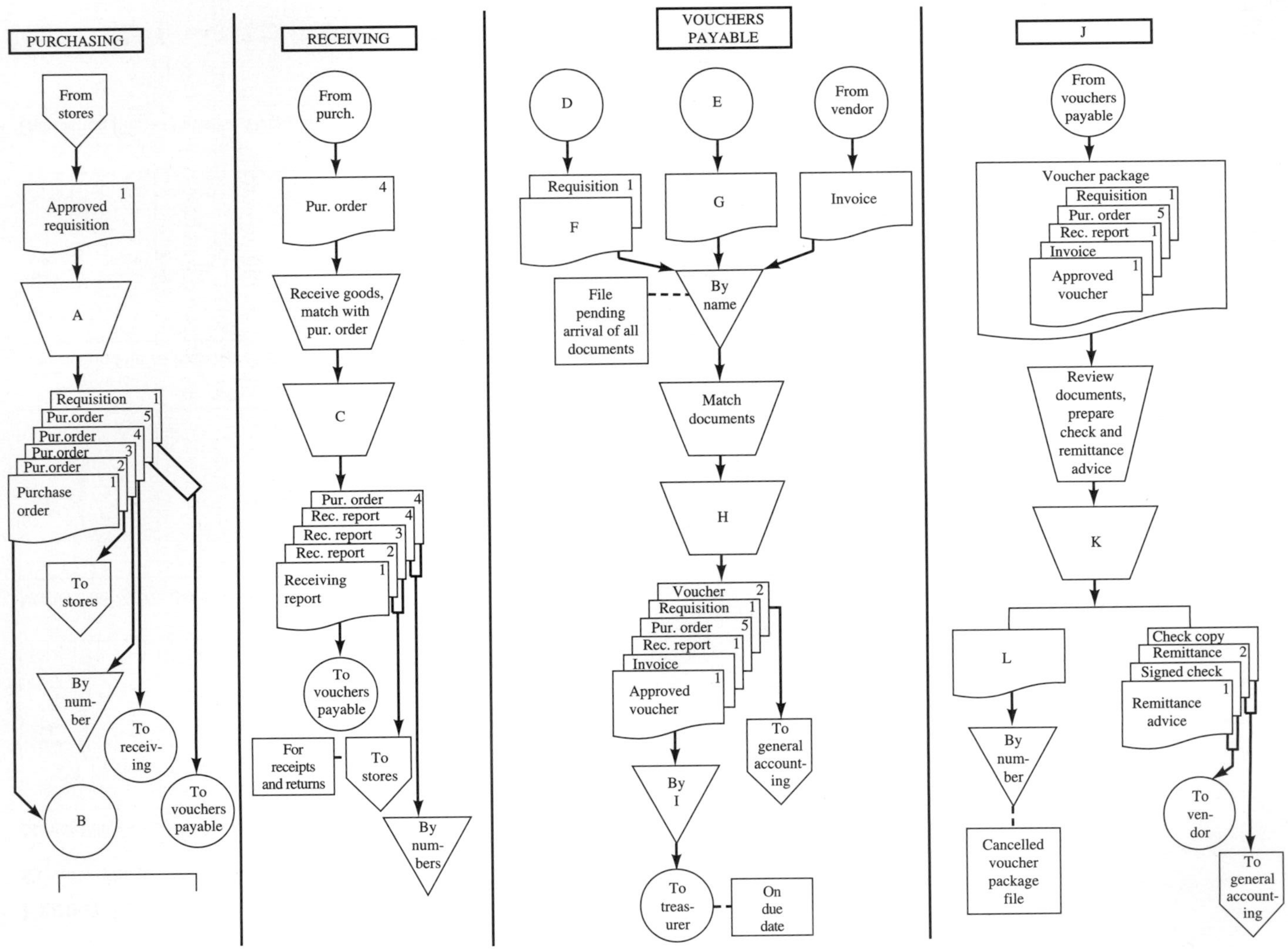

authorized to initiate or approve purchase requisitions for each active research project. A copy of this list is sent to the university's purchasing department regularly.

The purchase requisitions are prenumbered by department. The form provides spaces for the description and specification of each desired item, its quantity, and the suggested supplier. The requisitioner submits the purchase requisition to the Office of Sponsored Research, where the availability of funds is checked. Two copies of each approved requisition are sent to the purchasing department. The third copy is filed by a clerk in the office, and the last copy is sent back to the requisitioner.

Purchase Orders

Using the purchase requisitions, the purchasing department prepares purchase orders in 12 copies. Two are sent to the vendor, with the request that one be returned as an acknowledgment. Five copies (numbered 3 through 7) are forwarded to the receiving section. Two copies (11 and 12) are filed in the purchasing department. Other copies are sent to the Office of Sponsored Research (copy 8), accounts payable (copy 9), and the requisitioner (copy 10).

The purchasing department records the receipt of acknowledgments from vendors in the open purchase order file. It also follows up on orders for which no acknowledgment has been received or for which delivery is overdue. In the event that items received are damaged or incomplete or do not meet quality standards (as indicated on receiving reports), the purchasing department is responsible for contacting the vendor for appropriate adjustments.

In placing orders, buyers in the purchasing department must observe the regents' rules governing conflicts of interest. With respect to the purchasing policy, these rules state:

> Purchases are not permitted from any officer or employee of the university, or from a company or firm owned or partially owned by an officer or employee of the university unless the following conditions are met: (a) the relationship between the intended purchaser and any officer or employee is disclosed, (b) the cost is less than that from any other source, and (c) the purchase is approved by the vice president for business affairs, the president, or the board of regents as appropriate.

Generally, it takes about 15 days to process a routine purchase requisition. In many instances, however, the interval between making a requisition and placing a purchase order is longer. When this occurs, purchase orders have to be canceled or changed due to vendors' running out of stock or their inability to deliver on time. This results in dissatisfaction from researchers, who complain that they have been promised on-time delivery by these vendors when they prepared purchase requisitions.

The purchasing department's explanation is that often purchase requisitions have not been properly filled out, causing unnecessary delays. Another source of delay cited by the purchasing department is the poor intercampus mail delivery service.

Receiving Reports

Clerks in the receiving section file purchase orders numerically. When items are presented to the receiving section for acceptance, receiving personnel use copies of purchase orders on file as receiving reports. Separate receiving reports are prepared only when they receive a partial shipment.

After examining items for quantity and quality, the receiving section indicates acceptance or rejection on copies of purchase orders. One copy (number 3) is routed to the purchasing department for posting in its open purchase order file. Other copies are sent to the requisitioner (copy 4), accounts payable (copy 5), and Office of Sponsored Research (copy 6). Copy 7 is filed numerically in the receiving section.

Accounts Payable

The accounts payable department receives vendors' invoices in triplicate. Before approving these invoices for payment, accounts payable clerks check each invoice against its corresponding purchase order and receiving report. They also verify the accuracy of extensions on invoices. Once these steps are completed, a voucher is prepared authorizing cash disbursements in payment of the invoice. A copy of this voucher is sent to the Office of Sponsored Research, where the amount is subtracted from available balances for that project.

At the end of each month, the accounting department produces a monthly expense summary report. A copy of this summary report is sent to the Office of Sponsored Research. Another copy is sent to the principal investigators of all active research projects.

Required:

a. What are some of the strengths of the expenditure cycle procedures just described?
b. What are some of the weaknesses?
c. Which recommendations would you make to remedy these weaknesses?
d. Prepare a flowchart describing the foregoing procedures.

18–25.   *MANUAL VOUCHER SYSTEM*

ConSport Corporation is a regional wholesaler of sporting goods. The system flowchart in Exhibit 18–5 and the following description present ConSport's cash distribution system:

1. The accounts payable department approves for payment all invoices (I) for the purchase of inventory. Invoices are matched with purchase requisitions (PR), purchase orders (PO), and receiving reports (RR). Accounts payable clerks focus on vendors' names and skim the documents when they are combined.

2. When all the documents for an invoice are assembled, a two-copy disbursement voucher (DV) is prepared, and the transaction is recorded in the voucher register (VR). The disbursement voucher and supporting documents are then filed alphabetically by vendor.

3. A two-copy journal voucher (JV) that summarizes each day's entries in the voucher register is prepared daily. The first copy is sent to the general ledger department, and the second copy is filed in the accounts payable department by date.

4. The vendor file is searched daily for the disbursement vouchers of invoices due to be paid. Both copies of disbursement vouchers due are sent to the treasury department along with the supporting documents. The cashier prepares a check for each vendor, signs the check, and records it in the check register (CR). Copy one of

EXHIBIT 18–5

Exercise 18–25

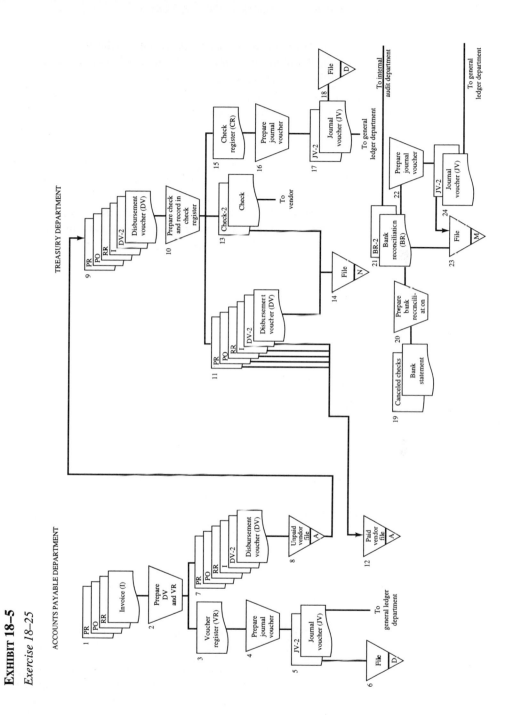

the disbursement voucher is attached to the check copy and filed by check number in the treasury department. Copy two and the supporting documents are returned to the accounts payable department and filed alphabetically by vendor.

5. A two-copy journal voucher that summarizes each day's checks is prepared. Copy one is sent to the general ledger department, and copy two is filed in the treasury department by date.

6. The cashier receives the monthly bank statement with canceled checks and prepares the bank reconciliation (BR). If an adjustment is required as a consequence of the bank reconciliation, a two-copy journal voucher is prepared. Copy one is sent to the general ledger department. Copy two is attached to copy one of the bank reconciliation and filed by month in the treasury department. Copy two of the bank reconciliation is sent to the internal audit department.

Required:

ConSport Corporation's cash disbursement system has some weaknesses. Review the cash disbursement system and for each weakness

a. Identify where the weakness exists by using the reference number that appears to the left of each symbol in Exhibit 18–5.
b. Describe the nature of the weakness.
c. Make a recommendation about how to correct the weakness.

(CMA Adapted)

18–26. FORMS DESIGN

Lynn Duncan, controller of Lankar Company, has decided that the company needs to redesign its purchase order form and to design a separate document to record the receipt of goods. Currently, a copy of Lankar's purchase order is serving as a receiving report, and the receiving clerk records the quantities received on the copy of the appropriate purchase order. Duncan has decided to implement these changes because there have been a number of errors in ordering materials and in recording the receipt of goods. She believes that these mistakes have resulted from the poor design of the current purchase order and the use of a copy of it as the receiving report. In addition to improved reporting, these new forms will provide Duncan with an excellent opportunity to reinforce the need for accuracy among the employees in the purchasing department.

The left column of Exhibit 18–6 shows the revised purchase order. The form will be letter size for ease in filing and will be used by several departments. The original and one copy will be mailed to the vendor. The clerical staff in the purchasing department will complete the form from the information provided on the purchase requisition, and the purchasing manager will sign it before mailing.

A draft of a new receiving report is shown in the right column of Exhibit 18–6. This form will be approximately 5 by 8 inches and will be prenumbered. Receiving clerks will fill out multiple copies of the receiving report.

Required:

a. Lynn Duncan believes that the errors experienced by Lankar Company were due in part to the use of a copy of the purchase order as a receiving report. Identify the problems that can occur as a result of this practice.

EXHIBIT 18–6

Case 18–26

A Draft Purchase Order

```
Lankar Company Purchase Order
       One Fordwick Palace
      Arion, Indiana  36999

To:                        Ship to:




Delivery Date:                  PO Date:

Shipping Instructions:
```

Item No.	Quantity	Lankar Part #	Vendor Part #	Description	Unit Cost

```
Special Instructions:



                           Purchasing Manager
```

A Draft Receiving Report

```
                                      No. NNNNNN
             Lankar Company
           One Fordwick Palace
          Arion, Indiana  36999

Received from:_____
(Name/Address)_____
              _____
              _____
              _____
```

Quantity	Description	Unit Price	Amount

	Subtotal	
	Frt. Charges	
	Total	
Remarks/Conditions	Dept. Delivered to:	

```
        BE SURE TO MAKE THIS RECORD
          ACCURATE AND COMPLETE
```

b. Review the new forms that Lynn Duncan has designed. Explain what should be added or deleted to improve the
   1. Purchase order.
   2. Receiving report.
c. Identify the departments that should receive a copy of the purchase order in order to provide good internal control. Explain why each department should receive a copy.

(CMA Adapted)

18–27.   *REENGINEERING THE EXPENDITURE CYCLE*

International Telephone and Telegraph Automotive (ITTA) is one of the world's largest automotive component suppliers, with 76 facilities in 16 countries on four continents.[2] It operates as a parent company for seven operating units, each with its own departments for administrative and service functions. Recently ITTA began an effort to streamline operations by restructuring the organization along product lines. As part of this effort, management formed a committee and hired a consultant to investigate the methods of processing accounts payable throughout the parent company and its subsidiaries.

----

[2]Adapted from "Reengineering Payables at ITT Automotive" by Richard J. Palmer, *Management Accounting*, July 1994, p. 38. Copyright by Institute of Management Accountants (1994), Montvale, N.J. 07645. Used by permission.

The Problem

The committee was given the responsibility to select software that would automate the matching process for purchase orders, receiving reports, and invoices in ITTA's expenditure cycle. As part of its evaluation process, the committee made a surprising discovery regarding the payables functions in the operating units. They discovered that purchases of material used in production, though accounting for 70 percent of the dollars spent, accounted for only 35 percent of the volume of documents processed. Thus automating only the purchases for production would have a relatively small impact on the activities of accounts payable personnel.

Other purchased items included supplies, small tools, indirect materials, utilities, insurance, services from various sources, and leases. Automating the purchase of these items would, the committee decided, not be cost-effective. ITTA management then hired the consultant to identify an efficient way to process these high-volume, low-dollar-value purchases.

Analysis

The consultant conducted interviews throughout the operating units and used flow-charting to analyze the value added to ITTA's products by existing purchasing processes. He found that operating units were using a traditional approach to processing payables transactions. The purchasing department would send a purchase order to a vendor, with a copy to accounts payable. When the goods arrived, a clerk at the receiving dock completed a receiving report and sent it to accounts payable. A clerk in accounts payable would then match the purchase order and receiving report with an invoice from the vendor before entering data into the computer to issue payment.

Often, however, the documents would not agree due to partial shipments or inaccurate information on the documents. Clerks would spend a considerable amount of time resolving these conflicts, sometimes requiring weeks of elapsed time. Additionally, accounts payable personnel spent a lot of their time performing activities that the consultant believed added no value to ITTA's products. Exhibit 18–7 summarizes some of these "nonvalue added" activities.

To measure the efficiency and cost of the expenditure cycle procedures, the consultant gathered data for the parent company and for each of its operating units. This data included head counts, operating costs for the accounts payable and purchasing departments, numbers of documents processed, mail volume, and unit cycle times (the number of days elapsed between identification of a need and order placement). Management concluded from this part of the analysis that improvements in efficiency were warranted and could be obtained.

Other data showed that 59 percent of all the manufacturing units' invoices were for noninventory items and that these constituted a relatively small dollar amount. Eighty percent of the noninventory invoices were below $1,000, accounting for 9 percent of total noninventory spending and 3.2 percent of spending on purchased goods. Conversely, 5 percent of noninventory invoices exceeded $3,000, and these accounted for 77 percent of all noninventory spending. Thus most noninventory purchases were for small amounts, and relatively few were large.

Despite this fact, ITTA operating units had the same controls in place for all transactions. The consultant determined that the average cost for ITTA to requisition, order,

EXHIBIT 18–7

Case 18–27: ITTA Expenditure Cycle—Nonvalue Added Activities

Maintaining suspense files for partially filled orders.
Checking for approvals and routing paperwork to obtain them.
Identifying and expediting invoices with early payment discounts.
Setting up new vendors on the computerized accounts payable system.
Answering supplier phone calls regarding the status of payment.
Verifying batch totals and invoice amounts.
Printing checks.
Obtaining signatures on checks or using a signature imprint machine.
Stuffing envelopes with the voucher package.
Filing paperwork.
Preparing end-of-month accruals for items received but not yet paid.

---

receive, and pay for an item was $142—a surprising amount since 34 percent of the purchases were for amounts less than $100. The average unit cycle time for the operating units varied between 2 and 10 days. From this analysis, management concluded that while stringent controls could be justified for high-dollar transactions, they were not cost-beneficial for low-dollar purchases.

Alternative Solutions

Management identified and tested three approaches to improving the expenditure cycle. First, they attempted to identify a single supplier for each noninventory item and arrange for monthly billing from that supplier. Although this decreased the number of payments to each supplier, it resulted in only minor improvement because of the wide variety of suppliers required for these items. Second, they allowed verbal orders rather than formal purchase orders on purchases below a specified dollar amount. Although this decreased the number of documents required, it likewise did not reduce significantly the workload in the accounts payable department.

The third solution implemented by ITTA involved procurement cards. A procurement card, or corporate purchasing card, is like an ordinary credit card in that it is issued by a bank and allows an employee to charge purchases to the card. The bank provides the company with a monthly bill that summarizes all purchases made by cardholding employees during that month. The company agrees to make full payment within 30 to 45 days, and the bank withholds 1 to 3 percent of the purchase price as a processing fee.

If procurement cards were issued to ITTA employees, the results could be dramatic. Major reductions in workload would result in the purchasing and accounts payable departments. Purchasing would no longer negotiate, order, or perform clerical activities for transactions placed on the card. Accounts payable would not match invoices, purchase orders, and receiving reports for these items. There would be a reduction in the number of checks written and associated check signing and reconciliation activities. A single monthly electronic funds transfer at a bank could replace thousands of checks.

Other advantages of using procurement cards would include a decrease in unit cycle time and increased empowerment for operating-level employees. The consultant estimated that, if procurement cards were used to purchase noninventory items costing less than $1,000, ITTA would eliminate 75 percent of its noninventory purchase orders and 81 percent of its invoices. This would allow a head-count reduction of 75 percent in accounts payable and 69 percent in purchasing.

After reviewing the information concerning procurement cards, ITTA management initiated four pilot programs in the Midwest. Encouraged by the results, they extended the program to another plant and to corporate headquarters. Current plans are to implement the card procedures at all North American locations.

Required:
- *a.* Do you think that ITTA should expand its use of procurement cards? What are the risks associated with this practice?
- *b.* What control procedures are appropriate for the use of procurement cards?

18–28.   TECHNOLOGICAL CHANGE

The King Company manufactures and distributes duplicating machines and related supplies.[3] The company has grown rapidly since its formation by the merger of two smaller manufacturing companies in 1970, and sales last year reached $80 million. This growth, combined with advances in technology, have caused King to consider changes to its accounts payable system. Because all manufacturing plants and warehouses now use desktop computers for word processing and spreadsheet applications, King management wants to investigate the feasibility of using them with existing accounting systems.

King's four manufacturing plants and 13 warehouses in the Midwest and western states are managed from corporate headquarters in Des Moines, Iowa. Initially, the duplicating machines were manufactured entirely in King Company factories. Rapid growth in machine sales, however, has forced the company to buy an increasing number of subassemblies from external sources and then assemble parts and subassemblies. All duplicating supplies are purchased from outside vendors. Sales are made through local sales agents who place orders with the nearest warehouse.

To provide greater flexibility in meeting local needs, purchases of parts, subassemblies, materials, and supplies are made by the individual plants and warehouses. Each manufacturing plant purchases raw materials and subassemblies for its own production requirements. Warehouses order machines from the factories and purchase duplicating supplies from the best local vendors. Corporate headquarters does not interfere with this decentralized purchasing function unless a plant or warehouse is not providing an adequate return on investment or shows other signs of difficulty. All cash disbursements for purchases, however, are centralized in the headquarters at Des Moines.

Processing at Purchase Locations

Existing accounts payable procedures have been in place for about 20 years. Purchases by manufacturing plants and warehouses are made with prenumbered purchase orders issued by the local purchasing section. One copy of each purchase order goes to the local factory or warehouse accounting department. It also receives and date-stamps a copy of each receiving report and all copies of vendors' invoices. The local accounting

---

[3]Adapted from a case prepared by Professors Frederick L. Neumann and Richard J. Boland, of the University of Illinois, under a grant from the Touche-Ross Foundation.

department keeps track of purchase order numbers, matches their detail to the receiving reports and vendors' invoices, and checks them for clerical accuracy.

When all the details agree, accounting prepares a prenumbered disbursement voucher summarizing the detailed information for each purchase. The plant controller or warehouse office manager reviews supporting documents and approves for payment these disbursement vouchers. The vouchers, together with the supporting documents, are then turned over to the approver's secretary who holds the vouchers, cancels the supporting documents, and returns them to accounting for filing. Periodically, the secretary batches the approved disbursement vouchers, attaches a transmittal slip indicating the number of vouchers in the batch, and forwards them to Des Moines for payment.

Once a week the corporate office at Des Moines prepares and mails the checks. It distributes to each plant and warehouse a report that lists the checks prepared that week, cross-referenced to the disbursement vouchers that the location submitted during the previous week. At each of the four manufacturing plants, the accounting office compares the list of checks to its copies of the disbursement vouchers. The warehouse accounting offices are severely understaffed and do not perform this reconciliation. The accounting department at the purchase location responds to inquiries about unpaid bills for those invoices it has not forwarded for payment. For vouchers that have been forwarded, it refers inquiries to Des Moines.

Centralized Processing

Corporate headquarters in Des Moines processes each disbursement voucher using the combination of manual and computerized processing flowcharted in Exhibit 18–8. The following table describes these activities.

Group	*Activity Performed*
Input	Open the mail containing approved disbursement vouchers and transmittal slips from the manufacturing plants and warehouses. Make test counts of disbursement vouchers against transmittal slips and forward both for further processing.
Vendor code	File transmittal slips. Sort disbursement vouchers alphabetically by vendor. Scan vouchers for completeness; check vendor's code, name, address, and terms against the vendor master file. Initiate changes or additions to vendor master file if warranted. Forward acceptable vouchers for further processing.
Batching	Scan vouchers for missing data and check calculations. Group acceptable vouchers by type, in batches of approximately 50. Create batch control totals on dollars and hash totals on quantities. Forward batches and control totals for processing.
Control desk	Scan batches for missing data and recalculate control totals. Assign control numbers to batches. Log them in with their control totals. Forward batches with control numbers and totals for further processing.
Data entry	Key data into disk files by batch. Transmit transaction batches to the data center for processing. Send batched documents to control desk for cancellation and return to accounting department for filing.
Data center	Perform program edits for completeness and reasonableness as well as appropriate limit and validity checks. Process acceptable data against vendor master file and transaction history file. Mechanically sign resulting prenumbered checks. Forward signed checks, reports, and unresolved rejects to control desk.
Control desk	Log and reconcile data center totals. Distribute data center output as appropriate. Foot, balance, and mail checks. Correct errors and otherwise resolve rejects.

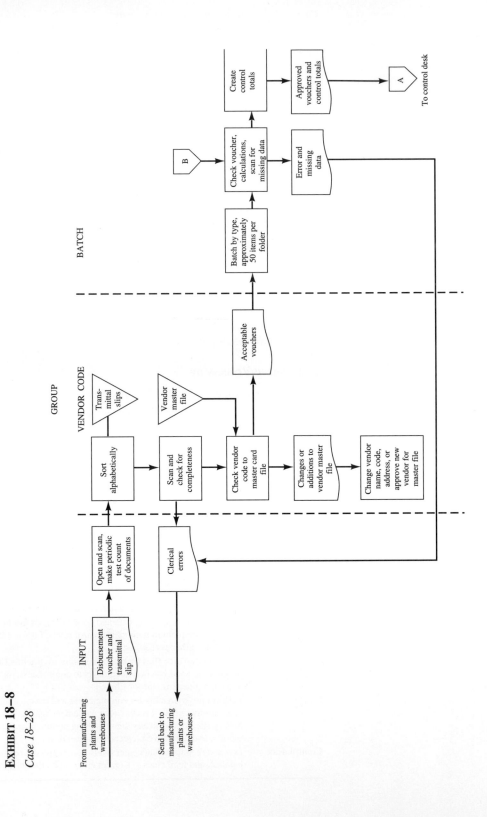

EXHIBIT 18–8
Case 18–28

From manufacturing
plants and
warehouses

INPUT

Disbursement
voucher and
transmittal
slip

Open and scan,
make periodic
test count
of documents

Send back to
manufacturing
plants or
warehouses

Clerical
errors

GROUP

VENDOR CODE

Trans-
mittal
slips

Sort
alphabetically

Scan and
check for
completeness

Vendor
master
file

Check vendor
code to
master card
file

Changes or
additions to
vendor master
file

Change vendor
name, code,
address, or
approve new
vendor for
master file

Acceptable
vouchers

BATCH

Batch by type,
approximately
50 items per
folder

B

Check voucher,
calculations,
scan for
missing data

Error and
missing
data

Create
control
totals

Approved
vouchers and
control totals

A

To control desk

646

EXHIBIT 18-8

Case 18–28 (concluded)

Required:

a. What additional information would you like to obtain before making your evaluation of the purchasing and cash disbursements systems?
b. What recommendations would you make to King Company management about the internal control over their centralized purchasing and disbursements systems?
c. How could King modernize its accounts payable procedures to take advantage of desktop computing at its plants and warehouses?

18–29.   INTEGRATIVE CASE—PART III

Agee Company is a manufacturer of large-diameter valves located in a major southwestern city. Management has engaged a local CPA firm to aid the company in updating its accounting systems, and you have been assigned to a design team responsible for developing the new processes. Members of the team include management accountants, Agee operating personnel, and representatives of the CPA firm's staff. The team leader is an experienced systems analyst from the CPA firm. In this chapter, you will complete assignments that allow you to participate in the design of application systems in Agee's expenditure cycle. For background information, you may refer to Part I of the case in Chapter 16.

Your team leader has given you the following preliminary system design (PSD) for four proposed systems in Agee's expenditure cycle. The PSD is incomplete, consisting of a short narrative and a system flowchart for each system. Make any assumptions necessary to complete the requirements, but state your assumptions.

Purchase Order System

Supervisors in the factory or in the office initiate purchasing procedures. They complete a material requisition and take it to the purchasing agent. The purchasing agent identifies a source and a price for the item and enters in the system the data necessary to prepare a purchase order. The system prints the purchase order, adds the record to the open purchase order file, and flags the appropriate record in the inventory file indicating that the item is on order.

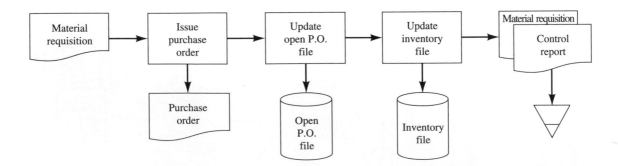

Receiving System

Material and supplies arrive at the receiving dock. A receiving clerk records on a receiving report the purchase order number, the items received, and the quantities of each item. The receiving report goes to the accounting department, where a payables clerk accesses the record in the open purchase order file and updates it to show receipt of material. The system then updates the inventory file and the general ledger master file.

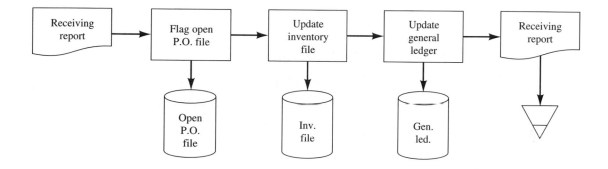

Accounts Payable System

Invoices from suppliers arrive in the mail. The receptionist, who opens the mail, forwards all invoices to the accounting department. There a payables clerk attaches to the invoice a prenumbered voucher form and records on the form the purchase order number, a payment due date, and the expense or asset account requiring a debit entry. The clerk then enters the data from this form and the invoice in the voucher file, and the system updates the general ledger master file.

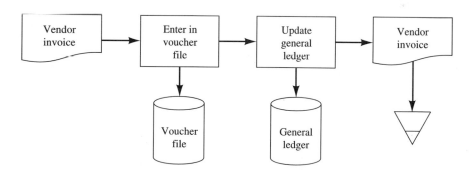

Cash Disbursements System

A payables clerk executes this system once each day after performing the accounts payable procedures. The system scans each record in the voucher file and identifies those vouchers that are due to be paid. Upon finding a voucher that is due, the system accesses the open purchase order record to determine if the full quantity of the items ordered has been received. If the items have been received, the system prints a check for the amount due and a disbursement listing showing all the checks printed. The system then deletes the voucher from the voucher file, deletes the purchase order from the open purchase order file, and updates the general ledger master file.

Required:

a. What observations do you have about this preliminary design? Do you think that modifications are needed?
b. Prepare a data flow diagram for the cash disbursements system.
c. Design a control report for the accounts payable system.
d. Design a register for the purchase order system.
e. Develop a record layout for the open purchase order file.
f. Design a data entry screen for the accounts payable system.
g. Design a receiving report for the receiving system.
h. What control procedures should you incorporate in the applications of Agee's expenditure cycle?

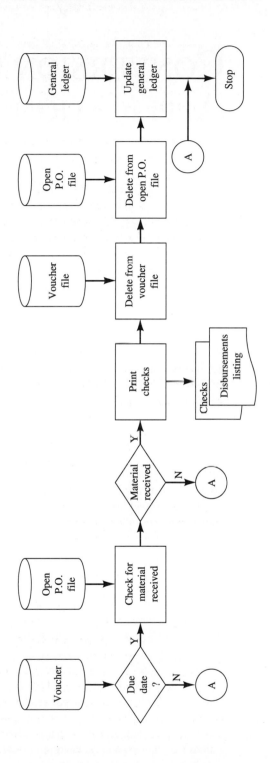

19 CONVERSION CYCLE APPLICATIONS

Learning Objectives

1. To review the accounting entries recorded in the conversion cycle.
2. To learn the documents, reports, and records used in the conversion cycle.
3. To understand how accounting transactions are processed by the application systems in the conversion cycle.
4. To see how control practices and procedures are applied in the conversion cycle.

Introduction

This chapter discusses the conversion cycle—one of the four transaction cycles used by accounting systems to record the activities of a business. This cycle differs, depending on whether the organization is a manufacturing, merchandising, or service firm.

In the conversion cycle, the accounting system records one economic event—the consumption of labor, material, and overhead to produce a salable product or service. In service organizations, this cycle consists of the payroll and the cost accounting systems. In merchandising companies, it contains the payroll and inventory systems. In manufacturing companies, the conversion cycle includes all three systems. Illustration 19–1 shows the application systems in the conversion cycle for each of these organizations.

Application systems in the conversion cycle process five types of transactions. Systems in the revenue and expenditure cycles also process two of these types. Illustration 19–2 summarizes these transactions and the documents recording them.

Inventory Systems

The inventory system maintains inventory records and notifies managers when the inventory level of a specific item requires replenishing. Manufacturing companies use inventory systems to control the levels of raw materials and finished goods inventories. Merchandising companies use them to ensure that goods are available for resale. Although service organizations maintain supplies inventories, most do not use a formal system to control them. They simply purchase supplies inventories as necessary and expense their costs.

ILLUSTRATION 19–1

Application Systems in the Conversion Cycle

System	Purpose	Type of Organization
Payroll	To calculate the pay due employees, to print paychecks, and to maintain cumulative earnings records	Service Merchandising Manufacturing
Inventory	To maintain inventory records and to notify managers when the inventory level of a specific item requires replenishing	Merchandising Manufacturing
Cost accounting	To determine the costs of products manufactured or services provided, and to record those costs in the accounting records	Service Manufacturing

Inventory System Transactions and Documents

An inventory system processes two types of transactions that originate in the revenue and expenditure cycles. These transactions are the purchase and sale of inventory.

Purchase of Inventory.   The expenditure cycle processes this type of transaction. However, the entry made to record the transaction depends on the method used for inventory accounting. The two methods are the periodic method and the perpetual method.

Periodic Method.   A company using the *periodic method* maintains no ongoing record of the amount of inventory on hand. Instead, it records the acquisition of inventory in a

ILLUSTRATION 19–2

Conversion Cycle Applications and Related Documents

Type of Transaction	Related Documents
Purchase of inventory*	Purchase order Receiving report Voucher
Sale of inventory†	Sales order Shipping notice Sales invoice
Transfer of material, labor and overhead into production	Material requisition Job ticket
Transfer of work in process into finished goods	Completed production order
Payroll	Timecard Salary authorization Other documents

*This transaction is processed in the expenditure cycle.
†This transaction is processed in the revenue cycle.

general ledger account entitled Purchases. The company determines beginning and ending inventory values by physical count. Periodically, it calculates Cost of Goods Sold from the Beginning and Ending Inventories and the Purchases account balance. The entry recording the acquisition of inventory is

```
Dr.   Purchases ............................. xxx
Cr.       Accounts Payable ............................. xxx
```

Merchandising companies used this method for many years. They have many transactions in inventory during each day, and implementing the perpetual method manually was impractical. Now, however, computerized inventory systems using the perpetual method are practical even for the smallest retailer.

Perpetual Method.   With the ***perpetual method,*** a company maintains an ongoing count of the inventory on hand. When it acquires inventory, it increases the quantity and cost of inventory. When inventory is sold, the company decreases quantity and cost. At any time it knows how much of each inventory item is available for sale. This allows the company to replenish inventory prior to completely depleting it.

Manufacturing companies use the perpetual method because they need to know if sufficient inventory is on hand for their manufacturing processes. Most merchandising companies with computer-based systems also use this method.

A company using the perpetual method has one or more inventory accounts in the general ledger. When inventory is acquired, it records the transaction by debiting the proper inventory account. For example, when a manufacturing company purchases raw material inventory for use in its factory, it makes the following entry:

```
Dr.   Raw Material Inventory ................... xxx
Cr.       Accounts Payable ............................. xxx
```

Because a merchandising company does not carry raw materials, it makes the debit in an account simply entitled Inventory. If the material is not to be resold, the debit is to the Supplies Inventory account.

The same documents record the purchase of inventory using both the periodic and the perpetual methods. They are purchase orders, receiving reports, and vouchers. A voucher documents the credit entry in Accounts Payable.

Sale of Inventory.   A company records the cost of inventory sold in the general ledger account entitled Cost of Goods Sold. How the firm determines this amount depends on the inventory method used.

With the periodic method, no entry is made at the time of the sale. Cost of Goods Sold is determined by adding the amount of the Purchases to the cost of the Beginning Inventory. This tells the cost of the goods available for sale. Subtracting from this amount the cost of the Ending Inventory gives the cost of the inventory sold.

With the perpetual method, the company records the sale by crediting an inventory account and debiting the Cost of Goods Sold account. At the end of a reporting period, the total in this account is the cost of the inventory that was sold during the period. In a manufacturing company, the credit entry is to an account containing the cost of all products manufactured during the period:

ILLUSTRATION 19–3

An Inventory Status Report

```
RUN DATE: 11/26/98                      W.D. Peachtree & Company                         PAGE  1
RUN TIME: 10:28 AM                          Inventory Control
                                         Inventory Status Report
```

DEPARTMENT: ELE

ITEM NUMBER	DESCRIPTION	BEGINNING BALANCE	SALES	RETURNS	RECEIPTS	ADJMTS.	COMPNTS	UNITS PENDING	UNITS AVAILABLE
8100000SPC	PORT. RADIO SPECIAL	0.00	0.00	0.00	10.00	0.00	0.00	0.00	10.00
8100001SPC	STEREO PACKAGE DEAL	0.00	0.00	0.00	20.00	0.00	0.00	0.00	20.00
810060PTV	COLORTRONIC TV	10.00	0.00	0.00	1.00	0.00	0.00	0.00	11.00
810104SPK	SPEAKERS	6.00	0.00	0.00	20.00	0.00	20.00	0.00	6.00
810229BLNK	BEACH BLANKET	50.00	0.00	0.00	0.00	0.00	10.00	0.00	40.00
810340TV	COLOR TELEVISION	0.00	1.00	0.00	4.00	0.00	0.00	0.00	3.00
810425RAD	PORTABLE RADIO	20.00	0.00	0.00	20.00	0.00	10.00	0.00	30.00
810522AMP	STEREO AMPLIFIER	20.00	0.00	0.00	20.00	0.00	20.00	0.00	20.00
810534BAT	BATTERIES	100.00	0.00	0.00	0.00	0.00	40.00	0.00	60.00
810544CDP	COMPACT DISC PLAYER	20.00	1.00	0.00	20.00	0.00	20.00	0.00	19.00
810549RAD	STEREO AM / FM RADIO	20.00	0.00	0.00	20.00	0.00	20.00	0.00	20.00
810555EQU	EQUALIZER	7.00	4.00	0.00	20.00	1.00-	0.00	0.00	22.00
810576REC	STEREO RECEIVER	20.00	1.00	0.00	20.00	0.00	0.00	0.00	39.00
810578CAS	DUAL CASSETTE DECK	20.00	0.00	0.00	20.00	0.00	20.00	0.00	20.00
810598EAR	EARPHONES	15.00	0.00	0.00	720.00	0.00	10.00	0.00	725.00
810698TRN	TURNTABLE	9.00	0.00	0.00	20.00	0.00	20.00	0.00	9.00

```
DEPARTMENT TOTALS                                                                    0.00      1054.00
        NUMBER OF ITEMS:     16.00                                               =========  ============
```

Copyright 1995 Peachtree Software, Inc. Reprinted by permission.

Dr.   Cost of Goods Sold xxx
Cr.   Finished Goods Inventory xxx

The documents used in the revenue cycle to record the sale are sales orders, shipping notices, and sales invoices.

Inventory System Reports

Like other applications, the inventory system produces control reports and registers. In addition, there are four special purpose reports: inventory status reports, query inventory reports, reorder reports, and physical inventory reports.

Inventory Status Report.   An inventory status report lists all items normally kept in inventory, the quantity on hand of each item, and the cost. It provides detail explaining the inventory amount shown on the balance sheet. A batch processing system prints this report daily or weekly. Employees use it to determine quantities that were available at the time of the most recent printing. Illustration 19–3 contains an inventory status report.

Query Inventory Items Report.   On-line real-time systems allow an employee to determine quantities on hand at the time of inquiry. A report such as that shown in Illustration 19–4 provides this information. Many systems provide employees the option of either printing the report or displaying it at a terminal.

ILLUSTRATION 19–4

A Query Inventory Report

```
RUN DATE: 11/26/98          W.D. Peachtree & Company             PAGE   1
RUN TIME: 11:47 AM               Inventory Control
                            Query Inventory Items Report
─────────────────────────────────────────────────────────────────────────
ITEM TYPE: P           DEPARTMENT: CLC          ITEM NUMBER: 436781G
─────────────────────────────────────────────────────────────────────────
ITEM DESCRIPTION..: GIRL'S BLUEJEANS
PRODUCT CODE......: C
LOCATION..........:
RECEIVING UNIT....: EACH
SELLING UNIT......: PAIR
CONVERSION FACTOR.:         1.00
NEGATIVE QUANTITY.: N
COSTING METHOD....: FIFO                      A/P   PERCENT      AMOUNT
CURRENT COST......:    5.4500000    PRICE A...: A   0.000      10.9900
LAST COST / UNIT..:    5.4500000    PRICE B...: A   0.000      12.5000
REORDER LEVEL.....:       10.00     PRICE C...: A   0.000      13.0000
REORDER QUANTITY..:       35.00     PRICE D...: A   0.000       0.0000
ON RO REPORT DATE.:    /  /         PRICE E...: A   0.000       0.0000

    VENDOR    ITEM #          NAME                    PHONE
─────────────────────────────────────────────────────────────────────────
1. NUMCO                  NUMCO CLOTHING, LTD.      212-555-0123
2.
3.
4.
5.

PTD ACTIVITY                       YTLP ACTIVITY

    SALES............:     87.50       SALES............:       0.00
    COST OF SALES....:     38.15       COST OF SALES....:       0.00

    BEGINNING QTY....:     35.00
    # SOLD...........:      7.00       # SOLD...........:       0.00
    # RECEIVED.......:     24.00       # RECEIVED.......:       0.00
    # RETURNED.......:      0.00       # RETURNED.......:       0.00
    # ADJUSTED.......:      0.00       # ADJUSTED.......:       0.00
    # COMPONENTS.....:      0.00       # COMPONENTS.....:       0.00
                                       ─────────────────
CURRENT QTY-ON-HAND..:     52.00
(-) # UNITS PENDING..:      2.00     ITEM VALUATION.......:    283.40
                      ───────
# UNITS AVAILABLE....:     50.00     UNITS ON ORDER.......:      0.00

────────────────── User Definable Fields ──────────────────
```

Reorder Report.   A reorder report identifies items in inventory that should be replenished. When the quantity on hand decreases to the reorder point, the inventory control system includes the item on this report. A purchasing agent uses the reorder report, such as the one in Illustration 19–5, to identify items for purchase. In a manufacturing company, a report of this type may identify items for manufacture.

Physical Inventory Report.   Periodically organizations physically count the number of each inventory item on hand. Called *taking the physical inventory,* this process allows

ILLUSTRATION 19–5

An Inventory Reorder Report

```
RUN DATE: 11/26/98                    W.D. Peachtree & Company                         PAGE  1
RUN TIME: 10:32 AM                       Inventory Control
                                        Reorder Items Report

        YOUR                                VENDOR  P                REORDER  DATE ON    REORDER  DATE      FIRST
        ITEM ID        DESCRIPTION    VENDOR  ITEM #  C   QTY AVAIL   LEVEL    REPORT     QUANTITY ORDERED   TIME?

   APP-0900120REF   COMMERCIAL REFRIGER. FRIGID 900120   A    0.00     8.00   11/26/96      6.00   _____   *YES*
   APP-0900121REF   COMMERCIAL REFRIGER. FRIGID 900121   A    5.00     8.00   11/26/96     10.00   _____   *YES*
   APP-0900122REF   COMMERCIAL REFRIGER. FRIGID 0900122  A    4.00     8.00   11/26/96      6.00   _____   *YES*
   APP-10040TRA    SUPERTRASH COMPACTOR ACME  COMP-XL    A    8.00    10.00   11/26/96      6.00   _____   *YES*
   APP-1200040DIS  DISHWASHER          MAYTAB DIS092721  A    8.00     8.00   11/26/96      8.00   _____   *YES*
   APP-1400040TRA  TRASH COMPACTOR     MAYTAB            A    0.00    10.00   11/26/96     15.00   _____   *YES*

   CLM-819608      SILK DESIGNER TIE   NUMCO             C   13.00    15.00   11/26/96     50.00   _____   *YES*

   ELE-8100000SPC  PORT. RADIO SPECIAL WD                E   10.00    10.00   11/26/96     20.00   _____   *YES*
   ELE-810060PTV   COLORTRONIC TV      CURTIS            E   11.00    20.00   11/26/96     10.00   _____   *YES*
   ELE-810340TV    COLOR TELEVISION    ELE001 340TV      E    3.00    20.00   11/26/96     10.00   _____   *YES*

   HDW-HDW020997   GUTTER STRAPS       WILSON               35.00    50.00   11/26/96    100.00   _____   *YES*
   HDW-HDW020999   ALUMINUM GUTTERS    WILSON               10.00    10.00   11/26/96     20.00   _____   *YES*

   SPO-0006BAG     SLEEPING BAG        WILSON BAG861-004  S    8.00    10.00   11/26/96     15.00   _____   *YES*
   SPO-1001WCA     BEG BACKPACK SPECIAL WD     SPECIAL    S    0.00     5.00   11/26/96     10.00   _____   *YES*
   SPO-2301DRI     FREEZE DRIED FOOD   HOLLYS            S   22.00    25.00   11/26/96     55.00   _____   *YES*

   TOTAL ITEMS BELOW REORDER LEVEL =  15


                              *** End of Reorder Items Report ***
```

Copyright 1995 Peachtree Software, Inc. Reprinted by permission.

computation of cost of goods sold when the periodic method is used. With the perpetual method, it allows the organization to correct errors in the inventory records.

A report such as that in Illustration 19–6 makes the process easier. This physical inventory report lists all items maintained in inventory and, with the perpetual method, the quantities on hand. An employee reconciles these quantities with item counts made by other employees in the inventory warehouse.

Inventory System Records

Noncomputerized Records.   In a manual system, a company using the perpetual inventory method requires an inventory ledger. It contains one page in a book, or one card in a card file, for each item maintained in inventory. A clerk records changes on the proper page or card each time items are added to or removed from inventory. The clerk also calculates the cost of the remaining quantity of the items after each transaction. The inventory ledger is a subsidiary ledger for the Inventory account in the general ledger.

Computerized Records.   Computerized records in a traditional data file system are similar to noncomputerized records in a manual system. They consist of both master files and transaction files. A database management system (DBMS) maintains the same data; however, the DBMS stores this data independently of the application.

ILLUSTRATION 19–6

A Physical Inventory Report

```
 RUN DATE: 11/26/98                    W.D. Peachtree & Company                          PAGE  1
 RUN TIME: 10:34 AM                        Inventory Control
                                        Physical Inventory Report
 ─────────────────────────────────────────────────────────────────────────────────────────────

 DEPARTMENT: APP

                    P                     VENDOR  VENDOR    SELL   |─── QTY-ON-HAND ───|
   ITEM NUMBER      C   DESCRIPTION   LOCATION  ID   ITEM #  UNIT   CALCULATED   ACTUAL      COMMENTS
 ─────────────      ─   ───────────   ────────  ──   ──────  ────   ──────────   ──────      ────────

   0900120REF       A  COMMERCIAL REFRIGER.  WRHS-1  FRIGID  900120    EACH        0.00  _____  _____
   0900121REF       A  COMMERCIAL REFRIGER.  WRHS-1  FRIGID  900121    EACH        5.00  _____  _____
   0900122REF       A  COMMERCIAL REFRIGER.  WRHS-1  FRIGID  0900122   EACH        6.00  _____  _____
   0900210REF       A  RESIDENTIAL REFRIG.   WRHS-1  FRIGID            EACH        7.00  _____  _____
   1001010VE        A  OVEN, COMMERCIAL      WRHS-1  TARPAN  TRPN11934 EACH       13.00  _____  _____
   10040TRA         A  SUPERTRASH COMPACTOR  BIN 2-2 ACME    COMP-XL   EACH        9.00  _____  _____
   1100101OVE       A  OVEN, COMMERCIAL      WRHS    TARPAN  TRPN11934 EACH       13.00  _____  _____
   1100102MOV       A  MICROWAVE OVEN                MAYTAB            EACH        7.00  _____  _____
                       MCRWV001214                                                      _____  _____
                       MCRWV001215                                                      _____  _____
                       MCRWV001216                                                      _____  _____
                       MCRWV001217                                                      _____  _____
                       MCRWV001218                                                      _____  _____
                       MCRWV001219                                                      _____  _____
                       MCRWV001244                                                      _____  _____
   1200040DIS       A  DISHWASHER            WRHS-1  MAYTAB  DIS092721 EACH       13.00  _____  _____
   1400040TRA       A  TRASH COMPACTOR       WRHS-1  MAYTAB            EACH        0.00  _____  _____


 DEPARTMENT TOTALS:            NUMBER OF ITEMS:     10.00     NUMBER OF UNITS:      73.00
```

The computerized equivalent of the inventory ledger is the ***inventory master file.*** It contains one record for each item maintained in inventory. Illustration 19–7 shows the contents of this record. If the company uses a DBMS, this illustration shows its subschema. The primary key field in the record, ITEM-NUMBER, uniquely identifies the kind of inventory item that the record describes. If the company uses a standard costing system, this record shows the item's standard cost rather than its actual cost.

ILLUSTRATION 19–7

Contents of an Inventory Master Record

ITEM-NUMBER*
ITEM-DESCRIPTION
UNIT-COST†
REORDER-POINT
REORDER-QUANTITY
VENDOR-FIRST
VENDOR-SECOND
VENDOR-THIRD
QUANTITY-ON-HAND
QUANTITY-ON-ORDER

*Designates the primary key.
†If a standard costing system is used, this is replaced by STANDARD-COST.

ILLUSTRATION 19–8

An Inventory Application

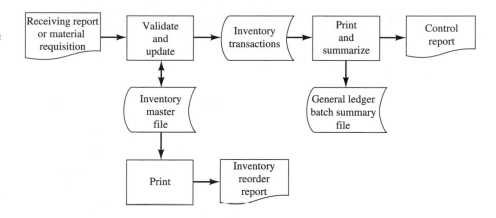

Inventory System Transaction Processing

Computerized Procedures.   Illustration 19–8 shows an on-line real-time system flow-chart of an inventory application. The receiving department prepares receiving reports and daily sends them to data entry. The inventory warehouse prepares materials requisitions that are also forwarded to data entry.

A validation program examines each transaction for errors and posts the transactions to the inventory master records, prints a control report, and adds summary records to the general ledger batch summary file. Another program then prints the inventory reorder report. Prior to the physical inventory count, a program prints the physical inventory report.

Application Controls.   Illustration 19–9 shows how input, processing, and output controls are implemented with an inventory system. The examples shown here consist of completeness and validity tests, record counts, and control total.

Cost Accounting Systems

The purpose of a cost accounting system is to determine the costs of products manufactured or services provided and to record those costs in the accounting records.

ILLUSTRATION 19–9

Example Application Controls in an Inventory System

Type	Control Procedure
Input	**Completeness tests.** Verify existence of item number and quantity on receiving report transactions. Verify existence of item number, quantity, and general ledger account number on materials requisition transactions.
	Validity test. Verify that the item number on a transaction exists in the inventory master record.
Processing	**Record counts.** Program verifies that the number of debits to the inventory account = the number of receiving reports. Program verifies that the number of credits = the number of materials requisitions.
Output	**Control total.** Clerk verifies from control report that all transactions were processed.

Cost Accounting Transactions and Documents

In a manufacturing company, a cost accounting system records two transactions in addition to those recorded in the inventory system. They are the transfer of material, labor, and overhead into production, and the transfer of completed production into finished goods inventory.

Transfer of Material, Labor, and Overhead.   A manufacturing company purchases raw material inventory and adds labor and overhead to it. This produces units of product that are in process. After the units are completed, the company sells the finished products.

The cost accounting system accumulates production costs—including those of material, labor, and overhead—in an inventory account called Work in Process. Labor costs include the pay earned by all workers directly involved in the process. Overhead costs include those required for manufacturing but not directly associated with the products. Examples are factory power, factory heating, manufacturing supplies, and pay for factory supervisors. Most companies allocate to products their fair share of these costs.

The entry recording this transaction is

Dr.	Work in Process Inventory xxx	
Cr.	Raw Material Inventory	xxx
Cr.	Direct Labor	xxx
Cr.	Factory Overhead	xxx

A manufacturing company uses a ***materials requisition*** to document the use of raw material in the process. A factory worker completes the requisition and submits it to the inventory warehouse. The inventory clerk accepts the requisition, issues the materials, and records on the requisition the cost of the materials issued. This is the source of the amount of the credit entry in the Raw Material Inventory account.

On a ***job ticket*** employees record the hours of labor devoted to manufacturing each kind of product. Daily or weekly, employees give their job tickets to a cost accountant, who computes the cost of their labor based on their pay rates. This becomes the source of the amount of the credit entry in the Direct Labor account. Periodically, someone reconciles all job tickets with the timecards used in calculating payroll.

Newer systems replace job tickets with automated data collection techniques. A case at the end of this chapter explores one such technique—-the use of magnetically encoded badges.

Most companies determine the amount of the credit entry to Factory Overhead from a predetermined allocation rate. The rate may be stated as the dollars of overhead allocated per labor hour worked or per machine hour worked. In a standard costing system, the rate is in dollars per unit produced. (A cost accounting course would teach you how to calculate and use this rate.)

Transfer of Completed Goods.   In a manufacturing company, when the production process is completed, workers transfer products to the inventory warehouse. The costs of these products are no longer associated with the units in process. Accountants transfer the cost of completed goods out of the Work in Process account with the entry

Dr.	Finished Goods Inventory xxx	
Cr.	Work in Process Inventory	xxx

ILLUSTRATION 19–10

A Job Cost Summary Report

```
RUN DATE: 11/27/98                      W.D. Peachtree & Company                    PAGE  1
RUN TIME:  5:42 PM                              Job Cost
                                        JOB COST SUMMARY REPORT


JOB RANGE ALL TO END


---------JOB---------   -REVISED-  -%-  -DUE-   --BILLINGS--   --PAYMENTS--   --COSTS--    --MARGIN--
NUMBER    DESCRIPTION      PRICE    COM  DATE   TOTAL     %    TOTAL     %    TOTAL    %    TOTAL    %


000123 INSTALL PRIVACY FENCE      1625.00 100 11/10/98    750.00 46    2250.00 138    2943.00 181    1318.00- 81-
005401 INSTALL PRIVACY FENCE      1180.00 100 06/30/98   1000.00 85    1000.00  85    2171.70 184     991.70- 84-
005999 INSTALL CHAIN LINK FENCE  13000.00     04/18/98  10000.00 77   10000.00  77    9597.50  74    3402.50  26
006100 INSTALL CHAIN LINK FENCE               05/28/98                                 7997.00         7997.00-
006650 INSTALL SPLITRAIL FENCE   15000.00     02/28/98  12500.00 83   10000.00  67   11485.00  77    3515.00  23
006668 INSTALL CHAIN LINK FENCE  10000.00     11/30/98  10000.00 100  10000.00 100    7565.50  76    2434.50  24
OFFICE IN HOUSE FOR UNBILL TIME                                                        3137.00         3137.00-

                                 =============        =============  =============  =============  =============
       RANGE TOTAL               40805.00              34250.00 84   33250.00  81   44896.70 110    4091.70- 10-

       NUMBER OF JOBS       7


                            *** END OF JOB COST SUMMARY REPORT ***
```

Companies determine the amount of this entry in different ways. Some use a *job costing system,* in which they identify products by job or batch number. They accumulate costs for the job, and these constitute the amount of the entry that is recorded when the job is complete. Other companies—for example, those that employ assembly lines—use a *process costing system.* They accumulate costs incurred in the factory and transfer these costs monthly to the Finished Goods account. With either system, a *completed production order* documents the completion of the products. A cost accountant or computerized cost accounting system calculates the amount of the entry.

This section described the accounting entries made by the cost accounting system and the documents that record the data for these entries. The next section describes typical cost accounting reports.

Cost Accounting System Reports

Cost accounting systems produce control reports and various production cost reports.

Control Reports.   Control reports provide evidence that transactions are not lost or improperly changed during processing. A cost accounting system typically uses control reports to summarize all jobs, or batches of products, that are added to or removed from the Work in Process Inventory account. They are also used to summarize the total additions of material and labor to all active jobs.

Production Cost Reports.   Cost accounting systems produce several different production cost reports. Some disclose total and unit costs by production cost center. Others disclose these for specific jobs. When a company uses a standard costing system, these reports compare actual costs with those budgeted.

Some periodic reports show costs incurred up to the date of printing for all jobs or cost centers. Illustration 19–10 contains a job cost summary report that summarizes the

ILLUSTRATION 19–11

A Job Inquiry Report

```
RUN DATE: 11/27/98                    W.D. Peachtree & Company                         PAGE  1
RUN TIME:  3:31 PM                            Job Cost
                                        JOB INQUIRY REPORT
-------------------------------------------------------------------------------------------------
JOB NUMBER 000123  INSTALL PRIVACY FENCE    START 11/05/98  P/O BT60241     ORIGINAL   1000.00  INVOICES    625.00
SUPERVISOR         JERRY HOBBS              DUE   11/10/98      1 CHG ORDS   REVISED    1125.00  BILLINGS    750.00
CUSTOMER # SMITHR  ROBERT M. SMITH          CLOSE 11/10/98    100% COMPLETE TOT COST    840.00  PAYMENTS    750.00
                                                              25.33% MARGIN             285.00  % DUE

           PHASE COST  ───────────────UNITS────────────────      ──────────────DOLLARS──────────────
           CODE  CODE  MEAS   ESTIMATE    ACTUAL    DIFFERENCE DIF%   ESTIMATE   ACTUAL   DIFFERENCED IF%
           ─────────── ────   ────────    ──────    ────────── ────   ────────   ──────   ─────────── ───

            03   BUILD  HOUR     1.00       1.53       0.53  53         75.00    115.00     40.00  53
            03   PREP   HOUR    10.00      10.00       0.00   0        120.00    120.00
            21   CHLINK FOOT    24.00      25.00       1.00   4        288.00    300.00     12.00   4
            27   FINISH HOUR     8.00       8.00                       160.00    160.00
            29   FINISH HOUR     8.00       7.25       0.75-  9-       160.00    145.00     15.00-  9-


     LABOR                      26.00      25.25       0.75-  3-       440.00    425.00     15.00-  3-
     MATERIAL                   24.00      25.00       1.00   4        288.00    300.00     12.00   4
     EQUIPMENT                   1.00       1.53       0.53  53         75.00    115.00     40.00  53
                              ==========  =========  =========       ========  ========   ==========
     JOB TOTAL                  51.00      51.78       0.78   2        803.00    840.00     37.00   5

                           *** END OF JOB INQUIRY REPORT ***
```

costs of all active jobs for a construction company. In a manufacturing company, this report provides detail supporting the balance in the Work in Process Inventory account.

In an on-line real-time system, employees can display at a terminal or print a report showing current costs recorded for a specific job or cost center. This provides better information for controlling costs than is available from a manual or batch processing system. Illustration 19–11 shows such a job inquiry report produced by a job costing system.

Three kinds of reports used in the cost accounting system are discussed here; in practice, you will see many others. This system frequently produces reports specially designed to suit management's preferences. The next section shows the accounting records needed to produce these reports.

Cost Accounting System Records

Manual accounting systems use books, card files, and filing cabinets to record and store accounting data. Computer-based systems replace books and cards with magnetic media such as disks and tapes. Although the data maintained by each form of technology are similar, computer-based systems use the data to produce more management reports than manual systems can generate.

Noncomputerized Records.   Manufacturing and service companies use a *production cost ledger.* It serves as a subsidiary ledger for the general ledger Work in Process Inventory account and exists in different forms in various industries.

If the company uses a job costing system, this ledger contains one page for each active job. If the company uses a process costing system, it contains one page for each cost center. A file of production orders is an efficient production cost ledger.

ILLUSTRATION 19–12

Contents of a Cost Center Record

RESPONSIBILITY-CODE*
COST-CENTER-NAME
COST-CENTER-MANAGER
LABOR-COST-ACTUAL
LABOR-HOURS-ACTUAL
LABOR-RATE-STANDARD†
STANDARD-HOURS-ALLOWED†
MATERIAL-COST-ACTUAL
MATERIAL-COST-STANDARD†
VARIABLE-OVERHEAD-ACTUAL
VARIABLE-OVERHEAD-BUDGET†
FIXED-OVERHEAD-ACTUAL
FIXED-OVERHEAD-BUDGET†

*Designates the primary key.
†Required with a standard costing system

Computerized Records.   Computerized records in a traditional data file system are similar to the noncomputerized records in a manual system. They consist of both master files and transaction files. A DBMS maintains the same data and provides the data to application programs. However, the DBMS stores these data independently.

In manufacturing companies, the cost accounting system processes those transactions that record the transfer of goods into or out of Work in Process Inventory. The computerized equivalent of a cost ledger in a manual system is a production cost file. Depending on the industry, this may exist in two forms.

A company that uses a process costing system establishes a *cost center file* containing one record for each factory cost center. The cost accounting system records in this file the costs of material, labor, and allocated factory overhead for the cost center during each month. From this data, the system calculates the cost of the units completed and the cost of the Work in Process Inventory in that cost center at the end of the month. Illustration 19–12 shows the contents of a cost center record. The primary key field, the field that uniquely identifies the applicable cost center, is RESPONSIBILITY-CODE.

A company that uses a job costing system establishes a *job cost file* containing one record for each job. In this record, the cost accounting system posts the costs of material, labor, and factory overhead for the job. Whenever the production control manager issues a new production order, the system creates a record in this file for it and assigns a job number. When production is complete and the products are transferred to the inventory warehouse, the system removes the job cost record. Illustration 19–13 shows its contents. The job number in this record is called PRODUCTION-ORDER-NUMBER, which is the primary key field.

If the company uses a standard cost system, then the cost center record or job cost record must store standard costs as well as actual ones. This allows the system to calculate variances. A batch processing system creates transaction files containing the data found on materials requisitions and job tickets. These transaction files contain records that the system posts to the inventory master, cost center, and job cost files. An on-line

ILLUSTRATION 19–13

Contents of a Job Cost Record

PRODUCTION-ORDER NUMBER*
ITEM-NUMBER
ITEM-DESCRIPTION
ORDER-SOURCE
ORDER-QUANTITY
ORDER-COMPLETION-DATE
LABOR-COST-ACTUAL
LABOR-COST-STANDARD†
MATERIALS-COST-ACTUAL
MATERIALS-COST-STANDARD†
LABOR-HOURS-ACTUAL
LABOR-HOURS-STANDARD†
TOTAL-VARIABLE-OVERHEAD†
TOTAL-FIXED-OVERHEAD†
TOTAL-COST
SALES-PRICE
MARGIN

---

*Designates the primary key.
†Required with a standard costing system

real-time system posts these transactions individually when they enter the system. Illustration 19–14 summarizes the contents of materials requisition and job ticket records. A materials requisition number uniquely identifies each materials requisition record; a job ticket number uniquely identifies each job ticket.

Like other application systems, a cost accounting system produces records for the general ledger batch summary file. These records summarize the transfers of material, labor, and overhead costs into work in process inventory. Other records summarize the transfer of completed units into finished goods inventory. The general ledger system

ILLUSTRATION 19–14

Contents of Materials Requisition and Job Ticket Records

Materials Requisition Record	Job Ticket Record
MATERIALS-REQUISITION-NUMBER*	JOB-TICKET-NUMBER*
TRANSACTION-CODE	TRANSACTION-CODE
RESPONSIBILITY-CODE	RESPONSIBILITY-CODE
GENERAL-LEDGER-ACCOUNT	GENERAL-LEDGER-ACCOUNT
PRODUCTION-ORDER-NUMBER	PRODUCTION-ORDER-NUMBER
DATE	DATE
ACTUAL-QUANTITY	ACTUAL-HOURS
STANDARD-QUANTITY†	STANDARD-HOURS†
ACTUAL-UNIT-COST	ACTUAL-RATE
STANDARD-UNIT-COST†	STANDARD-RATE†

*Designates the primary key.
†Required with a standard costing system

posts the records in this transaction file to the general ledger master file during the closing process.

This is how organizations record accounting data in both manual and computerized cost accounting systems. These records are similar even though the methods of recording them differ. The next section describes how this system processes transactions.

Cost Accounting Transaction Processing

Manual Processes.   Illustration 19–15 contains a document flowchart describing manual cost accounting procedures. Using these procedures, a production control manager initiates the process by scheduling a specific item for production. Many companies produce to order—that is, they schedule a product for manufacture when they receive a request for the product from a customer. In other companies, the production control manager may schedule production because an inventory reorder report indicates that a certain item needs replenishing. In either case, the manager prepares a production order.

A copy of this document, the production cost sheet, goes to cost accounting, where a clerk files it in the production cost ledger. When factory workers need material, they complete a materials requisition and exchange it for the material at the inventory warehouse. This document goes to cost accounting, where a clerk records the material on the production cost sheet. As work proceeds on the products, workers complete job tickets. A production supervisor forwards these to cost accounting daily or weekly, where a clerk records labor costs on the production cost sheet.

When production is complete in a job costing system, a cost accountant computes the unit cost of the goods and records the transfers of materials, labor, overhead, and Work in Process on journal vouchers. The accountant does this monthly for each cost center in a process costing system.

Control Procedures.   An adequate internal control structure requires proper segregation of duties and good control practices over transactions. Illustration 19–16 shows how to implement four types of control activities in a cost accounting system. It summarizes the control practices that should be applied to the documents and records just described.

Effective segregation of duties requires separating the custody of assets from the recordkeeping regarding them. This means that the employees keeping inventory records should not have access to the warehouse, and that employees performing timekeeping should not aid in preparing paychecks. Separating cost accounting functions from those of general accounting allows cost accountants to become more specialized and helps to prevent errors.

Computerized Processes.   Illustration 19–17 shows how computer-based job costing systems work. These costing systems are simpler than manual ones because transactions representing costs are posted only to a cost center file.

Data entry clerks create a new job cost record for each production order received from the production control manager. The system merges the new job cost records with the existing job cost file.

ILLUSTRATION 19–15

Manual Procedures for Cost Accounting

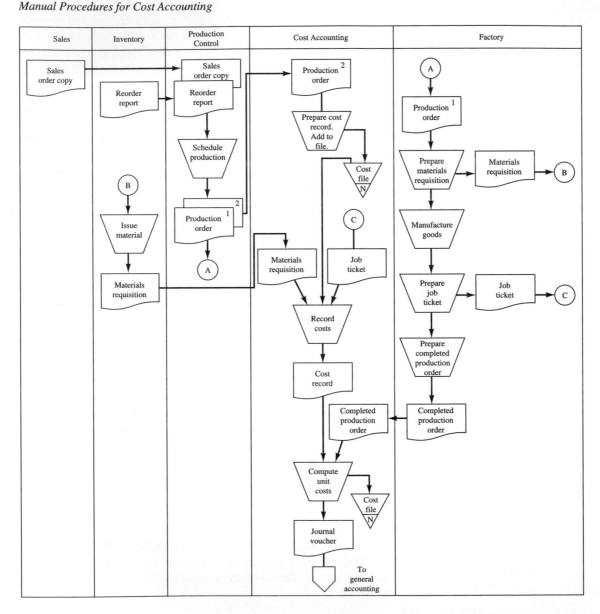

Each day data entry clerks create transaction records from materials requisitions and job tickets. In a batch system, these form transaction files. An on-line real-time system processes each transaction one at a time. The system records these material and labor transactions in the proper job cost record.

When production is complete, a factory supervisor records the number of units produced on the production order and sends it to cost accounting. Here clerks execute a

ILLUSTRATION 19–16

Control Activities for Cost Accounting Transactions

Activity	Materials	Labor	Transfer of Work in Process to Finished Goods
Transaction authorization	a. Production control manager authorizes, inventory control approves	a. Production control manager authorizes, production supervisor approves	a. Production supervisor authorizes and approves
Security for assets and records	Raw materials a. Initital quantity based on bill of materials b. Released only on receipt of materials requisitions		Finished goods a. Transfer based on finished goods report
Segregation of duties	a. Factory and production control b. Inventory records and warehouse c. Cost accounting and general accounting	a. Timekeeping and payroll b. Factory and timekeeping c. Cost accounting and general accounting d Payroll and personnel	a. Inventory records and warehouse b. Cost accounting and general accounting
Adequate documents and records	Production order request a. Based on reorder point and reorder quantity, or based on special customer order Production order a. Issued only on the basis of a production order request b. Prenumbered Job cost record a. Initiated only on receipt of production order b. Posted daily c. Control total established at month end Inventory record a. Numerical sequence of materials requisitions accounted for b. Control total established at month end General ledger a. Cost accounting integrated into financial accounting b. Control total from inventory records and cost accounting	Labor time a. Allowed time based on operations list b. Job ticket prepared with each assignment c. Data on job ticket and clock card compared Labor cost a. Updated employee list and pay rates provided by personnel department b. Posted with each pay period c. Control total established at month end General ledger a. Control total for direct labor compared to payroll total	Finished goods report a. Issued as soon as production process is completed b. Prenumbered Job cost record a. Removed from work in process records only on receipt of finished goods report b. Control total established at month end Inventory record a. Numerical sequence of finished goods report accounted for b. Control total established at month end General ledger a. Cost accounting integrated into financial accounting b. Control total from inventory

program that calculates unit costs for the job, produces summary records for the general ledger batch summary file, purges the completed job from the job cost file, and prints a job cost report. It also records in the inventory master file the transfer to work in process and finished goods inventory.

ILLUSTRATION 19–17

A Cost Accounting Application

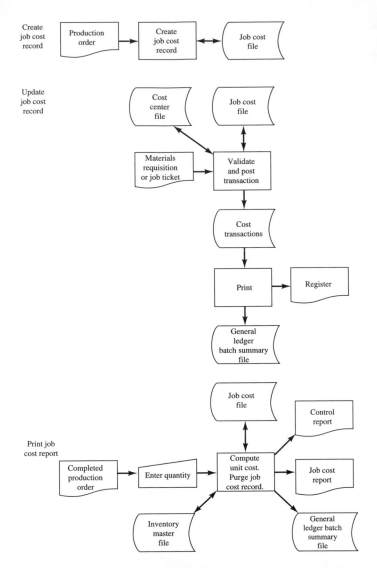

Application Controls.   Application controls prevent or detect errors and irregularities in an application system. They do this during input of data, during processing of data by the computer, and with the outputs from processing. Illustration 19–18 shows how a system design team implements input, processing, and output controls for the cost accounting system. These examples include completeness tests, control totals, record counts, and run-to-run controls.

Payroll Systems

The purposes of a payroll application are to calculate the pay due employees, to print paychecks, and to maintain cumulative earnings records. In theory, an organization could process payroll transactions by the cash disbursements application in the expenditure cycle. In practice, however, most process them by a separate payroll system for two reasons.

AIS in Practice

The **Simpson Investment Company** of Seattle, Washington, owns paper and lumber manufacturing operations in the northwestern United States and several other states. As part of a corporate restructuring, the company changed its information processing from mainframe-based systems to client/server processing. The new approach included implementation of an automated labor data collection system.

The new timekeeping software eliminated manual processes and provided companywide consistency, accuracy, and accessibility. Employees enter their time-worked data either by dedicated data collection devices or by a web browser. Supervisors use browsers on their desktop computers to view attendance reports, labor summaries, and electronic timesheets provided by a web server.

First, payroll systems must withhold amounts for deductions and taxes and summarize these in cumulative earnings reports. Such withholding and reporting are unnecessary when processing purchases transactions in the expenditure cycle. Second, payroll systems produce paychecks made out to employees. This makes fraud in payroll systems easier to conceal than in those systems that produce checks for vendors. Establishing a separate system for payroll allows greater control over these transactions.

Payroll Transactions and Documents

Payroll systems use different documents for hourly employees and salaried employees. Some companies also pay employees by other methods using specialized documents. Each document serves as authorization for the issue of a *paycheck*.

Hourly Employees.   Employers pay hourly employees a fixed rate per hour. Each day each employee records on a *timecard* the number of hours worked. Depending on the system, the employee may either enter the number by hand or insert the card into a clock that imprints it. A supervisor signs the timecard, verifying the total hours worked and authorizing issue of the paycheck by the payroll department. Illustration 19–19 shows a timecard. Fully computerized systems capture this data in magnetic form using terminals.

ILLUSTRATION 19–18

Example Application Controls in the Cost Accounting System

Type	Control Procedure
Input	**Completeness tests.** Verify that all fields exist in the materials transaction and labor transaction records.
Processing	**Control total.** Program verifies that total credits to work in process = total debits to finished goods.
	Control total. In the on-line real-time system, program verifies that total costs recorded in job cost file = total costs recorded in cost center file.
	Record count. Verify that the number of new job records + the number of records in the old job cost file = the number of records in the new job cost file.
Output	**Control totals.** Data control group verifies that total cost of jobs on job purge control report = total of job cost reports.
	Run-to-run controls. In batch system, data control group verifies that total on register = total transactions disclosed on error listings.

ILLUSTRATION 19–19

A Timecard

STORE	DAY	DAY	DATE	IN	OUT	HOURS WORKED	ABSENT EXPLAIN BY CODE
		1	16				
		2	17				
		3	18				
		4	19				
		5	20				
		6	21				
		7	22				
		8	23				
		9	24				
		10	25				
		11	26				
		12	27				
		13	28				
		14	29				
		15	30				
			31				

EMPLOYEE NAME   NUMBER

DATE TIME BEGINS: _____   DATE TIME ENDS: _____

TOTAL HOURS WORKED

CODE:
O-DAY OFF
S-SUNDAY
H-HOLIDAY
I-ILL
V-VACATION
P-PERSONAL
ANY OTHER
   EXPLAIN

OT HOURS WORKED _____   APPROVED BY _____

I HEREBY CERTIFY THAT THE ABOVE IS CORRECT

_____
EMPLOYEE SIGNATURE

APPROVED BY _____

Salaried Employees.   Employers pay salaried employees a fixed amount per biweekly or monthly pay period. For them, the employer authorizes the preparation of paychecks when employees are hired. The personnel department completes an *employment form* that documents the hiring and sends a copy to the payroll department, which prepares salaried paychecks. Different organizations give different names to this form, such as a "personnel action request" or a "salary authorization." Illustration 19–20 shows an employment form.

Other Pay Methods.   Some organizations use incentives, such as piecework rates or commissions, to determine employees' pay. For employees who are paid in these ways, other forms of documentation are used to support the payroll calculations. For example, a production supervisor may approve a production count card for a factory worker. A payroll clerk then computes the worker's pay based on the number of units produced rather than the hours worked. A payroll system may calculate a salesperson's commissions based on gross sales recorded in a sales order entry system.

ILLUSTRATION 19–20

An Employment Form

Used by permission of the University of Houston System.

Illustration 19–21 shows a paycheck. During system design, the design team determines how the check and its attached paycheck stub should look. The check itself must comply with the requirements of the banks that process it. The stub contains information to show the employee how the amount on the check was determined. It shows the calculations for determining gross pay, lists all deductions, and discloses net pay. Frequently it also shows these amounts accumulated for the year to date.

Accounting Entries.   The accounting entry recording payroll transactions recognizes the classifications of labor expenses in the chart of accounts. For most companies, the chart of accounts distinguishes between sales salaries, administrative salaries, indirect labor, and direct labor. It may make further distinctions if management wishes. The entry distributes total labor costs among these accounts and also among responsibility center accounts. For this reason, accountants call this entry the *labor expense distribution.* An accounting entry recording payroll is

ILLUSTRATION 19–21

A Paycheck

EARNINGS	HRS./UNITS	CURRENT AMOUNT	YEAR TO DATE	DEDUCTIONS	CURRENT AMOUNT	YEAR TO DATE
REGULAR	40.00	300.00	16845.00	SS	18.60	1045.09
OVERTIME 1		0.00	11.25	MCARE	4.35	244.41
OVERTIME 2		0.00	0.00	FEDERAL WH.	30.94	1992.38
SICK HOURS		0.77	43.12	CALIFORNIA	3.98	535.92
VACATION HOURS		1.54	86.24	CA/SDI	3.90	11.70

CLIC12 Cal Cline   430-83-9320   11/24/98   11/30/98   1465

PAY RATE	CURRENT EARNINGS	CURRENT DEDUCTIONS	NET PAY	YTD EARNINGS	YTD DEDUCTIONS	YTD NET PAY
7.500	300.00	61.77	238.23	16856.25	3829.50	13026.75

W.D. Peachtree & Company   1465
3900 Peachtree Street
Atlanta, GA 30309

PAY **** TWO HUNDRED THIRTY EIGHT & 23 /100 DOLLARS

DATE   AMOUNT

11/30/98   ******$238.23

TO THE
ORDER   Cal Cline
OF: 2301 Valley Heart Drive

Atlanta, GA   30345

CLIC12 Cal Cline   430-83-9320 11/24/98   11/30/98 1465

REGULAR	40.00	300.00	16845.00	SS	18.60	1045.09
OVERTIME 1		0.00	11.25	MCARE	4.35	244.41
OVERTIME 2		0.00	0.00	FEDERAL WH.	30.94	1992.38
SICK HOURS		0.77	43.12	CALIFORNIA	3.98	535.92
VACATION HOURS		1.54	86.24	CA/SDI	3.90	11.70
7.500	300.00	61.77	238.23	16856.25	3829.50	13026.75

Dr.	Sales Salaries		xxx	
Dr.	Administrative Salaries		xxx	
Dr.	Indirect Labor		xxx	
Dr.	Direct Labor		xxx	
Cr.		Wages and Salaries Payable		xxx

The following entry records the issue of paychecks:

Dr.	Wages and Salaries Payable		xxx	
Cr.		Cash		xxx
Cr.		Payroll Taxes Payable		xxx
Cr.		Other Deductions Payable		xxx

In this entry, the Payroll Taxes Payable account records the withholdings from the employee's salary for taxes. Amounts may also be voluntarily withheld for such items as insurance, contributions, or union dues.

Payroll Reports

Payroll systems produce three reports: the payroll register, control reports for paychecks, and various cumulative earnings reports.

Payroll Register.   Payroll systems produce a payroll register prior to printing paychecks. The register lists all employees for whom paychecks are due. For each employee, it shows the gross pay, lists all deductions, and shows the net pay.

Producing the payroll register is an important control practice. A payroll supervisor reviews the payroll register for errors before printing paychecks. Then a clerk corrects errors prior to printing the checks. This avoids printing erroneous checks that could be stolen and cashed. Illustration 19–22 contains a computer-printed payroll register.

Print Checks Control Report.   Because paychecks can easily be stolen or falsified, the system must control their preparation. The print checks control report aids in detecting missing or unauthorized checks.

The computer program that prints checks also produces this control report showing the number of checks printed and the total amount of these checks. The data control group compares these control totals with the checks. A payroll supervisor reconciles these amounts with those shown on the payroll register.

Cumulative Earnings Reports.   In the United States, employers are required to withhold taxes from employees' paychecks; quarterly they send these taxes to the government. Payroll systems aid in this process by producing several kinds of cumulative earnings reports, which summarize the gross pay and tax withheld for an employee during each quarter of the year. A report produced at year-end discloses this data for the entire year.

Payroll System Records

Noncomputerized Records.   Manual payroll systems maintain data in a filing cabinet about each individual employee. Payroll clerks use data in this file to calculate gross pay and to determine the amounts of deductions. They also record in this file cumulative earnings information for individual employees. Other files hold documents during or after processing them.

ILLUSTRATION 19–22

A Computer-Printed Payroll Register

```
RUN DATE: 11/30/98                      W.D. Peachtree & Company                              PAGE  1
RUN TIME:  4:46 PM                              Payroll
                                           Payroll Register

                                                                                  PERIOD ENDING 11/30/98

  DEPARTMENT 12
                    REGULAR   DISB.    NON-DISB   VOL.              SS/                                CHECK
  CODE      NAME    EARNINGS  MISC.INC MISC.INC   DEDUCT. FED.WH.   MCARE   TAX #1  TAX #2  TAX #3  TAX #4  NUMB   NET PAY


  12CLIC Cal Cline   300.00    0.00     0.00      0.00    30.94    18.60    3.98    3.90    0.00    0.00           238.23
                                                                   4.35
  12DELO Oscar DeLaren 300.00  0.00     0.00      0.00    30.94    18.60    3.98    3.90    0.00    0.00           238.23
                                                                   4.35

                     600.00    0.00     0.00      0.00    61.88    37.20    7.96    7.80    0.00    0.00           476.46
                                                                   8.70


  BREAKDOWN OF MISCELLANEOUS INCOME AND TAX CODES FOR DEPARTMENT 12

  DRAW          0.00      CALIFORNIA WH.     7.96      CURRENT DEF. DEDUCT.     0.00
  COMMISSION    0.00      CA/SDI     WH.     7.80      CURRENT ALLOC. DEDUCT.   0.00
   Tips         0.00
   MISC. #1     0.00
   BONUS        0.00
   MISC. #3     0.00
   MISC. #4     0.00
   MISC. #5     0.00
   MISC. #6     0.00
   EIC          0.00
```

Noncomputerized systems use a journal called the *payroll register,* in which a payroll clerk records the calculations for gross pay, deductions, and net pay. The payroll register provides an audit trail for the amounts shown on the paychecks. Illustration 19–23 shows the contents of a noncomputerized payroll register. Its contents are similar to those of the computer-printed payroll register.

Computerized Records.   Computerized payroll systems update a master file called the ***employee master file.*** This file contains one record for each current or past employee, and contains data necessary for determining payroll deductions and submitting earnings information required in government reports. Illustration 19–24 shows the contents of an employee master record. The primary key, EMPLOYEE-NUMBER, uniquely identifies the record. The secondary key, DEPARTMENT-NUMBER, allows the system to easily identify all workers in a department.

For hourly employees, the input to the payroll system is the file of timecards. For employees paid on piecework or commissions, payroll clerks create files of other documents. These are converted into computer-readable form and constitute the *payroll transaction file.* The system adds records to this file for any salaried employees whose paychecks are due during the pay period. The payroll system produces one paycheck from each record in this file.

ILLUSTRATION 19–23

A Manual Payroll Register

					Earnings			Deductions				
Employee		Name of Employee	Hours Worked	Base Rate	Regular	Over-time	Other	FICA	Income Tax With-held	Insur-ance	Other	Net Pay
Dept.	Number											

Page _____

The payroll system adds records to the *general ledger batch summary file* summarizing the transactions. Records placed in this file from the payroll system record a credit entry in Wages Payable, and debits to various labor expense accounts. The general ledger batch summary file accumulates summary records from many application systems. The general ledger system posts the records in this file to the general ledger.

Payroll Transaction Processing

Noncomputerized Procedures.   Illustration 19–25 contains a document flowchart showing manual payroll procedures. The personnel department screens applicants, authorizes the employee's initial pay rate, and creates the manual employment record. For salaried employees, this record authorizes a periodic paycheck.

During each pay period, hourly employees complete timecards. A supervisor approves these timecards and sends them to the payroll department, where clerks compute paycheck amounts and complete payroll records. The cash disbursements section in the treasurer's department prepares and distributes paychecks.

Imprest Accounts.   To improve control over payroll transactions, many organizations establish a separate bank checking account for the payroll system. All paycheck disbursements, but no other withdrawals, are made from this special bank account. Usually the payroll bank account is an *imprest account,* meaning that the balance in the account is always kept at a predetermined amount. This amount is usually sufficient to cover paychecks of all employees terminated between pay periods.

For example, suppose your company seldom fires more than one or two employees per month and no employee makes more than $5,000 in a month. You decide to create a payroll bank account separate from the regular account used for disbursements to suppliers. You decide to make the payroll bank account an imprest account and to maintain its balance at $10,000. When paychecks are written on this account, the payroll department determines their total amount. Then they request a

ILLUSTRATION 19–24

Contents of an Employee Master Record

EMPLOYEE-NUMBER*
EMPLOYEE-NAME
EMPLOYEE-ADDRESS
SOCIAL-SECURITY-NUMBER
MARITAL-STATUS
NUMBER-EXEMPTIONS
DEPARTMENT-CODE†
PAY-RATE
HOURLY/SALARY-CODE
INSURANCE-DEDUCTION
OTHER-DEDUCTION
DATE-EMPLOYED
DATE-TERMINATED
EARNINGS-DATA-CURRENT-PERIOD
  HOURS-WORKED
  REGULAR-EARNINGS
  OVERTIME-PREMIUM
  OTHER
  FICA-DEDUCTION
  INCOME-TAX-WITHHELD
  DEDUCTED-INSURANCE
  DEDUCTED-OTHER
EARNING-DATA-THIS-QUARTER
  HOURS-WORKED
  REGULAR-EARNINGS
  OVERTIME-PREMIUM
  OTHER
  FICA-DEDUCTION
  INCOME-TAX-WITHHELD
  DEDUCTED-INSURANCE
  DEDUCTED-OTHER
EARNINGS-DATA-THIS-YEAR
  HOURS-WORKED
  REGULAR-EARNINGS
  OVERTIME-PREMIUM
  OTHER
  FICA-DEDUCTION
  INCOME-TAX-WITHHELD
  DEDUCTED-INSURANCE
  DEDUCTED-OTHER

*Designates a primary key.
†Designates a secondary key.

cash disbursements check, drawn on the regular bank account, to reimburse the payroll account for the amount of the payroll. This maintains the payroll bank account balance at $10,000.

Why do organizations follow this procedure? Having a separate checking account for payroll makes reconciling this account easier. It also makes detecting certain frauds easier because all checks drawn on the payroll account should be payable to employees. Because checks payable to employees from the regular account are infrequent, they are

ILLUSTRATION 19–25

Manual Procedures for Payroll

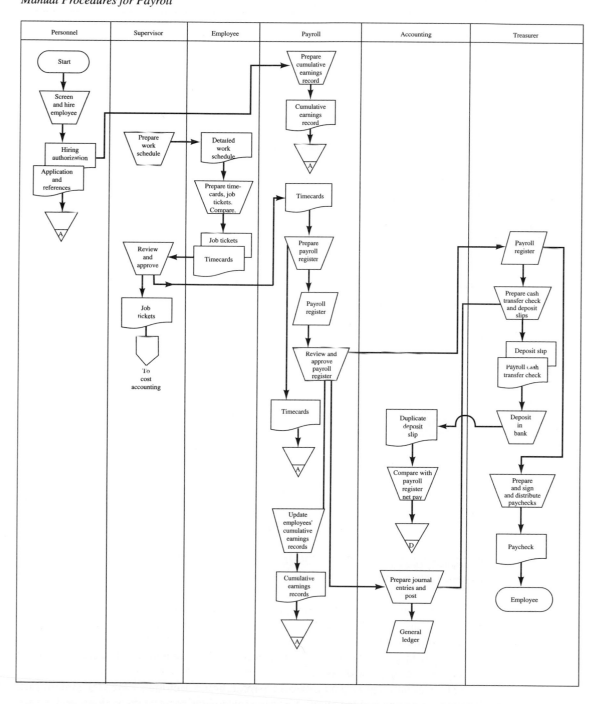

ILLUSTRATION 19–26

Control Activities for Payroll Transactions

Activity	Payroll
Transaction authorization	*a.* Supervisor authorizes, treasurer approves.
Security for assets and records	Paychecks *a.* Prepared only based on properly prepared payroll register *b.* Prenumbered *c.* Signed only if properly prepared *d.* Imprest bank account used *e.* Distributed by persons not involved in payroll process *f.* Voided checks kept *g.* Unclaimed checks listed
Segregation of duties	*a.* Timekeeping and payroll *b.* Payroll and cash disbursements *c.* Payroll and personnel
Adequate documents and records	Initial documentation *a.* Updated employee list and pay rates provided by personnel department *b.* Timecards reviewed *c.* Payroll preparation reviewed

examined closely. Also, should a dishonest employee find a way to embezzle from the payroll account, the employee's theft is limited to the imprest amount.

Control Procedures.   The use of imprest accounts is a procedure that prevents and detects errors and irregularities in payroll systems. It is appropriate regardless of whether the system uses computerized or manual processes. Other control procedures, called *application controls,* relate specifically to computerized processes.

Payroll registers, control reports, and imprest accounts improve control over payroll transactions. Illustration 19–26 summarizes effective segregation of duties and control practices applied to the documents for payroll transactions. Adequate segregation of duties requires that the timekeeping and personnel departments, which authorize paychecks and pay rates, are separate from the payroll department, which prepares paychecks. As discussed earlier, payroll employees and procedures should be separate from those used to process other cash disbursements checks.

Computerized Procedures.   Illustration 19–27 contains a system flowchart of a payroll system. Similar to the cash disbursements system, the payroll application uses batch processing.

In this system, a supervisor approves timecards for payment, batches them, and establishes a control total over the total hours worked in a batch. A data entry clerk enters the timecard data in a computer file. Some systems validate each data record during its data entry. Others create the transaction file and then validate them a batch at a time, producing an error listing.

The validation program produces a payroll transaction file, which the system sorts into employee number sequence. A program calculates pay and deductions, updates the

ILLUSTRATION 19–27

A Payroll Application

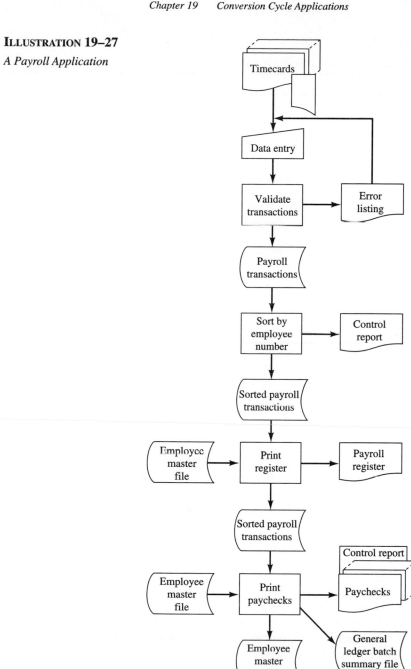

ILLUSTRATION 19–28

Example Application Controls in the Payroll System

Type	Control Procedure
Input	**Completeness test.** Program verifies existence of EMPLOYEE-NUMBER, EMPLOYEE-NAME, HOURS-WORKED. **Control total.** Program verifies that total number of hours on batch transmittal form = total number of hours on valid payroll transactions + total number of hours on erroneous payroll transactions.
Processing	**Record count.** Number of input transaction records = number of output transaction records. **Control total.** Total hours in input file = total hours in output file.
Output	**Limit test.** Program flags for review by data control group those transactions with amounts > $10,000. **Record count**. Program verifies that the number of paychecks = the number of payroll transaction records. **Control total.** Program verifies that total amount of paychecks = total debits to general ledger accounts = total credits to general ledger accounts. **Run-to-run controls.** Data control group compares control totals taken on paycheck amounts and disclosed on control report and payroll register.

cumulative earnings data in the employee master file, and prints the payroll register. After payroll clerks have reviewed the register for errors, another program prints paychecks and creates records for the general ledger batch summary file.

Application Controls.   Input, processing, and output controls help to prevent or detect errors during the processing of payroll transactions. Because most payroll systems use batch sequential processing, the data control group uses run-to-run controls to verify the total amounts for each pay period. Illustration 19–28 shows how record counts, control totals, and other validation procedures can be used in the payroll system.

Nonaccounting Applications

Companies with more advanced computer-based systems use computer applications in the conversion cycle to aid in controlling the production process. Although these systems do not process accounting transactions, they affect these transactions. Three such systems are production scheduling systems, material requirements planning (MRP) systems, and just-in-time (JIT) systems.

Production Scheduling Systems

In the system just described, a production control manager schedules jobs for production and authorizes them with production orders. Many manufacturing companies now use an on-line real-time computer-based system that replaces written production orders with computer records.

Such a system maintains two files, a *work order file* and a *work order detail file*. The work order file contains a record for each production order and shows its priority and desired completion date. A computer program schedules production by ranking active work orders by priority and date and disclosing this ranking on a computer report.

For each work order, there are several associated records in the work order detail file. Each represents one manufacturing operation required for production. As the factory completes operations, employees use terminals to record cost accounting data in the detail record. When production is complete, the cost accounting system summarizes costs using data in the work order detail file.

MRP Systems

A material requirements planning (MRP) system is actually a production information system rather than an accounting system. Its purpose is to minimize investment in inventory while ensuring that parts are available for production. This computerized system schedules not only finished products for production but also component parts and subassemblies.

When developing an MRP system, the design team creates a *bill of materials file*. This file contains one record for each product manufactured in the factory. This record shows all the components for the product and the quantities of each component needed. The system uses this information to schedule not only finished products but also the components for production. It arranges the production schedule so that all manufactured components are available when needed for producing the finished product. When the component must be purchased rather than produced, the MRP system produces a purchase requisition for the purchasing application system. It generates this requisition far enough in advance that the purchased material arrives shortly before it is needed for production.

Because a company with an MRP system produces or purchases components only when they are needed, the company avoids carrying inventories of these components. This decreases the financial investment in inventory and lowers storage and spoilage costs.

JIT Systems

The purposes of just-in-time (JIT) systems are to minimize work in process inventory and to eliminate raw materials inventories. This system expands the MRP concept by altering the production process to minimize inventory investments.

A JIT system schedules deliveries of raw materials so that they arrive just in time for the beginning of the production process. A truck delivering raw materials arrives at a receiving dock and unloads the material. Workers immediately move it to the factory and place it into production. In this way, a company using a JIT system avoids costs of carrying and storing raw material. This system requires close coordination between the company implementing JIT and its suppliers.

When a company implements a just-in-time system, its accounting application systems function differently from those you have learned about thus far. Procedures differ in the purchasing, receiving, and cost accounting applications.

Purchasing with JIT.   Many times, companies issue blanket purchase orders to suppliers. These identify the goods requested and create for the purchaser a legal obligation to pay for the goods. However, they do not specify quantities as do individual purchase orders. Instead, the purchasing company must specify quantities required, usually daily, in some other way.

Sometimes purchasing agents inform vendors of the desired quantity by telephone. Other companies use electronic data interchange (EDI) systems; these computer networks link their computerized purchasing systems to the computerized sales order entry systems of their suppliers. Rather than mailing individual purchase orders, the purchasing company transmits purchase order records to the supplier. The supplier's system is programmed to read this record and create from it a sales order detail record. This initiates the procedures in the supplier's order entry system. Usually with such systems, the supplier agrees to fill orders within a few hours of receipt.

Receiving with JIT.   When a company uses JIT, it does not use a single receiving dock. Instead, the company has multiple receiving points near the production facilities that use the material. The supplier must deliver the material not only at the proper time but also to the proper receiving point.

The supplier packages goods to speed the process of counting them on receipt. Usually the receiving personnel do not need to perform inspections because the supplier agrees to maintain certain quality standards prior to becoming an approved vendor. If the supplier does not meet these standards, the purchasing company finds another supplier.

Accounting with JIT.   Frequently, companies that use JIT find that their labor costs decrease. They may cease to report labor costs daily or weekly but instead provide monthly reports.

The company designs its assembly lines to produce one product, so production orders and job cost sheets may become unnecessary. Instead, the company calculates its costs at the end of a month from the quantities of finished goods produced. Since there are few raw materials inventories, the company combines the costs of purchased materials with those of units that are in process.

Similar to MRP, JIT systems are production rather than accounting systems, yet their existence affects how accounting systems process transactions. A case at the end of this chapter explores the implications of JIT for the cost accounting system.

Summary

The conversion cycle processes accounting transactions that record one economic event—the consumption of labor, material, and overhead to produce a salable product or service. This process is different depending on whether it occurs in a service, merchandising, or manufacturing organization.

The economic events in the conversion cycle are recorded by five types of transactions. Two of these, purchase and sale of inventory, are recorded in other transaction cycles. The other transactions are the transfer of material, labor, and overhead into production; the transfer of work in process into finished goods; and payroll.

There are three application systems in this cycle. The inventory system maintains perpetual inventory records and notifies managers when items require replenishing. The cost accounting system determines the costs of goods or services produced. The payroll system calculates the pay due employees, prints paychecks, and maintains cumulative earnings records. This chapter has explored methods of implementing segregation of duties and applying control practices in these systems.

Key Terms

cost center record   A record for a cost center containing data that identify the cost center and recording costs incurred during a reporting period.

employee master record   A record that contains data on each current and past employee that are used in determining payroll deductions and when preparing government reports.

imprest account   A bank checking account kept at a predetermined balance and frequently used for writing paychecks.

inventory master record   A record in a perpetual system for each item maintained in inventory. It shows reference data and the quantity on hand.

job costing system   A cost accounting system that accumulates production costs by job or batch number.

job cost record   In a job costing system, a record that exists for each job. It contains data identifying the job and recording the costs incurred on that job.

job ticket   A document used by factory employees to record the number of hours of their labor devoted to manufacturing each kind of product.

materials requisition   A document that, when completed by a production worker or supervisor, documents the issue of materials for use in production.

periodic method   A method of accounting for inventory that relies on a periodic physical inventory count to determine Cost of Goods Sold and ending inventories.

perpetual method   A method of accounting for inventory in which an organization maintains an ongoing count of each inventory item on hand.

process costing system   A cost accounting system that accumulates production costs by department or cost center.

timecard   A document on which employees record their hours worked. It is the basis for computing their pay.

Questions

19–1. Which economic events produce transactions in the conversion cycle?

19–2. Which types of transactions affect the accounting records in the conversion cycle? Which of them are processed in this cycle?

19–3. What is the purpose of each of the following documents:
    a. Materials requisition ?
    b. Job ticket?
    c. Timecard?
    d. Salary authorization?
    e. Production order?

19–4. What are the two methods of accounting for inventory? Which is most likely in a computer-based system?

19–5. What are two ways of calculating the cost of finished goods inventory? How do they differ?

19–6. Describe five special purpose reports produced in the conversion cycle.

19–7. Which forms do noncomputerized records take in the conversion cycle?

19–8. In a computerized accounting system, which data files are used in the conversion cycle? Identify the purpose of each file.

19–9. In a computer-based accounting system, what are the applications in the conversion cycle? What is the purpose of each?

19–10. Identify three nonaccounting computerized systems that affect the accounting applications in the conversion cycle.

Exercises and Cases

19–11.   *TRANSACTIONS AND DOCUMENTS*

The column on the left lists accounting transactions that affect the conversion cycle. The right column lists documents and reports. Identify the document(s) and report(s) associated with each transaction.

Transaction	Document or Report
a. Purchase inventory.	1. Journal voucher.
b. Sale of inventory.	2. Timecard.
c. Transfer of material and labor.	3. Purchase requisition.
d. Transfer of completed goods.	4. Job ticket.
e. Payroll.	5. Completed production order.
	6. Sales order.
	7. Materials requisition.

19–12.   *TRANSACTIONS AND APPLICATIONS*

The column on the left lists accounting transactions. The right column lists application systems used in the conversion cycle. Identify the application system associated with each transaction.

Transaction	Application System
a. Purchase inventory.	1. Cost accounting.
b. Sale of inventory.	2. Payroll.
c. Transfer of material, labor, and overhead.	3. Inventory.
d. Transfer of completed goods.	
e. Paycheck.	

19–13.   *TAKING PHYSICAL INVENTORY*

A company maintains its detailed inventory records and its general ledger inventory account on a perpetual basis. Thus, the cost of materials entering into production and the cost of inventory on hand for financial statement purposes can be readily determined. Nevertheless, the company takes periodic physical inventories.

Required:

State four reasons why the company should make periodic physical inventory counts.

(CIA Adapted)

19–14.   PERPETUAL INVENTORY METHOD

The year-end physical inventory of a large wholesaler of automotive parts has just been completed. The internal auditor reviewed the inventory-taking instructions before the start of the physical inventory, made and recorded test counts, and observed the controls over the inventory-taking process. No significant exceptions to the process were observed. After completion of the inventory count, the auditor compared quantities shown on count sheets with those listed on the physical inventory report. There were numerous discrepancies.

Required:

a. List five likely causes of such discrepancies.

b. List five inappropriate management actions that might have been taken as a result of relying on incorrect perpetual inventory data.

(CIA Adapted)

19–15.   DESKTOP COMPUTERS

Your company has procured a number of desktop computers for use in various locations and applications. One of these has been installed in the stores department, which has the responsibility for disbursing stock items and maintaining stores records. In this department a competent employee trained in computer applications receives the requisitions for stores, reviews them for completeness and for the propriety of approvals, disburses the stock, maintains the records, operates the computer, and authorizes adjustments to the total amounts of stock accumulated by the computer.

You have discussed the applicable controls with the department manager. The manager states that because the desktop computer is assigned exclusively to that department, it does not require the same types of controls applicable to large computer systems.

Required:

Comment on the manager's contentions. Discuss briefly five controls that would apply to this application.

(CIA Adapted)

19–16.   INVENTORY CONTROL

Alex Corporation manufactures several lines of machine tools for the automotive industry. As a consequence of the high demand for its products, the firm currently operates three shifts, five days a week. Maintenance work is done on the weekends unless breakdowns require immediate attention.

The production supervisors have complained that many times the maintenance work is not completed because parts have not been available in the storeroom. In reviewing the operating and accounting procedures of the maintenance crew and storerooms, the internal audit staff has identified the following procedures:

The maintenance crew consists of three persons, each of whom works 12 hours on most Saturdays and Sundays. Two of the three are on call during the week for breakdowns. Each person on the maintenance crew reports directly to the production supervisor. At the end of the week, the production supervisor leaves a list of maintenance work to be completed. At the end of the weekend, the maintenance crew leaves the list for the supervisor, indicating with a check mark the completed jobs and giving a reason for those not completed.

Maintenance parts and supplies are stored in a separate locked room. Many of the parts and supplies are very small in size and monetary value. However, a large number are very expensive and quite portable. The production supervisor, the receiving supervisor, and all maintenance crew members have keys to this room.

Perpetual inventory cards are maintained for all parts and supplies in the maintenance storeroom; the inventory cards are kept in the maintenance storeroom. When ordered parts and supplies are received, the receiving supervisor places them in the storeroom and records the receipt on the proper perpetual inventory card. The maintenance crew members record deductions on the inventory cards when they take parts and supplies. Parts and supplies are ordered by the receiving supervisor based on notes from the maintenance crew members indicating that quantities are low or depleted.

The accounting department uses the perpetual inventory cards at the end of the month to determine the value of the maintenance parts and supplies inventory. The balances indicated on the inventory cards are multiplied by the most recent prices to determine the carrying value of the maintenance inventory.

Required:

Identify the internal control weaknesses, and recommend improvements regarding the operating and accounting procedures of Alex Corporation's maintenance crew and storeroom.

(CMA Adapted)

19–17.   *PURCHASING AND INVENTORY CONTROL*

At Alden, Inc., raw materials consist mainly of high-cost electronic components kept in a locked storeroom. Storeroom personnel include a supervisor and four clerks. All are well trained, competent, and adequately bonded. Raw materials are removed from the storeroom only on written or oral authorization of one of the production supervisors.

There are no perpetual inventory records, so the storeroom clerks do not keep records of goods received or issued. To compensate for the lack of perpetual records, a physical inventory count is taken monthly by the storeroom clerks, who are well supervised. Appropriate procedures are followed in making the inventory count.

After the physical inventory count, the storeroom supervisor matches quantities counted against a predetermined reorder level. If the count for a given part is below the reorder level, the supervisor enters the part number on a materials requisition list and sends this list to the accounts payable clerk. The accounts payable clerk prepares a purchase order for the predetermined reorder quantity for each part and mails the purchase order to the vendor from whom the part was last purchased.

When ordered materials arrive at Alden, they are received by the storeroom clerks. The clerks count the items and compare the counts to the shipper's bill of lading. All vendors' bills of lading are initialed, dated, and filed in the storeroom to serve as receiving reports.

Required:

Describe the weaknesses in internal control and recommend improvements in Alden's procedures for purchase, receipt, storage, and issue of raw materials.

(AICPA Adapted)

19–18.   *COST ACCOUNTING SYSTEM*

The Phillips Foundry Company, a family-owned company in the greater Chicago area, is engaged in the manufacture of iron castings like barstool bases. It employs about 120 people and has annual sales of $1 million.

The production process for iron castings is composed of four steps: molding, casting, machining, and assembly. The company produces both to customer specifications and to inventory for several selected standard products. In either case, a production order is prepared showing the quantity and specifications of castings to be produced. A job order cost sheet is created to accumulate costs related to each production order. Costs are accumulated in the following manner:

Direct material. Materials requisition slips are filled out by supervisors when materials are needed. At the end of each month, requisitions are sorted by production order number and posted to job order cost sheets.

Direct labor. Employees are required to indicate on their timecards the production order numbers on which they have worked. These labor hours are converted to labor cost, summarized by production order number, and posted to job order cost sheets at the end of each month.

Factory overhead. Actual factory overhead incurred in the plant is totaled at the end of each month. An overhead costing rate is then established by dividing the total factory overhead by labor cost for the month. Concurrent with the posting of labor cost to job order cost sheets, factory overhead, computed by multiplying labor cost with the overhead costing rate, is entered in each job order cost sheet.

Unit costs. When posting to job order cost sheets at the end of the month, sheets marked "JOB COMPLETED" are removed and the costs of material, labor, and factory overhead posted on them are totaled. Unit costs are derived by dividing these total costs by the number of castings produced in these production orders.

During a slow period in April, Johnston Phillips, president and principal owner of the company, was scanning completed job order cost sheets for the past year or so to gain some understanding of the type of castings being produced by the company. He noted that production orders for Bar Stool X135 in lots of 100 came up most frequently. In an attempt to establish the total number of Bar Stool X135 produced during the past year, he pulled out its job order cost sheets. While pulling these sheets, Phillips was puzzled that none showed the same unit cost and that unit costs differed by as much as 60 percent between April and September. Unable to find an answer, he asked one of his golfing friends, management consultant Ronald Thompson, to come to his plant and take a look.

Required:

a. Make recommendations to Johnston Phillips as if you were Ronald Thompson. Present these recommendations in the form of a short letter.

b. In your letter, suggest several reasons why unit costs may differ by as much as 60 percent for the same product produced in different months.

19–19.   *PAYROLL PROCEDURES*

The Kowal Manufacturing Company employs about 50 production workers and has the following payroll procedures:

The factory supervisor interviews applicants and on the basis of the interview either hires or rejects them. An applicant who is hired prepares a W-4 form (Employee's Withholding Exemption Certificate) and gives it to the supervisor. The supervisor writes the hourly rate of pay for the new employee in the corner of the W-4 form and then gives the form to a payroll clerk as notice that the worker has been employed. The supervisor advises the payroll department of rate adjustments.

A supply of blank timecards is kept in a box near the entrance to the factory. Each worker takes a weekly timecard on Monday morning, fills in the name, and notes in pencil daily arrival and departure times. At the end of the week, the workers drop their timecards in a box near the door to the factory.

The completed timecards are taken from the box on Monday morning by a payroll clerk. Two payroll clerks divide the cards alphabetically, one taking the A to L section and the other the M to Z section. Fully responsible for a section of the payroll, each clerk computes the gross pay, deductions, and net pay; posts the details to the employee's earnings records; and prepares and numbers the payroll checks. Employees are automatically removed from the payroll when they fail to turn in timecards.

The payroll checks are manually signed by the chief accountant and given to the supervisor. The supervisor distributes the checks to the workers in the factory and arranges for the delivery of the checks to absent workers. The payroll bank account is reconciled by the chief accountant, who also prepares the various quarterly and annual payroll tax reports.

Required:

List suggestions for improving the Kowal Manufacturing Company's internal control procedures for factory hiring and payroll.

(AICPA Adapted)

19–20.   *TIMEKEEPING*

Olympia Manufacturing Company accounts for all production using job orders. All employees are paid hourly wages and receive time and one-half for overtime. The company's direct labor-hour input process for payroll and job cost determination is summarized in the system flowchart of Exhibit 19–1. Steps A and C are performed in timekeeping, step B in the factory operating departments, step D in payroll, step E in data entry, and step F in computer operations.

Required:

a. For each processing step, A through F, list the possible errors or discrepancies that may occur.
b. Cite the corresponding control procedure that should be in effect for each error or discrepancy.

(AICPA Adapted)

EXHIBIT 19–1

Exercise 19–20

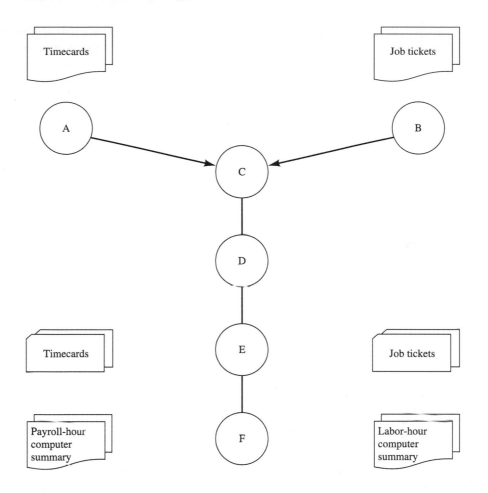

19–21.   INVENTORY SYSTEM

Beccan Company is a discount tire dealer that operates 25 retail stores in the Seattle metropolitan area. Both private brand and name brand tires are sold by Beccan. The company operates a centralized purchasing and warehousing facility and employs a perpetual inventory system. All purchases of tires and related supplies are placed through the company's central purchasing department to take advantage of quantity discounts. The tires and supplies are received at the central warehouse and distributed to the retail stores as needed. The perpetual inventory system at the central facility maintains current inventory records, designated reorder points, optimum order quantities, and continuous stock takings for each type of tire and other related supplies.

The following documents are employed by Beccan in their inventory control system:

> *Retail stores requisition.* This document is submitted by the retail stores to the central warehouse whenever tires or supplies are needed at the stores. The shipping clerks in the warehouse department fill the orders from inventory and have them delivered to the stores.

Purchase requisition. The inventory control clerk in the inventory control department prepares this document when the quantity on hand for an item falls below the designated reorder point. The document is forwarded to the purchasing department.

Purchase order. The purchasing department prepares this document when items need to be ordered. The document is submitted to an authorized vendor.

Receiving report. The warehouse department prepares this document when ordered items are received from vendors. The receiving clerk completes the document by indicating the vendor's name, the date the shipment is received, and the quantity of each item received.

Invoice. An invoice is received from the vendors specifying the amounts owed by Beccan.

The following departments are involved in Beccan's inventory control system:

Inventory control department. The inventory control department is responsible for the maintenance of all perpetual inventory records for all items carried in inventory. This includes current quantity on hand, reorder point, optimum order quantity, and quantity on order for each item carried.

Warehouse department. The warehouse department maintains the physical inventory of all items carried in inventory. All orders from vendors are received by a receiving clerk, and all distributions to retail stores are filled by shipping clerks in this department.

Purchasing department. The purchasing department places all orders for items needed by the company.

Accounts payable department. Accounts payable maintains all open accounts with vendors and other creditors. All payments are processed in this department.

Required:

a. Prepare a document flowchart showing how these documents should be used to provide adequate internal control over receipt, issue, replenishment, and payment.
b. Assume that Beccan plans to computerize its operations.
    1. Design the content of each master record required by your system.
    2. Prepare a system flowchart describing how these operations would occur in a computer-based system.
    3. Describe the control procedures Beccan would use in its system and indicate where these procedures would be placed.

(CMA Adapted)

19–22. *COST ACCOUNTING SYSTEM*

Valpaige Company is an industrial machinery and equipment manufacturer with several production departments. The company employs automated and heavy equipment in its production departments. Consequently, Valpaige has a large repair and maintenance department (R&M) for servicing this equipment.

The operating efficiency of the R&M department has decreased over the past two years. Further, repair and maintenance costs seem to be climbing more rapidly than other department costs. The assistant controller has reviewed the operations of the R&M department and has concluded that the administrative procedures used since the early days of the department are outmoded due in part to the growth of the company. The two major causes for the decrease in operating efficiency, in the opinion of the assistant controller, are an antiquated scheduling system for repair and maintenance work and the actual cost system to distribute the R&M department's costs to the production departments. The actual costs of the R&M department are allocated monthly to the production departments on the basis of the number of service calls made during the month.

The assistant controller has proposed that a formal work order system be implemented for the R&M department. The production departments would submit a service request to the R&M department for the maintenance, including a suggested time for having the work done. The supervisor of the R&M department would prepare a cost estimate on the service request for the work required (labor and materials) and indicate a suggested time for completing the work on the service request. The R&M department supervisor would return the request to the production department that initiated the request. Once the production department okays the work by returning a copy of the service request, the R&M supervisor would prepare a repair and maintenance work order and schedule the job. This work order provides the repair worker with the details of the work to be done and is used to record the actual maintenance hours worked and the materials and supplies used.

Production departments would be charged for actual labor hours worked at a predetermined standard rate for the type of work required. The parts and supplies used would be charged to the production departments at cost.

The assistant controller believes that only two documents are required in this new system. These are a maintenance service request initiated by the production departments and a maintenance work order initiated by the R&M department. These documents would be used to request maintenance work, to charge the production departments for completed work, and to evaluate the performance of the R&M department.

Required:

a. Which data items should be included on the maintenance work order?
b. How many copies of the maintenance work order would be required? How should each copy be distributed?
c. Prepare a document flowchart showing how the maintenance service request and the maintenance work order would be used.
d. Assume that Valpaige decides to develop a computer-based system for processing work orders. Design the record format for the
   1. Maintenance work order master record.
   2. Maintenance service request record.

(CMA Adapted)

19–23.   AUTOMATED DATA ENTRY

After a series of production-level increases, the management of a division of **ITT Space Communications** decided to introduce automated data collection techniques for the payroll and cost accounting systems at one of its plants.[1]

With this system, attendance and payroll records are automatically generated, edited, and summarized without the use of timecards. The system provides information for employee appraisals, unemployment insurance claims, and occasional disciplinary actions. It required changes to the existing manual systems in three areas: data entry, time and attendance reporting, and transaction editing and error corrections.

Data Entry

Each employee authorized to use the system is issued a plastic badge encoded with his or her employee number. This badge allows the employee access to the remote terminals used for data entry.

These terminals at various stations on the manufacturing floor are connected to a central processing unit (CPU) that is dedicated to this application. The dedicated CPU operates independently of the plant's main computer. During the day, the CPU accumulates data in a file. These transactions are off-loaded to the main computer at night. The main computer then produces labor distribution and efficiency reports.

A program executing on the dedicated CPU controls data entry at a terminal. It provides a display shown in Exhibit 19–2. As specific data input is required, individual blocks light up on the terminal. This tells the employee which data should be entered next. As employees became familiar with the operations at the terminals, they developed the ability to bypass the instructions on the screen and enter data without prompts. This greatly speeded up the recording of transactions.

When the CPU recognizes an attempt to enter erroneous data, the red REPEAT button lights up. The employee then presses the REPEAT button and reenters the data. An employee who continues to have trouble can consult with a supervisor who refers to a user's guide. The user's guide describes the procedure in a simple step-by-step format.

Transactions reported through the terminals are time attendance (clocking out and in), standard labor at the completion of each operation, multisequence standard labor (multiple operations against one part number), auxiliary direct labor, project orders (those for a nonstandard part number), transfer of labor to other departments, rework, and engineering change orders.

Time and Attendance Reporting

All time and attendance transactions are recorded in the attendance master file. It contains records similar to those in the payroll master file but omits the pay data. The attendance master file contains one record for each employee and shows such data as the employee number, the employee's supervisor's number, shift, lunch hours, and

---

[1]Adapted from an article by Quentin L. Karchner, Jr., "How One Plant Automated Its Collection of Data," *Management Accounting,* September 1980, pp. 45–48. Copyright by the National Association of Accountants (1980), Montvale, N.J. 07645. Used by permission.

EXHIBIT 19–2

Case 19–23

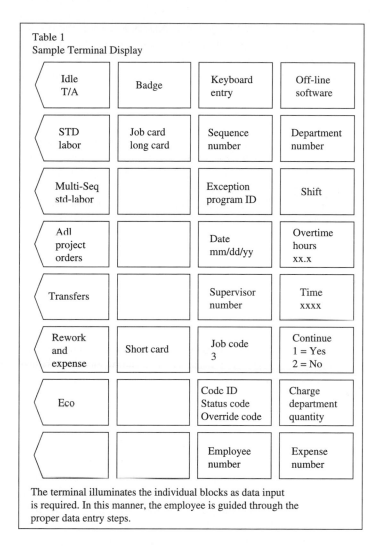

Table 1
Sample Terminal Display

Idle T/A	Badge	Keyboard entry	Off-line software
STD labor	Job card long card	Sequence number	Department number
Multi-Seq std-labor		Exception program ID	Shift
Adl project orders		Date mm/dd/yy	Overtime hours xx.x
Transfers		Supervisor number	Time xxxx
Rework and expense	Short card	Job code 3	Continue 1 = Yes 2 = No
Eco		Code ID Status code Override code	Charge department quantity
		Employee number	Expense number

The terminal illuminates the individual blocks as data input
is required. In this manner, the employee is guided through the
proper data entry steps.

department number. This allows updating the system about an individual employee more frequently than is done with the payroll system. Production supervisors are responsible for updating the attendance master file each day.

The attendance file provides up-to-date information to both the manufacturing and the accounting departments in the plant. To ensure its accuracy, timekeeping personnel are available to advise production supervisors and to review updates to the file. When timekeepers find discrepancies in the attendance master file, they report them to the cost accounting supervisor for correction.

Daily Reports. Twenty minutes after the start of each shift, the system produces the daily absentee report. This report identifies each absent employee, which shift the employee normally works, and the employee's current status (active, medical leave, vacation, etc.).

If an employee is shown as unaccounted for, the production supervisor determines the reason and reports it to timekeeping using the codes printed at the top of the report. Timekeeping personnel enter this information into the system and it is reflected in future reports. The system produces monthly and year-to-date reports showing employees' attendance history for use by management.

A daily labor-hours-worked report is generated and forwarded the next day to the production supervisor. This report discloses for each employee the number of hours worked, the time in, the time out, and the number of authorized overtime hours.

The system also produces daily efficiency reports. These show the supervisor how an employee performed on each different operation during the previous day. This makes the supervisor aware of any employee/job mismatches, unrealistic standards, special assembly problems, and high or low individual performance. The supervisor can take action to correct problems when they occur, rather than speculating about what happened a month later.

Editing Procedures

The system employs both expense editing and work in process editing procedures.

Expense Editing. The expense coding file is the basis for the expense editing. It consists of lists and tables of all acceptable expense and department numbers that can be entered at a terminal. This file is changed whenever changes are made to the direct labor procedures. Expense editing verifies the propriety of transaction expense accounts by comparing codes entered by an employee with codes in this file.

Work in Process Editing. Work in process editing procedures also verify the validity of transactions applied to a work order by employees. The edit program, for example, causes the system to reject a transaction that charges labor to a work order that is closed.

The edit program also determines the reasonableness of the production quantities entered at a terminal. It does this by maintaining a record of the quantity of items processed by the prior operation applied to the work order. If, for a current operation, a worker enters a quantity greater than that shown for the prior one, the transaction is rejected. This procedure also provides exact unit counts for all parts in production under a work order.

By extending these counts at the standard cost for each part, the system calculates the total cost of the work in process inventory located in each production department. When these totals are adjusted for known exceptions such as floor stock, they greatly aid in the process of taking a physical inventory.

Error Correction Procedures. Because of the possibility of errors in data entry, the system provides procedures for their correction. Examples of errors normally encountered include (1) an employee who failed to clock in; (2) an employee who inadvertently clocked out while entering a labor transaction; (3) an employee who clocked out twice; and (4) the failure to clock in or out at lunch hour.

Error correction procedures are called the *daily review routine.* Production supervisors record corrections on the form shown in Exhibit 19–3. They submit this form to timekeeping personnel who enter the corrections in the system. The form is flexible enough, and contains sufficient explanation, so that supervisors find error corrections easy to make.

EXHIBIT 19–3

Case 19–23

Table 2
Corrections to Weekly T & A Records

Date: _____   **Sample Input Form**

Employee number	Date	Hours worked	Shift	Clock time		Optional clock		Optional clock		Shift time		Optional lunch		Day code	Act code	Log day
				In	Out	In	Out	In	Out	Start	Stop	Start	Stop			
1-5	10-14	19-22	22	32-35	36-39	40-43	44-47	48-51		56-59	60-63	64-67	68-71	80	81	85

Action codes
A = Add to file
C = Change file
D = Delete from file
BLANK = Original

Day code
J = Monday-Friday
K = Saturday
L = Sunday

Logical day
Monday	= 1	Friday	= 5
Tuesday	= 2	Saturday	= 6
Wednesday	= 3	Sunday	= 7
Thursday	= 4		

INSTRUCTIONS

Employee number
An employee number is required for all transactions.

Date
A date is required for all transactions, i.e.,
                    10037
Month   Day   Year

Hours worked
Hours are required for all action codes except "D" and "F." Three digits are required, i.e., 02.5
                    tenths
                              hours

Shift
All transactions require a shift except a "D" and "F" action code.

Clock time
Times should be shown in military time, i.e., 0750, 1600. Not required for "D" and "F" action codes.

Optional clock
To be used when additional clock-in and clock-out is required. Not required for "D" and "F" action codes.

Optional lunch
Must be completed if lunch is taken out. If employee does not take lunch do not show hours. Hours should be in military time, i.e., 0850, 1740. Not required for "D" and "F" action codes.

Day code
J, K, or L code is required for all transactions.

Action code
A = Addition to file
C = Change file
D = Delete from file
BLANK = Data entered as terminal input
F = Flush (for timekeeping use only)

Logical day
Required for all transactions.

Benefits of the System

The elapsed time for the development of the system, from initial concept to implementation, was almost a year. Even during parallel operation with the previous manual system, the benefits of the new system began to appear.

During parallel operation, analysts noted differences between the outputs of the automated and the manual systems. These were investigated, and in most cases the manual system was faulty. Invalid shop orders were charged, labor was reported in error, and so forth. Thus the new system was probably producing more accurate results than the old manual one.

The automated collection system has provided more accurate information from the shop floor, reduced paperwork, increased productivity, reduced costs, and provided a means of integrating production data with other management information systems. It has been able to handle significantly higher production volume than the manual system with no increase in timekeeping personnel. Management has estimated that the benefits gained from this system paid for the cost of implementation in less than one year.

In addition, there were intangible benefits—better control of procedures for clocking in and out, error checks as data are entered at its source, daily attendance monitoring, and timely and accurate portrayal of operations.

Required:

What observations do you have concerning the company's automated data collection system?

19–24.   PAYROLL SYSTEM

The Vane Corporation is a manufacturing concern that has been in business for the past 18 years. During this period, the company has grown from a very small family-owned operation to a medium-sized manufacturing concern with several departments. Despite this growth, a substantial number of the procedures employed by Vane Corporation have been in effect since the business was started. Just recently, Vane Corporation has computerized its payroll operations.

The payroll function operates in the following manner: Blank timecards are kept near the factory entrance. After picking up their weekly timecards on Monday morning, workers write in their names and identification numbers. Each day they write on the timecards the time of their arrivals and departures. On the following Monday, the factory supervisors collect the completed timecards for the previous week and send them to data processing.

In data processing the timecards are used to prepare the weekly time file. This file is processed with the master payroll file that is maintained in a sequential file according to worker identification numbers. The checks are written by the computer on the regular checking account and imprinted with the treasurer's signature. After the payroll file is updated and the checks are prepared, the checks are sent to the supervisors who distribute them to the workers or hold them for absent workers to pick up later.

The supervisors notify data processing of new employees and terminations. Any changes in hourly pay rate or any other changes affecting payroll are usually communicated to data processing by the supervisors. The workers also complete a job time ticket for each individual job they work on each day. The job time tickets are collected daily and sent to cost accounting where they are used to prepare a cost distribution analysis.

Further analysis of the payroll function reveals the following:

a. A worker's gross wages never exceed $300 per week.

b. Raises never exceed $0.55 per hour for the factory workers.

c. No more than 20 hours of overtime are allowed each week.

d. The factory employs 150 workers in 10 departments.

The payroll function has not been operating smoothly for some time, but even more problems have surfaced since the payroll was computerized. The supervisors have indicated that they would like a weekly report indicating worker tardiness, absenteeism, and idle time so they can determine the amount of productive time lost and the reason for the lost time.

Required:

a. Identify the control weaknesses in the payroll procedures.

b. Suggest which application controls could be designed into Vane Corporation's payroll processing programs.

(CMA Adapted)

19–25.   JUST-IN-TIME SYSTEMS

Just-in-time (JIT) systems refer to a class of manufacturing systems that attempt to minimize inventories of raw and partially finished products.[2] When successfully implemented, such a system improves productivity by linking all production operations together in a smooth, uninterrupted flow.

Hewlett-Packard Company (HP) implemented a JIT system, which it calls repetitive manufacturing, in one of its plants recently. This system required significant changes to its methods of accounting for production costs.

JIT at Hewlett-Packard

Prior to developing the system, Hewlett-Packard management identified five goals for it: total quality control, reduction of inventory, cooperation with vendors, 100 percent on-time deliveries, and emphasis on cost reduction while maintaining employee satisfaction. No employees were unionized, none were paid on an incentive basis, and each was eligible for an annual bonus depending on overall company profits.

Production Control. As a new facility involved in the production of data storage devices, the plant's layout was designed to implement JIT concepts. The production line was set up in a U-shaped cell, so that one unit at a time would pass along the line. Exhibit 19–4 shows its arrangement.

---

[2]Adapted from "Kanban, ZIPS, and Cost Accounting: A Case Study," by B. R. Neumann and P. R. Jaouen. *Journal of Accountancy*, August 1986, pp. 132–41. Copyright © 1986 by American Institute of CPAs. Used by permission.

EXHIBIT 19–4

Case 19–25

HP production "U"

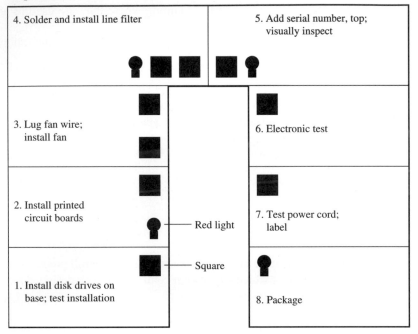

4. Solder and install line filter	5. Add serial number, top; visually inspect
3. Lug fan wire; install fan	6. Electronic test
2. Install printed circuit boards	— Red light 7. Test power cord; label
1. Install disk drives on base; test installation	— Square 8. Package

In this diagram, the squares represent the physical locations of bins, racks, or pallets near each worker. They provide a visible signal indicating when a given employee may pass a unit to the next worker.

If an employee's outgoing square is filled, the employee may either complete the unit being worked on, sit idle, or help another employee. However, he or she may not begin work on another unit. When a quality or production problem occurs, the entire line shuts down and a flashing red light attracts help from a supervisor, other employees, or engineers.

At all times the slowest workstation is being analyzed to make it faster. As soon as it improves, the next slowest station is analyzed, and so on. The result is a continual process of upgrading quality and making production a smooth process. The goal is to make the physical material "flow like water" through the production line.

Inventory Control. HP management desires to manage inventory on a real-time basis and minimize their investment in it. Inventory reduction is achieved by having many raw materials delivered straight to production lines, bypassing the storeroom. They use monthly rolling forecasts, long-term contracts, and a commitment to work together with vendors. This has resulted in vendors supplying 100 parts with a two-week lead time and daily deliveries.

Annual physical counts of inventory are no longer sufficient. These have been replaced by one-minute monthly physical inventories or perpetual cycle counts. The ultimate goal is to function in such a way that no physical verification is needed at year-end.

Because of these policies, warehouse space has been reduced by 50 percent, and units produced per square foot have doubled. The total inventory supply decreased from

2.8 months to 1.3 months within a six-month period. The number of vendors has decreased from 50 to 24, and there has been a 30 percent reduction in raw material inspections.

Cost Accounting Procedures

Historically, the cost accounting system used by HP had been a work order–based job costing system. With this approach, labor, materials, and overhead were assigned to work orders, and average unit costs were calculated for each work order.

With JIT, work orders have been eliminated and specific unit costs are deemphasized. The resulting cost accounting system is a hybrid containing some elements of both job and process costing. In addition, many of the traditional job and process cost accounts are eliminated.

Accounting for Material. After implementing JIT, Hewlett-Packard eliminated work orders and work in process inventory accounts. Unlike traditional manufacturing systems, at HP parts buildups are limited within each workstation. Therefore, the parts component of work in process is relatively immaterial. HP has combined it with the much-reduced raw materials inventories, creating a new account called raw and in process inventory (RIP).

To account for manufacturing costs without requisitions or work orders, HP uses a postmanufacturing deduction procedure. Raw materials costs (in RIP) are transferred to finished goods inventories when the unit is completed. Material usage variances are recognized after they are incurred by the use of a manual tracking system based on quantities of scrap.

Accounting for Labor. Prior to implementing JIT, management recognized that excessive resources were used to account for direct labor costs. Although simplicity was being emphasized in the manufacturing process, this had not translated into simplicity in the accounting records. Detailed records were kept assigning worker time to products, inspection, and training. These were no longer consistent with the team concept used in the manufacturing process.

Direct labor accounted for approximately 2.8 percent of total production costs and less than 1 percent of total inventory costs. So HP accountants decided to cease charging direct labor to manufacturing processes and to quit tracking them through the inventory accounts. Instead, they expense direct labor and overhead on a monthly basis. They also maintain in the RIP and finished goods inventory accounts a base level of labor and overhead costs.

Direct labor costs are still identified with groups of major products by summarizing the total direct labor costs and the number of units produced in each department. Accountants analyze direct labor costs quarterly or as needed, but unitary labor costs are not used to transfer costs between manufacturing processes.

Accounting for Overhead. In a traditional cost accounting system, overhead costs are allocated to products based on a direct labor activity measure such as hours or costs. HP determined that in this plant about half its overhead costs are more closely related to materials procurement and manufacturing support than to direct labor time. (Materials procurement activities include purchasing, receiving, stockroom, materials planning, and materials engineering. Manufacturing support entails manufacturing engineering, quality assurance, manufacturing management, and central EDP.) Using direct labor time as an allocation basis would, therefore, penalize departments with many small or inexpensive parts, but whose production line is longer than that of departments with relatively large parts but shorter production times.

Because of this, HP accountants identified three separate overhead allocation bases. For costs related to procurement activities, they allocate overhead according to department material costs. They allocate indirect overhead using total direct costs. Production overhead costs are allocated using estimated cycle times. The cycle time is the time to process one unit, and it equals the total time for production, waiting in squares, testing, and machine operation.

For accounting purposes, labor and overhead costs are lumped together. At the same time, detailed standards and actual costs are maintained for groups of products such that data is available for inventory valuation, performance measurement, and pricing decisions.

Results of JIT at HP

Because the data storage unit was never produced at this plant under a different manufacturing system, it is difficult to generalize about JIT's effects on reducing costs. However, accountants have been able to develop some specific comparisons concerning costs and efficiency.

Effects on Costs. The actual cost per unit for direct material, ignoring inflation, decreased by 33 percent over the first 18-month period. Because some additional investments were required, there has been no change in labor and overhead costs per unit. Period expenses, which include material scrap and rework, have decreased 39 percent per unit. This may have had a small impact on material usage.

Additional investments include those in training and in emphasizing teamwork on the production floor. In this environment, teamwork is essential so HP holds team meetings to discuss stress, quality, and line balancing issues. Educating employees about why HP converted to JIT has also been emphasized.

The per unit factory labor and overhead cost did not significantly improve during this first 18-month period. With a 500 percent increase in quantity produced, one would expect a per unit decrease. Failure to reduce factory overhead was due to the addition of new factory floor space and additional manufacturing, engineering, and support staff.

Effects on Efficiency. HP's JIT system has resulted in numerous benefits in other areas. Warehouse space has been reduced by 50 percent, while units produced per square foot have doubled. There has been a 48 percent reduction in the number of vendors, and a 30 percent reduction in incoming inspection. This accompanies a 300 percent increase in volume and a 10 percent increase in personnel.

Another positive result is the 60 percent reduction in raw material accounting transactions at this plant each month. This significant saving eliminates the collection and processing of work orders. Both product and raw material inventories have also been reduced. Although actual production time per unit has remained relatively constant, warranty costs are significantly below the average for all plants manufacturing this product.

Conclusions

Although HP has evolved many innovative techniques for cost accounting in a repetitive manufacturing environment, the evolution is not complete.

Undeniably, a major benefit of this system is the accounting time saved by reducing the number of transactions. The characteristics of repetitive manufacturing have led to simplified accounting. As physical material flows are smoothed, accounting material flows are streamlined. Production variances are recognized more through manufacturing process control techniques and less through accounting systems.

JIT has significantly affected cost accounting at HP. Nevertheless, this cost accounting system retains its basic objectives of providing information for inventory valuation, performance measurement, and pricing and operating decisions.

Required:

a. How do the inventory control and cost accounting systems at this factory differ from a traditional factory's systems?

b. Are the cost accounting methods described in this case consistent with generally accepted accounting principles? Why or why not?

19–26. *MANUFACTURING CONTROL SYSTEM—PART IV*

Lockheed Austin Division (LAD) was formed in August 1981 by Lockheed Missiles & Space Company, Inc., of Sunnyvale, California. Headquartered in Austin, Texas, LAD began operations in June 1982 with 30 employees, mostly scientists and engineers who worked on projects for the U.S. military. By 1984, the division had grown to over 2,000 people engaged in the development and manufacture of Navy and Air Force communications and surveillance systems.

LAD had become a melting pot of people, projects, and systems that had been added gradually with little planning or coordination. As a result, there was no integrated information system that allowed everyone access to the same information. A worker in one department who had a question about a project or operation had to go to several other departments for answers. Most of the systems being used in Austin were based in Sunnyvale, so employees at LAD had little input into how they worked. Furthermore, LAD couldn't operate unless the Sunnyvale computers were operating. In this environment, LAD could not predict when it was going to deliver its products. It had problems meeting schedules and budgets, and it was about to lose its competitive position in the marketplace.

It formed a system study team to analyze its information needs by business area. This team recommended a new manufacturing control system that would interface with LAD's budgeting, payroll, inventory, purchasing, and general ledger systems. Top management then formed a project team from all affected business areas to design and implement a new system—the operational support system (OSS).

Exhibit 19–5 shows a high-level diagram of the resulting system. As a defense contractor, LAD's cost accounting system was required to accumulate costs by government contract. Each contract was broken down into *work packages*—a work package was a set of related tasks required by the contract. Direct costs were traced to individual work packages and indirect costs allocated to them.

EXHIBIT 19–5

Case 19–26: LAD Financial Systems—High-Level Diagram of Modules

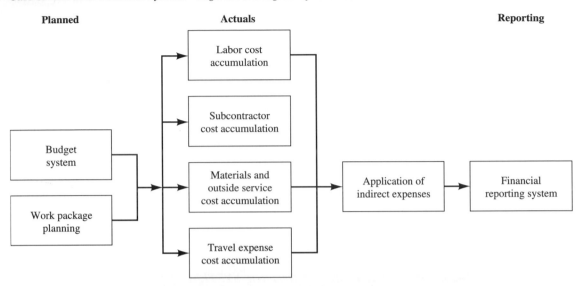

Four subsystems recorded actual cost data. These systems were labor cost accumulation, subcontractor cost accumulation, materials and outside service cost accumulation, and travel expense cost accumulation. To these direct costs the system allocated indirect expenses using overhead rates. Separate budget and work package planning systems allowed the financial reporting system to compare planned with actual activities and costs and report variances.

Exhibit 19–6 contains a diagram of the operational support system. It consisted of seven modules that rely on data from a centralized database management system. In this diagram, the shop floor control system assigned specific tasks to work centers or machines in the factory. The order management system kept track of the status of individual production orders. The configuration management system maintains data on the production facilities currently in place. The product assurance module maintained quality control data. The planning modules (materials requirements planning, master planning and scheduling, and asset and capacity planning) anticipate how to allocate current orders to existing production capacity and how to expand capacity in order to meet future needs.

Although significant time and resources are now devoted to satisfying system requirements, it now provides division-level management with more information and cost data than was available before. OSS is a real-time integrated system that provides better operating control throughout the company. Now minute by minute or day by day, a manager can check on project or employee data at any time, rather than relying on reports produced once a week or once a month. This reporting ability enables LAD management to react immediately to any kind of situation that arises.

Required:

a. What were the components of the cost accounting system at LAD? Is this a process costing or a job costing system? Explain your reasons.

EXHIBIT 19–6

Case 19–26: LAD Operational Support System—Overview of Modules

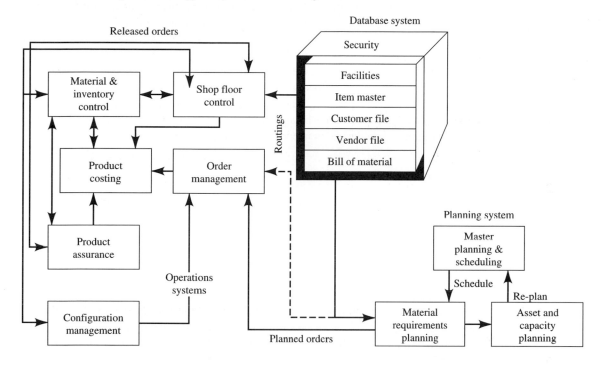

b. What were the nonaccounting modules that were a part of OSS? What kinds of data do you think these modules provided to the cost accounting system?

19–27. BAR CODING

Pillotex Corporation, located in Dallas, Texas, operates nine separate manufacturing plants throughout the United States. It sells a diverse line of pillows under both the Pillowtex and private labels to most major retailers in the country.[3] On average, it produces about 1.5 million pillows per month, but during the peak fall period a single location may produce as many as 20,000 per day. Pillowtex has developed systems to use bar coding and electronic data interchange (EDI) in order to shorten lead times and improve responsiveness to customers.

The Old System

Before automating its production capabilities, Pillowtex tracked its inventory manually. Workers on the shop floor packed finished goods into containers and were then respon-

---

[3]Adapted from "'Pillow Talk' for Productivity," by Lawrence Klein and Randy M. Jacques, *Management Accounting,* February 1991, pp. 47–49. Copyright by the Institute of Management Accountants (1991), Montvale, N.J. 07645. Used by permission.

sible for recording them on a written production order. As the order was shipped, the production order went to a data entry group where another employee would verify the information and use a terminal to key the data into an inventory transaction file. Later, batches of transactions were used to update the inventory system.

The old system's reliance on human processing provided opportunities for error. Often the shop floor worker counted the quantities within cartons inaccurately, and sometimes the data entry clerk entered this data incorrectly in the computer system. Even when these errors did not occur, the inventory records were not updated until after shipment of the order. The lag between shipment of the order and the file update process, which could sometimes be significant, meant that correct information was not readily available when decisions needed to be made.

Bar Codes in the Manufacturing Cycle

A few of Pillowtex's suppliers attach bar codes, according to preset specifications, to raw materials before shipping to the company. This marks the material with Pillowtex's own inventory item number in a form readable by a bar code reader. When materials that have not been coded arrive from other suppliers, Pillowtex personnel use a bar code printer to mark gummed labels and attach these to the raw material. Labels from either source are scanned when the materials arrive to update raw materials inventory records.

The manufacturing cycle begins when Pillowtex receives a customer's order, usually via EDI. Production personnel retrieve raw materials required for the order and scan the bar-coded labels, this time subtracting the material from inventory quantities. Production workers then fill the pillow, sew it, and mark it with a new bar code label. This label can be read with the basic point-of-sale bar code equipment used by many customers.

After completing the manufacturing process, another scan transfers the items from work in process to finished goods. Workers then pack the finished goods in containers. Another employee uses a bar code printer to prepare a container label that identifies the customer number, finished goods inventory item number, and quantity. Warehouse personnel use this code to track the boxed goods until they are shipped to the customer. At the time of shipment, they use it to create a shipping notice and close the customer order. This system enables the warehouse to determine exactly what was sent to each customer and assists in preventing premature shipment of incomplete orders.

Results

The new inventory control system significantly improves the integrity of the inventory database and gives management data on inventory levels in real time. It provides up-to-the-minute status on raw material, work in process, and finished goods inventories. Bar codes are the source for shipping information and are used by retailers in controlling their own inventories. The implementation of this technology has enabled Pillowtex to move to just-in-time manufacturing, which enables it to satisfy unique retailer requirements without disrupting its own processes.

For the retailer that cooperates with Pillowtex in establishing coding standards, the system means simplified inventory control, faster service at checkout, and an increase in sales due to quicker inventory replacement. The retailer can scan merchandise upon receipt and use the bar-coded labels to route it through the warehouse. At the point of sale, the bar code reader scans the label, deducts the item from inventory, verifies its price, and produces a customer receipt. The store manager can use this data to analyze sales and inventory levels knowing that the data are current and accurate. Some retailers use data on inventory levels to trigger automatic reorders of certain items.

Bar code and EDI technology has enabled the company to improve its competitive position by increasing the accuracy and speed of its data collection processes. The technology has produced better decisions and improved efficiency for Pillowtex and for its customers. This benefit is ultimately passed on to the consumer in the form of lower prices and better selections.

Required:

a. What procedures in a traditional inventory control system did Pillowtex's bar code system replace?
b. What control risks exist with bar code systems of the type described? Can you suggest some control procedures to minimize these risks?

19–28.   INTEGRATIVE CASE—-PART IV

Agee Company is a manufacturer of large diameter valves located in a major southwestern city. Management has engaged a local CPA firm to aid the company in updating its accounting systems, and you have been assigned to a design team responsible for developing the new processes. Members of the team include management accountants, Agee operating personnel, and representatives of the CPA firm's staff. The team leader is an experienced systems analyst from the CPA firm. In this chapter, you will complete assignments that allow you to participate in the design of application systems in Agee's conversion cycle. For background information, you may refer to Part I of the case in Chapter 16.

Your team leader has given you the following preliminary system design (PSD) for four proposed systems in Agee's conversion cycle. The PSD is incomplete, consisting of a short narrative and a system flowchart for each one. Make any assumptions necessary to complete the requirements, but state your assumptions.

Payroll System

The payroll system at Agee is a batch processing system that is executed each Friday. In the morning, supervisors collect a timecard from each hourly employee. The timecard shows the employee's name, job worked on, and the time the employee punched in and punched out for the workweek ending on Thursday. The supervisor examines the timecard for accuracy and signs it. A payroll clerk collects the timecards from all supervisors and brings them to the accounting department where checks are prepared. The clerk enters the hours worked for each employee in the system. Using data from the employee file, the system then calculates gross pay, deductions, and net pay. The system updates the employees' earnings records and prints the paychecks. After all checks are printed, the system prints a labor distribution control report that shows the labor expense accounts that should be debited.

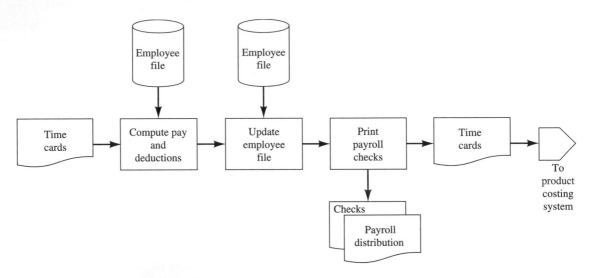

Material Issues System

Warehouse clerks execute this system to record the issue of material from inventory. When material is needed in the factory, a supervisor completes a stores request form and sends it to the warehouse. The warehouse clerk checks the inventory file to determine the location and quantity on hand. If the material is in stock, the clerk updates the inventory file, issues the material, notes on the stores request the quantity issued, and sends it to the cost accountant. The system compares the new quantity on hand to the inventory reorder point for that item. If the quantity is less than the reorder point, the system prints a material requisition for the purchasing agent.

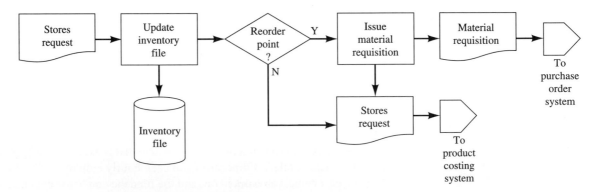

Work in Process System

Agee uses a job cost system that updates cost accounting records each Friday. The cost accountant examines the production orders for goods in process and from that estimates the number of equivalent units of production for each job. Using timecards and stores requests collected over the past week, the accountant enters into the system the costs for material, labor, and allocated overhead added to work in process inventory. The system uses this entry to update the production cost file and the general ledger.

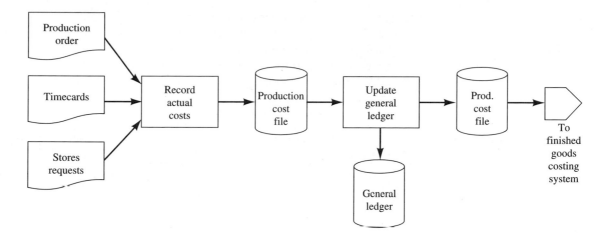

Finished Goods System

After determining work in process, the accountant executes the finished goods system to calculate the cost of goods transferred into finished goods inventory. The accountant enters in the system data from the production orders completed during the period. From this data and the production cost file, the system determines the cost of jobs completed and prints standard cost variance reports. It also makes an entry in the general ledger master file.

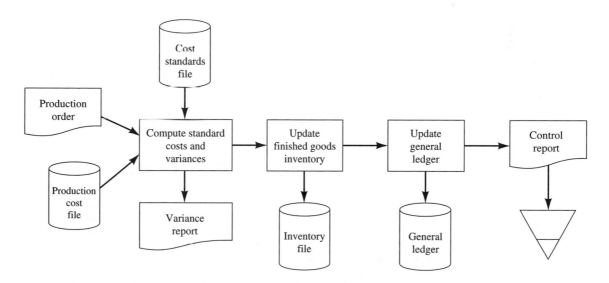

Required:

a. What observations do you have about this preliminary design? Do you think that modifications are needed?

b. Prepare a data flow diagram for the payroll system.

c. Design the payroll distribution control report for the payroll system.

    d. Design a register for the material issues system.

    e. Develop a record layout for the production cost file.

    f. Design a data entry screen for the material issues system.

    g. Design a variance report for the finished goods system.

    h. What control procedures should you incorporate in the applications of Agee's conversion cycle?

20 FINANCIAL CYCLE APPLICATIONS

Learning Objectives

1. To learn the kinds of transactions processed in the financial cycle.
2. To find out which reports and records are produced in the financial cycle.
3. To understand how accounting transactions are processed by the application systems in the financial cycle.
4. To see how control practices and procedures are applied in the financial cycle.

Introduction

Chapter 1 presented a conceptual model describing how accounting systems work. You reviewed the basic records in an accounting system and how to use the accounting cycle. For simplicity, this model assumed that all accounting records were in human-readable form. This chapter presents the activities in the accounting cycle with a computer-based system. These activities are a part of the financial cycle.

In this transaction cycle, the accounting system records two economic events. First, the business raises capital from owners and creditors. A journal entry system processes these and other infrequent transactions. Second, the business uses this capital to acquire the productive assets used to generate revenue. A property system records these transactions.

This transaction cycle also performs a third function that is not really an economic event—the financial reporting function. The financial cycle reports to the sources of capital and to managers concerning the results of its operations. A financial reporting system reports to external entities by summarizing accounting data and presenting them in financial statements. Sometimes it includes a responsibility accounting system that reports budgeted and actual costs to individual managers. The journal entry and financial reporting applications are sometimes called the components of a *general ledger system*. Illustration 20–1 summarizes the components of the financial cycle.

ILLUSTRATION 20–1

The Financial Cycle

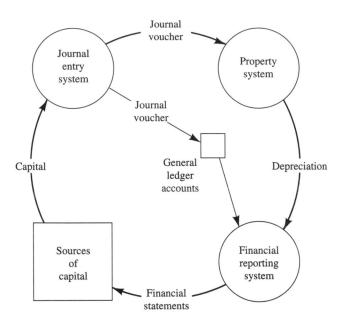

Debt and Equity Capital

Sources of an organization's capital include its owners and its creditors. The organization receives cash from these sources and invests this cash in productive assets. The journal entry system, described later in this chapter, processes the accounting transactions that record these events.

Capital Transactions

Organizations engage in three forms of capital transactions: bank loans, bond issues, and issues of capital stock.

Bank Loans.   Small organizations receive most of their debt financing in the form of bank loans. These may be medium- or long-term loans secured by mortgages on property, or they may be unsecured short-term loans. Large organizations usually rely on bank loans for short- or medium-term financing. If the organization has a good credit rating, these may be unsecured or they may be secured by mortgages. The journal entry system records bank loans in the Notes Payable account.

Bond Issues.   Large organizations acquire medium- and long-term capital by issuing bonds. When an organization issues bonds, it creates a contractual obligation to pay a fixed amount of interest to purchasers of the bonds at intervals specified in the contract. Ordinarily, the contract, or *bond indenture,* requires interest payments twice a year and repayment of the principal amount to the purchaser in 5 to 30 years.

   The journal entry system records each bond issue in a separate long-term liability account. The balance sheet summarizes bond issues under the heading Bonds Payable.

Stock Issues.   Corporations issue common and preferred stock in return for capital. Each share of stock represents an ownership interest in the corporation. A share of stock always has a *par* or *stated* value, which is commonly an even amount, such as $1 or $10 per share. The corporate charter and bylaws, legal documents created at incorporation, state the quantities, par or stated values, and classes of stock that the corporation may issue.

Corporations maintain different Capital Stock accounts for each class of stock. They record the par or stated value of issued shares in Common Stock and Preferred Stock accounts. They record amounts received that exceed the par or stated values in one or more accounts called *Paid-in-Capital in Excess of Par.*

Accounting Records for Debt and Equity Capital

Organizations keep separate subsidiary records for the Notes Payable, Bonds Payable, and Capital Stock accounts. When they are noncomputerized, accountants call them *subsidiary ledgers;* when computerized, they are master files.

Notes Payable Ledger.   If an organization has many notes outstanding, it may have a notes payable ledger. This ledger (or master file) is the subsidiary ledger for the Notes Payable account. It contains one page or record for each note outstanding. The record identifies the note, its holder, its maturity, its interest rate, and the original and current balance.

Bondholders Ledger.   The *bondholders ledger* maintains records of all the individuals or organizations that have purchased bonds. These records show their names and addresses, the bond certificate number, and the face value of the bonds they own. They provide the information necessary to issue interest checks.

A company with one outstanding bond issue has only one bondholders ledger. A large company has a separate bondholders ledger for each bond issue. Each is a subsidiary ledger for one Bonds Payable account. Frequently an organization employs a bank, called the *independent trustee,* to maintain the bondholders ledger.

Stockholders Ledger.   The *stockholders ledger* maintains data on all individuals or organizations that have purchased stock. It contains their names, addresses, the stock certificate number, the date the certificate was issued, and the number of shares. The stockholders ledger contains the information necessary to issue dividend checks.

A company maintains a separate stockholders ledger for each class of capital stock. Small corporations that issue only common stock have only one stockholders ledger. Larger companies may have multiple ledgers. Companies whose stock is traded on stock exchanges employ banks to maintain their stockholders ledgers. A bank performing this service is a *stock transfer agent.*

Controls for Debt and Equity Transactions

The most important control policies and procedures affecting debt and equity transactions concern authorization procedures for the transactions and segregation of duties over them.

Controls for Bank Loans.   An organization should have formal procedures for authorizing bank loans. The level of required management approval depends on the organization and the amount of the loan. Written company policies specify the level of approval required for loans of different amounts and durations.

Most organizations allow an appropriate officer, such as a treasurer, to authorize short-term loans. The board of directors should authorize large or long-term loans. The controller, as head of the accounting department, is responsible for recording the transactions.

Controls for Bond Issues.   The best control for bond issues is the use of an independent trustee. The trustee, a large bank, is experienced in handling these transactions. It has employees trained in processing bonds efficiently and safely. Most organizations that issue bonds consider the use of an independent trustee cost-beneficial.

An independent trustee performs four functions:

- It maintains the bondholders ledger, changing the records as bonds are sold, traded, or recalled.
- It has custody of bond certificates, issues new ones, and cancels old ones.
- It issues checks to bondholders representing interest payments and payments of principal at maturity.
- It represents the bondholders during the life of the bonds, ensuring that the borrowing organization complies with the terms of the bond indenture.

The board of directors should authorize any new bond issue and the selection of the independent trustee.

Controls for Stock Issues.   Large corporations usually employ an independent registrar and a stock transfer agent. Large banks provide these services, which are similar to those that independent trustees provide for bond issues. A single bank may serve in both capacities.

The independent registrar represents the interest of the stockholders. It monitors stock issues and determines that they do not exceed the quantities allowed by the corporate charter or bylaws. It verifies that all transactions in capital stock have been properly authorized by the board of directors or by vote of the stockholders.

The stock transfer agent maintains the stockholders ledger. It records changes in stock ownership, maintains custody of blank stock certificates, issues certificates to new owners, and cancels certificates when shares are sold. It also issues dividend checks to stockholders.

Smaller companies often do not use independent registrars and transfer agents. These companies should assign responsibilities so that no one individual has custody of blank stock certificates, signs the certificates, and maintains the stockholders ledger. The person who maintains the stockholders ledger should not sign dividend checks. All stock certificates and dividend checks should be prenumbered.

Often the treasurer of a small company maintains the stock certificates and signs dividend checks. The president signs stock certificates, and the controller maintains the stockholders ledger.

Because debt and equity transactions are relatively infrequent and represent large amounts, top management usually monitors them closely. Illustration 20–2 summarizes controls over these transactions.

ILLUSTRATION 20–2

Control Activities for Debt and Equity Transactions

Activity	Bank Loans	Bond Issues	Stock Issues
Transaction authorization	*a.* Executive management authorizes	*a.* Board of directors authorizes	*a.* Board of directors authorizes, stockholders approve
Security for assets and records		*a.* Independent trustee locks up certificates	*a.* Transfer agents locks up certificates
Segregation of duties	*a.* Authorization for bank loans separate from recordkeeping	*a.* Independent trustee	*a.* Independent registrar and stock transfer agent
			b. Custody of certificates, signing certificates, and maintain stockholders ledger.
			c. Sign dividence checks and maintain stockholders ledger
Adequate documents and records	*a.* Written, formal authoriza-tion procedures	*a.* Board of directors approves interest payments	*a.* Board of directors authorizes all dividends
	b. Higher-level approvals for larger or longer-term loans	*b.* Prenumbered certificates	*b.* Prenumbered certificates

Property Systems

The purpose of a property system is to maintain an accurate record of all depreciable property, plant, and equipment. It also maintains records of annual and accumulated depreciation on this property.

Property System Transactions and Documents

A property system records three types of transactions: the acquisition, depreciation, and disposition of property.

Acquisition of Property.   Companies use buildings and equipment when generating revenue. The expenditure cycle processes the acquisition transactions. Because of its long life, accountants treat property as an investment of capital. They record the acquisition of property in Property, Plant, and Equipment accounts. An example entry is

Dr.	Buildings	....	xxx
Cr.		Accounts Payable	....	xxx

Property acquisitions may represent significant amounts; thus, most organizations establish policies governing them. These policies require approval of all purchases; larger purchases require approvals at higher levels in the organization. For example, purchases of less than $10,000 may require a department head's approval. Those between $10,000 and $100,000 may require approval of an officer, and larger expenditures must be approved by the board of directors. Employees request the asset's acquisition and document its approval on a *capital acquisition request*.

Sometimes companies construct property and equipment themselves. In this case, a *capital work order*, approved by top management or the board of directors, authorizes construction. Material requisitions and job tickets document the costs of construction. The completed capital work order documents the preceding journal entry.

Depreciation.   Accountants use depreciation to approximate the consumption of property, plant, and equipment as the firm produces goods or services. For financial reporting, organizations compute depreciation using a method allowable by generally accepted accounting principles (GAAP). For computing their U.S. federal income tax, they use a method allowable by law. Accountants add each year's depreciation expense to an account called *Accumulated Depreciation* with an entry such as

```
Dr.   Depreciation Expense  . . . . . . . . . . . . . . . . . . .   xxx
Cr.       Accumulated Depreciation—Buildings . . . . . . . . . . . . .   xxx
```

Accountants usually make this entry at year-end while closing the books. A *journal voucher,* frequently a standard journal voucher, documents the entry.

Disposition of Property.   Ultimately a business disposes of all of its revenue-producing property. If the property has value, they sell it; otherwise, they abandon it. The accounting entry recording this transaction may take several forms. The simplest form occurs when an asset is sold for its net book value:

```
Dr.   Cash . . . . . . . . . . . . . . . . . . . . . . . . . . . . . . . . .xxx
Dr.       Accumulated Depreciation—Buildings . . . . . . .xxx
Cr.       Buildings . . . . . . . . . . . . . . . . . . . . . . . . . . . . . . . . .xxx
```

More frequently, the organization records a gain or loss on the sale. In some cases, no cash is received; these transactions require different accounting entries.

Because entries of this kind can take many different forms, accountants document them on journal vouchers. Many organizations authorize the disposition of property on a ***retirement work order.*** This document, which must be approved by top management, prevents employees from falsifying an entry on a journal voucher to cover the theft of an asset.

Property System Reports

Control Reports and Registers.   A system produces control reports to allow employees to monitor the actions of the system. By reviewing a control report, an accountant or data control clerk determines that a data entry clerk entered the proper number or amounts of transactions in a file or that a computer program executed correctly. Illustration 20–3 shows a control report used in a property system. It lists all deletions from property records made by a clerk and allows verification that they were made properly.

A register is a report listing the transactions of a specific type processed during a reporting period. It provides an audit trail by showing the changes that occurred in an account balance during the period. It also allows an accountant to review changes made to computer files by a program.

Illustration 20–4 contains a register used in the property system. Called an *asset acquisition schedule,* it shows the assets added to the Office Furniture account during the fiscal year. A similar register shows additions to other property, plant, and equipment accounts. Property systems also produce asset disposition schedules that show disposals of property, plant, and equipment.

ILLUSTRATION 20–3

A Property System Control Report

```
RUN DATE: 11/26/98        Fixed Assets Sample Co.              PAGE  1
RUN TIME:  2:02 PM            Fixed Assets
                           ASSET PURGE REPORT


   CLASS:  FURN    OFFICE FURNITURE

   ASSET                                  ACQ          DIS
   CODE         DESCRIPTION/SERIAL NO     DATE         DATE


   DESK2    WORK DESK AND ACCESSORIES   07/19/95    10/22/97


   TOTAL ASSETS PURGED        1
```

Special Purpose Reports.   Property systems produce two special purpose reports: property listings and depreciation schedules.

Property Listing.   The property listing identifies the location of all property, plant, and equipment. Employees produce this report periodically and use it when conducting a

ILLUSTRATION 20–4

A Property System Register

```
RUN DATE: 11/26/98                 Fixed Assets Sample Co.                        PAGE  1
RUN TIME:  1:25 PM                     Fixed Assets
                                  Asset Acquisition Schedule

CLASS: FURN
     OFFICE FURNITURE              Asset Acquisition Schedule        FOR FISCAL YEAR ENDING 12/31/98

       ----ASSET----    DEPT     ACQ/DIS              METHOD/  LIFE/ OPT REC  ORIG COST/   SEC 179/
  CODE  DESCRIPTION/SERIAL NO N/U  DATE   SALES PRICE BOOK ITC RATE TEFRA SW ST-L ACCUM DEP  TEFRA ADJ SALVAGE VAL

WDESK1 Walnut Desk        0    05/22/98    0.00  TAX  DBA    5.0    0     1500.00    0.00      0.00
                          N                            0      0     0      300.00    0.00
                                                 FIN  DBA    5.0    0     1500.00    0.00      0.00
            VENDOR                                     0      0     0      300.00    0.00
            LOCATION                             OPT  DBA    5.0    0     1500.00    0.00      0.00
                                                      0      0     0      300.00    0.00

CLASS:   OFFICE FURNITURE
TOTALS                                    0.00             TAX         1500.00    0.00      0.00
NUMBER OF ASSETS:    1                                                  300.00    0.00
                                                          FIN         1500.00    0.00      0.00
                                                                       300.00    0.00
                                                          OPT         1500.00    0.00      0.00
                                                                       300.00    0.00
```

physical count of property. A property listing provides detail that supports the balances in Property, Plant, and Equipment accounts. Illustration 20–5 contains a property listing.

Depreciation Schedule. The depreciation schedule shows annual depreciation amounts for items of property. In a manual system, an accountant prepares this report for each item when it is acquired. Periodically a batch processing system prints this schedule for all property. In an on-line real-time system, an employee can obtain this information for a specific item of interest and display it on a terminal or print it in a report.

ILLUSTRATION 20–5

A Property Listing

```
RUN DATE: 11/26/98                    Fixed Assets Sample Co.                      PAGE  1
RUN TIME:  1:37 PM                         Fixed Assets
                                      PROPERTY CONTROL REPORT
```

		Property Control Report		LOCATION RANGE ALL		
LOCATION	CODE	────ASSET──── DESCRIPTION	SERIAL NUMBER	VENDOR NAME	GL DEPT	ACQ DATE
	DESK2	WORK DESK AND ACCESSORIES			0	07/19/91
	WDESK1	Walnut Desk			0	05/22/96
ALPHARET	WHSBO	ORINGAL BUILDING			0	10/03/84
APPLE AV	705APP	RENTAL PROPERTY 705 APPLE			0	12/19/93
ELLIJAY	FARM1	FARM PROPERTY IN ELLIJAY			0	12/19/92
ELLIJAY	TRACTR	ALLIS-CHALMERS F100 TRACT	D983ID930E	ALLIS-CHALMERS	0	07/19/94
HOME	ACURAL	92 ACURA LEGEND	A3E465FY76	ACURA CARLAND	0	10/03/92
MARIETTA	MARET1	3250 AIRLINE RD		SPRINGFIELD WAY	0	06/19/94
ROSWELL	WHSE1	ROSWELL WAREHOUSE			0	12/19/92
WORK	18WHEL	FREIGHTLINER 18 WHEELER	0W93JDSWJ3	FREIGHTLINER IN	0	09/19/94
WORK	386-40	386 40MHZ 210MB		MAGITRONIC	0	11/21/91
WORK	486DXM	486DX MULTI-MEDIA 260MB	2842-JEF30		0	10/05/93
WORK	CONDEN	CONDENSOR	39DOD98E4P	SEARS	0	03/19/93
WORK	F150	76 FORD F150 FLATBED	DODJOJDWOW	FORD MOTOR CO.	0	10/01/86
WORK	FORKLF	FORKLIFT 312C 15 TON	3E943KIDI9	CASE	0	02/03/93
WORK	LJETIV	LASER JET IV PRINTER		HEWLETT PACKARD	0	09/17/94
WORK	RAM250	Ram 250 Diesel Heavy Duty	ace3483939	Chrysler	0	12/27/93

```
                        *** END OF - PROPERTY CONTROL REPORT ***
```

ILLUSTRATION 20–6

A Depreciation Schedule

```
RUN DATE: 11/26/98                    Fixed Assets Sample Co.                         PAGE  1
RUN TIME:  1:16 PM                         Fixed Assets
                                   Interim Depreciation Schedule
_____

CLASS:  AUTOS
        COMPANY AUTOMOBILES            Interim Depreciation Schedule - FIN      FOR THE 12 MONTHS ENDING 12/31/98

_____ASSET/CLASS_____     ACQ     ORIG COST/  N/   SECT 179/    _____DEPRECIATION_____
 CODE            DESCRIPTION   DATE    SALVAGE VAL U    TEFRA ADJ   LF  METH  DEPR BASIS   EXPENSE   ACCUMULATED  MO
                                                     -

ACURAL  92 ACURA LEGEND      10/03/92  29750.00  N       0.00     7.0  DBA     9293.01    2655.15    23112.14  12
AUTOS   COMPANY AUTOMOBILES             1000.00           0.00

CLASS: COMPANY AUTOMOBILES             _____        _____            _____    _____    _____
TOTALS                                 29750.00           0.00             9293.01    2655.15    23112.14
NUMBER OF ASSETS:    1                  1000.00           0.00
```

The depreciation schedule allows an accountant or computer program to determine the proper amount of annual depreciation each year without recalculating it. Illustration 20–6 shows a depreciation schedule.

Property System Records

Noncomputerized Records. A noncomputerized property system maintains a *property ledger* containing one page or card for each depreciable asset owned by the business. It is a subsidiary ledger for the Property, Plant, and Equipment account in the general ledger. Each page discloses an identifying number for the asset, its description, location, date of acquisition, and cost. A depreciation schedule for the asset is usually on this page.

Computerized Records. In a computerized system, the equivalent of the property ledger is the **property master record,** which contains data for each depreciable asset. Illustration 20–7 shows the contents of a property master record.

The system's designers develop a coding structure that assigns to each piece of property a unique identifying number, the ASSET-ID-NUMBER. It allows the property system to distinguish this asset from others and improves control over assets. The master record also shows the cost center that is assigned responsibility for the asset and the account classification code for the asset in the general ledger.

Property Transaction Processing

Manual Processes. Illustration 20–8 shows a document flowchart of manual procedures for a property system. When property is acquired, an accounting clerk adds a page recording it to the property ledger. Either a voucher or a completed capital work order documents the acquisition. The clerk records its cost and depreciation method and calculates the depreciation schedule. The clerk then prepares a journal voucher recording the acquisition in the general ledger. A retirement work order documents the disposition of property, which a clerk records in the property and general ledgers.

ILLUSTRATION 20–7

Contents of a Property Master Record

ASSET-ID-NUMBER*
ASSET-DESCRIPTION
RESPONSIBILITY-CODE
CUSTODIAN
LOCATION
GENERAL-LEDGER-CLASS
ACQUISTION-DATE
COST
DEPRECIATION-METHOD
DEPRECIATION-RATE
SALVAGE-VALUE
USEFUL-LIFE
ACCUMULATED-DEPRECIATION
VENDOR

*Denotes the primary key.

Control Procedures.   Illustration 20–9 summarizes the important control procedures for a property system. These procedures are similar to controls over purchase transactions in the expenditure cycle. However, for the purchase of property, a capital acquisition request (rather than a purchase requisition) initiates the procedures. As with other purchases, the important segregation of duties is between the purchasing department, which authorizes the transaction, and the accounts payable department, which maintains the accounting records.

Computerized Processes.   Illustration 20–10 contains system flowcharts showing a batch property system. In this system, accounts payable clerks code vouchers for depreciable assets with the proper account numbers. They forward batched copies of these vouchers to data entry. Employees complete capital work orders for constructed assets. These and retirement work orders constitute the transaction file that provides inputs to the system. The system posts these transactions to the property master file, produces asset transaction registers, and produces summary records for the general ledger batch summary file. Annually or monthly, another program prints the property listing.

   Many computerized systems receive inputs from the voucher system in the form of voucher records rather than documents. A program in the voucher system examines records added to the voucher file and identifies those recording debits to property accounts. The program places copies of these records in a batch file that is an input to the property system. This system is more reliable than one requiring human intervention.

Application Controls.   Application controls include control procedures applied to the input, the processing, and the output of computerized procedures. Illustration 20–11 shows application controls in the property system. They include completeness and validity tests, control totals, and run-to-run controls.

ILLUSTRATION 20–8

Manual Procedures for a Property System

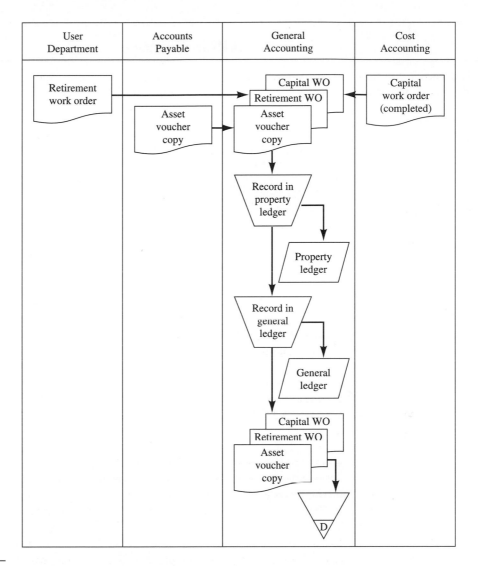

The Journal Entry and Financial Reporting Systems

The purpose of the journal entry system is to post to the general ledger transactions that are not processed by other application systems. These include transactions recording the acquisition of capital from the issue of stocks and bonds, obtaining cash from bank loans, and the acquisition and disposition of property.

The purpose of the financial reporting system is to close the general ledger and to produce financial statements and performance reports. It uses the journal entry system to record adjustments made to the accounts during the closing process. This is why some accountants identify the two systems together as the *general ledger system.*

Journal Entry and Financial Reporting Transactions

Businesses record transactions in the general ledger using three types of accounting entries: summaries of high-volume transactions, low-volume transactions, and closing entries.

AIS in Practice

Headquartered in New York, **Nathan & Lewis** is one of the largest independent broker–dealers in the United States. It provides accounting and marketing support to 1,000 financial advisers nationwide. Each adviser supplies individual and small business clients with financial advice, insurance products, mutual funds, and retirement plans.

A financial adviser may place several sales transactions per day. Nathan & Lewis's accounting system must process these transactions, which may route instructions and funds to any of the 3,463 mutual funds or dozens of insurance companies. Nightly, the system takes downloads from the funds and insurance companies showing commissions due the advisers. The system must match the large volume of sales information with the large volume of commission information and post it to the general ledger. To achieve this, Nathan & Lewis's chart of accounts posts 55,000 entries monthly to any of 28,000 accounts. In spite of the magnitude of the task, they routinely close their books daily rather than monthly.

Summaries of High-Volume Transactions. *High-volume transactions* are those a business has many times each day; they include sales, purchases, and manufacturing transactions. The accounting system records each of these with an accounting entry.

In computer-based systems, application systems process these high-volume transactions. For example, the application systems in the revenue cycle process sales transactions. These application systems are the order entry, shipping, billing, and cash

ILLUSTRATION 20–9

Control Activities for Property Transactions

Activity	Controls
Transaction authorization	*a.* Higher-level approvals required for higher-value purchases
Security for assets and records	Capital asset *a.* Receiving/inspection report prepared as asset is received *b.* Receiving report is prenumbered *c.* Accepted by user department
Segregation of duties	*a.* Purchasing and accounts payable
Adequate documents and records	Request for capital asset acquisition *a.* Initiated for user department *b.* Approved by higher-level management as needed Purchase order *a.* Prepared only on receipt of request for capital asset acquisition *b.* Prenumbered *c.* Vendor choice based on competitive bidding, if new project *d.* Checked for price, specifications, terms Voucher package *a.* Invoice sent directly to accounts payable *b.* Prenumbered *c.* Supported by request for capital asset acquisition, purchase order, receiving/inspection report, and original invoice *d.* Verified

ILLUSTRATION 20–10

A Property Application

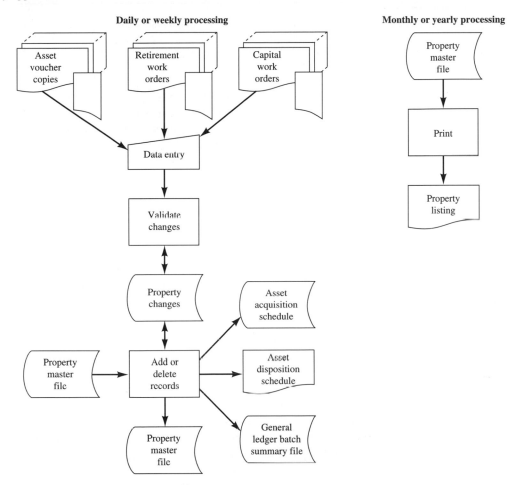

receipts systems. Application systems in the expenditure cycle process purchases transactions, and those in the conversion cycle process transactions related to manufacturing. Illustration 20–12 lists the applications in these cycles that produce summaries of high-volume transactions.

In a manual system, the equivalents of application systems are the special journals and subsidiary ledgers. Each day a bookkeeper totals the accounting entries made in special journals and posts these summaries to a ledger. In a computer-based system, an application system summarizes the results of its transactions in computer records daily and adds these records to the ***general ledger batch summary file.*** Then a journal entry system creates journal entries from these records and posts them to the computerized general ledger.

Low-Volume Transactions.   *Low-volume transactions* include those incurred to record changes in debt and equity capital, to dispose of depreciable property, and to pay

ILLUSTRATION 20–11

Application Controls in the Property System

Type	Control Procedure
Input	**Completeness test**. Verify that all master file fields are completed on the voucher or capital work order records. **Validity test**. Verify that an account number represents valid asset account.
Processing	**Record count**. Program verifies that the number of changes to the property master file = the number of vouchers + the number of retirement orders + the number of capital work orders. **Control total**. Program verifies that total debits to general ledger batch summary file = batch total of vouchers + batch total of capital work orders.
Output	**Control total**. Program verifies that total credits to general ledger batch summary file = total of retirement work orders.

taxes. They also include accruals and deferrals made as part of the closing process. These include interest accruals, bad-debt accruals, and accruals for warranty expenses.

Because a low-volume transaction occurs infrequently, accountants do not develop special journals or application systems for them. Instead, in a manual system they make these entries in the general journal. In a computer-based system, they make them using the journal entry system.

Accountants record a low-volume transaction on a journal voucher. A data entry clerk enters data from the journal voucher in the journal entry system. For repetitive low-volume transactions such as accruals, accountants create standard journal vouchers.

Illustration 20–13 shows a journal voucher. A clerk codes one entry on each line of the form. Each line contains space for an account description, an account code, a responsibility code, and an amount. With this system, credits to an account are shown by placing the amount in parentheses. Other systems use an entry code to designate debits and credits. This journal voucher form also has space for a data control clerk to enter a batch number for the set of transactions.

Closing Entries.   Accountants make closing entries when preparing the financial statements. In a manual system, bookkeepers use a general ledger account called *Income*

ILLUSTRATION 20–12

Applications that Produce Summaries of High-Volume Transactions

Transaction Type	Transaction Cycle	Applications
Sale	Revenue	Billing Cash receipts
Purchase	Expenditure	Voucher Cash disbursements
Production	Conversion	Inventory Cost accounting
Payroll	Conversion	Payroll

ILLUSTRATION 20–13

A Journal Voucher

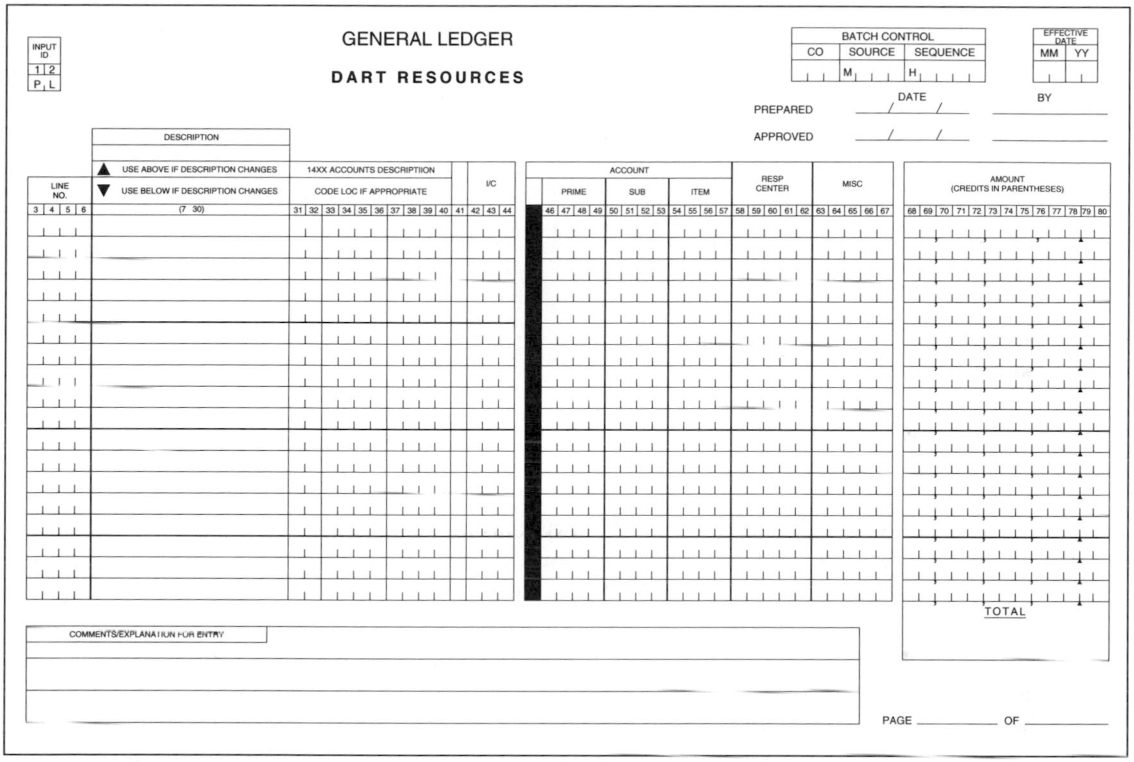
INPUT ID 1 2 P L

GENERAL LEDGER

DART RESOURCES

BATCH CONTROL: CO | SOURCE M | SEQUENCE H

EFFECTIVE DATE: MM | YY

DATE / BY

PREPARED / /

APPROVED / /

DESCRIPTION

LINE NO.	▲ USE ABOVE IF DESCRIPTION CHANGES ▼ USE BELOW IF DESCRIPTION CHANGES	14XX ACCOUNTS DESCRIPTION CODE LOC IF APPROPRIATE		I/C	ACCOUNT PRIME	SUB	ITEM	RESP CENTER	MISC	AMOUNT (CREDITS IN PARENTHESES)
3 4 5 6	(7 30)	31 32 33 34 35 36 37 38 39 40	41	42 43 44	46 47 48 49	50 51 52 53	54 55 56 57	58 59 60 61 62	63 64 65 66 67	68 69 70 71 72 73 74 75 76 77 78 79 80

TOTAL

COMMENTS/EXPLANATION FOR ENTRY

PAGE ______ OF ______

Summary. They credit each expense account, producing a zero balance, and debit Income Summary for equal amounts. They also debit each revenue account and credit Income Summary. After this procedure, the balance in Income Summary is Net Income.

In a computer-based system, a computer program in the financial reporting system makes this entry and uses the balances in the general ledger to produce financial statements. It transfers balances from revenue and expense accounts into the general ledger Income Summary account. In many systems, it also calculates and records depreciation, allocates overhead to responsibility centers, and posts final adjustments to the general ledger.

Another function of the financial reporting system is to prepare the general ledger for the next reporting period. Many computerized general ledgers record balances for both the current period and the prior period. In these, the financial reporting system transfers current period balances to the prior period fields. This system also may make reversing journal entries for accrual and deferral accounts.

Journal Entry and Financial Reports

Journal entry and financial reports include control reports, registers, financial statements, and performance reports.

Control Reports and Registers. Illustration 20–14 contains a control report produced by a journal entry system. It lists the summary entries from other applications contained

ILLUSTRATION 20–14

A General Ledger Control Report

```
RUN DATE: 11/30/98                          W.D. Peachtree & Company                          PAGE  1
RUN TIME:  4:54 PM                               General Ledger
                                      Transfer Summary Journals Control Report

ACCT.  DESCRIPTION         REF. SC   DATE      AMOUNT          ACTION

13500                        A    11/29/98   96,754.14  *** TRANSFERRED ***
20500                        A    11/29/98   96,754.14- *** TRANSFERRED ***


TOTAL TRANSACTIONS ENTERED:    2
TOTAL DEBITS..............:         96,754.14
TOTAL CREDITS.............:         96,754.14-
                                ================
DIFFERENCE................:              0.00

End Of - Transfer Summary Journals Control Report
```

in a general ledger batch summary file. An accounting clerk reviews it to ensure that the system properly summarized these entries.

Illustration 20–15 shows a transaction register that lists all transactions posted to specific general ledger accounts during a reporting period. Using this, an accountant or auditor can explain the changes in the account balance during the period.

Financial Statements. The reports in the financial reporting cycle are the trial balance, the balance sheet, the income statement, and the statement of cash flows. Examples of some of these familiar reports are in Illustrations 20–16, 20–17, and 20–18.

Performance Reports. Performance reports disclose performance measures for managers in the organization. Usually these performance measures include those revenues and costs that a manager can control. Performance reports disclose actual amounts, budgeted amounts, and their difference (called a *variance*). When the organization uses responsibility accounting, the financial reporting system produces performance reports for each responsibility center. (Chapter 2 contains several examples of these reports.)

The journal entry and financial reporting systems process three types of transactions and produce various reports. The next section describes the forms taken by the accounting records.

Journal Entry and Financial Reporting Records

Manual systems keep accounting records in books, card files, and filing cabinets. In addition, computer-based systems use computer files or a database management system.

Noncomputerized Records. A manual system keeps its records entirely in noncomputerized form. The general journal, any special journals, the general ledger, and any subsidiary ledgers are books or card files. Chapter 1 reviews these records.

ILLUSTRATION 20–15

A General Ledger Transaction Register

```
RUN DATE: 11/30/98        W.D. Peachtree & Company          PAGE   1
RUN TIME:  4:57 PM              General Ledger
                             Transaction Register


   ACCT  BATCH       DESCRIPTION        REF   S   DATE   PP PE    AMOUNT
   ===================================================================================

    110     1 Peachtree Realty          11495  2 11/01/98 11 11     2,500.00-
    110     1 Southern Bell             11560  2 11/04/98 11 11     3,967.55-
    110     1 Atlanta Gas Light         11561  2 11/04/98 11 11     1,123.55-
    110     1 Georgia Power Company     11562  2 11/04/98 11 11     4,033.88-
    110     1 Bryan's Office Supply     11577  2 11/10/98 11 11       176.88-
    110     1 Meyer's & Meyer's, CPA    11578  2 11/10/98 11 11       500.00-
    110     1 Jones, Smith & Jones      11622  2 11/20/98 11 11    11,000.00-
    110     1 U.S. Postmaster           11623  2 11/20/98 11 11       600.00-
    110     1 Burns Auto Repair         11624  2 11/20/98 11 11     1,189.54-
    110     2 Cash Sales W/E 11/5/96    JE33   1 11/05/98 11 11   102,553.31
    110     2 Serv. Sales W/E 11/5/96   JE33   1 11/05/98 11 11     3,455.00
    110     2 Returns for W/E 11/5/96   JE33   1 11/05/98 11 11     4,078.95-
                                                                 76,837.96 *

    130     4 Allowance for Bad Debts   JE50   3 11/30/98 11 11       500.00-

    135     3 Cost of Sales             JE34   3 11/05/98 11 11    38,240.78-

    160     5 VEH58  Accum Depreciation        F 11/30/98 11 11       240.16-
    160     5 BLD01  Accum Depreciation        F 11/30/98 11 11       284.70-
    160     5 EQP19  Accum Depreciation        F 11/30/98 11 11        11.86-
    160     5 EQP84  Accum Depreciation        F 11/30/98 11 11        44.73-
    160     5 EQP85  Accum Depreciation        F 11/30/98 11 11         8.03-
    160     5 EQP92  Accum Depreciation        F 11/30/98 11 11         4.01-
    160     5 EQP95  Accum Depreciation        F 11/30/98 11 11       404.24-
    160     5 DSK07  Accum Depreciation        F 11/30/98 11 11         0.85-
    160     5 DSK15  Accum Depreciation        F 11/30/98 11 11         7.71-
    160     5 VEH51  Accum Depreciation        F 11/30/98 11 11       118.20-
    160     5 VEH55  Accum Depreciation        F 11/30/98 11 11       362.33-
                                                                  1,486.82-*

    180     2 Magazine Ads w/Swain      ADVERT 6 11/01/98  1 11       350.00-
```

Computerized Records.   A computer-based system keeps accounting records in computer-readable form. These consist of five computer files.

General Ledger Master File.   The **general ledger master file** is the computerized equivalent of the general ledger, containing one record for each account in the chart of accounts. The record key is the account number, and the record shows the current balance in the account. In some systems, the record also shows a budgeted balance, a

ILLUSTRATION 20–16

A General Ledger Trial Balance

```
RUN DATE: 11/30/98        W.D. Peachtree & Company              PAGE      1
                              General Ledger
PERIOD END DATE: 11/30/98    SUMMARY TRIAL BALANCE


ACCOUNT                      ————————————— BALANCES —————————————
NUMBER       DESCRIPTION      BEGINNING       PERIOD         ENDING
============================================================================
 10500 Cash                       $0.00        $0.00          $0.00
 11000 Cash - Operating     $149,125.86   $76,837.96    $225,963.82
 11500 Cash on Hand           $1,500.00        $5.00      $1,505.00
 12000 Accounts Receivable  $120,869.86        $0.00    $120,869.86
 12500 Due from Employees         $0.00        $5.00-         $5.00-
 13000 Allowance for Bad Debts $5,500.00-     $500.00-     $6,000.00-
 13500 Inventory             $41,158.66   $58,513.36     $99,672.02
 14700 Furniture & Fixtures   $5,667.00        $0.00      $5,667.00
 15000 Machinery & Equipment $34,014.50        $0.00     $34,014.50
 15200 Buildings            $104,200.00        $0.00    $104,200.00
 15500 Land                  $25,000.00        $0.00     $25,000.00
 15700 Vehicles              $52,093.00        $0.00     $52,093.00
 16000 Accumulated Depreciation $47,841.23- $1,686.82-   $49,528.05-
 17200 Prepaid Expenses           $0.00        $0.00          $0.00
 17500 Prepaid Insurance          $0.00        $0.00          $0.00
 18000 Prepaid Advertising      $700.00-     $350.00-     $1,050.00-
 18500 Prepaid Uniforms         $148.42       $74.00-        $74.42
 19000 Deposits               $1,000.00        $0.00      $1,000.00
 20500 Accounts Payable      $28,307.40-  $98,881.64-   $127,189.04-
 21000 Accrued Payroll            $0.00        $0.00          $0.00
 21500 Notes Payable - Bank   $4,356.87-   $2,000.00      $2,356.87-
 22000 Payroll Taxes Payable      $0.00        $0.00          $0.00
 22100 Federal Withholding Taxes $7,151.40-    $0.00      $7,151.40-
 22200 State Withholding Taxes $2,240.40-      $0.00      $2,240.40-
 22400 FICA                   $8,377.51-       $0.00      $8,377.51-
 22600 Federal Unemployment Tax $5,634.44-     $0.00      $5,634.44-
 22800 State Unemployment Tax $1,667.80-       $0.00      $1,667.80-
 23000 Earned Income Credit       $0.00        $0.00          $0.00
 23100 Other Employee W/holding   $0.00        $0.00          $0.00
 23200 Fed. Income Tax Payable    $0.00        $0.00          $0.00
 23400 State Income Tax Payable   $0.00        $0.00          $0.00
 23600 Sales Tax Payable     $23,709.21-       $0.00     $23,709.21-
 23800 Industrial Ins. Payable    $0.00        $0.00          $0.00
 24000 Suspense                   $0.00        $0.00          $0.00
 25500 Notes Payable - Bank  $20,000.00-       $0.00     $20,000.00-
```

balance for the previous reporting period, and a balance for the same period in the previous year.

Illustration 20–19 shows the contents of a general ledger master record. When a database management system is used, this illustration shows the contents of the subschema for the journal entry and financial reporting applications.

ILLUSTRATION 20–17

A Balance Sheet

```
RUN DATE: 11/30/98                    W.D. Peachtree & Company                        PAGE   1
RUN TIME: 10:26 AM
                                           Balance Sheet
                                           AS OF 11/30/98

           **  THIS MONTH THIS YEAR **                 **  THIS MONTH LAST YEAR **
=================================================================================================

                                              ASSETS


CURRENT ASSETS
   Cash                     227,468.82                       464,644.00
   Accounts Receivable      120,869.86                       110,088.34
   Due from Employees            5.00-                             0.00
   Allowance for Bad Debts   6,000.00-                        20,045.00-
   Inventory                 99,672.02                         3,216.54

      Total Current Assets              442,005.70                         557,903.88

      Total Other Assets                    24.42                           1,000.00

         Total Assets                             613,476.57                         819,165.55
                                        ===============                     ===============


                                        LIABILITIES & EQUITY


CURRENT LIABILITIES
   Accounts Payable         127,189.04                       130,640.90-
   Notes Payable - Bank       2,356.87                         4,352.00-
   Payroll Taxes Payable     25,071.55                             0.00
   Sales Tax Payable         23,709.21                        21,809.25-

      Total Current Liabilities         178,326.67                         156,802.15-


LONG TERM LIABILITIES
   Notes Payable - Bank      20,000.00                             0.00

      Total Long Term  Liab.             20,000.00                             0.00

         Total Liabilities                        198,326.67                         156,802.15-

STOCKHOLDERS EQUITY
   Common Stock              75,000.00                             0.00
   Retained Earnings        221,876.76                             0.00
   Current Earnings         118,273.14                        975,967.70

      Total Equity                      415,149.90                         975,967.70

         Total Liab. & Equity                     613,476.57                         819,165.55
                                        ===============                     ===============
```

Copyright 1995 Peachtree Software, Inc. Reprinted by permission.

General Ledger Batch Summary File. The general ledger batch summary file is a sequential file. It contains transactions that, after further processing, are posted to the general ledger master file. The transactions in this file are summaries of high-volume transactions processed in other application systems. For example, many companies close their books monthly. In this case, the file contains one record summarizing sales transactions in each responsibility center for each workday during the month. It also

ILLUSTRATION 20–18

An Income Statement

```
RUN DATE: 11/30/98        W.D. Peachtree & Company              PAGE    1
RUN TIME:  2:56 PM
                         Department Income Statement
                       FOR THE MONTH ENDING 11/30/98

12  Men's Clothing
CURR. PERIOD RATIO: NET REVENUE
YTD RATIO.........: NET REVENUE    THIS MONTH   RATIO    11  MONTHS    RATIO
====================================================================================
INCOME
        Sales Men's Clothing        9,876.44    104.8     397,853.27    105.0
        Ret/Allow Men's Clothing      449.26-     4.8-     19,059.44-     5.0-

        Net Sales                   9,427.18    100.0     378,793.83    100.0


COST OF GOODS SOLD
        COS Men's Clothing          3,220.40     34.2     137,469.17     36.3

        Total Cost of Goods Sold    3,220.40     34.2     137,469.17     36.3


        Gross Profit                6,206.78     65.8     241,324.66     63.7

EXPENSES
        Salaries Men's Clothing         0.00      0.0     123,866.25     32.7

        Total Expenses                  0.00      0.0     123,866.25     32.7


        Net Operating Income        6,206.78     65.8     117,458.41     31.0


OTHER INCOME

        Total Other Income              0.00      0.0           0.00      0.0


OTHER EXPENSES

        Total Other Expenses            0.00      0.0           0.00      0.0


        Income Before Taxes         6,206.78     65.8     117,458.41     31.0


        Net Income                  6,206.78     65.8     117,458.41     31.0

                                ==============   ======  ==============   ======
```

contains summary transactions produced daily by other applications in the revenue, expenditure, and conversion cycles.

Illustration 20–20 shows the contents of this file. In a general ledger batch summary record, the TRANSACTION-CODE identifies the application system producing the record. The record contains two amount fields. TOTAL-AMOUNT is a control total that shows the total of the debits or credits for the summary transaction. POSTING-AMOUNT shows the amount of the entry in the account identified by ACCOUNT-CODE. At least two records should be in this file for each transaction code, date, and

ILLUSTRATION 20–19

Contents of a General Ledger Master Record

ACCOUNT-CODE*
ACCOUNT-NAME
BALANCE-CURRENT-MONTH
BALANCE-CURRENT-QUARTER
BALANCE-CURRENT-YEAR
BALANCE-LAST-YEAR-JANUARY
BALANCE-LAST-YEAR-FEBRUARY
*
*
*
BALANCE-LAST-YEAR-DECEMBER

*Denotes the primary key.

total amount. These records show each debit entry and each credit entry associated with the summary transaction.

Journal Voucher File.   This transaction file contains one record for each transaction affecting the general ledger. Each contains the data field TRANSACTION-CODE that identifies its source.

Systems analysts designate transaction codes when creating the journal entry and financial reporting application systems. They identify each transaction code with a standard journal entry. For example, they may designate a transaction code of 1 to represent a billing transaction. Then a journal voucher record with a transaction code of 1 indicates a summary transaction recorded in the billing system. It causes the journal entry system to make general ledger entries of the form

Dr.	Accounts Receivable	xxx	
Cr.	Sales		xxx
Dr.	Cost of Goods Sold	yyy	
Cr.	Inventory		yyy

The journal entry system creates the journal voucher file from two sources. An accountant may input entries manually, or the system may create them from the records in the general ledger batch summary file. Illustration 20–21 shows the contents of a journal voucher record.

ILLUSTRATION 20–20

Contents of a General Ledger Batch Summary Record

TRANSACTION-CODE*
DATE*
TOTAL-AMOUNT
ACCOUNT-CODE
RESPONSIBILITY-CODE
POSTING-AMOUNT

*Denotes the primary key.

ILLUSTRATION 20–21

Contents of Journal Voucher and Detail Posting Records

Journal Voucher Record	*Detail Posting Record*
JOURNAL-VOUCHER-NUMBER*	JOURNAL-VOUCHER-NUMBER*
DATE	ACCOUNT-CODE*
TOTAL-AMOUNT	DR-CR-CODE
TRANSACTION-CODE	POSTING-AMOUNT

*Denotes the primary key.

A journal voucher record contains only one amount—the total of the debits or credits in the transaction. The journal entry system uses this field as a control total. Another file, the detail postings file, contains records showing the amounts of entries in individual accounts.

Detail Postings File. The detail postings file contains data records showing the detailed entries in general ledger accounts. Each journal voucher record has associated with it two or more detail posting records. The journal entry system produces the records in this file from manual input or from the summary transactions in the general ledger batch summary file.

In the previous example, the journal entry system produces one journal voucher record and four detail posting records. It produces one detail posting record for each line in the journal entry. Illustration 20–21 shows the contents of a detail posting record. It contains data fields showing the account for the entry, its amount, and whether the entry is a debit or a credit.

Standard Postings File. Systems analysts create the ***standard postings file*** when developing the journal entry system. It shows the standard journal entries provided by the system; a transaction code identifies each standard journal entry.

For each transaction code, the standard postings file shows the required debit and credit accounts. The journal entry system reads a journal voucher record, identifies its transaction code, and then locates the code in the standard postings file. This file tells the journal entry system how many records to read from the detail postings file, which accounts these records affect, and whether to enter them as debits or credits in the accounts. The journal entry system then locates these detail posting records and posts their amounts to the general ledger master file.

Illustration 20–22 shows a standard postings file. This is how a computer-based system uses the transaction codes contained in the general ledger batch summary records.

You may wonder why a design team creates a separate standard postings file. After all, they could code these data as a table in a computer program and avoid using the file. However, using a standard postings file makes system changes simpler. If later an accountant decides to create another standard journal entry, the accountant creates another transaction code and adds this code and entry to the file. This avoids changes to the programs in the journal entry system.

ILLUSTRATION 20–22

A Standard Postings File

| | | **Posting Instruction** | | |
Transaction Code	Transaction Type	Dr/Cr	Account Code	Account Name
1	Billing	Dr	xxxx	Accounts Receivable
		Cr	xxxx	Sales
		Dr	xxxx	Cost of Goods Sold
		Cr	xxxx	Finished Goods Inventory
2	Cash receipts	Dr	xxxx	Cash
		Cr	xxxx	Accounts Receivable
3	Issue material to production	Dr	xxxx	Work in Process Inventory
		Cr	xxxx	Raw Material Inventory
4	Production labor	Dr	xxxx	Work in Process Inventory
		Cr	xxxx	Wages Payable
5	Apply factory overhead	Dr	xxxx	Work in Process Inventory
		Cr	xxxx	Factory Overhead
6	Complete production	Dr	xxxx	Finished Goods Inventory
		Cr	xxxx	Work in Process Inventory
7	Receive vendor invoice	Dr	——	Asset or Expense
		Cr	xxxx	Accounts Payable
8	Pay vendor invoice	Dr	xxxx	Accounts Payable
		Cr	xxxx	Cash
0	Journal voucher	Dr	——	Any account
		Cr	——	Any account

xxxx Indicates a general ledger account code from the chart of accounts. It is included in the standard postings file entry.

—— Indicates an account code that is not included in the standard postings file entry. The journal entry system obtains it from the general ledger batch summary record.

A DBMS does not maintain in separate files the accounting records used by computer-based applications in the financial cycle. Instead, the DBMS places them in the database at main storage locations known only to the DBMS software. It links a journal voucher record with its associated detail posting records. In a relational DBMS, each of these files is a separate relation.

Journal Entry and Financial Reporting Processing

Chapter 1 discusses how journal entry and financial reporting systems process transactions manually. In computerized systems, the same conceptual process is followed; however, procedures differ because different media are used to record the data.

Journal Entry System Processing.   The journal entry system updates the general ledger master file with low-volume transactions and with summaries of high-volume transactions. Illustration 20–23 shows a journal entry system that allows on-line data entry by an accounting clerk.

In this system, a computer program uses the information in the standard postings file to match the records in the general ledger batch summary file with accounting transactions. For each transaction, this program creates a record in the journal voucher file, creates two or more records in the detail postings file, and removes the associated

ILLUSTRATION 20–23

A Journal Entry System

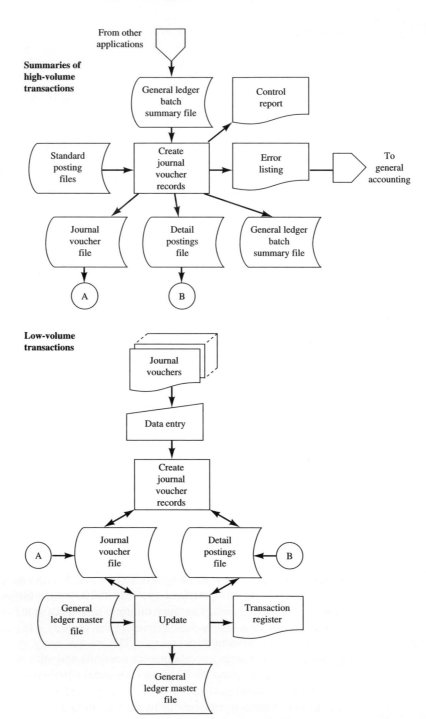

records from the general ledger batch summary file. Unmatched summary records remain in the general ledger batch summary file and are reported on an error listing. A clerk in the general accounting department corrects these erroneous entries before producing financial statements.

An accountant enters low-volume transactions from journal vouchers at a keyboard. The data entry program validates each journal voucher before adding records for it to the journal voucher and detail postings files. An update program posts the journal voucher transactions to the general ledger master file and produces a transaction register.

An organization usually executes the journal entry system monthly. This precedes execution of the second system in this transaction cycle, the financial reporting system.

Financial Reporting System Processing

Companies execute this application system only when they wish to produce financial statements. This may be monthly, quarterly, or annually, but it always follows execution of the journal entry system. Illustration 20–24 contains a system flowchart of a financial reporting system.

In a procedure many accountants call the *first closing,* the system prints a preliminary trial balance from the updated general ledger master file. Accountants then review this trial balance. The accountants examine the account balances and identify inconsistencies or incorrect amounts for correction. They also identify necessary accruals or deferrals and create journal vouchers documenting these changes.

Accountants or data entry clerks enter these journal vouchers, creating new journal voucher and detail posting files. A computer program posts these to the general ledger master file. Then in the *second closing*, the system produces a final trial balance and the financial statements. Finally, the system prepares the general ledger master file for the next reporting period.

Recording Depreciation

Accountants define *depreciation* as a systematic allocation of an asset's cost over its useful life. It is intended to represent the consumption of the asset during the conversion process. For this reason, many accountants consider depreciation to be a part of the conversion cycle.

Most computer-based accounting systems record depreciation not as this consumption occurs but rather immediately prior to the closing process.

Manual Systems.   In manual systems, accountants determine the amount of depreciation for each asset from the property ledger. They total this amount for each class of assets and create a journal voucher recording these totals in the general ledger. They also post the accumulated depreciation to individual records in the property ledger.

Computerized Systems.   With a computerized system, a depreciation program performs these procedures. The program calculates depreciation expense for each asset, totals these expenses for each asset class, and records this additional accumulated depreciation in the property master file. It then generates summary records for the general ledger batch summary file. These record depreciation expense in the general ledger master file.

ILLUSTRATION 20–24

A Financial Reporting System

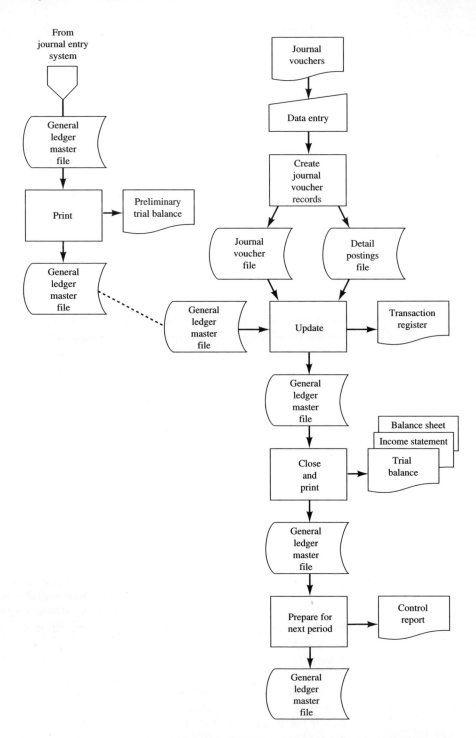

Application Controls   Application controls are those control procedures that the design team places in an application system during its development. They prevent or detect errors when processing transactions. Illustration 20–25 shows how application controls are used in the financial cycle. These examples include completeness tests, consistency tests, record counts, and run-to-run controls.

Responsibility Accounting   Many organizations implement a financial reporting system that produces not only financial statements but also performance reports for responsibility centers. These responsibility accounting systems associate costs and revenues with the responsibility center that best controls them. They produce monthly reports comparing controllable revenues and costs with those budgeted for each responsibility center.

A financial reporting system that provides responsibility accounting uses two additional files and two added sets of computerized procedures.

Files.   The files required by a responsibility accounting system are the general ledger batch summary file, the responsibility center file, and the budget file.

General Ledger Batch Summary File.   The journal entry system uses the general ledger batch summary file, which contains summary entries for the general ledger created by other application systems. These entries identify not only general ledger accounts but also the codes of the responsibility centers that create them. This allows the responsibility accounting system to summarize revenues and expenses by center.

ILLUSTRATION 20–25

Application Controls in the Journal Entry and Financial Reporting Systems

Type	System	Control Procedure
Input	Journal entry and financial reporting	**Completeness test.** Input program determines that all fields are provided.
		Consistency test. For any journal voucher, sum of debits = sum of credits.
Processing	Journal entry	**Record count.** Number of records from input general ledger batch summary file = number of records in detail postings file + number of records in output general ledger batch summary file.
	Journal entry and financial reporting	**Consistency test.** For each transaction, sum of debits = sum of credits.
Output	Journal entry	**Run-to-run control.** Data control group reconciles totals on control report, error listing, and transaction register.
	Financial reporting	**Run-to-run control.** Data control group uses transaction register to reconcile difference between first and second trial balances.

Responsibility Center File.   The responsibility center file contains one record for each center. During design of the system, analysts determine the data required on the performance report for each center and add to this file a record containing fields that accumulate these data. Data from general ledger batch summary records update these fields.

Budget File.   The budget file is similar to the responsibility center file because it contains one record for each responsibility center. Likewise it contains, in the budget record, a field for each revenue and expense category on that responsibility center's performance report. The only difference is that these fields contain budgeted rather than actual amounts. Budgetary accountants enter these budgeted amounts following the development of the annual budget.

Computerized Processes.   Processes in the responsibility accounting system include performance budgeting procedures and responsibility reporting procedures.

Performance Budgeting Procedures.   Performance budgeting procedures translate overall organizational objectives into goals for each responsibility center. In this way, they provide a top-down information flow. They include the procedures to develop budget goals and those used to enter them in the budget file.

Managerial accounting courses discuss typical procedures for developing budget goals. Nonaccounting managers take part in this process. Some companies implement *participative* budgeting, in which individual managers take part in setting goals for their responsibility centers. Others use *authoritative* budgeting whereby top management sets all budget goals. Regardless of the procedures used to develop them, budgetary accountants summarize the goals in a budgetary document and enter them in the budget file.

The system design team creates special data entry programs that create budgetary transactions. Fields in these records identify the budgeted amount, the general ledger account, and the responsibility center. A transaction code identifies them as budgetary transactions. An update program posts these transactions to the budget file.

Responsibility Reporting Procedures.   Responsibility reporting procedures summarize actual controllable revenues and costs by responsibility center and disclose them on performance reports. They provide a bottom-up information flow. Illustration 20–26 shows computerized responsibility reporting procedures.

The system sorts the general ledger batch summary records into responsibility code sequence. It then posts transactions from this file to the responsibility center file. Other programs then print performance reports by obtaining actual revenues and expenses from the responsibility center file and budgeted ones from the budget file. In this way, the system produces reports that compare actual and budgeted amounts for each responsibility center.

ILLUSTRATION 20–26

Responsibility Reporting Procedures

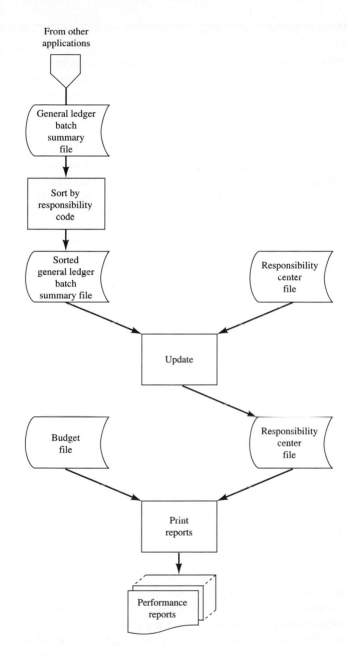

Summary

This chapter describes how computer-based accounting systems process transactions in the financial cycle. This cycle processes two economic events: the acquisition of capital and the use of that capital to acquire property. The financial cycle also performs the financial reporting function.

The three application systems in the financial cycle are the property system, the journal entry system, and the financial reporting system. The property system processes transactions recording the acquisition of property. The journal entry system records the acquisition of capital, depreciation, and the disposition of property.

The journal entry and financial reporting systems process three types of transactions. They are summary transactions from other application systems, low-volume transactions documented by journal vouchers, and closing entries. The files used by these systems are the general ledger master file, the general ledger batch summary file, the journal voucher file, the detailed postings file, and the standard postings file.

With a responsibility accounting system, the financial reporting system uses responsibility center and budget files to produce performance reports.

Key Terms

bondholders ledger   A subsidiary record containing data on all bondholders of an organization.

depreciation   A systematic allocation of the costs of property, plant, and equipment over their useful lives. It is recorded by a journal entry made in the financial cycle.

first closing   The process of printing a first trial balance; it occurs prior to the final accrual and deferral adjusting journal entries.

general ledger batch summary file   A computer file that accumulates summary transactions from the revenue, expenditure, and conversion cycles for posting to the general ledger.

general ledger master record   A record that exists for each account in the general ledger. It records the account number, description, and the balance in the account.

general ledger system   A name applied by many people to the combination of the journal entry and financial reporting application systems.

high-volume transactions   Accounting transactions that are processed by application systems in the revenue, expenditure, and conversion cycles. They are summarized by these applications for posting to the general ledger.

low-volume transactions   Accounting transactions recorded by the journal entry system. They include the acquisition of capital, the disposition of property, the accrual of revenues and expenses, and the payment of taxes.

property master record   A type of record that exists for each item of property, plant, and equipment in the organization. It identifies the property and serves as a record of its cost and accumulated depreciation.

retirement work order   A document used to authorize and record the disposition of property.

second closing   The process of printing a second trial balance and the financial statements after posting all adjusting journal entries.

standard postings file   A computer file containing all the standard journal entries that have been defined for an accounting system.

stockholders ledger   A subsidiary record containing information on all stockholders of a corporation.

Questions

20–1. Which economic events produce transactions in the financial cycle?

20–2. Which three types of transactions are processed in the financial cycle?

20–3. Which applications systems not in this cycle are sources of summary entries for the financial cycle?

20–4. What is the purpose of a journal voucher? How is it used by applications in the financial cycle?

20–5. What are the purposes of these property system reports:
   a. Control reports?
   b. Registers?

20–6. What are some sources of the low-volume transactions processed in the financial cycle?

20–7. In a computerized accounting system, which data files are used in the financial cycle? Identify the purpose of each file.

20–8. Why do computerized systems use a separate file that contains standard journal entries?

20–9. In a computer-based system, which application systems are in the financial cycle? What is the purpose of each system?

20–10. What is depreciation? How is it recorded in an accounting system?

Exercises and Cases

20–11.   LOW- AND HIGH-VOLUME TRANSACTIONS

Application systems in the financial cycle process both low-volume transactions and summaries of high-volume transactions. Classify each accounting transaction in the following list as a low-volume or high-volume transaction:

a. Cash sale.
b. Credit sale.
c. Increase allowance for doubtful accounts.
d. Sell common stock.
e. Acquire equipment.
f. Receive bank loan.
g. Reimburse payroll imprest account.

20–12. SUMMARY TRANSACTIONS

Other application systems provide summaries of transactions to the applications in the financial cycle. The following application systems are described in this text. For each one, identify the accounts debited and credited by its summary transactions. (*Hint:* Refer to the transactions described in Chapters 17 through 19.)

a. Cash receipts.
b. Cash disbursements.
c. Cost accounting.
d. Billing.
e. Voucher.

20–13. STANDARD JOURNAL ENTRIES

Standard journal entries are controls that prevent errors when transactions are recorded. Show how a standard journal entry would look for each of the following accounting transactions:

a. Record depreciation on a building.
b. Accrue wages owed for factory direct labor but unpaid at year-end.
c. Write-off of an account receivable.
d. Summary transaction for one day's credit sales.
e. Pay dividends.

20–14. JOURNAL VOUCHERS

Some of the transactions processed by a general ledger system originate from other application systems, and some originate on a journal voucher. Decide if each of the following transactions originates with this document. If it does not, identify the application system that originates it.

a. Payment of property taxes.
b. Repayment of bank loan.
c. Payment of vendor invoice.
d. Sale of a piece of machinery.
e. Customer payment on account.

20–15. TRANSACTION RECORDS

Pine & Apple Company, a retailer, uses a computerized general ledger system. On July 15, 1998, P&A had credit sales of $1,710. Its markup on inventory cost is 20 percent. The following account codes are from its chart of accounts.

Code	Account name
1100	Cash
1300	Accounts Receivable
1400	Inventory
2400	Equipment
3100	Accounts Payable
6100	Sales
7000	Cost of Goods Sold

Required:

Show the contents of all the following records that are necessary to make the preceding entry in P&A's computerized general ledger:

a. General ledger batch summary records.
b. Journal voucher records.
c. Detail posting records.

20–16.   TRANSACTION RECORDS

IPL, Inc., is a manufacturing company with a computerized general ledger. On April 21, IPL received vendor invoices for material totaling $2,467. The material had been properly ordered and has been received. The following accounts are a part of IPL's chart of accounts:

Code	Account name
1100	Cash
1300	Accounts Receivable
1400	Raw Material Inventory
2400	Equipment
3100	Accounts Payable
6100	Sales
7000	Cost of Goods Sold

Required:

Show the contents of all the following records that are necessary to record the preceding transaction in IPL's general ledger:

a. General ledger batch summary records.
b. Journal voucher records.
c. Detail posting records.

20–17.   APPLICATION CONTROLS

Illustration 20–25 shows some application controls that can be used in the journal entry and financial reporting systems of Illustrations 20–23 and 20–24. There are other application controls that can be used in these systems.

Required:

Identify one input control, one processing control, and one output control that can be used in these systems, in addition to those shown in Illustration 20–25.

20–18.   SYSTEM FLOWCHART

Illustration 20–23 contains a system flowchart of a journal entry system. This system shows on-line data entry and validation—that is, transactions are entered and validated one at a time.

Required:

Using standard flowchart symbols, show how the flowchart of the journal entry system would change if the system used batch processing data entry procedures.

20–19.   PROPERTY SYSTEM

Superior Company manufactures automobile parts for sale to the major U.S. automakers. You have been asked to review the internal controls over machinery and equipment and make recommendations for improvements where appropriate. You have obtained the following information:

Requests to purchase machinery and equipment are normally initiated by the supervisor in need of the asset. The supervisor discusses the proposed acquisition with the plant manager. A purchase requisition is submitted to the purchasing department when the plant manager is satisfied that the request is reasonable and that there is a remaining balance in the plant's share of the total corporate budget for capital acquisitions.

On receiving a purchase requisition for machinery or equipment, the purchasing department manager looks through the records for an appropriate supplier. A formal purchase order is then completed and mailed. When the machine or equipment is received, it is immediately sent to the user department for installation. This allows the economic benefits from the acquisition to be realized as early as possible.

The property, plant, and equipment ledger control accounts are supported by depreciation schedules organized by year of acquisition. These depreciation schedules are used to compute depreciation as a unit for all assets of a given type acquired in the same year. Standard rates, depreciation methods, and salvage values are used for each major type of fixed asset. These rates, methods, and salvage values were set 10 years ago during the company's initial year of operation.

When machinery or equipment is retired, the plant manager notifies the accounting department so that the appropriate entries can be made in the accounting records.

Since the company began operation there has been no reconciliation between the accounting records and the machinery and equipment on hand.

Required:

Identify the internal control weaknesses, and recommend improvements in the property system of Superior Company.

(CMA Adapted)

20–20.   STANDARD POSTINGS FILE

The Metropolitan Summer Light Opera Festival was organized to stage four musical shows during the summer. Each show was to last three weeks, and a three-week accounting period was adopted. Selected transactions during the first weeks of the festival were as follows:

June	1	Paid rent for 12 weeks, beginning June 9. The weekly rent was $1,000.
	2	Placed an advertisement in newspapers announcing the dates and programs of the festival. The expense was $200. Invoices were paid as received.
	3	Granted Theater Concessions, Inc., the privilege of selling refreshments during the 12-week festival in return for 5 percent of gross receipts payable within three days after the conclusion of each three-week period.
	4	Purchased liability insurance for the 12-week period at a total cost of $600. Payment is to be made when the policy is received.
	5	Four *Program Notes,* one for each show, were printed at a total cost of $400. Cash was paid.

7	Season tickets to the festival totaling $60,000 were sold. The season tickets permitted holders to attend each of the four shows on specified dates.
9	The first musical show, *The East Side Story,* had its premier. Cash sale of tickets to the performance amounted to $1,400.
28	The first musical show closed with this performance. Received a report from Theater Concessions, Inc., that total refreshment sales for the three-week period amounted to $20,000.

Required:

a. Assume that the festival uses a computerized accounting system. Decide whether each of the preceding transactions should be recorded by
   1. An application system.
   2. A journal voucher in the general ledger system.

b. Design a standard postings file appropriate for the festival's system.

20–21.   CLIENT/SERVER COMPUTING

Frisch's Restaurants, Inc., is a Cincinnati-based chain operating 100 eating establishments throughout the Midwest.[1] Frisch's property system keeps track of 45,000 assets—everything from bar stools to deep fryers. Recently they moved the system from their mainframe computer to a network of desktop computers connected to a file server.

Problems with the Mainframe

Management identified three major problems with the mainframe system. First, they felt that it cost too much money to operate. Second, its batch data entry process produced too many errors. And third, Frisch's accounting software vendor had informed them that it would no longer support the mainframe in future versions of the software. The vendor offered to install their own turnkey system in its place, but management rejected that alternative because the turnkey system could not be used by more than one person at a time.

The Solution

Instead, Frisch's management engaged a consulting firm to convert the accounting system to one that would run on desktop computers. The consulting firm converted the data, modified the existing COBOL programs, and produced a system that solved the problems of the old system while running twice as fast. They created data entry and edit screens, replacing the error-prone manual process that relied on paper forms and an outside service bureau to keypunch and update data in the system.

The consultants used microcomputer-based development tools to run the COBOL programs and to create a custom-designed interface program between the old programs and a database management system on the file server. The application worked the same way it did on the mainframe but ran on a desktop. In essence, Frisch's accountants then had miniature mainframes running on their desks. Frisch's information systems (IS) department programmed links between the property system and the general ledger

---

[1] Adapted from Doug van Kirk, "Frisch's Restaurants Cooks Up Downsizing Solution with Cobol," *Infoworld,* January 24, 1994, p. 56. Used with permission.

system, which still runs on the mainframe. The IS department also participated in the training, data conversion, and installation steps. Although technically the new system is client–server computing, it lacks the benefits of object-oriented programming or sophisticated query tools usually found on other such systems.

Benefits

Management observed several benefits resulting from the new system. It eliminated the need to keypunch data, which reduced data entry time and costs and the need to deal with the service bureau. It also eliminated time-consuming reviews of monthly control reports to detect data entry errors that would have caused the books not to balance. Errors are possible with the new system, but Frisch's accountants could find them earlier and correct them on-line. Because the new system used the application programs from the old one, the implementation and conversion process went quickly.

Frisch's property system isn't a glamorous one and, because it uses older programs coded in COBOL, is considered a "legacy" system. Yet it is simple and was implemented with a minimum of hassle. In the opinion of Frisch's management, the new system may be all the chain really needs.

Required:

a. What do you think of Frisch's solution to their problems? When is such a solution appropriate?
b. What risks are associated with the new system? What new controls are desirable?

20–22.   *DEVELOPING A SYSTEM*

Two years ago, East Coast Utility Co. (ECUCO) concluded that its manual general ledger system was no longer meeting the needs of its users.[2] Management decided to develop a new computerized general ledger system that would improve the accuracy and control of ECUCO's accounting data. This system was to provide a base for a more comprehensive computerized accounting system encompassing other applications.

Defining Inputs

The first step in developing this system was to identify the data elements necessary to support the general ledger system. The design team asked users to prepare lists of all the data they would like to see as outputs from this system. The team found that a number of the data items were processed by other systems, such as accounts payable, accounts receivable, and payroll. For this reason, they did not include them in this system. After repeated discussions with users, a list of general ledger system inputs was finally compiled.

Defining Outputs

The second step was to define the reports required from the system. After discussions with users, the design team determined that the system should produce a total of six reports. Four of these would be produced monthly; the remaining two would be produced after each execution of the system. These two reports allowed the accounting

---

[2]Adapted from D.P. Lubas, "Developing a Computerized General Ledger System," *Management Accounting,* May 1976, pp. 53–56. Copyright by National Association of Accountants (1976), Montvale, N.J. 07645. Used by permission.

department to monitor the system and to maintain adequate system controls. The following is a brief description of these reports:

General Ledger. The general ledger is normally produced at month-end, but it can be produced during the month if necessary. The design team decided that, in keeping with traditional general ledger layouts, each general ledger account and its detail would start on a new page. When the general ledger account is supported by a subsidiary ledger (or subledger), only totals appear in the general ledger. All details supporting the general ledger balance appear in the subledger.

The last page of the general ledger contains total debits for the month, total credits for the month, and trial balance figures. These figures can be reconciled with the most current summary control report printed prior to the printing of the general ledger. At year-end the system produces a pile-up general ledger, disclosing totals for all months rather than those for an individual month.

Exhibit 20–1 contains a schematic of the general ledger system showing how it captures data from both manual and mechanized sources, feeds summary data, and produces reports for top management.

EXHIBIT 20–1

Case 20–22

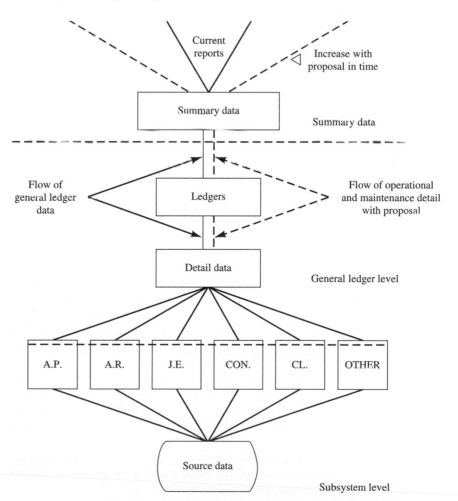

Subledgers. Similar to the general ledger, the subledgers are normally produced monthly; however, they can be produced at other times if necessary. Each subledger account and its detail starts on a new page and contains two types of information. First, the page contains a functional department breakdown by month and year. This shows each department that incurs a charge in that account. Second, it provides totals by charge classification (payroll, depreciation, taxes, and so forth).

Subledger Summary. The system prints the subledger summary at the end of each subledger. It contains the total debits and total credits for the account code range contained in the subledger. The accounting department reconciles these figures with the controlling general ledger account. The subledger summary also contains a functional department summary that lists, by department, totals for each charge classification by month and by year.

Operation and Maintenance Work Order Summary. An operation and maintenance work order identifies individual construction projects, types of project, or classes of expense. The system produces it monthly after the subledgers are printed. This summary contains detail totals by account for each operation and maintenance work order. It also contains a classification summary that lists monthly and year-to-date totals by charge classification.

Summary Control Report. The summary control report is printed at the end of each execution of the batch validation program. The report shows month-to-date totals for all accounts with subledgers and for all other accounts selected by the user. Frequently accountants use this to obtain a listing of totals for classification codes of interest to them. The report also shows total debits, total credits, trial balance amounts, and the amounts in any contra accounts.

Journal Register and Error List. The system produces these reports whenever transactions are submitted to the system. These reports list both valid and erroneous transactions. The error list identifies each erroneous transaction by printing the contents of the transaction and a description of the error.

The journal register and error list disclose both record counts and control totals. The record counts are provided when the batch is accepted as correct and added to the accepted records file.

System Procedures

The third step in the development of this general ledger system was determining how to collect and process the data. The design team identified methods for data collection, process flow, and procedures for data validation and correction.

Data Collection. Users record the data in one of three forms: manual input transactions, computerized interface input, and system control input.

1. *Manual input transactions.* Manual input transactions are all general journal entries. The accounts payable and accounts receivable entries are manual for two classes of users. Some do not have computerized systems, while others have computerized systems that are not interfaced with the new general ledger system. Management plans to integrate some of these systems with the new general ledger at some time in the future.

2. *Computerized interface transactions.* Computerized interface transactions consist of data passed automatically from the existing computerized system to the general ledger system for processing.

3. *System control input.* System control data is generated both manually by users and by computerized systems. Although individual users are responsible for submitting correct transactions, a central data control group coordinates their efforts.

Each user department maintains a control log of transaction batches that the control group reconciles with the journal register and error list. Batch control for computerized interface transactions is created automatically by the system; therefore, a control log is not required for these entries.

Processing Flow. After defining how data are gathered, the design team developed the processing flow. Source documents—including journal entries, accounts payable vouchers, and accounts receivable documents—are grouped by batch. Each batch contains documents of one source type and is numbered in sequence and then forwarded to data processing for data entry.

Batches are first processed by a validation program. Any number of batches can be submitted to one validation run, and all types of batches can be submitted simultaneously. Computerized entries from other systems are also validated; however, these maintain their original identity to simplify error correction procedures.

Data Validation and Correction. Batches submitted to the validation program pass sequentially through validity and compatibility checks. Records found to be in error are flagged with a descriptive error message, and all records of the batch are written to an error file. Erroneous records are assigned an identification key to enable the accounting clerk to locate them quickly. Batches that have no errors are then processed by a control program that accumulates data and prints account totals on the summary control report.

Users correct their errors with a separate error correction program. They use identification keys to locate erroneous records in the error file. They correct the erroneous records and then reprocess the entire error file through the validation program as if the errors were normal batch entries. Even when the erroneous transaction was produced by one of the computerized systems, the transaction is corrected by the general ledger system in this way.

Users execute the validation program whenever desired. On the last validation run of a month, however, the error file must be cleared of transactions. The system executes no general ledger or subledger programs if error records remain in this file. This is important because the system holds an entire batch in suspense whenever an error occurs in any record in the batch. Omitting an entire batch when printing the general ledger could seriously affect the accuracy of reported financial data.

System Controls

While the design team was developing processing flow, users requested numerous controls. After considering these requests, the design team developed controls in three basic areas: manual controls, automatic computerized controls, and manually initiated computerized controls.

Manual Controls. The design team instituted the following manual controls intended to ensure accurate submission of data and proper and complete acceptance of data by the system:

1. *Single source document.* All manual input, including corrections to the system, are in one standard format on a standard form. This simplifies submitting data, and auditing the system, and it eliminates errors arising from multiple forms and transactions.

2. *Control totals per batch.* The control total is calculated by totaling the amounts while ignoring their signs. Using this total ensures that all transactions in a batch are entered in the system.

3. *Month-to-date controls.* Each user location maintains month-to-date totals of amounts processed at that location. They reconcile these totals with those on the control report produced by the system.

4. *Review of output reports.* Both daily and monthly reports are reviewed. By reviewing key reports, users discover errors undetected by the system validation program. An example is recording a transaction in an incorrect expense account.

Automatic Computerized Controls. The system uses these controls during validation and updating, and in numerous other programs throughout the general ledger system.

1. *Detail element validation.* The system checks individual data elements for accuracy. These elements include the voucher number, accounting month, improper blanks, and alphabetic or numeric characters.

2. *Amount verification.* Computer programs determine that debits equal credits on all input transactions. Also, the total amounts of all transactions in a batch must equal the control totals submitted for the batch.

3. *Control file.* The control file contains current month totals by account code and by work order qualifier. From it, the system produces a monthly control report. Users verify the totals on this report to assess the accuracy of computerized procedures.

4. *Journal register and error list.* The system produces these reports whenever transactions enter it. They identify errors submitted to the system and suspense account entries created to eliminate the errors. The journal register provides a complete list of data submitted for validation and enables users to identify missing journal entries.

Manually Initiated Computerized Controls. Manual procedures provide audit capability and provide greater assurance of accuracy. They are initiated on request.

These control procedures check the various files of the system to ensure that they are in balance. All transactions processed are copied to a backup file. The total of all transactions in the backup file underlying a control file balance is checked against the total in the control file. These totals are also compared to the balance in the control accounts in the general ledger file.

Users initiate these procedures daily. They not only verify the accuracy of control file and general ledger file totals but also ensure accurate backup of the current day's transactions.

Responsibilities

The final step in the development of the general ledger system was establishing responsibilities. Two important job positions identified by the design team were those of site controller and system coordinator.

Site Controller. Management decided that users' groups would be responsible for the timely submission of transactions from their own departments or companies. To monitor and control system processing properly, each department and company was required to appoint a site controller.

The site controller accumulates and verifies transactions, develops batch totals, enters these batch totals on a transmittal form, and submits the batches for data entry. The site controller also reviews the journal register and error list and either corrects errors or initiates activity to resolve them. In addition, he or she reviews general and subledger reports.

System Coordinator. Although the system relies on data submitted by various locations, management desired a single, common accounting system using standardized procedures. For this reason, they appointed a system coordinator. This person reviews and approves policies and procedures and further coordinates processing between users' groups. The system coordinator is also responsible for reconciling system outputs with each users' group's site controller and serves as a centralized communication point for resolving inquiries regarding the system.

Conclusion

This computerized general ledger system makes standardized accounting information available throughout ECUCO. Besides enabling easier analysis and better decision making throughout the company, it eliminates manual preparation of many schedules, reports, and ledgers. It maintains system control while providing for future expansion of the computerized system into other application areas.

Required:

a. For this general ledger system, identify its
    1. Objectives.
    2. Outputs.
b. Describe the use of registers and control reports in this application.
c. Identify the following application controls in this system:
    1. Input controls.
    2. Processing controls.
    3. Output controls.
d. Draw a system flowchart showing the system's data validation and error correction procedures.

20–23.   INTEGRATIVE CASE—PART V

Agee Company is a manufacturer of large-diameter valves, located in a major southwestern city. Management has engaged a local CPA firm to aid the company in updating its accounting systems, and you have been assigned to a design team responsible for developing the new processes. Members of the team include management accountants, Agee operating personnel, and representatives of the CPA firm's staff. The team leader is an experienced systems analyst from the CPA firm. In Part V, you will complete assignments that allow you to participate in the design of application systems in Agee's financial cycle. For background information, you may refer to Part I of the case in Chapter 16.

Your team leader has given you the following preliminary system design (PSD) for four proposed systems in Agee's financial cycle. The PSD is incomplete, consisting of a short narrative and a system flowchart for each system. Make any assumptions necessary to complete the requirements, but state your assumptions.

Property System

Agee acquires fixed assets through its normal purchasing system. The process begins when a supervisor or manager completes either a materials acquisition or a capital acquisition request. Materials requisitions are used to obtain items costing less than $500. All supervisory personnel may initiate these without further approval. These purchases are considered supplies and are expensed rather than capitalized. Supervisors can also request capital expenditures of up to $2,000 using a capital acquisition request, which requires approval of the supervisors' immediate superior. Capital expenditures between $2,000 and $20,000 are initiated by department heads and require approval of an officer of the company. Expenditures of greater than $20,000 require approval by the board of directors. Once the request is approved, the purchasing department identifies a source and issues the purchase order.

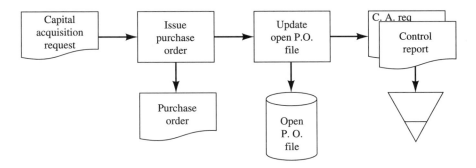

Journal Entry System

Agee uses its journal entry system to post to the general ledger accruals, deferrals, corrections, and other items that are not initiated from one of its other accounting systems. The chief accountant initiates a journal entry by completing a journal voucher form. The controller reviews the form to ensure that the entry is correct and justified and passes it to the general ledger clerk for data entry. The system records the journal entry in the general ledger master file and produces a journal voucher register listing all entries made at that time.

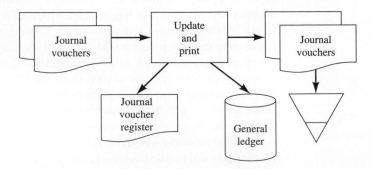

Financial Reporting System

Agee produces financial statements at the end of each month. However, only at year-end are accruals and deferrals made to comply with generally accepted accounting principles. At year-end, the general ledger clerk prints the contents of the general ledger master file in the form of a preliminary trial balance. The chief accountant and controller review this trial balance for obvious errors. They then prepare journal vouchers for adjusting entries and enter them in the general ledger using the journal entry system. The general ledger clerk then prints the final trial balance and the financial statements.

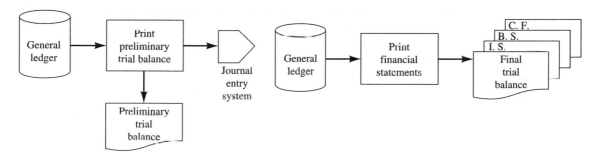

Budgeting System

Management develops its budgets for the upcoming calendar during the previous November and December. The general ledger clerk is responsible for entering budget targets in the budget file by the end of December. The budget file is identical to the general ledger master file except that it records budgeted rather than actual amounts. The budgeting system produces monthly reports that show actual and budgeted costs by general ledger account for the current month and for the year-to-date. Management may choose to revise the annual budget anytime during the year if unforeseen major events occur.

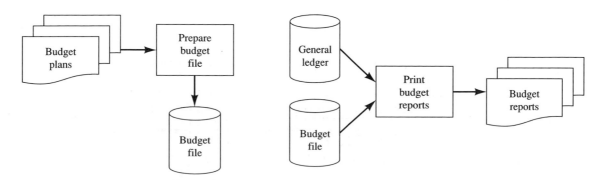

Required:

a. What observations do you have about this preliminary design? Do you think that modifications are needed?

b. Prepare a data flow diagram for the property system.

    c. Design the control report for the property system.

    d. Design a journal voucher register for the journal entry system.

    e. Develop record layouts for the budget and general ledger master files.

    f. Design a data entry screen for the journal entry system.

    g. Design a budget report for the budgeting system.

    h. What control procedures should you incorporate in the applications of Agee's financial cycle?